DIRECTORY
of
AFRICAN AMERICAN
RELIGIOUS BODIES

Howard University School of Divinity
Research Center on Black Religious Bodies

Lawrence N. Jones
*Dean, Principal Investigator
and General Editor*

Wardell J. Payne
Research Director and Editor

Kim Q. Boyd Leathers
*Senior Research Assistant
and Associate Editor*

Gail E. Bowman
Research Assistant

Gloria R. Shepherd
Secretary and Editorial Assistant

DIRECTORY
of
AFRICAN AMERICAN RELIGIOUS BODIES
A Compendium by the Howard University School of Divinity

Edited by **Wardell J. Payne**

Prepared under the Auspices of the
Research Center on Black Religious Bodies
Howard University School of Divinity
Washington, D.C.

Howard University Press
Washington, D.C.
1991

Howard University Press, Washington, D.C. 20008

Manufactured in the United States of America

This book is printed on acid-free paper.

10 9 8 7 6 5 4 3 2 1

No payment has been either solicited or accepted for the inclusion of entries in this publication.
Howard University School of Divinity has used its best efforts in collecting and preparing the
material for inclusion in this publication, but does not warrant that the information herein is
complete or accurate.

Library of Congress Cataloging-in-Publication Data

Directory of African American religious bodies : a compendium by the
  Howard University School of Divinity / Wardell J. Payne, editor :
  prepared and edited in the Research Center on Black Religious
  Bodies, Howard University School of Divinity.
      p.   cm.
    Includes bibliographical references and indexes.
    ISBN 0-88258-174-0 : $49.95.—ISBN 0-88258-066-3 (pbk.) : $29.95
      1. Afro-Americans—Religion—Directories.   2. United States—
  Religion—1960– —Directories.   3. Afro-Americans—Religious life.
  I. Payne, Wardell J., 1948–   .   II. Howard University. Research
  Center on Black Religious Bodies.
  BR563.N4D57   1991
  280′.089′96073—dc20   90–29313
                                                           CIP

TO
The Howard University School of Divinity Community
Past, Present, and Future

Contents

Introduction
The Organized Church

Part 1
African American Religious Bodies

Part 2
African American Religious Councils,
Ecumenical Organizations, and Service Agencies

Part 7
Appendixes

Part 8
Selected Bibliography

Part 9
Indexes

Preface

This inaugural edition of the *Directory of African American Religious Bodies: A Compendium by the Howard University School of Divinity* was made possible by a grant from the Lilly Endowment, Inc. Through the support of the Lilly Endowment, Inc., the Howard University School of Divinity established the Research Center on Black Religious Bodies to collect, compile, and publish the information in this volume.

The *Directory* provides comprehensive documentation of extant African American religious bodies, organizations, and agencies. The scope of coverage was defined by the following general operational criteria:

A *religious body* refers to an organizational entity that shares a common bond of fellowship or association. It should be an autonomous organization composed of at least 2,000 members and/or five related congregations. They should meet collectively or representatively on a regularly established basis for the purpose of sharing their religious practices, beliefs, and fellowship.

The term "religious body" is used to embrace the diverse religious communities in the United States. Because African Americans are represented in a multiple array of "faith communities," some of which extend beyond the Christian community and include "primitive" and "free thought" traditions, an effort has been made to create a classification scheme that recognizes a variety of self-definitions and structures. Some groups are clearly denominations, as this term is conventionally understood, whereas others are sects, or loosely gathered fellowships.

The *Directory* provides a selective listing of African American scholars in religion and provides abstracts on ancillary support services and auxiliary agencies that are not denominational in structure but are related to African American religious institutions (e.g., seminaries, Bible colleges, music resources, publishing companies, and community ministries).

In the *Directory* the term "church" is used to encompass a full range of religious experiences and structures, and extends beyond the "Christian" concept of the church to include groups that have no formal meeting house, as well as groups that do not use that word to describe their religious practices. Although a few individual congregations are included, this volume is devoted principally to aggregations of congregations.

African Americans are represented in virtually every religious body in the United States. The *Directory* is designed primarily to identify African American religious bodies. Non-African American religious groups and organizations are included if their ministry has organizational structures that serve persons of African American heritage. This category includes caucuses, conferences, conventions, standing committees, or permanent organizations in predominantly white American religious groups.

In summary, this publication includes groups that are

1. composed exclusively, or predominantly, of African Americans; or

2. predominantly white, but have a significant number of African American members; or
3. oriented toward increasing the participation of nonmajority group persons in the wider religious community of the United States.

The staff of the Research Center on Black Religious Bodies is grateful for the assistance of all persons who have contributed to the successful completion of this undertaking. Although every effort has been exerted to ensure the accuracy and completeness of all entries in this *Directory*, it is a certainty that this goal has not been fully achieved. Therefore, apologies are extended to any group or organization that might have been omitted or incompletely reported.

An additional grant from the Lilly Endowment, Inc., to the Howard University School of Divinity Research Center on Black Religious Bodies is underwriting the on-going process of updating and correcting the data in this volume. It is anticipated that a revised volume will be issued in three years. Listed in Appendix C are the religious bodies for which complete information was not available. Inquiries pertaining to this publication should be directed to the Howard University School of Divinity, Research Center on Black Religious Bodies. Persons who may have information that corrects or complements the entries in this *Directory* are encouraged to communicate with the editor. A form has been provided at the end of the book for updating information.

Acknowledgments

The Howard University School of Divinity Research Center on Black Religious Bodies acknowledges its profound indebtedness to the Lilly Endowment, Inc., particularly to Dr. Robert Wood Lynn, Vice President for Religion, and Ms. Jacqui Burton, Program Director, Religion.

The Research Center on Black Religious Bodies is also pleased to acknowledge a gift from the Kentucky Fried Chicken Corporation to assist in collecting information on music resource organizations serving the African American community. We thank Creative Connections, Inc., of Washington, D.C., which cooperated in this effort.

I extend particular appreciation to the staff of the Howard University School of Divinity Research Center. Kim Q. Boyd Leathers, senior research assistant and associate editor, and Gloria Read Shepherd, administrative secretary and editorial assistant, are due special recognition for their devotion in preparing this *Directory* for publication. Mrs. Leathers contributed creatively and invaluably through her work in establishing contact with religious leaders, scholars, and organizations as well as in editing, documenting, and writing historical narratives on the religious bodies. She also devised the charts that provide an organizational overview of the history and development of some religious bodies. Mrs. Shepherd and Mrs. Leathers have given of themselves without reservation in the herculean tasks of typing and indexing numerous drafts of the manuscript.

All of us here at the research center especially acknowledge the contributions of former staff members, the Reverends Gail E. Bowman, Esq., H. Lionel Edmonds, Charlotte J. Wing Moody, and Matthew Reese. These individuals contributed their time and energy to complete the preliminary tasks fundamental to this project. The Reverend Bowman is singled out for her contributions in developing profiles and narratives on organizations and bodies and for her thorough research assistance. We are grateful to the Reverend Mary Myers Montgomery, Esq., who assisted in early stages of the project; to the Howard University School of Divinity administrative staff, who supported this project in a variety of ways; to Irene Owens, former librarian, Howard University School of Divinity and to other members of the library staff, who have been a continuous source of information and support; to Alberta Johnson, Terence Leathers, and Rodney Sadler, Howard University School of Divinity students, who helped us to meet various project deadlines; to the Howard University School of Divinity faculty, who have assisted greatly in identifying issues and approaches from which to organize and to collect information on African American religious bodies, institutions, agencies, and scholars; and to the staff of the Howard University Press, who have been especially supportive in bringing this project to completion.

A special note of gratitude is due to the scholars who contributed extended essays to this volume. These persons include Cyprian Davis, O.S.B., Lawrence N. Jones, Calvin S. Morris, Clarence G. Newsome, and William C. Turner, Jr. We also appreciate the assistance of Father Elias Farajajé-Jones, who contributed informative narratives on the vodoun and spiritualist traditions.

We are especially appreciative of the following authors and their publications: Sherry S. DuPree, *Biographical Dictionary of African-American Holiness-Pentecostals*; Constant H. Jacquet, Jr., editor, *Yearbook of American and Canadian Churches*; Rayford W. Logan and Michael R. Winston, *Dictionary of American Negro Biography*; J. Gordon Melton, editor, *The Encyclopedia of American Religions*, Second and Third Editions, and *The Encyclopedia of American Religions: Religious Creeds*; and James C. Richardson, Jr., *With Water and Spirit: A History of Black Apostolic Denominations in the United States*. These publications were helpful in identifying various groups and clarifying facts about others.

Grateful appreciation is extended to Dean Lawrence N. Jones whose genius produced the proposal that resulted in the acquisition of funds to develop this project and whose steadfast encouragement and support have been highly instructive throughout all phases of this project. His vision of providing a means by which the opportunities for ecumenical ministries among African American religious bodies might be enlarged is realized in the publication of this *Directory*.

As editor of this volume I wish to express my personal appreciation to all who have assisted in this project. I especially thank my loving and understanding wife, Jennifer, and our children, Langston and Simone, who have tolerated innumerable inconveniences.

Wardell J. Payne

Contributors

Cyprian Davis, O.S.B., is the archivist and professor of church history at St. Meinrad Archabbey in St. Meinrad, Indiana. He holds the License of Sacred Theology degree from The Catholic University of America (1957) and the Ph.D. degree in historical sciences from The Catholic University of Louvain, Belgium (1977). His areas of interest include black Catholic history, medieval church history, and the history of black spirituality. He is a Benedictine monk.

Lawrence N. Jones is dean and professor of black church history at the Howard University School of Divinity in Washington, D.C. He holds a master's degree in American history from the University of Chicago (1948), a bachelor's degree in divinity from Oberlin Graduate School of Theology (1956), and a doctorate in religion from Yale University Graduate School (1961). His areas of specialization include African American church history and American religious history. Dr. Jones is an ordained minister in the United Church of Christ.

Calvin S. Morris is associate professor of pastoral theology at the Howard University School of Divinity in Washington, D.C. He has earned the Master of Arts degree in history (1964), the Bachelor of Sacred Theology degree (1967), and the Doctor of Philosophy degree in history (1982) from Boston University. His areas of interest include African American church history, American social and political history, and pastoral theology. Dr. Morris is an ordained minister in the United Methodist Church.

Clarence G. Newsome is associate dean and assistant professor of church history at the Howard University School of Divinity, Washington, D.C. He holds the Master of Divinity degree in church history (1975) and a doctorate in religious studies (1982) from Duke University. His areas of interest include church history, American religious thought, and the black experience in America. Dr. Newsome is president of the Society for the Study of Black Religion and an ordained Baptist minister.

William C. Turner, Jr., is assistant professor of theology and director of Black Church Affairs at the Duke University Divinity School in Durham, North Carolina. He earned the Master of Divinity degree (1974) and the Ph.D. degree in religion (1984) from Duke University. His areas of research include the black church in America, Christian theology, homiletics, and Pentecostalism. Dr. Turner is an ordained elder and pastor in the United Holy Church of America, Inc.

Consultants and Advisory Board

Consultants

Sherry DuPree, Reference Librarian, Sante Fe Community College, Gainesville, Florida

Bishop W. E. Howell, Bishop, United House of Prayer, Baltimore, Maryland

The late Constant H. Jacquet, Jr., Editor, *Yearbook of American and Canadian Churches*, and Staff Associate for Information Services, Communication Unit, National Council of the Churches of Christ in the U.S.A., New York, New York

The Rev. Dr. C. J. Malloy, Former General Secretary, Progressive National Baptist Convention, Inc., Washington, D.C.

Elder E. Myron Noble, Publisher, Middle Atlantic Regional Press, Washington, D.C.

The Rev. Dr. W. Franklyn Richardson, General Secretary, National Baptist Convention, U.S.A., Inc., Mt. Vernon, New York

Bishop Franklin C. Showell, Bishop, First Apostolic Faith Church of Jesus Christ, Inc., Baltimore, Maryland

The Rev. Stephen J. Thurston, Former General Secretary, National Baptist Convention of America, Inc., Chicago, Illinois

The Rev. Frank D. Tucker, President of the Council of Churches of Greater Washington and Chairman of the Church Association for Community Services of Washington, D.C. and Vicinity, Washington, D.C.

Advisory Board

Dr. Delores H. C. Carpenter, Associate Professor, Religious Education, Howard University School of Divinity, Washington, D.C.

Dr. Frank T. Cherry, Lecturer, Howard University School of Divinity, Washington, D.C.

Dr. Ed Dorn, Deputy Director of Research, Joint Center for Political Studies, Washington, D.C.

Dr. Joseph Eaglin, Former Executive Director, Congress of National Black Churches, Washington, D.C.

Dr. Lawrence Gary, Director, Institute for Urban Affairs, Howard University, Washington, D.C.

Dr. Lawrence N. Jones, Dean, Howard University School of Divinity, Washington, D.C.

Dr. C. Eric Lincoln, Department of Religion, Duke University, Durham, North Carolina

Dr. Lawrence H. Mamiya, Associate Professor, Religion and Africana Studies, Vassar College, Poughkeepsie, New York

Dr. Joseph McKinney, Treasurer, African Methodist Episcopal Church Finance Office, Washington, D.C.

Dr. Clinton D. McNair, Associate Professor, Practical Theology, Howard University School of Divinity, Washington, D.C.

Dr. Calvin S. Morris, Associate Professor, Pastoral Theology, Howard University School of Divinity, Washington, D.C.

Dr. Cheryl Sanders, Assistant Professor, Ethics, Howard University School of Divinity, Washington, D.C.

The late Rev. Dr. James S. Tinney, Professor, Journalism Department, School of Communications, Howard University, Washington, D.C.

Dr. Melvin Williams, Director, Department of Afro-American Studies, The University of Maryland, College Park, Maryland

Howard University School of Divinity Faculty, 1990–1991

Lawrence N. Jones, Ph.D., Dean
Clarence G. Newsome, Ph.D., Associate Dean
Mark A. Dennis, M.Div., Assistant to the Dean for Special Projects

Brown, Kelly D., Assistant Professor, Theology, Ph.D., Union Theological Seminary

Carpenter, Delores H. C., Associate Professor, Religious Education, Ed.D., Rutgers University

Crawford, Evans E., Professor, Homiletics, Ph.D., Boston University

Davis, D. H. Kortright, Professor, Theology, D.Phil., University of Sussex

Eubanks, John B., Visiting Professor, World Religions and Sociology of Religion, Ph.D., University of Chicago

Farajajé-Jones, Elias, Assistant Professor, World Religions, D.Th., University of Bern

Felder, Cain H., Professor, New Testament, Ph.D., Columbia University

Ferry, Henry J., Associate Professor, Church History, Ph.D., Yale University

McNair, Clinton D., Associate Professor, Practical Theology, Ph.D., Northwestern University

Morris, Calvin S., Associate Professor, Pastoral Theology, Ph.D., Boston University

Owens, Irene, Librarian, M.L.S., University of Maryland, M.A.R.S., Howard University

Rice, Gene, Professor, Old Testament Language and Literature, Ph.D., Columbia University

Sanders, Cheryl J., Assistant Professor, Ethics, D.Th., Harvard University

Taylor, Joseph E., Assistant Professor, Pastoral Theology, D.Min., Howard University

How to Use This Directory

This book is organized into nine sections preceded by the introductory essay, which provides an overview of the diversity and history of the African American religious experience. Parts 1, 2, 3, and 4 list African American religious bodies, agencies, institutions, and scholars, respectively. Part 5 provides a listing of predominantly white religious bodies and agencies with significant African American membership. Part 6 contains four historical reviews contributed by distinguished scholars in African American church history. These essays are overviews of African American religious traditions in the Baptist; Methodist; Holiness, Pentecostal and Apostolic; and Roman Catholic faith communities.

Part 7 provides three appendixes: a glossary of terms, charts on the historical organizational connections of selected African American religious bodies; and a listing of religious bodies for which the Research Center on Black Religious Bodies especially needs additional information. Part 8 presents a selected bibliography of written materials organized into four areas: denominational and historical profiles; biographical works; African American religious traditions, trends, expressions, and experiences; and general works. This material may assist the reader in further study of African American religious organizations. Part 9 consists of six indexes organized by: alphabet, categories, organizational classification, geographic location, personal names, and publications.

The listings are grouped into religious traditions in alphabetical order by their formal organizational name. Each entry includes the official organizational name and address along with the names of the respective organizational leader(s). Brief narrative descriptions on the group accompany each listing. The narratives are designed to provide the reader with additional insight into the history, purpose, and organizational structure of the respective religious entities.

The directory listings are organized in the following manner:

Official organizational name
Mailing address
Key denominational or organizational leader(s)
Narrative overview
Group type
Year the organization was founded
Membership
Major publications
Schedule of regular meetings

Each entry is classified by its primary function or organizational focus. Because each religious body or organization can have many functions, each group is distinguished by a maximum of three annotations. These categories are:

Administrative
Christian Education
Council of Churches or Groups
Denomination
Denomination Specific Organization
District Association or Annual Conference

Ecumenical or Nondenominational
Episcopal District
Lay
Lay and Clergy
Ministerial
Mission or Philanthropic
Music Resources
Publishing
Racial or Social Justice
Research or Education
State Group or Convention
Student
Women
Worship Resource
Youth

Introduction

The Organized Church
Its Historic Significance and Changing Role in Contemporary African American Experience

Lawrence N. Jones

From Earliest Beginnings To the Civil War

More than a century and a half passed from the first importation of Africans into America to the establishment of the organized African American church, which was the first institution that blacks controlled. It was nearly two centuries before a black denomination came into being. These facts suggest that a full understanding of the religious experience of blacks in America necessitates an investigation that is not restricted to the history of conventional ecclesiastical organizations. The religious experience of the minority of blacks who were involved in Christian institutions before emancipation was so closely intertwined with their total life experience that the starting point in understanding the meaning of that religious life must be the total life experience.

Paradoxically, those who initially founded this nation, who had left their homelands to escape religious, political, and economic oppression, introduced, almost immediately, one of the most oppressive systems of slavery that the world has witnessed. This paradox, in one way or another, has been both a source of guilt for whites and a goad to reforming actions throughout American history. The first efforts at Christianizing blacks had its source in this paradox.

Christianity had not taken root in Africa when the first slaves were brought from those shores.[1] Nevertheless, although Africans were not Christians when they came to America (this was later to be a rationalization for their enslavement), they were a religious people, because in their native land the totality of their lives was informed by what in western Europe was defined as "religion," but what, in Africa, was a basic part of life. Thus, they brought that "religion" with them; some, too, had been exposed to the Moslem faith before their capture.[2]

The earliest efforts to convert slaves were made within the context of family life, where master and mistress sought to share the liberating message of salvation. The irony of slaveholders seeking to win converts to Christianity, with its emphasis upon freedom, was only overcome by teaching that the freedom the Gospel promises is primarily spiritual in nature. This clear rationalization was given legal basis in the enactments of several of the colonial legislatures and later, in 1727, received the spiritual benediction of the bishops of London.[3] Later in the colonial period, individual clergymen felt called to preach the Gospel to slaves and did so with vigor but with minimal results.[4]

The first organized effort to Christianize slaves and Native Americans was the creation of the Society for the Propagation of the Gospel (SPG), by the Anglican Church in 1701. The SPG had indifferent success and frequently encountered considerable opposition, but it endured until the coming of the American Revolution.[5] The decades immediately preceding and following the revolutionary struggle were not distinguished as times of high religious fervor. By the end of the eighteenth century, only about 4 percent or 5 percent of blacks were enrolled on the rosters of the Christian churches. The impact of Christianity upon African Americans should not, however, be measured exclusively in terms of church statistics.

The delicate accommodation of slavery and Christianity, which some white Christians were able to achieve, was not acceptable to many others, who sensed that a deep contradiction existed between the Gospel and the practice of holding fellow human beings in thralldom. Persons in this latter group, whom I choose to call the "righteous remnant," initiated the first efforts to abolish the slave trade, organized the antislavery and abolition societies, and were intent upon ridding the church of the blight of slaveholding members. Individual Quakers, such as Anthony Benezet and John Woolman, led the way in these efforts, and as early as 1758, the Philadelphia Quaker Meeting passed legislation condemning the practice of trading in slaves.[6] A few other ministers and laymen, of whom the Congregationalists Samuel Hopkins of Newport and Samuel Sewall of Boston were typical, were in the vanguard of those who felt that Christianity and slavery were fundamentally incompatible.[7] They were not without their detractors. The relative success or failure of these efforts is not at issue here; their significance lies in the fact that these individuals were the first to contend that blacks and whites, slave and free, shared a common humanity, were creatures of a common Creator, and were the objects of the universal redemptive action of God in Christ. They were asserting that blacks, slave and free, were human beings.

Slaves were prohibited by custom and law from establishing organizations, or even from meeting for religious or other purposes without the inhibiting presence of their masters or representatives of that class. It was under these limitations that the first religious institution primarily controlled and administered by blacks was established at Silver Bluff, South Carolina, in the 1770s.[8] As might be expected, formal organizational activity was more frequent among free blacks in the urban North. These northern organizations were primarily mutual benefit societies that, in effect, sought to compensate for the neglect of blacks by the white government and institutions. The earliest of these societies was the Free African Society of Philadelphia, which was established in 1778. Richard Allen and Absalom Jones, two former slaves who had been frustrated in their efforts to establish a religious society by opposition from within the African American community, were the organizers.[9] The stated purpose of the society was to support "one another in sickness, and for the benefit of the [members'] widows and fatherless children."[10] A prime criterion for membership in all of these groups was an "orderly and sober life." Most of them were, in fact, quasi-religious bodies, and membership was heavily weighted with confessing African American Christians. Churches frequently came into existence from the memberships of these societies. The Free African Society of Philadelphia—that newly created independent body—was the mother of two African American churches, St. Thomas African Episcopal Church (later named the St. Thomas Protestant Episcopal Church) established in 1794, and the Bethel African Church, which was the first black congregation in the Philadelphia Methodist Conference. In 1796, by a special act of the legislature of the Commonwealth of Pennsylvania, Bethel African Church became an independent organization known as the African Methodist Episcopal Church. In a profound sense the benevolent, educational,

and literary societies that existed in great numbers in the first half of the nineteenth century were part of a search for community. The Masonic Lodge, which the Reverend Mr. Prince Hall succeeded in establishing for African Americans in 1787 with the help of British Masons, was also part of this search.

Black Religion in the Antebellum Period

During the antebellum period, organized African American Christianity was in its infancy: the ranks of its members were very thin, and on the national level, the bulk of black Christians belonged to predominantly white Methodist and Baptist bodies. The basic disability of the organized black congregations was lack of qualified leadership. Few of the clergy were theologically trained, and most of their constituents possessed no formal education. Daniel A. Payne reported that in the Mother Bethel African Methodist Episcopal Church in Philadelphia, fewer than one hundred persons in a congregation of fifteen hundred "could be found with a hymn-book in their hand."[11] In addition, the churches lacked the means of communicating with their constituents, because their publication boards were financially weak and had little prospect of developing, given the small readership they could hope to solicit. The management of organized institutions was a new thing for these northern freedmen, and they had a long apprenticeship to serve. Their institutional structures were weak and limited in effective power; their constituents existed on the edge of poverty, and their real estate was heavily mortgaged. When these disabilities were coupled with the overwhelming general-welfare needs of the community to which these pioneers were called to respond, their accomplishments appear all the more remarkable.

African Americans were, more often than not, second-class citizens in the predominantly Caucasian churches to which they belonged. It was common practice for pews to be provided for them in reserved sections of the churches. These benches were conventionally referred to as "nigger pews." In some churches, blacks could commune only after whites had done so; in others they could neither vote nor serve in any official capacity.[12] Segregated sections for African Americans were provided in church cemeteries so that the moldering dust of blacks and whites might not become mingled, even after death. Not every congregation followed every one of these discriminatory practices, but no major Protestant body was free from some taint of racist thought and practice.

The reasons for the rise of separate black congregations and the eventual emergence of black denominations in the North are complex. Viewed from one perspective, the independent black congregations were responses to, and accommodative of, white racism and practice. The separating African American brethren who formed the African Methodist Episcopal (A.M.E.) congregation in Philadelphia issued a public statement in which they asserted that they had taken this action to "obviate any offense our mixing with our white brethren might give them."[13] It is clear that the blacks, in addition to taking offense at the separate pews set aside for their use, were expressing their displeasure with the inhospitable reception their increasing numbers were receiving at St. George's Methodist Church.

The reason black Christians of New York City's John Street Methodist Church gave for their withdrawal and formation of the first A.M.E. Zion congregation was the failure of the Methodist parish to minister adequately to the needs of its increasing number of African American communicants.[14] Richard Allen, in Philadelphia, had offered a similar reason in partial explanation for the withdrawal of his group. There were other congregations that trace their origin to similar discontents.[15] Abyssinian Baptist Church in New York (1808) is a notable example. Its founders withdrew from the Gold Street Baptist Church in protest against the segregated practice of the church during worship services.[16]

Blacks also separated from white congregations because they felt that the souls of their fellows were being insufficiently attended to by white churchmen. The African American churchmen in Philadelphia offered as partial explanation for their withdrawal the need

> to preserve, as much as possible, from the crafty wiles of the enemy [the devil] our weak-minded brethren, taking offense at such partiality [segregated practice] as they might be led to think contrary to the spirit of the Gospel, in which there is neither male nor female, barbarian nor Scythian, bond nor free, but all are one in Christ Jesus.[17]

In a similar vein they argued that their worship would be more efficacious if they were separated. These pioneer African American evangelicals believed that if they were not worshipping with whites they could "more freely and fully hold the faith in unity of spirit and bonds of peace together, and build each other up in our most holy faith."[18]

To black Americans, one of the most galling aspects of their bondage was the fact that they were not considered to be human. They perceived very early that part of the American conception of humanness included the exercise of control over one's property. To be human was to be free, to some extent, to deploy the resources one owned. In the light of this perception, the rise of separate congregations must be seen fundamentally as an assertion by their founders of their own humanity. Separate congregations epitomized the desire to exert power and control over some area of their lives, which they understood was inherent in being human. Conversely, separate congregations were efforts to be free of the control of Caucasians. The African American congregations in New York and in Philadelphia included in their articles

of organization stipulations that excluded whites from official membership and from control of the churches' properties.[19] These were crucial provisos, for during the first twenty years of each of these groups' existence, they were integral parts of the Methodist conferences within whose jurisdictions they were located. In fact, Bethel Church withdrew from the Philadelphia conference when whites attempted to assert control over the pulpit and the property of their black brethren.[20] An additional source of irritation to blacks in the Methodist church was its failure to ordain African Americans to the itinerant ministry. In New York, this was the ostensible reason for the withdrawal of the Zion congregation from the Methodist Conference.[21]

In nearly every instance, the separating congregations of African Americans in the urban North were given financial assistance by benevolent whites. These benefactors frequently were not members of the congregations from which the blacks were withdrawing. The withdrawal of blacks from Caucasian churches did not result in their repudiation of the denomination as a denomination. The new congregations adopted the polity, doctrine, and structures of the parent Methodist body virtually intact, with few exceptions: the A.M.E. Zion group gave women the right to vote in their congregations and conference, and the A.M.E. Zion and the A.M.E. (Bethel) excluded Caucasians from membership.

The survival of these congregations and later denominations is remarkable. Although all the founders were individuals of deep religious faith, they were also of modest educational attainment and means, save for one or two who had financial resources in excess of their need. Of the nine men signing the A.M.E. Zion congregation's charter in 1801, four could not write their names and, presumably, could not read. Similarly, when the Philadelphia Bethel congregation was incorporated in 1796, three of the nine trustees signed the constituting documents with an "X." The fact that, in 1816, Richard Allen's fourteen-year-old son served as secretary of the constituting conference indicates the limited academic achievements of the A.M.E. church's founders.

In addition to those Methodist congregations that eventually became separate African American denominations, nearly a score of independent, non-Methodist local churches, mainly Baptist, were founded prior to 1820. Despite the appeal of the dissidents, a number of black members remained within the Methodist church. They formed the nuclei from which separate black congregations were formed within white institutional church structures.

In the antebellum South, blacks were not free to establish separate congregations, and all those who identified with institutionalized religion were affiliated with or supervised by white congregations. Whites were caught between their impulse to Christianize blacks, their need to exercise close control over the slaves and free blacks for reasons of security, and their distaste for being in the presence of too many blacks in a religious setting. Three patterns of congregational organization were employed to obviate the necessity of intimate association. Frequently, separate meeting times for blacks and whites were initiated. Another stratagem was to organize separate congregations supervised by a white minister. A third device was to create separate black congregations administered by blacks but with whites in attendance at all meetings. Black clergymen frequently were pastors of these churches and in some instances pastored white congregations as well for limited periods of time.[22] These means of dealing with the problem of race in the southern community prevailed until after the Civil War.

Although whites retained the reins of authority, blacks participated extensively in the ministry to the slaves. They were frequently deputized as "class leaders" in the Methodist church or as "watchmen" in the Baptist church and exercised oversight over the life and morals of the baptized black Christians. They also preached the Gospel and won many of their brothers and sisters to the faith.[23]

The A.M.E. church, which was organized as a denomination in 1816 with an initial membership of 8 clergy and 5 churches, grew in thirty years to 296 churches, 176 clergymen, and 17,375 members.[24] The A.M.E. Zion church did not grow as fast or cover as wide a geographical area as did the A.M.E. church. It was organized in 1821 with six congregations, 1,410 members, and 22 clergymen. By 1864, it had 113 clergy, 132 church buildings, and 13,702 members, including 2,654 in the newly liberated state of North Carolina.[25]

Given the inexperienced leadership of these organizations, much time and energy were directed to strengthening their internal structures, trying vigorously to train competent clergy for their increasing numbers of congregations, and striving to maintain the evangelical impulse. Because they were black, their concern for the slaves was axiomatic. The *Minutes* of the general and jurisdictional conferences of these African Methodist bodies are filled with references to the curse of slavery and to the many disabilities that blacks labored under in the free states. Like their counterparts in white denominations, they were concerned with temperance, moral reform, the care of superannuated clergy, and initiating missions in foreign lands. In the free states, the clergy waged a constant struggle to eradicate the residual effects of slavery upon newcomers. They deplored the absence of stable family life, the eroding effects of strong drink, and the indolence that characterized so many African Americans recently freed from the enforced labor of slavery. Hardly a conference convened that did not consider these matters.[26]

Black churchmen were also concerned about education, which they viewed almost with awe as the touchstone to acceptance into the American mainstream and as indispensable to personal and racial advancement. The Nineteenth Session of the Philadelphia Conference passed the following resolution, which is typical of the concerns of the church:

Resolved: That it shall be the duty of all the preachers of the Conference strictly and perseveringly to recommend that "Temperance Cause," in their respective circuits or stations, both by example and precept; and should a complaint of default in this particular be made against any preacher, he shall be dealt with by the senior, according to the provisions made for all such cases of imprudence and neglect of duty in our form of discipline.

Resolved: That as the subject of education is one that highly interests all people, and especially the colored people of this country, it shall be the duty of every minister who has charge of circuits or stations to use every exertion to establish schools wherever convenient, and to insist upon parents sending their children to school; and to preach occasionally a sermon on the subject of education; and it shall be the duty of all ministers to make returns yearly of the number of schools, the amount of scholars, the branches taught, and the places in which they are located; and that every minister neglecting so to do, be subject to the censure of the Conference.[27]

The slavery issue was also frequently deliberated by the A.M.E. church conferences. The *Discipline of the A.M.E. Church*, approved in 1817, included an article stating that "the buying and selling of men, women, and children with an intention to enslave them is prohibited by any member or members of this Church."[28] In the General Conference of 1856, the Committee on Slavery reported a resolution that would have forced the immediate expulsion of any slaveholding members, as well as that of any member who bought slaves and did not manumit them immediately.[29] However, it was frequently the practice of freedmen in the slaveholding states to buy their wives and children and then not free them legally, because some states required manumitted persons to leave their territories. At times a freedman would act as agent for a slave and purchase the individual with the slave's own earnings. These persons, too, were often technically held in bondage. In light of these facts, the conference affirmed its historic position of leaving local clergymen to decide if the letter and spirit of the church's regulations were being violated.

During the decade before the Civil War, there was considerable agitation among northern African Americans about the desirability of emigrating to Africa, Haiti, Central America, or Canada.[30] Although the A.M.E. church was officially opposed to emigration, the Philadelphia Conference, in response to the passage of the Fugitive Slave Law of 1850, passed a resolution in 1851 that eulogized the British people and their queen for opening Canada to blacks. In the text of the resolution, they recognized the fact that, given the situation of black people in America, sufficient reasons for emigration did exist:

Resolved: That, under existing circumstance, in our judgement, it is unwise and disadvantageous, as well as impolitic, for us to resolve that we will not leave the United States, as every such resolve only goes to stamp us as being willing to suffer anything that may be imposed upon us, rather than remove or emigrate; thereby encouraging our enemies to greater aggressions, and emboldening them in their encroachment on our liberty, and discouraging our friends, who are willing to receive us as part and parcel of their people, free and untrammelled from the powers of wicked laws.[31]

As a matter of general practice, the churches refrained from making official pronouncements in political matters unrelated to slavery. While the conferences were cautious, their leaders were sometimes less restrained. Bishop Paul Quinn, in his closing address to the New York A.M.E. Church Conference of 1851, remarked with some bitterness: "Nine times out of ten when we look into the face of a white man, we see our enemy. A great many like to see us in the kitchen, but few in the parlor."[32]

But, above all, these early black Christians were "evangelicals," deeply concerned with sharing the gospel of salvation with their brethren. They came into existence as much for this reason as for any other. If not phenomenal, their growth was steady. In A.M.E. church circles, W. Paul Quinn was called the "Missionary to the West." As the white denominations had their "Yale Bands" and their great home mission agencies, the African Americans had pioneer clergy who labored as valiantly as had Peter Cartwright, an early circuit-riding Methodist preacher, and Francis Asbury, first Methodist bishop in the United States, decades earlier. Quinn, as much as any, was responsible for the spread of the A.M.E. church into western territories. He reported to the General Conference of 1844 that, in a four-year period, he had helped establish forty-seven churches in the states of Indiana and Illinois (including 1,080 members, fifty-four clergymen, seventy congregations, fifty Sabbath schools, and forty temperance societies) and that he had conducted seventeen camp meetings. In addition, he had established congregations in St. Louis, Missouri, and Louisville, Kentucky, both slaveholding states. Commenting upon his new members, Quinn observed:

. . . [M]any of them within the last ten or fifteen years broke away from the fetters of slavery and settled with their families in those states, yet by dint of industry, they are not only supporting their families, schools and churches, but many of them are also acquiring wealth, amid opposing laws and chilling prejudice.[33]

Quinn was outstanding, but not unique. In these formative years, virtually every pastor was a missionary; a long list of men in the A.M.E., A.M.E. Zion, and Baptist churches did heroic pioneer work.

Despite the zeal of Quinn and others like him, the largest ingathering of blacks into the Christian fold occurred in the South under the aegis of white church bodies. In the period between the Nat Turner Rebellion of 1831 and the Civil War, Baptists, Presbyterians, Episcopalians, and Methodists expended considerable effort to win "black souls." After Turner's abortive attempt to exterminate Virginia whites, the slave states achieved what was virtually a monolithic defensive posture with respect to slavery, and proselytism of blacks received general public approval. Public antislavery agitation was muted, and individuals and institutions alike sought to commend slavery as a "positive good," no less for blacks than for whites. Slavery was, some white churchmen argued, entirely consonant with the will and purpose of God for blacks and for America.[34] Southern churchmen organized to evangelize the slaves, in part to assuage their guilt for acquiescing in the slave system; in part to answer the charge of some abolitionists and antislavery forces that slavery doomed slaves to remain in their "paganism"; in part as a response to their honestly held conviction that evangelization of all persons regardless of color was integral to Christianity; and in part as a means of controlling the bondsmen. An article in the *Methodist Review* puts the case quite succinctly:

. . . [R]eligious instruction administered by faithful and competent men lays the foundation of trustworthy morality; eradicates those tendencies to dissipation which destroy health and life: teaches principled contentment with the allotments of divine providence; puts into action a spring of industry and fidelity more powerful than the fear of corporeal punishment; and this, while it blesses the slave with the boon of that religion which is the poor man's chartered right, adds a thousand fold to the comfort and security of the master; and thus is largely instrumental in preserving and securing the public tranquility.[35]

Baptists and Methodists were most active in evangelizing the slaves and were the chief statistical beneficiaries in terms of converts. In relative terms, the effort to Christianize the slaves could not be counted as an unqualified success, nor were the effort and money expended in any way sufficient to the task. The African American population of the United States in 1860 was 4,444,830. Of this number, approximately 12 to 15 percent were enrolled as members of the churches—including men, women, and children with varying degrees of relationship to the congregations, and including the more than fifty thousand black Christians in the free states and territories.[36]

As has been indicated, the independent African American churches adopted forms of polity identical in virtually every respect to those of the churches from which they had withdrawn. A similar statement may be made about the orders of service and the rituals observed in the black Methodist congregations. However, because patterns of worship were not so uniformly prescribed in the free-church tradition of the Baptist bodies, the black Baptist congregations exhibited wide variety in worship.

A distinctive characteristic of the interior life of black congregations was the spontaneous participation of individual worshipers in all aspects of the service. Frequently this participation was marked by a high degree of emotionalism, which, in the period prior to the Civil War, was more characteristic of frontier revival services than of the formal worship of urban white churches. In addition, these churches frequently used spiritual folk songs drawn from the slave experience and the call-response style of congregational singing, neither of which were characteristic of worship in most European American congregations.

The differences of theological outlook between black churches and their white counterparts were related more to the life situations of the members than to deliberate choice. African Americans were an oppressed people, and although their traditional theology might be described as evangelical and their life-style as pietistic, they balanced the "promise of heaven's reward" with expectations that God would presently deliver their brethren from bondage and that He would liberate all blacks from social, political, and economic oppression.

Reference was previously made to the relatively minimal inroads that the organized church bodies were able to make in their efforts to win "black souls." One caveat should be made concerning the hazard of equating the influence of religious ideas with the statistics of ecclesiastical institutions. Christian ideas and teachings were carried among blacks far beyond the boundaries of the established churches. So pervasive were these teachings, and so extensive the quasi-religious groupings that developed around them, that one sociologist has referred to them as the "invisible institution."[37] African American Christians carried the "good news" into areas inaccessible to the organized churches, and they gathered bands of worshipers who met together as circumstances permitted to praise God and to pray for their expected deliverance from bondage. In short, African Americans themselves were doubtless the most effective evangelists among their own people—with and without official portfolio.[38]

It is easier to document the development of independent black Methodist bodies, yet many independent northern black Baptist congregations can trace their origins to the antebellum period as well. Most of these were located in the cities of the North and in the border states. Baptist polity permitted the organization of churches wherever the will existed among the people and wherever individuals were available to assume pastoral leadership. Because in Baptist polity authority is vested in local congregations, and these congregations were so widely scattered, African American Baptists were slow to gather into associations for purposes of cooperative action and consultation. The first associations among black Baptists were the Providence Association, which was formed in Ohio in 1834, and the Wood River Association, organized five years later in Illinois.[39] Unlike the Methodists, who met annually in conferences under the leadership of bishops, and who could speak for the churches on important issues when such statements were warranted, the

Baptists, lacking such structures, were local in influence and impact. The southern congregations remained under the close scrutiny of whites and were, thereby, effectually silenced.[40]

Like many U.S. benevolent institutions during the antebellum period, the A.M.E. church began to look to British philanthropy and churches for financial assistance. The first such initiative was made in 1846, when the church designated two of its clergy to attend the General World Convention of the Christian Church, held in London. Daniel Payne, one of the delegates, did not attend because his ship was forced to turn back by a violent storm. His colleague, the Reverend Mr. M. M. Clark, did succeed in reaching London, participated in the convention, and remained in England after its conclusion soliciting funds for the A.M.E. congregation in Washington, D.C. Later, Bishop Payne was to combine attendance at the meeting of the Evangelical Alliance in Amsterdam with a fund-raising effort on the behalf of Wilberforce University.[41] Wilberforce was a successor institution to the short-lived Union Seminary, which the Ohio Conference of the A.M.E. church had established in 1845. Wilberforce was the first institution devoted to higher education that was controlled exclusively by black Americans. It was founded in 1856 by white Methodists to educate both African and European Americans. By 1863, it was in danger of closing because its financial support had been eroded during the war. Payne, who had been a trustee of the institution since its opening, purchased the school for ten thousand dollars "in the name of God, for the A.M.E. Church," in March of 1862. He offered his personal note. He became its first president and remained its chief advocate in the church until his death in 1893.[42]

When the Civil War began, the African American churches could be encouraged by their organizational achievements. They had survived very tenuous beginnings. They had grown and expanded the territories within which they exercised jurisdiction. Schools had been established for the instruction of both adults and juveniles, and Sabbath schools were integral to the programs of most congregations. They had erected church edifices, evangelized their fellow African Americans, and established and maintained fraternal relations with Caucasian church bodies and with ecumenical groups. In most areas, church buildings were the only available places where meetings could be held, and the congregations were generous in offering their facilities for all sorts of gatherings—cultural, political, social, educational, and religious. As denominations or as congregations, they made pronouncements and passed resolutions concerning every pressing issue of the day. Even in this early period, the black churches were the most substantial institutions and the largest property owners in the black communities.

Although the institutions that black Christians had begun to develop represented a considerable achievement for persons of such limited organizational experience and material resources, the influence of Christianity beyond the churches was exerted primarily by individual Christians, particularly the clergy, rather than by the institutions. According to estimates, fully one-half of the African American leadership in pre-Civil War days were clergymen. Then, as now, the problems that confronted these individuals transcended denominational differences, and institutions to resolve these problems sprang up outside the church. Among the issues were such vital ones as ''What does it mean to be human?'' ''How can we achieve the rights that accrue to a person just because he or she belongs to the human race?'' ''Do blacks have a stake in America, or do we concur in the judgment of many whites and some blacks that we are aliens here?'' ''How do we change the conditions, and what strategies are appropriate to the effort?'' ''How can we be liberated from the oppression that afflicts us at every turn?'' Without question, the paramount sociopolitical issues were how an end could be brought to slavery and how the prejudice of whites could be overcome. In the North, the question of access to the rights inherent in U.S. citizenship were also discussed, including the right of access to the ballot box, the right to serve on juries, the right to public education, the right to receive service in public facilities and on transportation, and the right to work.[43]

Clergy were in the vanguard of the antislavery and abolitionist movements.[44] They contributed greatly to the success of the ''underground railroad''; they led the opposition to the American Colonization Society (ACS) organized in 1817 for the purpose of transporting free blacks to Africa.[45] A few clergymen supported the society as a poor but preferable alternative, for free blacks, to living in America.[46] Clergy and lay Christians alike fought for public education. They protested taxation without representation. In the North, they lobbied and petitioned for legislation to end slavery. In the decade just prior to the Civil War, some clergy were active in the political arena, particularly in New York State.[47]

African Americans were not in concord about the most appropriate strategies for dealing with their problems. At one extreme were those who advocated violent revolution as a means of ending slavery, including the alternative of ''dying with honor rather than living in bondage.'' At the other extreme were those of whom Frederick Douglass was typical, the so-called moral suasionists, who advocated various nonviolent strategies aimed at changing the attitudes and actions of the white oppressors. Even those blacks who affirmed the Bible to be the sole and authoritative source of guidance in all things were of divided minds. Denmark Vesey, in South Carolina, and Nat Turner, in Virginia, had found in their religion a mandate for violent revolution. The Reverend Henry Highland Garnet and David Walker took similar positions, with careful qualifications. Douglass championed

political means as a solution to the problem of slavery, although his position underwent some change in the decade before the war. The literature of the period reflects a variety of positions in between the two poles of Turner and Douglass.[48] No black was unaware of his or her powerlessness, and the issue resolved itself into the question of whether blacks, in the assertion of their humanity, should give their lives in one violent, probably futile, battle for freedom, or conversely, devote themselves to the tortuously slow process of appealing to the assumed innate sense of right within their oppressors. The question was unresolved then, and it has remained so.

Coping with Realities

Despite the vigorous efforts of African American Christians and the spate of organizational activity,[49] when the Civil War began, the great majority of blacks in America were not Christian in any formal sense. The several African American religious institutions, however, were on the brink of unparalleled expansion in the decade ahead. During the war, the churches wholeheartedly supported the Union cause, as did most blacks, and cooperated vigorously in raising troops. Later, they joined in pressuring President Lincoln to issue the Emancipation Proclamation. Freedom, the prize they long had sought, seemed within reach.

The decade between 1860 and 1870 was a period of accelerated growth for organized religion among African Americans. The A.M.E., A.M.E. Zion, and Baptist churches sent missionaries into the South hard on the heels of the conquering Union armies and found among the recently freed slaves many who were anxious to affiliate with their black brethren. Most of these new members, although not all, had previously been members of the churches of their masters. For example, the Methodist Episcopal (M.E.) church (South) lost some 130,000 of its black members during the decade. The exodus from white Baptist churches was comparable. Of course, numerous African American Baptist congregations were already in existence in the South, some of them pastored by African Americans and all of them under the fairly strict control of white ecclesiastical bodies. These churches now became entirely free from white supervision.

The dimensions of the harvest of new members is evident in the following statistics: The A.M.E. church began the decade with fewer than 20,000 members and within six years had grown to include some 50,000 souls.[50] The A.M.E. Zion church had 46,000 members in 1860 and achieved a membership of 125,000 by 1870.[51] This precipitous expansion created tremendous strains on the resources of the churches. The experience of the Reverend Dr. Henry McNeal Turner, a presiding elder in Georgia and the first black chaplain in the U.S. Army, is instructive at this point. In his letter of resignation from the presiding eldership in 1872, he reported:

> I had to preach three times every Sunday and every night in the week, month after month, then come out of the pulpit and explain the history and character, purpose and object of our Church, for hours, to satisfy the colored and whites, who would often look at me as if I were a bear or a lion; sometimes just commencing the organization of the church about twelve or one at night. . . .
>
> Since I have been trying to preach the Gospel, I have had the inestimable pleasure of receiving into the Church on probation, fourteen thousand, three hundred and eighteen persons which I can account for, besides some three or four thousand I cannot give an account of. And I would guess . . . that I have received during and since the war about sixteen or seventeen thousand full members in the A.M.E. Church, by change of church relations, making in all nearly forty thousand souls that I have in some manner been instrumental in bringing to religious liberty.[52]

As Dr. Turner's report indicates, the churches grew through vigorous evangelistic campaigns as well as through the accession of members who were effecting a "change of church relations."

As might be supposed, the rapid expansion of these African American denominations created immediate and pressing problems. Although new congregations were frequently granted permission by the Freedmen's Bureau or army commanders to take over buildings abandoned by whites, the problem of adequate housing persisted. Moreover, for all churches the supply of clergy was extremely limited. Turner often resorted to radical and irregular means to fill the pulpits:

> I have been accused of recklessly licensing preachers by the cargo, etc., because I had to license such a number. I admit that I did, on several occasions, exercise rather extraordinary powers in this respect, but in no instance where the emergency in the case would not justify such actions. I was for a longtime elder, superintendent and everything else, and sometimes had to make preachers of raw material at a moment's notice. I have licensed preachers while riding on the cars, but I always put [them] through an examination.[53]

Although many other church leaders lacked the audacity and flamboyance of H. M. Turner, his activities with respect to filling pulpits was, without a doubt, duplicated in South Carolina, Alabama, and Mississippi. Turner's Georgia Conference, in its first session in 1871, admitted forty-one men to the ranks of its clergy. The 1872 conference admitted an additional forty-eight men, with the list of those being admitted on trial being too long to include in the *Minutes*.[54]

The freedmen not only joined existing religious bodies but also, in some instances, with the support and encouragement of the white brethren, created new ones. In 1865, the African American members of the Primitive Baptist churches in the South withdrew and organized the Colored Primitive Baptists of America.[55] The black members of the M.E. church (South) were constituted as the Colored M.E. church, with some seventy thousand members, in 1870. In 1869, the General Assembly of the Cumberland Presbyterian Church organized its Negro membership as the Colored Cumberland Presbyterian Church.[56]

The missionaries of northern Caucasian churches also followed the Union armies into the South and enjoyed some success in recruiting among the freedmen. But virtually every church body, North and South, in which Caucasians were in the majority began to segregate African Americans in separate judicatories and congregations, and at the national level, agencies were established to oversee the "colored" work and to deal with matters of race.[57] Nondenominational agencies, such as the Young Men's Christian Association (YMCA) and the Young Women's Christian Association (YWCA), were no exception. However, the major energies of white northern Christians were expended initially not in proselytizing but in developing and staffing educational institutions for the freedmen.[58] African American church bodies shared this concern for education and worked with equal vigor. By 1900, Baptist bodies were supporting some eighty schools and eighteen academies and colleges. The A.M.E. church had raised over $1,100,000 for educational purposes between 1884 and 1900 and supported twenty-two institutions providing education above the elementary level. At the turn of the century, the A.M.E. Zion church was supporting, as a denomination, eight colleges and/or institutes, while the Colored Methodist Episcopal church had established five schools during its thirty-year history.[59]

While they were far from being affluent themselves, African American Christians in the North were actively involved in seeking to provide for the physical necessities of their recently liberated brethren.

> Among the outstanding Negro freedman's aid societies were the Contraband Relief Association and the Union Relief Association of Israel Bethel Church (A.M.E.) in Washington; the Contraband Committee of Mother Bethel Church in Philadelphia . . . Between 1862 and 1869 the African Methodist Episcopal Church contributed nearly $167,000 towards freedmen's relief.[60]

The agenda of African American churches has been mandated not only by the Gospel and by institutional considerations, but also by the historical situation of their members. This was clearly the case in the years between the end of the Civil War and the dawning of the twentieth century. Although the Thirteenth, Fourteenth, and Fifteenth Amendments to the Constitution were supposed to guarantee the rights of African Americans as citizens and to ensure their freedom, the historical reality was vastly different. In the years immediately following the war, African Americans in the South picked up the agenda on which their brothers had been working in the North— education, civil rights, economic equality, and the amelioration of the corrosive effects of prejudice and naked racism. Church meetings frequently addressed these questions, but for the most part, they were dealt with by clergy and laypersons working as individuals or in secular organizations.

During Reconstruction, African Americans began to develop alternative structures as the means for dealing with their perennial problems. Involvement in political parties, particularly in the South, and the establishment of labor unions, commercial banks, and insurance companies, along with other types of voluntary associations, took some of the pressure off the churches. Moreover, for the first time, the federal government began to develop agencies devoted to the welfare of the freedmen, and northern religious bodies were going all out to provide educational opportunities.[61] The black churches did not flag in their devotion to these concerns, yet they benefited from being liberated to a degree to attend to their own internal problems and to their "mission" as churches. These internal problems were many, including assimilating new members, training clergy, providing houses of worship, maintaining discipline among clergy and laypersons alike, and developing structures appropriate to their new national status.

From the standpoint of ecclesiastical organization, no event was of more importance in the postwar decades than gathering the majority of black Baptists, the largest denominational grouping, under one roof. The congregational polity of Baptist bodies has historically made it extremely difficult for them to achieve unification. The Providence Baptist Association and the Wood River Association, which were founded in the late 1830s, began this unification process when they merged in 1853 to form the Western Colored Baptist Association. The unified organizations included some, but not all, of the churches in Ohio, Illinois, Kentucky, Missouri, Indiana, Michigan, and Connecticut. Thirteen years earlier, in 1840, the American Baptist Missionary Convention had been established among the churches of New England and the Middle Atlantic states.[62]

In the interim between these early beginnings and 1895, when the National Baptist Convention, U.S.A. (NBCUSA) was incorporated, several associations were organized mainly for the purpose of advancing foreign missions and education. In 1897, a large segment of Virginia Baptists seceded from the NBCUSA to form the Lott Carey Missionary Convention. Yet another schism occurred in 1915, when a sizable group led by the Reverend Richard Henry Boyd split off from the NBCUSA to form the National Baptist Convention, Unincorporated, the second largest black Baptist body in America. A third secession from the NBC took place in 1961, when the Progressive National Convention was organized.[63] In 1988 the National Missionary Baptist Convention emerged out of the National Baptist Convention of America, Inc., constituting the fourth major African American Baptist body in America.

As the nineteenth century drew to a close, African American Christians had achieved a high degree of institutionalization. The Atlanta University census of black churches and churchmen, issued in 1906, reported that the A.M.E. church had expanded its rolls to include 494,777 persons, and the A.M.E. Zion church reported a membership of 184,542. The Colored Methodist Episcopal church had more than doubled its membership to 172,996. The NBCUSA was by far the largest denomination with 2,201,549 members, while 474,880 blacks retained membership in the predominantly Caucasian denominations.[64] Virtually every black group could count some of its missionaries in Africa and in the islands of the Western Hemisphere, and all had educational institutions to which they gave their support. Unlike their white counterparts, they continued to be concerned with the oppression of African Americans and the constraints placed upon them. The chilling physical presence of this oppression was evident in the escalating number of lynchings in the South and in state legislation and federal court decisions reflecting a climate of increasing hostility toward blacks.[65]

Organized Religion in the Twentieth Century

The single most important factor bearing upon the organized church in the twentieth century has been the movement of African Americans from rural areas to the urban centers of the North and South.

> At every census from 1790 to 1900, at least 90 percent of the Negro population of the United States lived in the South. In 1910, 89 percent of Negroes still lived in the South, but the percentage fell in succeeding decades, to 85 percent in 1920, 77 percent in 1940, and 60 percent in 1960.[66]

The greatest percentage of these immigrants moved into the cities of the Eastern Seaboard, the Midwest, and the Far West. By 1970, only 45 percent of all African Americans remained in the old Confederate states.[67] In 1969, 70 percent of Americans lived in metropolitan areas, with 55 percent concentrated in the inner cities, while 52 percent still lived in the South. The significance of these facts is that increasingly the ministry had to address persons for whom humane survival in the urban environment was problematic. The brutal fact is that people migrating out of the South were, for the most part, inadequately prepared to survive in an urban environment. The legacy of discrimination and segregation in the United States has been most conspicuously and dramatically manifested in its cities. To compound the problems of the religious establishment, African American immigrants settled in already crowded inner cities that had been abandoned by previous generations of immigrants. The churches, like the immigrants, had to move into previously occupied spaces, into buildings that white congregations had abandoned in their flight from blacks. In New York City, for example, the black community, before it settled in Harlem in the early decades of this century, was twice pushed out of the space it occupied.[68] In many respects, this relocation pattern was like trying to fit too many square pegs into an inadequate number of round holes. Because African American communities are notable for the greater number of churches they support per capita compared to white communities, the number of church buildings available within the community was inadequate to the needs of its new inhabitants. The rise of the so-called storefront church is, in part, a land-use and architectural response to this situation. In addition to being centers of community, these smaller churches are also outlets for the leadership ambitions of individuals who are denied access to other means for expressing their aspirations.

The city, too, as a sociological environment, was equally decisive insofar as worship and the structures of congregations are concerned. Persons moving from the intimacy of the rural South had a greater need for supportive relationships in the matrix of the hostile city. Even today, city congregations are frequently transplanted rural southern churches in form of worship, in patterns of personal relationships, and in the internal structures of congregational life.

A number of black churches made determined attempts to deal with the massive problems that mass migration and urbanization thrust upon them in the twentieth century. They usually possessed the following characteristics: a sizable middle-class constituency, college-trained clergy leadership, and a much larger-than-average congregation, frequently numbering as many as twelve thousand members.[69] In comparison to conventional black churches, they included many "secular" concerns in their agenda. In Chicago, for example, Quinn Chapel A.M.E. Church, as early as 1902, operated a kindergarten, a reading room and library, a savings bank, and an employment bureau. In 1905, the Olivet Baptist Church in Chicago "had a complete roster of girls' clubs, boys' clubs, athletic activities and three years later, in 1908, sponsored a program for the relief of the unemployed."[70] Also in Chicago, Reverdy C. Ransom established the A.M.E. Institutional Church and Social Settlement in 1900. This innovative church operated a whole range of social services. "Institutional operated a day nursery, a kindergarten, a mothers' club, an employment bureau, a print shop, and a fully equipped gymnasium; it offered a complete slate of club activities and classes in sewing, cooking and music, its Forum featured lectures by leading white and Negro figures; and its facilities were always available for concerts, meetings, and other civic functions."[71]

In New York, Harlem was still "in the making" at the turn of the century, and the movement of the churches to new locations "uptown" was incomplete. By 1930,

however, the migration was complete, and Harlem had become an African American "Mecca."[72] There were several institutional churches that sought to minister to the community in nontraditional ways. Notable among them were the Abyssinian Baptist, Salem Methodist, Mother A.M.E. Zion, St. Philip's Protestant Episcopal, and St. James Presbyterian churches. An innovative example of church participation in social change occurred in 1937 when A. Philip Randolph, the Reverend Adam C. Powell, Jr., Arnold J. Johnson, and the Reverend William Lloyd Imes joined together to form the Greater New York Coordinating Committee for the Employment of Negroes. For nearly a decade, this coalition of clergy and secular leaders labored to improve the economic situation of blacks. They took on Consolidated Edison and other utilities in an effort to open up employment opportunities. The Reverend A. Lorenzo King, pastor of St. Mark's Methodist Episcopal Church, declared on one occasion during this period, "We're tired of religion that puts us to sleep. We've got to put religion to work for us!"[73]

The examples cited from Chicago and New York could be duplicated on a less grand scale in other areas, but it is clear that such churches were the exceptions rather than the rule. That this should be the case is not difficult to understand. No matter how devoted the leadership or committed the membership, without training, financial resources, and sufficient "mass," no congregation can make a dent in the complex problems of the urban environment. In addition to its traditional ministries, perhaps the greatest service the African American church rendered in the period following the Civil War was that it enabled some blacks to establish identities, to participate in stable institutions, and to develop a sense of self-worth guaranteed by the Creator of the universe. In the twentieth century, it continues to serve in this way, while providing the additional function of being one means by which affiliated African Americans have been able to preserve a sense of their individual uniqueness in the maelstrom of the city.

Catholics

Historically, the majority of African Americans have been Protestant, although there have been African American Catholics here from the earliest times. Because slaves tended to adopt the religious affiliation of their masters, the majority of these converts were to be found in the Catholic population centers of Louisiana and Maryland. Consistent with this pattern, the Archbishop of Baltimore reported that in 1785 there were three thousand black Catholics in Maryland. Most of these had doubtlessly entered the church under the aegis of their masters, because the hierarchy did not encourage the aggressive proselytization of blacks. Nevertheless, when black concentrations developed, the church endorsed special ministries to and for them. The Oblate Sisters of Providence, established in Baltimore, Maryland, in 1829, had the specific mission of catechizing Maryland blacks whose population had been dramatically increased by an influx of some five hundred slaves from San Domingo. These slaves accompanied their masters who were fleeing the slave uprising of 1793. This black order established several schools and performed works of charity among African Americans.

In Louisiana, the concern for the Christianization of blacks was pursued more vigorously. The *Code Noir* promulgated in 1724 by Governor M. Bienville specially provided that masters should take their slaves to church and have them instructed and baptized into the Catholic religion. As in Maryland, the political upheavals and slave revolts in San Domingo gave rise to a sudden increase in the slave population in 1801, when two thousand black refugees arrived in the colony. In response to the growing number of slaves, the Christian Doctrine Society, an order of African American women, was organized in 1818 in New Orleans to carry out a ministry of evangelism. Less well-organized initiatives occurred in Kentucky, South Carolina, and several other southern states with far fewer members of the Catholic faith in their populations. By the end of the Civil War, there were approximately 100,000 black Catholics in the United States, of whom 16,000 were in Maryland and approximately 63,000 in Louisiana.[74]

Catholic race relations tended to duplicate those of other white religious groups. Like their Protestant neighbors, white Catholics established separate schools, segregated catechistic instruction, and other instrumentalities designed specifically to deal with the "Negro problem." In some parishes, separate masses were said for black communicants. In the years following the Civil War, the establishment of separate churches for African Americans was accelerated.

There were three ordained black Catholic priests in America before Lee surrendered at Appomattox. All were brothers, the sons of Michael Morris Healy, a wealthy Georgia Irish immigrant, and a mulatto slave woman referred to by Healy as his "Trusty Woman Eliza." Each of the Healy brothers carved out a distinguished career in the church. James became Bishop of Portland, Maine; Sherwood was a highly respected priest-theologian and for five years was rector of the Boston Cathedral; and Patrick, a Jesuit, became rector of Georgetown University (1873–82) and is sometimes referred to as its "second founder." The Healy brothers were not "race men" (i.e., African Americans committed to advancing the race through all of their endeavors, often at great personal sacrifice). Their singular distinction for the purposes of this study lies in the fact that they were the first men of color to be ordained priests and to function within the American Catholic church. Not one of these men was ordained by an American bishop. Their ordinations set no trend in the American Catholic church, nor did their ministries greatly affect the situation of black Catholics.[75]

In the years immediately following the Civil War, a number of blacks defected from the ranks of the Catholic church, particularly in Louisiana. This phenomenon paralleled the defection of black Protestants from predominantly white churches. The American hierarchy made no effort to counter these losses. It was not until 1871 that the Mill Hill Fathers of England began an apostolate to the freedmen. The first missionaries from Mill Hill disembarked in Baltimore, Maryland, and established their work in that city. Subsequently, several other Catholic societies began ministries among African Americans, but it was not until the Third Plenary Council in 1884 that the national church launched the Commission for Catholic Missions among the Colored People and the Indians. The appointed purpose of the commission was to propagate the faith. The effectiveness of these varied Catholic initiatives is difficult to assess, because of limited documentation of their efforts and because no statistics were compiled prior to 1928. In 1929 (according to the *Statistical Profile of Black Catholics* by Shuster and Kearns published in 1976), 200,000 African Americans were listed on Catholic membership rolls. Seventy-five percent of them were in the southern or border states. By 1975, there were 916,584 black Catholics. Consistent with the continuing migration of blacks from the South, the largest gains were in eastern and midwestern urban centers.

The African American Catholic population nearly doubled between 1940 and 1975, rising from 2.3 percent of the total black population to 4.0 percent.[76] The reasons for this dramatic increase might be the appeal of Catholicism to a growing African American middle class, coupled with dissatisfaction with traditional African American Protestant churches. The increased numbers of blacks seeking to avoid segregated public schools and the assumed superiority of parochial education contributed to this dramatic growth as well. In addition, the displacement of immigrant groups by African Americans in the urban centers changed the ethnic character of Catholic parishes and had the same impact on parochial school populations as it did on public school systems. The inevitable result was that many schoolchildren and their parents became Catholics. Another significant factor contributing to the growth of Catholicism among blacks was the practice of the church neither to segregate nor to exclude worshipers on the basis of color. Moreover, the Catholic churches did not abandon the inner city as their Protestant counterparts frequently have done, and they reaped a harvest of new converts as a result.

At present the voices of African American Catholics are being heard with increasing urgency throughout the American church. Rising black consciousness and self-awareness are expressed both at the parish level and through the National Office of Black Catholics.[77] Efforts are being made to increase the representation of blacks in the decision-making centers of church structures and to "indigenize" worship so that the cultural heritage of ethnic groups can be affirmed. Increasingly, African American Catholics and Protestants find themselves addressing the same agenda in their respective church groups and in the world outside the churches. There is a developing ecumenism among these black Christians that has its origins in nontheological and nonecclesiastical considerations. This growing unity arises out of a concern to improve the quality of life for persons whom the churches serve. As African American Catholics and Protestants abandon the historical suspicions and antagonisms that they appropriated from their white mentors, the Christian community among this minority group is being radically altered.

Pentecostals

Pentecostalism, which is a term covering a broad range of groups, became a vigorous competitor for the allegiance of African Americans early in the twentieth century. The movement is called Pentecostalism because of its emphasis upon the gifts of the spirit, particularly that of glossolalia, or "speaking in tongues." William J. Seymour, a Holiness preacher, is credited with triggering the revival that instituted the movement in the United States. The so-called Azusa Street Revival took place in Los Angeles in 1906 and launched what was originally an integrated movement; by 1914 it had split into black and white branches.[78] This rapidly growing movement was soon organized into church bodies.

Today there are approximately two hundred separate Pentecostal groups; the largest African American one is the Church of God in Christ, with headquarters in Memphis, Tennessee. Accurate statistics for these bodies are very difficult to obtain because few records are kept, and polity is rather loose. However, in 1970, there were estimated to be 425,000 members in the Church of God in Christ. The reported growth of the Church of God in Christ—from 53,558 members and 1,444 congregations in 1926 to an estimated membership of 413,000 and 4,000 congregations in 1963—is an index of its broadening appeal. The church estimated its worldwide membership in 1970 to be 3 million.[79]

African American Pentecostal churches are primarily an urban phenomenon, although their existence in rural areas of the South is not uncommon. Pentecostalism is frequently the doctrinal affiliation of so-called storefront churches, although many of these smaller churches may be a Pentecostal-style worship service without holding to the primary doctrine of classical Pentecostalism, that is, speaking in tongues and spiritual rebirth. The denominational affiliation of these churches, at least nominally, may be Baptist or any of a number of less well-known church bodies.

The significance of the rise of Pentecostalism among African Americans for this study is that these churches do not explicitly trace their roots to any of the major denominational sources of black religion. Many of their converts, however, were originally members of Baptist and Methodist churches who were apparently drawn to Pentecostals by their strict moral teachings and discipline, and by the intimacy of their worship and congregational life style.

Marcus Garvey

In the twentieth century aggressive alternatives to institutionalized Christianity also emerged. One of the first of these alternatives was under the leadership of Marcus Garvey and his Universal Negro Improvement Association (UNIA), a movement that was primarily nationalistic and economic in character, but which functioned as a veritable religion for many of its adherents. Its religious arm was the African Orthodox church, founded in 1920, with its membership consisting of a substantial number of Garveyites.

The African Orthodox church was not officially tied to the UNIA and never matched its mass membership. The number of African Americans who abandoned orthodox Christianity for Garvey's black nationalism cannot be determined, but the opposition of established clergymen to the movement suggests that it was a significant figure. A number of explanations are offered for the clerical opposition, among which is Garvey's insistence that God is black.[80] Whatever the reasons, Garvey's movement was too short-lived and too soon deprived of his charismatic leadership to allow any prediction of the extent to which his popularity might have eroded support for traditional religious institutions.

The Nation of Islam

A much more potent competitor for the religious allegiance of urban African Americans is the Nation of Islam, which was organized in Detroit in 1930. While Garvey's followers reinterpreted the Christian faith to harmonize it with their economic and nationalistic aims, the members of the Nation of Islam, or Black Muslims, were initially aggressive in their denunciation of Christianity as a part of the slave-making strategy of white men to deceive and subjugate blacks. The Muslims have a carefully planned social and economic theory working in conjunction with their theology and have been particularly successful in winning urban blacks to their banner. Their membership is of "undetermined thousands."[81]

The Honorable Elijah Muhammad, who for forty-one

years was the spiritual leader of the Nation of Islam, had begun to soften his criticism of Christianity and its African American adherents prior to his death in 1975. This fostered a tentative rapprochement between black Christians and Muslims in the larger urban centers. The climate for this rapprochement was created on the Christian side by the fact that most African Americans had begun to accept as axiomatic some of the teachings of Elijah Muhammad with respect to black self-awareness, and by the pervasive appeal of black liberation as a rallying point. The Black Muslims did not place their greatest emphasis upon theology when they came into prominence in the 1960s. They emphasized, rather, their social, economic, and ethnic tenets. C. Eric Lincoln, an authority on the history of the Nation of Islam, has said that it is "a dynamic social protest that moves upon a religious vehicle."[82]

With the accession of the Honorable Wallace Muhammad to the leadership of the Nation of Islam, perceptible changes have been taking place in its attitude toward non-Muslim blacks. Supreme Minister Wallace Muhammad has argued, for example, that the Nation of Islam is that "Body-Christ (Jesus) in your midst that the world has been awaiting for almost two thousand years."[83] In this view, the Nation of Islam is the fulfillment of the kingdom of God as understood in Christian theology. Muhammad writes further that

> it is time for the Black Man and the Black Woman of America to stand up and take on their Divine appointment as the Resurrected Christ, the World Saviour. You cannot escape the Divine Dictate of Almighty God, the Originator of all creation.[84]

Under the leadership of Wallace Muhammad, some of the racial exclusivism of the Nation of Islam has been repudiated, and there is a spirit of openness not characteristic of the group during the tenure of his father. The full import of the new leadership is not yet clearly apparent, but it would appear to signal a clear turn toward the development and explication of Muslim theology as interpreted by the Nation of Islam.

Judaism

Judaism has the fewest number of African American adherents of any of the major religious traditions in the United States. The reason, which is not hard to deduce, is that Judaism is essentially an ethnic and cultural religion, invested in the popular mind with social, economic, and, especially, political interests. Nevertheless, a small number of African Americans are Jews. The origins of these black Jews are quite diverse:

> Black Jewish congregations are made up of Caribbean Island Negroes who are descendants of miscegenous marriages between Sephardic Jews and blacks, descendants of slaves of Jewish-owned southern plantations, leftovers

from the Back-to-Africa Movement in the 1920s and recent recruits. The conversions began with the Great Migration in 1915 and hit their peak in the thirties and forties. They are almost solely a northern urban phenomena[sic].[85]

New York City, Detroit, Los Angeles, and Philadelphia have significant numbers of black Jews. If their origins are diverse, so are the practices of the individual congregations, which range from rigorous orthodoxy in all phases of public, family, and personal life, to impressionistic versions of Jewish ritual only. The most widely known group, the Commandment Keepers, with headquarters in Harlem, is but one among several relatively small all-black congregations. A limited number of converts to Judaism are members of integrated congregations. In the larger urban centers, some children of black Jews receive their elementary education in Hebrew day schools. African American Jews have made modest beginnings in the development of institutions that parallel those of the larger Jewish religious community, such as the Israelite Board of Rabbis in Brooklyn, organized by African Americans in 1971.

Signs that the numbers of black Jews will increase dramatically are not apparent, largely because black Jews tend to be relatively inconspicuous in the population, are not identified with popular race causes, and because their teachings run so directly counter to the rising tide of African American self-affirmation.

Other Groups

Although this essay has concentrated upon the major religious groupings among blacks, a number of smaller bodies do not fit conveniently into any of the conventional classifications. The great diversity of cults and sects, some of which number members in the thousands, are too numerous and too amorphous to be dealt with in depth here. Some of these groups have been in existence for more than half a century and are well established. Others are of more recent origin and have quite tenuous existences. The majority of these groups are Protestant in tone, derivation, spirit, and lineage, although a growing number claim African origins and purport to be unadulterated importations of black African worship, ritual, and belief. Still others have only peripheral relations to historic Protestantism or Catholicism.

One common characteristic of sect and cult groups is that they invariably are led by charismatic leaders. Father Divine, Daddy Grace, and Prophet Jones are notable examples of such leadership. These men had great numbers of followers and left behind well-established institutions with sizable constituencies. The most prominent sect leader of the television era is the Reverend Frederick J. Eikerenkoetter—better known as "Reverend Ike"—whose United Church Science of Living Institute, Inc., was founded in 1966. Reverend Ike teaches that the Bible is a "psychology book" that helps persons to believe in the fact that God lives within them, after which all things are possible. "The love of money is not the root of all evil," Reverend Ike asserts, "but the lack of money is."[86] The United Church Science of Living Institute has its headquarters in New York, but Reverend Ike carries on a nationwide ministry via television and public appearances. Membership statistics are not available, but if conspicuous wealth may be taken as an index, the number of contributors to this church must be substantial.

During the twentieth century, many African American social, political, and economic institutions and movements continued to develop. These organizations and movements earlier had taken over many of the tasks that the church had assumed because alternatives did not exist. The National Association for the Advancement of Colored People and the Urban League began to dominate the struggle for economic and civil justice early in the century. Moreover, the towering figure of Booker T. Washington and his pervasive influence, as well as the organizations that he fathered, dwarfed the efforts of groups led by less powerful men. Garvey followed Washington and was perhaps the last national leader prior to the arrival of the Reverend Martin Luther King, Jr., who could claim a mass following. Thus, as the race developed more institutions with diversified functions and purposes, the importance of the role the church had exercised in black affairs declined. The status of the clergy also was eroded during these years. Organized religion took its place as chief among many ideologies, cults, sects, and movements competing for the allegiance of urban black Americans, and seeking to minister, insofar as it could, to the ills to which they were subjected. The Christian church's distinctiveness lay in the fact that 1) it had been among the earliest of the institutions laboring for the freedom and humanity of African Americans; 2) it had the longest history in the African American community; and 3) it continued to be the most stable institution that African Americans controlled.

The civil rights struggles of the 1950s and 1960s have eclipsed all other events involving African Americans in this century. Between the years 1955 and 1966, the preeminent person in that struggle was Martin Luther King, Jr. King, a Baptist preacher with a deep Christian commitment, galvanized great numbers of persons of all races with his philosophy of social change through nonviolent means. He succeeded in mobilizing churchmen and people outside the churches in quest of his vision of social justice. He pioneered the founding of the Southern Christian Leadership Conference (SCLC) and the Student Nonviolent Coordinating Committee (SNCC). His campaigns were characterized by mass meetings reminiscent of revivals and, in the early years, he led a successful assault upon some of the more conspicuous forms of racial discrimination and segregation. King's movement was nondenominational, but it was Christian in its premises and religious in its character.[87]

On the march to Selma in 1966, the cry for "Black Power" was raised, marking the civil rights movement's turn from its conspicuous religious and Christian character. The men contesting the preeminence of Martin Luther King, Jr., were more secular, more pragmatic, and less idealistic than the preacher from Montgomery.[88]

The African American clergy's responses to the secularized initiatives of the new aspirants to leadership were ambiguous at first. King himself applauded the objectives of the black power movement, but deplored its lack of a substantive program and its violent connotations. But whatever else could be said, it was clear that African Americans, particularly the young, were impatient with the passive, patient, long-suffering strategies that King articulated and implemented. Clear, too, was the fact that the institutionalized character of racism in the United States would finally yield neither to demonstrations in the street nor to civil disobedience strategies. Moreover, when Dr. King courageously declared his opposition to the Vietnam War, he lost whatever leverage he had held in high places, and his critics were quick to cry, "I told you so!—The [King] man is not going to change." In the intervening years, the nationally organized and coordinated struggle for civil rights has virtually evaporated. However, at the local level a large share of the leadership in the struggle is still exercised by members of the clergy.

One of the consequences of the popularization of the black power slogan was the organization of the National Committee of Black Churchmen (NCBC), which came to national attention with their "Declaration on Black Power" in July of 1966. This loose organization of members of the clergy, drawn from all denominations, held conventions annually and began several projects designed to fight racism in the nation and within ecclesiastical structures, and to make common cause with Pan-African concerns.[89] Two of its most active substructures were the African Commission, which recruited and sent black Americans to Africa with the skills needed in the emerging black nations of Africa, and its Theological Commission, which developed the parameters of a black theology and spun off the Society for the Study of Black Religion, whose membership consists of persons engaged primarily in academic communities and in theological education.[90]

Another phenomenon among black Christians that was a direct result of the civil rights movement and the urban riots of the mid-1960s was the emergence of black caucuses within virtually every white denomination with blacks in their membership. Eleven of these caucuses came into existence with the avowed purpose of fighting racism within the churches. They have been funded by their own churches and have been accorded official status by them. In addition, black Christians have raised their voices within the various ecumenical bodies where they hold membership and have challenged the "benign neglect: and tacit paternalism of these bodies."[91]

As has been apparent throughout this essay, the efforts of blacks to improve their lot has more often than not been rooted in solid Christian motivation, but has found expression beyond the institutional church. This has continued to be the pattern, as it has been in the white religious community as well. SCLC, the Montgomery Improvement Association, and SNCC were conspicuously, and by design, Christian in their conception and strategies. In part, these extra-ecclesiastical bodies were founded as a means of transcending denominational allegiances, and as organizations that dropped religious qualifications for membership, yet retained a Christian posture.

SCLC, as its concerns became more and more focused on issues of economic justice, created "Operation Breadbasket," with the aggressive and charismatic Reverend Jesse Jackson as its national coordinator. In 1972, Jackson resigned this post and organized Operation PUSH (People United to Save Humanity). SCLC has continued Operation Breadbasket, but the resignation of Jackson deprived it of his creative leadership and amputated one of its strongest units—the Chicago Operation Breadbasket.[92] In Philadelphia, the Reverend Leon Sullivan founded the Opportunities Industrialization Centers (OIC), whose operations have become international in scope. OIC has remained in the hands of the clergy, and it has expanded to many cities where it is an effective instrument for training individuals for positions in industry.[93] These organizations are national in the scope of their operations and, except for the moribund SNCC, are still effective initiatives for social change. As has been suggested, there are others—less well-known—that operate on local levels.

Black Theology

The emergence of the black power slogan as a rallying point for persons and groups committed to work for the liberation of black people also signaled the beginning of the development of black theology. Black theology is clearly an effort on the part of African Americans to investigate the relationship between the black quest for power and the Gospel. The African American religious community has not produced many theologians in the formal sense of that term. African Americans clearly have had operative theologies. However, those doctrines have been informal and largely produced by clergymen in the course of their ministries; rarely have they been systematized. At the present time, several theologians, teaching in seminaries and in universities, are writing in this field.

Organized African American Christian religion has always had its detractors. Many slaves and freedmen refused to "hear" the Gospel because, as manipulated by white Christians, it appeared to rob them of their humanity and to sacralize an unjust status quo. Skepticism directed toward the church today has several aspects. Some of its critics reiterate the points raised by their forebears. Others disparage the leadership of the church, viewing it as being primarily self-serving and exploitative of its membership. Still others reject Christianity because of its identification with the white U.S. majority. They view the Christian church as collusive in a system that oppresses its nonwhite minorities and benefits from that oppression. They point to the segregated structures of the Christian establishment and cannot reconcile the Christian faith with these manifestations of prejudiced racial attitudes.

In the context of the drive for African American liberation, African American churches are arraigned for failing to contribute to that drive in proportion to their numerical strength and financial resources. These are serious charges, indeed, in a time when all institutions are being evaluated in functional terms relative to the African American's struggle for empowerment. In a narrow, present-day sense, these criticisms have a certain validity, but viewed through the spectrum of history their merit is limited. To appraise properly the contribution of black organized religion, it is necessary to recognize that it, too, has shared in the powerlessness of all African Americans. It has suffered from a leadership that, though dedicated, has been poorly prepared to cope with problems of institutionalized racism and the complex demands that an ever-growing urban constituency has laid upon it. On the whole, African American churches are poor, small, fragmented, in debt, and excluded from the sources of power that could effect change. Even so, the contribution that African American Christians are making to the struggle through their churches is substantial. They have organized and opened their facilities for community activities, such as Head Start programs, day-care centers, senior citizen programs, credit unions, employment offices, parochial schools, after-school tutorial programs, drug abuse centers, and many other programs designed to make the communities more humane. Virtually every major city has church-sponsored housing projects. Moreover, one observes a new awareness among members of the clergy of the need to equip themselves with secular skills appropriate to the demands of urban existence.

If African American churches are to remain viable in the years immediately ahead, they will require leadership that is theologically better trained and better equipped with the secular knowledge and skills requisite for dealing with the chronic problems that persist in the areas they serve, e.g., poverty, substandard housing, substance abuse, limited employment opportunities, deteriorating family structures, AIDS, injustice within law enforcement agencies and the courts, declining rates of completion at all levels of education, and the crippling lack of social infrastructures. Moreover, African American Christian believers will have to overcome, as individuals, as congregations, and as denominations, the petty differences, the self-interested activities, and the excessive religious privatism that prevent them from studying, planning, and acting together to carry out the Gospel mandates that enjoin "feeding the poor, clothing the naked, visiting prisoners, and preaching freedom to the captives." Unified strategies involving the spiritual, human, and financial assets of all groups are necessary for any effective ministry. To this end common cause must be made with persons and groups seeking to effect constructive change without sacrificing Christian integrity and faithfulness.

Institutions in the African American community that have long traditions and history have to take account of the transformed consciousness of the young who demand that they validate their existence by contributing to the resolution of problems that are both perennial and emergent. Reciting past service, remembered glory, and even present contributions will not be enough to win the allegiance of a rising generation that is struggling to rectify historic injustices in an increasingly unfavorable social, political, and economic climate. The churches have consistently nurtured the humane spirit and life of the African American community. Presently, under the dehumanizing impact of institutionalized racism, rampant substance abuse and the violence it engenders, deteriorating urban cultures, and social dislocation attributable to the technological, political, and social revolution, coupled with escalating rates of incarceration among black males, the viability of African American communities as inhabitable environments has been brought into serious question. Historically, churches have sought, as the only indigenous institutions in their communities, to combat the destructive impact of these accelerating forces. They must continue to do so, for it has long been clear that the existence of the churches, which are voluntary gatherings, is contingent upon the extent to which they contribute to the enhancement of the quality of life in the communities they serve.

Notes

1. Christianity in Africa was restricted mainly to the coastal areas around the forts during the period of the slave trade; it penetrated the interior, from which most slaves were collected for export, only very superficially. Christopher Fyfe, "Peoples of the Windward Coast A.D. 1000-1800," in J. F. Ade Ajayi and Ian Espie, *A Thousand Years of West African History* (Ibadan, Nigeria: Ibadan University Press, 1965), 161-62; and, in the same volume, A. C. F. Ryder, "Portuguese and Dutch in West Africa before 1800," 225-26.

2. J. O. Hunwick, "Islam in West Africa," in Ajayi and Espie, 113-31.

3. See John C. Hurd, *The Law of Freedom and Bondage in the United States*, 2 vols. (New York: Negro Universities Press, 1968). See also Edmund Gibson, "Two Letters of the Bishop of London" (London, 1727), as quoted in Winthrop D. Jordan, *White over Black* (Chapel Hill: University of North Carolina Press, 1968), 191.

4. Marcus J. Jernegan, "Slavery and Conversion in the Colonies," *American Historical Review* 21 (April 1916):504-37.

5. Frank J. Klingberg, *Anglican Humanitarianism in Colonial New York* (Philadelphia: 1940); and his *An Appraisal of the Negro in Colonial South Carolina* (Washington, D.C.: Associated Publishers, 1941).

6. Carter G. Woodson, *The History of the Negro Church* (Washington, D.C.: Associated Publishers, 1941), 14-16.

7. Lorenzo J. Greene, *The Negro in Colonial New England* (New York: Atheneum, 1968), 288.

8. Woodson, 35ff.; Walter H. Brooks, "The Priority of the Silver Bluff Church and Its Promoters," *The Journal of Negro History* 7, no. 2 (April 1922):172-96.

9. Richard Allen, *The Life Experience and Gospel Labors of the Rt. Rev. Richard Allen* (New York: Abingdon Press, 1970).

10. "A Minute to Be Handed to the Abolition Society for the Convention, Philadelphia, Nov. 3, 1794," as quoted in Benjamin T. Tanner, *An Apology for African Methodism* (Baltimore, 1867), 144-45.

11. Daniel A. Payne, *A History of the African Methodist Episcopal Church*, vol. 1 (Nashville, Tenn.: A.M.E. Sunday School Union, 1891), 335ff.

12. Donald J. Matthews, *Slavery and Methodism* (Princeton: Princeton University Press, 1965), 64-65.

13. "A Minute to Be Handed," 145.

14. David H. Bradley, Sr., *A History of the A.M.E. Zion Church 1796-1872* (Nashville, Tenn.: Parthenon Press, 1956), 45ff.

15. Allen, 25.

16. Adam Clayton Powell, Sr., *Upon This Rock* (New York: n.p., 1949), 2.

17. "A Minute to Be Handed," 145.

18. Ibid., 145.

19. *Articles of Association of the African Methodist Episcopal Church of the City of Philadelphia in the Commonwealth of Pennsylvania*, art. 7 (Philadelphia, 1799), 7.

20. Bradley, 52-53.

21. Payne, 1-8. The Supreme Court of Pennsylvania affirmed the right of blacks to control these aspects of their church life in 1816.

22. Matthews, 64-65.

23. Luther P. Jackson, "Religious Development of the Negro in Virginia from 1760-1860," *Journal of Negro History* 16, no. 2 (April 1931): 168-239. See also Woodson, 34-60.

24. "A Minute to Be Handed," 179.

25. Bradley, 146.

26. Few accessible records of the conferences of the A.M.E. Zion church are available covering this period. Their growth was relatively slow, and they were beset by internal problems as well. Daniel A. Payne was the first official historian of the A.M.E. church, and although his reports are abbreviated, one gets a detailed insight into its history. His volume has already been cited. For a discussion of early Baptist history, see Lewis G. Jordan, *Negro Baptist History U.S.A., 1750-1930* (Nashville, Tenn.: Sunday School Publishing Board, National Baptist Convention, n.d.).

27. "A Minute to Be Handed," 157.

28. *Discipline of the A.M.E. Church*, sec. 1, art. 3 (Nashville, Tenn.: Sunday School Union, 1948), 81.

29. For full discussion of this historic issue, see George A. Singleton, *The Romance of African Methodism* (New York: Exposition Press, 1952), 45-46, and Payne, 336ff.

30. Howard H. Bell gives a succinct account of this agitation in the introduction to the two-volume edition by Holly and Harris, which deals with proposals for emigration to Africa and to the Caribbean. James T. Holly and J. Dennis Harris, *Black Separatism and the*

Caribbean, 1860 (Ann Arbor: University of Michigan Press, 1970), 1-16. See also M. R. Delaney and Robert Campbell, *Search for a Place: Black Separatism and Africa, 1860* (Ann Arbor: University of Michigan Press, 1969), 1-22.

31. "Minutes of the Philadelphia Conference of the A.M.E. Church, 1851." Quoted in Payne, *History of A.M.E. Church*, 251.

32. Ibid., 257.

33. Tanner, 175.

34. A documentary summary of the arguments is contained in Eric L. McKittrick, *Slavery Defended: The View of the Old South* (Englewood Cliffs, N.J.: Prentice-Hall, 1963).

35. *The Methodist Review*, 1 (July 1847):321.

36. Exact figures are difficult to obtain. This educated estimate is based upon a compilation of statistics derived from numerous sources.

37. E. Franklin Frazier, *The Negro Church in America* (New York: Schocken Books, 1963), 28.

38. This fact is documented in numerous slave narratives as well as in the literature dealing specifically with the religious instruction of the slaves. See the "Reports of the Association for the Religious Instruction of Negroes in Liberty County, Georgia, 1835-1847," in which frequent allusion is made to "Watchmen" and "exhorters" among the blacks. Note also the legal restrictions imposed in several states against preaching to blacks in other than supervised situations.

39. The American Baptist Missionary Convention was organized in 1840 as a home-missions body. It was incorporated in 1848, having added a ministers Widow's Fund in 1845. Jordan contains the constitution of this body, 66-70. The concerns of this body were later broadened to include foreign territories. The members also declared themselves relative to temperance, education, and morals. "Report of the Nineteenth Anniversary of the American Baptist Missionary Convention" (New Bedford: n.p., 1959), cited in Jordan, 70.

40. Woodson, 106.

41. Daniel A. Payne, *Recollecting Seventy Years* (New York: Arno Press and *New York Times*, 1969), 82-91, 166-81.

42. Payne, *History of A.M.E. Church*, 151ff.

43. Leon F. Litwack, *North of Slavery* (Chicago: University of Chicago Press, 1961), 153-86.

44. Benjamin Quarles, *Black Abolitionists* (New York: Oxford University Press, 1969).

45. Ibid., 1-14.

46. Payne, *History of A.M.E. Church*, 28. The A.M.E. church was divided over this issue. Daniel Coker, for example, was among the first immigrants to Liberia in 1820. At the Philadelphia Conference of 1853, Dr. J. G. Bigs advised his associates not to go to Africa, but rather to go to Canada, Haiti, or the British West Indies: At various times in A.M.E. history, Bishops James A. Handy, Willis Mazrey, Daniel Payne, and H. M. Turner endorsed emigration schemes.

47. Quarles, 183-96.

48. Howard H. Bell discusses these positions as they came in to focus in national meetings in *A Survey of the Negro Convention Movement 1830-1861* (New York: Arno Press and *New York Times*, 1964). See also Carleton Mabee, *Black Freedom: The Nonviolent Abolitionists from 1830 through the Civil War* (New York: Macmillan, 1970).

49. In addition to the Methodist and Baptist churches already mentioned, there were several other groups that came into existence during the first half of the nineteenth century. One of these was the African Union First Colored Methodist Protestant Church, Inc., which was created by the merger of the African Union Church and the First Colored Methodist Protestant Church in 1866 and which is still in existence. Its founder in Wilmington, Delaware, the Reverend Peter Spencer, was at the conference at which the A.M.E. church was constituted as a denomination, but he chose not to maintain affiliation with that body because of a dispute over the discipline and polity. His congregation withdrew from the Methodist church in Wilmington for the sake of "religious liberty" in 1813. See Woodson, 93.

50. George W. Williams, *History of the Negro Race in America from 1619 to 1880* (New York: G. P. Putnam's Sons, 1883), 454.

51. Bradley, 163.

52. Richard R. Wright, Jr., *The Bishops of the African Methodist Episcopal Church* (Nashville, Tenn.: A.M.E. Sunday School Union, 1963), 333 ff.

53. Ibid., 334.

54. Charles S. Smith, *History of the A.M.E. Church 1856-1922* (Philadelphia: Book Concern of the A.M.E. Church, 1922), 94.

55. Woodson, 93.

56. Andrew E. Murray, *Presbyterians and the Negro—A History* (Philadelphia: Presbyterian Historical Society, 1966), 152-56.

57. For a full discussion of this phase of American church life, see David M. Reimers, *White Protestantism and the Negro* (New York: Oxford University Press, 1965), 25-83.

58. Henry A. Bullock, *A History of Negro Education in the South: From 1619 to the Present* (Cambridge, Mass.: Harvard University Press, 1967), 25-35.

59. Lawrence N. Jones, "They Sought a City: Black Churches and Churchmen in the Nineteenth Century," *Union Seminary Quarterly Review* 26, no. 3 (Spring 1971):271.

60. August Meier and Elliott M. Rudwick, *From Plantation to Ghetto* (New York: Hill and Wang, 1966), 142.

61. Bullock, 25ff.

62. Jordan, 63-112.

63. Ibid., 114-20. Edward A. Freeman, *The Epoch of Negro Baptists and the Foreign Missions Board* (Kansas City, Kans.: Central Seminary Press, 1953), 81-99; R. H. Boyd, *A Story of the National Baptist Publishing Board* (Nashville, Tenn.: 1924); Lauris B. Whitman, ed., *1969 Yearbook of American Churches* (New York: National Council of Churches, 1969), 59.

64. See W. E. B. Du Bois, *The Negro Church*, Atlanta University Report no. 8, 1903 (reprinted by Arno Press and *New York Times*, 1969), for a compilation of statistics relative to these matters.

65. Constance Baker Motley, "The Legal Status of the Negro in the United States" in *The American Negro Reference Book*, John P. Davis, ed. (Englewood Cliffs, N.J.: Prentice-Hall, 1966), 516.

66. Karl E. Taeuber and Alma F. Taeuber, "The Negro Population in the United States," in Davis, 102.

67. *Britannica Book of the Year, 1972*, 22.

68. James Weldon Johnson, *Black Manhattan* (New York: Atheneum, 1968), 59-159; Seth M. Scheiner, *Negro Mecca: The History of the Negro in New York City, 1865-1920* (New York: New York University Press, 1965), 15-44.

69. Benjamin E. Mays and John W. Nicholson, *The Negro's Church* (New York: Institute of Social and Religious Research, 1933), 119-23.

70. Allan H. Spear, *Black Chicago: The Making of a Negro Ghetto, 1890-1920* (Chicago: University of Chicago Press, 1969), 92.

71. Ibid., 99.

72. Scheiner, 119-23.

73. Roi Ottley and William J. Weatherby, eds., *The Negro in New York: An Informal Social History* (New York: New York Public Library, 1967), 289.

74. Joe L. Feagen, "Black Catholics in the United States: An Exploratory Analysis," in *The Black Church in America*, Hart M. Nelsen, Raytha L. Yokely, and Annie K. Nelson, eds. (New York: Basic Books, 1971), 248.

75. See Albert S. Foley, *God's Men of Color* (New York: Farrar, Straus, and Co., 1955) for a discussion of early black ordinations in the Catholic church.

76. George Shuster and Robert M. Kearns, *Statistical Profile of Black Catholics* (Washington, D.C.: Josephite Pastoral Center, 1976), 34.

77. See Fr. Lawrence Lucas, *Black Priest, White Church* (New York: Random House, 1970), for a discussion of rising black awareness in the church by an articulate spokesman and black activist.

78. John T. Nichols, *The Pentecostals* (Plainfield, N.J.: Logos International, 1966), contains a compact account of this development. See also Walter J. Hollenweger, ''Black Pentecostal Concept,'' *Concept*, special issue no. 30 (June 1970).

79. Nichols, 104.

80. E. David Cronon, *Black Moses: The Story of Marcus Garvey and the Universal Negro Improvement Association* (Madison: University of Wisconsin Press, 1969), 182.

81. C. Eric Lincoln, *The Black Muslims in America* (Boston: Beacon Press, 1961) provides a comprehensive account of the rise of the Nation of Islam. See also E. U. Essien-Udom, *Black Nationalism: A Search for an Identity in America* (New York: Dell Publishing Co., 1964).

82. C. Eric Lincoln, *Black Muslims in America*, 246.

83. Interview with C. Eric Lincoln, 29 June 1972.

84. Wallace D. Muhammad, *Muhammad Speaks*, 9 May 1975.

85. Lenora E. Berson, *The Negro and the Jews* (New York: Random House, Inc., 1971), 210.

86. Frederick J. Eikerenkoetter, *Action Magazine* 8 (July 1974):5.

87. Martin Luther King, *Stride Toward Freedom* (New York: Ballantine Books, 1958). Cf. David L. Lewis, *King: A Critical Biography* (New York: Praeger, 1970).

88. King, *Where Do We Go From Here: Chaos or Community?* (New York: Bantam Books, 1967), 27-37. Stokely Carmichael was one of the leaders of the black power movement. He delineates his views in a book that he coauthored with Charles Hamilton, *Black Power: The Politics of Liberation in America* (New York: Vintage Books, 1967).

89. The entire issue of *Renewal*, 10, no. 7 (October-November 1970), is devoted to the National Committee of Black Churchmen. It includes several of the initial documents that the NCBC issued. The NCBC has been renamed the National Conference of Black Churchmen.

90. The Society for the Study of Black Religion was organized in 1971 at the meeting of the American Academy of Religion in Atlanta.

91. Leon Watts, ''Caucuses and Caucasians,'' *Renewal* 10, no. 7 (October-November 1970):4-6.

92. *Wall Street Journal*, 16 March 1972; *New York Times*, 21 December 1971; *Amsterdam News*, 11 December 1971.

93. Leon H. Sullivan, *Build, Brother, Build* (Philadelphia: Macrae, 1969).

Bibliography

Allen, Richard. *The Life Experience and Gospel Labors of the Right Reverend Richard Allen*. New York: Abingdon Press, 1960.

Berson, Lenora. *The Negroes and the Jews*. New York: Random House, 1971.

Bradley, David H., Sr. *A History of the A.M.E. Zion Church, Vol.I 1796-1872*. Nashville: Parthenon Press, 1956.

Bragg, George F. *History of the Afro-American Group of the Episcopal Church*. Baltimore: Church Advocate Press, 1922.

Bullock, Henry A. *A History of Negro Education in the South*. Cambridge, Mass.: Harvard University Press, 1967.

Cleage, Albert E., Jr. *Black Messiah*. New York: Sheed and Ward, 1968.

————— . *Black Christian Nationalism: New Directions for the Black Church*. New York: William Morrow and Co., 1972.

Cone, James H. *Black Theology and Black Power*. New York: Seabury Press, 1969.

————— . *Liberation: A Black Theology of Liberation*. New York: J. B. Lippincott Co., 1970.

Davis, John P., ed. *The American Negro Reference Book*. Englewood Cliffs, N.J.: Prentice Hall, Inc., 1966.

Du Bois, William E. B., ed. *The Negro Church*. Atlanta University Report no. 8. 1903. Atlanta: Atlanta University Publications, II, 1903. Reprint. New York: Arno Press and *New York Times*, 1969.

Fauset, Arthur H. *Black Gods of the Metropolis*. 1944. Reprint. New York: Octagon Books, 1970.

Foley, Albert S.J. *God's Men of Color: The Colored Priests of the United States 1854-1954*. New York: Farrar, Straus, and Co., 1955.

Frazier, E. Franklin. *The Negro Church in America*. New York: Schocken Books, 1963.

Freeman, Edward A. *The Epoch of Negro Baptists and Foreign Missions Board*. Kansas City, Kans.: Central Seminary Press, 1953.

Gardiner, James A., and Deotis Roberts, eds. *Quest for a Black Theology*. Philadelphia: Pilgrim Press, 1971.

Gillard, John T., S.J. *The Catholic Church and the American Negro*. Baltimore: St. Joseph's Society Press, 1929.

————— . *Colored Catholics in the United States*. Baltimore: Josephite Press, 1941.

Greene, Lorenzo J. *The Negro in Colonial New England*. New York: Atheneum, 1968.

Hood, James W. *One Hundred Years of the African Methodist Episcopal Zion Church*. New York: A.M.E. Zion Book Concern, 1895.

Johnson, James Weldon. *Black Manhattan*. New York: Atheneum, 1968.

Jordan, Winthrop D. *White over Black: American Attitudes toward the Negro, 1550-1812*. Chapel Hill: University of North Carolina Press, 1968.

Jordon, Lewis G. *Negro Baptist History U.S.A. 1750-1930*. Nashville: Sunday School Publishing Board, National Baptist Convention, 1931.

King, Martin L., Jr. *Stride toward Freedom*. New York: Ballantine Books, 1958.

————— . *Where Do We Go from Here: Chaos or Community?* New York: Bantam Books, 1967.

Lincoln, C. Eric. *The Black Muslims in America*. Boston: Beacon Press, 1961.

Lucas, Lawrence. *Black Priest/White Church: Catholics and Racism*. New York: Random House, 1970.

Mabee, Carlton. *Black Freedom: The Nonviolent Abolitionists from 1830 through the Civil War*. New York: Macmillan, 1970.

Matthews, Donald J. *Slavery and Methodism*. Princeton: Princeton University Press, 1965.

Mays, Benjamin E. *The Negro's God*. New York: Chapman and Grimes, Inc., 1938.

Mays, Benjamin E., and John W. Nicholson. *The Negro's Church*. New York: Institute of Social and Religious Research, 1933.

Meier, August, and Elliott M. Rudwick. *From Plantation to Ghetto*. New York: Hill and Wang, 1966.

Murray, Andrew E. *Presbyterians and the Negro—A History*. Philadelphia: Presbyterian Historical Society, 1966.

Myrdal, Gunnar. *The Negro Social Structure*. Vol. 2 of *An American Dilemma*. New York: McGraw Hill Book Co., 1964.

Nelen, Hart M., Raytha L. Yokley, and Anne K. Nelsen, eds. *The Black Church in America*. New York: Basic Books, 1971.

Nichols, John T. *The Pentecostals*. Plainfield, N.J.: Logos International, 1966.

Payne, Daniel A. *A History of the African Methodist Episcopal Church 1816-1856*. Nashville: A.M.E. Sunday School Union, 1891.

Otley, Roi, and William J. Weatherby, eds. *The Negro in New York: An Informal Social History*. New York: New York Public Library, 1976.

Phillips, Charles H. *History of the Colored Methodist Episcopal Church in America*. Jackson, Tenn.: Publishing House of the C.M.E. Church, 1925.

Powell, Adam Clayton, Sr. *Upon This Rock*. New York: n.p., 1949.

Quarles, Benjamin. *Black Abolitionists*. New York: Oxford University Press, 1969.

Reimers, David M. *White Protestantism and the Negro*. New York: Oxford University Press, 1965.

Scheiner, Seth M. *Negro Mecca: The History of the Negro in New York City, 1865-1920*. New York: New York University Press, 1965.

Shuster, George, and Robert M. Kearns. *Statistical Profile of Black Catholics*. Washington, D.C.: Josephite Pastoral Center, 1976.

Singleton, George A. *The Romance of African Methodism*. New York: Exposition Press, 1952.

Smith, Charles S. *A History of the African Methodist Episcopal Church, 1856-1922*. Philadelphia: Book Concern of the A.M.E. Church, 1922.

Spear, Allan H. *Black Chicago: The Making of a Negro Ghetto, 1890-1920*. Chicago: University of Chicago Press, 1969.

Tanner, Benjamin T. *An Apology for African Methodism*. Baltimore: n.p., 1867.

Washington, Joseph R., Jr. *Black Religion: The Negro and Christianity in the United States*. Boston: Beacon Press, 1966.

————— . *The Politics of God*. Boston: Beacon Press, 1967.

Williams, George W. *History of the Negro Race in America from 1619 to 1880*. New York: G.P. Putnam's Sons, 1883.

Woodson, Carter G. *The Negro Church*. Washington, D.C.: Associated Publishers, 1921.

Wright, Richard R., Jr. *The Bishops of the African Methodist Episcopal Church*. Nashville: A.M.E. Sunday School Union, 1963.

Part 1
African American Religious Bodies

The following religious bodies are African American in origin, and are both Christian and non-Christian. Most are classified as a *denomination*, a religious group or community that maintains a corporate fellowship, shares basic doctrinal beliefs, and has a distinctive name. The growth and development of a denomination is generally stable and is not under the influence of charismatic individuals. Some of the religious bodies might be considered a *sect*, an autonomous religious group whose adherents recognize a special set of teachings or practices. All have been included as equally important and viable religious bodies. They are presented in letter-by-letter alphabetical order within each respective category.

Baptist

Black Primitive Baptists

c/o Primitive Baptist Library
Route 2
Elon College, NC 27244
Mrs. Mabel Berry

Black Primitive Baptists organized into separate congregations after the Civil War, before which time they were members of predominantly white Primitive Baptist associations worshipping in separate, segregated meeting houses. The doctrine and practices of black Primitive Baptists are the same as regular Primitive Baptists. In the early 1950s, the late Elder W. J. Berry, editor of *Old Faith Contender*, partially underwrote *The Primitive Messenger*, but it was published for only four years.

Group Type: Denomination
Membership: In the early 1970s, approximately 5 churches (with 20 members each) in each of 43 associations; about 3,000 persons

General Association of Baptists in Kentucky

1715 West Chestnut Street
Louisville, KY 40203
(502) 583-6939
Dr. H. B. Harris, Moderator

The General Association of Baptists in Kentucky was founded on August 16, 1865 (the Wednesday before the third Sunday), at the Fifth Street Baptist Church in Louisville, Kentucky. Twelve "messengers" from Fifth Street Baptist Church, Green Street Baptist Church of Louisville, York Street Baptist Church of Louisville, First Baptist Church of Danville, First Baptist Church of Greensburg, and Pleasant Green Baptist Church of Lexington met with the Reverend H. Adams, pastor of Fifth Street, to form the State Convention of Colored Baptists in Kentucky. The organization purchased its first piece of property in 1866, according to a deed dated August 21 of that year. Its first report of missionary work was made by the Reverend R. Martin, who collected $22.98. At the meeting in August 1868, the reported membership was 6,260 persons from 27 churches. The name was changed to its current one at this meeting.

The purpose of the association is to promote Christian education, stewardship, missions, and sound doctrine. It also attempts to inspire generations to build upon a solid foundation. The organization meets annually in August with approximately 1,500 persons attending. It also holds the Annual Black Baptist Pastors' Conference, which averages over three thousand participants. It has published commemorative volumes of the association's history in 1915, 1943, and 1968, and currently publishes *The American Baptist*, a weekly newspaper. Various brochures and pamphlets are also regularly published. The association founded the Simmons Bible College in Louisville in 1879. It is an accredited Bible college and offers four certificate and degree programs.

Group Type: Denomination specific; state group or convention
Founded: August 16, 1865
Membership: 160,000 persons in 639 congregations
Publications: *The American Baptist*, a weekly religious newspaper; *The Golden Jubilee* (1915); *The Diamond Jubilee* (1943); *The Centennial Volume* (1968)
Meetings: Annual Black Pastors' Conference in February

Lott Carey Baptist Foreign Mission Convention

1501 11th Street, NW
Washington, DC 20001
(202) 667-8493

The Reverend Dr. Wendell C. Somerville, Executive
  Secretary-Treasurer

The Lott Carey Convention was named for the Reverend Lott
Carey, a former slave, who was born near Richmond, Virginia.
Carey sailed for West Africa on January 16, 1821, as the first
American missionary to Africa. The convention was founded
in a meeting at Shiloh Baptist Church in Washington, D.C. in
December, 1897. The founders of the convention included many
of the distinguished black Baptist pastors of the time: the Rev-
erends C. S. Brown, Richard Spiller, P. F. Morris, H. L. Barco,
W. T. Johnson, A. B. Collins, C. C. Somerville, J. H. Carter,
R. H. Walker, W. M. Alexander, J. M. Armstead, A. W.
Pegues, Z. D. Lewis, and Joseph E. Jones.

The Lott Carey Convention is the only distinct African American foreign mission convention in the United States. Unlike
other missionary bodies, this organization is completely autonomous from a denominational convention. It includes individuals and representatives from local Baptist congregations,
associations, and state organizations. Sixteen states and the
District of Columbia are affiliated with Lott Carey. The parent
body and the auxiliaries have separate officers who are elected
annually.

The Convention supports 133 missionaries in Guyana, India,
Kenya, Liberia, and Nigeria. The work of Lott Carey is performed 1) through evangelism—teaching non-Christians how
to know Jesus Christ, 2) through education—enlightening minds
by training nationals of various lands for leadership; 3) through
the creation of Ministries of Healing Communities, including
three leprosariums in India, and clinics at each mission station;
and 4) by contributing substantial sums to numerous hunger
crisis areas. Most recently, the Convention has begun contributing to AIDS research, in light of its devastating effects on
Africans.

The Convention consists of the Parent Body, the Women's
Auxiliary, the Laymen's League, the Youth Department, and
the Annual Christian Youth Seminar. The Parent Body and
Auxiliaries meet jointly on an annual basis. The Convention
meets annually in various cities on the Tuesday before the first
Sunday in September. It also publishes the *Lott Carey Herald*.

Group Type: Denomination specific; mission/philanthropic
Founded: December, 1897
Publications: *Lott Carey Herald*, a quarterly publication
Meetings: Meets annually on the Tuesday before the first
               Sunday in September

National Baptist Convention of America, Inc.

1540 Pierre Avenue
Shreveport, LA 71103
(318) 221-2629
The Reverend Dr. E. Edward Jones, President
The Reverend Dr. E. E. Stafford, Corresponding Secretary

The National Baptist Convention of America, Inc. (commonly
referred to as the "unincorporated" Baptist Convention and for-
merly known as the Boyd convention), traces its history to the
November 24, 1880, founding of the Baptist Foreign Mission
Convention of the United States in Montgomery, Alabama. The
National Baptist Convention, U.S.A., was formally established

in 1895 by the merger of the Baptist Foreign Mission Convention
of the United States with two other conventions—the National
Baptist Educational Convention founded in 1893 and the American National Baptist Convention founded in 1886.

In 1896, the National Baptist Convention, U.S.A., instructed
its Home Mission Board to establish a publishing house and
begin printing a series of Sunday School materials for use in
its various churches. The publishing house was established in
Nashville, Tennessee, with the Reverend Dr. Richard Henry
Boyd in charge.

When the convention met in Chicago for its annual meeting
in 1915, two problems prompted immediate controversy. The
first was the disagreement over whether the Reverend E. C.
Morris was to continue in office as president of the convention,
and whether he had, as some accused, arranged to have non-
supporters barred from the convention hall.

The second problem was confusion relating to the publishing
house, then alleged to be worth some $350,000. A series of
efforts to bring it more closely under the control of the convention had revealed that the publishing house and its copyrights were probably not the property of the convention, but
of the Reverend Richard Henry Boyd, chairman of the board
of the publishing house. Since the publishing house was incorporated under Tennessee law while the convention operated
as an unincorporated body, the National Baptist Convention,
U.S.A., was hard-pressed to elect members to the board or to
control the board.

Under the shadow of these two clouds, Boyd's supporters
began meeting at Salem Baptist Church in Chicago, Illinois.
They successfully sought an injunction against the Morris faction, but it was subsequently overturned; the Boyd faction was
eventually ruled a "rump" convention. Nevertheless, on September 9, 1915, the National Baptist Convention, Unincorporated, was born out of the Boyd faction and is now identified
as the National Baptist Convention of America, Inc. The directorate of the National Baptist Convention of America, Inc.,
was incorporated in Shreveport, Louisiana, in 1987. One of
the convention's first acts was to determine that the publishing
house was not the property of any convention.

Over the summer of 1988, controversy over the control of
the National Baptist Sunday Church School and Baptist Training Union Congress and the National Baptist Publishing Board,
Inc., became an issue, as it had been in 1915. This congress,
started by the Reverend Richard Henry Boyd in 1906, was a
part of the National Baptist Convention of America, Inc. Some
members of the convention wanted to gain greater control over
the planning, execution, and profits of the convention's annual
Sunday School leader training meeting. This ultimately resulted
in the formation of a new convention—the National Missionary
Baptist Convention of America.

The division resulted from an official convention session of
the National Baptist Convention of America, Inc., in San Antonio, Texas, in 1988, attended by over seven hundred church
leaders from across the country. It was determined that the
National Baptist Convention of America, Inc., would start a
Sunday school congress to be controlled by the convention
itself. This, in effect, severed ties with the Boyd-controlled
congress and publishing house. Five hundred church leaders
subsequently met in Dallas, Texas, in November 1988 to form
a new organization, intended to remain committed to the National Baptist Publishing Board, Inc., and the National Baptist

Sunday Church School and Baptist Training Union Congress, still controlled by the Boyd family. The parent body—the National Baptist Convention of America, Inc.—thus attempted to gain control over the publishing aspect of the convention, ironically after declaring upon its own inception that the publishing house would not be the property of any convention.

The National Baptist Convention of America, Inc., assumes the same doctrinal position as the National Baptist Convention, U.S.A., Inc. The members accept the scripture as divinely inspired and infallible, and they believe in justification through faith and salvation by grace. To be saved, sinners must be born again through the baptism of the Holy Spirit.

The National Baptist Convention of America, Inc., has eight boards and eleven auxiliaries. The boards include: Foreign Mission, Benevolent, National Baptist Congress of Christian Workers, Union Congress, Evangelical, Home Mission, Education, and the Board of Managers. These boards, although affiliated with the convention, are autonomous in governing structure. The auxiliaries include: the Senior Women's Missionary Auxiliary, the Junior Women's Missionary Auxiliary, the Brotherhood Auxiliary, the Ushers' Auxiliary, the Nurses' Auxiliary, the National Baptist Youth Convention, Field Missionaries, Men on Christian Assignment, the Pastor's Conference, the Ministers' Wives Conference, and the Matrons' Auxiliary.

The National Baptist Convention of America, Inc., maintains missions in Ghana, West Africa; Cameroon, West Africa; Haiti; St. Ann, Jamaica; Kingston, Jamaica; the Virgin Islands; and Panama. With an annual disbursement running over three-quarters of a million dollars, foreign missions constitute the single largest disbursement item in the Convention. The Foreign Mission Board publishes a newsletter, *Go Preach*. The Evangelism Board of the Convention holds its own annual meeting as well as miniconferences. It publishes a newsletter, *The Crier*. Additionally, the Convention office produces *The Lantern*, the presidential newsletter.

Currently, the Convention is working in concert with the Progressive Baptists and the National Baptists, U.S.A., in a project to explore issues of African American survival. The Convention's Commission on Social Justice is devoting its time and effort to this undertaking and is developing papers on African American women's issues; African American male issues; alcohol, drugs and violence; human sexuality; ministries with single adults and with prisoners; marriage enrichment; homeless families; pastoral care and stress; global issues including South Africa, Nicaragua, and the Middle East; and racism and racial violence.

The National Baptist Convention of America, Inc., helps to support fifteen institutions of higher learning including Union Baptist Seminary, Florida Memorial College, and Morris College. Today, the total membership of the Convention is approximately 3,500,000 persons, representing over twenty-five hundred churches and eight thousand ordained clergy. It is strongest in California, South Carolina, Texas, Mississippi, Florida, and Louisiana. The Reverend Dr. E. Edward Jones is the president and the Reverend Dr. E. E. Stafford is the corresponding secretary.

Group Type: Denomination
Founded: Organized November, 1880; incorporated September 9, 1915
Membership: 3,500,000 persons in 2,500 churches with 8,000 ordained clergy, as of September, 1987

Publications: *The Lantern*, the presidential newsletter; *The Crier*, a newspaper published by the Evangelical Board; *Go Preach*, a newsletter published by the Foreign Mission Board; the *Official Journal*, published by the convention; for cassette copies of the convention proceedings (includes sermons, musicals, lectures, etc.), contact the Reverend Stephen Thurston, third vice-president, at (312) 846-3799, or write in care of the New Covenant Baptist Church, 740 E. 77th Street, Chicago, IL 60619 (catalogs are available)
Meetings: Annual board meeting in February; Congress and Board meeting in June; Foreign Mission Board meeting in December; Evangelical Board meeting in December; and the annual session in September

State Conventions and District Associations of the National Baptist Convention of America, Inc.

American Baptist District Association—Texas

7121 Parker Road
Houston, TX 77016
The Reverend Dr. R. S. Thomas, Moderator

Group Type: Denomination specific; district association/annual conference

American Baptist Eastern District Association—Texas

6319 Laura Koppe Road
Houston, TX 77016

Group Type: Denomination specific; district association/annual conference

American Baptist Progressive State Convention of Texas

7121 Parker Road
Houston, TX 77016
The Reverend Dr. R. S. Thomas, President

Group Type: Denomination specific; state group or convention

American Baptist State Convention—Texas

92826 Lawton Street
Corpus Christi, TX 78405
The Reverend Dr. H. C. Dilworth, President

Group Type: Denomination specific; state group or convention
Membership: 256 churches and 16 associations as of September, 1987

Argenta District Association—Arkansas

5100 Summertree Court, SA 25
N. Little Rock, AR 72116
The Reverend Arnette Dotson, Moderator

Group Type: Denomination specific; district association/annual conference

Baptist Education and Missionary Convention of South Carolina

1315 Bunche Avenue
Greenwood, SC 29646
The Reverend Edward F. Johnson, President

Group Type: Denomination specific; state group or convention

Baptist Missionary and Educational Convention of Louisiana

P.O. Box 37265
Shreveport, LA 71103
(318) 221-2629
The Reverend Dr. E. Edward Jones

Group Type: Denomination specific; state group or convention
Founded: 1953
Membership: 10,000 persons, 33 churches, and 50 ordained clergy as of October 12, 1987
Publications: Baptist Missionary and Educational Journal
Meetings: Annual meeting the last week in June

Baptist Missionary District Association—Texas

7101 Laura Koppe Road
Houston, TX 77028
The Reverend G. T. Hutchinson

Group Type: Denomination specific; district association/annual conference

Bossier Education District Association—Louisiana

5000 McDaniel Drive
Shreveport, LA 71109
c/o Ms. Edna Morgan

Group Type: Denomination specific; district association/annual conference

California Baptist State Convention

719 Crosby Street
San Diego, CA 92113
(619) 233-6487
The Reverend Dr. S. M. Lockridge, President

Group Type: Denomination specific; state group or convention
Membership: 175,000 persons, 9 associations, and 344 churches as of September, 1987

Capitol City District Association—Indiana

1048 W. 73rd Street
Indianapolis, IN 46260
The Reverend J. C. Davis, Moderator

Group Type: Denomination specific; district association/annual conference

Central Baptist District Association—Illinois

1517 W. 79th Street
Chicago, IL 60620
(312) 994-7911
The Reverend W. D. Collins, Moderator

Group Type: Denomination specific; district association/annual conference
Founded: 1920
Meetings: Annual meeting in July

Central District Association—Texas

Route 3, Box 146
Caldwell, TX 77836
The Reverend D. N. Jones, Moderator

Group Type: Denomination specific; district association/annual conference

Central District Association—Texas

P. O. Box 656
La Marque, TX 77568
The Reverend J. P. Davis, Moderator

Group Type: Denomination specific; district association/annual conference

Central Missionary Baptist Convention of Texas

5902 Beall Street
Houston, TX 77091
(713) 692-5333
The Reverend Floyd N. Williams, Sr., President

Group Type: Denomination specific; state group or convention
Founded: 1981
Membership: 30,000 persons, 75 churches, and 75 ordained clergy as of August 11, 1987
Publications: A newsletter
Meetings: Annual meeting on the Monday after the third Sunday in October

Central Missionary Baptist District Association—Texas

1101 N. Walters Street
San Antonio, TX 78202
The Reverend J. J. Rector, Moderator

Group Type: Denomination specific; district association/annual conference

Christian Ministers Missionary Baptist Association—Louisiana

Carlisle Post Office
Phoenix, LA 70042
(504) 333-4402
The Reverend Percy Murphy Griffin, Moderator

Group Type: Denomination specific; district association/annual conference
Founded: 1951
Membership: 2,015 persons, 13 churches, and 22 ordained clergy as of September, 1987
Publications: The Plaquemines Parish Gazette and The Plaquemines Watchman, newspapers
Meetings: Group meets quarterly in January, April, July, and November

Cumberland River, South Kentucky, Middle Tennessee Baptist District Association

1325 Dodd Street
Clarksville, TN 37040
(615) 648-3424
The Reverend Leroy Burgess, Moderator

Group Type: Denomination specific; district association/annual conference
Founded: 1875
Membership: 5,000 persons, 40 churches, and 60 ordained clergy as of November 9, 1987
Meetings: Annual meeting and Women's Convention meet the third week in August; Sunday School and B.T.U. Congress meets the third week in June; Pastor's Conference meets the second week in April

Dal-Worth District Association—Texas

2837 Prosperity Avenue
Dallas, TX 75216
The Reverend W. H. Harlan, Moderator

Group Type: Denomination specific; district association/annual conference
Founded: 1962
Membership: 2,400 persons, 16 churches, and 32 ordained clergy as of September 18, 1987
Publications: Cedars of Dal-Worth
Meetings: Annual meeting the Tuesday after the first Sunday in August; Christian education meeting the first Tuesday in June

Eastern Progressive District Association—Michigan

1361 Harry Street
Ypsilanti, MI 48198
The Reverend Dr. H. E. Leggett, Moderator

Group Type: Denomination specific; district association/annual conference

Eastern Seventh District Association—Louisiana

410 E. Long Street
Ville Platte, LA 70586
The Reverend Dr. M. L. Thomas, Moderator

Group Type: Denomination specific; district association/annual conference

East Florida Bethany Baptist District Association

4820 Lockley Street
Jacksonville, FL 32200
The Reverend B. H. Hartley, Moderator

Group Type: Denomination specific; district association/annual conference

East Pearl River District Association—Mississippi

Route 3, Box 280
Foxworth, MS 39483
The Reverend Dr. L. Z. Blankenship, Moderator

Group Type: Denomination specific; district association/annual conference

Education and Missionary Baptist State Convention—South Carolina

Columbia, SC 29208
The Reverend Dr. J. O. Rich, President

Group Type: Denomination specific; state group or convention
Membership: 400,000 persons, 170 associations, and 1,700 churches as of September 1988

Education Missionary Baptist Association—Louisiana

130 Howard Road
Pineville, LA 71360
The Reverend W. Williams, Moderator

Group Type: Denomination specific; district association/annual conference

Equal Right District Association—Florida

3007 Forrestal Street
Pensacola, FL 32506
The Reverend Deaser Smith, Moderator

Group Type: Denomination specific; district association/annual conference

First South Florida Missionary Baptist Association

1521 Providence Road
Lakeland, FL 33805
(813) 680-2312
The Reverend Paul H. Jackson, Moderator

Group Type: Denomination specific; district association/annual conference
Founded: 1889
Membership: Approximately 35,000 persons, 96 churches, and 158 ordained clergy as of October 1, 1987
Publications: A History of First South Florida, a history by A. S. Bentley, and *The First South Florida Associational Voice*
Meetings: Annual meeting on the Wednesday before the third Sunday in November

First Sweet Pilgrim District Association—Mississippi

Route 2, Box 130 B
Seminary, MS 39479
The Reverend Dr. S. L. Johnson, Moderator

Group Type: Denomination specific; district association/annual conference

Friendship District Association—Illinois

3352 W. Fifth Avenue
Chicago, IL 60624
The Reverend J. R. McCoy, Moderator

Group Type: Denomination specific; district association/annual conference

Garden State Convention of New Jersey

522 E. 7th Street
Plainfield, NJ 07060
The Reverend John P. Terry, President

Group Type: Denomination specific; state group or convention

General Baptist Convention of Missouri and Kansas

2310 East Linwood Boulevard
Kansas City, MO 64109
(816) 923-3689
Dr. Wallace S. Hartsfield

Group Type: Denomination specific; state group or convention
Founded: 1918
Membership: 17,081 persons, 75 churches, and approximately 300 ordained clergy as of August 15, 1987
Publications: Whence Came They, a history published in 1968, Thelma Dumas, editor; *Official Journal [of] the General Baptist Convention of Missouri, Kansas, and Nebraska*, Jessie Mae Egans
Meetings: Annual meeting in October

General Baptist Convention of the Pacific Northwest

3138 N. Vancouver Avenue
Portland, OR 97227
The Reverend Dr. O. B. Williams, President

Group Type: Denomination specific; state group or convention

Membership: 6,000 persons, 50 churches, and 3 associations as of September, 1987

General Baptist State Convention of New York, Inc.

1515 Bedford Avenue
Brooklyn, NY 11216
The Reverend Dr. J. D. Washington, President

Group Type: Denomination specific; state group or convention

General Baptist State Convention of North Carolina, Inc.

603 South Wilmington Street
Raleigh, NC 27601
The Reverend J. B. Humphrey, President
(704) 372-1075
The Reverend Dr. C. C. Craig, Executive Director
(919) 821-7466

Group Type: Denomination specific; state group or convention
Founded: 1867; incorporated in 1947
Membership: 425,000 persons, 1,700 churches, and 1,200 ordained clergy as of December 8, 1987
Publications: *The Baptist Informer*, a general newspaper
Meetings: Annual meeting held in July

General Bowen Missionary Baptist District Association—Texas

1283 Cedar Street
Beaumont, TX 77701
The Reverend Dr. G. W. Daniels, Moderator
(409) 833-3945

Group Type: Denomination specific; district association/annual conference
Founded: 1900
Membership: 18,000 persons, 50 churches, 60 ordained clergy, and 15 licentiates as of September, 1987
Meetings: Spring board meeting the first Tuesday through Thursday in April; Fall board meeting the second Tuesday through Thursday in November; and annual session the second week in August

General Missionary Baptist Convention of Colorado

605 Plaid
Colorado Springs, CO 80901
The Reverend E. Ray Johnson, President

Group Type: Denomination specific; state group or convention
Membership: 2,091 persons, 13 churches, and 2 associations as of September, 1987

General Missionary Baptist Convention of Oklahoma

1409 N.E. 9th Street
Oklahoma City, OK 73117
The Reverend Dr. E. H. Hill, President

Group Type: Denomination specific; state group or convention
Membership: 6,000 persons, 127 churches, and 7 associations as of September, 1987

General Missionary Baptist State Convention of Arizona

2006 E. Broadway Road
Phoenix, AZ 85040
The Reverend Dr. Bernard Black, President

Group Type: Denomination specific; state group or convention
Membership: 6,000 persons and 44 churches as of September, 1987

General Missionary Baptist State Convention of Arkansas

1722 Gaines Street
Little Rock, AR 72206
The Reverend Clyde E. Kelly, President

Group Type: Denomination specific; state group or convention
Membership: 3,200 persons, 40 churches, and 2 associations

General Progressive State Convention of Mississippi, Inc.

Route 3, Box 164-C
Aberdeen, MS 39730
(601) 369-6260
The Reverend L. C. Cook, President

Group Type: Denomination specific; state group or convention
Founded: 1916
Membership: 26,527 persons, 117 churches, 3 associations, and 91 ordained clergy as of August 18, 1987
Meetings: Annual meeting from Wednesday through Saturday after the second Sunday in July

Good Hope Western District Association—Texas

P.O. Box 644
Killeen, TX 76541
The Reverend R. A. Abercrombie, Moderator

Group Type: Denomination specific; district association/annual conference

Greater South Florida Missionary Baptist Association

609 S.W. 9th Street
Belle Glade, FL 33403
The Reverend J. B. Adams, Moderator

Group Type: Denomination specific; district association/annual conference

Greater Unity District Association—Texas

4445 Woodhollow Drive, #360
Dallas, TX 75237
The Reverend C. L. Veasy, Moderator

Group Type: Denomination specific; district association/annual conference

Harmony District Association—Texas

2612 Willis Point Court
Fort Worth, TX 76110
The Reverend T. W. Pope, Moderator

Group Type: Denomination specific; district association/annual conference

Illinois District Association

1049 W. Marquette Road
Chicago, IL 60621
The Reverend Clifford Bolden, Moderator

Group Type: Denomination specific; district association/annual conference

Illinois National Baptist State Convention

3993 South King Drive
Chicago, IL 60653
(312) 536-2619
The Reverend Luke W. Mingo, President

Group Type: Denomination specific; state group or convention
Founded: 1914
Membership: Approximately 3,500 persons, 104 churches, and 250 ordained clergy as of September, 1987
Publications: INBSC Newsletter
Meetings: Annual meeting during the third week in July

Independent Baptist District Association—Louisiana

2011 Weinstock Street
Shreveport, LA 71103
The Reverend Dr. J. E. Martin, Moderator

Group Type: Denomination specific; district association/annual conference

Independent Missionary Baptist General Association—Texas

3221 Southmore Boulevard
Houston, TX 77004
The Reverend Dr. E. S. Branch, Moderator

Group Type: Denomination specific; state group or convention
Membership: 353,798 persons, 1,157 churches, and 60 associations as of September, 1987

Independent 13th District Association #2—Louisiana

2519 Milam Street
Shreveport, LA 71103
The Reverend L. Jones, Moderator

Group Type: Denomination specific; district association/annual conference

Indiana Missionary Baptist State Convention

3148 E. Fall Creek Parkway North Drive
Indianapolis, IN 46205
The Reverend Dr. F. Benjamin Davis, President
(317) 636-6622

Group Type: Denomination specific; state group or convention
Membership: 18,706 persons, 109 churches, and 5 associations as of September, 1987

Kansas General Missionary Baptist State Convention

1902 N. Chautauqua Street
Wichita, KS 67214
(316) 685-2917
The Reverend D. D. Miller, President

Group Type: Denomination specific; state group or convention
Founded: 1979
Membership: 5,276 persons, 18 churches, and 27 ordained clergy as of August 16, 1987
Publications: Religion, published by Kansas State Globe, 2225 E. 21st Street, Wichita, KS 67214, the Reverend D. D. Miller, associate editor
Meetings: Annual meeting the week following the third Sunday in August

Kentucky State Baptist Convention

1226 Algonquin Parkway
Louisville, KY 40208
The Reverend A. J. Elmore, President

Group Type: Denomination specific; state group or convention

Kissimmee Valley District Association—Florida

1321 N.W. Sistrunk Boulevard
Fort Lauderdale, FL 33313
The Reverend Wilson Davis, Moderator

Group Type: Denomination specific; district association/annual conference

Lincoln District Association—Texas

609 W. Benkins
Hearne, TX 77859
The Reverend C. M. Roach, Moderator

Group Type: Denomination specific; district association/annual conference

Long Island Progressive Missionary Baptist Association—New York

147 Wright Street
North Babylon, NY 11704
The Reverend Dr. R. Hamilton, Moderator

Group Type: Denomination specific; district association/annual conference

Louisiana Freedmen Missionary Baptist General Convention

2108 Jackson Avenue
New Orleans, LA 70113
The Reverend Dr. W. E. Hausey, President
(504) 238-0572

Group Type: Denomination specific; state group or convention
Founded: June 18, 1880
Membership: Approximately 50,000 persons, 75 churches, and 2,000 ordained clergy as of August 20, 1987
Meetings: Annual meeting on the Monday after the third Sunday in May

Louisiana Home and Foreign Mission Baptist State Convention

307 LaSalle Street
New Orleans, LA 70151
The Reverend Dr. F. H. Dunn, President

Group Type: Denomination specific; state group or convention
Founded: 1917
Membership: 47,000 persons, 205 churches, and 17 associations as of July, 1987
Meetings: Annual session the last Sunday in July

Maryland Baptist State Convention

1220 N. Chester Street
Baltimore, MD 21213
(301) 732-3494
The Reverend Dr. Harlie W. Wilson II, President

Group Type: Denomination specific; state group or convention
Membership: 4,000 persons and 18 churches as of September, 1987

Michigan General Baptist State Convention

1361 Harry Street
Ypsilanti, MI 48198
The Reverend Dr. H. E. Leggett, President

Group Type: Denomination specific; state group or convention
Membership: 162,000 persons, 42 churches, and 4 associations as of September, 1987

Missionary General State Convention of Tennessee

2501 Meharry Boulevard
Nashville, TN 37208
The Reverend James Thomas, President

Group Type: Denomination specific; state group or convention

Mount Hermon Baptist District Association—Louisiana

c/o 5821 Ledbetter Street
Shreveport, LA 71108
(318) 636-4930
The Reverend Joe Roscoe Gant, Jr., Moderator

Group Type: Denomination specific; district association/annual conference
Founded: 1941
Membership: 4,000 persons, 14 churches, and 25 ordained clergy as of October 12, 1987
Meetings: Annual meeting from Tuesday through Saturday following the fourth Sunday in October

Mount Olive Baptist District Association—Illinois

1026 Newby Avenue
Mt. Vernon, IL 62864
(618) 242-3145
The Reverend William R. Lash, Moderator

Group Type: Denomination specific; district association/annual conference
Founded: 1837
Membership: 22 churches and 27 ordained clergy as of December 3, 1987
Publications: An official journal
Meetings: Annual meeting the third week in August

Mount Pilgrim Missionary Baptist District Association— Florida

1130 N. Webster Avenue
Lakeland, FL 33805
The Reverend N. S. Sanders, Moderator

Group Type: Denomination specific; district association/annual conference

Mount Zion Cossa Valley District Association—Alabama

1600 First Court, W.
Birmingham, AL 35222
The Reverend J. Whetstone, Moderator

Group Type: Denomination specific; district association/annual conference

Mount Zion District Association—California

928 24th Street
Oakland, CA 44607
The Reverend E. L. Thomas, Moderator

Group Type: Denomination specific; district association/annual conference

Mount Zion District Association —Texas

P.O. Box 961
Cuero, TX 77054
The Reverend Dr. J. D. White, Moderator

Group Type: Denomination specific; district association/annual conference

Mount Zion Missionary Convention—Delaware

Dover, DE
The Reverend Dr. J. H. Williams, President

Group Type: Denomination specific; state group or convention
Membership: 2,800 persons in 9 churches as of September, 1987

Nashville City District Association—Tennessee

1303 Hawkins Street
Nashville, TN 37203
The Reverend James C. Turner, Moderator

Group Type: Denomination specific; district association/annual conference

Nashville City Mothers Baptist District Association— Tennessee

907 15th Avenue, S.
Nashville, TN 37212
The Reverend James C. Turner, Moderator

Group Type: Denomination specific; district association/annual conference

New Bethel District Association—Alabama

2219 21st Street, SE
Birmingham, AL 35211
The Reverend Q. E. Hammonds, Moderator

Group Type: Denomination specific; district association/annual conference

New Central Missionary Baptist District Association— Florida

107 4th Street
Winter Garden, FL 32787
The Reverend D. L. Washington, Moderator

Group Type: Denomination specific; district association/annual conference

New Era Progressive Baptist State Convention of Alabama

3405 31st Place, North
Birmingham, AL 35207
The Reverend Dr. J. E. Townsend, President

Group Type: Denomination specific; state group or convention
Membership: 21,852 persons, 138 churches, and 7 associations as of September, 1987

New Gulf Coast District Association—Florida

3815 2nd Drive
Panama City, FL 32401
The Reverend H. C. McCray, Jr., Moderator

Group Type: Denomination specific; district association/annual conference

New Light District Association—Louisiana

632 Robinson Street
DeRidder, LA 70634
The Reverend W. W. Battier, Moderator

Group Type: Denomination specific; district association/annual conference

New Unity District Association—Illinois

643 N. Cicero Avenue
Chicago, IL 60644
The Reverend Samuel Evans, Moderator

Group Type: Denomination specific; district association/annual conference

North Mount Olive District Association—Mississippi

Route 2, Box 222D
Houston, MS 38851
The Reverend Dr. M. D. Bowen, Moderator
(601) 456-2936

Group Type: Denomination specific; district association/annual conference
Founded: 1886
Membership: 4,400 persons, 43 churches, and 30 ordained clergy as of September, 1987
Meetings: Spring session held the fourth Saturday in April; general session held Wednesday through Saturday after the third Sunday in July

North Texas District Association—Texas

2823 N. Houston Street
Fort Worth, TX 76106
The Reverend A. E. Chew, Moderator

Group Type: Denomination specific; district association/annual conference

Northeastern District Baptist Association—Indiana

705 West 26th Street
Marion, IN 46953
(317) 664-1731
The Reverend Dr. J. D. Williams, Moderator

Group Type: Denomination specific; district association/annual conference
Founded: 1907
Membership: 9,000 persons, 36 churches, 76 ordained clergy, and 25 licentiates as of August 13, 1987
Meetings: Annual meeting in April

Northwestern District Association—Indiana

2211 North Olive Street
South Bend, IN 46628
(219) 234-2776
The Reverend Booker T. West, Moderator

Group Type: Denomination specific; district association/annual conference
Founded: 1967
Membership: 17 churches as of October 19, 1987
Meetings: Quarterly meetings; annual meeting for one week beginning on the second Saturday in May

Northwood River District Association—Illinois

415 W. Englewood Avenue
Chicago, IL 60621
(312) 873-4433
The Reverend Dr. W. N. Daniel, Moderator

Group Type: Denomination specific; district association/annual conference

Ohio Baptist General Convention

48 Parkwood Avenue
Columbus, OH 43203
(614) 253-5563
The Reverend Dr. George W. Lucas, President
The Reverend Dr. A. Wilson Wood, Executive Director

Group Type: Denomination specific; state group or convention
Founded: 1896
Membership: 750,000 persons, 468 churches, and 500 ordained clergy as of December 7, 1986
Meetings: Annual meeting held the third Sunday in August

Ohio State Baptist Convention

5428 Laconia Street
Cincinnati, OH 45237
The Reverend P. L. Brown, President

Group Type: Denomination specific; state group or convention

Orthodox Woodriver District Association—Illinois

1155 W. Forest Avenue
Decatur, IL 62522
The Reverend Oliver Johnson, Moderator

Group Type: Denomination specific; district association/annual conference

Pacific District Association—California

1404 E. Firestone Boulevard
Los Angeles, CA 90001
The Reverend Dr. W. T. Snead, Moderator

Group Type: Denomination specific; district association/annual conference

Pennsylvania State Convention

5627 Woodcrest Ave.
Philadelphia, PA 19131
(215) 879-5249
The Reverend Robert Lovett, President

Group Type: Denomination specific; state group or convention

Perriton District Association—Texas

6610 Wileyvale Road
Houston, TX 77028
The Reverend P. L. Williams, Moderator

Group Type: Denomination specific; district association/annual conference

Progressive Baptist State Convention of New York, Inc.

207-15 48th Avenue
Bayside, NY 11364
(718) 428-9031
The Reverend Dr. Lynnwood T. Deans, President

Group Type: Denomination specific; state group or convention

Founded: 1932

Membership: Approximately 4,570 persons, 23 churches, 3 associations, 34 ordained ministers, and 15 licentiates as of August 27, 1987

Meetings: Meets twice a year in April and August

Progressive District Association—California

719 Crosby Street
San Diego, CA 92113
(619) 233-6487
The Reverend Dr. S. M. Lockridge, Moderator

Group Type: Denomination specific; district association/annual conference

Progressive Educational and Missionary Baptist State Convention of Florida

2968 Breve Drive
Jacksonville, FL 32209
The Reverend H. T. Rhim, President

Group Type: Denomination specific; state group or convention

Membership: 70,000 persons, 203 churches, and 14 associates as of September, 1987

Progressive Missionary Baptist District Association—Florida

709 Nutmeg Avenue
Niceville, FL 35278
The Reverend E. B. Williams, Moderator

Group Type: Denomination specific; district association/annual conference

Progressive State Missionary Baptist Convention—New Mexico

1401 E. White
Hobbs, NM 88240
The Reverend H. R. Watkins, Moderator

Group Type: Denomination specific; state group or convention

Membership: 560 persons, 13 churches, and 2 associations as of September, 1987

Progressive West Texas District Association—Texas

1305 N.W. 9th Avenue
Amarillo, TX 79107
The Reverend D. Hill, Moderator

Group Type: Denomination specific; district association/annual conference

Saint John Regular District Association—Texas

7519 Blessing Avenue
Austin, TX 78752
The Reverend Dr. C. V. Clark, Moderator

Group Type: Denomination specific; district association/annual conference

Saint Luke District Association—New Mexico

1521 Pitt Street, N.E.
Albuquerque, NM 87112
(505) 296-8951
The Reverend Dr. Frank H. Cates, Moderator

Group Type: Denomination specific; district association/annual conference

Founded: 1966

Membership: 800 persons, 6 churches, 10 ordained clergy, and 12 licentiates as of August 19, 1987

Meetings: Annual meeting held the third Wednesday in July

Salem Baptist General Association—Pennsylvania

3 Meadowbrook Drive
Coatesville, PA 19320
(215) 384-6982
The Reverend Dr. Joshua Grove II, Moderator

Group Type: Denomination specific; district association/annual conference

Founded: 1929

Membership: 1,930 persons, 13 churches, and 22 ordained clergy as of September 26, 1987

Meetings: Annual meeting from Wednesday through Friday after the third Sunday in June

Salt River Valley General Association of Arizona

4436 S. 20th Street
Phoenix, AZ 85040
The Reverend C. N. Hall, President

Group Type: Denomination specific; state group or convention

Second Sweet Pilgrim District Association—Mississippi

Route 12, Box 507
Laurel, MS 39440
The Reverend M. L. Sampson, Moderator

Group Type: Denomination specific; district association/annual conference

Shiloh Missionary Baptist District Association—Mississippi

437 East Division Street
Biloxi, MS 39532
The Reverend A. A. Dickey, Moderator

Group Type: Denomination specific; district association/annual conference

Southern District Association—Texas

P.O. Box 236
Galveston, TX 77553
The Reverend A. S. Johnson, Moderator

Group Type: Denomination specific; district association/annual conference

Southern General Missionary Baptist Association—Louisiana

P.O. Box 124
Belle Chase, LA 70037
The Reverend D. J. Sullen, President

Group Type: Denomination specific; district association/annual conference

Membership: 9,000 persons and 40 churches as of September, 1987

South Mississippi Baptist State Convention

Route 3, Box 280
Foxworth, MS 39483
The Reverend Dr. L. Z. Blankenship, President

Group Type: Denomination specific; state group or convention

Membership: 9,802 persons, 259 churches, and 12 associations as of September, 1987

Spring Hill District Association—Mississippi

Route 1, Box 67
Aberdeen, MS 39730
The Reverend W. R. Sims, Moderator

Group Type: Denomination specific; district association/annual conference

Stones River District Association—Tennessee

P.O. Box 5763
Nashville, TN 37208
The Reverend Dr. W. J. Curry, Moderator

Group Type: Denomination specific; district association/annual conference

Sunflower District Association—Kansas

1100 Madison Street, NE
Topeka, KS 66608
The Reverend M. C. Caraway, Moderator

Group Type: Denomination specific; district association/annual conference

Sunshine District Association—Missouri

4600 Cleveland Avenue
Kansas City, MO 64130

Group Type: Denomination specific; district association/annual conference

Third District Bogue Chitto Baptist Association—Louisiana

406 S. 3rd Street
Amite, LA 70422
The Reverend W. Vernon, Moderator

Group Type: Denomination specific; district association/annual conference

Union District Association—Missouri

4300 E. 18th Street
Kansas City, MO 64127
The Reverend J. J. Woods, Moderator

Group Type: Denomination specific; district association/annual conference

Union District Association—Oregon

3200 N.E. 21st Avenue
Portland, OR 97212
The Reverend E. Boyd, Jr., Moderator

Group Type: Denomination specific; district association/annual conference

Union District Association—Texas

1125 Sherman Street
Waco, TX 76704
The Reverend R. McClain, Moderator

Group Type: Denomination specific; district association/annual conference

Union General Baptist State Convention—California

P.O. Box 11370
Los Angeles, CA 90011
The Reverend T. T. Turner, President

Group Type: Denomination specific; state group or convention

United Missionary Baptist District Association of Kansas

1902 N. Chautauqua Street
Wichita, KS 67214
(316) 685-2914
The Reverend D. D. Miller, Moderator

Group Type: Denomination specific; district association/annual conference
Founded: 1974
Membership: 3,700 persons, 14 churches, and 21 ordained clergy as of August 18, 1987
Meetings: Board meeting the first Tuesday through Thursday in February; Sunday School and Baptist Training Union Congress the first Tuesday through Friday in May; and District Convention held the first Tuesday through Friday in August

United Progressive District Association—Louisiana

2415 S. Claiborne Avenue
New Orleans, LA 70125
The Reverend L. E. Landrium, Moderator

Group Type: Denomination specific; district association/annual conference

Unity District Association—Texas

1930 Dennison Street
Dallas, TX 75212
The Reverend W. Bookman, Moderator

Group Type: Denomination specific; district association/annual conference

Virginia Baptist State Convention

111 Confier Lane
Salem, VA 24153
The Reverend Dr. J. A. Braxton, President

Group Type: Denomination specific; state group or convention

Washington State Baptist Convention

2001 South Jay Street
Tacoma, WA 98405
(206) 572-7054
The Reverend Dr. Joseph Andrew Boles, President

Group Type: Denomination specific; state group or convention
Founded: 1985
Membership: 966 persons, 33 churches, and 1 association as of October 16, 1987
Meetings: Annual meeting held the third week in August

West Nashville District Association—Tennessee

3201 Holland Lane
Nashville, TN 37218
The Reverend Dr. A. M. Walker, Moderator

Group Type: Denomination specific; district association/annual conference

Western District Association—Michigan

2032 Reynolds Street
Muskegon Heights, MI 49444
The Reverend Jones, Moderator

Group Type: Denomination specific; district association/annual conference

Zion Spring Leaf District Association—Mississippi

Route 1, Box 140
Collins, MS 39428
The Reverend Dr. V. M. McGee, Moderator

Group Type: Denomination specific; district association/annual conference

National Baptist Convention, U.S.A., Inc.

World Center Headquarters
1720 White Creek Pike
Nashville, TN 37207
(615) 228-6292
The Reverend Dr. Theodore Jemison, President
The Reverend Dr. W. Franklyn Richardson, General
    Secretary
Ms. Louise McClellan, Executive Director

The National Baptist Convention, U.S.A., Inc., is part of an African American Baptist convention tradition that predates the Civil War. In the antebellum era, there were two general Baptist associations, east and west. These extended into the South after the war. Then, in 1880, the Baptist Foreign Mission Convention of the United States was formed.

In a September, 1895 meeting in Atlanta, Georgia, the Baptist Foreign Mission Convention of America, the American National Baptist Convention (organized in St. Louis in 1886), and the National Baptist Educational Convention (organized in Washington, D.C. in 1893) agreed on a resolution to merge as the National Baptist Convention of the United States of America. The founding date most frequently attributed to the National Baptist Convention, U.S.A. is September 28, 1895.

Within the National Baptist Convention, U.S.A., Inc., the Baptist Foreign Mission Convention became the National Baptist Foreign Mission Board (although some who opposed this absorption eventually split with the Convention and joined the Lott Carey Convention). The Home Mission Board (established in 1886) and the Educational Board (1893) were continued within the Convention. A Sunday School Publishing Board (1896), Baptist Temperance Union Board (1899), and Women's Convention (1900) were subsequently established. The Baptist Convention of Western States and Territories joined with the National Baptist Convention, U.S.A., Inc., in 1896.

In 1896, the National Baptist Convention, U.S.A. instructed its Home Mission Board to establish a publishing house and begin printing a series of Sunday School materials for use in its various churches. The publishing house was established in Nashville, Tennessee, with the Reverend Richard Henry Boyd in charge.

When the Convention met in Chicago for its annual meeting in 1915, two problems prompted immediate controversy. The first was the disagreement over whether the Reverend E. C. Morris was to continue in office as president of the convention, and whether he had, as some accused, arranged to have non-supporters barred from the convention hall.

The second problem was confusion relating to the publishing house, then alleged to be worth some $350,000. A series of efforts to bring the house more closely under the control of the convention had revealed that the house and its copyrights were probably not the property of the convention, but of the Reverend Boyd, chairman of the board of the publishing house. Since the publishing house was incorporated under Tennessee law while the convention operated as an unincorporated body, the National Baptist Convention, U.S.A. was hard-pressed to elect members to the board or to control it.

Under the shadow of these two clouds, Boyd's supporters began meeting at Salem Baptist Church in Chicago, Illinois. They successfully sought an injunction against the Morris faction, but it was subsequently overturned; the Boyd faction was eventually ruled a "rump" convention. Nevertheless, on September 9, 1915, the National Baptist Convention, Unincorporated was born out of the Boyd faction and now carries the name National Baptist Convention of America, Inc. (the directorate of the organization was incorporated in Shreveport, Louisiana, in 1987). The directorate of the National Baptist Convention, U.S.A. incorporated in 1915 following the resolution of these issues.

Members of the National Baptist Convention, U.S.A., Inc., perceive scripture as divinely inspired and infallible, and believe in salvation by grace, and justification through faith. To be saved, sinners must be born again through the baptism of the Holy Spirit. The church is the congregation of baptized believers but only those who endure to the end will be saved.

Currently, the National Baptist Convention, U.S.A., Inc., has three auxiliaries and three boards. The auxiliaries include the National Baptist Laymen's Movement; the National Baptist Congress of Christian Education; and the Women's Convention that represents four million women and publishes *The National Baptist Woman*. The boards include the Sunday School Publishing Board (operations assumed from the National Baptist Temperance Union Board in 1984), the National Baptist Home Mission Board, and the National Baptist Foreign Mission Board. The missionary focus includes work in Sierra Leone, Liberia, Lesotho, South Africa, Malawi, Nicaragua, Swaziland, Barbados, Jamaica, and the Bahamas.

The National Baptist Convention, U.S.A., Inc., is supportive of a number of institutions of higher learning. They include: Shaw University, Shaw Divinity School, National Baptist College, Central Baptist Theological Seminary, Morehouse School of Religion, Selma University, and American Baptist Theological Seminary. The Convention also publishes *The National Baptist Voice*, a newspaper.

With the opening of its World Center Headquarters, the National Baptist Convention, U.S.A., Inc., has established its first permanent administrative facility. It opened on May 1, 1989, and was dedicated on June 21, 1989. Housed in this facility are all official offices of the convention. The convention represents thirty thousand churches, with a membership in excess of 7,500,000. The Reverend Dr. Theodore Jemison is president of the convention and is assisted by the Reverend Dr. W. Franklyn Richardson, who serves as general secretary. Ms. Louise McClellan is the executive director.

Group Type: Denomination
Founded: September, 1895
Membership: 30,000 churches with a membership in excess of 7,500,000 as of September, 1988
Publications: *The National Baptist Voice*, a newspaper, the Reverend Roscoe D. Cooper, Jr., executive editor, 2800 Third Avenue, Richmond, VA 23222,

(804) 329-5544; and *The National Baptist Woman* published by the Women's Auxiliary

Meetings: Annual meeting is held during the first week in September following Labor Day

State Conventions and District Associations of the National Baptist Convention, U.S.A., Inc.

Alabama Baptist Missionary State Convention

P.O. Box 2156
Selma, AL 36701
(205) 262-1002
The Reverend Dr. W. F. Alford, President

Group Type: Denomination specific; state group or convention
Founded: 1880
Membership: 800 churches as of December 8, 1987
Publications: *Baptist Leader*, Dr. W. H. Rodney, manager
Meetings: Annual meeting on the Monday after the second Sunday in November

Bahamas National Baptist Missionary and Educational Convention

Baillou Hill Road
P.O. Box N4435
Nassau, Bahamas
(809) 325-0729
The Reverend Dr. Charles W. Saunders, President

Group Type: Denomination specific; state group or convention
Founded: 1935
Membership: 60,000 persons, 214 churches, and 250 ordained clergy as of July, 1987
Meetings: Annual meeting on the fourth Monday in May

Baptist Associations and Auxiliaries of Southern Maryland and Vicinity

No current address

Group Type: Denomination specific; district association/annual conference
Founded: 1936

Baptist Brotherhood District Association—Illinois

1111 S. Laflin Street
Chicago, IL 60607
(312) 942-0143
The Reverend O. C. Nicks, Moderator

Group Type: Denomination specific; district association/annual conference
Founded: 1941
Membership: Between 3,000 and 5,000 persons, 14 churches, and approximately 20 ordained clergy as of September, 1987
Meetings: Annual meeting during the second week in May every year

Baptist Congress of Christian Education—Maryland

1434 McCulloh Street
Baltimore, MD 21217
(301) 523-0983
Arlene E. C. White, President

Group Type: Denomination specific; state group or convention; Christian education

Baptist Convention of Maryland/Delaware

1313 York Road
Lutherville, MD 21093
Minor Davidson, President

Group Type: Denomination specific; state group or convention

Baptist Convention of Washington, D.C., and Vicinity

c/o Providence Baptist Church
526 15th Street, SE
Washington, DC 20003
(202) 723-1156
The Reverend Carey E. Pointer, President
The Reverend George C. Gilbert, Sr., Secretary

Group Type: Denomination specific; state group or convention
Founded: 1872
Membership: 115,000 persons, 105 churches, and 237 ordained clergy as of December 15, 1987
Publications: Proceedings and directory; newsletter and help book for pastors and churches forthcoming
Meetings: Annual meeting from Monday through Friday before the third Sunday in October

Baptist General Convention of Virginia

1500 N. Lombardy Street
Richmond, VA 23220
(804) 359-4067
Dr. Cessar L. Scott, Executive Minister

Group Type: Denomination specific; state group or convention

Baptist Ministers Conference of Washington, D.C., and Vicinity

1615 Third Street, NW
Washington, DC 20001
(202) 667-1833
The Reverend George C. Gilbert, Sr., President
The Reverend Eugene O. Wright, Recording Secretary

Group Type: Denomination specific; ministerial

Baptist Ministers Union of Chicago and Vicinity

5657 Lafayette Avenue
Chicago, IL 60621
(312) 314-2753
The Reverend Dr. C. V. Johnson, Jr., President

Group Type: Denomination specific; ministerial

Baptist Missionary and Educational Convention of Michigan, Inc.

8811 East Forest Avenue
Detroit, MI 48214
(313) 923-1050
The Reverend W. W. Williams, President

Group Type: Denomination specific; state group or convention
Founded: 1947
Membership: About 35,000 persons, 99 churches, and 290 estimated ordained clergy as of December 8, 1987
Meetings: Annual meeting from Monday through Friday after the first Sunday in August

Baptist Pastors and Ministers Conference of Oakland and the East Bay

8500 A Street
Oakland, CA 94621
(415) 569-9492
The Reverend Dr. J. Alfred Smith, Sr., President

Group Type: Denomination specific; ministerial

Baptist State Convention of Illinois, Inc.

5657 Lafayette Avenue
Chicago, IL 60621
(312) 324-2750
The Reverend Dr. C. Sugar Hampton, President

Group Type: Denomination specific; state group or convention

Berean District Association—Missouri

1849 Cass Avenue
St. Louis, MO 63106
(314) 421-2487
The Reverend Jimmy L. Brown, Moderator

Group Type: Denomination specific; district association/annual conference
Founded: September, 1878
Membership: 63 churches as of September 8, 1988
Meetings: The Congress meets monthly on the second Monday; Evangelist Outreach every third Saturday; Board the first Monday in March; and an annual session in mid-July

Bethlehem Baptist District Association #1—Alabama

3728 Hickory Avenue, SW
Birmingham, AL 35221
(205) 925-5260
The Reverend Cephus Simmons, Sr., President

Group Type: Denomination specific; district association/annual conference

Bethlehem Baptist District Association #2—Alabama

1623 Lapsley Street
Selma, AL 36701
(205) 874-8037
The Reverend W. G. Lett, President

Group Type: Denomination specific; district association/annual conference
Founded: 1917
Membership: Approximately 13,000 persons, 42 churches, and 35 ordained clergy as of September 8, 1987
Meetings: Annual meeting on the Wednesday and Thursday before the second Sunday in October

Big Creek and Reedville Baptist District Association—Arkansas

606 North Porter Street
Stuttgart, AR 72160
(501) 673-2129
The Reverend D. L. O'Neil, Moderator

Group Type: Denomination specific; district association/annual conference
Founded: 1924
Membership: Approximately 2,000 persons, 26 churches, and 31 ordained clergy as of September 9, 1987

Meetings: Annual meeting on the Wednesday before the fourth Sunday in September
Publications: Big Creek and Reedville Baptist District Association Newsletter

Bluegrass State Baptist Convention—Kentucky

P.O. Box 11067
Louisville, KY 40211
(502) 778-6063
The Reverend Dr. A. Russell Awkard, President

Group Type: Denomination specific; state group or convention
Founded: 1986
Membership: 30 churches as of August 27, 1987
Meetings: Meets in June and November

Bowen-East District Association—Georgia

Route 1, Box 430
West Point, GA 31833
(404) 645-2620
The Reverend O. C. Stiggers, Moderator
The Reverend Eugene Cookes, Secretary

Group Type: Denomination specific; district association/annual conference

Brotherhood Missionary Baptist and Educational Association—Mississippi

P.O. Drawer 610
Mount Bayou, MS 38762
(601) 741-2313
The Reverend H. Y. Ward, Moderator

Group Type: Denomination specific; district association/annual conference
Founded: 1959
Membership: 7,000 persons, 15 churches, and 20 ordained clergy as of September 9, 1987
Meetings: Annual meeting before the third Saturday in July

Calcasieu Union Missionary and Educational Baptist Association—Louisiana

1120 Sixth Street
Mamou, LA 70554
(318) 468-3573
The Reverend Mack C. Guillory, Moderator

Group Type: Denomination specific; district association/annual conference
Founded: 1910
Membership: 7,578 persons, 36 churches, and 53 ordained clergy as of August 25, 1987
Meetings: Annual meeting in the week following the first Sunday in July; boards meet on the Thursday following the first Sunday in October, January, and April; Congress of Christian Education meets the week following the second Sunday in June

California State Baptist Convention, Inc.

684 Erlandson Street
Richmond, CA 94804
(415) 232-1058
The Reverend Dr. A. H. Newman, President

Group Type: Denomination specific; state group or convention
Founded: 1941
Membership: 15,000 persons, 325 churches, and 1,100 ordained clergy as of June 19, 1987
Publications: Two newsletters through its auxiliaries for young people and young adults
Meetings: Annual meeting the week following the third Sunday in October

Central District #2 Association—Arkansas

606 North Porter
Stuttgart, AR 72160
(501) 673-2129
The Reverend D. L. O'Neil, Moderator

Group Type: Denomination specific; district association/annual conference
Founded: 1964
Membership: 1,200 persons, 5 churches, and 12 ordained clergy as of September 9, 1987
Meetings: Annual meeting on the Thursday after the third Sunday in August

Central District Association—California

P.O. Box 233
Ventura, CA 93001
(805) 643-1976
The Reverend John Baylor, Moderator

Group Type: Denomination specific; district association/annual conference
Founded: 1954
Membership: 3,000 persons, 13 churches, and 20 ordained clergy as of October 5, 1987
Meetings: Annual meeting on the third Friday and Saturday of July

Central Hope Baptist District Association—Ohio

67 East North Street
Akron, OH 44304
(216) 253-3534
The Reverend Dr. Leonard T. King, Moderator

Group Type: Denomination specific; district association/annual conference
Founded: 1937 or 1939
Membership: 2,000 persons and 10 churches as of September 6, 1988
Meetings: Annual meeting every fourth Monday in July

Central Hudson Baptist Association—New York

409 Union Street
Schenectady, NY 12305
(518) 374-8679
The Reverend Carl B. Taylor, Moderator

Group Type: Denomination specific; district association/annual conference
Founded: 1919
Membership: 42 churches as of September 6, 1988
Publications: An annual report
Meetings: Meets quarterly with an annual session in July

Chain Lake District Missionary Baptist Association—Michigan

339 E. Prospect
Jackson, MI 49203
(517) 784-7026
The Reverend Amos Polk Williams, Moderator

Group Type: Denomination specific; district association/annual conference
Founded: 1843
Membership: 40,000 persons in south-Central Michigan, 54 churches, and 55 ordained clergy with 5 ministers not pastoring as of September 13, 1987
Meetings: Meets three times a year

Christian Fellowship Missionary Baptist Association—New Jersey

17-21 East Kinney Street
Newark, NJ 07102
(201) 642-8336
Dr. Mitchell Douglas, Moderator

Group Type: Denomination specific; district association/annual conference
Founded: 1971
Membership: 24 churches as of August 28, 1987
Meetings: Annual meeting the last Sunday in July through the first Sunday in August; semiannual meeting for a week beginning the Monday after the last Sunday in February

Cincinnati Ohio District Association

1556 John Street
Cincinnati, OH 45214
(513) 579-1133
The Reverend Daniel Smith, Moderator

Group Type: Denomination specific; district association/annual conference
Founded: 1923
Membership: 32 churches in Hamilton County as of September 8, 1988
Meetings: Meets annually in July; board meets in April

Cleveland District of Baptist Women—Ohio

4400 Clarkwood Parkway
Warrensville Heights, OH 44128
Mrs. Daisy G. Horne, President

Group Type: Denomination specific; women

Colorado Baptist Southern District Association

1032 Lawrence Avenue
Colorado Spring, CO 80906
(303) 576-5847
The Reverend Lewis W. Harvey, Moderator

Group Type: Denomination specific; district association/annual conference
Founded: 1965
Membership: 3,000 persons, 8 churches, and 15 ordained clergy as of September 9, 1987
Meetings: Annual meeting on the Tuesday after the fourth Sunday in July

Consolidated Missionary State Convention of Arkansas, Inc.

1600 Bishop Street
Little Rock, AR 72202
(501) 763-8653
The Reverend Dr. P. J. James, President

Group Type: Denomination specific; state group or convention
Founded: 1868
Membership: 115,896 persons, 100 churches, 95 ordained clergy, 60 unordained clergy
Publications: The Baptist Vanguard, Dr. C. L. Horn, managing editor, Dr. P. J. James, editor-in-chief
Meetings: Meets annually in November

Creek District Baptist Association—Oklahoma

419 N. Elgin Avenue
Tulsa, OK 74120
(918) 584-0510
The Reverend G. Calvin McCutcheon, Moderator

Group Type: Denomination specific; district association/annual conference
Membership: 52 churches, 59 ordained clergy as of September 9, 1987
Meetings: Annual meeting in late August

Cypress District Baptist Association—Texas

P.O. Box 253
Como, TX 75431
(214) 488-3457
The Reverend John W. Williams, Moderator

Group Type: Denomination specific; district association/annual conference
Founded: 1873

Dallas County District Association—Alabama

Route 1, Box 244
Browns, AL 36724
(205) 628-8152
The Reverend John L. Ward, Moderator

Group Type: Denomination specific; district association/annual conference
Founded: 1888
Membership: 26 churches in Dallas County, Alabama, as of September 6, 1988
Meetings: Meets annually

East Dallas District Association—Alabama

3006 Kingsley Drive
Selma, AL 36701
(205) 872-6108
The Reverend L. L. Ruffin, Moderator

Group Type: Denomination specific; district association/annual conference
Founded: 1886
Meetings: Wednesday after the fourth Sunday in October

East Mississippi State Baptist Convention, Inc.

1223 Marion Avenue
Columbia, MS 39429
(601) 736-6494
The Reverend R. Sylvester Porter, President

Group Type: Denomination specific; state group or convention
Founded: 1899
Membership: 19,000 persons and 75 churches as of June 18, 1987
Meetings: Annual meeting in October

East Texas Bethel Association

Route 3, Box 109
Carthage, TX 75633
(214) 693-4644
The Reverend J. T. Harris, Moderator

Group Type: Denomination specific; district association/annual conference
Founded: 1950
Membership: 75 ministers in 23 churches in East Texas as of September 8, 1988
Meetings: Meets annually for one week beginning after the second Sunday in September; district meets quarterly

East Texas Mount Zion Missionary Association

P.O. Box 102
Timpson, TX 75975
(409) 564-4351
The Reverend Reggie L. Cotton, Moderator

Group Type: Denomination specific; district association/annual conference
Founded: 1903
Membership: 12,000 persons in Nacogdoches, Shelby, and St. Augustine counties and 24 churches as of September 9, 1988
Meetings: Meets quarterly

Eastern Baptist Association of New York

275 Kingston Avenue
Brooklyn, NY 11233
(718) 622-7295
The Reverend Washington L. Lundy, Moderator

Group Type: Denomination specific; district association/annual conference
Founded: 1921
Membership: 10,000 persons, 206 churches, and 400 ordained clergy as of September 8, 1987
Meetings: Annual meeting in the week of the second Sunday in July

Eastern Ohio District Association

3216 McGuffy Road
Youngstown, OH 44505
(216) 746-5580
The Reverend Ralph Burton, Moderator

Group Type: Denomination specific; district association/annual conference
Founded: 1925
Membership: 10,000 persons, 46 churches, and 50 ordained clergy as of September 8, 1987
Meetings: Annual meeting on the second Monday in July

Educational and Missionary Baptist Convention of South Carolina

2334 Elmwood Avenue
Columbia, SC 29204
(803) 277-0364
The Reverend Dr. S. C. Cureton, President

Group Type: Denomination specific; state group or convention
Founded: 1877
Publications: *Baptist Informer, Speaking the Truth in Love, Accenting Baptist Leadership in South Carolina*
Meetings: Annual meeting the first week in May

Educational Progressive Association—Mississippi

1221 13th Avenue
Meridian, MS 39301
(601) 482-4892
The Reverend Dr. A. M. Thomas, Moderator

Group Type: Denomination specific; district association/annual conference
Founded: 1928
Membership: 8 churches as of September 6, 1988
Meetings: Meets annually

Emmanuel Progressive Baptist Association—Florida

2103 W. 40th Street
Jacksonville, FL 32209
(904) 764-3695
The Reverend E. I. Norman, Moderator

Group Type: Denomination specific; district association/annual conference
Founded: 1923
Membership: 6,600 persons, 22 churches, and 30 ordained clergy as of September 9, 1987
Meetings: Annual meeting on the Thursday after the third Sunday in October

Empire Baptist Missionary Convention of New York

63-65 West 125th Street
New York, NY 10027
(212) 427-2443
The Reverend Allen A. Stanley, Moderator

Group Type: Denomination specific; state group or convention
Founded: 1897
Membership: 7,578 persons, 36 churches, and 53 ordained clergy as of August 25, 1987
Meetings: Annual meeting the third week in October

Eureka Association—Tennessee

1525 Willison
Memphis, TN 38106
(901) 774-0685
The Reverend C. J. Patterson, Moderator

Group Type: Denomination specific; district association/annual conference
Founded: 1976
Membership: 3,500 persons, 6 churches, and 8 ordained clergy as of September 8, 1987
Meetings: Annual meeting on the Tuesday after the second Sunday in July

First Bethlehem Baptist Association, Inc.—Florida

P.O. Box 61
Live Oak, FL 32060
(904) 362-3182
The Reverend C. C. Curry, Moderator

Group Type: Denomination specific; district association/annual conference
Founded: 1865
Membership: 3,000 persons, 87 churches, 87 ordained clergy, 6 missionaries, and 2 evangelists as of September 8, 1987
Publications: *Bugle State*, a newsletter
Meetings: Annual meeting on the Monday after the first Sunday in October

First Interprise District Association—Mississippi

P.O. Box 323
Heidelburg, MS 39439
(601) 787-3250
The Reverend L. D. Ducksworth, Moderator

Group Type: Denomination specific; district association/annual conference
Founded: 1871
Membership: 2,800 person, 49 churches, and 63 ordained clergy as of 1987
Meetings: Annual meeting on the fourth Friday of each October

Florida General Baptist Convention

3455 Second Avenue South
St. Petersburg, FL 33711
(813) 327-0656
The Reverend Dr. Henry J. Lyons, President

Group Type: Denomination specific; state group or convention
Founded: 1879
Membership: 500,000 persons, 728 churches, and 946 ordained clergy as of July 14, 1987
Publications: *The Baptist Bugle* through the Florida Convention Press
Meetings: Annual meeting during the week after the first Sunday in April

Fowlstown Missionary Baptist Association—Georgia

Route 8, Box 850
Baxley, GA 31513
(912) 367-4989
The Reverend H. M. Moss, Sr., Moderator

Group Type: Denomination specific; district association/annual conference
Founded: 1875
Membership: 15,979 persons, 23 churches, 28 ordained clergy, and 8 licentiates as of September 8, 1987
Publications: *Georgia Baptist Witness*
Meetings: Annual meeting on the Wednesday before the fourth Sunday in October

Franklin County Sunday School and Baptist Training Union Convention—North Carolina

Route 3, Box 243
Louisburg, NC 27549
Dr. Arthur Williams, President

Group Type: Denomination specific; district association/annual conference

Fundamental Baptist Fellowship Association

No current address

Group Type: Denomination specific; district association/annual conference

Gaston Baptist Missionary Association—North Carolina

2702 Bradford Street
Gaston, NC 28054
(704) 864-6145
The Reverend Theodore Armstrong, Jr.

Group Type: Denomination specific; district association/annual conference
Meetings: Meets quarterly

General Baptist Association of West Germany

Albrecht-Durer Platz 7
Schweinfort, West Germany
(49) 09721-186198
The Reverend Elijah Mitchell, Moderator

Group Type: Denomination specific; district association/annual conference
Founded: 1986
Membership: 8 churches as of September 7, 1988
Meetings: Meets quarterly; board meeting in January; Congress of Christian Education meeting in April; annual session in August

General Baptist State Convention of New Jersey, Inc.

604 Martin Luther King Street
Newark, NJ 07010
(201) 938-2428
The Reverend Caleb E. Oates, President

Group Type: Denomination specific; state group or convention
Founded: 1903
Membership: 69,000 persons, 234 churches, and 250 ordained clergy as of July 18, 1987
Publications: Convention Press
Meetings: Annual meeting first week in October

General Baptist State Convention of North Carolina, Inc.

603 South Wilmington Street
Raleigh, NC 27601
The Reverend J. B. Humphrey, President
(704) 372-1075
The Reverend Dr. C. C. Craig, Executive Director
(919) 821-7466

Group Type: Denomination specific; state group or convention
Founded: 1867; incorporated in 1947

Membership: 425,000 persons, 1,700 churches, and 1,200 ordained clergy as of December 8, 1987
Publications: The Baptist Informer, a newspaper
Meetings: Annual meeting held in July

General Baptist State Convention of Wisconsin, Inc.

1442 N. 21st Street
Milwaukee, WI 53205
(414) 342-0292
The Reverend H. K. Henderson, President

Group Type: Denomination specific; state group or convention
Founded: 1956
Membership: About 15,000 persons, 35 churches, and 50 ordained clergy as of September 9, 1987
Meetings: Annual meeting during the first week in August

General Missionary Baptist and Educational State Convention of Mississippi

140 S. 8th Street
Greenville, MS 38701
(601) 332-8353
The Reverend J. B. Woods, President

Group Type: Denomination specific; state group or convention
Founded: 1904
Membership: About 50 churches and 60 ordained clergy as of October 8, 1987
Meetings: Annual meeting on the second Tuesday in July

General Missionary Baptist State Convention of Indiana, Inc.

2400 Virginia Street
Gary, IN 46407
(219) 938-1301
The Reverend Dr. F. Brannan Jackson, President

Group Type: Denomination specific; state group or convention
Founded: 1922
Membership: 70,000 persons, 90 churches, 90 ordained clergy, and 30 licentiates as of June 18, 1987
Publications: The Missionary Study Guide and Sunday school literature through the Sunday School Publishing Board
Meetings: Annual meeting every second Monday in July

General Missionary Baptist State Convention of Indiana, Inc. #2

663 S. Elliott Street
Evansville, IN 47713
(812) 425-3498
The Reverend Dr. W. R. Brown, Sr., President

Group Type: Denomination specific; state group or convention
Founded: 1920
Membership: 60,000 persons, 103 churches, and 250 ordained clergy as of June 28, 1987
Meetings: Annual meeting first full week in July
Publications: Voice of Indiana Baptist through the General Missionary Baptist State Convention

General Missionary Baptist State Convention of Mississippi

P.O. Box 627
Indianola, MS 38751
(601) 887-1587
The Reverend Dr. David Matthews, President

Group Type: Denomination specific; state group or convention
Founded: 1869
Membership: 300,000 persons, 540 churches, 340 ordained clergy, and 300 pastors as of July 29, 1987
Meetings: Annual meeting on the Monday after the third Sunday in July

Greater Hartford Baptist District Association

24 Kenny Terrace
Hartford, CT 06112
(203) 549-7019
The Reverend Dr. Judge Lee, Moderator

Group Type: Denomination specific; district association/annual conference
Founded: 1980
Membership: 10,000 persons and 9 churches as of September, 1987
Publications: Greater Hartford Weekly Circular
Meetings: Annual meeting on the second Wednesday after the first Saturday in July

Greatland State Baptist Convention of Alaska

P.O. Box 200156
Anchorage, AK 99520-0156
(907) 276-6673
Dr. Alonzo B. Patterson, President

Group Type: Denomination specific; state group or convention
Founded: 1984
Membership: 14 churches, 11 ordained clergy, and 3 licentiates as of January 12, 1988
Meetings: Annual convention meets the fourth Monday in July

Grenada District Missionary Baptist Association— Mississippi

799 Pearl Street
Grenada, MS 38901
(601) 226-4290
Dr. Jim H. Purnell, Moderator

Group Type: Denomination specific; district association/annual conference
Membership: Approximately 3,000 persons, 20 churches, and 35 ordained clergy as of September 8, 1987
Meetings: Annual meeting every third Monday in July

Guyan Baptist Association—West Virginia

P.O. Box 183
Sharpres, WV 25183
(304) 369-3169
The Reverend Ron Hamilton, Moderator

Group Type: Denomination specific; district association/annual conference

Hudson River Frontier Missionary Baptist Association— New York

813 Strong Street
Schenectady, NY 12307
(518) 374-9016
The Reverend Albert J. Holman, Moderator

Group Type: Denomination specific; district association/annual conference
Meetings: Meets quarterly

Indiana Brotherhood Missionary Baptist District Association

5601 East 4th Avenue
Gary, IN 46406
(219) 938-8126
The Reverend Charles N. Burnside, Moderator

Group Type: Denomination specific; district association/annual conference
Founded: 1953
Membership: 1,500 people in 15 churches as of September 7, 1988
Meetings: Meets in March, May, and October with occasional call meetings

Iowa Missionary and Educational Baptist State Convention

1315 10th Street
Des Moines, IA 50314
(515) 282-1197
The Reverend Dr. George H. Parrish, President

Group Type: Denomination specific; state group or convention
Founded: 1877
Membership: 7,000 persons, 42 churches (33 in Iowa, 6 in Nebraska, and 3 in Illinois), 80 ordained clergy, and 70 licentiates as of September 7, 1988
Meetings: Meets quarterly in April, June, August, and October; annual meeting on the Monday after the second Sunday in August

Kaw Valley District Association—Kansas

3030 Farrow Avenue
Kansas City, KS 66104
(913) 621-4510
The Reverend Stacy E. Hopkins, Moderator

Group Type: Denomination specific; district association/annual conference
Founded: 1902
Membership: 54 churches as of September 7, 1988
Meetings: Meets three times a year

Kingston Lake Missionary Baptist Association—South Carolina

P.O. Box 1318
Conway, SC 29526
(803) 756-1781
The Reverend Allen B. Nichols, Moderator

Group Type: Denomination specific; district association/annual conference
Founded: 1887

Membership: 3,500 persons, 37 churches, 64 ordained clergy, and 19 licentiates as of September 7, 1987

Meetings: Annual meeting the third week in October

Liberty Hill Baptist Association—Louisiana

Old Grambling Road, Box 288
Grambling, LA 71245
(318) 247-6170
The Reverend C. C. McLain, Moderator

Group Type: Denomination specific; district association/annual conference
Founded: 1882
Membership: 7,400 persons, 39 churches, 46 ordained clergy, and 7 licentiates as of September 1, 1987
Meetings: Annual meeting on the Wednesday after the third Sunday in October; extra session held the Friday after third Sundays

Macedonia Baptist Association—South Carolina

P.O. Box 171
Barnwell, SC 29812
(803) 259-3280
The Reverend C. F. Mitchell, Moderator

Group Type: Denomination specific; district association/annual conference

Memphis District Association—Tennessee

1797 S. Parkway East
Memphis, TN 38114
(901) 276-5295
The Reverend O. C. Collins, Sr., Moderator

Group Type: Denomination specific; district association/annual conference
Founded: 1937
Membership: 10,000 persons, 34 churches, and 34 ordained clergy as of September 9, 1987
Meetings: Annual meeting on the Monday after the first Sunday in August

Miami Valley District Association—Ohio

700 Southwestern Avenue
Dayton, OH 45407
(513) 263-6969
The Reverend Al Peters, Moderator

Group Type: Denomination specific; district association/annual conference
Founded: 1986
Membership: 3,000 persons, 8 churches, and 13 ordained clergy as of September, 1987
Meetings: Annual meeting on the fourth Monday in July

Middlesex Central Baptist Association—New Jersey

111 Perry Street
Trenton, NJ 08618
(609) 396-8722
The Reverend W. J. Sanders, Moderator

Group Type: Denomination specific; district association/annual conference
Founded: 1906

Membership: 100,000 persons, 60 churches, and 75 ordained clergy as of September 8, 1987

Meetings: Annual meeting after the second Sunday in July

Middlesex Central District Association of New Jersey

2426 Springfield Avenue
Vauxhall, NJ 07088
(201) 686-5437
The Reverend Alfonzo Williams, Moderator

Group Type: Denomination specific; district association/annual conference
Founded: 1907
Membership: 10 churches in southern and northern New Jersey as of September 7, 1988
Meetings: Meets semiannually

Missionary Baptist State Convention of Kansas

2600 North Grove
Wichita, KS 67219
(316) 684-1443
The Reverend Dr. W. C. Williams, President

Group Type: Denomination specific; state group or convention
Founded: 1899
Membership: 28,748 persons and 117 churches as of June 20, 1987
Publications: *The Kansas Missionary*, Mrs. Paula Pyles, publisher
Meetings: Annual meeting on the Monday following the first Sunday in October

Missionary Baptist State Convention of Missouri

2315-17 East 12th Street
Kansas City, MO 64130
(816) 924-4963
The Reverend Dr. McKinley Dukes, President

Group Type: Denomination specific; state group or convention
Founded: 1889
Membership: Approximately 17,000 persons and 313 churches as of September, 1987
Publications: *Grapevine Express*
Meetings: Annual meeting on the Monday following the second Sunday in October

Montgomery Antioch District Association—Alabama

915 Ridgemont Avenue
Montgomery, AL 36105
(205) 265-5931
The Reverend G. W. Bozeman, Moderator

Group Type: Denomination specific; district association/annual conference
Founded: 1893
Membership: 5,000 persons, 53 churches, and 64 ordained clergy as of September 9, 1987
Meetings: Meets quarterly; annual meeting the week after the third Sunday in October

Mount Calvary Missionary Baptist Association—Ohio

2867 Keystone Drive
Columbus, OH 43209
(614) 491-0268
The Reverend Dr. Joseph Freeman, Jr., Moderator

Group Type: Denomination specific; district association/annual conference

Founded: 1957

Membership: 5,000 persons, 10 churches, and 12 ordained clergy as of August 18, 1987

Meetings: Annual meeting begins the second Monday in July

National Baptist Student Union Retreat

c/o Springfield Baptist Church
600 East McBee Avenue
Greenville, SC 29601
(803) 271-3494
Dr. John H. Corbitt, National Director

Group Type: Denomination specific; student

National Capitol Baptist Congress of Christian Education—D.C.

c/o St. Phillips Baptist Church
1001 North Capitol Street, NE
Washington, DC 20002
(202) 789-0840
The Reverend Dr. Andre H. Owens, President

Group Type: Denomination specific; district association/annual conference; Christian education

National Capitol Convention (Baptist)—D.C.

3501 Martin Luther King Avenue, SE
Washington, DC 20032
The Reverend James Edward Lewis, President

Group Type: Denomination specific; state group or convention

Nevada and California Interstate Missionary Baptist Convention

1265 Montello Street
Reno, NV 89512
(702) 786-1017
The Reverend William C. Webb, President

Group Type: Denomination specific; state group or convention

Founded: 1947

Membership: 27 churches as of September, 1987

Meetings: Annual meeting during the week before the third Sunday in August

New Antioch Bethlehem Association—Alabama

3432 Glen Drive
Tuscaloosa, AL 35401
(205) 345-5135
The Reverend J. L. Simpson, Moderator

Group Type: Denomination specific; district association/annual conference

Founded: 1813

Membership: 37 churches and 32 ordained clergy as of September, 1987

New Ashley Baptist Association—South Carolina

2069 Arbutus Avenue
Charleston, SC 29405
(803) 554-1509
The Reverend Alfred Williams, Moderator

Group Type: Denomination specific; district association/annual conference

New Educational State Convention of the State of Mississippi

1028 Denny Avenue
Pascagoula, MS 39567
(601) 769-1044
The Reverend Dr. John W. Davis, Sr., President

Group Type: Denomination specific; state group or convention

Founded: 1971

Membership: 10,000 persons, 35 churches, and 45 ordained clergy as of June 15, 1987

Meetings: Annual meeting on the Tuesday following the 4th of July

New Era Baptist State Convention of Alabama

2923 Norwood Boulevard
Birmingham, AL 35234
(205) 251-8306
The Reverend P. T. Williams, President

Group Type: Denomination specific; state group or convention

Founded: 1894

Membership: 30 churches as of June 28, 1987

Publications: Proceedings of its annual conference in the *Baptist Leader*

Meetings: Annual meeting every second Wednesday in November

New Hope Missionary Baptist Association—New Jersey

675 South 20th Street
Newark, NJ 07103
(201) 923-9766
The Reverend William Irving, Moderator

Group Type: Denomination specific; district association/annual conference

Founded: April 21, 1898

Membership: 38 churches and 46 ordained clergy as of September, 1987

North Arkansas District Association

P.O. Box 141
Madison, AR 72359
(501) 637-2387
The Reverend R. B. Bland, Moderator

Group Type: Denomination specific; district association/annual conference

Founded: 1885

Membership: Approximately 3,000 persons, 33 churches, and 36 ordained clergy as of September 9, 1987

Meetings: Annual meeting on the Monday after the second Sunday in August

Northeastern District Association—Kansas

3909 Mission Road
Kansas City, KS 66103
(913) 432-9999
The Reverend Dr. H. L. Jarrett, Moderator

Group Type: Denomination specific; district association/annual conference

Founded: 1902
Membership: 9 churches in north Kansas as of September 6, 1988
Meetings: Meets monthly

North Eastern District Association—New York

233 Lincoln Avenue
Syracuse, NY 13204
(315) 478-0475
The Reverend Dr. Louis C. Walker, Moderator

Group Type: Denomination specific; district association/annual conference
Founded: June 19, 1959
Membership: Approximately 15,000 persons and 11 churches in the Syracuse area as of September 6, 1988
Meetings: Meet in retreat each February; congress meets annually; semiannual meeting each third week in April; annual session second week in October

Northeast Mississippi Baptist State Convention

P.O. Box 1331
Corinth, MS 38834
(601) 286-5131
The Reverend O. C. Brand, President

Group Type: Denomination specific; state group or convention
Founded: 1945
Membership: 28,000 persons, 205 churches, and 9 associations as of December 15, 1987
Publications: Northeast Baptist Voice, Mary Henly, publisher/editor
Meetings: Wednesday through Friday following the first Sunday in July

Northern District Baptist Association of Colorado

2677 Ash Street
Denver, CO 80207
(303) 332-9198
The Reverend Leon V. McGuire, Moderator

Group Type: Denomination specific; district association/annual conference
Founded: 1949

Northern Virginia Baptist Association, Inc.

6626 Costner Drive
Falls Church, VA 22042
(703) 533-3217
The Reverend Dr. James E. Browne, Moderator

Group Type: Denomination specific; district association/annual conference

North Mississippi Baptist Education Convention

P.O. Box 37
Hernando, MS 38632
(901) 942-0015
The Reverend Coleman Crawford, Jr., President

Group Type: Denomination specific; district association/annual conference
Founded: 1887
Membership: 50 churches and 50 ordained clergy as of July 13, 1987

Meetings: Annual meeting Monday through Friday of the first week in November

North Missouri Baptist Association

P.O. Box 682
Hannibal, MO 63401
(314) 769-3830
The Reverend Clay Taite, Moderator

Group Type: Denomination specific; district association/annual conference
Founded: September 1865
Membership: 840 persons, 14 churches, and 11 ordained clergy as of September 4, 1987
Meetings: Annual meeting the first week in August

Ohio Baptist State Convention, Inc.

3212 Reading Road
Cincinnati, OH 45229
(513) 221-4006
The Reverend Dr. H. L. Harvey, Jr., President

Group Type: Denomination specific; state group or convention
Founded: January 21, 1918
Membership: 300,000 persons, 300 churches, and 400 ordained clergy as of July 14, 1987
Meetings: Annual meeting first week in August; meets quarterly

Oklahoma Missionary Baptist State Convention, Inc.

1014 East Pine Street
Tulsa, OK 74106
(918) 582-8668
The Reverend Dr. T. Oscar Chappelle, President

Group Type: Denomination specific; state group or convention
Founded: 1907
Membership: 43,000 persons, 210 churches, 325 ordained clergy, and 25 licentiates as of September, 1987

Original Mount Carmel Baptist Association—Georgia

P.O. Box 11
Woodland, GA 31836
(404) 674-2319
The Reverend Alfred McCrary, Moderator

Group Type: Denomination specific; district association/annual conference

Pacalet River Baptist Association—South Carolina

338 Crestview Drive
Spartansburg, SC 29301
(803) 574-0104
The Reverend Dr. B. T. Sears, Sr., Moderator

Group Type: Denomination specific; district association/annual conference
Founded: October, 1873
Membership: 31 churches in Union County, SC, as of September 9, 1988
Meetings: Meets annually from Tuesday through Thursday after the second Sunday in October; union of churches meets quarterly; laymen meet monthly

Peace Baptist District Association—Alabama

721 12th Street Ensley
Birmingham, AL 35218
(205) 788-0543
The Reverend Eugene Jones, Moderator

Group Type: Denomination specific; district association/annual conference
Founded: 1938
Membership: 40 churches as of September 6, 1988
Meetings: Meets about four times a year

Pleasant Grove District Association—Michigan

8806 Mack Avenue
Detroit, MI 48221
(313) 571-9797
The Reverend Robert E. Starghill, Moderator

Group Type: Denomination specific; district association/annual conference
Membership: 15 churches as of September, 1987
Meetings: Annual meeting the third Monday in July

Pleasant Grove District Association—Tennessee

797 Laurel Street
Memphis, TN 38112
(901) 452-7993
The Reverend Sampson Townsend, Moderator

Group Type: Denomination specific; district association/annual conference
Meetings: Annual meeting in September

Post Range, Hines and Joining Counties Association—Mississippi

1129 Pleasant Avenue
Jackson, MS 39203
(601) 969-4199
The Reverend Dr. James C. Matthew, Moderator

Group Type: Denomination specific; district association/annual conference
Founded: 1933
Membership: 3,000 persons and 22 churches in Hines and adjoining counties as of September 7, 1988
Meetings: Meets semiannually

Potomac River Baptist Association—D.C.

712 Randolph Street, NW
Washington, DC 20011
(202) 541-5000
The Reverend Frank D. Tucker, Moderator

Group Type: Denomination specific; district association/annual conference

Progressive District Association—Michigan

14516 W. Chicago Boulevard
Detroit, MI 48228
(313) 336-2928
The Reverend Robert Linsey, Moderator

Group Type: Denomination specific; district association/annual conference
Membership: 600 persons, 6 churches, and 10 ordained clergy of September 8, 1987

Meetings: Annual meeting on the second fifth Sunday of the year

Progressive Education District Association—California

2595 San Jose Avenue
San Francisco, CA 94112
(415) 333-0427
The Reverend Ray Howland, Moderator

Group Type: Denomination specific; district association/annual conference
Founded: 1952
Membership: 10,000 persons, 62 churches, and 72 ordained clergy as of September 8, 1987
Meetings: Annual meeting on the Monday after the third Sunday in August

Pure Light Association—Louisiana

4442 America Street
New Orleans, LA 70126
The Reverend Dr. Rene Powe, Moderator

Group Type: Denomination specific; district association/annual conference

Regular Arkansas Baptist Convention, Inc.

2200 Willow Street
North Little Rock, AR 72114
(501) 758-1190
The Reverend Dr. O. C. Jones, President

Group Type: Denomination specific; state group or convention
Founded: October 1, 1934
Membership: 16,900 persons, 544 churches, and 21 associations as of July 1, 1987
Meetings: Annual meeting on the second Sunday in November

Riverside District Association—Tennessee

1612 May Street
Memphis, TN 38108
(901) 274-3531
The Reverend Dr. R. E. Plunkett, Moderator

Group Type: Denomination specific; district association/annual conference

Saint Marion District Association—Arkansas

2809 Mississippi Street, Route 3
Pine Bluff, AR 71601
(501) 534-0128
The Reverend R. C. Pierce, Moderator

Group Type: Denomination specific; district association/annual conference
Founded: 1867
Membership: 3,000 persons, 31 churches, and 40 ordained clergy as of September 8, 1987
Meetings: Annual meeting in the third week of August

Sardis District Baptist Association—Mississippi

Route 2, Box 546
Highway 315
Sardis, MS 38666
(601) 563-8258
The Reverend Ezra Jowner, Moderator

Group Type: Denomination specific; district association/annual conference
Founded: 1875
Membership: 250 persons, 34 churches, 34 ordained clergy as of September 4, 1987
Publications: *The Southern Reporters—Sardis*, Mrs. Fletcher, editor; *Panolian—Batesville*, Mr. John Howell, editor
Meetings: Sunday School and Baptist Training Union Congress meets the week after the first Sunday in August; an extended session is held the Friday after Thanksgiving; the midspring session is the Friday before the first Sunday in June

Seacoast Missionary Baptist Association—New Jersey

311 Hillside Avenue
Navesink, NJ 07752
(201) 291-0105
The Reverend Henry P. Davis, Jr., Moderator

Group Type: Denomination specific; district association/annual conference
Founded: 1900
Membership: 10,000 persons and 40 churches as of September, 1988
Meetings: Annual meeting during the week following the second Sunday in September

Second District Missionary Baptist Association of Louisiana

P.O. Box 1402
Gonzales, LA 70707-1402
(504) 644-0446
The Reverend Charles B. Bell, Jr., Moderator

Group Type: Denomination specific; district association/annual conference
Founded: 1880
Membership: 47 churches as of September 7, 1988
Meetings: Meets monthly

Snow Creek District Baptist Association—Alabama

P.O. Box 1102
Anniston, AL 36202
(205) 237-2773
The Reverend Eugene Leonard, Moderator

Group Type: Denomination specific; district association/annual conference
Founded: 1870
Membership: 32 churches as of September 8, 1988
Meetings: Annual meeting the Wednesday after the first Sunday in April

Southeast Alabama District Baptist Association

406 Alabama Avenue
Dothan, AL 36303
(205) 792-8467
Mrs. Ruth P. Brackins, Moderator

Group Type: Denomination specific; district association/annual conference
Founded: 1873

Membership: Over 4,000 persons and 12 churches as of September 8, 1988
Meetings: Meets twice a year

Southeast District Association—Kansas

718 East 7th Street
Coffeyville, KS 67337
(316) 251-4769
The Reverend C. H. Littlejohn, Moderator

Group Type: Denomination specific; district association/annual conference
Membership: 750 persons, 11 churches, and 8 ordained clergy as of September 8, 1987

Southern Arizona Missionary Baptist District Association

P.O. Box 27321
Tucson, AZ 85726
(602) 624-0882
The Reverend Hosea Hines, Moderator

Group Type: Denomination specific; district association/annual conference
Founded: 1954
Membership: 9 churches as of September, 1987
Meetings: Annual meeting on the Tuesday before the second Sunday in August

South West Baptist Association—Missouri

1517 Hill Street
Joplin, MO 64801
(417) 781-8935
The Reverend Harry F. Givens, Moderator

Group Type: Denomination specific; district association/annual conference
Founded: 1886
Meetings: Association has three one-day sessions and one full-week session

Southwestern District Association—Kansas

300 E. 2nd Street
Hutchinson, KS 67505
(316) 662-7497
The Reverend W. C. Tillman, Moderator

Group Type: Denomination specific; district association/annual conference
Founded: 1898

Spring Hill Missionary Baptist Association—Mississippi

Rankin and Simpson Streets
Florence, MS 39208
(601) 932-1355
The Reverend A. J. Taylor, Moderator

Group Type: Denomination specific; district association/annual conference

State Congress of Christian Education, Bluegrass Baptist Convention—Kentucky

1159 Algonquin Parkway
Louisville, KY 40208
(502) 635-7906
Dr. T. Vaughn Walker, Dean

Group Type: Denomination specific; state group or convention; Christian education

Storm Branch Association—South Carolina

685 Edrie Street
Aiken, SC 29801
(803) 648-5457
The Reverend Alfred Holmes, Moderator

Group Type: Denomination specific; district association/annual conference

Swan Lake Missionary Baptist Association—Mississippi

P.O. Box 200
Jonestown, MS 38639
(601) 627-2679
The Reverend Arthur Lee, Moderator

Group Type: Denomination specific; district association/annual conference
Founded: 1873
Membership: 1,519 persons, 25 churches, and 25 ordained clergy as of September 6, 1988
Meetings: Annual meeting from Wednesday through Friday before the second Sunday in August; semiannual session on the third Saturday in December

Tallahatchie-Oxford Missionary Baptist Association, Inc.—Mississippi

P.O. Box 412
Oxford, MS 38655
(601) 563-9580
The Reverend Walter L. Nash, Moderator

Group Type: Denomination specific; district association/annual conference
Founded: 1900
Membership: Between 300 and 500 persons, 20 churches, and 22 ordained clergy as of September 2, 1987
Meetings: Annual meeting from Monday through Wednesday following the second Sunday in August

Tennessee Baptist Missionary and Education Convention

900 Jefferson Street
P.O. Box 5645
Nashville, TN 37208
(615) 254-3115 or 255-9931
The Reverend Dr. V. J. Caldwell, President

Group Type: Denomination specific; state group or convention
Founded: 1872
Membership: 110,396 persons and 386 churches as of June 16, 1987
Publications: Tennessee Baptist Missionary and Education Newsletter
Meetings: Annual meeting on the Monday after the third Sunday in October

Tennessee Regular Baptist Convention

652 Lipford Street
Memphis, TN 38112
(901) 452-9582
The Reverend L. R. Donson, President

Group Type: Denomination specific; state group or convention

Founded: 1948
Membership: 15,500 persons, 37 churches, and 50 ordained clergy as of September, 1987
Meetings: Annual meeting on October 26th

Tri-County District Association—California

610 Lillian Drive
Barstow, CA 92311
(619) 256-2508
The Reverend Wayman Brown, Sr., Moderator

Group Type: Denomination specific; district association/annual conference
Meetings: Meets four times yearly; annual meeting the second week after the first Sunday in July

Trinity Valley Missionary Baptist District Association—Texas

2190 Bourbon Street
Beaumont, TX 77705
(409) 842-2249
The Reverend Holmon T. Tatman, Moderator

Group Type: Denomination specific; district association/annual conference
Founded: 1874
Membership: 58 churches as of September 17, 1987
Meetings: Annual meeting in the week after the first Sunday in August

True Friendship Missionary Baptist and Educational Association—Louisiana

2533 Washington Avenue
New Orleans, LA 70113
(504) 436-2546
The Reverend Ernest L. Porter, Sr., Moderator

Group Type: Denomination specific; district association/annual conference
Founded: 1954
Membership: 900 persons, 10 churches, and 20 ordained clergy as of September 8, 1987
Meetings: Annual meeting begins the Monday after the first Sunday in August

Union District Association—Ohio

11210 Union Avenue
Cleveland, OH 44112
(216) 751-9834
The Reverend Edward Smalls, Moderator

Group Type: Denomination specific; district association/annual conference
Founded: 1920
Membership: 10,000 persons, 50 churches, and 50 ordained clergy as of September 8, 1987
Publications: Quarterly notes
Meetings: Annual meeting on the fourth Sunday in July

United Baptist Convention of Delaware, Inc.

13 East Salisbury Drive
Wilmington, DE 19809
(302) 764-1571
The Reverend Tommie L. Brown, Sr., President

Group Type: Denomination specific; state group or convention

Founded: 1932
Membership: 3,928 persons and 19 churches as of August 26, 1987
Meetings: Annual meeting every second Tuesday in May

United Baptist Convention of Massachusetts, Rhode Island, and New Hampshire, Inc.

717 Main Street
Worcester, MA 02140
(413) 783-7608
The Reverend Gordon D. O'Neal, President

Group Type: Denomination specific; state group or convention
Founded: 1922
Membership: Approximately 18,000 persons, 55 churches, 48 ordained clergy, and 15 assistant and associate ministers as of September 9, 1988
Meetings: Annual meeting from Wednesday through Friday after July 4th

United Baptist Missionary Convention of Maryland, Inc.

1434 McCulloh Street
Baltimore, MD 21217
(301) 523-0983
The Reverend Dr. Olin P. Moyd, President

Group Type: Denomination specific; state group or convention
Founded: 1926
Membership: Approximately 100,000 persons, 130 churches, 200 ordained clergy, and 200 licentiates as of July 27, 1987
Meetings: Annual meeting during the week following the third Sunday in May

United Missionary Baptist Association—New York

20 W. 116th Street
New York, NY 10026
(212) 996-0334
The Reverend Hunson Greene, Moderator

Group Type: Denomination specific; district association/annual conference

West Mount Olive District Association—Mississippi

Route 1
Woodland, MS 39776
(601) 262-7280
The Reverend Joe Henson, Moderator

Group Type: Denomination specific; district association/annual conference
Founded: 1897
Membership: Approximately 2,000 persons, 13 churches, and 12 ordained clergy as of September 8, 1987
Meetings: Annual meeting the second week in August

Western District Missionary Association, Inc.—Oklahoma

P.O. Box 2545
Lawton, OK 73502
(405) 357-9161
The Reverend Dr. Charles Whitlow, Moderator

Group Type: Denomination specific; district association/annual conference

Founded: 1894
Membership: 3,000 persons, 29 churches, and 35 ordained clergy as of September 9, 1987
Meetings: Annual meeting in August

Western States Baptist Convention of Colorado and Wyoming

195 South Monaco Parkway
Denver, CO 80224
(303) 388-7533
The Reverend Dr. Acen L. Phillips, President

Group Type: Denomination specific; state group or convention
Founded: 1908
Membership: 33 churches, 155 ordained clergy, and 45 licentiates as of September, 1987
Publications: Western States Convention and monthly newsletter
Meetings: Meets the Tuesday following the second Sunday in August each year

Whitehaven District Association—Tennessee

P.O. Box 9593
Memphis, TN 38109
(901) 948-6511
The Reverend Lester Bastien, Moderator

Group Type: Denomination specific; district association/annual conference
Founded: 1883
Membership: 2,000 persons, 27 churches, and 27 ordained clergy as of September 8, 1987
Meetings: Annual meeting on the Monday after the third Sunday in August

Wills Creek District Missionary Baptist Association— Alabama

1431 Chestnut Street
Gadsden, AL 35901
(205) 547-6271
The Reverend W. H. Granger, Moderator

Group Type: Denomination specific; district association/annual conference
Founded: 1870
Membership: 40 churches and 40 ordained clergy as of September 9, 1987
Meetings: Annual meeting from Wednesday through Friday after the second Sunday in October

Woodriver Baptist District Association—Illinois

1324 W. Macon Street
Decatur, IL 62522
(217) 428-7654
The Reverend H. L. McClendon, Jr., Moderator

Group Type: Denomination specific; district association/annual conference
Founded: 1857
Membership: 5,000 persons, 45 churches, and 50 ordained clergy as of September 8, 1987
Meetings: Annual meeting on the third Monday in July

Zion District Association—Illinois

515 20th Street
Cairo, IL 62914
(618) 734-1028
The Reverend S. W. Oliver, Moderator

Group Type: Denomination specific; district association/annual conference
Founded: 1915
Membership: 500 persons and 10 churches, in Jackson, Alexander, Pulaski, and Williamson counties as of September 8, 1988

National Baptist Evangelical Life and Soul Saving Assembly of the U.S.A.

441-61 Monroe Avenue
Detroit, MI 48226

The National Baptist Evangelical Life and Soul Saving Assembly of the U.S.A. began as a city mission and evangelical movement of the National Baptist Convention of America in Kansas City, Missouri, in 1920. Founded by A. A. Banks, the assembly went independent in Birmingham, Alabama, in 1936, as a result of differences with the convention throughout the 1930s. Subsequently, centers have been established in cities across the country.

Its doctrine is generally that of the National Baptist Convention of America. The assembly conducts charitable activities, relief work, and evangelism. Members are urged to bring in a new member each year. Degrees are given for correspondence courses in pastoral ministry, missions, evangelism, and lay work. No current membership figures are available, but, as of 1951, there were 57,674 persons in 264 churches and 137 ministers across the country.

Group Type: Denomination
Founded: 1920
Membership: 57,674 persons, 264 churches, and 137 ministers as of 1951

National Missionary Baptist Convention of America

719 Crosby Street
San Diego, CA 92113
(619) 233-6487
The Reverend Dr. S. M. Lockridge, President
The Reverend Dr. S. J. Gilbert, General Secretary

The National Missionary Baptist Convention of America was organized as a separate entity from the National Baptist Convention of America, Inc., in 1988. It traces its origin to the founding of the first African American Baptist convention, the Baptist Foreign Mission Convention of the United States, on November 24, 1880, in Montgomery, Alabama. In 1895, the Baptist Foreign Mission Convention of the United States merged with two other conventions—the National Baptist Educational Convention founded in 1893 and the American National Baptist Convention founded in 1886—to form what is now known as the National Baptist Convention, U.S.A., Inc. On September 9, 1915, the National Baptist Convention of America, Inc., was born out of the National Baptist Convention, U.S.A., Inc.

Over the summer of 1988, control of the National Baptist Sunday Church School and Baptist Training Union Congress and the National Baptist Publishing Board, Inc. became controversial, as it had in 1915. This congress was a part of the National Baptist Convention of America, Inc. Some members of the convention wanted to gain greater control over the planning, execution, and profits of the convention's annual Sunday School leader training meeting. This ultimately resulted in the formation of a new convention—the National Missionary Baptist Convention of America.

The division resulted from an official session of the National Baptist Convention of America, Inc., in San Antonio, Texas, in 1988 attended by over seven hundred church leaders from across the country, where it was determined that the Convention would start a Sunday school congress to be controlled by the body itself. This, in effect, severed ties with the Boyd-controlled congress and publishing house. Five hundred church leaders subsequently met in Dallas, Texas, in November 1988 to form a new organization, intended to remain committed to the National Baptist Publishing Board, Inc., and the National Baptist Sunday Church School and Training Union Congress, still controlled by the Boyd family. The parent body, the National Baptist Convention of America, Inc., thus attempted to gain control over the publishing aspect of the convention, ironically after declaring that the publishing house would not be the property of any convention.

The purpose of the National Missionary Baptist Convention of America is to serve as an agency of Christian education, church extension, and missionary efforts. It seeks to maintain and safeguard full religious liberty and engage in social and economic development.

The National Missionary Baptist Convention of America, also known as the Boyd Convention, meets three times annually. The winter board meeting is held in February; the summer board meeting is held in June; and the annual convention is held in September. There are also regular executive committee meetings. Membership of the convention is in excess of 2,142,150 persons in 14,281 churches. The Reverend Dr. S. M. Lockridge is president and the Reverend Dr. S. J. Gilbert serves as general secretary.

Group Type: Denomination
Founded: November, 1988
Membership: Approximately 3,200,000 persons organized in churches, district associations, and state conventions
Meetings: Annual convention held in September; winter board meeting in February and summer board meeting in June; annual National Baptist Sunday Church School and Baptist Training Union Congress held in June in conjunction with the National Baptist Publishing Board, Inc.

National Primitive Baptist Convention, U.S.A.

P.O. Box 2355
Tallahassee, FL 32301
(904) 222-5218 or 5549
Elder F. L. Livingston, President

The National Primitive Baptist Convention, U.S.A., was the result of a 1906 call to black clergy by Elders Clarence Francis

Sams, George S. Crawford, James H. Carey, and others to meet in Huntsville, Alabama, in 1907 in order to establish a national convention. Eighty-seven elders representing seven southern states attended, thus the convention was organized, breaking from traditional Primitive Baptist polity—there would be no organization above the associations that served several counties.

The doctrine of the convention is the same as the Regular Primitive Baptists. Its creeds avow the belief of the "particular election of a definite number of the human race." The polity of the church is congregational, with the offices of pastor or elder, and deacon or deaconess (mother) on the local level. There are annual meetings of the convention, which also sponsors a publishing board and Sunday school.

Group Type: Denomination
Founded: 1907
Membership: 250,000 persons and 636 ministers in 606 churches as of 1975

New England Missionary Baptist Convention

c/o Berean Baptist Church
924 Madison Street, NW
Washington, DC 20011
The Reverend O. B. J. Burson, President

The New England Missionary Baptist Convention is the oldest African American Baptist organization in the United States. It was founded on May 16, 1874, at a meeting at the Congdon Street Baptist Church in Providence, Rhode Island. J. Horatio Carter, Rufus L. Perry, William T. Dixon, Robert D. Wynn, T. Doughty Miller, Joseph O. Johnson, George T. Tucker, Henry P. Thomas, and William H. Holloway were the nine pastors who founded the convention. According to the convention's history, "the particular business and object of the said society is to foster and maintain home and foreign missionary and benevolent work, and to establish and maintain educational institutions or chapels or places of Christian worship, or parsonages, and to receive, the charge of and disburse any property or funds which at any time and from time to time may be entrusted to said society for the aforesaid purpose." The convention also sought to serve as a type of "religious railroad," aiding those blacks leaving the South and moving North or traveling the Eastern Corridor.

The convention covers the New England and Middle Atlantic states—Maine, New Hampshire, Vermont, Massachusetts, Rhode Island, Connecticut, Pennsylvania, New York, New Jersey, Delaware, Maryland, and the District of Columbia. It has convened each year since 1875 without interruption or lapse of program. At its peak, there were four hundred member churches.

Throughout its history, the New England Missionary Baptist Convention has lent financial support to foreign missions, home missions, widows' funds, needy churches, aged ministers, and educational institutions such as the Northern School of Religion, Virginia Seminary and College, National Training School, and Shaw University.

Group Type: Denomination specific; state group or convention
Founded: May 16, 1874

Progressive National Baptist Convention, Inc.

601 50th Street, NE
Washington, DC 20019
(202) 396-0558
The Reverend Dr. Charles G. Adams, President
The Reverend Tyrone Pitts, General Secretary

Limited tenure for the president of the National Baptist Convention, U.S.A., Inc., has been an issue for a number of years and is at least partially responsible for a split in that convention in 1915 that gave rise to the National Baptist Convention of America. In 1922, the National Baptist Convention, U.S.A., voted to adopt a resolution limiting the president to a four-year term. However, the next president to take office remained in the position for eighteen years. In 1952, the constitution was revised to provide for a four-year term, but when the incumbent president, Dr. J. H. Jackson, reached the end of his four-year term in 1953, he refused to step down and attempted to have the four-year term ruled out-of-order.

During the 1960 annual meeting, more than two thousand delegates remained in the hall during a recess and elected Dr. Gardner C. Taylor president. In 1961, Jackson refused to let Taylor take office and, some allege, tried to block the Taylor supporters from the hall. Also, at that same time, there was disagreement over whether the convention should lend denominational support to the Civil Rights Movement and Dr. Martin Luther King, Jr., a member of the convention.

On September 11, 1961, Dr. L. V. Booth, pastor of Zion Baptist Church in Cincinnati, issued a press release announcing a meeting in his church, on November 14th and 15th, for the purpose of forming a new convention. Thirty-three delegates from fourteen states responded to the call, and the Progressive National Baptist Convention was born. The preamble to its constitution provides a clear statement of its doctrine and polity:

> The people called Progressive Baptists believe in the principles, tenets, and doctrines proclaimed or advocated in the New Testament as sufficient for their polity and practices. In Church government, Baptists believe in the rule of the people, by the people, and for the people, and in the vestment of the authority and power to act in the majority. Therefore, we, the members of the Progressive National Baptist Convention, U.S.A., Inc., federate ourselves together in the name of and under the direction and guidance of God, sharing our common faith in Jesus Christ and our concern for strengthening God's work through our common activities, and establish this Constitution for the Progressive National Baptist Convention, U.S.A, Inc.

Like most Baptists, Progressive Baptists endorse the general concept that individuals are able and expected to discern religious truth in communion with God and in fellowship with Jesus. Baptists emphasize individual discernment in the life of local, state, and national church structures as well.

The PNBC comprises four regions: southern, southwest, midwest, and east. Each region conducts yearly meetings in addition to participating in the annual meeting of the convention. Three of the four regions have a Congress of Christian Education that meets during the regional meeting. The Congress of Christian Education constitutes one of the largest auxiliaries of the convention.

The Progressive National Baptist Convention, Inc. has several auxiliaries. The Women's Auxiliary, established in 1962, is active in support of missions, evangelism, education, citizenship, child welfare concerns, and civil rights. The Home and Foreign Mission Boards are developing a pastoral counseling center in inner-city Philadelphia, cosponsoring *Healing Word* convocations, and have encouraged the member churches of the convention to participate in "One Church, One Child," whereby at least one person or couple in each church would adopt a child. The convention is also active in Haiti, Liberia, Nigeria, and West Africa. It also has a Youth Auxiliary, Laymen's Auxiliary (which meets twice yearly in support of special programs), Ushers and Nurses Auxiliary, and a Moderators' Auxiliary. In addition to the Home and Foreign Mission Boards, there are the Christian Education, Publication, and Pension Boards.

PNBC members are politically and socially active in other ways. For example, members have picketed and been arrested protesting South African apartheid. The convention is a participant supporter of the NAACP, Urban League, SCLC, Martin Luther King, Jr. Center for Nonviolent Social Change, Baptist World Alliance, North American Baptist Fellowship, Baptist Joint Committee on Public Affairs, National Council of Churches, and the General Commission of Chaplains and Armed Forces Personnel. The convention financially supports a number of institutions of higher learning, including Chicago Baptist Theological Seminary, Morehouse School of Religion, Virginia Union University School of Theology, Shaw Divinity School, Morris College, and Howard University School of Divinity. It also publishes *Baptist Progress*, a bimonthly journal of the convention.

From its modest beginning of thirty-three members from fourteen states, the PNBC has grown remarkably. Its churches now total more than 1,800, with membership of 1,800,000, in forty-six states and the District of Columbia. Its president is the Reverend Dr. Charles G. Adams and the general secretary is the Reverend Tyrone Pitts.

Group Type: Denomination
Founded: 1961
Membership: 1,200,000 persons in over 1,000 churches
Publications: *Baptist Progress*, 1477 Copley Road, Akron, OH 44320
Meetings: An annual convention the first week in August

State Conventions and District Associations of the Progressive National Baptist Convention, Inc.

Air Force Chaplain Fund

Headquarters, U.S. Air Force
Washington, DC 20330

Group Type: Ecumenical/nondenominational; ministerial

Allegheny Union Baptist Association—Pennsylvania

2700 Centre Avenue
Pittsburgh, PA 15219
The Reverend Jessie L. McFarland, Moderator

Group Type: Denomination specific; district association/annual conference

Antioch District Association—Illinois

8426 South Elizabeth Street
Chicago, IL 60620
The Reverend John Digby, Moderator

Group Type: Denomination specific; district association/annual conference

Atlanta Baptist Association—Georgia

205 Oakcliff Court, NW
Atlanta, GA 30331

Group Type: Denomination specific; district association/annual conference

Baptist Convention of the District of Columbia and Vicinity

1600 13th Street, NW
Washington, DC 20009
The Reverend David Durham, Moderator

Group Type: Denomination specific; state group or convention

Baptist Men of Philadelphia

354 Osceola Avenue
Elkins Park, PA 19117

Group Type: Denomination specific; state group or convention; lay/clergy

Baptist Ministers Conference of Los Angeles

c/o True Way Baptist Church
9122 South San Pedro Avenue
Los Angeles, CA 90003
(213) 777-9575
The Reverend Frank J. Higgins, President

Group Type: Denomination specific; ministerial; state group or convention

Baptist State Convention of Illinois

7925 South Chicago Avenue
Chicago, IL 60617
The Reverend John Conner, President

Group Type: Denomination specific; state group or convention

Baptist State Missionary Convention—Kentucky

2300 West Madison Street
Louisville, KY 40211

Group Type: Denomination specific; state group or convention

Bethlehem Baptist District Association—Illinois

3722 Martin Luther King Drive
Chicago, IL 60653
The Reverend E. R. Williams, Moderator

Group Type: Denomination specific; district association/annual conference

Charleston Association—South Carolina

2678 Meeting Street Road
Charleston, SC 29405

Group Type: Denomination specific; district association/annual conference

Christian Fellowship District Association—California

1572 7th Street
Oakland, CA 94607
The Reverend Eugene Lumpkin, Jr., Moderator

Group Type: Denomination specific; district association/annual conference

Cincinnati District Association—Ohio

2297 Gephart Road
Hamilton, OH 45011
The Reverend Dr. Charles Brown, Moderator

Group Type: Denomination specific; district association/annual conference

City Union Number 1 State of Tennessee District Association

682 South Lauderdale Street
Memphis, TN 38126

Group Type: Denomination specific; district association/annual conference

Cleveland District of Baptist Women

4400 Clarkwood Parkway
Warrensville Heights, OH
Mrs. Daisy G. Horne, President

Group Type: Denomination specific; district association/annual conference; women

Connecticut Baptist Missionary Convention

1324 Chapel Street
New Haven, CT 06511
The Reverend Dr. C. M. Coffield II, President

Group Type: Denomination specific; state group or convention

County Line Baptist Convention Association—North Carolina

Route 3, Box 243
Louisburg, NC 27549
The Reverend Moses Hardy, Moderator

Group Type: Denomination specific; district association/annual conference

D.C. Ministers' Conference

601 50th Street, NE
Washington, DC 20019

Group Type: Denomination specific; ministerial; state group or convention

D.C. Progressive Laymen

1129 Tewksbury Place, NW
Washington, DC 20012
Mr. Clarence E. Barker, President

Group Type: Denomination specific; lay

District Federation of Young People—D.C.

3341 D Street, SE
Washington, DC 20019

Group Type: Denomination specific; state group or convention; youth

Eastern Keystone Baptist Association—Pennsylvania

2500 W. Columbia Avenue
Philadelphia, PA 19121
The Reverend Robert Lovett, Moderator

Group Type: Denomination specific; district association/annual conference

Fellowship Baptist District Association, Inc.—Illinois

1805 South Pulaski Road
Chicago, IL 60623
The Reverend Lee H. Ivy, Moderator

Group Type: Denomination specific; district association/annual conference

Fellowship Missionary Baptist District Association—Missouri

5604 Garfield Avenue
Kansas City, MO 64130
The Reverend Dr. James A. Howard, Moderator

Group Type: Denomination specific; district association/annual conference

Franklin County Sunday School and Baptist Training Union Convention—North Carolina

Route 3, Box 243
Louisburg, NC 27549
Dr. Arthur Williams, Moderator

Group Type: Denomination specific; district association/annual conference

General Baptist State Convention of North Carolina, Inc.

603 South Wilmington Street
Raleigh, NC 27601
The Reverend J. B. Humphrey, President
(704) 372-1075
The Reverend Dr. C. C. Craig, Executive Director
(919) 821-7466

Group Type: Denomination specific; state group or convention
Founded: 1867; incorporated in 1947
Membership: 425,000 persons, 1,700 churches, and 1,200 ordained clergy as of December 8, 1987
Publications: *The Baptist Informer*, general newspaper
Meetings: Annual meeting held in July

Gethsemane Baptist Association, Inc.—South Carolina

2221 Maguerette Street
Columbia, SC 29204
The Reverend Frank Young, Moderator

Group Type: Denomination specific; district association/annual conference

Indiana State Convention

4525 Lesley Avenue
Indianapolis, IN 46226

Group Type: Denomination specific; state group or convention

*Interdenominational Minister District Association—
Mississippi*

P.O. Box 4516
Greenville, MS 38704
The Reverend W. L. Newton, Moderator

Group Type: Denomination specific; district association/annual conference

Kentucky State Fellowship

470 W. 6th Street
Lexington, KY 41011
The Reverend A. A. Hester, President

Group Type: Denomination specific; state group or convention

*Kingston Lake Missionary Baptist Association—South
Carolina*

P.O. Box 1318
Conway, SC 29526
(803) 756-1781
The Reverend Allen B. Nichols, Moderator

Group Type: Denomination specific; district association/annual conference
Founded: 1887
Meetings: Annual meeting held during the third week in October

Louisiana Progressive Baptist Fellowship

6112 West Bank Expressway
Marrero, LA 70072
Mrs. Valarie Taylor, President

Group Type: Denomination specific; district association/annual conference

Louisiana Progressive Baptist State Convention

650 Blount Road
Baton Rouge, LA 70807
The Reverend H. B. Williams, President

Group Type: Denomination specific; state group or convention

Marine Corps Development and Educational Convention

Office of Command Chaplain
Quantico, VA 20390
Captain Charles L. Keyser

Group Type: Ecumenical/nondenominational; lay/clergy

Martin Luther King, Jr. State Convention—Indiana

3902 Alexander Street
East Chicago, IN 46312
The Reverend Dr. Vincent L. McCutcheon, President

Group Type: Denomination specific; state group or convention

*Metropolitan Missionary District Baptist Association—
California*

1001 W. 69th Street
Los Angeles, CA 90044
The Reverend Jack B. Richardson, Moderator

Group Type: Denomination specific; district association/annual conference

Michigan Progressive Baptist Convention

20056 Cherrylawn Street
Detroit, MI 48221
The Reverend Dr. Charles W. Butler, President

Group Type: Denomination specific; state group or convention

Middlesex Central Baptist Association—New Jersey

34 Sweets Avenue
Trenton, NJ 08618

Group Type: Denomination specific; district association/annual conference

Missouri Progressive Missionary Baptist Convention

2627 Jackson Avenue
Kansas City, MO 64127
The Reverend J. B. Randolph, President

Group Type: Denomination specific; state group or convention

Missouri Progressive Missionary Baptist State Convention

5604 Garfield Avenue
Kansas City, MO 64130
(816) 444-7174
The Reverend James A. Howard, President

Group Type: Denomination specific; state group or convention

Mount Carmel Missionary Baptist Association—Georgia

P.O. Box 46
Talbotton, GA 31827
The Reverend H. Herring, Moderator

Group Type: Denomination specific; district association/annual conference

Mount Moriah Baptist Association—South Carolina

P.O. Box 158
Liberty Hill, SC 29074

Group Type: Denomination specific; district association/annual conference

Mount Zion Baptist Association, Inc.—New York

36 Vassar Street
Poughkeepsie, NY 12601
The Reverend H. Austin, Moderator

Group Type: Denomination specific; district association/annual conference

New Era District Association—Indiana

3902-06 Alexander Avenue
East Chicago, IN 46312
The Reverend Vincent L. McCutcheon, Moderator

Group Type: Denomination specific; district association/annual conference

New Era Missionary Baptist Convention—Georgia

395 Chamberlin Street, SE
Atlanta, GA 30312
The Reverend Dr. Charles Hamilton, President

Group Type: Denomination specific; state group or convention

New Hope Christian Baptist Association—New York

147 W. 131st Street
New York, NY 10027
The Reverend J. M. Dawson, Moderator

Group Type: Denomination specific; district association/annual conference

New Jersey Convention Progressive

P.O. Box 370
Cranford, NJ 07103
The Reverend W. Marcus Williams, President

Group Type: Denomination specific; state group or convention

New York Missionary Baptist Association

340-44 Malcolm X Boulevard
Brooklyn, NY 11233
(718) 773-1650
(516) 867-3278
The Reverend Irvin Wilson, Moderator

Group Type: Denomination specific; district association/annual conference

New York Progressive Baptist State Convention

15 Wallace Street
Tuckahoe, NY 10707
The Reverend Charles E. Houston, President

Group Type: Denomination specific; state group or convention

Northern Virginia Baptist Association, Inc.

6626 Costner Drive
Falls Church, VA 22042
The Reverend Dr. James E. Browne, Moderator

Group Type: Denomination specific; district association/annual conference

Ohio Baptist Women's Convention

48 N. Parkwood Avenue
Columbus, OH 43203
Mrs. Bernice Troy, President

Group Type: Denomination specific; state group or convention; women

Oklahoma City District Association

5816 North Rhode Island Avenue
Oklahoma City, OK 73111
The Reverend Willard Dallas, Moderator

Group Type: Denomination specific; district association/annual conference

Old Landmark District Association—California

15609 S. Sandel Avenue
Gardena, CA 90248
The Reverend Willie Island, Jr., Moderator

Group Type: Denomination specific; district association/annual conference

Pee Dee Baptist Association—North Carolina

Route 1, Box 197
Wagram, NC 28396
The Reverend J. H. Ferguson, Moderator

Group Type: Denomination specific; district association/annual conference

Pee Dee Baptist Association—South Carolina

92 Chestnut Street
Cheraw, SC 29520

Group Type: Denomination specific; district association/annual conference

Pennsylvania Baptist Association

1701 Bainbridge Street
Philadelphia, PA 19146
The Reverend Dr. T. C. Killebrew, Moderator

Group Type: Denomination specific; district association/annual conference

Pennsylvania State Baptist Convention

6556 Shetland Avenue
Pittsburgh, PA 15206
The Reverend Dr. Elmer L. Williams, President

Group Type: Denomination specific; state group or convention

Progressive Baptist Association—Tennessee

Larmer Avenue
Memphis, TN 38114

Group Type: Denomination specific; district association/annual conference

Progressive Baptist Convention of Maryland

612-18 North Gilmor Street
Baltimore, MD 21217
The Reverend Dr. Raymond Kelly, Jr., President

Group Type: Denomination specific; state group or convention

Progressive Baptist Convention of Mississippi

P.O. Box 55
Tutwiler, MS 38963
The Reverend Dr. J. L. Featherstone, President

Group Type: Denomination specific; state group or convention

Progressive Baptist Council—Tennessee

682 South Lauderdale Street
Memphis, TN 38126
The Reverend W. C. Holmes, President

Group Type: Denomination specific; district association/annual conference

Progressive Baptist District Association—Illinois

5533 Wentworth Avenue
Chicago, IL 60621
The Reverend Clifford Tyler, Moderator

Group Type: Denomination specific; district association/annual conference

Progressive Baptist District Association—Ohio

3028 Vine Street
Cincinnati, OH 45219
The Reverend Douglas Jones, Moderator

Group Type: Denomination specific; district association/annual conference

Progressive Baptist Fellowship Association—Louisiana

6112 Westbank Expressway
Marrero, LA 70772

Group Type: Denomination specific; state group or convention

Progressive Baptist Missionary and Educational Convention—Alabama

39-20 Avenue South
Birmingham, AL 35205
The Reverend J. W. Taylor, President

Group Type: Denomination specific; state group or convention

Progressive Baptist State Convention—California

2057 W. Century Boulevard
Los Angeles, CA 90047
The Reverend Willie Williams, President

Group Type: Denomination specific; state group or convention

Progressive Baptist State Convention of Illinois

7701 South Ridgeland Avenue
Chicago, IL 60649
The Reverend James Fair

Group Type: Denomination specific; state group or convention

Progressive Baptist State Convention—Texas

9702 Rosehaven Drive
Houston, TX 77051
The Reverend J. R. Jackson, President

Group Type: Denomination specific; state group or convention

Progressive District Association of Oklahoma

P.O. Box 11321
Oklahoma City, OK 73136
The Reverend Willard Dallas, Moderator

Group Type: Denomination specific; district association/annual conference

Progressive National Baptist Convention Youth Department—Illinois

1005 N. Lamon Avenue
Chicago, IL 60651
Mrs. Elsie Nelson, Coordinator

Group Type: Denomination specific; youth

Progressive National Baptist Convention Youth Department—National

3414 Aberdeen Street
Suitland, MD 20746
Mr. Kenneth E. Barksdale, Coordinator

Group Type: Denomination specific; youth

Progressive Oklahoma Baptist State Convention

4621 NE 23rd Street
Oklahoma City, OK 73121
The Reverend Jayel Jacobs, President

Group Type: Denomination specific; state group or convention

Progressive Western District Association—Oklahoma

4621 NE 23rd Street
Oklahoma City, OK 73121
(415) 732-7521
The Reverend I. L. LeFall, Moderator

Group Type: Denomination specific; district association/annual conference

Ready River Baptist Association—South Carolina

107 Fleming Street
Greenville, SC 29607
The Reverend Robert E. Dennis, Moderator

Group Type: Denomination specific; district association/annual conference

Rocky River Association—South Carolina

Johnson Street
Anderson, SC 29624

Group Type: Denomination specific; district association/annual conference

Saint John Baptist Association—North Carolina

706 Raleigh Street
Laurinburg, NC 28352
The Reverend Dr. J. J. Johnson, Moderator

Group Type: Denomination specific; district association/annual conference

Saint Louis Progressive Missionary Baptist Convention—Missouri

1617 N. Euclid Avenue
St. Louis, MO 63113
The Reverend Eddie Sennie, President

Group Type: Denomination specific; state group or convention

Saint Louis Progressive Missionary Baptist District Association—Missouri

1617 N. Euclid Avenue
St. Louis, MO 63113
The Reverend Eddie Sennie, Moderator

Group Type: Denomination specific; district association/annual conference

Shoal Creek Baptist Association—Georgia

727 Charlotte Place, NW
Atlanta, GA 30318
The Reverend E. J. Jester, Sr., Moderator

Group Type: Denomination specific; district association/annual conference

South Carolina Baptist Education and Missionary Convention

2334 Elmwood Avenue
Columbia, SC 29204
The Reverend Dr. J. O. Rich, President

Group Type: Denomination specific; state group or convention

Southern Nevada Progressive Baptist State Convention

501 Alexander Avenue
Las Vegas, NV 89106
The Reverend C. C. Smith, President

Group Type: Denomination specific; state group or convention

Tennessee Baptist Missionary and Education Convention

900 Jefferson Street
P.O. Box 5645
Nashville, TN 37208
(615) 254-3115
The Reverend Dr. V. J. Caldwell, President
(615) 629-3277

Group Type: Denomination specific; state group or convention
Founded: 1872
Publications: Tennessee Baptist Missionary and Education Newsletter
Meetings: Annual meeting is held on the Monday after the third Sunday in October

Union District Association—Illinois

1048 N. Lavergne Avenue
Chicago, IL 60651
The Reverend August Minor, Moderator

Group Type: Denomination specific; district association/annual conference

United Baptist District Association of California

1735 W. 57th Street
Los Angeles, CA 90062
The Reverend Dr. R. D. Jordan, Moderator

Group Type: Denomination specific; district association/annual conference

United Shiloh Missionary Baptist Association—North Carolina

500 E. Grand Avenue
Rocky Mount, NC 27802
The Reverend Dr. Elbert Lee, Moderator

Group Type: Denomination specific; district association/annual conference

Virginia Baptist State Convention

745 Park Avenue Place
Norfolk, VA 23504
The Reverend Dr. J. H. Foster, President

Group Type: Denomination specific; state group or convention

Wateree Association—South Carolina

7 Stark Street
Sumter, SC 29150

Group Type: Denomination specific; district association/annual conference

Zion Sunday School and Baptist Training Union Congress—Mississippi

Route 3, Box 182
Winona, MS 38967
The Reverend A. C. Cade, Moderator

Group Type: Denomination specific; district association/annual conference

United American Free Will Baptist Denomination, Inc.

1011 University Street
P.O. Box 3303
Kinston, NC 28501
(919) 527-0120
Dr. J. E. Reddick, Presiding General Bishop

The Free Will Baptists of North Carolina derived from the General Baptists of England. The United Free Will Baptist Church subsequently derived from the Free Will Baptists of North Carolina in 1867. A small group of visionaries met in Green County, North Carolina, and used a bush shelter for their services until the first church, Shady Grove, was built.

The church has a varied form of congregational polity, and has district, quarterly, annual, and general conferences. Local churches are autonomous in government, but the conferences decide questions of doctrine. Its theology is taken from the parent body, and is Armenian in origin. The church practices anointing the sick with oil, footwashing, and baptism. The church is currently building a multipurpose facility at its headquarters with short-range goals that include a Free Will Baptist Bible College and retirement home for the elderly. It supports Kinston College in Kinston, North Carolina, and publishes *The Free Will Baptist Advocate*.

Group Type: Denomination
Founded: 1867
Membership: Approximately 50,000 persons in 250 congregations
Publications: The Free Will Baptist Advocate
Meetings: District, quarterly, annual and general conferences

Methodist

African Methodist Episcopal Church

1134 11th Street, NW
Washington, DC 20001
(202) 371-8700
Bishop John Hurst Adams, Senior Bishop
Dr. Joseph C. McKinney, Treasurer
Dr. O. Urcille Ifill, General Secretary
Dr. Dennis C. Dickerson, Historiographer

The African Methodist Episcopal Church was founded in Philadelphia on April 12, 1787, as a result of discrimination against the black members of the St. George's Methodist Episcopal Church and in protest of slavery. Richard Allen, along with Absalom Jones and others, organized the Free African Society, a beneficial and mutual aid society, which eventually spread to other cities. The society issued a plan for a nondenominational church, which was organized on July 7, 1791. The

Bethel Church was formalized in Philadelphia on July 17, 1794. The denomination was officially established on April 16, 1816, with Richard Allen named its first bishop on April 11, 1816.

The A.M.E. Church has always accepted the standards of Methodism. Its standards of faith are the Twenty-Five Articles of Religion adopted by John Wesley from the Thirty-Nine Articles of the Church of England, and the Apostles' Creed. The church believes in justification through faith and personal repentance toward Jesus Christ. It does not believe in apostolic succession or extreme ritualism in services. Additionally, it proposes faith in the Holy Trinity, belief in Jesus Christ and His resurrection, the sacraments of Baptism and the Lord's Supper, law and leadership of the country, and support of the poor.

The Articles of Religion are the basis for the church's position on biblical interpretation and political involvement. The Bible is considered to provide "all things necessary for salvation, so that what is not read therein nor may be proved thereby is not to be required of any man . . . as an article of faith or be thought requisite or necessary to salvation." The sixty-six books of the Bible are considered canonical. The church also acknowledges the leadership of the United States as such, and it is believed to be the duty of ministers and all Christians to obey the laws of the country.

Based on the principle that local A.M.E. bodies "shall be engaged in carrying out the spirit of the original Free African Society out of which the A.M.E. Church evolved," A.M.E. churches seek to find and save the lost and to serve those in need through preaching, caring for the needy, sick, and elderly, and encouraging economic advancement. The denomination emphases educational opportunity and mission work; therefore, the A.M.E. Church sponsors seven colleges and universities (Wilberforce, Morris Brown, Paul Quinn, Edward Waters, Allen, Shorter, and Bonner Campbell). The Church has established and continues to supports two seminaries: Payne Theological Seminary in Xenia, Ohio, and Turner Theological Seminary in Atlanta, Georgia. In addition, three Job Corps centers are located on A.M.E. sites, and more than thirty percent of local A.M.E. congregations sponsor housing, facilities for the elderly, or schools.

Overseas, the A.M.E. Church supports many projects, including Monrovia College and Industrial Training School, Inc., in Monrovia, Liberia; the Jordan Agricultural Institute in Royesville, Liberia; the A.M.E. Church Publishing House in South Africa; the James Center (a multipurpose facility) in Mesuru, Lesotho; schools in Malawi and Zimbabwe; and a School of Religion in Johannesburg, South Africa. In the Caribbean, the A.M.E. Church sponsors numerous schools in Jamaica, St. Croix, and Haiti. There are also three active A.M.E. congregations in London, England.

The polity structure of the A.M.E. Church is based upon that of the Methodist Church. The General Conference is the supreme body and meets every four years to address matters of concern to the church. The Council of Bishops, the executive branch of the body, is charged with the general oversight of the church during the interim between general conferences. The General Board of Trustees supervises in trust all connectional (church) property and acts on behalf of the church on such matters when necessary. The General Board serves as the administrative body of the church and is composed of various departmental representatives. The Judicial Council is the highest judiciary body, serving as an appellate court chosen by the General Conference and is amenable to it. In addition to these, each of the nineteen districts is responsible for annual, district, and quarterly conferences as well as church meetings in each congregation.

Much of the denomination work of the A.M.E. Church is handled through its commissions. There are commissions on finance and statistics, pensions, publications, minimum salary, church extension and evangelism, missions, higher education, research and development, Christian education, social action, and lay organization.

The A.M.E. Church continues to serve others through its 3,500,000 members and eight thousand churches in the United States, and in Africa, Canada, the Caribbean, and South America. The church recently celebrated its bicentennial.

Group Type: Denomination
Founded: April 12, 1787 (officially established as a denomination April 16, 1816)
Membership: 3,500,000 persons in 8,000 churches
Publications: *A.M.E. Christian Recorder* [the oldest continuing African American church periodical in the world], Dr. Robert H. Reid, Jr., editor, 500 Eighth Avenue, South Nashville, TN 37203, (615) 256-8548; *A.M.E. Review*, Dr. Jayme C. Williams, editor, 500 Eighth Avenue, South Nashville, TN 37203, (615) 320-3500; *Voice of Missions*, Dr. Frederick C. Harrison, editor and secretary-treasurer, Missions Department 475 Riverside Drive, Suite 1926 New York, NY 10027, (212) 870-2258; *Women's Missionary Magazine*, Mrs. Delores L. Kennedy Williams, president, Women's Missionary Society, P.O. Box 2624, Indianapolis, IN 46206; *Secret Chamber*, Dr. G. H. J. Thibodeaux, editor, 1150 Portland Avenue, Shreveport, LA 71103; *Journal of Christian Education*, Dr. Y. Benjamin Bruce, director, Department of Worship and Evangelism, 8128 Banyan Boulevard, Orlando, FL 32819, (305) 352-6515; and other religious literature, Dr. Cyrus S. Keller, Sr., editor, Religious Literature, P.O. Box 5327, St. Louis, MO 63115
Meetings: A General Conference every 4 years as well as annual, district, and quarterly conferences

Episcopal Districts of the African Methodist Episcopal Church

1st Episcopal District—A.M.E. Church

3801 Market Street
Philadelphia, PA 19143
(215) 662-0506
Bishop Frank Curtis Cummings

Group Type: Denomination specific; episcopal district
Geographic Areas: Bermuda; Delaware; New England; New Jersey; New York; Philadelphia

2nd Episcopal District—A.M.E. Church

1134 11th Street, NW
Washington, DC 20001
(202) 371-8700
Bishop H. Hartford Brookins

Group Type: Denomination specific; episcopal district
Geographic Areas: Baltimore; North Carolina; Washington, D.C.; Western North Carolina

3rd Episcopal District—A.M.E. Church

700 Bryden Road, Suite 135
Columbus, OH 43215
Bishop Richard Allen Hildebrand
(614) 461-6496

Group Type: Denomination specific; episcopal district
Geographic Areas: Pittsburgh; Ohio; North Ohio; South Ohio; West Virginia

4th Episcopal District—A.M.E. Church

7220 North Illinois Street
Indianapolis, IN 46260
(317) 373-6587
Bishop J. Haskell Mayo

Group Type: Denomination specific; episcopal district
Geographic Areas: Canada; Chicago; Illinois; Indiana; Michigan

5th Episcopal District—A.M.E. Church

4144 Lindell Boulevard, Suite 222
St. Louis, MO 63108
(314) 534-4274
Bishop Vinton R. Anderson

Group Type: Denomination specific; episcopal district
Geographic Areas: California; Colorado; Kansas-Nebraska; Missouri; Northwest Missouri; Puget Sound

6th Episcopal District—A.M.E. Church

208 Auburn Avenue, NE
Atlanta, GA 30303
(404) 524-8279
Bishop John Hurst Adams

Group Type: Denomination specific; episcopal district
Geographic Areas: Atlanta-North Georgia; Augusta; Macon, Georgia; Old Georgia; South Georgia; Southwest Georgia

7th Episcopal District—A.M.E. Church

Landmark East, Suite 402
3700 Forest Drive
Columbia, SC 29204
Bishop Frederick C. James

Group Type: Denomination specific; episcopal district
Geographic Areas: Central South Carolina; Columbia; Palmetto; Piedmont; Northeast South Carolina; South Carolina

8th Episcopal District—A.M.E. Church

2138 St. Bernard Avenue
St. Louis, MO 70119
(504) 948-4251
Bishop Donald G. K. Ming

Group Type: Denomination specific; episcopal district
Geographic Areas: Central-Louisiana; Central-North Mississippi; East Mississippi; Louisiana; Mississippi; Northeast-West Mississippi

9th Episcopal District—A.M.E. Church

737 Oneida Drive
Birmingham, AL 35214
(205) 791-1908
Bishop Cornelius E. Thomas

Group Type: Denomination specific; episcopal district
Geographic Areas: Alabama; Central Alabama; East Alabama; North Alabama; South Alabama; West Alabama

10th Episcopal District—A.M.E. Church

Oak Cliff, Suite 813
400 South Zang Boulevard
Dallas, TX 75208
(214) 943-3001
Bishop John R. Bryant

Group Type: Denomination specific; episcopal district
Geographic Areas: Central Texas; North Texas; Northeast Texas; Northwest Texas; Southwest Texas; Texas; West Texas

11th Episcopal District—A.M.E. Church

101 Riverside Avenue
Jacksonville, FL 32202
(904) 355-8262
Bishop Philip Robert Cousin

Group Type: Denomination specific; episcopal district
Geographic Areas: Bahamas; Central Florida; East Florida; Florida; Orlando; South Florida; Tampa, Florida

12th Episcopal District—A.M.E. Church

604 Locust Street
Little Rock, AR 72114
(501) 375-4310
Bishop Henry A. Belin, Jr.

Group Type: Denomination specific; episcopal district
Geographic Areas: Arkansas; Central Arkansas; Central Oklahoma; East-Northeast Oklahoma; South Arkansas

13th Episcopal District—A.M.E. Church

500 Eighth Avenue, South
Nashville, TN 37203
(615) 242-6814
Bishop Vernon R. Byrd

Group Type: Denomination specific; episcopal district
Geographic Areas: East Tennessee; Kentucky; Tennessee; West Kentucky; West Tennessee

14th Episcopal District—A.M.E. Church

4000 Bedford Road
Baltimore, MD 21207
(301) 484-7508

P.O. Box 4191
Monrovia, Liberia, West Africa
011-231-225-828#
Bishop John R. Bryant

Group Type: Denomination specific; episcopal district
Geographic Areas: Ghana; Liberia; Nigeria; Sierra Leone

15th Episcopal District—A.M.E. Church

17751 Hamilton Road
Detroit, MI 48203

28 Walmer Road
Woodstock 7925
Capetown, Republic of South Africa
011-27-021-475-786#
Bishop Robert Thomas, Jr.

Group Type: Denomination specific; episcopal district
Geographic Areas: Cape; Eastern Cape; Kalahari; Namibia; Queenstown

16th Episcopal District—A.M.E. Church

604 Locust Street
North Little Rock, AR 72214
(501) 375-4310
Bishop Henry A. Belin, Jr.

Group Type: Denomination specific; episcopal district
Geographic Areas: Dominican Republic; Haiti; Jamaica; London; Cuba; Surinam-Guyana; Virgin Islands; Windward Islands

17th Episcopal District—A.M.E. Church

P.O. Box 183
St. Louis, MO 63166

P.O. Box 36628
Lusaka, Zambia, Central Africa
Bishop Richard Allen Chappelle

Group Type: Denomination specific; episcopal district
Geographic Areas: Malawi; Northeast Zimbabwe; Northeast Zambia; Northwest Zambia; South Zambia; Southwest Zimbabwe

18th Episcopal District—A.M.E. Church

P.O. Box 183
St. Louis, MO 63166

P.O. Box 223
Maseru, Lesotho, Southern Africa
Bishop Richard Allen Chappelle

Group Type: Denomination specific; episcopal district
Geographic Areas: Botswana; Lesotho; Mozambique; Northeast Lesotho; Swaziland

19th Episcopal District—A.M.E. Church

P.O. Box 12
Residensia, 1980
Republic of South Africa
011-2716-351655#
Bishop Harold Ben Senatle

Group Type: Denomination specific; episcopal district
Geographic Areas: East Transvaal; Natal; Northern Transvaal; Orangia; West Transvaal

Annual Conferences of the African Methodist Episcopal Church

Alabama Annual Conference, 9th Episcopal District

737 Oneida Drive
Birmingham, AL 35214
Bishop Cornelius E. Thomas

Group Type: Denomination specific; district association/annual conference

Arkansas Annual Conference, 12th Episcopal District

604 Locust Street
Little Rock, AR 42114
Bishop Henry A. Belin, Jr.

Group Type: Denomination specific; district association/annual conference

Atlanta—North Georgia Annual Conference, 6th Episcopal District

208 Auburn Avenue, NE
Atlanta, GA 30303
Bishop John Hurst Adams

Group Type: Denomination specific; district association/annual conference

Augusta, Georgia Annual Conference, 6th Episcopal District

208 Auburn Avenue, NE
Atlanta, GA 30303
Bishop John Hurst Adams

Group Type: Denomination specific; district association/annual conference

Bahama Islands Annual Conference, 11th Episcopal District

101 Riverside Avenue
Jacksonville, FL 32202
Bishop Philip Robert Cousin

Group Type: Denomination specific; district association/annual conference

Baltimore Annual Conference, 2nd Episcopal District

1134 11th Street, NW
Washington, DC 20001
Bishop H. Hartford Brookins

Group Type: Denomination specific; district association/annual conference

Bermuda Annual Conference, 1st Episcopal District

3801 Market Street
Philadelphia, PA 19143
Bishop Frank Curtis Cummings

Group Type: Denomination specific; district association/annual conference

Botswana Annual Conference, 18th Episcopal District

P.O. Box 183
St. Louis, MO 63166
Bishop Richard Allen Chappelle

Group Type: Denomination specific; district association/annual conference

California Annual Conference, 5th Episcopal District

4144 Lindell Boulevard, Suite 222
St. Louis, MO 63108
Bishop Vinton R. Anderson

Group Type: Denomination specific; district association/annual conference

Canadian Annual Conference, 4th Episcopal District

7220 North Illinois Street
Indianapolis, IN 46260
Bishop J. Haskell Mayo

Group Type: Denomination specific; district association/annual conference

Cape Annual Conference, 15th Episcopal District

17751 Hamilton Road
Detroit, MI 48203
Bishop Robert Thomas, Jr.

Group Type: Denomination specific; district association/annual conference

Central Alabama Annual Conference, 9th Episcopal District

737 Oneida Avenue
Birmingham, AL 35214
Bishop Cornelius E. Thomas

Group Type: Denomination specific; district association/annual conference

Central Arkansas Annual Conference, 12th Episcopal District

604 Locust Street
Little Rock, AR 72214
Bishop Henry A. Belin, Jr.

Group Type: Denomination specific; district association/annual conference

Central Florida Annual Conference, 11th Episcopal District

101 Riverside Avenue
Jacksonville, FL 32202
Bishop Philip Robert Cousin

Group Type: Denomination specific; district association/annual conference

Central Louisiana Annual Conference, 8th Episcopal District

2138 St. Bernard Avenue
St. Louis, MO 70119
Bishop Donald G. K. Ming

Group Type: Denomination specific; district association/annual conference

Central-North Mississippi Annual Conference, 8th Episcopal District

2138 St. Bernard Avenue
St. Louis, MO 70119
Bishop Donald G. K. Ming

Group Type: Denomination specific; district association/annual conference

Central Oklahoma Annual Conference, 12th Episcopal District

604 Locust Street
Little Rock, AR 72214
Bishop Henry A. Belin, Jr.

Group Type: Denomination specific; district association/annual conference

Central South Carolina Annual Conference, 7th Episcopal District

Landmark East, Suite 402
3700 Forest Drive
Columbia, SC 29204
Bishop Frederick C. James

Group Type: Denomination specific; district association/annual conference

Central Texas Annual Conference, 10th Episcopal District

Oak Cliff, Suite 813
400 South Zang Boulevard
Dallas, TX 75208
Bishop John R. Bryant

Group Type: Denomination specific; district association/annual conference

Chicago Annual Conference, 4th Episcopal District

7220 North Illinois Street
Indianapolis, IN 46260
Bishop J. Haskell Mayo

Group Type: Denomination specific; district association/annual conference

Colorado Annual Conference, 5th Episcopal District

4144 Lindell Boulevard, Suite 222
St. Louis, MO 63108
Bishop Vinton R. Anderson

Group Type: Denomination specific; district association/annual conference

Columbia Annual Conference, 7th Episcopal District

Landmark East, Suite 402
3700 Forest Drive
Columbia, SC 29204
Bishop Frederick C. James

Group Type: Denomination specific; district association/annual conference

Cuba Annual Conference, 16th Episcopal District

604 Locust Street
North Little Rock, AR 72214
Bishop Henry A. Belin, Jr.

Group Type: Denomination specific; district association/annual conference

Delaware Annual Conference, 1st Episcopal District

3801 Market Street
Philadelphia, PA 19143
Bishop Frank Curtis Cummings

Group Type: Denomination specific; district association/annual conference

Dominican Republic Annual Conference, 16th Episcopal District

604 Locust Street
North Little Rock, AR 72214
Bishop Henry A. Belin, Jr.

Group Type: Denomination specific; district association/annual conference

East Alabama Annual Conference, 9th Episcopal District

737 Oneida Drive
Birmingham, AL 35214
Bishop Cornelius E. Thomas

Group Type: Denomination specific; district association/annual conference

Eastern Cape Annual Conference, 15th Episcopal District

17751 Hamilton Road
Detroit, MI 48203
Bishop Robert Thomas, Jr.

Group Type: Denomination specific; district association/annual conference

East Florida Annual Conference, 11th Episcopal District

101 Riverside Avenue
Jacksonville, FL 32202
Bishop Philip Robert Cousin

Group Type: Denomination specific; district association/annual conference

East Mississippi Annual Conference, 8th Episcopal District

2138 St. Bernard Avenue
St. Louis, MO 70119
Bishop Donald G. K. Ming

Group Type: Denomination specific; district association/annual conference

East-Northeast Arkansas Annual Conference, 12th Episcopal District

604 Locust Street
North Little Rock, AR 72214
Bishop Henry A. Belin, Jr.

Group Type: Denomination specific; district association/annual conference

East Tennessee Annual Conference, 13th Episcopal District

500 Eighth Avenue, South
Nashville, TN 37203
Bishop Vernon R. Byrd

Group Type: Denomination specific; district association/annual conference

East Transvaal Annual Conference, 19th Episcopal District

P.O. Box 12
Residensia, 1980
Republic of South Africa
Bishop Harold Ben Senatle

Group Type: Denomination specific; district association/annual conference

Florida Annual Conference, 11th Episcopal District

101 Riverside Avenue
Jacksonville, FL 32202
Bishop Philip Robert Cousin

Group Type: Denomination specific; district association/annual conference

Ghana Annual Conference, 14th Episcopal District

Oak Cliff, Suite 813
400 South Zang Boulevard
Dallas, TX 75208
Bishop John R. Bryant

Group Type: Denomination specific; district association/annual conference

Haiti Annual Conference, 16th Episcopal District

604 Locust Street
North Little Rock, AR 72214
Bishop Henry A. Belin, Jr.

Group Type: Denomination specific; district association/annual conference

Illinois Annual Conference, 4th Episcopal District

7220 North Illinois Street
Indianapolis, IN 46260
Bishop J. Haskell Mayo

Group Type: Denomination specific; district association/annual conference

Indiana Annual Conference, 4th Episcopal District

7220 North Illinois Street
Indianapolis, IN 46260
Bishop J. Haskell Mayo

Group Type: Denomination specific; district association/annual conference

Jamaica Islands Annual Conference, 16th Episcopal District

604 Locust Street
North Little Rock, AR 72214
Bishop Henry A. Belin, Jr.

Group Type: Denomination specific; district association/annual conference

Kalahari Annual Conference, 15th Episcopal District

17751 Hamilton Road
Detroit, MI 48203
Bishop Robert Thomas, Jr.

Group Type: Denomination specific; district association/annual conference

Kansas-Nebraska Annual Conference, 5th Episcopal District

4144 Lindell Boulevard, Suite 222
St. Louis, MO 63108
Bishop Vinton R. Anderson

Group Type: Denomination specific; district association/annual conference

Kentucky Annual Conference, 13th Episcopal District

500 Eighth Avenue, South
Nashville, TN 37203
Bishop Vernon R. Byrd

Group Type: Denomination specific; district association/annual conference

Lesotho Annual Conference, 18th Episcopal District

P.O. Box 183
St. Louis, MO 63166
Bishop Richard Allen Chappelle

Group Type: Denomination specific; district association/annual conference

Liberia Annual Conference, 14th Episcopal District

Oak Cliff, Suite 813
400 South Zang Boulevard
Dallas, TX 75208
Bishop John R. Bryant

Group Type: Denomination specific; district association/annual conference

London Annual Conference, 16th Episcopal District

604 Locust Street
North Little Rock, AR 72214
Bishop Henry A. Belin, Jr.

Group Type: Denomination specific; district association/annual conference

Louisiana Annual Conference, 8th Episcopal District

2138 St. Bernard Avenue
St. Louis, MO 70119
Bishop Donald G. K. Ming

Group Type: Denomination specific; district association/annual conference

Macon, Georgia Annual Conference, 6th Episcopal District

208 Auburn Avenue, NE
Atlanta, GA 30303
Bishop John Hurst Adams

Group Type: Denomination specific; district association/annual conference

Malawi Annual Conference, 17th Episcopal District

P.O. Box 183
St. Louis, MO 63166
Bishop Richard Allen Chappelle

Group Type: Denomination specific; district association/annual conference

Michigan Annual Conference, 4th Episcopal District

7220 North Illinois Street
Indianapolis, IN 46260
Bishop J. Haskell Mayo

Group Type: Denomination specific; district association/annual conference

Mississippi Annual Conference, 8th Episcopal District

2138 St. Bernard Avenue
St. Louis, MO 70119
Bishop Donald G. K. Ming

Group Type: Denomination specific; district association/annual conference

Missouri Annual Conference, 5th Episcopal District

4144 Lindell Boulevard, Suite 222
St. Louis, MO 63108
Bishop Vinton R. Anderson

Group Type: Denomination specific; district association/annual conference

Mozambique Annual Conference, 18th Episcopal District

P.O. Box 183
St. Louis, MO 63166
Bishop Richard Allen Chappelle

Group Type: Denomination specific; district association/annual conference

Namibia Annual Conference, 15th Episcopal District

17751 Hamilton Road
Detroit, MI 48203
Bishop Robert Thomas, Jr.

Group Type: Denomination specific; district association/annual conference

Natal Annual Conference, 19th Episcopal District

P.O. Box 12
Residensia, 1980
Republic of South Africa
Bishop Harold Ben Senatle

Group Type: Denomination specific; district association/annual conference

New England Annual Conference, 1st Episcopal District

3801 Market Street
Philadelphia, PA 19143
Bishop Frank Curtis Cummings

Group Type: Denomination specific; district association/annual conference

New Jersey Annual Conference, 1st Episcopal District

3801 Market Street
Philadelphia, PA 19143
Bishop Frank Curtis Cummings

Group Type: Denomination specific; district association/annual conference

New York Annual Conference, 1st Episcopal District

3801 Market Street
Philadelphia, PA 19143
Bishop Frank Curtis Cummings

Group Type: Denomination specific; district association/annual conference

Nigeria Annual Conference, 14th Episcopal District

Oak Cliff, Suite 813
400 South Zang Boulevard
Dallas, TX 75208
Bishop John R. Bryant

Group Type: Denomination specific; district association/annual conference

North Alabama Annual Conference, 9th Episcopal District

737 Oneida Drive
Birmingham, AL 35214
Bishop Cornelius E. Thomas

Group Type: Denomination specific; district association/annual conference

North Carolina Annual Conference, 2nd Episcopal District

1134 11th Street, NW
Washington, DC 20001
Bishop H. Hartford Brookins

Group Type: Denomination specific; district association/annual conference

Northeast Lesotho Annual Conference, 18th Episcopal District

P.O. Box 183
St. Louis, MO 63166
Bishop Richard Allen Chappelle

Group Type: Denomination specific; district association/annual conference

Northeast South Carolina Annual Conference, 7th Episcopal District

Landmark East, Suite 402
3700 Forest Drive
Columbia, SC 29204
Bishop Frederick C. James

Group Type: Denomination specific; district association/annual conference

Northeast Texas Annual Conference, 10th Episcopal District

Oak Cliff, Suite 813
400 South Zang Boulevard
Dallas, TX 75208
Bishop John R. Bryant

Group Type: Denomination specific; district association/annual conference

Northeast-West Mississippi Annual Conference, 8th Episcopal District

2138 St. Bernard Avenue
St. Louis, MO 70119
Bishop Donald G. K. Ming

Group Type: Denomination specific; district association/annual conference

Northeast Zambia Annual Conference, 17th Episcopal District

P.O. Box 183
St. Louis, MO 63166
Bishop Richard Allen Chappelle

Group Type: Denomination specific; district association/annual conference

Northeast Zimbabwe Annual Conference, 17th Episcopal District

P.O. Box 183
St. Louis, MO 63166
Bishop Richard Allen Chappelle

Group Type: Denomination specific; district association/annual conference

Northern Transvaal Annual Conference, 19th Episcopal District

P.O. Box 12
Residensia, 1980
Republic of South Africa
Bishop Harold Ben Senatle

Group Type: Denomination specific; district association/annual conference

North Louisiana Annual Conference, 8th Episcopal District

2138 St. Bernard Avenue
St. Louis, MO 70119
Bishop Donald G. K. Ming

Group Type: Denomination specific; district association/annual conference

North Ohio Annual Conference, 3rd Episcopal District

700 Bryden Road, Suite 135
Columbus, OH 43215
Bishop Richard Allen Hildebrand

Group Type: Denomination specific; district association/annual conference

North Texas Annual Conference, 10th Episcopal District

Oak Cliff, Suite 813
400 South Zang Boulevard
Dallas, TX 75208
Bishop John R. Bryant

Group Type: Denomination specific; district association/annual conference

Northwest Missouri Annual Conference, 5th Episcopal District

4144 Lindell Boulevard, Suite 222
St. Louis, MO 63108
Bishop Vinton R. Anderson

Group Type: Denomination specific; district association/annual conference

Northwest Texas Annual Conference, 10th Episcopal District

Oak Cliff, Suite 813
400 South Zang Boulevard
Dallas, TX 75208
Bishop John R. Bryant

Group Type: Denomination specific; district association/annual conference

Northwest Zambia Annual Conference, 17th Episcopal District

P.O. Box 183
St. Louis, MO 63166
Bishop Richard Allen Chappelle

Group Type: Denomination specific; district association/annual conference

Ohio Annual Conference, 3rd Episcopal District

700 Bryden Road, Suite 135
Columbus, OH 43215
Bishop Richard Allen Hildebrand

Group Type: Denomination specific; district association/annual conference

Oklahoma Annual Conference, 12th Episcopal District

604 Locust Street
Little Rock, AR 72214
Bishop Henry A. Belin, Jr.

Group Type: Denomination specific; district association/annual conference

Old Georgia Annual Conference, 6th Episcopal District

208 Auburn Avenue, NE
Atlanta, GA 30303
Bishop John Hurst Adams

Group Type: Denomination specific; district association/annual conference

Orangia Annual Conference, 19th Episcopal District

P.O. Box 12
Residensia, 1980
Republic of South Africa
Bishop Harold Ben Senatle

Group Type: Denomination specific; district association/annual conference

Orlando, Florida Annual Conference, 11th Episcopal District

101 Riverside Avenue
Jacksonville, FL 32202
Bishop Philip Robert Cousin

Group Type: Denomination specific; district association/annual conference

Palmetto Annual Conference, 7th Episcopal District

Landmark East, Suite 402
3700 Forest Drive
Columbia, SC 29204
Bishop Frederick C. James

Group Type: Denomination specific; district association/annual conference

Philadelphia Annual Conference, 1st Episcopal District

3801 Market Street
Philadelphia, PA 19143
Bishop Frank Curtis Cummings

Group Type: Denomination specific; district association/annual conference

Piedmont Annual Conference, 7th Episcopal District

Landmark East, Suite 402
3700 Forest Drive
Columbia, SC 29204
Bishop Frederick C. James

Group Type: Denomination specific; district association/annual conference

Pittsburgh Annual Conference, 3rd Episcopal District

700 Bryden Road, Suite 135
Columbus, OH 43215
Bishop Richard Allen Hildebrand

Group Type: Denomination specific; district association/annual conference

Puget Sound Annual Conference, 5th Episcopal District

4144 Lindell Boulevard, Suite 222
St. Louis, MO 63108
Bishop Vinton R. Anderson

Group Type: Denomination specific; district association/annual conference

Queenstown Annual Conference, 15th Episcopal District

17751 Hamilton Road
Detroit, MI 48203
Bishop Robert Thomas, Jr.

Group Type: Denomination specific; district association/annual conference

Sierra Leone Annual Conference, 14th Episcopal District

Oak Cliff, Suite 813
400 South Zang Boulevard
Dallas, TX 75208
Bishop John R. Bryant

Group Type: Denomination specific; district association/annual conference

South Alabama Annual Conference, 9th Episcopal District

737 Oneida Drive
Birmingham, AL 35214
Bishop Cornelius E. Thomas

Group Type: Denomination specific; district association/annual conference

South Arkansas Annual Conference, 12th Episcopal District

604 Locust Street
North Little Rock, AR 72214
Bishop Henry A. Belin, Jr.

Group Type: Denomination specific; district association/annual conference

South Carolina Annual Conference, 7th Episcopal District

Landmark East, Suite 402
3700 Forest Drive
Columbia, SC 29204
Bishop Frederick C. James

Group Type: Denomination specific; district association/annual conference

Southern California Annual Conference, 5th Episcopal District

4144 Lindell Boulevard, Suite 222
St. Louis, MO 63108
Bishop Vinton R. Anderson

Group Type: Denomination specific; district association/annual conference

South Florida Annual Conference, 11th Episcopal District

101 Riverside Avenue
Jacksonville, FL 32202
Bishop Philip Robert Cousin

Group Type: Denomination specific; district association/annual conference

South Georgia Annual Conference, 6th Episcopal District

208 Auburn Avenue, NE
Atlanta, GA 30303
Bishop John Hurst Adams

Group Type: Denomination specific; district association/annual conference

South Ohio Annual Conference, 3rd Episcopal District

700 Bryden Road, Suite 135
Columbus, OH 43215
Bishop Richard Allen Hildebrand

Group Type: Denomination specific; district association/annual conference

Southwest Georgia Annual Conference, 6th Episcopal District

208 Auburn Avenue, NE
Atlanta, GA 30303
Bishop John Hurst Adams

Group Type: Denomination specific; district association/annual conference

Southwest Texas Annual Conference, 10th Episcopal District

Oak Cliff, Suite 813
400 South Zang Boulevard
Dallas, TX 75208
Bishop John R. Bryant

Group Type: Denomination specific; district association/annual conference

South-West Zimbabwe Annual Conference, 17th Episcopal District

P.O. Box 183
St. Louis, MO 63166
Bishop Richard Allen Chappelle

Group Type: Denomination specific; district association/annual conference

South Zambia Annual Conference, 17th Episcopal District

P.O. Box 183
St. Louis, MO 63166
Bishop Richard Allen Chappelle

Group Type: Denomination specific; district association/annual conference

Surinam-Guyana Annual Conference, 16th Episcopal District

604 Locust Street
North Little Rock, AR 72214
Bishop Henry A. Belin, Jr.

Group Type: Denomination specific; district association/annual conference

Swaziland Annual Conference, 18th Episcopal District

P.O. Box 183
St. Louis, MO 63166
Bishop Richard Allen Chappelle

Group Type: Denomination specific; district association/annual conference

Tampa, Florida Annual Conference, 11th Episcopal District

101 Riverside Avenue
Jacksonville, FL 32202
Bishop Philip Robert Cousin

Group Type: Denomination specific; district association/annual conference

Tennessee Annual Conference, 13th Episcopal District

500 Eighth Avenue, South
Nashville, TN 37203
Bishop Vernon R. Byrd

Group Type: Denomination specific; district association/annual conference

Texas Annual Conference, 10th Episcopal District

Oak Cliff, Suite 813
400 South Zang Boulevard
Dallas, TX 75208
Bishop John R. Bryant

Group Type: Denomination specific; district association/annual conference

Virginia Annual Conference, 2nd Episcopal District

1134 11th Street, NW
Washington, DC 20001
Bishop H. Hartford Brookins

Group Type: Denomination specific; district association/annual conference

Virgin Islands Annual Conference, 16th Episcopal District

604 Locust Street
North Little Rock, AR 72214
Bishop Henry A. Belin, Jr.

Group Type: Denomination specific; district association/annual conference

Washington, D.C., Annual Conference, 2nd Episcopal District

1134 11th Street, NW
Washington, DC 20001
Bishop H. Hartford Brookins

Group Type: Denomination specific; district association/annual conference

West Alabama Annual Conference, 9th Episcopal District

737 Oneida Drive
Birmingham, AL 35214
Bishop Cornelius E. Thomas

Group Type: Denomination specific; district association/annual conference

West Arkansas Annual Conference, 12th Episcopal District

604 Locust Street
North Little Rock, AR 72214
Bishop Henry A. Belin, Jr.

Group Type: Denomination specific; district association/annual conference

Western North Carolina Annual Conference, 2nd Episcopal District

1134 11th Street, NW
Washington, DC 20001
Bishop H. Hartford Brookins

Group Type: Denomination specific; district association/annual conference

West Florida Annual Conference, 11th Episcopal District

101 Riverside Avenue
Jacksonville, FL 32202
Bishop Philip Robert Cousin

Group Type: Denomination specific; district association/annual conference

West Kentucky Annual Conference, 13th Episcopal District

500 Eighth Avenue, South
Nashville, TN 37203
Bishop Vernon R. Byrd

Group Type: Denomination specific; district association/annual conference

West Tennessee Annual Conference, 13th Episcopal District

500 Eighth Avenue, South
Nashville, TN 37203
Bishop Vernon R. Byrd

Group Type: Denomination specific; district association/annual conference

West Texas Annual Conference, 10th Episcopal District

Oak Cliff, Suite 813
400 South Zang Boulevard
Dallas, TX 75208
Bishop John R. Bryant

Group Type: Denomination specific; district association/annual conference

West Transvaal Annual Conference, 19th Episcopal District

P.O. Box 12
Residensia, 1980
Republic of South Africa
Bishop Harold Ben Senatle

Group Type: Denomination specific; district association/annual conference

West Virginia Annual Conference, 3rd Episcopal District

700 Bryden Road, Suite 135
Columbus, OH 43215
Bishop Richard Allen Hildebrand

Group Type: Denomination specific; district association/annual conference

Winward Islands Annual Conference, 16th Episcopal District

604 Locust Street
North Little Rock AR 72214
Bishop John R. Bryant

Group Type: Denomination specific; district association/annual conference

African Methodist Episcopal Ministerial Alliance

606 17th Street, NE
Washington, DC 20002
(202) 396-8582
The Reverend Gregory L. Edmond, President

Group Type: Denomination specific; ministerial

African Methodist Episcopal Zion Church

Office of the General Secretary
P.O. Box 32843
Charlotte, NC 28232
(704) 332-3851
Bishop William Milton Smith, Senior Bishop
Bishop Cecil Bishop, President, Board of Bishops
The Reverend Dr. W. Robert Johnson, General Secretary-Auditor

Founded in October, 1796, after blacks were denied the sacraments and full participation in the John Street Methodist Church (a white church in New York City), the African Methodist Episcopal Zion Church became a reality through the efforts of James Varick and others who were dissatisfied with the condition and treatment of blacks in New York City. They petitioned Bishop Francis Asbury for permission to meet among themselves. The Bishop visited the black classes. After a series of meetings at the home of James Varick, they met again with Bishop Asbury in August, 1796, and received approval to hold separate meetings and a meeting house was rented.

Eventually, this humble beginning emerged into the African Methodist Episcopal Zion Church, which was chartered by the name African Methodist Episcopal Church in New York City on April 6, 1801. ''Zion'' was added to the church's original name by vote of the General Conference in 1848. This was because the African Methodist Episcopal Church emerged in

Philadelphia at about the same time, with the same name, which caused a great deal of confusion. Zion refers to the first church of the denomination. The church claims to be the oldest Methodist organization to separate from the Methodist Episcopal Church in the United States, having voted itself out of the Methodist Episcopal Church on July 26, 1820.

Like most Methodist bodies, the standards of faith for the African Methodist Episcopal Zion Church are the Twenty-Five Articles of Religion extracted from the Thirty-Nine Articles of the Church of England by the founder of Methodism, John Wesley. The Apostles' Creed is the only formal creed accepted. Other beliefs of the church include: sanctification, a witness of the Spirit, a life of joy and obedience, Christian experience, means of grace, and conversion. Love feasts are also practiced. The Articles of Religion are the basis for biblical interpretation and the church's political stance. The church believes that teachings not found in the Bible should not be required of anyone nor should they be considered as necessary for salvation. The Old Testament as well as the New Testament in its entirety are considered canonical. The church also recognizes the leaders of the United States as such and believe it to be the duty of ministers and all Christians to obey the laws of the country.

From its inception, the A.M.E. Zion Church adopted the fundamental form of polity of the American Methodist Church. The church is governed by a General Conference, which meets every four years. The A.M.E. Zion church divides its territory into thirteen districts, each of which is presided over by a bishop. The bishops of the church govern the body and interpret its laws and mandates in the interim of the General Conference. The presidency of the Board of Bishops changes at six-month intervals. Each district is divided into conferences. Annual meetings are held on the district and conference level. A District Convention is established where the church schools' organizations are separate from the District Conference. Quarterly Conferences are held to assess the condition of the local churches within a specific area. The members' meetings consider business within the local churches.

The church formed the Bureau of Evangelism in 1920 to ensure close adherence to the teachings of Christ and accomplishment of the chief end of the Gospel—the salvation of souls. The church established the A.M.E. Zion Health Center in Hot Springs, Arkansas, in 1956, the Laymen's Council in 1916 (which became a part of the constitutional structure in 1952), the Ministers' and Laymen's Association in 1938, and the Historical Society in 1956. There is also a Woman's Home and Overseas Missionary Society. The A.M.E. Zion Church supports Livingstone College and Hood Theological Seminary in Salisbury, North Carolina; Clinton Junior College in Rock Hill, South Carolina; and Lomax-Hannon Junior College in Greenville, Alabama.

There have been several unsuccessful attempts to merge between the African Methodist bodies. The A.M.E. Zion and the Christian Methodist Episcopal Churches tried from 1902 to 1903, and the A.M.E., A.M.E. Zion, and the C.M.E. churches attempted again to unite in 1918. After careful consideration of the aborted attempts, the African Methodist Episcopal Zion Church and the Christian Methodist Episcopal Church are in the midst of implementing the union between the two churches. A detailed plan of union has been developed in several stages, and each church body will have an opportunity to ratify these recommendations made by the steering committee of each church and the joint commission before moving on to the next stage. Principles of and reasons for union have been established, and after final approval of the last phases of the merger by each church's annual conferences in January of 1991 and 1992, it is expected and hoped that the new church will celebrate its inaugural general conference in July of 1992.

The general conference of each church will meet in the same city, but in different locations, from Wednesday to Friday, then come together for the inaugural general conference, to convene on Friday and Saturday. The service of union of the new church will tentatively be held on the Sunday of the conference, from 11:00 a.m. to 3:00 p.m., and will be designed so that the declaration of union and the birth of the new church would be made promptly at 12:00 noon. A city will be chosen that will allow maximum exposure and publicity as well as attendance of between twenty thousand and thirty thousand members of the two churches. At this time, a plan to select the new name of the church has not been delineated, but the working title is "The Varick/Miles Methodist Episcopal Church," in honor of James Varick, the founder of the A.M.E. Zion Church, and William H. Miles, the first bishop of the C.M.E. Church.

The African Methodist Episcopal Zion Church is proud of both its ecclesiastical and freedom principles. It feels that it is in accord with John 8:32—"And ye shall know the truth, and the truth shall make you free." With a membership of approximately 1,200,000 persons, over 6,275 ordained clergy, and over six thousand churches worldwide, the church has spread from its humble beginnings in New York City. The church first expanded into the South and West, especially after the Civil War, then it moved quickly into Canada. After World Wars I and II, migration of African Americans to the North led to the growth of the church in large northern cities. Over the years it expanded into Haiti, the Bahamas, Liberia, South America, Jamaica, and England.

Group Type: Denomination
Founded: 1796
Membership: Over 6,275 ordained clergy, 6,000 churches, and approximately 1,200,000 persons in 13 episcopal districts
Publications: *Star of Zion* (weekly), the Reverend Morgan W. Tann, editor, P.O. Box 31005, Charlotte, NC 28231, (704) 377-4329; *Missionary Seer* (monthly), Dr. Kermit DeGraffenreidt, editor, 475 Riverside Drive, Room 1910, New York, NY 10115, (212) 870-2952; *Church School Herald* (quarterly); *A.M.E. Zion Quarterly Review*, the Reverend James D. Armstrong, editor, P.O. Box 31005, Charlotte, NC 28231
Meetings: A General Conference every 4 years as well as annual, district, and quarterly conferences

Episcopal Districts of the African Methodist Episcopal Zion Church

1st Episcopal District—A.M.E. Zion Church

3753 Springhill Avenue
Mobile, AL 36608
(205) 344-7769
Bishop William Milton Smith

Group Type: Denomination specific; episcopal district
Geographic Areas: Bahamas; India; New York; Western North Carolina

2nd Episcopal District—A.M.E. Zion Church

Presidential Commons, A521
City Line and Presidential Boulevard
Philadelphia, PA 19131
(215) 877-2659
Bishop Alfred G. Dunston, Jr.

Group Type: Denomination specific; episcopal district
Geographic Areas: Albemarle; New England; New Jersey; North Carolina; Virgin Islands

3rd Episcopal District—A.M.E. Zion Church

1511 K Street, NW, Suite 1100
Washington, DC 20005
(202) 347-1419 or 347-1473
Bishop J. Clinton Hoggard

Group Type: Denomination specific; episcopal district
Geographic Areas: Arlington, Virginia; Baltimore, Maryland; Barbados; Guyana; Philadelphia, Pennsylvania; Washington, D.C.; Western New York

4th Episcopal District—A.M.E. Zion Church

3513 Ellamont Road
Baltimore, MD 21215
(301) 466-2220
Bishop Clinton R. Coleman

Group Type: Denomination specific; episcopal district
Geographic Areas: Michigan; Tennessee; Trinidad-Tobago; Virginia

5th Episcopal District—A.M.E. Zion Church

8604 Caswell Court
Raleigh, NC 27612
(919) 848-6915
Bishop John H. Miller, Sr.

Group Type: Denomination specific; episcopal district
Geographic Areas: Central North Carolina; Kentucky

6th Episcopal District—A.M.E. Zion Church

1238 Maxwell Street
P.O. Box 986
Salisbury, NC 28144
(704) 637-1471
Bishop Rueben L. Speaks

Group Type: Denomination specific; episcopal district
Geographic Areas: Blue Ridge; Cape Fear; Colorado; East Tennessee-Virginia; Missouri

7th Episcopal District—A.M.E. Zion Church

7013 Toby Court
Charlotte, NC 28213
(704) 598-7419
Bishop Herman L. Anderson

Group Type: Denomination specific; episcopal district
Geographic Areas: Florida; Jamaica; Ohio; South Florida; West Alabama

8th Episcopal District—A.M.E. Zion Church

5401 Broadwater Street
Temple Hills, MD 20748
(301) 894-2165
Bishop Cecil Bishop

Group Type: Denomination specific; episcopal district
Geographic Areas: Allegheny; Georgia; North Alabama; South Georgia; West Central North Carolina

9th Episcopal District—A.M.E. Zion Church

607 N. Grand Avenue, Suite 701
St. Louis, MO 63103
(314) 531-1112
Bishop Richard L. Fisher

Group Type: Denomination specific; episcopal district
Geographic Areas: Arizona; Indiana; Louisiana; Palmetto; Pee-Dee

10th Episcopal District—A.M.E. Zion Church

10 Hardin Lane
Glastonbury, CT 06033
(203) 633-3089
Bishop Alfred E. White

Group Type: Denomination specific; episcopal district
Geographic Areas: Alabama; Cahaba; Central Alabama; South Alabama; South Mississippi; West Tennessee

11th Episcopal District—A.M.E. Zion Church

3654 Poplar Road
Flossmoor, IL 60422
(312) 799-5599
Bishop George W. Walker, Sr.

Group Type: Denomination specific; episcopal district
Geographic Areas: Alaska; Arkansas; California; North Arkansas; Oklahoma; Oregon/Washington; Southwest Rocky Mountain; Texas; Washington

12th Episcopal District—A.M.E. Zion Church

1140 Greenway Drive East
P.O. Box 975
Mobile, AL 36608
(205) 344-4745
Bishop Milton A. Williams

Group Type: Denomination specific; episcopal district
Geographic Areas: East Ghana; London - Birmingham; West Ghana

13th Episcopal District—A.M.E. Zion Church

9-11 School Road
P.O. Box 1149
Owerri, Nigeria
West Africa
083-231-303
Bishop S. Chuka Ekemam

Group Type: Denomination specific; episcopal district
Geographic Areas: Central Nigeria; Liberia; Nigeria; Rivers

Annual Conferences of the African Methodist Episcopal Zion Church

Akim Mansa District—Ghana West Africa Annual Conference, 13th Episcopal District

P.O. Box 28
Akim Mansa
Ghana, West Africa
The Reverend K. P. Hanson

Group Type: Denomination specific; district association/annual conference

Akron District—Allegheny Annual Conference, 8th Episcopal District

104 N. Prospect Street
Akron, OH 44304
The Reverend Dr. Eugene Morgan, Jr.

Group Type: Denomination specific; district association/annual conference

Alaska Annual Conference, 11th Episcopal District

3356 New Comb Drive
Anchorage, AK 99504
The Reverend Theodore Moore

Group Type: Denomination specific; district association/annual conference

Albany District—Western New York Annual Conference, 3rd Episcopal District

2037 Arkona Court
Schenectady, NY 12309
The Reverend Allen Brown

Group Type: Denomination specific; district association/annual conference

Arizona Annual Conference, 9th Episcopal District

1607 E. South Mountain Avenue
Phoenix, AZ 85040
The Reverend Windle Tucker

Group Type: Denomination specific; district association/annual conference

Ashville District—Blue Ridge Annual Conference, 6th Episcopal District

P.O. Box 2921
Asheville, NC 28802
The Reverend Dr. Samuel L. Brown

Group Type: Denomination specific; district association/annual conference

Atlanta/Summerville District—Georgia Annual Conference, 4th Episcopal District

1616 Ezra Church Drive, SW
Atlanta, GA 30314
The Reverend William A. Potter

Group Type: Denomination specific; district association/annual conference

Augusta/Winder District—South Georgia Annual Conference, 8th Episcopal District

3448 Morgan Road
Hepzepiah, GA 30815
The Reverend Dr. Robert L. Postell

Group Type: Denomination specific; district association/annual conference

Bahamas Annual Conference, 1st Episcopal District

Nassau, BA
The Reverend Wilbert Rolle

Group Type: Denomination specific; district association/annual conference

Barbados Annual Conference, 3rd Episcopal District

2228 George's Lane
Philadelphia, PA 19131
The Reverend Dr. William Kennedy, Jr.

Group Type: Denomination specific; district association/annual conference

Batesville District—West Tennessee/Mississippi Annual Conference, 10th Episcopal District

Route 2, Box 198
Como, MO 38619
The Reverend W. S. Johnson

Group Type: Denomination specific; district association/annual conference

Bay Cities District—California Annual Conference, 9th Episcopal District

709 Leats Drive
Vallejo, CA 94590
The Reverend Dr. John E. Watts

Group Type: Denomination specific; district association/annual conference

Beaufort District—North Carolina Annual Conference, 2nd Episcopal District

112 1/2 Kerr Street
Jacksonville, NC 28540
The Reverend Jeremiah Asbury

Group Type: Denomination specific; district association/annual conference

Birmingham District—North Alabama Annual Conference, 8th Episcopal District

4933 Huntsville Avenue
Bessemer, AL 35020
The Reverend Dr. F. D. Mayweather

Group Type: Denomination specific; district association/annual conference

Birmingham/Manchester District—London/Birmingham Annual Conference, 12th Episcopal District

185 Broomwood Road
London, SW 11
England
The Reverend L. B. Simpson

Group Type: Denomination specific; district association/annual conference

Black River District—Cornwall Jamaica Annual Conference, 7th Episcopal District

Middlesex
P.A. Elizabeth Parish
Jamaica
The Reverend Obediah Seymour

Group Type: Denomination specific; district association/annual conference

Bluefield District—East Tennessee/Virginia Annual Conference, 6th Episcopal District

200 Chestnut Street
Greenville, TN 37743
The Reverend James H. Jackson

Group Type: Denomination specific; district association/annual conference

Boston District—New England Annual Conference, 2nd Episcopal District

22 Crowley Drive
Randolph, MA 02368
The Reverend Dr. Warren M. Brown

Group Type: Denomination specific; district association/annual conference

Brewton District—South Alabama Annual Conference, 10th Episcopal District

Route 5, Box 40
Brewton, AL 36426
The Reverend H. K. Matthews

Group Type: Denomination specific; district association/annual conference

Bristol District —East Tennessee/Virginia Annual Conference, 6th Episcopal District

616 Oakview Avenue
Bristol, TN 24201
The Reverend Dr. Raymond Dickerson

Group Type: Denomination specific; district association/annual conference

Brooklyn District—New York Annual Conference, 1st Episcopal District

889 Hecscher Avenue
Bayshore, NY 11706
The Reverend John E. Durham

Group Type: Denomination specific; district association/annual conference

Camden District—New Jersey Annual Conference, 2nd Episcopal District

540 East Brinton Street
Philadelphia, PA 19144
The Reverend Victor L. Carson, Sr.

Group Type: Denomination specific; district association/annual conference

Canton/Jackson District—South Mississippi Annual Conference, 10th Episcopal District

329 1/2 Bell Street
Crystal Springs, MS 39059
The Reverend Jimmie Hicks

Group Type: Denomination specific; district association/annual conference

Central Demerara District—Guyana Annual Conference, 3rd Episcopal District

150 Regent Street
Lacytown
Georgetown Demerara, Guyana
The Reverend V. L. Adams

Group Type: Denomination specific; district association/annual conference

Central Nigeria Annual Conference, 13th Episcopal District

No current address

Group Type: Denomination specific; district association/annual conference

Central Valley District—California Annual Conference, 11th Episcopal District

27 Pulsar Circle
Sacramento, CA 95822
The Reverend E. Eugene Parker

Group Type: Denomination specific; district association/annual conference

Charlotte District—Western North Carolina Annual Conference, 1st Episcopal District

6210 Coach Hill Lane
Charlotte, NC 28212
The Reverend Smith Turner III

Group Type: Denomination specific; district association/annual conference

Chattanooga District—Tennessee Annual Conference, 4th Episcopal District

251 Glenwood Drive
Chattanooga, TN 37404
The Reverend Dr. O. R. Hayes

Group Type: Denomination specific; district association/annual conference

Cheraw/Bennettsville District—Pee Dee Annual Conference, 9th Episcopal District

P.O. Box 96
Richburg, SC 29729
The Reverend Dr. G. C. Johnson

Group Type: Denomination specific; district association/annual conference

Chicago District—Michigan Annual Conference, 4th Episcopal District

7540 South Indiana Avenue
Chicago, IL 60619
The Reverend Dr. Dorocher Blakey

Group Type: Denomination specific; district association/annual conference

Clarkton District—Cape Fear Annual Conference, 6th Episcopal District

1107 North 7th Street
Wilmington, NC 28401
The Reverend Dr. C. R. Thompson

Group Type: Denomination specific; district association/annual conference

Columbia/Camden District—Palmetto Annual Conference, 9th Episcopal District

2912 Grimes Street
Charlotte, NC 28206
The Reverend Dr. R. Pyant

Group Type: Denomination specific; district association/annual conference

Columbus/Cincinnati District—Ohio Annual Conference, 8th Episcopal District

3596 Van Antwerp Place
Cincinnati, OH 45229
The Reverend Dr. George Kendall

Group Type: Denomination specific; district association/annual conference

Concord District—West Central North Carolina Annual Conference, 8th Episcopal District

P.O. Box 109
Granite Quarry, NC 28072
The Reverend Dr. O. C. Dumas

Group Type: Denomination specific; district association/annual conference

Dallas District—Texas Annual Conference, 11th Episcopal District

2312 E. Illinois Avenue
Dallas, TX 75216
The Reverend Ralph V. Washington

Group Type: Denomination specific; district association/annual conference

Denver District—Colorado Annual Conference, 6th Episcopal District

1142 Salida Way
Aurora, CO 80017
The Reverend Willie Long, Jr.

Group Type: Denomination specific; district association/annual conference

Detroit District—Michigan Annual Conference, 4th Episcopal District

711 LaFayette Towers East
Detroit, MI 48207
The Reverend Dr. William M. Poe

Group Type: Denomination specific; district association/annual conference

Durham District—Central North Carolina Annual Conference, 5th Episcopal District

Route 3, Box 180
Silver City, NC 27344
The Reverend Dr. E. J. Alston

Group Type: Denomination specific; district association/annual conference

East Demerara/West Berbice District—Guyana Annual Conference, 3rd Episcopal District

No current address
The Reverend George McDonald

Group Type: Denomination specific; district association/annual conference

East Ghana Annual Conference, 12th Episcopal District

No current address

Group Type: Denomination specific; district association/annual conference

East Montgomery District—Central Alabama Annual Conference, 10th Episcopal District

P.O. Box 8115
Montgomery, AL 36110
The Reverend Dr. J. E. Fields

Group Type: Denomination specific; district association/annual conference

East Pensacola District—Cahaba Annual Conference, 10th Episcopal District

1018 E. Yonge Street
Pensacola, FL 32503
The Reverend Dr. C. H. Little

Group Type: Denomination specific; district association/annual conference

East West Demerara and Essequibo District—Guyana Annual Conference, 3rd Episcopal District

Lot A/B Grove Public Road
East Bank, Demerara
Guyana
The Reverend H. V. Craig

Group Type: Denomination specific; district association/annual conference

Edenton District—Albemarle Annual Conference, 2nd Episcopal District

P.O. Box 115
Winfall, NC 27985
The Reverend Dr. H. F. Simons

Group Type: Denomination specific; district association/annual conference

Elizabeth City District—Albemarle Annual Conference, 2nd Episcopal District

Route 2, Box 21
Edenton, NC 27932
The Reverend J. A. Elliot

Group Type: Denomination specific; district association/annual conference

Evansville District—Indiana Annual Conference, 9th Episcopal District

310 Fagan Street
Henderson, KY 40211
The Reverend Anthony Anguish, Sr.

Group Type: Denomination specific; district association/annual conference

Fayette/Jasper District—North Alabama Annual Conference, 8th Episcopal District

213 10th Street, West
Warrior, AL 35180
The Reverend C. T. Berry

Group Type: Denomination specific; district association/annual conference

Fayetteville District—Central North Carolina Annual Conference, 5th Episcopal District

502 Burton Street
Fuquay-Varina, NC 27526
The Reverend Dr. W. M. Freeman

Group Type: Denomination specific; district association/annual conference

Goldsboro District—Cape Fear Annual Conference, 6th Episcopal District

602 South Chestnut Street
Mount Olive, NC 28365
The Reverend Dr. Morris Newkirk

Group Type: Denomination specific; district association/annual conference

Grange Hill District—Cornwall Jamaica Annual Conference, 7th Episcopal District

Geneva Fullersfield, P.O.
Westmoreland Parish
Jamaica

Group Type: Denomination specific; district association/annual conference

Greensboro/Demopolis District—Cahaba Annual Conference, 10th Episcopal District

1517 Weaver Street
Selma, AL 36701
The Reverend Dr. Joshua Bettis

Group Type: Denomination specific; district association/annual conference

Greensboro District—West Central North Carolina Annual Conference, 8th Episcopal District

1913 Bellcrest Drive
Greensboro, NC 27406
The Reverend Dr. A. E. Harris

Group Type: Denomination specific; district association/annual conference

Greenville District—South Alabama Annual Conference, 10th Episcopal District

Route 3, Box 397 - AA
Wetumpa, AL 36092
The Reverend Dr. R. L. George

Group Type: Denomination specific; district association/annual conference

Hartford District—New England Annual Conference, 2nd Episcopal District

12 Eldridge Street
Waterbury, CT 06704
The Reverend Harrison D. Bonner

Group Type: Denomination specific; district association/annual conference

Hendersonville District—Blue Ridge Annual Conference, 6th Episcopal District

306 South French Broad
Asheville, NC 28801
The Reverend Dr. N. H. Hicklin

Group Type: Denomination specific; district association/annual conference

Hot Spring District—North Arkansas Annual Conference, 11th Episcopal District

5 British Colonia Drive
Little Rock, AR 72206
The Reverend James A. Vault

Group Type: Denomination specific; district association/annual conference

Houston District—Texas Annual Conference, 11th Episcopal District

4301 Hull Street
P.O. Box 14776
Houston, TX 77221
The Reverend Richard G. Stewart

Group Type: Denomination specific; district association/annual conference

Hudson River District—New York Annual Conference, 1st Episcopal District

8 Hillside Close
White Plains, NY 10603
Elder C. Guita McKinney

Group Type: Denomination specific; district association/annual conference

Indianapolis District—Indiana Annual Conference, 9th Episcopal District

1208 Glendale Drive
Anderson, IN 46011
The Reverend Dr. I. C. Weatherly

Group Type: Denomination specific; district association/annual conference

Jackson District—West Alabama Annual Conference, 7th Episcopal District

2864 Whistler Street
Whistler, AL 36612
The Reverend Dr. Thomas C. Gill

Group Type: Denomination specific; district association/annual conference

Jacksonville District—South Florida Annual Conference, 7th Episcopal District

1111 South East 9th Street
Gainesville, FL 32601
The Reverend Lawrence Coward

Group Type: Denomination specific; district association/annual conference

Jefferson District—West Alabama Annual Conference, 7th Episcopal District

Route 1, Box 531
Greensboro, AL 36744
The Reverend Otha L. Thomas

Group Type: Denomination specific; district association/annual conference

Jersey District—New Jersey Annual Conference, 2nd Episcopal District

32 Trebling Lane
Willingboro, NJ 08046
The Reverend Enoch B. Rochester

Group Type: Denomination specific; district association/annual conference

Johnson City District—East Tennessee/Virginia Annual Conference, 6th Episcopal District

421 W. Locust Street
Johnson City, TN 37601
The Reverend J. P. Keaton

Group Type: Denomination specific; district association/annual conference

Kansas City District—Missouri/Colorado Annual Conference, 6th Episcopal District

6409 E. 109 Terrace
Kansas City, MO 64134
The Reverend Dr. Joseph Jones, Sr.

Group Type: Denomination specific; district association/annual conference

Kingston District—Surrey Jamaica Annual Conference, 7th Episcopal District

127 1/2 Mountain View
P.O. Box 51
Kingston 3, Jamaica
The Reverend L. A. Forrester

Group Type: Denomination specific; district association/annual conference

Knoxville/Maryville District—Tennessee Annual Conference, 4th Episcopal District

303 N. Chilhowie Drive
Knoxville, TN 37914
The Reverend Dr. M. L. Walker

Group Type: Denomination specific; district association/annual conference

Lancaster District—Pee Dee Annual Conference, 9th Episcopal District

P.O. Box 173
Salisbury, NC 28144
The Reverend Dr. B. W. Moncur

Group Type: Denomination specific; district association/annual conference

Laurinburg District—Central North Carolina Annual Conference, 5th Episcopal District

1142 Evans Road
Cary, NC 27511
The Reverend Dr. S. J. Farrar

Group Type: Denomination specific; district association/annual conference

Liberia Annual Conference, 13th Episcopal District

No current address

Group Type: Denomination specific; district association/annual conference

Lincolnton District—Western North Carolina Annual Conference, 1st Episcopal District

Route 2, Box 737
Newton, NC 28658
The Reverend S. I. Clement

Group Type: Denomination specific; district association/annual conference

Little Rock District—North Arkansas Annual Conference, 11th Episcopal District

5 British Colonia Drive
Little Rock, AR 72206
Elder James A. Vault

Group Type: Denomination specific; district association/annual conference

London District—London/Birmingham Annual Conference, 12th Episcopal District

26 Courcey Road, Hornsey
London N8 ORH, England
The Reverend H. A. Gordon

Group Type: Denomination specific; district association/annual conference

Long Island District—New York Annual Conference, 1st Episcopal District

High Street
Elmsford, NY 10523
Elder David Pharr

Group Type: Denomination specific; district association/annual conference

Los Angeles District—Southwest Rocky Mountain Annual Conference, 11th Episcopal District

4015 Elizabeth Street
Compton, CA 90221
The Reverend Dr. Harriet O. Hooks

Group Type: Denomination specific; district association/annual conference

Louisville District—Kentucky Annual Conference, 5th Episcopal District

2910 Virginia Avenue
Louisville, KY 40211
The Reverend Dr. Joseph L. Walton

Group Type: Denomination specific; district association/annual conference

Madisonville District—Kentucky Annual Conference, 5th Episcopal District

178 Woodburne Drive
New Albany, IN 47150
The Reverend Dr. James H. Dunlap

Group Type: Denomination specific; district association/annual conference

Manchester District—Middlesex Jamaica Annual Conference, 7th Episcopal District

Pulsey Hill D. Prattville
Manchester Parish
Jamaica
The Reverend John Crawford

Group Type: Denomination specific; district association/annual conference

May Pen District—Middlesex Jamaica Annual Conference, 7th Episcopal District

York Town, P.O.
Clarendon Parish
Jamaica
The Reverend Canute Clair

Group Type: Denomination specific; district association/annual conference

Memphis/Mark/Glendora District—West Tennessee/ Mississippi Annual Conference, 10th Episcopal District

229 West Frank Avenue
Memphis, TN 38109
The Reverend Amanda Ballard

Group Type: Denomination specific; district association/annual conference

Miami District—South Florida Annual Conference, 7th Episcopal District

702 Whitehead Street
Key West, FL 33040
The Reverend Dr. F. Isaac Lowe

Group Type: Denomination specific; district association/annual conference

Mobile District—West Alabama Annual Conference, 7th Episcopal District

262 Cubia Street
Mobile, AL 36603
The Reverend James H. Taylor

Group Type: Denomination specific; district association/annual conference

New Bern District—North Carolina Annual Conference, 2nd Episcopal District

Route 1, Box 170
Havelock, NC 28532
The Reverend O. R. Ellis

Group Type: Denomination specific; district association/annual conference

New Haven District—New England Annual Conference, 2nd Episcopal District

10 Wendy Road
Trumbull, CT 06611
The Reverend George Sanders, Sr.

Group Type: Denomination specific; district association/annual conference

New Orleans District—Louisiana Annual Conference, 9th Episcopal District

1410 Hano Road
Independence, LA 70443
The Reverend Dr. Francis Williams

Group Type: Denomination specific; district association/annual conference

Nigeria Annual Conference, 13th Episcopal District

No current address

Group Type: Denomination specific; district association/annual conference

Norfolk District—Virginia Annual Conference, 4th Episcopal District

902 Parkview Drive
Elizabeth City, NC 27909
The Reverend Dr. R. R. Purnell

Group Type: Denomination specific; district association/annual conference

North Charlotte District—Western North Carolina Annual Conference, 1st Episcopal District

5631 Lake Side Drive
Pfafftown, NC 28040
The Reverend Horace C. Walser

Group Type: Denomination specific; district association/annual conference

Oklahoma City District—Oklahoma Annual Conference, 11th Episcopal District

2424 North Kelly Street
Oklahoma City, OK 73111

Group Type: Denomination specific; district association/annual conference

Opelika District—Alabama Annual Conference, 10th Episcopal District

605 Torbert Boulevard
Opelika, AL 36801
The Reverend Dr. A. L. Wilson

Group Type: Denomination specific; district association/annual conference

Osborne Store District—Middlesex Jamaica Annual Conference, 7th Episcopal District

Rocky Point District
Lionel P.O.
Clarendon Parish
Jamaica

Group Type: Denomination specific; district association/annual conference

Petersburg District—Virginia Annual Conference, 4th Episcopal District

5601 Germain Road
Richmond, VA 23223
The Reverend Dr. J. A. Strange

Group Type: Denomination specific; district association/annual conference

Philadelphia District—Philadelphia/Baltimore Annual Conference, 3rd Episcopal District

2239 Kensington Street
Harrisburg, PA 17104
The Reverend Dr. A. Addison Cash

Group Type: Denomination specific; district association/annual conference

Pine Bluff District—Arkansas Annual Conference, 11th Episcopal District

808 Cherry Street
Pine Bluff, AR 71601
The Reverend G. Bernard Crawford

Group Type: Denomination specific; district association/annual conference

Pittsburgh District—Allegheny District, 8th Episcopal District

1757 Crestline Street
Pittsburgh, PA 15221
The Reverend Arizona Nicholson

Group Type: Denomination specific; district association/annual conference

Portland District—Surrey Jamaica Annual Conference, 7th Episcopal District

Moore Town, Portland Parish
Jamaica
The Reverend Magnus McFarlane

Group Type: Denomination specific; district association/annual conference

Raleigh District—Central North Carolina Annual Conference, 5th Episcopal District

305 Wilmington Avenue
Dunn, NC 28337
The Reverend Dr. P. J. Stroud

Group Type: Denomination specific; district association/annual conference

Rivers Annual Conference, 13th Episcopal District

No current address

Group Type: Denomination specific; district association/annual conference

Rochester/Syracuse/Buffalo District—Western New York Annual Conference, 3rd Episcopal District

6 Hamlin Road
Buffalo, NY 14208
The Reverend Dr. Joseph D. Kerr

Group Type: Denomination specific; district association/annual conference

Rock Hill District—South Carolina Annual Conference, 9th Episcopal District

1082 Allendale Circle
Rock Hill, SC 29730
The Reverend Dr. C. J. Jenkins

Group Type: Denomination specific; district association/annual conference

Rockingham District—West Central North Carolina Annual Conference, 8th Episcopal District

116 S. Ledbetter Street
Rockingham, NC 28379
Elder Reverend Dr. Grady W. Beard

Group Type: Denomination specific; district association/annual conference

Rocky Point District—Middlesex Jamaica Annual Conference, 7th Episcopal District

Portland Cottage
Clarendon Parish
Jamaica
The Reverend Herman Thomas

Group Type: Denomination specific; district association/annual conference

Roseland District—Louisiana Annual Conference, 9th Episcopal District

412 Magnolia Street
Amite, LA 70422

Group Type: Denomination specific; district association/annual conference

Saint James District—Cornwall Jamaica Annual Conference, 7th Episcopal District

Mt. Carey Anchovy
P.O. Box 2
Saint James Parish
Jamaica
The Reverend Myra Samuels

Group Type: Denomination specific; district association/annual conference

Saint Louis District—Missouri/Colorado Annual Conference, 6th Episcopal District

6409 E. 109 Terrace
Kansas City, MO 64134
The Reverend Dr. Joseph Jones, Sr.

Group Type: Denomination specific; district association/annual conference

Salisbury District—Philadelphia/Baltimore Annual Conference, 3rd Episcopal District

10412 Capehart Court
Gaithersburg, MD 20879
The Reverend Dr. Rena Karefa-Smart

Group Type: Denomination specific; district association/annual conference

Salisbury District—Western North Carolina Annual Conference, 1st Episcopal District

Route A, Box 725 Sells Road
Salisbury, NC 28144
The Reverend L. C. Siler

Group Type: Denomination specific; district association/annual conference

San Diego District—Southwest Rocky Mountain Annual Conference, 11th Episcopal District

735 Olivewood Terrace
San Diego, CA 92114
The Reverend Reuben Winston

Group Type: Denomination specific; district association/annual conference

Sanford District—Central North Carolina Annual Conference, 5th Episcopal District

General Delivery
Cumnock, NC 27237
The Reverend Dr. C. V. Flack

Group Type: Denomination specific; district association/annual conference

Selma District—Cahaba Annual Conference, 10th Episcopal District

920 Hibernarian
Birmingham, AL 35214
The Reverend Willie J. Lewis

Group Type: Denomination specific; district association/annual conference

Spartanburg District—Palmetto Annual Conference, 9th Episcopal District

501 Arch Street
Spartanburg, SC 29301
The Reverend David L. Scott

Group Type: Denomination specific; district association/annual conference

Statesville District—Western North Carolina Annual Conference, 1st Episcopal District

2126 Rice Planter Road
Charlotte, NC 28210
The Reverend G. L. Godfrey

Group Type: Denomination specific; district association/annual conference

Tampa District—South Florida Annual Conference, 7th Episcopal District

702 Whitehead Street
Key West, FL 33040
The Reverend Dr. F. Isaac Lowe

Group Type: Denomination specific; district association/annual conference

Trinidad/Tobago District—Virginia Annual Conference, 4th Episcopal District

D'Abadie
Trinidad, West Indies

Group Type: Denomination specific; district association/annual conference

Tuscaloosa District—North Alabama Annual Conference, 8th Episcopal District

2618 39th Court
Tuscaloosa, AL 35401
The Reverend Dr. James Hendrix

Group Type: Denomination specific; district association/annual conference

Tuskegee District—Alabama Annual Conference, 10th Episcopal District

P.O. Box 883
Tuskegee Institute, AL 36088
The Reverend Dr. R. M. Richmond, Sr.

Group Type: Denomination specific; district association/annual conference

Union Springs District—Alabama Annual Conference, 10th Episcopal District

Route 3, Box 186
Tuskegee, AL 36083
The Reverend S. H. Chatman

Group Type: Denomination specific; district association/annual conference

Virgin Island Annual Conference, 2nd Episcopal District

St. Croix, Virgin Islands

Group Type: Denomination specific; district association/annual conference

Wadesboro Monroe District—West Central North Carolina Annual Conference, 8th Episcopal District

P.O. Box 5606
High Point, NC 27262
The Reverend James Robertson, Jr.

Group Type: Denomination specific; district association/annual conference

Washington District—North Carolina Annual Conference, 2nd Episcopal District

54 Kerr Street
Jacksonville, NC 28540
The Reverend W. H. Thomas

Group Type: Denomination specific; district association/annual conference

Washington District—Philadelphia/Baltimore Annual Conference, 3rd Episcopal District

1516 Emerson Street, NW
Washington, DC 20009
The Reverend Dr. Frederick Barnes

Group Type: Denomination specific; district association/annual conference

Washington/Oregon Annual Conference, 11th Episcopal District

1716 23rd Avenue
Seattle, WA 98122
The Reverend Dr. B. Leon Carson

Group Type: Denomination specific; district association/annual conference

West Ghana Annual Conference, 12th Episcopal District

No current address

Group Type: Denomination specific; district association/annual conference

West Montgomery District—Central Alabama Annual Conference, 10th Episcopal District

2538 Westgate
Montgomery, AL 36108
The Reverend Dr. R. L. Lyons

Group Type: Denomination specific; district association/annual conference

West Pensacola District—Florida Annual Conference, 8th Episcopal District

421 N. Reus Street
Pensacola, FL 32501
The Reverend M. S. Chatman

Group Type: Denomination specific; district association/annual conference

West Virginia District—Allegheny Annual Conference, 8th Episcopal District

Homewood and Bennett Streets
Pittsburgh, PA 15208
The Reverend George A. Fitch

Group Type: Denomination specific; district association/annual conference

Wilmington District—Cape Fear Annual Conference, 6th Episcopal District

619 South 14th Street
Wilmington, NC 28401
The Reverend Dr. T. D. Robinson

Group Type: Denomination specific; district association/annual conference

Wilmot District—Arkansas Annual Conference, 11th Episcopal District

609 E. McCloy
Monticello, AR 71655
The Reverend E. P. Boyce

Group Type: Denomination specific; district association/annual conference

Wilson District—Cape Fear Annual Conference, 11th Episcopal District

310 Brentwood Drive
Dudley, NC 28333
The Reverend Henry A. Gregory

Group Type: Denomination specific; district association/annual conference

Winston-Salem District—Western North Carolina Annual Conference, 1st Episcopal District

P.O. Box 183
Wilkesboro, NC 28697
The Reverend R. J. Harris

Group Type: Denomination specific; district association/annual conference

York Chester District—South Carolina Annual Conference, 9th Episcopal District

Route 5, Box 600
Forest City, SC 28043
The Reverend Dr. M. B. Robinson

Group Type: Denomination specific; district association/annual conference

African Methodist Episcopal Zion Ministerial Alliance

4113 18th Place, NE
Washington, DC 20018
(202) 526-8282
The Reverend Wilmer T. Frazier, President

Group Type: Denomination specific; ministerial

African Union First Colored Methodist Protestant Church

602 Spruce Street
Wilmington, DE 19801

The African Union First Colored Methodist Protestant Church, also known as the African Union First Colored Methodist Protestant Church of America or Elsewhere, is the product of the union between the African Union Church and the First Colored Methodist Protestant Church.

The African Union Church resulted from a lawsuit between Asbury Methodist Church, the parent and predominantly white church in Wilmington, Delaware, and Ezion Methodist Episcopal Church, which was a predominantly black Methodist congregation. Peter Spencer, William Anderson, and forty other black members of Asbury withdrew in 1805, and formed Ezion Church after being denied church rites because of their race. They remained under the supervision of Asbury Church. The suit arose when a white elder was appointed to preach at Ezion because Spencer and Anderson were laypersons, and the congregation rejected this. The suit was quickly abandoned because of the time and expense involved, and the group led by Spencer and Anderson left Ezion Church to form the Union Church of African Members, which was incorporated three years before Richard Allen incorporated the A.M.E. Church in Philadelphia. Spencer was present at the 1816 meeting to organize the A.M.E. Church, but chose not to unite with Allen's followers. In 1850 (shortly after Spencer's death), a faction left the church and formed another with an episcopal government. This group later became the Union American Methodist Episcopal Church, Inc. The schism resulted in the Union Church of Africans becoming the African Union Church.

It is believed that the First Colored Methodist Protestant Church resulted from a schism within the A.M.E. Church because little is known of its origin. Its representatives met with those of the African Union Church on November 25, 1865, to finalize plans for a merger.

The church's polity reflects that of the Methodist Protestant Church before 1939. Its doctrine is Wesleyan. The church has no foreign mission program, but home missions are the responsibility of the women of the church. The last reported membership figures, in 1957, listed five thousand persons in thirty-three churches.

Group Type: Denomination
Founded: 1865
Membership: As of 1957, 5,000 persons in 33 churches

Black Methodist Clergy Association

Varick Memorial A.M.E. Zion Church
255 Anacostia Avenue, NE
Washington, DC 20019
(202) 399-9221
The Reverend Lewis Anthony

The Black Methodist Clergy Association is an amalgamation of black ministers from A.M.E., C.M.E., A.M.E. Zion, and United Methodist churches in metropolitan Washington, D.C. The group meets on the first Monday of each month to consider justice, advocacy, and civil rights issues.

Group Type: Denomination specific; ministerial

Christian Methodist Episcopal Church

531 South Parkway East
Memphis, TN 38106
(901) 947-3135
The Right Reverend Caesar D. Coleman, Senior Bishop
Dr. W. Clyde Williams, Executive Secretary
The Reverend Edgar L. Wade, Secretary, General
    Conference

The issue of slavery created a schism in the Methodist Episcopal Church in America. The resulting division of the church into the Methodist Episcopal Church (i.e., the northern segment of the church) and the Methodist Episcopal Church, South (MECS) led to greater consideration of the role of blacks in the church, whether free or enslaved. Accordingly, in 1866, the Methodist Episcopal Church, South was petitioned by its African American members for a separate church that would be governed by the MECS. This was done primarily because of the rejection of African Methodist churches and the affinity felt with southern whites. At the 1870 General Conference of the MECS, the committee that had studied the question at the previous conference recommended that the black members be constituted as an independent church, rather than a subordinate group. This change in opinion reflected the social climate of the times. Thus, the Colored Methodist Episcopal Church was born on December 15, 1870. It changed its name in 1954 to the Christian Methodist Episcopal Church.

The C.M.E. Church adopted the Discipline of the MECS at its organizing conference in 1870, and made changes to suit its name and "the peculiarities of their condition." Thus, the Twenty-Five Articles of Religion as extracted from the Thirty-Nine Articles of the Church of England by John Wesley serve as the guiding doctrines. Accordingly, the polity structure of the church was adopted from the MECS and that of American Methodism. It is governed by bishops and holds general, annual, and quarterly conferences.

The evangelization of the black race, primarily by preaching and education, is the C.M.E. Church's philosophy. Because of its precarious position between the white Methodist body and black Methodists, it has taken the position that its property would not be used for political purposes or assemblages. However, many of its leaders were prominent in the civil rights movement of the 1960s and serve the church now as administrators of its colleges and schools. The 1970 General Conference approved the establishment of the Department of Christian Social Action and Concerns to address social problems of the era. A Social Creed was adopted in 1966 as well.

There have been several unsuccessful attempts to merge the African Methodist bodies. The A.M.E. Zion and the C.M.E. churches tried from 1902 to 1903, and the A.M.E., A.M.E. Zion, and C.M.E. churches attempted again to unite in 1918. After careful consideration of the abortive attempts, the Christian Methodist Episcopal Church and the African Methodist Episcopal Zion Church are in the midst of implementing the union between the two churches. A detailed plan of union has been developed in several stages, and each church body will have an opportunity to ratify the recommendations made by the steering committee of each church and the joint commission before moving on to the next stage. Principles of and reasons for union have been established, and after final approval of the last phases of the merger by each church's annual conferences in January of 1991 and 1992, it is expected and hoped that the new church will celebrate its inaugurating general conference in July of 1992.

The general conference of each church will meet in the same city, but in different locations, from Wednesday to Friday, then come together for the inaugurating general conference, to convene on Friday and Saturday. The service of union of the new church will tentatively be held on the Sunday of the conference, from 11:00 a.m. to 3:00 p.m., and will be designed so the declaration of union and the birth of the new church would be made promptly at 12:00 noon. A city will be chosen that will allow maximum exposure and publicity as well as attendance of between twenty thousand and thirty thousand members of the two churches. At this time, a plan to select the new name of the church has not been delineated, but the current working title is "The Varick/Miles Methodist Episcopal Church," in honor of James Varick, the founder of the A.M.E. Zion Church, and William H. Miles, the first bishop of the C.M.E. Church.

Group Type: Denomination
Founded: December 15, 1870
Membership: Estimated at over 1,000,000 persons worldwide
Publications: *The Christian Index* (bimonthly), the Reverend L. L. Reddick III, editor, P.O. Box 665 Memphis, TN 38101; *The Missionary Messenger* (monthly), Mrs. P. Ann Pegues, editor, 2309 Bonnie Avenue, Bastrop, LA 71220
Meetings: General Conferences are held every four years; District and Annual Conferences meet on a regular basis

Episcopal Districts of the Christian Methodist Episcopal Church

1st Episcopal District—C.M.E. Church

564 E. Frank Avenue
Memphis, TN 38106
(901) 947-6180
Bishop William H. Graves

Group Type: Denomination specific; episcopal district
Geographic Areas: Arkansas; Tennessee

2nd Episcopal District—C.M.E. Church

6322 Elwynn Drive
Cincinnati, OH 45236
(513) 984-6825
Bishop Othal H. Lakey

Group Type: Denomination specific; episcopal district
Geographic Areas: Kentucky; Ohio

3rd Episcopal District—C.M.E. Church

5925 W. Florissant Avenue
St. Louis, MO 63136
(314) 381-3111
Bishop Dotcy I. Isom, Jr.

Group Type: Denomination specific; episcopal district
Geographic Areas: Illinois; Indiana; Kansas; Michigan; Missouri; Wisconsin

4th Episcopal District—C.M.E. Church

109 Holcomb Drive
Shreveport, LA 71103
(318) 222-6284
Bishop Marshall Gilmore

Group Type: Denomination specific; episcopal district
Geographic Areas: Louisiana; Mississippi

5th Episcopal District—C.M.E. Church

1723 Third Avenue North
Birmingham, AL 35203
Bishop Richard O. Bass, Sr.

Group Type: Denomination specific; episcopal district
Geographic Areas: Alabama; Florida

6th Episcopal District—C.M.E. Church

2780 Collier Drive, NW
Atlanta, GA 30318
(404) 794-0096
Bishop Joseph C. Coles, Jr.

Group Type: Denomination specific; episcopal district
Geographic Areas: Georgia

7th Episcopal District—C.M.E. Church

P.O. Box 56125
Washington, DC 20012
(202) 723-2660
Bishop Oree Broomfield, Sr.

Group Type: Denomination specific; episcopal district
Geographic Areas: Connecticut; Delaware; District of Columbia; Maryland; Massachusetts; New Jersey; New York; North Carolina; Pennsylvania; South Carolina

8th Episcopal District—C.M.E. Church

2323 West Illinois Avenue
Dallas, TX 75224
Bishop Caesar D. Coleman, Senior Bishop

Group Type: Denomination specific; episcopal district
Geographic Areas: Texas

9th Episcopal District—C.M.E. Church

P.O. Box 11687
Los Angeles, CA 90011
(213) 216-9278
Bishop E. Lynn Brown

Group Type: Denomination specific; episcopal district
Geographic Areas: Alaska; Arizona; California; New Mexico; Oklahoma; Oregon; Washington

10th Episcopal District—C.M.E. Church

P.O. Box 170127
Atlanta, GA 30317-0127
Bishop Nathaniel L. Linsey

Group Type: Denomination specific; episcopal district
Geographic Areas: Ghana; Liberia; Nigeria

Annual Conferences of the Christian Methodist Episcopal Church

Alaska-Pacific Annual Conference, 9th Episcopal District

P.O. Box 11687
Los Angeles, CA 90011
(213) 216-9278
Bishop E. Lynn Brown

Group Type: Denomination specific; district association/annual conference

Arizona-New Mexico Annual Conference, 9th Episcopal District

P.O. Box 11687
Los Angeles, CA 90011
(213) 216-9278
Bishop E. Lynn Brown

Group Type: Denomination specific; district association/annual conference

Birmingham Annual Conference, 5th Episcopal District

1723 Third Avenue North
Birmingham, AL 35203
Bishop Richard O. Bass, Sr.

Group Type: Denomination specific; district association/annual conference

Carolina Annual Conference, 7th Episcopal District

P.O. Box 56125
Washington, DC 20012
(202) 723-2660
Bishop Oree Broomfield, Sr.

Group Type: Denomination specific; district association/annual conference

Central Georgia Annual Conference, 6th Episcopal District

2780 Collier Drive, NW
Atlanta, GA 30318
(404) 794-0096
Bishop Joseph C. Coles, Jr.

Group Type: Denomination specific; district association/annual conference

Central Texas Annual Conference, 8th Episcopal District

2323 West Illinois Avenue
Dallas, TX 75224
Bishop Caesar D. Coleman

Group Type: Denomination specific; district association/annual conference

Dallas-Ft. Worth Annual Conference, 8th Episcopal District

2323 West Illinois Avenue
Dallas, TX 75224
Bishop Caesar D. Coleman

Group Type: Denomination specific; district association/annual conference

East Mississippi Annual Conference, 4th Episcopal District

109 Holcomb Avenue
Shreveport, LA 71103
(318) 222-6284
Bishop Marshall Gilmore

Group Type: Denomination specific; district association/annual conference

East Tennessee Annual Conference, 1st Episcopal District

564 E. Frank Avenue
Memphis, TN 38106
(901) 947-6180
Bishop William H. Graves

Group Type: Denomination specific; district association/annual conference

East Texas Annual Conference, 8th Episcopal District

2323 West Illinois Avenue
Dallas, TX 75224
Bishop Caesar D. Coleman

Group Type: Denomination specific; district association/annual conference

Florida Annual Conference, 5th Episcopal District

1723 Third Avenue North
Birmingham, AL 35203
Bishop Richard O. Bass, Sr.

Group Type: Denomination specific; district association/annual conference

Georgia Annual Conference, 6th Episcopal District

2780 Collier Drive, NW
Atlanta, GA 30318
(404) 794-0096
Bishop Joseph C. Coles, Jr.

Group Type: Denomination specific; district association/annual conference

Ghana Annual Conference, 10th Episcopal District

P.O. Box 170127
Atlanta, GA 30317-0127
Bishop Nathaniel L. Linsey

Group Type: Denomination specific; district association/annual conference

Kansas-Missouri Annual Conference, 3rd Episcopal District

5925 W. Florissant Avenue
St. Louis, MO 63136
(314) 381-3111
Bishop Dotcy I. Isom, Jr.

Group Type: Denomination specific; district association/annual conference

Kentucky Annual Conference, 2nd Episcopal District

6322 Elwynn Drive
Cincinnati, OH 45236
(513) 984-6825
Bishop Othal H. Lakey

Group Type: Denomination specific; district association/annual conference

Lagos Annual Conference, 10th Episcopal District

P.O. Box 170127
Atlanta, GA 30317-0127
Bishop Nathaniel L. Linsey

Group Type: Denomination specific; district association/annual conference

Liberia Annual Conference, 10th Episcopal District

P.O. Box 170127
Atlanta, GA 30317-0127
Bishop Nathaniel L. Linsey

Group Type: Denomination specific; district association/annual conference

Louisiana Annual Conference, 4th Episcopal District

109 Holcomb Drive
Shreveport, LA 71103
(318) 222-6284
Bishop Marshall Gilmore

Group Type: Denomination specific; district association/annual conference

Michigan-Indiana Annual Conference, 3rd Episcopal District

5925 W. Florrisant Avenue
St. Louis, MO 63136
(314) 381-3111
Bishop Dotcy I. Isom, Jr.

Group Type: Denomination specific; district association/annual conference

Mississippi Annual Conference, 4th Episcopal District

109 Holcomb Avenue
Shreveport, LA 71103
(318) 222-6284
Bishop Marshall Gilmore

Group Type: Denomination specific; district association/annual conference

New York-Washington Annual Conference, 7th Episcopal District

P.O. Box 56125
Washington, DC 20012
(202) 723-2660
Bishop Oree Broomfield, Sr.

Group Type: Denomination specific; district association/annual conference

Nigeria, Eastern Zone Annual Conference, 10th Episcopal District

P.O. Box 170127
Atlanta, GA 30317-0127
Bishop Nathaniel L. Linsey

Group Type: Denomination specific; district association/annual conference

Nigeria, Western Zone Annual Conference, 10th Episcopal District

P.O. Box 170127
Atlanta, GA 30317-0127
Bishop Nathaniel L. Linsey

Group Type: Denomination specific; district association/annual conference

North Arkansas Annual Conference, 1st Episcopal District

564 E. Frank Avenue
Memphis, TN 38106
(901) 947-6180
Bishop William H. Graves

Group Type: Denomination specific; district association/annual conference

North Central Alabama Annual Conference, 5th Episcopal District

1723 Third Avenue North
Birmingham, AL 35203
Bishop Richard O. Bass, Sr.

Group Type: Denomination specific; district association/annual conference

Northern California Annual Conference, 9th Episcopal District

P.O. Box 11687
Los Angeles, CA 90011
(213) 216-9278
Bishop E. Lynn Brown

Group Type: Denomination specific; district association/annual conference

North Mississippi Annual Conference, 4th Episcopal District

109 Holcomb Avenue
Shreveport, LA 71103
(318) 222-6284
Bishop Marshall Gilmore

Group Type: Denomination specific; district association/annual conference

Northwest Texas Annual Conference, 8th Episcopal District

2323 West Illinois Avenue
Dallas, TX 75224
Bishop Caesar D. Coleman

Group Type: Denomination specific; district association/annual conference

Ohio Annual Conference, 2nd Episcopal District

6322 Elwynn Drive
Cincinnati, OH 45236
(513) 984-6825
Bishop Othal H. Lakey

Group Type: Denomination specific; district association/annual conference

Oklahoma-Muskogee Annual Conference, 9th Episcopal District

P.O. Box 11687
Los Angeles, CA 90011
(213) 216-9278
Bishop E. Lynn Brown

Group Type: Denomination specific; district association/annual conference

South Arkansas Annual Conference, 1st Episcopal District

564 E. Frank Avenue
Memphis, TN 38106
(901) 947-6180
Bishop William H. Graves

Group Type: Denomination specific; district association/annual conference

Southeast Alabama Annual Conference, 5th Episcopal District

1723 Third Avenue North
Birmingham, AL 35203
Bishop Richard O. Bass, Sr.

Group Type: Denomination specific; district association/annual conference

Southeast Missouri, Illinois and Wisconsin Annual Conference, 3rd Episcopal District

5925 W. Florissant Avenue
St. Louis, MO 63136
(314) 381-3111
Bishop Dotcy I. Isom, Jr.

Group Type: Denomination specific; district association/annual conference

Southeast Texas Annual Conference, 8th Episcopal District

2323 West Illinois Avenue
Dallas, TX 75224
Bishop Caesar D. Coleman

Group Type: Denomination specific; district association/annual conference

Southern California Annual Conference, 9th Episcopal District

P.O. Box 11687
Los Angeles, CA 90011
(213) 216-9278
Bishop E. Lynn Brown

Group Type: Denomination specific; district association/annual conference

South Georgia Annual Conference, 6th Episcopal District

2780 Collier Drive, NW
Atlanta, GA 30318
(404) 794-0096
Bishop Joseph C. Coles, Jr.

Group Type: Denomination specific; district association/annual conference

South Louisiana Annual Conference, 4th Episcopal District

109 Holcomb Drive
Shreveport, LA 71103
(318) 222-6284
Bishop Marshall Gilmore

Group Type: Denomination specific; district association/annual conference

South Mississippi Annual Conference, 4th Episcopal District

109 Holcomb Drive
Shreveport, LA 71103
(318) 222-6284
Bishop Marshall Gilmore

Group Type: Denomination specific; district association/annual conference

Southwest Georgia Annual Conference, 6th Episcopal District

2780 Collier Drive, NW
Atlanta, GA 30318
(414) 794-0096
Bishop Joseph C. Coles, Jr.

Group Type: Denomination specific; district association/annual conference

West Tennessee Annual Conference, 1st Episcopal District

564 E. Frank Avenue
Memphis, TN 38106
(901) 947-6180
Bishop William H. Graves

Group Type: Denomination specific; district association/annual conference

Free Christian Zion Church of Christ

1315 Hutchinson
Nashville, AR 71852

The Free Christian Zion Church of Christ was founded by the Reverend E. D. Brown on July 10, 1905, in Redemption, Arkansas. The Reverend Brown, an African Methodist Episcopal Zion conference missionary, and several other Methodist ministers disagreed with "taxing" or assessing individual churches to support the central church body. Rather, they believed that the church's primary interests should be directed toward support of the poor.

The polity of the church is essentially Episcopal and its doctrine is Wesleyan. The head of the church is the chief pastor (bishop) who appoints ministers and church officers. Each local church has a pastor and deacons as its officers, and evangelists are appointed for communities where there are no churches. The church produces the *Zion Trumpet*.

Group Type: Denomination
Founded: July 10, 1905
Membership: In 1965, 16,000 persons in 60 churches
Publications: Zion Trumpet

Reformed Methodist Union Episcopal Church

1136 Brody Avenue
Charleston, SC 29407
(803) 776-3534, 723-8857
The Right Reverend Leroy Gethers, Presiding Bishop
The Reverend Fred H. Moore, General Secretary

The founding of the Reformed Methodist Union Episcopal Church by withdrawn members of the African Methodist Episcopal Church in 1885 resulted from a dispute concerning the election of ministerial delegates to the annual conference. The first president of the church was the Reverend William E. Johnson. The new church's nonepiscopal structure was well-received, but in 1896, an effort was made to change its polity. E. Russell Middleton was elected bishop in 1899 after the death of the Reverend Johnson, and after his death, another bishop was consecrated by seven elders of the church.

The church shares the doctrine of the Methodist Episcopal Church. Its polity shifted toward that of an episcopacy and was adopted in 1899. Love feasts and class meetings, common in traditional Methodism, are held.

Group Type: Denomination
Founded: 1885
Membership: As of 1976, 3,800 persons in 17 churches with 26 ministers
Publications: The Doctrines and Discipline, Reformed Methodist Union Episcopal Church, Charleston, SC, 1972

Union American Methodist Episcopal Church, Inc.

772-74 Pine Street
Camden, NJ 08103
(609) 963-4530, 963-0434
Bishop Earl L. Huff, President and Presiding Bishop, 2nd and 3rd Episcopal Districts

Bishop George W. Poindexter, Secretary and Presiding
   Bishop, 1st and 4th Episcopal Districts
Dr. M. O. Jones, Connectional Secretary

The Union American Methodist Episcopal Church, Inc. (UAMEC), traces its origins to the movement of Peter Spencer, William Anderson, and forty other black members of the Asbury Methodist Church (Wilmington, DE) who left that church in 1805, because of having been denied the rites of the church on the basis of race. The group established itself as Ezion Methodist Episcopal Church, under the supervision of Asbury Church.

When a white elder was appointed to preach at the church in 1812 (Spencer and Anderson were both lay leaders), another dispute arose and quickly ended up in court. The African American members abandoned the lawsuit because of time and money, and left Ezion. The group purchased a lot from a Quaker, constructed another building, and dedicated it in the fall of 1813. They severed their ties with the Methodist Episcopal Church and established and incorporated the Union Church of African Members (three years before Richard Allen incorporated the African Methodist Episcopal Church in Philadelphia, Pennsylvania). Spencer was present at the 1816 organizing conference of the African Methodist Episcopal Church, but decided not to join with the Allen group.

Some time after 1816, thirty congregations of the Union Church of Africans were led out of that denomination by Ellis Saunders and Isaac Barney. Twenty-four of the congregations continued on their own under the same name (Union Church of Africans) for several years, eventually incorporating in 1865, as the African Union American Methodist Episcopal Church in the United States of America and Elsewhere. The denomination is known today as the Union American Methodist Episcopal Church. The other wing of the original group merged in 1866 with the First Colored Methodist Protestant Church and is known today as the African Union First Colored Methodist Protestant Church (see narrative).

The Union American Methodist Episcopal Church, Inc., is Methodist in doctrine, emphasizing the freedom of humankind's will. However, the church is episcopal in governmental structure and general practice, allowing the authoritative rule of chief pastors (i.e., bishops), according to Hebrews 13:24. Bishops are elected to ensure that all points of faith and general church programmatic concerns and polity are followed. They are assisted by district superintendents appointed from the ranks of seasoned elders. District superintendents serve at the bishop's request. Operational departments of the church include the Book Room (under the direction of Dr. Irene C. Dutton), Education (under the direction of Dr. Clyde J. B. Bowman, Sr.), Evangelism, the Church School, Statistical Division, Connectional Historian, and Publications.

The Union American Methodist Episcopal Church, Inc., has a strong tradition of lay participation and responsibility. Coupled with this tradition is the church's long-standing position in favor of licensing women to preach.

The Articles of Religion are considered the fundamentals of the faith and the essence of true doctrine. The denomination believes in the Holy Trinity, the Son of God as the Word, the bodily resurrection of Christ, His ascension into heaven and His eventual return. Union American Methodist Episcopals believe the holy scriptures are sufficient for salvation, and believe that everlasting life is offered to humankind by Christ in the Old and New Testaments of the Bible.

The Union American Methodist Episcopal Church, Inc., maintains that original sin is attributable not to Adam's fall, but to the corruption of the nature of every person. Doctrine also provides that fallen persons cannot of themselves, without the assisting grace of God, turn away from sin. People are accounted righteous before God through the merit of the Lord and Saviour Jesus Christ, by faith. Good works are the fruits of faith and follow after justification, but cannot put away sin. With repentance, all sins committed after justification are forgiven (with the exception of sins against the Holy Spirit).

The church also believes that the visible Church of Christ is a congregation of faithful men and women where the pure word of God is preached and the sacraments duly administered. The sacraments are signs of grace and God's goodwill toward the faithful. The two sacraments are Baptism and the Lord's Supper. Baptism is a sign of profession and a mark of difference, a sign of regeneration and rebirth. Baptism of young children is practiced. The Lord's Supper is a sacrament of redemption by the Lord's death received with faith. According to the Articles of Faith, Union American Methodist Episcopals maintain that the concept of purgatory is foolish and that glossolalia is plainly repugnant to the Word of God.

The General Conference of the Union American Methodist Church, Inc., composed of elected delegates representing all UAME churches, meets quadrennially (the next meeting is in October, 1994 in the New Jersey/New York area). The first and fourth districts' annual conference is held in April, and the second and third districts convene annually in May. The brotherhood meets every three months, and the sisterhood meets twice yearly.

Today, the Union American Methodist Episcopal Church, Inc., comprises between twelve thousand and fifteen thousand persons in fifty-five congregations. Its greatest concentrations are in Delaware, Jamaica, Maryland, New England, New Jersey, New York, and Pennsylvania. They are proud of their Pan-Methodist involvement. At the 1986 General Conference, the bishops were authorized by the body to meet with authorized representatives of the African Methodist Episcopal Zion Church to discuss and implement ways and means to strengthen the fellowship and affiliation between the two churches. The UAME Church has established a Home for the Aged and hopes to make provision for additional homes sometime in the near future. Headquartered in Camden, New Jersey, it is led by Bishop Earl L. Huff, the Presiding Bishop for the Second and Third Episcopal Districts, and Bishop George W. Poindexter, Presiding Bishop for the First and Fourth Episcopal Districts. The church news is published in *The Union Messenger*. The church also publishes a UAME Church catechism and maintains a UAME bookstore in Wilmington, Delaware.

Group Type: Denomination
Founded: 1805
Membership: Between 12,000 and 15,000 persons in 55 congregations primarily on the East Coast
Publications: *The Mark of a Man: Peter Spencer and the African Union Methodist Tradition*, by Lewis V. Baldwin; *The Union Messenger*, a newsletter; the UAME Church catechism
Meetings: General Conferences are held quadrennially; next general conference is October 1994; first and fourth districts' annual conference is held in April, second and third districts' annual conference is

held in May; brothers meet every three months, sisters meet twice annually

United Wesleyan Methodist Church of America

270 W. 126th Street
New York, NY 10027
The Reverend David S. Bruno

The United Wesleyan Methodist Church of America was founded in 1905 by immigrants from the West Indies. They wanted to continue the practices of the Methodist Church in the Caribbean and the Americas, which had British Methodism as its historical base. The church's doctrine adheres to Wesleyan principles, and it does not have a governing episcopacy. According to the *Encyclopedia of American Religions* (2nd ed.), the Methodist Church in the Caribbean and the Americas entered into an agreement with the United Methodist Church in 1976, and this has led to several jointly supported projects in the Caribbean. The church belongs to the Caribbean Conference of Churches and the World Council of Churches.

Group Type: Denomination
Founded: 1905
Membership: In 1978, 4 congregations in New York City; in 1982, 68,898 persons in the West Indies
Meetings: Meets biennially

Pentecostal/Apostolic, Holiness, and Deliverance

The pentecostal/apostolic, holiness, and deliverance religious traditions are listed in alphabetical order by each respective organizational name. All groups identified in this section are considered to be trinitarian in doctrine unless otherwise specified. The trinitarian doctrine maintains that there is a union of the Father, Son, and Holy Ghost in one divine nature.

Many of the pentecostal/apostolic, holiness, and deliverance bodies are difficult to categorize. Their doctrinal emphasis suggests a general means for appreciating the religious traditions practiced by the respective bodies. Whereas the Pentecostals are generally trinitarian, Holiness traditions emphasize a sinless life of moral and spiritual purity, and Deliverance traditions emphasize the use of spiritual gifts, especially healing and miracles. Apostolic/pentecostals may be grouped according to whether their doctrine is ''Jesus Only'' (i.e., oneness/apostolic) or trinitarian.

This listing includes some bodies that have fewer than five congregations or less than two thousand persons. In many instances, it has been difficult to obtain membership data. Therefore, information is included on as many viable organizations as possible.

African Universal Church

No current address
Archbishop Clarence C. Addison, Founder

The African Universal Church was founded in Jacksonville, Florida, in 1927, by Archbishop Clarence C. Addison. The movement, which later became the African Universal Church, credits its beginnings to a number of tribal chiefs in Gold Coast (Ghana), West Africa, where Princess Laura Adorkor Koffey was a leader. She was the daughter-in-law of an African king and was married to Joseph Koffey, although no mention is found of him in the United States. Mother Koffey, as she was known to her followers, was assassinated on March 8, 1928, in Miami, Florida. Captain Maxwell Cook, a captain of the African Legion of the Universal Negro Improvement and Conservation Association (UNIA), was also stabbed and beaten to death during the same incident. According to some reports, her assassination was attributed to her appeal as a powerful preacher to both blacks and whites, and it was suspected that the assassin was a member of a rival spiritual church in Miami. In the United States, she and her followers were involved with the UNIA led by Marcus Garvey. The building where her followers met was also used for UNIA meetings.

The Commercial League Corporation, formed in 1934 as an outreach of the church, serves as an insurance company for pastors and members of the church. This can be seen as a direct influence of the black nationalistic teachings and beliefs of Marcus Garvey, whose movement was strong at that time. Addison, the founder of the church, was outspoken on Garvey's beliefs, and because of his opposition to integration and civil rights, he was considered an acceptable speaker for conservative white groups.

The church is trinitarian Pentecostal in its theology and believes in healing and the Second Coming of Christ. Baptism of the Holy Ghost, justification, sanctification, and baptism with fire are the four spiritual experiences of the church. The latter, according to the church, is described as a definite scriptural experience, obtainable by faith on the part of the Spirit-filled believer. Baptism of the Holy Ghost is only for the sanctified. Wine is not used for the Lord's Supper, nor is water used for baptism.

The polity of the church is episcopal, and a senior mother and district mothers are in charge of a network of parish mothers (deaconesses). A general assembly meets every four years, and the church is divided into state districts headed by overseers. The last reported membership of the church was in 1970, with fewer than one hundred congregations. The organization is not affiliated with the African Universal Church, Inc., a group of seven independent churches in Florida and Alabama that also considers Mother Koffey as its inspirational leader.

Group Type: Denomination
Founded: 1927
Membership: In 1970, fewer than 100 congregations

Alpha and Omega Pentecostal Church of America, Inc.

c/o St. John Alpha and Omega Pentecostal Church
1950 West North Avenue
Baltimore, MD 21216
(301) 366-2253
The Right Reverend Magdalene Phillips, Founder and
    National President

The Alpha and Omega Pentecostal Church of America, Inc., was organized in 1945 by its founder, the Reverend Magdalene Phillips. Five congregations comprise the body. Three churches are located in Baltimore, Maryland. The remaining two churches are located in St. Augustine, Florida, and Philadelphia, Pennsylvania. An annual missionary convention, initially organized in 1962, is conducted in April. The national conference convenes in August.

Group Type: Denomination
Founded: 1945
Membership: 5 churches
Meetings: Annual national conference is held in August; annual missionary convention is held in April

Apostolic Assemblies of Christ, Inc.

No current address

The Apostolic Assemblies of Christ, Inc., was founded in 1970 by former members of the Pentecostal Churches of the Apostolic Faith. The administrative skills of the presiding bishop, Willie Lee, were questioned by both church leaders and members, and questions arose concerning the church charter. Before these questions were resolved, he died, and in the resulting confusion the church split. Those who formed the Apostolic Assemblies of Christ, Inc., were led by Bishop G. N. Boone. Its polity is congregational and it has kept the doctrines of the parent body.

Group Type: Denomination
Founded: 1970
Doctrine: Oneness/Apostolic
Membership: As of 1980, approximately 3,500 persons in 23 churches with 70 ministers

Apostolic Assemblies of Our Lord and Savior Jesus Christ

1200 West Girard Avenue
Philadelphia, PA 19123
(215) 765-6305
Bishop W. B. Selby

Group Type: Denomination
Doctrine: Oneness/Apostolic
Meetings: Meets annually in the last week of August

Apostolic Church of Christ, Inc.

2044 Stadium Drive
Winston-Salem, NC 27107
(919) 784-5836
Bishop Johnnie Draft, Founder and Bishop

The Apostolic Church of Christ, Inc., was founded on May 12, 1969, by Bishop Johnnie Draft and Elder Wallace Snow in Winston-Salem, North Carolina. It is the result of an amicable split from the Church of God (Apostolic), one of the oldest Apostolic churches, which is also headquartered in Winston-Salem.

Bishop Draft had served as an overseer in the Church of God (Apostolic) in the states of Pennsylvania, Virginia, North Carolina, and South Carolina prior to forming his own church. He was also pastor of the denomination's headquarters, St. Peter's Church. He believed that the Spirit of the Lord led him to form his own church, not that he differed with the parent body—the usual reason for separation.

The doctrine of the Apostolic Church of Christ, Inc., is like that of its parent body. It has a centralized church polity—final decisions rest with the executive board. All local churches are deeded to the central body in order to avoid defections. The church has purchased a headquarters church where Bishop Draft is pastor and has built an affiliated church in Mullins, South Carolina, in addition to acquiring a church in Hampton, Virginia, and adding congregations to the fold. It meets annually during the fourth week in August and publishes *The Nationalist Spiritualist Reporter*. Its last reported membership (1980) included three hundred members in six churches served by fifteen ministers and one bishop.

Group Type: Denomination
Founded: May 12, 1969
Doctrine: Oneness/Apostolic
Membership: 300 members, 6 churches, 15 ministers, and 1 bishop
Publications: *The Nationalist Spiritualist Reporter*
Meetings: Meets annually in the fourth week of August

Apostolic Church of Christ in God

1217 East 15th Street
Winston-Salem, NC 27105
(919) 722-6715
Bishop James C. Richardson, Sr., Presiding Bishop

In 1940, the Apostolic Church of Christ in God was formed from a schism in the Church of God (Apostolic), which was headed by its founder, Bishop Thomas J. Cox. The Church of God (Apostolic), founded in 1897, was one of the oldest Apostolic churches. Bishop Cox had been its leader for over four decades. Because of poor health, Bishop Cox was forced into inactivity; therefore, his duties were assumed by Bishop Eli Neal, a state bishop. As acting presiding bishop, Neal would not accept assistance or input from other ministers and members of the church. In addition, there were questions about his personal life.

For these reasons, a group decided to leave the church. Affiliation with another Apostolic body was considered, but because the church was only affiliated with a regional body, those who wanted to leave did not know about other Apostolic churches, most of which were in the Midwest and in the North. Elders James C. Richardson, Sr., J. W. Audrey, Jerome Jenkins, J. M. Williams, and W. R. Bryant started the Apostolic Church of Christ in God, headquartered in Winston-Salem, North Carolina. There were three affiliated churches: St. Paul Apostle Church in Rudd, North Carolina, of which Audrey was pastor; Mt. Sinai Apostle Church in Martinsville, Virginia, where Richardson was pastor; and Bethlehem Apostle Church in Winston-Salem, North Carolina, where Williams was pastor. Audrey was elected as the first presiding bishop. Elder Walter J. Jackson, another minister, soon joined the original five.

In 1952, Richardson was elected as the second bishop at the general assembly. By the next year, the first split occurred. Elder Robert O. Doub, state overseer of Pennsylvania, was not pleased with Audrey's performance as presiding bishop, feeling that he did not possess the ability and competence to lead the church. By this time, the church had spread to New York, Pennsylvania, and across Virginia and North Carolina. Because of this growth, the board decided to keep Audrey as presiding bishop. Doub, then, used his local congregation to form and incorporate Shiloh Apostolic Temple, Inc., in Philadelphia. Only a few churches of the parent body went with Doub.

Audrey stepped aside, and Richardson, whom Doub had supported against Audrey, became the presiding bishop in 1956, the position he continues to hold. The church has reached its greatest levels of success through Richardson's leadership. Under his guidance, the church produced a bimonthly publication, *The Apostolic Gazette*, later renamed the *Apostolic Journal*, that was very beneficial before it was discontinued. Richardson also initiated a fund to assist members of affiliated churches with their postsecondary education programs. He set an example for the church when, in 1961, he entered the seminary at the age of fifty-one. Many of the clergy and laity of the church followed this example.

In 1962, there was another schism. Elder George H. Wiley of Yonkers, New York, presented to the official board of the church his qualifications for the office of bishop. When the board refused his request, he left the church to form the Mount Hebron Apostolic Temple of Our Lord Jesus Christ. Wiley's wife had been active with youth, and he was well-respected in the church. However, few chose to leave with him. Even his brother, an elder (later bishop) in the church, stayed with the parent body.

In 1971, there was yet another split, the repercussions of which would be felt for a long time. Personality attacks, old feuds, and envy seemed to be instrumental in the conflict. Most of the ministers and congregations who left the church formed a new church under the leadership of Bishop Audrey, who led the break. Several other ministers and bishops, including Bishop Joseph Wiley, left the church after the departure of Bishop Tilman Carmichael in 1974.

The church shares the doctrine and congregational polity of its parent body, the Church of God (Apostolic). In 1980, its population was 2,150 members in thirteen congregations, with five bishops and twenty-five ministers.

Group Type: Denomination
Founded: 1940
Doctrine: Oneness/Apostolic
Membership: In 1980, 2,150 persons in 13 congregations, 5 bishops, and 25 ministers

Apostolic Faith Churches Giving Grace, Inc.

Route 3, Box 111G
Warrenton, NC 27589
(919) 257-2120
Bishop Geanie Perry

The Apostolic Faith Churches Giving Grace, Inc., formerly the New Jerusalem Apostolic Faith Church of God, was reorganized in 1975. Its founders were Bishop Rufus A. Easter and Mother Lillie Williams. It operates the New Jerusalem Rest Home for Senior Citizens and the Helping Hand Food Bank. There are twenty-five churches and small missions affiliated with the church. It holds its annual convention during the first week in August in Garysburg, North Carolina.

Group Type: Denomination
Founded: 1975
Membership: 25 churches and small missions
Meetings: An annual convention is held the first week of August

Apostolic Faith Churches of A Living God, Inc.

3416 Carver Street
Columbia, SC 29203
Bishop Richard C. Johnson, Sr., Traveling Overseer

The Apostolic Faith Churches of A Living God, Inc., grew out of the Apostolic Faith Churches of God (AFCsOG). The founder, Bishop LeRoy Williams, was the president of the South Carolina District Young People's Union of the Apostolic Faith Churches of God, Inc. There were several splits in the AFCsOG from 1965 to 1970. The seven churches comprising the body are located in South Carolina. The headquarters are located in Estill, South Carolina. The denomination adheres to the doctrine of the AFCsOG. An annual convention is held in South Carolina in mid-July. It publishes the *Union Newsletter*.

Group Type: Denomination
Founded: 1979
Membership: 7 churches in South Carolina
Meetings: Annual convention in South Carolina in mid-July
Publications: Union Newsletter

Apostolic Faith Churches of God, Inc.

700 Charles Street
Franklin, VA 23851
Bishop Stephen Douglas Willis, Sr., President and Presiding Bishop

The Apostolic Faith Churches of God, Inc. (AFCsOG), developed out of the original Azusa Street Revival, under the leadership of Bishop William Joseph Seymour. The headquarters are in Franklin, Virginia, under the direction of Bishop Stephen Douglas Willis, Sr. The previous leaders of this body include: William J. Seymour, Charles W. Lowe, Bishop Rossie Cleveland Grant, Bishop George Buchanan White, Bishop George W. Parks, Bishop Lois Cleveland Grant, Bishop Abraham Urquhart, and Bishop Stephen Douglas Willis, Sr.

Apostolic Faith Churches of God, Inc., is one of five Pentecostal organizations that have united to create a Fellowship Convention. The other bodies are: the Apostolic Faith Church of God (Bishop Oree Keyes, Jefferson, Ohio); the Apostolic Faith Church of God Live On (Bishop Richard H. Cross, Hopewell, Virginia); the Apostolic Faith Church of God in Christ (Bishop R. A. Griswould, Hertford, North Carolina); and the Church of Christ Holiness unto the Lord, Inc. (Bishop Moses

Lewis, Savannah, Georgia). These comprise the United Fellowship Convention of the Original Azusa Street Mission (Bishop Oree Keyes, Jefferson, Ohio). This fellowship convention is considered the first step leading toward a merger of these bodies. Each of the respective bodies has its roots in the original Azusa Street Revival. Bishop Oree Keyes is the leading figure in this reunion effort. In May, 1988, a Board of Directors, consisting of representatives from each of the five Pentecostal groups was appointed. Bishop Oree Keyes is the chairman of this board.

Bishop Stephen Douglas Willis, Sr., was installed as president and presiding bishop of the Apostolic Faith Churches of God, Inc., during the annual church convention on August 11, 1989, in the church where he serves as pastor (the East End Apostolic Faith Church, 410 East Street, Franklin, Virginia).

Group Type: Denomination
Founded: 1909
Meetings: Annual convention begins on the Tuesday preceding the second Sunday in August and ends on the second Sunday in August

Apostolic Faith Churches of God in Christ, Inc.

330 King Street
Hertford, NC 27944
Bishop R. A. Griswould

The Apostolic Faith Churches of God in Christ, Inc., was organized in 1936 by Bishop John Henry Tucker. It has thirteen congregations and holds its annual convention during the last week in September in Hertford, North Carolina. The National Women's Convention and the National Youth Convention are held in conjunction with it. It publishes a discipline.

Apostolic Faith Churches of God in Christ, Inc., is one of five Pentecostal organizations that have united to create a Fellowship Convention. The other bodies are: the Apostolic Faith Churches of God, Inc. (Bishop Stephen Douglas Willis, Sr., Franklin, Virginia); the Apostolic Faith Church of God (Bishop Oree Keyes, Jefferson, Ohio); the Apostolic Faith Church of God Live On (Bishop Richard H. Cross, Hopewell, Virginia); and the Church of Christ Holiness unto the Lord, Inc. (Bishop Moses Lewis, Savannah, Georgia). These comprise the United Fellowship Convention of the Original Azusa Street Mission (Bishop Oree Keyes, Jefferson, Ohio). This fellowship convention is considered the first step leading toward a merger of these bodies. Each of the respective bodies has its roots in the original Azusa Street Revival. Bishop Oree Keyes is the leading figure in this reunion effort. In May, 1988, a Board of Directors, consisting of representatives from each of the five Pentecostal groups was appointed. Bishop Oree Keyes is the chairman of this board.

Group Type: Denomination
Founded: 1936
Membership: 13 churches
Publications: A discipline
Meetings: An annual convention is held during the last week in September

Apostolic Faith Church of God

Headquarters:
Apostolic Faith Church of God and True Holiness
Franklin, VA 23851

825 Gregg Road
Jefferson, OH 44047
Bishop Oree Keyes, Presiding Bishop

The Apostolic Faith Church of God developed from the Azusa Street Revival in Los Angeles, California, in 1906, under the dynamic leadership of Bishop William Joseph Seymour. The body was founded in 1909 by William Joseph Seymour and Charles W. Lowe. The headquarters office is located in Franklin, Virginia. The presiding bishop is Bishop Oree Keyes of Jefferson, Ohio.

Circa 1945, there were approximately forty churches in the organization. In 1946, Charles W. Lowe separated from the original organization taking one church with him. This resulted in two groups on the East Coast that stemmed from the ministry of William Joseph Seymour and maintained in varying forms the original name adopted by Seymour, Apostolic Faith Mission. Bishop Lowe kept the name Apostolic Faith Church of God but added the distinguishing suffix "and True Holiness." Bishop Rossie Cleveland Grant served as vice-bishop under Bishop Lowe. Bishop Grant was later elected presiding bishop. Grant's local church in Baltimore was incorporated as Apostolic Faith Church of God, Number 1. Both groups claimed to be the major root, dating back to 1909. Following the death of Bishop Rossie Cleveland Grant, George Buchanan White became presiding bishop. Bishop White's church became the incorporating body for the convention, incorporating under the name "Apostolic Faith Church of God of Washington, D.C." The convention agreed to operate under the charter of the local church in 1965 (at the time that the local church was incorporated). Upon the death of Bishop White, Bishop George W. Parks of Franklin, Virginia, assumed leadership of the body. This group dissociated itself from the charter of the Washington church and operated as an independent and unincorporated convention. Following the death of Bishop George W. Parks, Bishop Lois Cleveland Grant became the presiding bishop. Under his leadership, the group was incorporated in North Carolina as the Apostolic Faith Churches of God, Inc. Bishop Lowe's branch was succeeded by Bishop Levi Butts of Baltimore, Maryland. Bishop Oree Keyes became presiding bishop following the administration of another bishop, whose name is not known.

The Apostolic Faith Church of God is one of five Pentecostal organizations that have established a Fellowship Convention. The other bodies are: the Apostolic Faith Churches of God, Inc. (formerly under the leadership of the late Bishop Lois Cleveland Grant, Baltimore, Maryland, now headed by Bishop Stephen Douglas Willis, Sr., Franklin, Virginia); the Apostolic Faith Church of God Live On (Bishop Richard H. Cross, Hopewell, Virginia); the Apostolic Faith Churches of God in Christ (Bishop R. A. Griswould, Hertford, North Carolina); and the Church of Christ Holiness unto the Lord, Inc. (Bishop Moses Lewis, Savannah, Georgia). These comprise the United Fellowship Convention of the Original Azusa Street Mission (Bishop Oree Keyes, Jefferson, Ohio). This fellowship convention is considered the first step leading toward a merger of these bodies. Each of the respective bodies has its roots in the original Azusa Street Revival. Bishop Oree Keyes is the leading figure in this reunion effort. In May, 1988, a board of directors, consisting of representatives from each of the five Pentecostal groups was appointed. Bishop Oree Keyes is the chairman of this board.

Group Type: Denomination
Founded: Circa 1946

Apostolic Faith Church of God, Live On

2300 Trenton Street
Hopewell, VA 23860
(804) 458-5688
Bishop Richard H. Cross, Presiding Officer

The Apostolic Faith Church of God, Live On, was founded in 1952 in Franklin, Virginia, by the late Bishop Willie P. Cross, Elder R. T. Butts, and the late Bishop Jesse Hanshaw (the Presiding Bishop). It is also known as The Live On Church. It separated from The Apostolic Faith Church of God, led by the late Bishop Charles W. Lowe.

The church currently has approximately three hundred members in fifteen churches and missions primarily in Virginia, North Carolina, and New York. Future plans include the construction of a convention center/headquarters building that will seat nine hundred persons and provide office space, a fellowship/dining area, a nursery and a home for the aged. Presently, the church issues pensions to disabled persons through the Apostolic Faith Disability Society, a ministry of the organization.

The Apostolic Faith Church of God, Live On, meets six times annually in addition to its normal services. In January and June, there are business conferences with the elders of the church and the membership. The women's conference is held in April, and the junior (youth) conference is held in August, as is the general convention. Homecoming is held in Suffolk, Virginia, each year in November. The church publishes *The Crusade*, a bimonthly newsletter, *The Guiding Light*, youth training literature, and its annual yearbooks. The church's manual, containing by-laws, amendments, and doctrine, is produced through these publications. Bishop Richard H. Cross is the presiding officer of the church.

The Apostolic Faith Church of God, Live On, is one of five Pentecostal organizations that have established a Fellowship Convention. The other bodies are: the Apostolic Faith Church of God (Bishop Oree Keyes, Jefferson, Ohio with headquarters in Franklin, Virginia); the Apostolic Faith Churches of God, Inc. (Bishop Stephen D. Willis, Sr., Franklin, Virginia); the Apostolic Faith Churches of God in Christ (Bishop R. A. Griswould, Hertford, North Carolina); and the Church of Christ Holiness unto the Lord, Inc. (Bishop Moses Lewis, Savannah, Georgia). These comprise the United Fellowship Convention of the Original Azusa Street Mission (Bishop Oree Keyes, Jefferson, Ohio). This fellowship convention is considered the first step leading toward a merger of these bodies. Each of the respective bodies has its roots in the original Azusa Street Revival. Bishop Oree Keyes is the leading figure in this reunion effort. In May, 1988, a board of directors, consisting of representatives from each of the five Pentecostal groups was appointed. Bishop Oree Keyes is the chairman of this board.

Group Type: Denomination
Founded: 1952

Membership: 300 persons in 15 churches
Publications: *The Crusade*, a bimonthly newsletter; *The Guiding Light*; youth training literature; and annual yearbooks
Meetings: Business conferences held in January and June; women's conference held in April; junior conference and general convention held in August; homecoming held in Suffolk, VA., each year in November

Apostolic Faith Mission Church of God

3344 Pearl Avenue North
Birmingham, AL 36101
(904) 587-2332
Bishop Houston Ward

The Apostolic Faith Mission Church of God was founded on July 10, 1906, by F. W. Williams. Williams attended the Azusa Street Revival in Los Angeles and received the baptism of the Holy Spirit under William Joseph Seymour. He went back to the South and started a branch of the Apostolic Faith Mission in Mississippi. This was not successful, and he went to Mobile, Alabama, to conduct a revival. When a complete congregation of Primitive Baptists was converted, it gave Williams its building to become the first meeting house for the new mission.

Williams, now bishop of the church, embraced the Apostolic or Oneness doctrine in 1915. Thus, he broke ties with William Seymour and adopted the church's current name. It was incorporated on October 9, 1915. Bishop Williams died in 1932.

The doctrine of the church is Apostolic. It practices footwashing with communion, emphasizes healing, and baptizes in the name of the Lord Jesus Christ. The church prohibits the use of alcohol, drugs, and tobacco and encourages marriage only to those who are saved. It also allows women preachers. It is headed by a senior bishop and a cabinet of executive officers, which includes bishops, overseers, and the general secretary.

Group Type: Denomination
Founded: July 10, 1906
Doctrine: Oneness/Apostolic
Membership: In 1982, 16 congregations
Meetings: Meets annually in the third week of June

Apostolic Holiness Church of America

P.O. Box 353
Freemont, NC 27830
(919) 242-6208
Bishop Isaac Ryals

This denomination was founded in November, 1927, and later reorganized in 1929. Its founders were Elders J. M. Barns, W. M. D. Atkins, Ernest Graham, J. W. McKinnon, and Sisters Sarah Artis and Emma Spruel.

Group Type: Denomination
Founded: November, 1927
Membership: 10 churches
Publications: A discipline

Apostolic Ministers Conference of Philadelphia and Vicinity

1516 W. Master Street
Philadelphia, PA 19121
(215) 763-7335
the late Bishop Robert O. Doub, Jr., Founder and President

The Apostolic Ministers Conference of Philadelphia and Vicinity was organized by Bishop Robert O. Doub, an outstanding leader and organizer in his denominational affiliation. The conference was established in 1971 to promote greater unity and communication among Apostolic ministers in the Philadelphia, Pennsylvania, metropolitan area. It fosters fellowship with ministers in the Apostolic faith tradition. Bishop Robert O. Doub, Jr., served as president. The conference consists of fifty to sixty ministers. In 1986, Bishop Doub organized the National Apostolic Fellowship, a similar fellowship for ministers on the Eastern Seaboard. Bishop Robert O. Doub served as president of both groups.

Group Type: Denomination specific; ministerial
Doctrine: Oneness/Apostolic
Founded: January, 1972

Apostolic Overcoming Holy Church of God, Inc.

1120 N. 24th Street
Birmingham, AL 35234
(205) 324-2202
The Right Reverend Jasper Roby, Senior Bishop

In 1912, William Thomas Phillips became convinced that holiness was a system through which God wanted him to serve. When Phillips was called to the ministry in the next year, he undertook evangelistic work in Alabama. By 1916, Bishop Phillips had organized the Ethiopian Overcoming Holy Church of God (incorporated in Alabama on July 14, 1920). The name was changed later to reflect Phillips's understanding that the word of God was for all people, and the denomination was reincorporated in 1941 as the Apostolic Overcoming Holy Church of God (AOH). Following the death of Bishop Phillips in 1974, the Executive Board elected Bishop Jasper Roby as Senior Bishop and Executive Head of the AOH. The church has never experienced a schism.

Members of the Apostolic Overcoming Holy Church of God believe in water baptism (in Jesus' name only), in the Lord's Supper, and observe footwashing as in John 13:4-17. They believe in sanctification through the blood of Christ, justification by faith, the resurrection of the dead, and the second coming of Christ. The Bible is perceived as the inspired word of God, and every portion of scripture is to be adhered to. The AOH believes in the triune Godhead (Father, Son, and Holy Ghost) and states that the three are one, manifested in the person of Jesus Christ. Faith in what was revealed through Christ will lead to loving obedience and good works. Godly living should characterize the life and work of all saints, according to the pattern and example of Jesus and His apostles.

In addition, members of the AOH believe in baptism of the Holy Ghost (as on Pentecost) and that those who receive the Holy Ghost will speak in tongues. They also believe in divine healing, and that women have the right to preach and teach.

The church carries on foreign mission work in Haiti and other locations.

The Apostolic Overcoming Holy Church of God, although concentrated mainly in Alabama, is represented throughout the United States. There are more than twelve thousand members (not including ministers) in 173 churches. Among its proudest accomplishments have been construction of a Saint's Home (this nursing facility is no longer standing, but the church plans to replace it with a senior citizens apartment building in Birmingham, Alabama) and establishment of the Theological Seminary and Christian School. The AOH publishes its own youth materials as well as an outreach magazine, *The People's Mouthpiece*, issued quarterly. The church's National Convention meets annually during Pentecost (June 1-10).

Group Type: Denomination
Founded: March, 1916
Doctrine: Oneness/Apostolic
Membership: 12,000 persons in 173 congregations
Publications: *The People's Mouthpiece* (a quarterly magazine), Phillips Printing Company, Mobile, AL
Meetings: The National Convention meets annually during Pentecost (June 1-10); a national youth convention meets in July; the National Sunday School Convention meets in August; and seven Regional Ministers Councils meet during the year

Bible Church of Christ, Inc.

1358 Morris Avenue
Bronx, NY 10456
(212) 588-2284
Bishop Roy Bryant, Sr., President
Elder Alice Jones, Contact Person

The Bible Church of Christ, Inc., was founded by Bishop Roy Bryant, Sr., on March 1, 1961. The body is trinitarian in doctrine and accepts the Bible as the divinely inspired Word of God. Its doctrine includes miracles of healing and the baptism of the Holy Spirit. The church holds its annual meeting in March and supports mission work in Africa and India.

Group Type: Denomination
Founded: March 1, 1961
Membership: In 1989, approximately 6,405 persons in 6 churches, with 46 ministers
Publications: *The Voice*, a periodical, Mr. Montrose Bushrod, editor, 1358 Morris Avenue, Bronx, New York 10456 (212) 588-2284; and a directory through the main office
Meetings: Annual meeting in March

Bible Church of God, Inc.

718 N. 14th Street
Erwin, NC 28339
(919) 897-7105
Pastor C. C. McNeil

Group Type: Denomination
Founded: 1919
Doctrine: Oneness/Apostolic
Meetings: Meets annually during the last week in May

Bible Way Church of Our Lord Jesus Christ World Wide, Inc.

1100 New Jersey Avenue, NW
Washington, DC 20001
(202) 789-0700
Apostle Smallwood E. Williams, Presiding Bishop

Bible Way Church of Our Lord Jesus Christ World Wide, Inc., was born in 1957, out of a dispute within the Church of Our Lord Jesus Christ of the Apostolic Faith. Elder Smallwood E. Williams, executive secretary of the denomination, and others were concerned about the unwillingness of Bishop Robert Clarence Lawson to appoint a board of bishops to assist him. Elder Williams, for example, had been preaching for forty-three years, had been ordained in the denomination for thirty-two years, had been executive secretary for twenty-five years, and was pastor of the second largest congregation in the denomination, yet held little hope of ever becoming a bishop.

At the thirty-eighth Convocation of the Church of Our Lord Jesus Christ of the Apostolic Faith, an unsuccessful attempt was made to address these concerns. Elder Williams and other ministers left the Convocation and the denomination and met in a National Pentecostal Ministerial Conference in Washington, D.C., from September 25 to 27, 1957. The result of the conference was the consecration of Williams and four others as bishops and the creation of Bible Way Church of Our Lord Jesus Christ World Wide, Inc., to be headquartered in Williams's church.

Prior to the changes in 1957, Williams's association with the Church of Our Lord Jesus Christ of the Apostolic Faith (COOLJC) under the administration of Bishop Robert Clarence Lawson was long and rich. It was Lawson, in fact, who sent Williams to Washington, D.C., in July, 1927 to establish the first church of COOLJC in the city.

The denomination is headed by a presiding bishop (Apostle Williams), three vice-presiding bishops, a general board of bishops (9) and junior bishops (10), and officers that include the executive and general secretaries and assistants, the treasurer and assistants, sergeant-at-arms, chairman of the United Deacon's Association, general president of the Women's Council, president of the Youth Department, superintendent of the Sunday School Department, president of the International Missionary Department, and president emeritus. There are sixteen committees: finance, credentials, adjustment, publication board, resolution, convocation/council program planning, home mission and church extension, examination and ordination, foreign mission board, registration, board of education, social action, convocation/council coordinating, national broadcast, evangelistic board, and proofreading.

Bible Way maintains a television ministry in Washington, D.C., and publishes ''The Bible News Voice'' biweekly. Its theology is Pentecostal, but the denomination believes in baptism in the name of Jesus only. There are approximately 250,000 members in three hundred churches.

Group Type: Denomination
Founded: September 1957
Doctrine: Oneness/Apostolic
Membership: 250,000 persons in 300 churches
Publications: The Bible News Voice, a biweekly newsletter
Meetings: Meets annually the second week in July

Bible Way Pentecostal Apostolic Church

No current address

The Bible Way Pentecostal Apostolic Church was founded in 1960 by Curtis P. Jones, a minister in the Church of Our Lord Jesus Christ of the Apostolic Faith headed by Bishop Robert Clarence Lawson. Jones began as a state bishop in Winston-Salem, North Carolina, for the Church of God (Apostolic) under the direction of Bishop Eli Neal. In 1933, he was sent to Roanoke, Virginia, to start a church. Having become disillusioned with the leadership of the church's presiding bishop, T. J. Cox, Jones split from the Church of God (Apostolic) in 1938 and aligned himself with Bishop Lawson.

He became pastor of St. Paul Apostle Church in Axton, Henry County, Virginia, and, although he had worked harmoniously with the church's founder, the Reverend Sister Phanelson, his alignment with Bishop Lawson demanded that he denounce women in the ministry. In 1957, when Bishop Smallwood E. Williams left to form the Bible Way Church of Our Lord Jesus Christ World Wide, Jones initially intended to go with Williams, but opted to form his own church in 1960. He returned to pastor the congregation in Roanoke. This congregation, with the Henry County church and a new mission in Franklin County, Virginia, formed the base of the new church. A fourth congregation was soon added.

After Bishop Jones's death in 1960, it was expected that Elder Edward Martin (who had assumed the pastorate of the Henry County church) would be named the presiding bishop, were it not for strong opposition to his candidacy. Nevertheless, he declared himself bishop, but the church does not accept him as such. As of 1980, he remained bishop of his own congregation only. There is continued fellowship among the four churches and their leadership, and a reconciliation is desired.

Group Type: Denomination
Founded: 1960
Doctrine: Oneness/Apostolic
Membership: As of 1980, 4 churches in Virginia
Meetings: Annual meeting every second Wednesday in November

Christ Holy Sanctified Church of America, Inc.

5204 Willie Street
Fort Worth, TX 76105
Bishop E. L. McBride, President

Christ Holy Sanctified Church of America, Inc., was organized, incorporated, and chartered by Judge and Sarah King in Keatchie, Louisiana, in 1910. The group had previously conducted informal meetings in Mansfield, Louisiana, starting in 1907. Sarah King was introduced to the doctrines of sanctification and holiness through a group of white missionaries who came into Lousiana in 1903 to spread their religious convictions. Through her ministry, Judge King was later converted and became a preacher in the church.

The white missionaries who influenced the Kings were part of a group who petitioned to be released from their membership in a Methodist Episcopal church in Chincoteague Island, Virginia, in 1867. They left because of their belief that salvation required sanctification in the form of some clear evidence of in-filling with the Holy Spirit (such as glossolalia). Missionaries from this body were sent to Louisiana, and they formed the church in Mansfield, but were soon dropped from the Pentecostal rolls over differences of opinion. Judge and Sarah King were converts who, under the influence of this ministry, established a black congregation.

Christ Holy Sanctified Church of America, Inc., differs from the Christ's Sanctified Holy Church and other Pentecostal groups because its sacraments include: baptism with water in the name of the Trinity; celebration of communion with cooked grape juice; and footwashing.

Christ Holy Sanctified Church of America, Inc., includes more than two hundred fifty individual churches with the highest concentration in the South (particularly Louisiana, East Mississippi, and Texas) and California. Following the death of Bishop Judge King in 1946, his son, the late Bishop Ulysses S. King, Sr., became presiding bishop and president of the body. Upon the death of Bishop Ulysses S. King, Sr., in 1985, Bishop E. L. McBride was elected senior bishop and president of Christ Holy Sanctified Churches of America, Inc. Bishop E. L. McBride is the pastor of Gospel Temple in Fort Worth, Texas.

Group Type: Denomination
Founded: 1910
Doctrine: Holiness
Membership: Over 250 churches in North America and Africa
Meetings: An annual convention
Publications: A discipline and a history booklet

Christ's Sanctified Holy Church

1310 South Cutting Avenue
P.O. Box 513
Jennings, LA 70546
Celestine Gilbeaux, Secretary/Treasurer

Christ's Sanctified Holy Church was organized in 1904 by Christ's Sanctified Holy Church (headquartered in South Carolina), a white Holiness religious body. Its parent body intended it to be a ministry to serve black persons. Its founding leaders were Dempsey Perkins, A. C. Mitchell, James Briller, Sr., and Leggie Pleasant.

The church has been known by two other names—the Colored Church South (its original name), and Christ's Sanctified Holy Church Colored (a modification of its present name, derived from its identification with its parent body). The church's doctrine is trinitarian and it places primary emphasis on sanctification. The headquarters are in Jennings, Louisiana.

Membership is divided into two categories: probationary and full. Persons who are justified and awaiting sanctification are considered as probationary members. Once they have received sanctification, they are considered full members. The body observes the ordinances of water baptism and the Lord's Supper. They contend that no rite is essential to a relationship between God and man. All full members are given equal rights and privileges. Women are accepted into the clergy. A strict code for clothing and jewelry is enforced.

Group Type: Denomination
Founded: 1904
Doctrine: Holiness

Churches of God, Holiness

848 Martin Luther King Drive, SW
Atlanta, GA 30314
Bishop Titus Paul Burruss

The Churches of God, Holiness, were founded circa 1920 by the late Bishop King Hezekiah Burruss, who died in 1963. The denomination developed from the Church of Christ (Holiness) U.S.A., of which Bishop Burruss was a member. It started as a local congregation in Atlanta, Georgia, in 1914 and experienced rapid growth. Its doctrine is identical with that of its parent body—the Church of Christ (Holiness) U.S.A.

The church conducts its business through national conventions (its highest authority) and state conventions. The bishop is the primary administrator, whose authority includes the appointment of state overseers. These overseers are responsible for appointing pastors within their jurisdictions. The current bishop is Bishop Titus Paul Burruss, who is also the pastor of the headquarters church, Bethlehem Church of God. According to the *Encyclopedia of American Religions* (2nd ed.), and Bishop Titus Paul Burruss, the churches are located primarily on the East Coast.

Group Type: Denomination
Founded: 1920
Doctrine: Holiness
Membership: In 1967, there were approximately 25,600 members in 42 congregations with 16 ministers

Church of Christ (Holiness), Inc.

Bethel Church of Christ (Holiness), Inc.
1302 E. Adams Boulevard
Los Angeles, CA 90011
(213) 773-7263
Bishop Matthew N. Richardson, President

The Church of Christ (Holiness), Inc., also known as the Associated Churches of Christ (Holiness), was organized in 1915 by the late Bishop William A. Washington in Los Angeles, California. For several years he ministered on the West Coast separately from the original movement, founded by the late Charles Price Jones in Jackson, Mississippi. Prior to coming West, Washington was pastor in the Church of Christ (Holiness) U.S.A., under the direction of Charles Price Jones. After pioneering the Bethel Church, he invited Jones to come to Los Angeles to conduct a series of meetings and, through these meetings, William A. Washington rejoined the Church of Christ (Holiness), U.S.A., Convention in Jackson, Mississippi, under the leadership of Charles Price Jones.

When Jones returned later to the West Coast, he worked out an agreement with Washington to organize Christ Temple Church of Christ (Holiness) U.S.A., in Los Angeles, California. The two prelates entered into a private agreement to work together under the Church of Christ (Holiness), U.S.A., Convention, which was located predominantly east of the Mississippi. However, the Bethel Church of Christ (Holiness), Inc., pastored by William A. Washington, was incorporated in 1915 in California, prior to this private agreement.

According to Otho B. Cobbins in the *History of Church of Christ (Holiness) U.S.A. 1895-1965* (1966):

The general constituency of the church was never made fully aware of this agreeable understanding between the two clergymen.

This agreement continued for thirty years until the convention year of 1946-47. The manipulating of some administrative problems in the upper circles of the church, finally resulted in an organizational eruption. The 1945 convention yearbook shows Bishop Charles Price Jones, President Emeritus, and Bishop William A. Washington, President. As a result of the eruption, Bishop William A. Washington was no longer in the Church of Christ (Holiness) U.S.A. He was still legally entitled to continue under his continued incorporation—as Church of Christ, Holiness, Incorporated, dated 1915. The end result was two organizational administrative units, but one in doctrine and practice.

As of September, 1989, the Church of Christ (Holiness), Inc., is an extension of the Church of Christ (Holiness) U.S.A., in its doctrine and practices. The Church of Christ (Holiness), Inc., continues to emphasize Holiness doctrine. This includes acceptance of the Methodist Articles of Religion and an emphasis on sanctification through the Holy Spirit. No information is available on the administrative structure and operational viability of the body.

Group Type: Denomination
Founded: 1915
Doctrine: Holiness

Church of Christ Holiness unto the Lord, Inc.

General Headquarters
1650 Smart Street
P.O. Box 1642
Savannah, GA 31401
Bishop Moses Lewis, President and General Overseer
(912) 857-3797
Bishop Ernest Kelly, Assistant Presiding Bishop
District Supervisor Elder James C. Hagan, General Secretary

The Church of Christ Holiness unto the Lord, Inc. (CCHL), established in Savannah, Georgia, on January 8, 1926, was founded under the auspices of the late Bishop Milton Solomon Bennett, who served as General Overseer for twenty-six years. Elder Bennett was ordained an elder by Bishop Davis in the Apostolic Holiness Church. In 1925, he withdrew from this group and began holding services in a little building on Indian Lane and Ann Street in Savannah, Georgia. In 1952, following the death of Bishop Bennett, Bishop Benjamin Franklin Colty was elected General Overseer. In 1960, Bishop James Kelly assumed the position of General Overseer and served in this capacity for approximately eighteen years.

Since its inception, the Church of Christ Holiness unto the Lord, Inc., has conducted an annual meeting known as the General Assembly of the Church of Christ Holiness unto the Lord, Inc. In 1979, the body reconstituted its organizational structure. The Church of Christ Holiness unto the Lord, Inc., is one of five Pentecostal organizations that have united to create a Fellowship Convention. The other bodies are: the Apostolic Faith Churches of God, Inc. (Bishop Stephen Douglas Willis, Franklin, Virginia); the Apostolic Faith Church of God (Bishop Oree Keyes, Jefferson, Ohio); the Apostolic Faith Church

of God Live On (Bishop Richard H. Cross, Hopewell, Virginia); and the Apostolic Faith Churches of God in Christ (Bishop R. A. Griswould, Hertford, North Carolina). These constitute the United Fellowship Convention of the Original Azusa Street Mission (Bishop Oree Keyes, Jefferson, Ohio). This fellowship convention is considered the first step leading toward a merger of these bodies. Each of the respective bodies has its roots in the original Azusa Street Revival. Bishop Oree Keyes is the leading figure in this reunion effort. In May, 1988, a Board of Directors, consisting of representatives from each of the five Pentecostal groups was appointed. Bishop Oree Keyes is the chairman of this board.

Group Type: Denomination
Founded: January 8, 1926
Publications: *Discipline Manual of The Church of Christ Holiness unto the Lord, Inc.*, 1983, Savannah, Georgia

Church of Christ (Holiness) U.S.A.

329 East Monument Street
Jackson, MS 39202
(601) 353-4033
Bishop M. R. Conic, Senior Bishop and President
(601) 982-8420
Elder Bobbye Sutton, Recording Secretary
(601) 969-7193

The Church of Christ (Holiness) U.S.A., was founded in 1894 by Charles Price Jones and Charles Harrison Mason, former Baptist ministers, who left the Baptist fellowship because of their emphasis on sanctification through the Holy Spirit. The initial organizational meeting was held in Jackson, Mississippi. The late Bishop Charles Price Jones was ratified as the leader of this, initially, interdenominational body. In 1898, it became a full-fledged Holiness denomination, led by Bishop Charles Price Jones. In 1907, many followers left the body to establish the Church of God in Christ, under the leadership of Charles Harrison Mason. Those who remained followed the original Holiness teachings of Charles Price Jones.

The body believes that salvation is possible only through divine grace and that baptism must be performed in the name of Jesus only. The organizational structure of the church is episcopal. The highest office is senior bishop. The church has seven dioceses, each headed by a bishop. It has a biennial convention, which establishes governing policies for the organization. The church operates its own publishing house, the National Publishing House, located in Chicago, Illinois, Mr. R. W. Lee, manager; the Boydton Institute in Boydton, Virginia; and the Industrial College in Jackson, Mississippi.

The senior bishop and president is Bishop M. R. Conic, whose office is the Jackson, Mississippi, headquarters.

Group Type: Denomination
Founded: 1894/1898
Doctrine: Holiness
Publications: *Truth*, Mrs. Alberta Bunton, editor, 8536 S. Justine Street, Chicago, IL 60620; National Publishing House, 8222 S. Ashland Avenue, Chicago, IL 60620, Mr. R. W. Lee, Manager

Church of God (Apostolic), Inc.

1031 North Highland Avenue
Winston-Salem, NC 27101
(919) 722-2285
Bishop Ruben K. Hash, General Overseer

The Church of God (Apostolic), Inc., was organized in 1897, by Elder Thomas J. Cox. At the time of its founding in Danville, Kentucky, it was known as the Christian Faith Band and was incorporated in 1901. In 1915, a meeting of the General Overseer and the Board of Elders discussed adopting a new, more "scriptural" name. The "Church of God (Apostolic)" was accepted although it was not incorporated as such until 1919, in Paris, Kentucky, its headquarters at that time.

The church subsequently changed its headquarters to the location of each new general overseer. St. Peter's Church of God (Apostolic) in Winston-Salem, North Carolina, became the organization's headquarters in 1948, the home city of its General Bishop and Overseer, Eli N. Neal, elected in 1950. In 1966, the church's General Assembly proclaimed St. Peter's Church of God (Apostolic) to be the official headquarters, where it remains today.

Admission into the Church of God (Apostolic), Inc., depends upon repentance for sin, confession of faith, and baptism by immersion in the name of Jesus for the remission of sin. Its members believe in Holiness and sanctification and practice the ordinance of footwashing. They celebrate communion with unfermented grape juice and unleavened bread.

Under the leadership of Bishop Ruben K. Hash, General Overseer, the church is constructing a headquarters building, an education building, and a community outreach center in Winston-Salem, North Carolina. The church is governed by a board of bishops. It publishes its discipline and a ministerial training manual. A newsletter is being planned and organized for the near future. There are currently forty-five congregations throughout the United States. The church meets twice a year—in June and August—for general church conferences.

Group Type: Denomination
Founded: 1897, incorporated in 1901
Doctrine: Oneness/Apostolic
Membership: 45 congregations throughout the United States with approximately 15,000 persons
Publications: Newsletter to be published in the future; a discipline
Meetings: General church conferences in June and August

Church of God by Faith, Inc.

3220 Haines Street
P.O. Box 3746
Jacksonville, FL 32206
(904) 353-5111
Bishop James E. McKnight, Presiding Bishop

This body was established in Jacksonville, Florida in 1914. Its founders were Crawford Bright, Aaron Matthews, Sr., Elder John Bright, Mother Delia Scippio, and Nathaniel Scippio. The founding principles emphasize that the "church" refers to an assembly of people gathered together for the purpose of glorifying God. Special attention is devoted to the means by which the believers are to encourage, sustain, and grow spiritually through a unified bond of Christian fellowship. The first As-

sembly Meeting was held in 1917, in White Springs, Florida. The charter was drafted in 1922, in Alachua, Florida. In December, 1941, the General Assembly moved from Alachua, Florida to Ocala, Florida, and annual assemblies were held there for forty years. In December, 1986, the General Assembly moved to Atlanta, Georgia.

The denomination is concentrated primarily on the East Coast, with its greatest numbers in the Southeast. There are eleven districts headed by a District Superintendent.

Group Type: Denomination
Founded: 1914
Publications: The Spiritual Guide
Meetings: Semiannual sessions held in Atlanta, GA

Church of God in Christ, Congregational

918 Bond Avenue
East St. Louis, IL 62201
(618) 271-7780
Bishop George Slack

The Church of God in Christ, Congregational, is a result of a 1932 split from its parent body, the Church of God in Christ, over the issue of polity. Bishop J. Bowe believed that the polity of the church should be congregational rather than episcopal. He organized the church and in 1934 was joined by George Slack, who had been barred from the parent church because he did not believe that tithing was essential for salvation. He also believed that tithing was not a New Testament teaching. Slack, who had served as junior bishop to Bishop Bowe, became the senior bishop in 1945, when Bowe rejoined the Church of God in Christ.

The church has retained the doctrine of its parent body, but disagrees with the issues of polity and tithing. Its members are conscientious objectors.

Group Type: Denomination
Founded: 1932
Membership: As of 1971, 33 churches in the United States, 6 in Mexico, and 4 in England
Publications: A manual
Meetings: Meets annually during the fourth week in October

Church of God in Christ, Inc.

272 South Main Street
Memphis, TN 38103
(901) 578-3838
Bishop Louis H. Ford, Presiding Bishop
Bishop G. R. Ross, General Secretary

The Church of God in Christ, Inc. (COGIC), was established by Charles Harrison Mason and Charles Price Jones during the late nineteenth century. After Mason and Jones were rejected by Baptist groups because they overemphasized Holiness, they separated from the Baptists and formed the Church of God in Christ.

Mason attended the Arkansas Baptist College in 1893 for about three months, but left because he believed the Lord showed him that salvation was not to be found in schools or colleges. He preached on his own initiative until he met Charles Price

Jones in Mississippi, in 1895. The two, along with several others, called a revival meeting in 1896, at Jackson, Mississippi. This led to a second meeting in 1897, at Lexington, Mississippi, where the Church of God in Christ was formally established. It was incorporated as a chartered denomination in Memphis, Tennessee, in late 1897, thereby becoming the first, legally chartered southern Holiness denomination. By 1906, a brick edifice had been raised to replace an earlier, temporary structure. By 1907, however, significant changes occurred.

Jones heard of the activities begun in 1906, at the Azusa Street Mission in Los Angeles under William Joseph Seymour. In 1907, he encouraged Mason to go there to receive the Holy Spirit, thus sanctifying him for the ministry. When Mason returned from California, having received the Holy Spirit, he encouraged entire sanctification in the congregation. Jones and Mason disagreed over the necessity of speaking in tongues as proof of baptism of the Holy Spirit and sanctification.

According to some accounts, Mason and his followers were either voted out of the church or left, while others say that Jones and the non-Pentecostal faction withdrew. Regardless of these questions, the split between the leaders and congregants resulted in separate churches. Jones reorganized his followers into the Church of Christ (Holiness), U.S.A., adhering to the Holiness perspective. Mason retained the name of the original church, and the church began its phenomenal growth and popularity under his leadership. He continued as bishop until his death in 1961.

In the mid-1960s, a question arose as to where the COGIC constitution placed the authority of the Senior Bishop, relative to the Executive Board. Legal struggles followed from November, 1964 to November, 1968. On October 13, 1967, a consent decree was issued from the Chancery Court of Shelby County, Tennessee. Under the consent decree, it was agreed that "all rights, powers, and duties of the Senior Bishop and the Executive Board shall remain status quo until a final determination by the constitutional convention of the General Assembly," and that Bishop Mason's authority reverted to the Board of Bishops upon his death.

The Constitutional Convention met from January 30 to February 2, 1968. The Convention abolished the office of Senior Bishop (although, at the discretion of the Board and sanction of the General Assembly, Bishop O. T. Jones, Sr., was honored as the ceremonial head of the church and given the title Senior Bishop). The Convention also provided for the election of an Executive Board of twelve that replaced the Executive Commission of seven; the Executive Board has a presiding bishop, and first and second assistant presiding bishops. The task of the Executive Board is to conduct the administrative affairs of the church during and between meetings of the General Assembly, "keeping the General Assembly informed of its actions."

Today, the ecclesiastical structure of the church includes the Executive Board, the General Assembly, the Board of Bishops, the Women's Department, the General Council, Jurisdictional Assemblies, and local churches. The General Assembly is the supreme legislative and judicial authority of the COGIC, and is composed of all bishops, pastors, elders, missionaries, and qualified lay members. It is the only tribunal that has power to express the doctrines and creeds of the church, and its decisions are binding on all church members.

The national structure of the church is governed by a presiding Bishop, who heads the eleven-man General Board of Bishops. The General Board of Bishops is elected, as is the presiding Bishop, by the General Assembly, for a tenure of four years. The General Board members are jurisdictional Bishops, elected from the board to the General Board by the General Assembly.

Jurisdictional assemblies are composed of members in or affiliated with designated ecclesiastical jurisdictions, which include the jurisdictional bishops, supervisor of women's department, all pastors of local churches, ordained elders, district missionaries, jurisdictional department heads, and one lay delegate selected from each jurisdictional district. Each state is presided over by a bishop who organizes his jurisdiction into districts presided over by superintendents, made up of local pastors.

The Women's Department of the Church of God in Christ is under the supervision of the national supervisor of women with her cabinet. There are nine other departments in addition to the Women's Department: National Youth, International Sunday School, Home and Foreign Mission, National Music, Urban Affairs, Evangelism, the Board of Education, the National Publishing Board, and the National Banking Committee. The Youth, Music, Evangelism, Sunday School, and Missions departments all have annual conventions.

The Church of God in Christ is basically trinitarian, teaching the infallibility of scripture, the need for regeneration, and subsequent baptism of the Holy Ghost. It emphasizes Holiness as God's standard for Christian conduct. Holy Communion, footwashing, and baptism are recognized as ordinances. The church also stresses repentance, justification, sanctification, speaking in tongues (glossolalia), and the gift of healing as evidence of baptism of the Spirit.

Articles of Faith of COGIC outline the belief in angels, demons, the church, the second coming of Christ, divine healing, miracles, and baptism of the Holy Spirit. The church is Pentecostal (members ascribe to and believe in the charismatic experience of speaking in tongues and are taught that every believer must do so at least once) rather than Apostolic (refuting belief in the doctrine of the Trinity, baptizing in the name of Jesus Christ only).

The Church of God in Christ believes in marriage and is opposed to divorce or separation. The church opposes homosexuality, abortion, and pre- or extramarital sex. Women in the ministry must serve in a subservient or support role.

The presiding bishop of the church, Bishop Louis H. Ford, was elected in April, 1990 following the death of Bishop James Oglethorpe Patterson, Sr., on December 29, 1989. The general secretary is Bishop G. R. Ross. There are Church of God in Christ congregations throughout the United States and in Jamaica, Canada, and West Germany. The denomination numbers approximately four million.

Group Type: Denomination
Founded: 1897
Membership: 4,000,000 persons in 982 congregations with 10,425 ministers
Publications: *Whole Truth*, 67 Tennyson, Highland Park, MI 48203; *The Voice of Missions*, 1932 Dewey Street, Evanston, IL 60201
Meetings: Meets annually during the second week in November

Church of God in Christ, International

584 Myrtle Avenue
Brooklyn, NY 11025
(718) 857-3444
Bishop Carl Williams, Sr., Presiding Bishop
Bishop David J. Billings, Executive Secretary

The Church of God in Christ, International, is the result of a major split from the Church of God in Christ. The question of centralized authority in the reorganization of the parent body, following its 1969 constitutional convention, caused fourteen bishops to leave the church. Led by Bishop Illie L. Jefferson, they rejected the polity of the newly reorganized church and left to form the Church of God in Christ, International, in Kansas City. It retains the doctrine of its parent body but developed a new denominational structure.

Group Type: Denomination
Founded: 1969
Membership: As of 1982, 200,000 persons in 300 congregations with 1,600 ministers
Publications: *Message* and *Holiness Code*, both periodicals

Church of God (Sanctified Church)

1044 Jefferson Street
Nashville, TN 37208
(615) 255-5579
Elder Jerry E. Gordon, Assistant Central District Overseer and Assistant Financial Officer

Church of God (Sanctified Church) was founded in 1901 in Columbia, Tennessee, by Elders Charles W. Gray (1861-1945) and John C. Brown. The church has been known as the "Church of God" and the "Holiness Church." The church was incorporated following a schism relating to Pentecostalism. After Bishop C. H. Mason persuaded most of the believers to follow Pentecostal doctrine, some of those that remained adhered to the belief in "holiness through sanctification by the Holy Spirit" and became the Church of Christ (Holiness) U.S.A. The Church of God (Sanctified) is one of a small number of independent groups that remained faithful to the "holiness" movement. This church differs from the Church of Christ (Holiness) U.S.A., only in its polity, which is congregational. The local church has authority to appoint its own ministers. In 1927, there was a schism that resulted in Elder Gray establishing another religious body, known as the Original Church of God (or Sanctified Church). The church incorporated under a board of elders in 1927. The incorporating leaders were Elders J. L. Rucker, R. A. Manter, M. S. Martin, B. Smith Sowell, and G. A. Whitley.

Group Type: Denomination
Founded: 1901
Doctrine: Holiness

Church of God (Which He Purchased with His Own Blood)

1628 NE 50th Street
Oklahoma City, OK 73111
(405) 427-8264
Bishop William J. Fizer, Chief Bishop
Evangelist Alsie Mae Fizer, General Secretary

The Church of God (Which He Purchased with His Own Blood) [W.H.P.W.H.O.B.] was founded in Oklahoma City, Oklahoma, in 1953 by Bishop William Jordan Fizer. According to the *Yearbook of American and Canadian Churches* (1989 ed.), the church was formed after Bishop Fizer's excommunication from the Church of the Living God (Christian Workers for Fellowship) over disagreements of doctrine relating to the Lord's Supper. The Church of God (W.H.P.W.H.O.B.) believes that grape juice or wine and unleavened bread should be used instead of water, which is used by its parent body.

The body considers itself non-Pentecostal in doctrine, but does take a stance on traditional Pentecostal elements. It does not practice speaking in tongues, but rather believes that the Holy Ghost is given to those who obey the Lord. Members also observe footwashing as an act of humility. Baptism (by immersion) is administered in the trinitarian formula.

The church believes that it is the body of Christ and, through scriptural doctrine and practices, the church formed by Christ. Members of the church generally abstain from tobacco and alcohol. Divine healing is considered an article of faith, but it does not exclude the value of medical professionals.

Group Type: Denomination
Founded: 1953
Publications: *Gospel News* (a monthly periodical), a Bible doctrine book, and religious tracts, all written by Bishop Fizer
Meetings: Annual meeting (a four-day session) is held in Oklahoma City, Oklahoma; annual Sunday School Teachers' Union Convention is held from Friday to Sunday, ending on the fourth Sunday in July; bishops' council is held the first weekend in May

Church of Our Lord Jesus Christ of the Apostolic Faith

2081 Adam Clayton Powell Boulevard
New York, NY 10027
(212) 866-1700
Bishop William Bonner

The Church of Our Lord Jesus Christ of the Apostolic Faith was founded in 1919 in Columbus, Ohio, by the Reverend Robert Clarence Lawson. A sickly child, he was taken in 1913 to the Apostolic Faith Assembly Church where G. T. Haywood served as pastor of this branch of the Pentecostal Assemblies of the World. Lawson soon joined the Pentecostal Assemblies of the World and eventually served as a pastor, founding congregations in Ohio, Missouri, and Texas. In 1919, he left his thriving church in Columbus, Ohio (under the Reverend G. T. Haywood's jurisdiction), and moved to New York City, where he started his own church, Refuge Temple. In addition to beginning other congregations, he also started a day nursery, a radio ministry, a periodical, and several businesses. Among his accomplishments was the opening of the Church of Christ Bible Institute in 1926, to train ministers and pastors. The school was fully accredited in 1950.

In the 1930s and 1940s, the church spread to the West Indies. Lawson continued to serve as bishop and nurtured other ministers, who eventually would split from the church when Lawson would not share the bishopric nor divide the leadership within the church. Sherrod C. Johnson left the church in 1930 to eventually form the Church of the Lord Jesus Christ of the

Apostolic Faith in 1933, partly over the dress code for female members. Smallwood E. Williams left in 1957 to form the Bible Way Church of Our Lord Jesus Christ World Wide, Inc. Bishop Henry C. Brooks also left the church to form the Way of the Cross Church of Christ in 1927 because he wanted no organizational affiliations in the church. Hubert J. Spencer succeeded Bishop Lawson after his death in 1961. He served as a stabilizing force for the church after forty-one years of one man's leadership and the major split from the church by Bishop Smallwood E. Williams in 1957. The current presiding apostle, Bishop William Bonner, succeeded Bishop Spencer. Bishop Bonner has initiated two new programs not usually found among African American Apostolics—the development of a retirement plan and the beginning of new churches by ordained elders with denominational support.

The church maintains the doctrine of the Pentecostal Assemblies of the World, from which it grew. The baptism of the Holy Spirit is believed necessary for salvation, and footwashing is practiced. Missions, health clinics, and churches have been established in Africa, Trinidad, England, and Germany. In addition to the presiding apostle or bishop, there are four regional apostles. An annual convocation is held in New York City.

Group Type: Denomination
Founded: 1919
Doctrine: Oneness/Apostolic
Membership: As of 1980, 30,000 persons in 450 churches in the United States, Africa, Germany, the West Indies, and England
Publications: *Contender of the Faith*, a monthly magazine
Meetings: An annual convocation in New York City in August

Church of the Living God (Christian Workers for Fellowship)

801 NE 17th Street
Oklahoma City, OK 73105
(405) 427-3701
Bishop F. C. Scott

The Church of the Living God (Christian Workers for Fellowship) was founded in 1889 by the Reverend William Christian, a former slave who had been influenced by C. H. Mason, the founder and bishop of the Church of God in Christ, when they both were members of the Baptist faith. According to the Reverend Christian, he received a revelation from God concerning Baptists—that they preached or believed in a sectarian doctrine. Christian left the Baptists and founded a church wherein the truth would be taught. His wife said that she too received the revelation. Christian became the "chief" of the church and remained in this position until his death on April 11, 1928. Chief Christian's rule served as the power and law of the organization, and along with his wife, he served as the executive head of the church. Nothing could be done by local organizations without their prior approval. He was succeeded by his wife, who was later succeeded by their son.

Several factions of the church have split from the original body. In 1902, the Church of the Living God, Apostolic Church emerged, and changed its name to the Church of the Living God, General Assembly, in 1908. It was led by the Reverend C. W. Harris. A second, smaller splinter group merged with this one in 1924. A third church, Church of the Living God, the Pillar and Ground of Truth, led by the Reverend E. J. Cain, split from the original body in 1925. The Church of the Living God, General Assembly, and the Church of the Living God, the Pillar and Ground of Truth, merged in 1926 to form the House of God Which Is the Church of the Living God, the Pillar and Ground of Truth.

It should be noted that this church is different from the original Church of the Living God, the Pillar and Ground of the Truth, Inc. [Lewis Dominion], founded by Mary L. Tate in 1903, in Tennessee. The leadership of Tate's church was divided into three segments after her death in 1930. In addition to the original body, there is the House of God Which is the Church of the Living God, the Pillar and Ground of the Truth *Without Controversy* [Keith Dominion], founded in 1931 and originally led by Bishop Mary Frankie Lewis Keith, and the Church of the Living God, the Pillar and Ground of the Truth Which He Purchased with His Own Blood, Inc., founded in 1931 and originally led by Bishop Bruce L. McLeod.

The church's doctrine is trinitarian, and it believes in some Pentecostal tenets. Footwashing, the Lord's Supper (with water and unleavened bread), and speaking in tongues are considered ordinances. Unlike most Pentecostal bodies, speaking in tongues is *not* considered to be the initial evidence of the baptism of the Holy Spirit. Rather, "tongues" are allowed but must be recognizable languages instead of mere utterances. Baptism by immersion is also observed.

Of interest is the church's belief that Jesus was black because of David's and Abraham's lineage. Biblical references include David referring to himself becoming as a bottle in the smoke (Psalms 119:83 KJV) and Job's, Jeremiah's, and Moses's wives being black (see Job 30:30, Jeremiah 8:21, and Numbers 12:1-11). The church asserts that the saints of the Bible were black, whereas Baptists taught that blacks were not human, but rather the product of a human father and a female beast.

Although the polity of the church is episcopal, its organization is modeled after fraternal organizations (extremely popular in the black community during the church's early years), having many auxiliaries that are particularly important in sickness and burial. As in secret and fraternal organizations, the church has several points of doctrine known only to its members. Local organizations are called temples. Publications of the church include *Fellowship Echoes* and *National Bulletin*.

Its last reported membership in 1964 was 43,320 persons in 276 churches with 376 ministers.

Group Type: Denomination
Founded: 1889
Membership: As of 1964, 43,320 persons in 276 churches with 376 ministers
Publications: *Fellowship Echoes* and *National Bulletin*

Church of the Living God, the Pillar and Ground of the Truth, Inc. [Lewis Dominion]

4520 Hydes Ferry Pike, Box 5735
Nashville, TN 37208
(615) 255-0401
Bishop Helen M. Lewis, Chief Overseer and President
Dr. Meharry H. Lewis, General Secretary and Treasurer

Founded in 1903 in Dickson, Tennessee, by Mary Magdalena Lewis Tate, the Church of the Living God, the Pillar and Ground of the Truth, Inc., grew to become a national denomination that is strongest in the eastern United States. The church was established upon a fundamental doctrine of Holiness, and upon the principles of conversion, sanctification, water baptism, and reception of the Holy Ghost as evidenced by speaking in unknown and other tongues. The name of the church was divinely inspired, and its foundations ("Living God," "Pillar," "Ground," and "Truth") are supported in I Timothy 3:15 and Genesis 28:16-22.

The church began as a street and door-to-door ministry in Dickson, Steele Springs, and Paris, Tennessee, and spread to Kentucky, Georgia, Alabama, Ohio, and Illinois. Mary Tate served as chief apostle of the church and was ordained to the bishopric by the church elders in 1908. She was set apart as chief overseer of the formally incorporated body and reportedly became the first woman to attain the rank of bishop in a nationally recognized religious body.

"Mother Lewis's" church experienced many splits, the first in 1919. The initial group left to become the House of God, Which Is the Church of the Living God, the Pillar and Ground of Truth, Inc., and is headquartered in Philadelphia, Pennsylvania. Many of the resulting bodies use names similar to that of the parent body, and some still recognize their origins in the founding efforts of Mother Tate.

After the death of Bishop Tate in 1930, a committee appointed by the executive council of bishops formulated a recommendation to the church's general assembly to determine its future leadership. It was decided that three competent persons should be duly recognized and ordained to constitute the office of chief overseer of the church. The "1931 Agreement," as it has come to be known, resulted in a triumvirate, with each member overseeing sixteen of the (then) forty-eight states of the United States. This ruling evolved into the dominion rule of the church.

The body discussed in this narrative is the continuation of the original denomination. Its leadership was assumed by Bishop Felix Early Lewis (Mother Tate's younger son) until his death in 1968. The body is also known as the "Lewis Dominion." Under the leadership of Mrs. Mary Frankie Lewis Keith (the widow of Bishop Walter Curtis Lewis, Mother Tate's older son), the House of God Which Is the Church of the Living God, the Pillar and Ground of Truth Without Controversy was formed. Bishop Keith led the organization until her death in 1962. This is also known as the "Keith Dominion." The third segment of the original church was led by Bishop Bruce L. McLeod, who died in 1936. It became the Church of the Living God, the Pillar and Ground of the Truth, Which He Purchased with His Own Blood, with its headquarters in Indianapolis, Indiana. It is led by Bishop Mattie Lou McLeod Jewell, Bishop McLeod's widow.

The polity of the church is episcopal. Women have always been prominent in the denomination and have been encouraged in the ministry. Many have served and continue to serve with distinction and continue to serve as chief overseers, bishops, and deaconesses. Remarriage is allowed, although it is not known whether divorce is permitted.

Today, the church has approximately two thousand members in twenty churches. There is a general assembly that meets the last week in July in Nashville, Tennessee, and an annual Holiness Young People's Assembly (November), in addition to state assemblies. Its yearbook, church newsletter, and *General Assembly Journal* are published through its New and Living Way Publishing House in Nashville, Tennessee.

Currently, the Church of the Living God, the Pillar and Ground of the Truth, Inc., is building a national headquarters in Nashville, which will include an educational facility, a youth activity center, and an outreach program facility. The church publishing house will also be located in the new national headquarters. The church is associated with the United Churches of the Living God, the Pillar and Ground of the Truth, Inc., in Nashville, of which Bishop Helen Lewis is General Overseer. The church's Chief Overseer and President, Bishop Helen M. Lewis, succeeded her husband, Bishop Felix Early Lewis, in April 1969, following his death in 1968. The General Secretary/Treasurer is (Bishop) Dr. Meharry H. Lewis, their son. Five of Bishop Helen Lewis's nine children serve as ministers in the church.

Group Type: Denomination
Founded: 1903
Doctrine: Holiness
Membership: Approximately 2,000 persons in 20 churches
Publications: *General Assembly Journal*; *Seventy-Fifth Anniversary Yearbook of the Church of the Living God, the Pillar and Ground of the Truth, Inc., 1903-1978*, The New and Living Way Publishing House, Inc., P.O. Box 5735, Nashville, TN 37208; and a church newsletter
Meetings: General Assembly, which meets the last week in July in Nashville, TN; an annual Holiness Young Peoples' Assembly in November; and state assemblies

Church of the Living God, the Pillar and Ground of the Truth, Which He Purchased with His Own Blood, Inc.

3359 North Ruckle Street
Indianapolis, IN 46205
Bishop Mattie Lou McLeod Jewell, Chief Overseer

The Church of the Living God, the Pillar and Ground of the Truth, Inc. [Lewis Dominion], was founded in 1903 in Dickson, Tennessee, by Mary Lena Lewis Tate. After the death of Bishop Tate in 1930, a committee appointed by the church's executive council of bishops formulated a recommendation to the general assembly to determine its future leadership. It was decided that three competent persons should be duly recognized and ordained to constitute the office of chief overseer of the church. The "1931 Agreement," as it has come to be known, resulted in a triumvirate, with each member overseeing sixteen of the (then) forty-eight states of the United States. This ruling evolved into the dominion rule of the church.

The leadership of the parent church was assumed by Bishop Felix Early Lewis (Mother Tate's younger son) in 1931. He held this position until his death in 1968. Under the leadership of Bishop Mary Frankie Lewis Keith (the widow of Bishop Walter Curtis Lewis, Mother Tate's older son), the second segment, the House of God Which Is the Church of the Living God, the Pillar and Ground of Truth Without Controversy, was formed (this is also known as the "Keith Dominion"). Bishop

Keith led the body until her death in 1962. The third segment of the original church was led by Bishop Bruce L. McLeod. It became the Church of the Living God, the Pillar and Ground of the Truth, Which He Purchased with His Own Blood, Inc. Bishop McLeod died in 1936 and was succeeded by his widow, Bishop Mattie Lou McLeod Jewell. It is headquartered in Indianapolis, Indiana.

Group Type: Denomination
Founded: 1931

Church of the Lord Jesus Christ of the Apostolic Faith

22nd and Bainbridge Streets
Philadelphia, PA 19146
(215) 735-8982
Bishop J. McDowell Shelton

The Church of the Lord Jesus Christ of the Apostolic Faith grew out of the Church of *Our* Lord Jesus Christ of the Apostolic Faith in 1933. Founded by Bishop Sherrod C. Johnson, this faction took a more conservative stance than did the Reverend Robert Clarence Lawson, the founder of its parent body. Lawson allowed women to wear jewelry and makeup, whereas Bishop Johnson, considered ultraconservative among Apostolics, insisted on calf-length dresses, unstraightened or natural hair with head coverings, cotton stockings, and no makeup or jewelry for women. In addition to this, Johnson opposed the celebrations of Christmas, Easter, and Lent.

The doctrine is Apostolic or oneness, believing that members must be sanctified or filled with the Holy Ghost in order to be born again. Baptism is administered in the name of either "Jesus Christ" or the "Lord Jesus," not in the mere name of "Jesus," to distinguish the Christ from Bar-Jesus (Acts 13:6) and Jesus Justus (Colossians 4:11) of the Bible. Women preachers, the wearing of expensive or worldly attire, and remarriage after divorce are prohibited.

The church's polity is episcopal, with lay persons in many administrative positions. The church has missions in Africa, England, Portugal, Jordan, the Caribbean, and the Maldives, and it has a radio ministry, "The Whole Truth," that broadcasts over fifty stations. There is also an annual national convention held at the church's headquarters in Philadelphia. The current presiding officer is Bishop S. McDowell Shelton, who succeeded Bishop Johnson after his death in 1961.

Group Type: Denomination
Founded: 1933
Doctrine: Oneness/Apostolic
Membership: As of 1980, over 100 congregations
Publications: *The Whole Truth*, a periodical, 22nd and Bainbridge Streets, Philadelphia, PA 19146
Meetings: Annual convention in Philadelphia

Church of Universal Triumph—The Dominion of God

8317 LaSalle Boulevard
Detroit, MI 48206
The Reverend James Shaffer

The Church of Universal Triumph—The Dominion of God is a Holiness religious body founded by the late Reverend James Francis Marion Jones, who was internationally known as Prophet Jones (1908–1971). His religious title was "His Holiness the Reverend Dr. James F. Jones, D.D., Universal Dominion Ruler."

Prophet Jones organized this group in 1938, following a schism from Triumph the Church and Kingdom of God in Christ, the Holiness body that initially recognized his ministry. His departure was related to problems resulting from his phenomenal success as a child preacher. He reputedly initiated a regular preaching schedule at the age of eleven.

In 1938, he was sent by his former denomination to conduct missionary work in Detroit, Michigan. A controversy developed over ownership of property that had been lavishly bestowed upon Prophet Jones. Rather than relinquish the property to the leadership of Triumph the Church and Kingdom of God in Christ, he started his own church. As in the cases of Daddy Grace and Father Divine, his church's growth and development were linked to his unique personality. He was renowned for his tremendous wealth and his healing ability. Grateful supporters showered him with material wealth and resources. His reputation suffered following a 1956 incident at his home when he was arrested for gross indecency. Although he was exonerated of these charges, his ministry never flourished to the heights that he had gained during the 1940s and early 1950s.

Most of his followers were located in large northern metropolitan areas. He routinely commuted between Chicago and Detroit until his death in 1971. The church adhered to very strict standards, prohibiting members from the use of tobacco, alcohol, coffee or tea, and from entering into marriage without approval of the church leadership. Men were required to wear health belts, and women were instructed to wear girdles. The Reverend Lord James Schaffer succeeded Prophet Jones as Dominion Ruler in 1971. He reports to a dominion council and board of trustees. No information is available on the current membership or activity of the church.

Group Type: Denomination
Founded: 1938
Doctrine: Holiness

Deliverance Evangelistic Centers, Inc.

621 Clinton Avenue
Newark, NJ 07108
(201) 824-7300
Ms. Denise Holmes

Group Type: Denomination
Founded: 1956
Doctrine: Deliverance
Publications: *Deliverance Voice*

Deliverance Evangelistic Church

4732 North Broad Street
Philadelphia, PA 19141
(215) 456-2151
The Reverend Dr. Benjamin Smith, Sr., Founder and Pastor
The Reverend Dr. Joseph L. Ross, Sr., Administrator

The Deliverance Evangelistic Church, also known as the Time of Deliverance Ministry, was founded on December 16, 1961, by the Reverend Dr. Benjamin Smith, Sr., in Philadelphia. The Reverend Dr. Smith had served as the leader of ten persons who banded together as a prayer group that did evangelistic witnessing to the public in 1960. As the group grew, it moved to several locations until it settled in its current facility.

The goal of the church is threefold: to evangelize souls to Christ; to teach the word of God toward spiritual maturity; and to prepare for worship and Christian service. The emphasis and efforts of the eighty-three thousand members in thirty-two independent congregations, primarily in Pennsylvania and New Jersey, continue to focus on an extensive outreach program that includes provision for the needy through clothing, food, shelter, and funds as well as evangelism in hospitals, prisons, nursing homes, and for the shut-in population. It also sponsors a radiobroadcast and various departmental interests of the church, especially that of Christian education, which includes the Deliverance Evangelistic Bible Institute and the Youth Bible School. These educational endeavors reach over two thousand persons yearly through general and Christian education and ministers' preparatory programs. Missions are supported in Haiti, India, and Liberia.

Dr. Smith is the founder and president of the future "Deliverance Village," a multipurpose complex that will include a church auditorium to seat between seven thousand and ten thousand persons, a Christian medical center, a Christian school for grades kindergarten through twelve, and a home for the aged to accommodate approximately five hundred persons. Hope Plaza, a shopping center that is part of the complex, is complete. Construction on the new church building began in 1989.

In addition to the quarterly church newsletter and several record albums produced by the church's choirs, the Deliverance Evangelistic Church publishes *Evangel* magazine, as well as an annual Christmas magazine and an annual Bible Institute graduation book. The church holds its annual convention in Philadelphia during the last week in June and has its regional fellowship during the first week of September. Dr. Benjamin Smith, Sr., serves as the pastor of the church and Dr. Joseph L. Ross, Sr., is the administrator and associate minister.

Group Type: Denomination
Founded: 1961
Doctrine: Deliverance
Membership: 83,000 persons in 32 congregations with 81 ministers
Publications: *Evangel*, a magazine; an annual Christmas magazine; a quarterly church newsletter; an annual Bible Institute graduation book
Meetings: Annual Convention held the last week in June in Philadelphia; the Regional Fellowship held the first week in September

Deliverance Miracle Revival Center, Inc.

P.O. Box 268
Gainesville, FL 32602

Group Type: Denomination
Doctrine: Deliverance

Emmanuel Tabernacle Baptist Church Apostolic Faith

329 North Garfield Avenue
Columbus, OH 43203
(614) 253-2535

Bishop H. C. Clark, Presiding Bishop
Elder John J. Duff, General Secretary

The Emmanuel Tabernacle Baptist Church Apostolic Faith was organized in 1916 and incorporated in 1917 by Bishop Martin Rawliegh (*sic*) Gregory (1885-1960) in cooperation with Lela Grant and Bessie Dockett (two faithful workers of the church) in Columbus, Ohio. Gregory was called to the ministry at the age of seventeen. He studied law and medicine at Colgate University and worked in the Baptist church for nine years before coming to Columbus in 1914.

Apostolic in theology, the ordinances of the church include baptism by immersion in the name of Jesus only, footwashing, and the Lord's Supper. According to its bylaws, the ruling power of the church is found in Matthew 18:1-35.

Located primarily in the North and the South, it comprises approximately thirty churches and seeks to evangelize the world for Christ. The organization meets quarterly in different locations, but it always convenes at its headquarters in Columbus for its June meeting. The church is currently erecting its first multipurpose building.

Bishop Gregory was the first Apostolic bishop to give women a place equal to men in the church, believing that "all persons may be granted equal rights in preaching God's word." Accordingly, women have been on the Board of Bishops, from which the succeeding leader of the church is chosen upon the death of its presiding bishop. The church's current presiding bishop is a woman, Bishop H. C. Clark.

Group Type: Denomination
Founded: 1916
Doctrine: Oneness/Apostolic
Membership: 30 congregations
Meetings: Quarterly meetings are held; the June meeting is always in Columbus, OH

Evangel Temple, Inc.

P.O. Box 4187
Upper Marlboro, MD 20772
(202) 635-8000 (Washington, DC listing)
Bishop John L. Meares, Bishop and President
Virgil Meares, Secretary

Group Type: Denomination
Meetings: Men's Conference held in June, Women's Conference held in May; National Pastors Conference held in mid-March
Publications: *Bridgebuilder*, R. Anthony, editor; *Communicator*, M. L. Meares, editor; *Kingdom Lifeline*, Bishop John L. Meares, editor

Faith Tabernacle Council of Churches, International

7015 NE 23rd Avenue
Portland, OR 97211
(503) 282-8071
Bishop Louis W. Osborne, Sr., Founder and Presiding Officer

The Faith Tabernacle Council of Churches, International (FTCC), was founded in 1962 by Bishop Louis W. Osborne, Sr., in Portland, Oregon, and was incorporated in 1963. It was formerly known as the Faith Tabernacle Corporation of Churches, Inc., until the name was changed at the July 1989 Annual Conference. The 55 member churches are found across the United States, in Zimbabwe, and South Africa.

The FTCC was founded after Bishop Osborne received a vision from the Lord. In his vision, he caught and carried a light that grew in intensity, thus enabling him to lead people down the pathway they had stopped traveling. The organization seeks to spread the message of the Gospel, not to one denomination—Apostolic—but to all. The emphasis, then, is on fellowship and freedom. Each church in the FTCC is autonomous, and the internal affairs of each remain within its purview, unless otherwise requested. Guidelines for Christian development are provided to member churches merely as helpful tools. The churches are not bound to use them. Conformity is not imposed. As an organization, ministers are licensed and ordained by the Faith Tabernacle Council of Churches, International.

The organization meets yearly the first week in July. It publishes *The Light of Faith* and yearbooks. The church is currently building two churches in Zimbabwe. Bishop Osborne continues to serve as the presiding officer.

Group Type: Denomination specific; council of churches/groups
Founded: 1962
Membership: 55 churches
Publications: *The Light of Faith* and yearbooks
Meetings: Annual meeting the first week in July

Faith Temple Pentecostal Church, Inc.

P.O. Box 447
Salt Lake City, UT 84118

Group Type: Denomination

Federated Pentecostal Church International, Inc.

315 26th Avenue
Seattle, WA 98122
Bishop S. D. Leffall, Presiding Officer
(206) 641-5820

Bishop Richard E. Taylor, Executive Secretary
14250 SE 13th Place
Bellevue, WA 98008

Founded by Bishop E. F. Morris in 1934, the Federated Pentecostal Church International, Inc. (FPCI), is an umbrella organization of eight independently incorporated Pentecostal bodies. The eight have pledged full fellowship to one another, feel related to one another, and have agreed to help one another. The primary purposes of the body are to "engage in religious activities in churches, halls, on radio and television broadcasts and the printed page as deemed advisable" and to "promote missionary endeavors and raise funds for missionary support by accepting free will donations and bequests from the membership and friends." The Women's National Evangelistic Union is an auxiliary of the body.

Members of the church believe in the Godhead, salvation, sanctification, baptism by immersion, baptism of the Holy Ghost (Acts 2:4), and are adverse to spiritualism (communion with the dead).

The FPCI is active in Nigeria, where it has established a school and helps support 134 pastors. Its membership there is 22,000. A cathedral, which will also serve as its headquarters, is being developed in Calabar, Nigeria.

The Federated Pentecostal Churches International, Inc., includes four hundred churches in North America and Africa. The organization meets annually during the fourth week in August (beginning on the Thursday preceding Labor Day and ending on the Tuesday following Labor Day). The current presiding officer is Bishop S. D. Leffall.

Group Type: Denomination
Founded: 1934
Membership: 400 churches in the United States and Africa; 22,000 persons in Nigeria
Meetings: Annual meeting during the fourth week in August

Fire Baptized Holiness Church of the Americas

556 Houston Street, NE
Atlanta, GA 30312

Mrs. Delores Morgan, Contact Person
6912 Valley Park Road
Capitol Heights, MD 20743

The Fire Baptized Holiness Church of the Americas, formerly known as the Colored Fire Baptized Holiness Church, was founded in 1908 by Bishop and Sister W. E. Fuller. The church holds a national convention every four years during the second week in June. There are approximately fifty-three congregations in the United States with 9,088 persons, as of 1968.

Group Type: Denomination
Founded: 1908
Membership: In 1968 approximately 53 churches in the United States with 9,088 persons
Publications: *True Witness*, a semiannual newspaper, and a discipline book
Meetings: Annual meeting is held every four years; the next scheduled meeting is in 1990 during the second week in June

First Born Church of the Living God

Waycross, GA

The First Born Church of the Living God is the result of the first split from the Church of the Living God, the Pillar and Ground of the Truth, Inc., founded by Bishop Mary Lena Lewis Tate in 1903 in Tennessee. The split was lead by Bishop C.H. Bass, Quincy Crooms, Simon Crooms, and Clarence Blakley.

Group Type: Denomination

First Church of Love, Faith and Deliverance

3101 Ridge Avenue
Philadelphia, PA 19121
(215) 769-1275
The Reverend Rosie Wallace Brown, Founder and Pastor

Group Type: Denomination
Doctrine: Deliverance

First United Church of Jesus Christ (Apostolic), Inc.

5150 Baltimore National Pike
Baltimore, MD 21229
(301) 945-0664
Bishop Monroe R. Saunders, Founder and Presiding Bishop

The First United Church of Jesus Christ (Apostolic) was founded in 1965 by Bishop Monroe R. Saunders in Baltimore, Maryland. Bishop Saunders had served as the pastor of the Washington church and as general secretary in the Church of God in Christ (Apostolic), founded by Bishop Randolph Carr in 1945. Bishop Carr left the Pentecostal Assemblies of the World to found the new church, which grew to include more than sixty churches in the West Indies, Canada, and England as well as in the United States.

The schism occurred because of Bishop Carr's precise instructions and interpretations concerning marriage and divorce. His own actions, however, contradicted his teachings, and, as a result, many members of the church did not continue to support his leadership. Bishop Carr asked Saunders to leave the church, and because of this, most of the church defected to Saunders. The church's name was changed to First United Church of Jesus Christ (Apostolic) in 1965 with Saunders serving as the first (and present) presiding bishop.

Bishop Saunders is an innovator in strengthening the role that formal academic training plays in the ministry within Pentecostal/Apostolic traditions. Through his example, greater emphasis has been placed on an educated ministry and laity. The church operates the Institute of Biblical Studies from the headquarters church in Baltimore and the Center for a More Abundant Life. Among its programs are a senior citizens' complex and a community social service department to treat substance-abuse clients and to provide day care and a baby clinic. The Creative Learning Center teaches children from kindergarten to sixth grade, and a secondary school is planned for the future.

Under the leadership of Bishop Saunders, the church has worked with Third World Apostolic ministers and ecumenical groups on racial issues. This work is enhanced by the church's missionary efforts in Trinidad-Tobago, Jamaica, and Mexico.

The church emphasizes open doors of communication in all areas of church life, including missionary work, financial matters, and doctrine. Individual congregations are free to join or leave the church at any time in the spirit of Christian love. As of 1980, there were over 75,000 members in fifty-two churches, with 150 ministers and five bishops.

Group Type: Denomination
Founded: September, 1965
Doctrine: Oneness/Apostolic
Membership: In 1980, over 75,000 persons in 52 churches with 150 ministers and 5 bishops
Meetings: Annual meeting the third week in June

Free Church of God in Christ

No current address

Group Type: Denomination
Founded: 1925

Free Church of God in Christ in Jesus' Name, Inc.

1940 E. Wier Avenue
Phoenix, AZ 85040
(602) 276-5902
Bishop Robert B. Johnson

In 1927, Earl Evans was called to the ministry and traveled to Taylor, Texas. The Free Church of God in Christ in Jesus' Name, Inc., was founded in 1928 by Bishop Evans, the first senior bishop, with his wife, Mother Elizabeth Annie Mae Evans as cofounder, in Taylor, Texas. It was incorporated in 1939 in Austin, Texas. Bishop Evans died June 13, 1987, and was succeeded by the current presiding bishop, Robert Bailey Johnson. The church is spread throughout the Midwest and West.

Group Type: Denomination
Founded: 1928
Doctrine: Oneness/Apostolic

Free Church of God True Holiness

1900 N. 3rd Street
Kansas City, KS 66101
Bishop C. W. Burchette

Group Type: Denomination

Free Gospel Church of The Apostle's Doctrine

c/o The Free Gospel Church of Christ
4702 Marlboro Pike
Coral Hills, MD 20743
(301) 420-9300
Bishop Ralph E. Green, Founder and Presiding Bishop

The Free Gospel Church of The Apostle's Doctrine was founded in 1962 in Washington, D.C., by Bishop Ralph E. Green. Also known as the Free Gospel Church of Christ and Defense of the Gospel Ministries, the church currently seeks to preach the gospel of Jesus Christ to every person, to heal the sick, to cast out devils, and to ready the church for the coming of the Lord, baptizing them in the name of Jesus Christ with the receiving of the Holy Ghost.

Apostolic in nature, the church traces its historical roots back to the apostles and prophets of the first century, A.D. Historically, it is associated with Charles Parham and the early beginnings of the Holiness/Pentecostal movement in the early 1900s, and from there traces its background to William J. Seymour and the Azusa Street Movement of 1906. All Holiness/Pentecostal and Apostolic movements in America were born of these ministries. Following this association, the church's next predecessor was the Pentecostal Assemblies of the World, in 1906, which fathered many independent ministries. The establishment of the Refuge Churches of Our Lord and Savior Jesus Christ led by Bishop Robert Clarence Lawson is one result. Bishop Lawson's ministry also fathered other ministries, one being the Way of the Cross Church of Christ led by Bishop Henry C. Brooks (established in 1928). The Way of the Cross ministry fathered Ralph E. Green as a son in the ministry. In

1962, Bishop Green was inspired to form the Free Gospel Church of Christ of the Apostle's Doctrine.

The church has an active program of community service. Among these activities are an extensive prison and outreach ministry in the Washington metropolitan area and a twenty-seven- year-old radio ministry that reaches Washington, D.C.; Annapolis and Waldorf, Maryland; Culpeper, Portsmouth/Virginia Beach, Virginia; portions of North and South Carolina; and Jacksonville, Florida. Two newsletters are produced in its printing shop: *From Prison to Praise*, distributed in prisons, and *The Defense of the Gospel Newsletter*. In addition, the church produces various gospel tracts as well as gospel music record albums that feature the church's choirs. Bishop Green also has recorded over 1,000 sermons. The church manages a bookstore and a federal credit union. In addition, for seven years the church has held tent revivals in a one-thousand seat tent, and in 1985, it began development of a Christian retreat in King George, Virginia. Recently, the church held six successful retreats, ministering to the needs of persons of all ages. The retreats provide informal, therapeutic, and relaxing environments for recreation, education, and worship.

There are 2,500 active members currently in the church headquarters, and five other congregations located in Leonardtown and Bryans Road, Maryland; Wallace, North Carolina; Culpeper, Virginia; and Clarenden, Jamaica. There are over fifty elders, deacons, and ministers in the church body. It is currently in the midst of a $2.3 million building/renovation project.

Group Type: Denomination
Founded: 1962
Doctrine: Oneness/Apostolic
Membership: Over 2,500 persons, 5 congregations, and over 50 elders, deacons, and ministers
Publications: *From Prison to Praise* and *Defense of the Gospel Newsletter* (newsletters); and gospel tracts

Free Temple Revival Center

P.O. Box 208
Windsor, NC 27983
Apostle T. L. Bayler

Group Type: Denomination
Doctrine: Deliverance

Full Gospel Pentecostal Association, Inc.

1032 North Sumner
Portland, OR 97217
Bishop Adolph A. Wells, Presiding Bishop

The Full Gospel Pentecostal Association (FGPA) was founded in 1970 by Overseer Adolph A. Wells, Pastor Edna Travis, and Elder S. D. Leffall. It is a collection of Pentecostal churches, and it operates a prison ministry. It is designed to minister to all community needs. The national headquarters serves as a clearinghouse for ministers and members. It provides a central point for doctrinal discussion and education and disseminates publications about meetings, seminars, and workshops pertaining to Full Gospel Pentecostal churches.

Group Type: Denomination specific; council of churches/groups
Founded: 1970

Publications: *The Epistle*, The Reverend Clarence R. Hill, executive editor, 1300 North LaBrea Avenue, Inglewood, CA 90302; *Five Point-Five Year Projection* (a booklet); *Ministers Guideline Handbook*

Glorious Church of God in Christ Apostolic Faith

Roanoke, VA
Bishop Perry Lindsey

The Glorious Church of God in Christ Apostolic Faith was founded by C. H. Stokes in 1921. Stokes served as the first presiding bishop until 1928, when Bishop S. C. Bass became head of the church. He served in that capacity for over twenty-five years. After his wife's death in 1952, Bass married a divorcée, which was against church doctrine and generally unacceptable in Apostolic and Pentecostal groups. There were fifty congregations in the church, and Bass's personal situation split the church in half. Bishop Bass's supporters retained the name of the church. The founding charter of the organization (originally obtained by Bishop Stokes) was retained by the other half of the church, which changed its name to the Original Glorious Church of God in Christ Apostolic Faith. As of 1980, the presiding bishop was Perry Lindsey.

Group Type: Denomination
Founded: 1921
Doctrine: Oneness/Apostolic
Membership: As of 1980, approximately 25 congregations

God's House of Prayer for All Nations, Inc.

1801 NE Madison Street
Peoria, IL 61603
Bishop Tommie Lawrence, Founder

God's House of Prayer for All Nations, Inc., was founded by Bishop Tommie Lawrence in Peoria, Illinois, in 1964. The church's theology is Apostolic and Pentecostal—Jesus Christ is identified with God the Father. Its government is episcopal. Healing is considered one of the signs of the spirit. There are several congregations in northern Illinois.

Group Type: Denomination
Founded: 1964
Doctrine: Oneness/Apostolic
Membership: Several congregations in northern Illinois

Gospel Spreading Church of God

1522 R Street, NW
Washington, DC 20009
(202) 387-8233
Elder James Jehu Riddick, General Overseer

The Gospel Spreading Church of God was established in 1919 in Hopewell, Virginia, under the leadership of its charismatic founder, the late Elder Lightfoot S. Michaux, also known as the "Happy Am I Preacher." Elder Michaux was introduced to Christ the Savior from sin, through his wife, the late Mary E. Michaux. The primary mission of the Gospel Spreading Church of God is saving souls for Christ by spreading the Word of God to the world. Its ministry has operated under the banner of the Church of God and now the Gospel Spreading Church of God.

The Gospel Spreading Church of God has distinguished itself by initiating several innovative ministries. Elder Michaux, under the inspiration of the Holy Spirit, originated during the Depression the "common plan," which provided for the church's members. He opened the Happy News Cafe in Washington, D.C., to feed the hungry. He also purchased a block of houses on 7th Street in Northwest Washington from S to T streets to house the evicted. In 1953, at the risk of his life, he was the first person to fly over the Arctic Circle, where he dropped the Holy Bible (written in Russian) on Soviet soil.

The Church of God is on the East Coast with most of its congregations concentrated between Newport News, Virginia, and New York City. Its major edifice, "The Temple of Freedom Under God," is in the District of Columbia. Elder Michaux purchased a parcel of land in Virginia, now known as the National Memorial Park. It houses a campsite, "Camp Lightfoot," on the historic James River where the first slaves debarked. It maintains a farm on the shores of the James River below historic Williamsburg, Virginia. During the 1940s, the church was the first to erect a major housing development for African Americans. Elder Michaux's prophetic leadership and administrative skills were well-known. He served as an adviser to U.S. presidents and was renowned for his oratorical skills. Under his guidance, the church began a highly significant and successful radio ministry that continues to flourish in many cities throughout the United States. The Gospel Spreading Church of God still continues its unique annual tradition of conducting a mass public baptism in the District of Columbia, where the famed "Happy Am I Cross Choir" sings.

The church believes in and practices the doctrine of living a life above sin, founded on the precepts of Christ. The church's largest congregation, at 2030 Georgia Avenue, N.W., Washington, D.C. 20001, is under the leadership of Elder Wendell M. Green, Pastor.

Group Type: Denomination
Founded: 1919
Doctrine: Holiness
Membership: Approximately 4,000 persons in 12 congregations between North Carolina and New York
Publications: *Happy News*, a magazine, Deacon J. Walker Sturdivant, editor, Happy News Publishing Co., 2030 Georgia Avenue, NW, Washington, DC 20001
Meetings: Four quarterly meetings held on New Year's Day in Philadelphia, PA; Easter Monday in Newport News, VA; July 4th in Williamsburg, VA; and Thanksgiving Day in Newport News, VA; and annual baptismal service in September in Washington, D.C.

Greater Emmanuel Apostolic Church, Inc.

Portsmouth, OH
Bishop Quander Wilson

Group Type: Denomination
Doctrine: Oneness/Apostolic

Greater Mount Zion Pentecostal Church —of America

735 Hancock Street
Brooklyn, NY 11233
Bishop Ida Robinson

Group Type: Denomination
Founded: 1944

Henry L. Porter Evangelistic Association, Inc.

P.O. Box 4321
Sarasota, FL 34230
(813) 365-7543
Bishop Henry L. Porter, Founder and Pastor
The Right Reverend R. Vincent Smith III, Assistant to the Bishop
The Reverend Wallace T. Murray, Presiding Elder

The Henry L. Porter (HLP) Evangelistic Association was founded June 11, 1969, and incorporated in 1971 by Bishop Henry L. Porter, who currently serves as pastor. Also known as "Westcoast," "Westcoast Gospel Chorus of Florida," and "Westcoast Center for Human Development," its mission is to educate, prepare, and ordain Christian men and women for the ministry of the gospel of Jesus Christ. It also seeks to enhance spiritual growth and enlightenment, moral and personal purity, and to aid in the spread of the gospel of Jesus Christ around the world through a ministry of preaching, teaching, praying, miracles, and healing.

The ministry includes the "HLP Love Campaign" initiated in 1987, a television ministry featuring the programs "Reflections" and "Smiling with Henry Porter;" radiobroadcasts; and the Westcoast School for Human Development (grades kindergarten through twelve), which opened in 1981. In 1980, it instituted the "Fortunate Ones Orchestra," the first of its kind in the United States. Its membership numbers over six hundred people located primarily in Tampa, Tallahassee, Panama City, Miami, Titusville, and Gainesville, Florida, but its scope is worldwide. Regular services are held at headquarters and local churches on Sundays, Wednesdays, and Saturdays. In addition, there are campus and community prayer meetings, and outreach programs in Europe and Africa.

There are several publications: *Sword of the Spirit*, the official newsletter; *Black Action*, the monthly international newspaper; *First Steps in Christ* and *A Sure Thing*, books written by Dr. Porter. The Right Reverend R. Vincent Smith is the Assistant to the Bishop. The Reverend Wallace T. Murray is the presiding elder.

Group Type: Denomination
Founded: June 11, 1969
Doctrine: Deliverance
Membership: Over 600 persons in Florida
Publications: *Sword of the Spirit*, a newsletter; *Black Action*, the monthly newspaper; *First Steps in Christ* and *A Sure Thing*, books by Bishop Porter; forthcoming: *Child of the Thought* and *Leaders*

Highway Christian Churches of Christ, Inc.

432 W Street, NW
Washington, DC 20001
(202) 234-3940
Bishop J. V. Lomax, General Chairman
(202) 926-3076
Elder W. Bryant, Acting General Secretary
(202) 926-3076
Elder Herman Ginwright, Treasurer
(202) 269-1417

The Highway Christian Church of Christ, Inc., organized in Washington, D.C., was founded in 1927 by James Thomas Morris. It is an Apostolic body that emphasizes Holiness and teaches its members to observe a life-style and dress code that conform to these teachings. Although the church does not ordain women into the ministry, it maintains fellowship with women pastors, and ordained female ministers from other denominations are accepted into the church. The church is governed by an executive board, under the direction of the head bishop, who serves as the general chairman.

Group Type: Denomination
Founded: 1927
Doctrine: Oneness/Apostolic
Membership: Approximately 3,000 persons in 13 congregations
Meetings: Annual meeting the fourth week of August

Holiness Church of God, Inc.

Box 541
Galax, VA 24333
Mrs. Nana B. Hash, General Secretary

Group Type: Denomination
Founded: 1917

Holiness Community Temple

5536 South Indiana Avenue
Chicago, IL 60637
(312) 667-9825

Group Type: Denomination
Founded: 1937

Holiness Ministers' Alliance, Inc.

4628 Minnesota Avenue, NE
Washington, DC 20019
Elder Chester Plummer

The Holiness Ministers' Alliance, Inc., was established on September 4, 1965, in Washington, D.C. Its founders were the late Bishop Arthur E. Brooks and the late Bishop Arthur R. Christian. Bishop Brooks was the first president; he was succeeded by Bishop Christian. The current president is Bishop John S. Young, Jr.

The Holiness Ministers' Alliance has denominational affiliations in the District of Columbia, Maryland, Virginia, and West Virginia. The group adheres to trinitarian doctrine. There are approximately ten denominational groups represented in the

alliance. Associated with the Holiness Ministers' Alliance, Inc., is the Holiness Ministers' Wives and Widows Council, a separately organized entity founded by the late Dr. Lillian W. Christian, which addresses the concerns and interests of the ministers' wives.

Group Type: Denomination specific; ministerial
Founded: 1965
Membership: 10 churches
Meetings: Annual meeting held during the third weekend in January

Holy Church on the Rock

707 Division Avenue, NE
Washington, DC 20019
Bishop Clifton McNair, Pastor

The Holy Church on the Rock was established as a denomination by the late Bishop Carrie Bailey. There are approximately eight congregations; although, during the 1960s, there were approximately sixteen. These are located primarily in the District of Columbia, North Carolina, and Virginia. Following the death of Bishop Bailey, there was a schism that resulted in the reduction of the number of churches affiliated with the group. The Church on the Rock conducts an annual meeting in Newport News, Virginia, in October, that is presided by Mother Willis of Newport News, Virginia. The son of the late founder, Bishop Clifton McNair, serves as pastor.

Group Type: Denomination
Founded: 1950
Doctrine: Holiness
Meetings: Meets annually in October

Holy Temple Church of Christ, Inc.

439 12th Street, SE
Washington, DC 20003
(202) 547-8364
Bishop Joseph Weathers, Founder and Presiding Bishop

The Holy Temple Church of Christ, Inc., was born at the request of some members of the Way of the Cross Church of Christ, following the death of their Bishop, Henry C. Brooks, in 1967. There was some controversy over who should replace Bishop Brooks. During the interim year (1968), Elders Joseph Weathers, Walter Thompson, and James Davis each served as Elder-in-Charge for four months. At the end of their service, a decision was made by the presiding officer, some officials, and church members that none of the elders would serve as acting pastor or pastor of the Way of the Cross Church of Christ. In January, 1969, Elder Joseph Weathers left this body to establish the Holy Temple Church of Christ, Inc. The congregation initially held its services at the True Grace Memorial House of Prayer for All People (205 V Street, N.W., Washington, D.C.) with the cooperation and assistance of the late Elder T. O. Johnson. The church was organized with a membership of 120 persons and incorporated in Washington, D.C., on April 15, 1979.

The purpose of the Holy Temple Church of Christ is to carry out the great commission of evangelization and Christianization of the world as commanded by our Lord and Saviour Jesus Christ to the apostles, confirming with miracles and signs following (see Mark 16:15-18). The body, a New Testament believing community of faith, is committed to establishing churches through the process of preaching, teaching, evangelizing, and witnessing. According to its official manual, membership consists of persons or congregations who have obeyed the gospel of Jesus Christ and his teachings about how to become a Christian, having heard the scriptural testimony of Christ. They believe in the Word of God; have repented of their sins; and were, or are willing to be, baptized in water in the name of Jesus Christ for the remission of sins and to receive the gift of the Holy Ghost. They are requested to abide by the teachings of Christ as presented in the New Testament.

The body teaches its members to be loyal to its civil authority and to obey civil governmental laws. It does not endorse nor actively advocate participation in violence or in combat training for violence. The church is governed by a Presiding Bishop and a Joint Board. An annual convocation is held during the last week in July or the first week in August at the headquarters church, 429 12th Street, SE, Washington, DC 20003.

Group Type: Denomination
Founded: 1969
Doctrine: Oneness/Apostolic
Meetings: Annual meeting the last week of July or the first week of August

Holy Temple, First Pentecostal Church of Deliverance

Selma, NC 27576
(919) 965-6534
Clair Sanders

Group Type: Denomination
Founded: 1974

Holy Temple of Jesus Christ Church, Inc.

8409 Hoffman Street
Houston, TX 77016
Minister Anita Walls, Contact Person
Overseer Annie Mae Lee
(713) 631-6685

This denomination was organized by Overseer Annie Mae Lee, Minister Anita Walls, and Bishop Howard C. Manuel and was incorporated in Houston, Texas, in 1958. It operates a food bank program.

Group Type: Denomination
Founded: 1954
Membership: 12 congregations
Meetings: Annual meeting held during the fourth week in June in Houston, Texas

House of God, Holy Church of the Living God, the Pillar and Ground of the Truth House of Prayer for All People (Hebrew Pentecostal)

New Bern, NC 28560
Reverend Simon Peter Rawlings, Chief Apostle

The House of God, Holy Church of the Living God, the Pillar and Ground of the Truth House of Prayer for All People (Hebrew Pentecostal) is the result of a 1914 split from the Church of the Living God, the Pillar and Ground of the Truth, Inc. [Lewis Dominion], founded by Mary Lena Lewis Tate in 1903. The Chief Apostle is Reverend Simon Peter Rawlings.

Group Type: Denomination
Founded: 1914

House of God Which Is the Church of the Living God, the Pillar and Ground of the Truth, Inc.

7070 Whitney Street
Hartford, CT 06105
Bishop Jesse J. White, Presiding Bishop

Correspondence Office:
Church of the Living God
P.O. Box 21559
Philadelphia, PA 19139

The House of God Which Is the Church of the Living God, the Pillar and Ground of Truth, Inc., was founded on June 28, 1919, in Philadelphia, Pennsylvania, by Bishop Archie H. White. It was originally associated with the Church of the Living God, the Pillar and Ground of the Truth, Inc. [Lewis Dominion], organized in 1903 by the late Mother Mary Lena (Magdalena) Lewis Tate. Its structure is episcopal in form with the presiding bishop serving as the corporate and spiritual leader. Bishop Jesse J. White, the son of the founder, serves as presiding bishop.

Group Type: Denomination
Founded: June 28, 1919
Membership: Approximately 110 churches in the United States and abroad, exceeding 26,000 persons
Publications: Previously published *The Spirit of Truth Magazine*, 3943 Fairmont Avenue, Philadelphia, PA 19104; a discipline manual
Meetings: Annual meeting is held in October

House of God Which Is the Church of the Living God, the Pillar and Ground of Truth

No current address

The House of God Which Is the Church of the Living God, the Pillar and Ground of Truth is the result of a split from the Church of the Living God (Christian Workers for Fellowship, CLGCWF) founded by the Reverend William Christian, a former slave. In 1902, a group split from the parent body and adopted the name Church of the Living God, Apostolic Church. Led by the Reverend C. W. Harris, this faction changed its name to Church of the Living God, General Assembly in 1908. A second, small splinter group united with this faction in 1924. In 1925, there was yet another split from the parent body (CLGCWF), and this group (led by the Reverend E. J. Cain) adopted the name Church of the Living God, the Pillar and Ground of Truth. Harris's group and Cain's group merged in 1926 and adopted the name House of God Which Is the Church of the Living God, the Pillar and Ground of Truth. The church shares the doctrine of its parent body and is episcopal in polity.

It meets on an annual basis. Its current membership and headquarters are unknown.

This church is often confused with the House of God, Which Is the Church of the Living God, the Pillar and Ground of Truth, Inc., the church of the same name, which is an outgrowth of Bishop Mary L. Tate's movement.

Group Type: Denomination
Founded: 1926
Meetings: An annual general assembly

House of God Which Is the Church of the Living God, the Pillar and Ground of Truth Without Controversy [Keith Dominion]

P. O. Box 9113
Montgomery, AL 36108
Bishop J. W. Jenkins, Chief Overseer

This body is the result of a division of administration within the Church of the Living God, the Pillar and Ground of the Truth, Inc., founded in 1903 by Bishop Mary Lena Lewis Tate. After the death of Bishop Tate in 1930, a committee appointed by the executive council of bishops formulated a recommendation to the church's general assembly to determine its future leadership. It was decided that three competent persons should be duly recognized and ordained to constitute the office of chief overseer of the church. The "1931 Agreement," as it has come to be known, resulted in a triumvirate, with each bishop overseeing sixteen of the (then) forty-eight states of the United States. This ruling of 1931 evolved into the dominion rule of the church.

The three segments eventually became independent of one another and were soon called "dominions." Bishop Tate's younger son, Felix Early Lewis, assumed the leadership of the parent body. Under the leadership of Bishop Mary Frankie Lewis Keith (the widow of Bishop Walter Curtis Lewis, Mother Tate's older son), the House of God Which is the Church of the Living God, the Pillar and Ground of Truth Without Controversy was formed. Bishop Keith led the organization until her death in 1962. This is also known as the "Keith Dominion." The third segment of the original church was led by Bishop Bruce L. McLeod. It became the Church of the Living God, the Pillar and Ground of the Truth, which He Purchased with His Own Blood, Inc. Bishop McLeod died in 1936 and was succeeded by his widow, Bishop Mattie Lou McLeod Jewell. The church is headquartered in Indianapolis, Indiana.

The current chief overseer, Bishop J. W. Jenkins, succeeded Bishop Keith and is assisted in governing the body by a Supreme Executive Council.

Group Type: Denomination
Founded: 1931

House of Prayer, Church of God, Inc.

Route 9, Box 131
Charles Town, WV 25414
Bishop Walter Newman, Presiding Bishop

The House of Prayer, Church of God, Inc., was founded in 1929 by the late Bishop and Mrs. James P. Simms. There are five congregations that meet during the second week in July at the headquarters church in Landover, Maryland. Affiliated churches are located in Maryland, Virginia, and West Virginia. The body adheres to trinitarian doctrine. Bishop Walter Newman is the presiding bishop.

Group Type: Denomination
Founded: 1929
Membership: 5 churches
Meetings: Annual meeting is held during the second week in July in Landover, Maryland

House of Prayer for All Nations

868 9th Avenue
Longview, WA 98632
(206) 577-5219
Bishop E. M. Jackson

The House of Prayer for All Nations is a member of the Federated Pentecostal Church International, Inc. The body has five churches.

Group Type: Denomination
Membership: 5 churches

House of the Lord

No current address

The House of the Lord was founded by Bishop W. H. Johnson in 1925, in Detroit, Michigan. Its doctrine is Pentecostal.

Group Type: Denomination
Founded: 1925

House of the Lord and Church on the Mount, Inc.

415 Atlantic Avenue
Brooklyn, NY 11217
(718) 596-1991
Bishop Herbert D. Daughtry

The House of the Lord and Church on the Mount, Inc., was founded and incorporated in 1930 by Bishop Alonzo Austin Daughtry in Augusta, Georgia. Bishop Daughtry had been saved by the founder of the House of Prayer for All People, Bishop C. M. Grace, in Savannah, Georgia. After reading II Corinthians 12, Daughtry felt that "man should not ascribe to man's divine prerogatives" but should worship Christ. Because of this difference in beliefs, he left Grace's church and moved to Harlem in 1942. He subsequently formed churches there.

Also known as the House of the Lord Church and the House of the Lord Pentecostal Church, the church came under the leadership of Mother Inez Cain after the death of Bishop Daughtry on February 17, 1952. She was succeeded by the current National Presiding Minister, Bishop Herbert D. Daughtry, the founder's fourth son. Bishop Daughtry is also the president of the African Peoples' Christian Organization (APCO), which was founded in October 1982.

The church's national youth convention is held from the first Thursday through Sunday in August, and the annual general convocation is held from the first Thursday through Sunday in October in Brooklyn, NY.

Group Type: Denomination

Founded: 1930
Meetings: National youth convention is held from the first Thursday through Sunday in August, and the annual general convocation is held from the first Thursday through Sunday in October in Brooklyn, NY

Intercollegiate Pentecostal Conference International, Inc.

100 Bryant Street, NW
Seymour House at Howard University
P.O. Box 90646
Washington, DC 20090-0646
(202) 232-5918
The Reverend Stephen N. Short, Founder and Executive Director
Bishop David J. Billings III, President

Founded in 1975 by the Reverends Stephen N. Short and Betty Lancaster Short, the Intercollegiate Pentecostal Conference International, Inc. (IPCI) seeks "to establish a network of collegiate Christians dedicated to the nurture and spiritual development of students, faculty and staff; the cultivation of the relationship between Christian bodies and their collegiate constituency; and, in general, to sensitize collegiate Christians and, in particular, collegiate Pentecostals and their judicatories to [their] socio-political responsibility." The ministry of IPCI includes counseling, Bible study, recreation, fellowship, social services, and referrals, all conducted from the William J. Seymour House located on the Howard University campus in Washington, D.C.

In the future, IPCI aspires to establish a national Pentecostal information research center, to serve as a training agency for Christian campus ministers, promoting unity among Pentecostals and between Pentecostals and other religious groups, and stimulating appreciation for and understanding of the Pentecostal dynamic. The organization has published the book *In the Tradition of William J. Seymour.*

Group Type: Denomination specific; student
Founded: 1975
Publications: In the Tradition of William J. Seymour

International Evangelical Church and Missionary Association

610 Rhode Island Avenue, NE
Washington, DC 20002
(202) 635-8000
The Reverend Vergil Meares

Group Type: Denomination
Publications: The Message and *The Holiness Call*
Meetings: Annual meeting is held during the second week in March

International Gospel Center

375 Calliotle, P.O. Box 9556
Ecorse, MI 48229
Apostle Charles O. Miles

Group Type: Denomination

King's Apostle Holiness Church of God, Inc.

101 W. Marl Street
Ranson, WV 25438
Bishop Eugene Baltimore, Presiding Bishop

The King's Apostle Holiness Church of God, Inc., is a trinitarian Pentecostal denomination founded in 1929 by Evangelist Mother Carrie V. Gurrey. The headquarters church, established in Baltimore, Maryland, was founded in 1907, and it is reputed to be the oldest Black Holiness Church in Baltimore. King's Apostle Holiness Church of God, Inc., holds an annual convention during the second week in August. There are approximately ten congregations in the organization. Membership churches are located primarily in the District of Columbia, Maryland, Virginia, and West Virginia. The presiding leader and bishop is Bishop Eugene Baltimore, 101 W. Marl Street, Ranson, West Virginia.

Group Type: Denomination
Founded: 1929
Membership: 10 congregations
Publications: King's Messenger and a discipline book
Meetings: Annual convention during the second week in August

Kodesh Church of Immanuel

Killingsworth Temple
51st and Brown Street
Philadelphia, PA 19139
(215) 473-9863
The Reverend Alphonso L. Benjamin

The Kodesh Church of Immanuel was founded in 1929 by the Reverend Frank Russell Killingsworth, who was a former member of the African Methodist Episcopal Church. The church adheres to Holiness doctrine, teaching its followers to live a consecrated life exemplifying sanctification. In particular, members are required to refrain from the use of alcoholic beverages, tobacco, lavish attire, and membership in secret societies. Members are expected to observe the Sabbath and restrict their activities in order not to profane the day.

The church was organized in 1929 with 120 adherents. In 1934, it merged with the Christian Tabernacle Union of Pittsburgh. The church operates through a quadrennial general assembly and annual regional assemblies. It maintains mission activity in Liberia.

Group Type: Denomination
Founded: 1929
Doctrine: Holiness
Membership: Information on membership is not available, but according to *Encyclopedia of American Religions* (1987 edition) there are fewer than 12 churches located on the East Coast, primarily around the District of Columbia, Philadelphia, and Pittsburgh

Latter House of the Lord for All People and the Church of the Mountain, Apostolic Faith

No current address

The Latter House of the Lord for All People and the Church of the Mountain, Apostolic Faith, was organized in 1936 by Bishop L. W. Williams. The church observes Pentecostal doctrine, and it substitutes water for wine during the Lord's Supper. There is a chief overseer, who is given a lifetime appointment.

Group Type: Denomination
Founded: 1936
Membership: In 1947, approximately 4,000 persons

Living Witness of Apostolic Faith, Inc.

3520 West Ogden Avenue
Chicago, IL 60623
(312) 762-6702
Bishop Charles E. Poole

Group Type: Denomination
Doctrine: Oneness/Apostolic

Mount Calvary Holy Church of America

1214 Chowan Road
Durham, NC 27713
Bishop Harold I. Williams

Mount Calvary Holy Church of America was founded by Bishop Broomfield Johnson in 1928, in Boston, Massachusetts. It is currently led by Bishop Harold I. Williams, the husband of gospel singer and evangelist Shirley Caesar. Its headquarters are in Durham, North Carolina. There are fifty churches in the United States and abroad. The church's annual convention is held the fourth week in August. A discipline is published by the church.

Group Type: Denomination
Founded: 1928
Membership: 50 churches in the United States and abroad
Publications: A discipline
Meetings: An annual convention is held the first week in August

Mount Calvary Pentecostal Faith Church, Inc.

1204 Eutaw Place
Baltimore, MD 21217
(301) 728-9681
Bishop Gladys Brandhagen

The Mount Calvary Pentecostal Faith Church, Inc. (also known as the Emmanuel Temple Pentecostal Faith Church, Inc., and the Mount Calvary Assembly Hall of the Pentecostal Faith of All Nations), was founded in 1932 by Bishop Rosa Artemus Horne in New York City. The first meeting place was 400 Lenox Avenue, on the corner of 130th Street, in Harlem. The bishop began the church after she was called to the ministry but was rejected, probably because of gender. Her oldest daughter, Jessie Horne, succeeded her as bishop. A son, Eddie,

served as a minister in the church. The church is currently headed by Bishop Gladys Brandhagen, the founder's adopted daughter. The church meets annually on Pentecost Sunday at its Baltimore location.

Group Type: Denomination
Founded: 1932

Mount Hebron Apostolic Temple of Our Lord Jesus Christ of the Apostolic Faith, Inc.

27 Vineyard Avenue
Yonkers, NY 10703
Bishop George H. Wiley III, Founder and Presiding Bishop

The Mount Hebron Apostolic Temple of Our Lord Jesus Christ was founded in 1963. The Mount Hebron Church was an affiliate of the Apostolic Church of Christ in God, after it began in 1957, in Yonkers, New York. Its pastor, the Reverend George H. Wiley III felt that, because of his accomplishments in the denomination, especially in youth work (where his wife served as president of the Department of Youth Work), he should be named to the office of bishop. His request to do so was denied, and he and his followers left to form a new Apostolic denomination.

In response to the need "to build the vision the Lord gave me" and to have better outreach to youth, the ministry of the church, under the leadership of Bishop Wiley, has emphasized and focused on youth work and radio outreach, establishing centers in South Carolina, North Carolina, and New York. There are also Bible schools in each local church and plans for homes for senior citizens and children. Bishop Wiley has also started an interdenominational youth forum designed to get input from youth in church programs and planning.

The doctrine and polity of the church are those of its parent body, the Apostolic Church of Christ in God, which adopted its own from the Church of God (Apostolic). Footwashing and the Lord's Supper are ordinances of the church. There are over 3,000 members in ten congregations with fifteen ministers and two bishops.

Group Type: Denomination
Founded: 1963
Doctrine: Oneness/Apostolic
Membership: Over 3,000 persons in 10 congregations with 15 ministers and 2 bishops

Mount Sinai Holy Church of America, Inc.

1601 South Broad Street
Philadelphia, PA 19148
Bishop Mary E. Jackson, Presiding Bishop

The Mount Sinai Holy Church of America was founded by Bishop Ida Robinson in 1924, in Philadelphia, Pennsylvania. After her conversion at age seventeen, she joined the United Holy Church of America. She moved from her home in Georgia to Philadelphia, Pennsylvania, and became the pastor of the Mount Olive Holy Church. She established the Mount Sinai Holy Church in obedience to a divine revelation from what she believed to be the Holy Spirit.

The church's doctrine is Pentecostal and stresses sanctification before the baptism of the Holy Spirit. Conversion must occur before membership is granted. According to the *Encyclopedia of American Religions* (2nd ed.), Bishop Robinson delineated four types of persons: 1) *the chosen of God*; 2) *the compelled*—persons who could not help themselves from being saved; 3) *the who so ever will* who can be saved; and 4) *the damned* (those ordained for hell). The church also stresses spiritual healing and practices footwashing. Behavior of the membership (especially sexual) follows a strict code, and worldly amusements, short dresses, and neckties are disfavored.

The polity of the church is episcopal. Women have played an integral role in its governance. Bishop Elmira Jeffries, the original vice-president of the church, succeeded as senior bishop upon the death of Bishop Robinson in 1946 and was in turn succeeded by Bishop Mary E. Jackson (the current presiding officer) in 1964. A board of presbyteries is composed of elders of the church, and a bishop heads each of four administrative districts. The entire church holds an annual conference, and each district has an annual conference as well. The church supports foreign mission work.

Group Type: Denomination
Founded: 1924
Membership: As of 1968, 2,000 persons in 92 churches

National Tabernacles of Deliverance, Inc.

547 Winchester Avenue
New Haven, CT 06511
The Reverend Ardell E. Tucker

The National Tabernacles of Deliverance, Inc., was organized in 1971 and incorporated in 1972 in New Haven, Connecticut, by two African American women, Overseer Ardell E. Tucker and the late Reverend Dorothy O. Austin. Overseer Tucker was a former member of the Apostolic Faith Church of God of Washington, D.C., which was pastored by her father, the late Bishop George B. White. The church is Pentecostal and adheres to trinitarian beliefs. Its annual convention is held the fourth week in August. There is a national youth and young adult convention that convenes the last week in November.

Group Type: Denomination
Founded: 1972
Membership: 17 churches
Publications: A manual
Meetings: Annual meeting held during the fourth week in August in New Haven, Connecticut; youth and young adult convention held the last week in November

New Bethel Church of God in Christ (Pentecostal)

San Francisco, CA

The New Bethel Church of God in Christ (Pentecostal) was founded by the Reverend and Mrs. A. D. Bradley and Lonnie Bates. The denomination grew out of the Church of God in Christ, the parent body from which the Reverend Bradley was ostracized for preaching the "Jesus Only" doctrine. The church adheres to similar practices and beliefs of "Jesus Only" denominations. The presiding bishop serves as the executive of-

ficer. There is a board of bishops that serves as the judicatory body and a general assembly that serves as the legislative component of the church.

Group Type: Denomination
Founded: 1927
Doctrine: Oneness/Apostolic

New Faith Chapel Holiness Church, Inc.

1419 Waughtown Street
Winston-Salem, NC 27107
(919) 784-7699
Bishop and Mrs. L. S. Tate
Sister Lenora McClain, Secretary

The New Faith Chapel Holiness Church, Inc., was founded in Winston-Salem, North Carolina, by Bishop and Mrs. L. S. Tate. No information is available on its doctrine or membership.

Group Type: Denomination

New Jerusalem Cathedral

1905 Linwood Drive
P.O. Box 20832
Greensboro, NC 27420
(919) 272-1105
Bishop Frank Williams

The New Jerusalem Cathedral was founded in 1963 in Greensboro, North Carolina, by Bishop Frank Williams. Its doctrine is Pentecostal. No information is available on its membership and organizational structure.

Group Type: Denomination
Founded: 1963

Original Church of God (or Sanctified Church)

2214 E. 17th Street
Chattanooga, TN 37404
Elder J. L. Rucker

The Original Church of God (or Sanctified Church) was founded prior to 1907 by the Reverend Charles W. Gray in Nashville, Tennessee. It holds to its legacy of being the original church that predates the incorporation of the Church of Christ (Holiness) U.S.A. and the Church of God (Sanctified Church), the latter of which retains the original name of the denomination after a 1927 dispute and subsequent split. The church's doctrine is identical to that of the Church of Christ (Holiness) U.S.A., stressing sanctification. The church's polity is congregational. Each local church has authority to appoint its own ministers and direct its own administrative affairs. Its polity differs from the Church of Christ (Holiness) U.S.A., which has an episcopal structure headed by a senior bishop. Its polity is distinguished from the Church of God (Sanctified Church), which is under the direction of a Board of Elders led by a general overseer.

Group Type: Denomination
Founded: 1927
Doctrine: Holiness

Original Glorious Church of God in Christ, Apostolic Faith, Inc.

No current address
Bishop I. W. Hamiter

The Original Glorious Church of God in Christ Apostolic Faith, founded by Bishop W. O. Howard in 1952, traces its roots to the Glorious Church of God in Christ Apostolic Faith, which was founded in 1921. It resulted from a doctrinal disagreement pertaining to the remarriage of its bishop to a divorced woman. The church adopted the name "Original" to claim symbolically its rights to the founding charter. Under the leadership of its presiding bishop, I. W. Hamiter, it has developed mission programs in Haiti, Jamaica, and India. The church is developing a convention center in Columbus, Ohio, to host its annual convention, according to the *Encyclopedia of American Religions* (3rd edition).

Group Type: Denomination
Doctrine: Oneness/Apostolic
Founded: 1952
Membership: 25,000 persons in 165 churches (55 in the U.S.; 110 elsewhere), with approximately 300 ministers and 25,000 persons
Meetings: Annual convocation in Columbus, Ohio

Original United Holy Church International

P.O. Box 263
Durham, NC 27702
(919) 682-3498
Bishop Hudson W. Fields, President

The Original United Holy Church International is the result of a split from its parent body, the United Holy Church of America, Inc., wherein it originally represented the Southern District. For some time, the Southern District, led by its president, Bishop James A. Forbes, felt that it was not treated fairly. A separate charter of incorporation was drawn up for the district on April 5, 1972, that nullified, in essence, the incorporation of the United Holy Church of America. Questions arose as to whether Bishop Forbes (who also served as vice-president of the church) and others had planned the split or whether it was in direct response to the strife between him and Bishop W. N. Strobhar, the general president of the church. Only seven of the 107 churches of the district remained loyal to the parent body.

At the first signs of trouble, efforts were made to reunite the two factions. The Southern District wanted to be accepted with its own charter in order to rejoin the parent body, with the understanding that the words "of the United Holy Church of America" established its relationship to the general body. Several administrative changes were also demanded, as well as an apology to its leadership and members. Because the Southern District did not pay its assessments to the general body for two years and would not agree to be bound with all other districts and auxiliaries under the original charter, the Board of Bishops recommended that the split be effective immediately. On May 2, 1977, when Bishop Forbes addressed the General Convocation it was in effect a farewell address because the Southern District delegation walked out of the meeting following the

speech. On June 29, 1977, those who left the church met in Raleigh, North Carolina, and formed the new body.

Land in Goldsboro, North Carolina, which had been deeded to the Southern District of the original church, also became an issue, because the parent body wanted the deed changed so that it would revert to the general body if the Southern District should disband. Although the Southern District disagreed, a court struggle between the two groups in 1984 ended with dismissal and the return of the land to the parent body.

On January 29, 1984, an agreement with the International Pentecostal Holiness Church was signed in Wilmington, North Carolina, that began a close, cooperative relationship between the two bodies.

The Original United Holy Church International is Pentecostal in doctrine and essentially shares the theology of the United Holy Church of America, Inc., which took its beliefs from the Church of God (Cleveland, Tennessee). Members believe in the baptism of the Holy Spirit as evidence of sanctification and divine healing. The church's ordinances include the Lord's Supper, footwashing, and baptism by immersion.

In 1985, the church had over fifteen thousand members in 210 congregations. It is found primarily on the East Coast from South Carolina to Connecticut, with additional congregations in Texas, California, and Kentucky. Mission work is supported in Liberia. It also runs the United Christian College in Goldsboro, North Carolina, and publishes *Voice of the World*, a periodical. Bishop Forbes resigned as president of the church in September, 1985, due to declining health, and the presidency was assumed by Bishop Hudson W. Fields.

Group Type: Denomination
Founded: 1977
Membership: In 1985, 15,000 persons in 210 congregations
Publications: *Voice of the World*, a periodical
Meetings: Meets annually during the third week in September

Overcoming Saints of God

Archer, FL
Pastor A. T. Mobley

This Pentecostal body was founded in Archer, Florida, by Pastor A. T. Mobley. There are nine churches on the East Coast from Boston to Florida.

Group Type: Denomination

Pentecostal Assemblies of the World, Inc.

3939 Meadows Drive
Indianapolis, IN 46205
(317) 547-9541
Bishop James A. Johnson, Presiding Bishop
Bishop Paul A. Bowers, Assistant Presiding Bishop
Mr. John E. Hampton, Administrator

The Pentecostal Assemblies of the World, Inc. (PAW), is the oldest Apostolic/Pentecostal organization professing the "Jesus Only" doctrine. It is a general federation of Oneness/Pentecostal religious bodies. Its doctrine holds that Holiness is an important unifying factor in the life of the church. It stresses sanctification as essential to salvation.

The group has been a racially mixed organization from its inception in Los Angeles, California, in 1906. The first general superintendent was J. J. Frazee (sometimes referred to as Frazier). Bishop Garfield Thomas Haywood of Indianapolis, Indiana, was the first prominent African American leader in the PAW. He was a chief proponent of the "Oneness" doctrine and worked with other leaders such as H. A. Goss, F. J. Ewart, and J. J. Frazee to develop the doctrinal positions espoused by the organization. Bishop Robert Clarence Lawson, another outstanding leader of this group, later left to create his own Apostolic organization. Other outstanding African American trailblazers include Joseph M. Turpin, P. J. F. Bridges, and F. I. Douglas.

The PAW holds that speaking in tongues is vital to rebirth in the church. It distinguishes itself from other Pentecostal religious bodies by its Oneness doctrine, which places emphasis on the unity of the trinity as one. Believers are baptized in the name of "Jesus Only." In addition to its historical roots as an integrated organization, PAW has, since its inception, accepted the ordination of women in the ministry and approves of women as pastors.

The Pentecostal Assemblies of the World, Inc., is headquartered in Indianapolis, Indiana. It holds an annual general assembly and is divided into forty districts or dioceses each headed by a bishop. The following bishops serve on the Board of Directors: David L. Ellis; C. Watkins; R. P. Paddock; P. A. Bowers; Arthur Brazier; B. T. Moore; James A. Tyson; M. E. Golder; J. A. Johnson; R. W. McMurray; and L. E. Brisbin. A missionary board governs mission activities. The body is composed of the following auxiliaries: Young People, Sunday School, Home Missions, Women's Missionary, Usher Board, Brotherhood, and Minister's Wives. It also supports Aenon Bible College and publishes *The Christian Outlook* and *Apostolic Light*.

Group Type: Denomination
Founded: 1906
Doctrine: Oneness/Apostolic
Membership: In 1989, 500,000 persons in 1,005 churches in the United States; 850 mission churches in foreign fields
Publications: *The Christian Outlook* and *Apostolic Light*, Mr. John Hampton (Administrator), PAW, Headquarters, 3939 Meadows Dr., Indianapolis, IN 46205

Pentecostal Churches of Apostolic Faith

Detroit, MI
Bishop Elzie Young, Presiding Bishop

The Pentecostal Churches of Apostolic Faith (PCAF) was founded in 1957 under the leadership of such African American Apostolic pioneers as Elder David Collins and Bishops Samuel N. Hancock, Willie Lee, and Heardie Leaston. Bishop Hancock served as presider until his death in 1963; he was succeeded by Bishop Willie Lee. In 1964, while under Bishop Lee's leadership, the organization split over the doctrine of the Godhead. A splinter group led by Bishop Elzie Young strongly urged that the denomination return to its original Oneness doctrine, which it subsequently did. Although departure from the Oneness teachings was associated with Bishop Hancock, (who

emphasized that Jesus was merely the son of God and not God), it was Bishop Lee's teachings that were challenged.

Under the guidance of Bishop Young, PCAF has expanded its ministry. Member churches contribute a proportionate share of their budget to the national office, and missionaries are supported by the church. Its major missionary efforts are in Haiti and Liberia, where it has built a school. According to membership data for 1980, the PCAF had approximately 25,000 members in 115 churches with 380 ministers.

Group Type: Denomination
Founded: 1957
Doctrine: Oneness/Apostolic
Membership: In 1980, approximately 25,000 persons in 115 churches with 380 ministers

Pentecostal Church of God

9244 Delmar Street
Detroit, MI 48211
(313) 865-0510
Apostle Willie James Peterson

The Pentecostal Church of God was founded in Detroit, Michigan, by Apostle Willie James Peterson. It is Pentecostal in doctrine. No information is available on its membership, history, and organizational structure.

Group Type: Denomination

Pentecostal Miracle Deliverance Centers, Inc.

2603 Whitaker Street
Savannah, GA 31401
(912) 233-7045
Prophetess Idell Cheever, President and General Overseer

The Pentecostal Miracle Deliverance Centers, Inc., was founded by Prophetess Idell Cheever and Elder Christopher Cheever (husband and wife) in 1970 in Savannah, Georgia. It adheres to Pentecostal doctrine. Its general convention is held the first two weeks in September beginning on Labor Day and ending on the third Sunday. There are also ordination services on the first Sunday in February and a youth convention beginning the third Sunday in June. It also operates a radio ministry. No current information is available on membership.

Group Type: Denomination
Founded: 1970
Publications: Publishes the following tracts: "We Need Them Both," "Point of No Return," and "Hell Requires No Reservations"
Meetings: Meets annually during the first two weeks in September

Perry Community Holiness Church

Norfolk, VA

The Perry Community Holiness Church was founded in 1934, in Norfolk, Virginia, by Bishop Laura L. R. Perry. Its doctrine is Pentecostal. No information is available on its polity or membership.

Group Type: Denomination
Founded: 1934

Powerhouse of Deliverance Church

1800 Bothwell Street
Greensboro, NC 27401
(919) 274-9924
Bishop J. H. Covington

Group Type: Denomination
Doctrine: Oneness/Apostolic

Prayer Band Fellowship Union

Gospel Temple Community Holiness Church
P.O. Box 9101
Bridgeport, CT 06601
Bishop Curtis E. Mouning, Founder, and Presiding Officer
(203) 333-3308
The Reverend Lucille Fogg, Founder

The Prayer Band Fellowship Union is a group of seven New England Pentecostal churches. It was established in 1976 by Bishop Curtis E. Mouning and the Reverend Lucille Fogg. The group continues under the leadership of Bishop Mouning, who is the pastor of Gospel Temple Community Holiness Church in Bridgeport, Connecticut. An annual convention is held on the third Saturday night in January in Bridgeport, where all members dress in white and participate in a candlelight communion service.

Group Type: Denomination specific; council of churches/groups
Founded: 1976
Membership: 7 churches
Meetings: Annual convention held in Bridgeport, Connecticut on the third Saturday in January

Redeemed Assembly of Jesus Christ, Apostolic

734 First Street, SW
Washington, DC 20024
Bishop Douglas Williams

The Redeemed Assembly of Jesus Christ, Apostolic, was founded by two bishops of the Highway Christian Church, Douglas Williams of Washington, D.C. and James Frank Harris of Richmond, Virginia, in 1979. Bishops Williams and Harris disapproved of the management of the Highway Christian Church by its leader, Bishop J. V. Lomax, who conferred and made decisions with the elders of his Washington, D.C. church rather than with the bishops and pastors of other churches in the denomination. Most of those elders were laity, which alienated the clergy and divine leadership. It was also felt that Bishop Lomax was closed to new ideas and that the church had become stagnant as a result.

The polity of the Redeemed Assembly of Jesus Christ, Apostolic is episcopal, with a presiding bishop, an assistant presiding bishop, and an executive council made up of bishops and pastors in the church. It maintains the doctrine of the parent body. There are six churches—one each in Richmond, Virginia, and New York City, and four in the Washington, D.C. area.

Group Type: Denomination

Founded: 1979
Doctrine: Oneness/Apostolic
Membership: As of 1980, 6 congregations

Reformed Zion Union Apostolic Churches of America

P.O. Box 207
South Hill, VA 23970
(804) 447-3374
Deacon James C. Feggins, General Secretary of the Executive Board

The Reformed Zion Union Apostolic Church was formed in April, 1869 by members of the African Methodist Episcopal Church who were interested in Christian union and Holiness. The members met in Boydton, Virginia, to form the new church. The Reverend James Howell, who had led the group, was elected president and served until 1874, when a change in the church's polity led to his election as bishop with the tenure changed from a four-year term to life. This decision generated such disapproval that, even with the resignation of Bishop Howell, the church almost disbanded. In 1882, the church was reorganized, resulting in reinstatement of the four-year term and the adoption of the present name.

The church emphasizes holiness and has kept the traditional Methodist governing structure. General conferences are held quadrennially. Since the church's reorganization, the bishop's tenure has changed again to life. The church's board of publication controls its literature.

Group Type: Denomination
Founded: April 1869
Membership: As of 1965, 1,832 persons and 27 churches
Publications: *General Rules and Discipline of the Reformed Zion Union Apostolic Church*, Creecy's Good-Will Printery, Norfolk, VA, 1966
Meetings: A general conference every four years; annual conference every year

Saints of the Solid Rock Holiness

Fayetteville, NC

The Saints of the Solid Rock Holiness was founded in 1928 by Elder Holland Goff in Fayetteville, North Carolina. He had been an evangelist in Milwaukee before coming to North Carolina.

Group Type: Denomination
Founded: 1928

Shiloh Apostolic Temple, Inc.

1516 W. Master Street
Philadelphia, PA 19121
(215) 763-7335
the late Bishop Robert O. Doub, Jr., Founder and Presiding Bishop

The Shiloh Apostolic Temple, Inc., was organized by Elder Robert O. Doub on August 22, 1948. The church was incorporated in Philadelphia in 1954. Elder Doub was ordained a bishop by his spiritual mentor and pastor, the late Bishop Melvin Robinson of the Highway Church of Christ. Assisting in this ordination were Bishops L. Gravely and D. M. Jones.

Under the leadership of Bishop Doub, Shiloh Apostolic Temple, Inc., has operated a radio ministry for over thirty years and has established a television ministry. The church has extended its work from New England to Florida, Europe, and the West Indies. Because of Doub's commitment and efforts, the church has enjoyed considerable growth and has increased from one to twenty-three churches with over 4,500 persons around the world. In addition to Bishop Doub, there are two other bishops and thirty ministers.

Shiloh Apostolic Temple, Inc., has developed the Shiloh Promised Land Camp in Winston-Salem; Heavenly Mountain Camp in Montrose, Pennsylvania; and a seventy-acre camp and retreat in Florida. The church publishes *Shiloh Gospel Wave* and the *Shiloh Mid-Week Message*. The church maintains fellowship with the Highway Christian Church and the Apostle Church of Christ in God.

Bishop Robert O. Doub was an outstanding leader and organizer. He served as a leader to other ministries within his denominational affiliation. In 1971, he started the Apostolic Ministers' Conference of Philadelphia and Vicinity, organizing Apostolic ministers for greater unity, and continued to serve as its president until his death. The Apostolic Ministers' Conference of Philadelphia and Vicinity has fifty to sixty ministers. In 1986, he organized the National Apostolic Fellowship. This organization consists of ministers on the East Coast, and Bishop Doub served as its first president.

Group Type: Denomination
Founded: 1954
Doctrine: Oneness/Apostolic
Membership: As of 1980, 4,500 persons in 23 congregations with 3 bishops and 30 ministers
Publications: *Shiloh Gospel Wave* (a periodical), 1516 West Master, Philadelphia, PA 19121; *Shiloh Mid-Week Message*

Sought Out Church of God in Christ and Spiritual House of Prayer, Inc.

Brunswick, GA 31520

This organization was founded in 1947 by Mother Mozella Cook, who left the Church of God in Christ to establish this church in Brunswick, Georgia. Current membership information is unavailable.

Group Type: Denomination
Founded: 1947
Membership: In 1949, 60 persons in 4 congregations

Soul Saving Station for Every Nation, Christ Crusaders of America

644 Fillmore Avenue
Buffalo, NY 14212
(716) 856-4040

This denomination was founded in 1940 in Buffalo, New York, by Billy Roberts and its second leader, Bishop Jessie F. Winley. It is affiliated with the Pentecostal Holiness Church.

Group Type: Denomination
Founded: 1940
Membership: In 1973, approximately 11,000 persons

Triumph the Church and Kingdom of God in Christ (International)

Headquarters:
213 Farrington Avenue, SE
Atlanta, GA 30315

The Right Reverend A. J. Scott, Chief Bishop
1323 N. 36th Street
Savannah, GA 31404
(912) 236-2877

Bishop C. H. Whittaker, National General Recording Secretary
9200 Miles Avenue
Cleveland, OH 44105

This Holiness body was founded as the Triumph Church in 1902 by the late Apostle Elias Dempsey Smith. The church's history states that the late Apostle Elias Dempsey Smith experienced a divine revelation that inspired him to establish the church. This vision occurred on October 20, 1897, at 12:00 noon when Smith was a Methodist pastor in Issaquena County, Mississippi. The first meeting of the congregation was held at noon on January 20, 1904, after five years of planning.

The body is commonly known as the "Triumph Church," although its full name has been amended to "Triumph the Church and Kingdom of God in Christ (International)." Its operation was formally started in 1904 and confirmed in Birmingham, Alabama, in 1915, with 225 members. In 1918, the body was incorporated in Washington, D.C.

Its membership now extends to thirty-eight states as well as overseas. The church's administrative operation is divided into eighteen episcopal districts, including South America and Africa. General overseers are the chief officers. The church conducts a quadrennial International Religious Congress. The official staff consists of the Senior Bishop, who serves a four-year term; the Bishops for each Episcopal District, the General Recording Secretary; and other officials, as designated by the Congress. Other administrative work of the body is transacted by its state, county, and local officers.

The objectives and purposes of the body are numerous. They include deepening the spiritual life of its members; putting man in closer touch with the Creator; educating its youth to a fuller understanding of God; establishing funds for pensioning the elderly; and appointing elders, pastors, and missionaries, who are divinely called and set apart to conduct their work. The basis of the Union is as follows:

> We believe that Jesus's blood was shed for the remission of sin, we believe in the doctrine of Justification of faith, we believe that Christ dwells in the heart and mind of the justified believer, we believe in sanctification for the complete cleansing of sin. We believe in the Baptism of the Holy Spirit and the experience of Fire which is a more complete knowledge of God's Word.

Triumphant doctrine emphasizes Life, Truth, and Knowledge. It provides its members with a theology for understanding the reality of God in man and a clarifying perspective on how God's presence is expressed through man. The doctrine and philosophy further consider such concepts as manifested wisdom, complete and full understanding, and constant new revelations. These teachings emphasize the qualities of "goodness" and highlight "the second coming of Christ." The believers, known also as Triumphians, place strong significance on the revelation that God is the God of the living—not the God of the dead. As in other Holiness bodies, the church's doctrine teaches cleansing from sin in all "justified" believers through the shed blood of Christ, the Second Coming of Christ, sanctification as an instantaneous, definite work of second grace, and baptism by fire.

Group Type: Denomination
Founded: 1902
Doctrine: Holiness
Membership: Unavailable, but the body operates in 38 states in the United States and has 18 episcopal districts, including districts in Africa and South America
Meetings: Quarterly and annual conferences; International Religious Congress (quadrennial)

True Fellowship Church of America, Inc.

4236-4238 Pimlico Road
Baltimore, MD 21215
(301) 367-7716
Bishop Carroll Waldron Jones, Sr., Pastor and General Chief Overseer

The True Fellowship Church of America, Inc., also known as the True Fellowship Church of the Pentecostal Assemblies of the World and True Fellowship Pentecostal Church of God of America, Inc., was founded in July 1964 by Bishop Charles E. Waters, Sr., who died on December 12, 1986. Bishop Waters was affiliated with the Alpha and Omega Pentecostal Church (from 1947) and connected with the Church of God in Christ.

The True Fellowship Church of America, Inc., adheres to the belief of the Godhead as recorded in the Bible in Acts 17:29, Romans 1:20, and Colossians 2:9, and to its definition and explanation as found in I John 5:6-8. It believes in the completeness of the Godhead and that everything is derived from God. The church also accepts women into the ministry.

Believers are baptized in accordance with Acts 2:38, in the name of Jesus Christ upon the profession of their faith. The words of institution are:

In obedience to the command of our Lord and Saviour Jesus Christ, recorded in the Gospel according to St. Matthew 28:19 and upon the profession of your faith, in the name of the Father and of the Son, and of the Holy Ghost, which is one Spirit, I baptize you according to Acts 2:38 to baptize in the name of Jesus Christ, I baptize you my brother/sister in Jesus name.—Amen

The True Fellowship Church of America, Inc., is under the leadership of Bishop Carroll Waldron Jones, Sr., who is the son-in-law of the late Bishop Charles Emory Waters, Sr. Bishop Jones was installed as pastor in June, 1984 by the late Bishop Charles Emory Waters.

Group Type: Denomination
Founded: July, 1964
Membership: Membership not reported; however, in 1989, there were 2 congregations

True Grace Memorial House of Prayer for All People

911 6th Street, NW
Washington, DC 20001

The True Grace Memorial House of Prayer for All People is the result of a schism from the United House of Prayer for All People, Church on the Rock of the Apostolic Faith founded by "Sweet Daddy Grace" in 1926. Walter McCullough was elected bishop following the death of Daddy Grace in 1960, but after about six months, he was questioned about his unauthorized use of church funds. A lawsuit was brought that ordered a new election, and McCullough was relieved of his position. However, he was reelected to the bishopric. There was still concern over McCullough's doctrinal stance, such as his claim that he had the power to condemn or redeem people and that only he was doing God's work. After the second election, several church leaders were dismissed. Among them was Elder Thomas O. Johnson, who had served as a pastor for over twenty years. He and twelve dissenting members left the church to form the True Grace Memorial House of Prayer.

The True Grace Memorial House of Prayer is Pentecostal in doctrine. Its last reported membership included eight congregations on the East Coast.

Group Type: Denomination
Founded: 1962
Membership: As of the 1970s, 8 congregations on the East Coast

True Vine Pentecostal Churches of Jesus

New Bethel Apostolic Church
931 Bethel Lane
Martinsville, VA 24112
(703) 632-7290
Dr. Robert L. Hairston, Presiding Bishop

The True Vine Pentecostal Churches of Jesus was founded in 1961 by Dr. Robert L. Hairston. Hairston had been a minister and pastor in various Pentecostal bodies and, with William Monroe Johnson, had founded the True Vine Pentecostal Holiness Church. But in 1961, Hairston accepted Apostolic or "Jesus Only" teachings and baptism, believing them to be biblically correct. Johnson and Hairston also differed over church polity and taxation of local congregations to pay for the annual convocation. There were also questions about Hairston's marital status—he was divorced and had remarried. This was unacceptable to many Pentecostals and Apostolics alike. During his divorce, Bishop Hairston became disillusioned because of the lack of understanding and support from church members.

Hairston has stated that he formed the new church because of his concern over its continuation after his death. Therefore, the charter does not allow a person or group to take over the church. The church enjoyed a fellowship with Bishop Willie Giles of North Carolina, but the issue of women in the ministry severed that relationship. After a chance meeting in 1976 and extensive interaction, Bishop Thomas C. Williams's churches merged with the True Vine Pentecostal Churches of Jesus. Bishop Williams serves as senior bishop and Bishop Hairston serves as presiding bishop. The church has expanded to include ten churches and missions with 900 members and fourteen ministers. One of its major accomplishments is its music department. The convention choir, primarily from the New Bethel Church Choir and musicians, is noted to be among the best among Apostolics.

Group Type: Denomination
Founded: 1961
Doctrine: Oneness/Apostolic
Membership: As of 1980, 900 persons in 10 churches and missions with 2 bishops and 14 ministers
Meetings: Annual meeting on the second Sunday in November

True Way Resurrection Pentecost Holiness Church of God in Christ

Old Stage Road
Raleigh, NC 27603
(919) 779-2627
Bishop Geraldine Bailey

This church was founded by Pastor Geraldine Bailey in either Hamlet or Gibson, North Carolina. The church adheres to Pentecostal teaching. No information is available on its polity and membership.

Group Type: Denomination

United Churches of Jesus, Apostolic, Inc.

No current address
Bishop J. W. Audrey, General Bishop

The United Churches of Jesus, Apostolic, Inc., is the result of a separation from the Apostolic Church of Christ in God led by Bishop James C. Richardson, Sr. Richardson discussed his decision to marry a divorcée with several bishops in November, 1970. He offered to marry the woman then step down as presiding bishop, or to retain his position and not marry. He received support from all but one bishop. Several of those who did support his decision, however, chose to leave the church. There was also conflict between the bishops, several of whom had been founders of the church.

Bishop J. W. Audrey, who had served as presiding bishop before Richardson (the second bishop), was opposed by many, including Elder Robert O. Doub, who left the church to form the Shiloh Apostolic Temple, Inc., with the local congregation in Philadelphia as his base. Richardson, whom Doub had supported, subsequently succeeded Audrey as presiding bishop. In 1971, Bishop Audrey and several others left to form a new denomination. Much of the split is attributed to jealousy and old personality conflicts and feuds.

The new church retained the doctrine of its parent body. It has developed a strong youth department and it tithes to charity. Scholarships are given to college-bound students. As of 1980, the church had grown to approximately two thousand members in twenty churches with six bishops and thirty ministers.

Group Type: Denomination
Founded: 1971
Doctrine: Oneness/Apostolic
Membership: As of 1980, 2,000 persons in 20 churches with 6 bishops and 30 ministers

United Church of Jesus Christ Apostolic, Inc.

2226 Park Avenue
Baltimore, MD 21217
(301) 728-9679
Bishop James B. Thornton, Presiding Bishop
Bishop E. M. Williams, Presiding Bishop

The United Church of Jesus Christ Apostolic, Inc., was founded in 1961 by Bishop James B. Thornton. Its doctrine is Apostolic. There are affiliated congregations in Washington, D.C., Maryland, Pennsylvania, New York, and South Carolina. It meets annually at the end of August. The church publishes *United News*, a newsletter. The presiding bishops are James B. Thornton, whose church is in Baltimore, and E. M. Williams, whose church is in Philadelphia.

Group Type: Denomination
Founded: 1961
Doctrine: Oneness/Apostolic
Publications: *United News*, a newsletter
Meetings: An annual convocation beginning the last Monday of August to the first Monday of September, in Baltimore, MD

United Crusade Fellowship Conference, Inc.

14250 SE 13th Place
Bellevue, WA 98008
(206) 641-5820
Bishop Richard E. Taylor

The United Crusade Fellowship Conference, Inc., was founded by Bishop Richard E. Taylor in 1973 and was incorporated in 1986. It is a Pentecostal conference of six churches with an annual convention held the second week in August. The United Crusade Fellowship Conference, Inc., operates a Christian Bible Institute and a licensed children's day-care center. The mailing address is: Christian Bible Institute, P.O. Box 7042, Bellevue, WA 98008. United Crusade Fellowship Conference, Inc., also operates a mission outreach program in the Philippines, which encompasses several missions.

Group Type: Denomination
Founded: 1973
Meetings: Annual meeting is held during the second week in August

United Fellowship Convention of the Original Azusa Street Mission

825 Gregg Road
Jefferson, OH 44047
Bishop Oree Keyes, Founder and Presiding Officer

The United Fellowship Convention of the Original Azusa Street Mission is an umbrella fellowship organization that unites various bodies that have separated from the original organization from 1936 to the present. The original organization, the Apostolic Faith Church of God, was founded in 1909 by William J. Seymour and Charles W. Lowe in Hansome, Virginia.

The United Fellowship Convention of the Original Azusa Street Mission was established in 1987, under the leadership of Bishop Oree Keyes. It was founded to promote communication, fellowship, and information exchange on the growth and development of churches stemming from the ministry of William J. Seymour, the founder of the Apostolic Faith Church of God and the pastor of the Azusa Street Mission. The United Fellowship Convention of the Original Azusa Street Mission consists of the following bodies: the Apostolic Faith Church of God, the Apostolic Faith Churches of God, Inc., Apostolic Faith Church of God in Christ, Inc., Apostolic Faith Church of God, Live On, and Church of Christ Holiness unto the Lord, Inc.

Group Type: Denomination specific; council of churches/groups
Membership: 100 congregations
Founded: 1987
Meetings: Annual convention held during the last weekend in May

United Holy Church of America, Inc.

312 Umstead Street
Durham, NC 27707
(919) 682-1819
Bishop Joseph T. Bowens, General President

The United Holy Church of America, Inc. (UHCA), was the result of a Holiness revival conducted by the Reverend Isaac Cheshier in the town of Method, North Carolina, near Raleigh. The first meeting was held on the first Sunday in May, 1886, with three men in addition to the Reverend Cheshier. It was the first meeting of its kind in the state. On October 13, 1894, in Durham, North Carolina, the first convocation was organized, and on October 15, 1900, a convention was called in Durham to prepare a discipline for those churches that had come together. It was first known as the "Holy Church of North Carolina" and then, as it expanded, the "Holy Church of North Carolina and Virginia." In September, 1916, the body met and changed the name to its current one, and it was incorporated under this name in North Carolina on September 25, 1918.

The Southern District of the church was organized in 1894 and became the largest of several districts organized by the church. The church has experienced only one schism. A separate charter of incorporation was drawn up for the Southern District on April 5, 1972, and this, in essence, nullified the incorporation of the United Holy Church of America. Bishop James A. Forbes, at the time vice-president of the UHCA and president of the Southern District, was instrumental in the split, which was feared to truly break the unity of the general body. Questions arose as to whether he and others had actually planned to form a new body or whether the split was in direct response to conflict between Bishop Forbes and Bishop W. N. Strobhar, the general president of the church. In any case, seven churches remained loyal to the parent body, whereas one hundred aligned themselves with the new body.

On May 2, 1977, at the General Convocation in Cleveland, Ohio, Bishop Forbes delivered a speech, which was, in effect, a farewell address because the Southern District's delegation walked out of the assembly after his speech. There were several reasons for the split, among them the feeling by the Southern District that its membership had not been treated fairly. From 1975, when the first signs of a split became evident, efforts were made to reunite the two factions. The Southern District wanted to be accepted with its own charter in order to rejoin the parent body, with the understanding that the words "of the United Holy Church of America" established its relationship to the general body. They also demanded several administrative changes and an apology for mistreatment of its leadership and members. Because the Southern District did not pay its assessments to the general body for two years and would not agree to be bound with all other districts and auxiliaries under the single and original charter, the Board of Bishops recommended that the split be effected immediately.

On November 4, 1933, property purchased by early members of the church, D. V. and Fannie Butler, was conveyed to the church. In addition to the aforementioned charges, there was a question over this land in Goldsboro, North Carolina, to which the Southern District had the deed. The Board of Bishops ordered the Southern District to revise the language of its deed so that the property would revert back to the parent body in the event of the dissolution of the district. The Southern District refused to do so. Eventually the United Holy Church of America and the new body, the Original United Holy Church of the World, went to court over the controversies existing between the two groups. In 1984, the case was dismissed and the land was returned to the parent body. The new church is now the Original United Holy Church International under the leadership of Bishop Hudson W. Fields.

The church is Pentecostal in doctrine, and its theology is similar to that of the Church of God (Cleveland, Tennessee). Members believe in the Baptism of the Holy Spirit as the gift of power on a sanctified life, divine healing, and the observance of the Lord's Day as a day of rest and worship. Ordinances of the church include baptism by immersion, the Lord's Supper, and footwashing.

The church publishes a periodical, *The Holiness Union*. It is under the leadership of Bishop Joseph T. Bowens, general president, who served as vice-president and general supporter to Bishop Strobhar. He was named to the office in 1980.

Group Type: Denomination
Founded: 1886
Publications: The Holiness Union, a monthly periodical

United House of Prayer for All People, Church on the Rock of the Apostolic Faith, Inc.

1721-1/2 7th Street, NW
Washington, DC 20001
(202) 289-1916
The late Bishop Walter McCollough, former Presiding Bishop

Headquarters:
601 M Street, NW
Washington, DC 20001

The United House of Prayer for All People was founded by Bishop Marcelino Manoel de Graca, better known as "Sweet Daddy Grace." The church and Daddy Grace reached their greatest popularity in the 1930s and 1940s. Grace was born in 1884 on Brava, Cape Verde Islands, and began preaching in 1925 after migrating to the United States and working as a railroad cook. He also proclaimed himself a bishop and adopted a Holiness/Pentecostal format for his church. The one difference was that he also proclaimed himself God. He is often quoted as saying: "Salvation is by Grace only . . . Grace has given God a vacation, and since He is on vacation, don't worry Him. If you sin against God, Grace can save you, but if you sin against Grace, God cannot save you."

Daddy Grace was a charismatic, flamboyant leader, often remembered for his long hair and fingernails, who demanded total loyalty from his followers. Members of the church worshipped him as God, genuflecting before him and praying before pictures of him. The church often sponsored large parades and meetings that drew thousands. Grace controlled the financial management of the church and provided employment and financial benefits to the African American community through the production of "Daddy Grace Products," which included healing-power products, soap, cookies, facial creams, talcum powder, hair dressing, toothpaste, coffee, tea, stationery, and the *Grace Magazine*.

After the death of Daddy Grace, in 1960, Bishop Walter McCollough became the head of the church, although several court battles intervened and a split ensued, resulting in the True Grace Memorial House of Prayer. The church continues to grow and opened a major housing project near the headquarters church in Washington, D.C. in 1974 that bears McCollough's name. Its doctrine has come closer to that of traditional Pentecostal bodies.

Group Type: Denomination
Founded: 1926
Membership: As of 1974, 4,000,000 members
Meetings: An annual convocation

United Pentecostal Council of the Assemblies of God, Inc.

211 Columbia Street
P.O. Box 308
Cambridge, MA 02139
(617) 648-0808

The Reverend Edgar L. Lashley, President
44 Victor Court
Milford, CT 06406
The Reverend Herman Greene, Secretary
The Reverend Roderick R. Caesar, National Bishop

The United Pentecostal Council of the Assemblies of God, Inc., was established in Cambridge, Massachusetts, with the Reverend George Allan Phillip as its founder and first president. It was founded in 1919 to assist and sustain missionary activities. The Council is made up of churches adhering to Pentecostal teachings. The Reverend Alexander and Margaret Howard, who arrived in Cape Palmas, Liberia, on December 21, 1920, were its first missionaries. This body was initially organized to raise funds to transport the mission to Liberia.

The United Pentecostal Council of the Assemblies of God, Inc., has no direct relationship with other Pentecostal bodies. Although it shares in doctrinal beliefs, it is not affiliated with the General Council at Springfield, Missouri, nor the United Pentecostal Church of Tennessee. Its membership has grown from three churches in Cambridge, Massachusetts, to numerous churches in the cities of Chicago, New York, and Louisville;

the states of Florida, North Carolina, South Carolina, and Iowa; and the Caribbean and Panama.

Group Type: Denomination
Founded: 1919

United Way of the Cross Churches of Christ of the Apostolic Faith

Bethel United Way of the Cross
Mount Cross Road
Danville, VA 24521
Bishop Joseph H. Adams

The United Way of the Cross Churches of Christ of the Apostolic Faith was founded in 1974 by Bishop Joseph H. Adams of the Way of the Cross Church of Christ and Elder Harrison J. Twyman of the Bible Way Church of Our Lord Jesus Christ World Wide, Inc. Both men discovered that each had received a vision to leave their respective churches and form a new denomination. In addition to this, Bishop Adams had some concerns about administrative matters with the Way of the Cross Church, led at the time by Bishop J. L. Brooks, brother-in-law of the founder.

The church grew as other Apostolic bodies that had left their respective denominations aligned with the new denomination. As of 1980, the church had approximately 1,100 members in fourteen churches with thirty ministers and four bishops. It is a regional Apostolic organization, located primarily in five or six states.

Group Type: Denomination
Founded: 1974
Doctrine: Oneness/Apostolic
Membership: As of 1980, 1,100 persons in 14 churches with 30 ministers and 4 bishops

Universal Christian Spiritual Faith and Churches for All Nations

Last known address:
545 West 92nd Street
Los Angeles, CA 90044

The Universal Christian Spiritual Faith and Churches for All Nations was founded by Dr. David William Short in 1952 with the merger of three denominational groups: the National David Spiritual Temple of Christ Church Union (Inc.) U.S.A.; St. Paul's Spiritual Church Convocation; and King David's Spiritual Temple of Truth Association. The National David Spiritual Temple of Christ Church Union (Inc.) U.S.A. was established in Kansas City, Missouri, in 1932 by a former Baptist minister, Bishop David William Short. The church is Pentecostal in belief and doctrine. Membership is approximately 40,000 persons. The church publishes a monthly magazine, *The Christian Spiritual Voice*.

The church teaches that, although a full and complete Baptism of the Holy Spirit is evidenced by the gift of speaking in tongues and other gifts of the Holy Ghost, it is possible to receive the Spirit without these outward expressions. This distinguishes it from most Pentecostal bodies. Its polity is similar to other Pentecostal groups, with the bishop serving as the primary leader.

Group Type: Denomination

Founded: 1952
Membership: Over 40,000 persons and 60 churches in the mid-1960s
Publications: *The Christian Spiritual Voice*, a monthly magazine
Meetings: An annual assembly

Universal Church of Christ, Inc.

19-23 Park Street
P.O. Box 146
Orange, NJ 07050
(201) 673-4424
The Reverend Robert C. Jiggetts, Jr., Chief Apostle,
  Founder, and President

The Universal Church of Christ, Inc., was founded in 1972 in Orange, New Jersey, through the ministry of the Reverend Dr. Robert C. Jiggetts, Jr., with the support of Elder Nathaniel Kirton and Elder Carl Winckler. There are twenty temples located throughout the United States and the West Indies.

The doctrine of the church is Apostolic. The ordinances of the church include the Lord's Supper, marriage, and baptism. The church believes in the infallibility of scripture and divine healing. In keeping with its beliefs, it started a soup kitchen in 1984, staffed by Dr. Jiggetts's mother, church volunteers, and welfare recipients earning their subsidies through ''workfare'' programs. The kitchen operates from the Orange, New Jersey, Church and provides over 1,300 meals a month to the indigent and homeless. This successful effort has been subsidized by grants from the government, surplus government food, and generous donations of food and money from area businesses and organizations.

Dr. Jiggetts is the Chief Apostle and serves as president and general overseer of the church. He is the author of several booklets and pamphlets concerning Christian life. The church's annual convention is held the fourth week in August in Orange, New Jersey.

Group Type: Denomination
Founded: 1972
Doctrine: Oneness/Apostolic
Membership: 20 temples throughout the United States and the West Indies
Publications: Several pamphlets and booklets by Dr. Jiggetts
Meetings: Annual convention the fourth week in August in Orange, NJ

Way of the Cross Church of Christ

819 D Street, NE
Washington, DC 20002
(202) 543-0500
Bishop Alphonzo Brooks, Presiding Bishop
Elder Ronald A. Frazier, Administrator

The Way of the Cross Church of Christ was founded by Henry C. Brooks in Washington, D.C. in February, 1927. Bishop Brooks went to New York to receive his credentials from Bishop Robert Clarence Lawson of the Church of Our Lord Jesus Christ of the Apostolic Faith, but was instructed to return to Washington and gain some experience working with Elder James T. Morris (later the founder of the Highway Christian Church). However, he chose to start a church in Washington and soon started a second near Henderson, North Carolina. Bishop Lawson granted him charter credentials on June 1, 1928.

Bishop Brooks remained a part of the fellowship with Bishop Robert Clarence Lawson and the Church of the Lord Jesus Christ of the Apostolic Faith from 1928 to 1933. In December, 1933, the Way of the Cross Church of Christ was incorporated, taking on the authority to establish and organize other churches and to ordain ministers. Elder Henry C. Brooks was consecrated as bishop in 1933.

Bishop Brooks served as pastor and bishop from 1927 to 1967, in the headquarters church in Washington, D.C. The church was not without schisms, although only one group left under his administration—Ralph Green formed the Free Gospel Church of Christ, Inc., in 1962. After Bishop Brooks's death in 1967, three ministers were used on a four-month trial basis at the headquarters church during the first year. Among them were Elders Joseph Weathers, Walter Thompson, and Willie James Davis. A decision was made to offer the pastorate to Bishop John L. Brooks (the brother-in-law of the late Bishop Henry C. Brooks). Bishop John L. Brooks left his church in Henderson, North Carolina, and assumed the pastorate as well as the presiding bishop office for the body. Elder Joseph Weathers left in 1969 to form the Holy Temple Church of Christ, Inc., believing that he had not been fairly considered for the pastorate. In 1974, Joseph Adams left to form the United Way of the Cross Churches of the Apostolic Faith, Inc. In 1978, Bishop Henry Brooks's son, Alphonzo, became pastor of the headquarters church upon the retirement of Bishop John L. Brooks from the pastorate.

Under the leadership of Bishop Alphonzo Brooks, the Way of the Cross Church of Christ, Inc., has established the Sound of Pentecost radio ministries, which are transmitted across the United States and to four provinces in Canada. The church operates the Apostolic Educational Center, established in 1987, and it maintains a highly visible social outreach mission program.

In 1979, the church became an international body, adding thirteen churches and missions in Ghana and Liberia. As of 1980, there were approximately fifty thousand persons in forty-eight congregations and missions around the world.

Group Type: Denomination
Founded: 1928
Doctrine: Oneness/Apostolic
Membership: As of 1980, 50,000 persons in 48 congregations and missions

OTHER CHRISTIAN BODIES

Catholic

African American Catholic Congregation

P.O. Box 91700
Washington, DC 20090-1700
(202) 371-0800
FAX (202) 371-0808
Bishop George Augustus Stallings, Jr., Senior Pastor and
    Founder
Mrs. Catherine Boucree, Executive Administrator
Mr. William E. Marshall, Jr., Director of Communications

Imani Temple
Friendship Educational Center
Livingston Road and South Capitol Street, SE
Washington, DC
The Reverend Charles F. Stephney, Assistant Pastor

Kujichagulia Temple
Holiday Inn
Norfolk, VA 23501-1291
(804) 640-1455
The Reverend H. Randolph Caines, Assistant Pastor

Kuumba Temple
Philadelphia, PA

The African American Catholic Congregation (AACC) was formed by the Reverend George Augustus Stallings, Jr., and others in response to the Roman Catholic Church's insensitivity to spiritual and cultural needs of African American Catholics. After unsuccessful discussions with Cardinal James A. Hickey, Archbishop of the Archdiocese of Washington, D.C., Father Stallings (who served formerly as director of evangelism for the Archdiocese of Washington and as pastor of St. Teresa of Avila Parish, Washington, D.C.) sought to form a separate entity to meet the needs of African American Catholics. When Stallings celebrated his experimental Mass in defiance of warnings from the Archdiocese, Cardinal Hickey formally suspended him from preaching, celebrating Mass, or administering the sacraments of the church, which include Baptism, Matrimony, and Holy Communion.

In July 1989, the black Catholic bishops of the United States announced plans to begin "very preliminary" studies about the feasibility for an African American rite in the U.S. The first step, according to Bishop John H. Ricard, auxiliary bishop of Baltimore and chairman of the Committee for Black Catholics of the National Conference of Black Catholics, is to determine whether there is consensus among black Catholics for a distinctly black-oriented and black-controlled unit within the church. However, the black bishops had issued a document in 1984, strongly supporting cultural adaptation of the church's liturgy "according to the genius of the gifts of our African American spiritual heritage." According to articles in the *Washington*

Post and the *Charlotte Observer*, and by religious experts, what is actually at issue is the creation of a semiautonomous unit in communion with the Roman Catholic Church, which would have its own bishops, liturgy, canon law, and traditions. This would be similar to the church's Armenian and Ukrainian rites, which recognize the pope's authority but have their own hierarchy and their own particular liturgy. There are about twenty such rites worldwide. However, no group, already a part of the Roman church, has actually moved out to create such a rite in the 1,900-year history of the church.

The inaugural service of Imani Temple was held on Sunday, July 2, 1989, at the Dumbarton Chapel of the Howard University Law School, with more than 3,000 persons attending. The Mass included an experimental liturgy used in the Republic of Zaire. Ancestral spirits were also invoked, thus recognizing the cultural continuum with traditional African religion. The services of the African American Catholic Congregation are similar to those sanctioned by the Roman Catholic Church for black communities throughout the nation. They include traditional elements of the black Protestant experience and encourage spontaneous interaction between the celebrant and the congregation. African music and black literature are also included in worship services. The Mass celebrated by Father Stallings is legitimate in form, but it is *not* considered legitimate by the Roman Catholic Church because it is not sanctioned by the church.

The AACC is committed to the following general principles: 1) the formation of programs in the areas of Bible study and spiritual development; membership development and reclamation; lay development; tithing and finance; youth culture and behavior; African and African American spirituality and heritage; employment, training and economic development; communication (audio- and tele-evangelization); crisis intervention and counseling; disability and access; worship; and senior citizen security and other issues of aging; 2) the development of liturgies that are both authentically Catholic and African American; 3) the formation and development of a sensitive indigenous African American clergy and leadership that springs from the people and is designed to serve the people; 4) the development of models that will seek to advance the commitment to view Catholic schools as appropriate locations for both education and evangelization; 5) support of growth and development of African American businesses; and 6) the development of new directions and services regarding preparation of white priests who work in African American parishes. Many of these principles reflect the sense of community and traditional support systems found in the African American community, especially as expressed through the black church.

The temples of the AACC are named after the seven principles of the African/African American value system (the Nguzo Saba), which are given in Swahili. Scriptural correlations are given for each principle. The name of the mother church, Imani, means faith. The second temple, Umoja, means unity. The name of the third temple, *Kujichagulia*, means self-determination. The other principles are: *ujima* (collective work and responsibility); *ujamaa* (cooperative economics); *nia* (purpose); and *kuumba* (creativity). It should be noted that *Imani* has been interpreted as the Swahili word for faith, but East Africans have said that there is no such word in the language. The Swahili word *Amani*, literally translated, means peace, and can refer to faith in some contexts. A similar word in the Kinyarwandi language, *Imana*, means God.

Father Stallings formally declared the African American Catholic Congregation's independence from the Roman Catholic Church on Tuesday, January 30, 1990, during an appearance on the "Donahue Show." According to Stallings, the formal split from the church was caused by the "intolerable institutionalized racism in the Roman Catholic Church," and it recognizes that "within the context of Catholic [universal], there are expressions of one truth," that being the Gospel of Jesus Christ. As a result of Father Stallings's decision, he and his Roman Catholic followers face automatic excommunication from the Roman Catholic Church.

Although, for the most part, the doctrine, discipline, faith, and moral teachings of the AACC will be in accord with those of the Roman Catholic Church, Father Stallings has stated that the African American Catholic Congregation will "do everything that the Roman Catholic Church is afraid to do." Specifically, the new church will relax the traditional Roman stance on abortion, believing that, although there is sanctity in human life from the moment of conception, abortion is ultimately a decision of conscience. It will support abortion in cases of rape and incest. The church will welcome divorced and remarried persons into full membership. It will also open communion, or the Lord's Supper, to all baptized Christians, whereas the Roman Catholic Church believes that only members of the Catholic faith may receive communion in the Catholic church. The church will also let priests choose between celibacy or marriage, and will encourage the ordination of women to the ministry.

Father Stallings caused a major controversy when he proclaimed Dr. Martin Luther King, Jr., a saint on Sunday, January 14, 1990. In the Roman Catholic Church, only baptized Catholics can be canonized, and the process involves extensive research and proof of miracles. According to church officials, martyrdom for God can weigh heavily in this process. The pope has sole authority to canonize saints after papal procedures are exhausted. Candidates must be "elevated" through three levels before attaining sainthood—servant of God, venerable, and blessed. Father Stallings suspects that donations to the Vatican have eased the way for some to become saints. He also believes that God has the sole authority to declare sainthood, rather than the Holy Father. In the African American Catholic Congregation, Dr. King will be venerated on the same day each year.

Initial plans for expansion included the development of a total of seven temples by July 1990, with temples in other cities. Plans are also underway for the Imani Temple Academy, which will provide day-care and classes for grades K-12. Mass is celebrated on Sundays at 8:00 a.m. and 11:00 a.m. at Imani Temple and at 11:00 a.m. at Kujichagulia Temple. The Reverend George Augustus Stallings, Jr., serves as the senior pastor of the denomination. The Reverend Charles F. Stephney serves as assistant pastor for the Imani Temple. The Reverend H. Randolph Caines serves as the assistant pastor for the Kujichagulia Temple. Stallings is currently writing a book entitled,

"Take Courage, My Soul," a series of reflections on living a successful and fulfilling life.

On February 8, 1990, the three hundred congregants of the second temple, Umoja Temple, led by the Reverend Bruce Edward Greening, left the African American Catholic Congregation to seek reconciliation with the Roman Catholic Church. The decision was made to leave the AACC after Father Stallings declared that the African American Catholic Congregation would become an independent body, thus inviting automatic excommunication from the Roman Catholic Church. The fourth temple, Kuumba (meaning creativity in Swahili), began services in West Philadelphia on April 4, 1990. These services will be held on Sunday evenings with Father Stallings conducting them. On May 12, 1990, Stallings was consecrated a bishop by the Reverend Richard W. Bridges, archbishop of the American Independent Orthodox Church on the West Coast.

Group Type: Denomination
Founded: July 2, 1989
Membership: Approximately 1,500 persons in 3 congregations

Independent African American Catholic Rite

Church of St. Martin de Porres
P.O. Box 41449
Washington, DC 20018
(202) 544-5234
Bishop Bruce E. Greening, BMdP, Pastor
The Reverend Lewis T. Tait, Jr., Associate Pastor
Mrs. Yetta W. Galiber, President, Executive Board

The Independent African American Catholic Rite is the result of the desire among African American Catholics for self-determination and self-government as well as a commitment to empower African Americans religiously, socially, politically, and economically on the basis of racial solidarity.

In July 1989, the black Catholic bishops of the United States announced plans to begin "very preliminary" studies about the feasibility of an African American rite in the U.S. The first step, according to Bishop John H. Ricard, auxiliary bishop of Baltimore and chairman of the Committee for Black Catholics of the National Conference of Black Catholics, is to determine whether there is consensus among black Catholics for a distinctly black-oriented and black-controlled unit within the church. However, the black bishops had issued a document in 1984 strongly supporting cultural adaptation of the church's liturgy "according to the genius of the gifts of our African American spiritual heritage."

According to religious experts and articles in the *Washington Post* and the *Charlotte Observer*, what is actually at issue is the creation of a semiautonomous unit in communion with the Roman Catholic Church, that would have its own bishops, liturgy, canon law, and traditions. This would be similar to the church's Armenian and Ukrainian rites, which recognize the pope's authority but have their own hierarchy and their own particular liturgy. There are about twenty such rites worldwide. However, no group, already a part of the Roman church, has actually moved out to create such a rite in the 1,900-year history of the church.

The African American Catholic Congregation was formed by the Reverend George Augustus Stallings, Jr., and others in July 1989 in response to the Roman Catholic Church's insensitivity to spiritual and cultural needs of African American

Catholics. The Reverend Stallings formally declared the African American Catholic Congregation's independence from the Roman Catholic Church on Tuesday, January 30, 1990, during an appearance on the "Donahue Show." This decision meant automatic excommunication from the Roman Catholic Church for Reverend Stallings and his Roman Catholic followers.

The second temple of the African American Catholic Congregation, Umoja Temple, was led by the Reverend Bruce Edward Greening. After Reverend Stallings declared his movement's independence, the three hundred congregants of Umoja Temple subsequently left the African American Catholic Congregation to seek reconciliation with the Roman Catholic Church on February 8, 1990. In the attempted reconciliation, the body wanted permission for a five-year period of experimentation with liturgy as well as the reinstatement of Father Greening to the priesthood. There was no response to the request.

Umoja Temple was renamed the Church of St. Martin de Porres after St. Martin de Porres, a black Dominican priest born in Lima, Peru. Canonized by the Roman Catholic Church in 1963, he is acknowledged as an apostle of charity, patron of social justice, father of the sick and poor, and helper in hopeless cases. He is considered a powerful intercessor for those in need. The church declared its independence from the local archdiocese, Rome, and the authority of the pope on June 15, 1990. Father Greening was then unanimously elected bishop by the congregants, and permission was sought to raise him to the episcopate from the African Orthodox Church. Archbishop Stafford J. Sweeting, patriarch of the African Orthodox Church, consecrated Greening to the office of bishop in an impressive ceremony on September 28, 1990.

The Independent African American Catholic Rite has emerged as a response to the inability of the Roman Catholic Church to live up to the ideals of universality and inclusion. Thus, the denomination is committed to the empowerment of African American Catholics, the development of institutional ownership, and the emergence of a new leadership model based on the presence of a participatory and democratic spirit.

The Independent African American Catholic Rite is committed to forming strong programs of Bible study and spiritual development; membership development; lay leadership; tithing and finance; youth culture and behavior; African American spirituality and heritage; employment training and economic development; worship; and programs that address access and other issues of the disabled, as well as security for senior citizens and other problems of aging. These initiatives are concrete embodiments of the National Black Pastoral Plan. The church is also committed to the formation and development of a sensitive, indigenous African American clergy and lay leadership who come from the people themselves. The church believes that native vocations are essential and critical if it is to be universal. The church also supports the growth and development of African American businesses.

Services of the Independent African American Catholic Rite are held at McKinley High School in Washington, D.C. each Sunday at 10:30 a.m. Bishop Bruce Edward Greening, BMdP, serves as pastor of the body and is assisted by the Reverend Lewis T. Tait, Jr., the associate pastor. Mrs. Yetta W. Galiber serves as president of the executive board.

Group Type: Denomination
Founded: June 15, 1990
Membership: Approximately 500 persons

Churches of Christ (Disciples of Christ)

General Assembly Churches of Christ (Disciples of Christ)

330 Warwick Avenue
Mount Vernon, NY 10553
(914) 667-8234
Bishop MacDonald Moses, General Bishop
Elder Joseph M. Baum, Secretary

The Church of Christ (Disciples of Christ) was founded in 1871, and it was known initially as the Disciples Church. The church was called the "Disciples of Christ" according to conference records of 1886, at the Vine Swamp Church, Lenoir County, North Carolina. Four men were instrumental in developing the church: Joe Whitley, Bill Ant'ly, Offie Pettiford, and Easom Green. They realized that Alexander Campbell wanted to take the church back to the teaching and structure of the New Testament church, which included going back to the name "Disciple." They felt that they needed no other name—such as "Christian"—to identify the church. The name was modified to "Church of Christ, Disciples of Christ" in 1931, at its tenth quadrennial assembly. It should be noted that this is a predominately African American religious body, which is autonomous from the majority white Christian Church (Disciples of Christ).

In an effort to follow the New Testament Church, the founding fathers emphasized the need to institute the following sacraments: footwashing (which imitated the practices of the Freewill Baptist Church); baptism; and the Eucharist (or Communion).

The church is organized into five District Assemblies that make up the General Assembly. It conducts two major meetings: 1) the biennial meeting of the General Assembly during the third week in May of odd years; and 2) the ministers' retreat, a biennial retreat session during even years, designed to serve the ministers of the General Assembly of the church.

In May 1988, the General Council Board and staff of the General Assembly agreed to accept the Liberian Church into its fellowship. This decision was pending ratification by the full assembly in its May, 1989 session.

Group Type: Denomination
Founded: 1871
Membership: 5 District Assemblies comprise the General Assembly, which has a total of approximately 50,000 persons
Publications: *The Disciples' Herald*, a quarterly bulletin focusing on the news from the district assemblies; *The Disciples' Voice*, published by Dr. Oscar S. Lucas, since 1950; *Disciple of Christ Church*

Manual, by Beryl Smith Garrett, published in 1977; General Assembly's *Guide to Christian Living* with the constitution and bylaws, initially printed in 1971 and revised in 1983

Meetings: General Assembly of the Churches of Christ (Disciples of Christ) held during the third week in May of odd years; ministers' retreat—biennial retreat session occurring during the third week in May of even years

National Convocation of the Christian Church (Disciples of Christ)

P.O. Box 1986
222 South Downey Avenue
Indianapolis, IN 46206
(317) 353-1491, x406
The Reverend John R. Foulkes, Administrative Secretary

At the close of the Civil War, black and white Disciples, who had been worshipping together, divided into separate bodies. The denomination continued, divided along racial lines, for many years, and the African American congregations formed their own assemblies. The yearbook of the white branch listed the black congregations but without annual reports, which were not submitted. In 1954, separate listing of "Negro" congregations was discontinued, and all congregations were listed together by county and city.

In 1969, the Christian Church (Disciples of Christ) restructured itself when the National Christian Missionary Convention (the African American congregations) merged with the International Convention (the predominantly white congregations). The National Convocation of the Christian Church was formed to ensure the continued and fair representation of African Americans (who compose four percent of the overall group) in the denomination. The National Convocation seeks to be a forum for total church life, fellowship, worship, program promotion, leadership training, and congregational strengthening. It promotes the interpretation and discussion of issues, concerns, and needs related to African American congregational life. The National Convocation of the Christian Church (Disciples of Christ) is considered to be *both* a denomination *and* a convocation of churches.

Christian Churches (Disciples of Christ) are generally noncreedal, and take the Bible as their standard of faith and practice. They are resistant to the codification of doctrinal affirmations into summary articles of belief. They allow and evidence a wide variety of theological opinions.

Members of the Christian Church (Disciples of Christ) embrace Christ as the Son of God and Savior of humankind, and as the giver of a mission to spread the good news throughout the world. God is perceived as Creator and as the source of the love that binds people together and to God. Members of the Christian Church (Disciples of Christ) believe that people are made new through Baptism and also believe that the communion of the Holy Spirit joins Christians in discipleship and obedience to Christ. The saving acts and the presence of Christ are celebrated through communion. Members of the Christian Church also believe that the gift of ministry and the light of scripture are received within the universal church.

The church emphasizes evangelism, particularly through program services to Hispanic American and bilingual congregations. Its Black and Hispanic Concerns Committee reviews the ministries of the units of churches with African American and Hispanic American congregations and gives advice and counsel to enhance those ministries. The General Reconciliation Committee, created in the 1960s as the church's response to racism and poverty, continues to operate today. Its primary concern is the systemic victimization of women and children.

Through its Office of Church in Society, religious liberties, human rights, criminal justice issues (particularly the need to break the cycles of violence and vengeance), and church and community issues (e.g., migrant farm-worker housing conditions, and resettlement of immigrants) are explored. The Christian Church (Disciples of Christ) monitors national security, economic development, the United Nations, and international conflict resolution issues through its Office of International Affairs.

The educational programs of the Christian Church (Disciples of Christ) are handled through its Office of Christian Education. Educational leader development, racial/ethnic educational ministries, youth ministry, youth and young adult ministries, family and children's ministry, education for mission, and educational program development are all administered from that office.

The Christian Church's (Disciples of Christ) Division of Overseas Ministries operates through sixty-eight churches and councils of churches worldwide. Its Division of Homeland Ministries works in the areas of evangelism, social action, Christian education, lay involvement, and ministerial concerns.

As of August, 1986, there are approximately 538 African American congregations in the National Convocation of the Christian Church. The highest concentrations are in North Carolina, South Carolina, Texas, and New York. The Reverend John R. Foulkes, Sr., is the current administrative secretary of the National Convocation and the deputy general minister and vice-president for inclusive ministries.

Group Type: Denomination; council of churches/groups
Founded: 1969
Membership: 538 congregations
Meetings: A biennial assembly

Nondenominational/Ecumenical

African Universal Church, Inc.

2336 Southwest 48th Avenue
West Hollywood, FL 33023
(305) 921-5392
Elder Andrew B. Lane, Sr., Pastor
Deacon Audley Sears, Chairman of Trustees

The African Universal Church, Inc., was founded by followers of Princess Laura Adorkor Koffey shortly after her assassination on March 8, 1928, in Miami, Florida. According to some reports, she was assassinated because of her popularity with both blacks and whites as a powerful preacher, and it was suspected that the assassin was a member of a rival spiritual church in Miami. Captain Maxwell Cook, a captain of the

African Legion of the Universal Negro Improvement and Conservation Association and African Communities League (UNIA), was also stabbed and beaten to death during the same incident.

"Mother Koffey" or "Saint Adorkor," as she is affectionately remembered, came to the United States (via Canada) from the small village of Asofa (near Accra, Ghana), where there is a small mission. She was married to Joseph Koffey, the son of an African King. However, there is no mention of Koffey found in the United States. She traveled, preaching and spreading the gospel until she reached Alabama, South Carolina, and Florida, believing that God had inspired her to evangelize through revelation by divine grace. It seems that she was involved with the UNIA, led by Marcus Garvey, because the building where her followers met was also used by the UNIA.

After Mother Koffey's assassination, her followers sought leaders who would continue her work, and several native Africans were identified to do so. In addition, a delegation was sent to the Gold Coast of West Africa in search of Mother Koffey's relatives, but they were not found.

In 1931, a meeting was held in Jacksonville, Florida, that resulted in a separation of the congregations of the church. Ernest Bethel and Ernest Sears, two church leaders, sought other congregations in 1953, and one was found in East Jacksonville, Florida. In March of the same year, a meeting was held to decide the future of the church. It was agreed that three bodies would be incorporated, namely: St. Adorkor African Universal Church of Miami; St. Adorkor African Universal Church of Hollywood, Florida; and African Universal Church of Jacksonville. The first chairman of the assembly was Elder John Dean, who held office from 1953 to 1958. These three congregations worked together for fifteen years, withstanding many problems.

Deacon Clifford Hepburn served as general assembly chairman from 1958 to 1970, but two major disputes arose, leaving the African Universal Church of East Jacksonville and the African Universal Church of West Hollywood, Florida, incorporated. Brother Ernest Sears, a long-standing member of the church, went to Ghana in 1968 to attempt to find Mother Koffey's family and establish communication with them. This time, he was successful. The family had not known anything of her whereabouts or her death in the forty-two years since they last saw her. The church in Ghana was still standing, although in need of extensive repair. Mother Koffey's nephew was brought back to the United States.

From 1970 to 1974 Sister Gloria Hepburn was general assembly chairwoman. During this time a third African trip was made, and plans were carried out to incorporate the church in the Asofa village in Accra, Ghana. Deacon Audley Sears, Sr., became chairman in 1975 (the position he continues to hold) and early in his tenure, communication with the African Universal Church of Daphne, Alabama, was established.

The African Universal Church is composed of seven independent churches, most located in the southern United States, particularly Florida and Alabama. It seeks to teach and preach the gospel of Jesus Christ as well as to teach African Americans about themselves and self-sufficiency. It is also instrumental in the establishment of businesses that trade goods with Africa. Finally, it seeks to maintain a viable line of communication with Africans.

Over the years, the church has been involved in numerous activities. During the 1930s, a school was operated for children from kindergarten through the twelfth grade. From 1946 to 1953 and again from 1956 to 1975, a sundry was operated to train youth in business management. The church has also assisted the African church and community in Asofa, Ghana, providing for church repairs and the establishment of a school. In 1977, the first discipline of the church was published. At one time, there was a commercial league, but exact information concerning its activities is not available.

The church is nondenominational and believes in healing and the Second Coming of Christ. Baptism of the Holy Ghost, justification, sanctification, and confession are the four spiritual experiences of the church. Wine is used for the Lord's Supper, and water is used for baptism.

Ministers are referred to as elders (although the title Reverend is acceptable). Elders are spiritual advisors to their congregations. Deacons and trustees, along with members of the congregation, govern policies about the allocation of resources. The churches operate autonomously, with the elders serving as the spiritual heads. An independent assembly meets annually in August. The church does not have any districts or associational suborganizations. Regular worship services are held on Sunday. Fellowship with other churches is held annually during the memorial observance of Mother Koffey's death on March 8 and on other occasions during the year.

Group Type: Ecumenical/nondenominational
Founded: 1928
Membership: 7 independent churches
Meetings: Annual memorial observance of Mother Koffey's death held in March and annual meetings held in August

Crenshaw Christian Center

P.O. Box 90000
Los Angeles, CA 90009
(213) 758-3777
Dr. Frederick K. C. Price III, Founder and Pastor
Ms. Angela M. Evans, Executive Vice President

After spending seventeen years in the ministry in the Baptist, African Methodist Episcopal, Presbyterian, and Christian Missionary Alliance denominations, the Reverend Frederick K. C. Price, D.D., read *The Authority of the Believer* by Kenneth E. Hagin. Dr. Hagin's book inspired Dr. Price to begin teaching his West Washington Community Church congregation of 125 members about the power of the Holy Spirit. The affiliate of the Christian Missionary Alliance grew rapidly from this point and in 1973 purchased a three-acre site on Crenshaw Boulevard in Inglewood, California.

The Crenshaw Christian Center held its first service in November 1973, with three hundred persons attending. The sanctuary was soon filled to its capacity of 1,400, and the schedule was changed to accommodate this growth, first with two morning services, and finally with three.

Quickly outgrowing this space, the Crenshaw Christian Center purchased the urban campus of Pepperdine University, a thirty-two-acre site, in 1981. By 1984, the Sunday services and most of the church's activities were held there. Because of the church's growth, the erection of a new 10,145-seat sanctuary was necessary, and its doors were opened on Sunday, September 10, 1989. The Faith Dome is the largest church sanctuary in the continental United States.

The Crenshaw Christian Center's outreach program includes the Ever Increasing Faith Ministries, a national television broadcast that reaches approximately two million persons over ninety-three cable and network stations in the United States, Australia, Haiti, the West Indies, the Virgin Islands, and the Bahamas. A radio program is broadcast over sixty-eight stations across the country. In addition, annual crusades are held in cities such as New York, Washington, D.C., Atlanta, New Orleans, Houston, and Los Angeles over two-day periods. These crusades help to provide financial support for the Ever Increasing Faith Ministries, which is designed to sustain itself rather than to rely on the congregation.

The Center's School of Ministry opened in 1985 to train those called to the ministry. Its three-year program operates concurrently with the School of the Bible, which opened in September, 1988. The course of study for the School of the Bible is either one or two years and is the same for those in the School of Ministry, who will be trained in the ministry in the third year. In addition to these, there is the Frederick K. C. Price III Elementary and Junior High School, and a child-care center.

The ministry also sponsors a weekly alcohol and drug abuse program and a twenty-four-hour, on-site intercessory prayer network. In addition to Dr. Price, there are eight associate ministers—five assistant pastors and one female minister who conduct weddings, memorial services, and counseling sessions; and two ministers who teach primarily in the School of Ministry.

Group Type: Ecumenical/nondenominational
Founded: 1973
Membership: 16,000 persons
Publications: Ever Increasing Faith Messenger

Faith Bible Church, Inc.

1350 Maryland Avenue, NE
Washington, DC 20002
(202) 398-4400
Dr. Lewis T. Tait, Sr., Founder and Presiding Bishop
The Reverend Lewis T. Tait, Jr., General Secretary

Faith Bible Church, Inc., was organized in 1959 in Washington, D.C. by the Reverend Lewis T. Tait, Sr. It is a non-denominational movement with an episcopal polity. The Reverend Lewis T. Tait, Sr., its founder and presiding bishop, was consecrated by Bishop Samuel Kelsey, Presiding Bishop of the Church of God in Christ, District of Columbia Jurisdiction, in 1962. Bishop Tait is responsible for the development and the administrative affairs of the churches. Local pastors provide spiritual guidance for their respective congregations.

Faith Bible Church started as an independent congregation under the name of Faith Church of God in Son in Washington, D.C. The name was changed later to Faith Bible Church, Inc. The movement now consists of six churches located in South Carolina and Washington, D.C. Each church is led by a founding pastor whose ministry developed through his or her association in Faith Bible Church. Women are accepted into all facets of ministry in the church, including the pastorate. Currently three of the six churches comprising the body are pastored by women.

The movement's doctrine is fundamentally Bible based. Membership requires baptism through immersion; all believers are baptized and infants are christened. The church believes in salvation by grace through faith (see Ephesians 2:8). No physical or outward sign is required. The movement's religious traditions developed out of trinitarian doctrine. Conversion of believers is deemed a personal matter and believers make a personal confession of their faith. The basic tenets of the church are salvation, communion, and baptism (Romans 10:9; 10:10; and 10:13).

Faith Bible Church, Inc., incorporates the following beliefs in its doctrine: 1) We believe the Bible is the inspired, infallible and authoritative word of God; 2) We believe that there is one God manifested in three persons, God the Father, God the Son, and God the Holy Spirit; 3) We believe in the deity of our Lord and Saviour, Jesus Christ; 4) We believe in His virgin birth, in His sinless life, in His miracles, in His vicarious atoning death. We believe in His bodily resurrection, in His ascension to the right hand of the Father, and in His personal return; 5) We believe that we are saved by grace through faith; and that not of ourselves, it is the gift of God; 6) We believe that regeneration is the work of the Holy Spirit and is absolutely essential for personal salvation; 7) We believe that the Baptism of the Holy Spirit occurs when a sinner trusts Christ as Saviour, and receives Him by faith into his heart; 8) We believe in the resurrection of both the saved and the lost; the saved to everlasting life, the lost to everlasting torment; and 9) God loves you; Jesus died for you that you might be saved. Trust Jesus, receive Him by faith into your heart today and be saved.

The administrative work of the movement is conducted at its annual national convention, held in Washington, D.C., beginning on the Thursday preceding the first Sunday in October and ending on the first Sunday in October. An annual four-day Women's Convention is held in South Carolina and provides fellowship, training, and edification for women. It is a forum for expressing concerns of Christian women in the church, the community, and the wider society.

Group Type: Ecumenical/nondenominational
Membership: Approximately 40 ministers in 6 congregations with 3,000 persons
Meetings: Annual national convention held in Washington, D.C., beginning on the Thursday preceding the first Sunday in October and ending on the first Sunday in October; annual women's convention held in South Carolina

Father Abraham Temple

645 E. 79th Street
Los Angeles, CA 90001
(213) 750-2817
The Reverend Nellie White

Group Type: Ecumenical/nondenominational

Father Divine's "Kingdom" and Peace Mission

Divine International Evangelical Peace Mission Hotel
1808 Ridge Avenue
Philadelphia, PA 19130

Father Divine, born George Baker about 1880, worked as an itinerant garden laborer in Baltimore in his late teens and preached on the side. He apprenticed as a latter-day Messiah under St. John the Divine Hickerson. He also worked under Samuel Morris, who proclaimed himself "the Father Eternal" and adopted the name "Father Jehovia." Morris anointed George Baker the "Messenger" and "God in the Sonship Degree." Baker and several of his followers moved to Valdosta, Georgia, in 1914, where he proclaimed himself God.

After being found guilty of being a public menace because of his noisy, outdoor congregation, he moved to Harlem. There he established his operation and refined his techniques, while serving under Hickerson. He later established his own church in Brooklyn and proclaimed himself the only living God. Complete loyalty was demanded from his followers and was maintained through strict moral codes. Baker forbade sexual relations between even husband and wife, as his followers became "sisters and brothers" in the faith. No children were born into the body; any children from families were reared together at the church's farm by surrogate parents. Communal living was promoted. Men and women lived dormitory-style on separate floors in hotels and were separated in worship. Peninah (later known as Sister Penny), one of his followers, had come with Baker from Georgia, and they later married.

Because of the increase in membership, Baker and his wife bought a home in Sayville, Long Island, in 1919. The organization began with twenty converts, but quickly grew when Baker started recruiting Harlem residents as domestic workers for wealthy, white Long Island residents. Many followers stayed in the home with Father and Mother Divine, which eventually became a shrine for the movement. Many were also attracted because of the small, free dinners begun by Sister Penny that evolved into lavish affairs, which the "Kingdom" provided at little or no cost. These dinners were incorporated into the worship services. During this time, Baker attracted several wealthy white converts as well. He formally took the name Father Divine in 1930.

On November 15, 1931, eighty followers in Sayville were arrested for disorderly conduct, the result of a noisy demonstration that offended white residents. Fifty-five persons pleaded guilty and paid the five-dollar fine. Although Father Divine and twenty-five others pleaded innocent, he was found guilty. Father Divine was sentenced to a year in the county jail and a five-hundred-dollar fine in the spring of 1932, but three days later, the sentencing judge died of a heart attack. Divine is quoted as saying "I hated to do it." The conviction was later overturned. Since the time of the incident, the group's newspaper, the *New Day*, has printed incidents of death and suffering predicted to occur or that had occurred, supposedly caused by opposition to Father Divine and his program. Also during this time, his deity and following were solidified. Upon his release, a "Monster Glory to Our God" reception was held at Rockland Palace in Harlem, and Divine decided to expand his operation in Harlem.

The positive impact Father Divine had on Harlem and the lives of African Americans is undeniable, especially during the Depression. He became one of the largest landlords in Harlem, owning apartment buildings, hotels, grocery stores, restaurants, barbershops, and a coal business. In addition to feeding and providing housing for numerous persons, these enterprises provided employment for his followers. During the 1930s, he also acquired businesses in other East Coast cities. His kingdoms and missions expanded to large cities across the country, and

eventually to Australia, Sweden, England, Germany, Austria, and Switzerland. Father Divine's personal wealth was unknown, because he neither filed nor paid income tax. Some sources state that neither Divine nor his church actually owned properties, but rather that several followers would come together to purchase or form a business. Father and Mother Divine were always provided for by each church. Each had a separate apartment for their personal use when visiting a church.

On November 4, 1933, Fiorello LaGuardia, then a candidate for mayor, came to a vespers banquet held at the Rockland Palace to seek Father Divine's advice and counsel, which further solidified his influence. He encouraged his followers to register and vote to benefit their community. Such was the strength of the organization that members were allowed to register under assumed names rather than their given names.

On April 20, 1937, two white men (one a process server) were beaten after a confrontation with Father Divine and one of his followers, "Faithful Mary." Although money and sex were not to be discussed in his kingdom, allegations had been made that Divine received money from businesses to keep his followers complacent and content with their positions, and to supply competent domestic workers for the elite of New York. Allegations about his own relationships with women had also been raised. Father Divine and three of his "angels" were sought to answer charges of felonious assault. He was found three days later in Connecticut and brought back to New York. During the same week, John West Hunt, a wealthy follower, was arrested under the Mann Act for the interstate transportation for sexual purposes of a young follower named "Miss Delight Jewel." Faithful Mary, who was considered the star angel of the movement, defected after making sensational charges about Divine's sex life and the alleged blackmailing of his followers. Although the movement recovered from these allegations and Faithful Mary rejoined it, more allegations would occur that would damage the image and work of Father Divine.

In 1938, the Kingdom acquired the Krum Elbow estate in Hyde Park, New York. This acquisition received national attention because Father Divine became a neighbor of President Franklin D. Roosevelt. In 1941, Father Divine moved to a thirty-two-room mansion near Philadelphia, the gift of John De Voute, a white disciple. Father Divine was found in contempt of court after defying an order to pay almost $5,000 to an angel who accused him of defrauding her, and he fled to Philadelphia to escape prison. He abandoned his headquarters in Harlem, and his organization began to decline. Father Divine's image was further tarnished when he married Ednah Rose Ritchings (known as "Sweet Angel"), a Canadian-born white follower, in April, 1946. He claimed that she was the reincarnation of his deceased wife, Sister Penny. This was decried in both the black and white press. Finally, in 1944, a court ruling denied a large bequest made by a follower based upon the fact that she had been of unsound mind.

Father Divine died in 1965. A shrine was built between 1965 and 1966 at a cost of $300,000 to house his body at the Woodmount estate near Philadelphia. In 1978, many followers still came to the estate and shrine, where Mother Divine led daily worship services over communion banquets in the chapel.

The polity of the movement is linked directly to the continued charisma of Father Divine. Although he is gone, Father Divine was and still is considered the true leader of the organization. He personally chose the leadership of many local groups and designated women as his secretaries. Much of the business of the organization has always been handled by a lay lawyer not affiliated with the organization. The incorporated churches have annual open meetings when a president, secretary, treasurer, and board of trustees are elected. These officers are subject to approval by Father Divine and the current Mother Divine. Financial issues are not discussed; rather, treasurer's reports are given, delineating physical improvements, acquisitions, and all cash transactions. Only the names of officers are published in the *New Day* newspaper, and no membership lists are available.

The current strength of the organization is unknown, but in 1978, the *New Day* had a production rate of nine thousand copies. The newspaper continues to print Father Divine's messages from the 1930s and 1940s. Most of the followers are believed to be women and have been members of the group for many years.

Group Type: Ecumenical/nondenominational
Founded: 1919
Publications: New Day, a weekly newspaper

Gospel Mission

1637 S. Pulaski Road
Chicago, IL 60623
(312) 522-9572

Group Type: Ecumenical/nondenominational
Founded: 1940

Holy Temple of God, Inc.

Big Apple Road
East Palatka, FL 32031
Mr. Walter Camps

Group Type: Ecumenical/nondenominational

Missionary Church of America

Route 7
Morganton, NC 28655

Group Type: Ecumenical/nondenominational

Refuge Church of Christ

3618 Route 108
P.O. Box 9
Olney, MD 20832
(301) 924-4847
Elder R. Lamont Settles, Pastor

The Refuge Church of Christ was founded in 1954, in Montgomery County, Maryland, by Bishop Rufus Amos Settles. It is based on the principles in Isaiah 6:1-3. After Bishop Settles's death on October 5, 1985, he was succeeded by Elder Rufus Lamont Settles. In addition to regular services, the church has an extensive program including Bible study, a tape ministry, community outreach programs, and a daily radio broadcast, "Now Hear This," on WBZE-AM radio. The sacraments of the church are baptism and communion.

Group Type: Ecumenical/nondenominational
Founded: 1954

Salvation and Deliverance Church

37 West 116th Street
New York, NY 10026
(212) 722-5488
Apostle William Brown, Founder and Pastor

Although originally it began in 1975 as a ministry of the African Methodist Episcopal Church, Salvation and Deliverance Church is now a nondenominational, interracial, international, Holiness ministry.

The founder and pastor of the church, Apostle William Brown, was raised as a Roman Catholic and came to the ministry from the corporate world, where he served as a marketing vice-president. Under his leadership, Salvation and Deliverance Church has grown in membership and number of projects. The church has missions in forty-six countries (including churches in Ghana, Nigeria, Liberia, India, Haiti, Jamaica, and Canada); it provides leadership and focus for the International Youth Movement for Christ; and it has sixteen elementary schools, five Bible colleges (see St. Paul's Bible Institute, Part 3, this vol.), two orphanages, and two trade schools. In 1987, Apostle Brown won the "Ethnic New Yorker Award" for the church's extensive addiction rehabilitation project in Harlem, where the church is headquartered.

The church maintains a Christian retreat and resort center on sixty acres in New York's Catskill Mountains (Ellensville, New York). The center, "Miracle Mountain," includes a chapel specifically designed to meet the special needs of the residents of New Horizons for the Retarded Educational Campus and clients of the Sullivan and Ulster County Association for Retarded Citizens.

Salvation and Deliverance is made up of more than 140 member churches. They de-emphasize denominationalism and emphasize the attainment of "holy perfection."

Group Type: Ecumenical/nondenominational
Founded: 1975
Membership: More than 140 churches
Meetings: An annual convocation in mid-June

Sanctuary Church of the Open Door

1601 North 72nd Street
Philadelphia, PA 19510
(215) 877-7312
The Reverend Audrey Bronson

Group Type: Ecumenical/nondenominational
Publications: National Bulletin and *Fellowship Echoes*

Tabernacle of Prayer

Brooklyn, NY

Group Type: Ecumenical/nondenominational

United Christian Evangelistic Association ["Reverend Ike"]

United Church
4140 Broadway
New York, NY 10033
The Reverend Frederick Eikerenkoetter II ("Reverend Ike")

The United Christian Evangelistic Association was formed in 1966 by the Reverend Frederick Eikerenkoetter II, a 1956 graduate of the American Bible School in Chicago and a former Baptist minister. Upon graduation, he was involved in evangelization and faith healing, but was subsequently influenced by New Thought philosophy. His ministry changed to teach positive mind power to his followers. According to the *Encyclopedia of American Religions* (3rd ed.), his teaching is called the "science of living."

Popularly known as "Reverend Ike," his ministry encourages positive and practical thinking for this life, not the hereafter. Reverend Ike believes that the lack of money is the root of all evil, and that one should focus on God as the real person within one's self. According to him, the belief in God's work allows one to see one's self as worthy of God's success. He encourages his followers initially to project their desires into the conscious mind, and then to follow a prosperity "blessing plan"—emphasizing belief, giving, and prosperity.

Also known as the United Church and Science of Living Institute, the ministry uses the media as one of its primary outreach mechanisms, and services (including testimonies of successful believers) are broadcast over eighty-nine radio and twenty-two television stations primarily in the eastern United States and in California and Hawaii.

Group Type: Ecumenical/nondenominational
Founded: 1966
Membership: 2 congregations, 1 each in New York and Boston with over 5,000 in average attendance as of 1974
Publications: *Action*, a periodical; *Pool of Bethesda*, a newsletter, P.O. Box 9000, Boston, MA 02205-9933; *Health, Happiness and Prosperity for You!*, by Reverend Eikerenkoetter

Universal Foundation for Better Living, Inc. [Johnnie Coleman]

11901 South Ashland Avenue
Chicago, IL 60643
(312) 568-2282
The Reverend Dr. Johnnie Coleman, Founder

The Universal Foundation for Better Living (UFBL) was organized on June 14, 1974, in Illinois as the Unity Foundation for Better Living. The name was changed in January 1976 to the Universal Foundation for Better Living. It is organized exclusively for religious and religious educational purposes.

The Universal Foundation for Better Living is an association of independent New Thought (Metaphysical) churches. It is dedicated to coordinating assistance to member churches and strengthening them. These churches are committed to spreading the abundant-living message of Jesus Christ throughout America and the rest of the world. Membership is open to groups, organizations, ministers, laypersons, Christian educators, business and professional people, artists, musicians, and persons of all races, creeds, and ethnic backgrounds.

The Universal Foundation for Better Living is a springboard for positive action to bring the Kingdom of God on the earth. It elicits this consciousness so that all men will know "there is but one presence and one power in the universe—God, the good omnipotent, the everywhere principle of absolute good."

The New Thought Movement—positive thinking—is an approach that stems from the conscious awareness of humankind's sameness with God. It teaches persons to discover the power of God that is within everyone. UFBL views itself as the vehicle through which God has chosen to bring freedom to the world. Its mission develops out of the universal hunger for practical techniques that demonstrate how to fulfill the good desires of the heart. The organization is directed by its founder, Dr. Johnnie Coleman. She has developed and conducted workshops and seminars designed to assist members to become more "actualized" in using their spiritual consciousness to effect personal change.

Group Type: Ecumenical/nondenominational
Founded: June 14, 1974
Publications: *Truth for Better Living*

World's Gospel Feast

New York, NY

Group Type: Ecumenical/nondenominational

Yahweh's Temple

No current address
Bishop Samuel E. Officer, Church Leader

Initially called the Church of Jesus, Yahweh's Temple was founded in 1947. In 1953 it was changed to the Jesus Church, and in 1981 its present name was adopted. The church's name has been augmented to reflect its primary doctrinal concern, which is to link the identification of Jesus with Yahweh, God of the Old Testament.

The church's theological orientation is "oneness" or Apostolic, baptizing in the name of Jesus only. It is similar to that of the Church of God (Cleveland, Tennessee), but differs in its acceptance of the use of Hebrew transliterations of the name of God or the Creator. The church's name is a reflection of the belief that Jesus is the proper name of God, Christ, and the church. Names such as Churches of Christ, Church of God, and Pentecostal are rejected. The church also observes Saturday as the Sabbath.

Under the leadership of Bishop Samuel E. Officer, a former member of the Church of God (Cleveland, Tennessee), the church maintains an intricate structure of four wheels within wheels, based on Ezekiel 10:10. Because its organization is founded upon the belief that each member has a special place to work within the body, each wheel has a "hub" of elders, "spokes" of helpers, a "band" for service, and the "rim" of membership. At the center is the international bishop, who is the theocratic and episcopal authority. There are bishops on both the national and state levels, with deacons serving locally.

At this time, it is not known whether the organization remains active. The last reported membership, in 1973, listed about ten thousand members.

Group Type: Ecumenical/nondenominational
Founded: 1947
Membership: In 1973, 10,000 persons
Publications: *The Light of the World*

Orthodox

African Orthodox Church

112 West 129th Street
New York, NY 10027
The Reverend Stafford J. Sweeting, Archbishop and
Patriarch

The African Orthodox Church was established at a meeting of African American clergy at the Church of the Good Shepherd in New York City on September 2, 1921. Black suffragan bishops (who had no right to succession and no vote in the house of bishops) had been established in 1910 because of unacknowledged discrimination in the Protestant Episcopal Church. The church had a significant African American membership, which grew after the Civil War. It took the position that because the church did not recognize racial differences, there was no need to raise blacks to the bishopric simply on the basis of race or because of the demands of African American church members.

Dr. George A. McGuire, an Episcopal priest from the West Indies, had served parishes in Antigua and the United States, but opted to study medicine at Jefferson Memorial College (he graduated with an M.D. in 1910). He hoped to be considered for the post of Suffragan Bishop of Arkansas. After completing his M.D. program, he served at St. Bartholomew's Episcopal Church in Cambridge, Massachusetts. He then became the Secretary of the Commission for Work among Blacks under the church's Board of Missions.

McGuire returned to Antigua after several years to build St. Paul's Church in Sweets, where he was baptized. He returned to the United States after six years to support Marcus Garvey, who had established the Universal Negro Improvement Association (UNIA) by this time.

The meeting of independent black clergy in New York City in 1921 resulted in the establishment of the first Synod of the new African Universal Church and the designation of Dr. McGuire as its bishop-elect. The Synod then began discussions with the Russian Orthodox Church in America to secure Episcopal orders for the new bishop. However, the Russian Orthodox Church wanted to control the newly established jurisdiction if they consecrated McGuire. Archbishop Joseph Rene Vilatte of the American Catholic Church was then contacted, and he was willing to confer orders without seeking to control the new church. Dr. McGuire was consecrated as the first bishop of the new church on September 29, 1921, in the Church of the Lady of Good Death in Chicago.

Bishop McGuire emphasized education of the clergy (who often did not serve full-time) and led efforts to organize Endich Theological Seminary in New York City (although it is still in existence, it has not sought to become an accredited degree-granting institution). He also encouraged at least some support of clergy by each congregation. The church's growth throughout his administration was slow but steady, and the church was stable in both leadership and membership until his death on November 10, 1934.

Archbishop William E. J. Robertson had been appointed to succeed McGuire after his death, but dissatisfaction among the clergy resulted in a schism and the establishment of the African

Orthodox Church of New York and Massachusetts, led by Bishop Richard Grant Barrow, McGuire's closest associate. In 1935, controversy surrounding the Very Reverend Monsignor Fred A. Toote resulted in the suspension of several bishops, priests, and ministers who took sides against the church's administration. Efforts to establish a new church led to a court battle, and on June 8, 1938, the New York Superior Court granted a permanent injunction to the African Orthodox Church against the new schismatic group. The group was forbidden to use the name of the church or to acknowledge George Alexander McGuire as founder of the new church. The judge, asking for the cooperation of the African Orthodox Church Primate, Bishop Robertson, in order to avoid further litigation, called for a hearing for those who wanted to return to the parent body. Each case was heard individually. At a conclave of bishops held at Holy Cross Pro-Cathedral on September 13, 1938, Robertson was unanimously elected Patriarch, succeeding the late Patriarch, Bishop McGuire. On April 30, 1941, the Patriarchate of the African Orthodox Church was incorporated, giving the church legal status in the state of New York and allowing for solicitation of funds from the general public.

Bishop Fred A. Toote and Bishop Gladstone St. Claire Nurse eventually succeeded Bishop Barrow as leaders of the new church. Nurse began an effort to reunite the two factions of the church. The two bodies joined together on February 22, 1964, under Bishop Robertson (head of the original church) who had taken the patriarchal name of James I. However, in an obvious effort to maintain control of the reunited church, Bishop Robertson consecrated several bishops just before the merger. After Robertson's death, Bishop Nurse (who had not protested Robertson's consecration) was elected as the new leader of the church. His efforts to realign all elements of the church were successful, and upon his death Archbishop William R. Miller succeeded him and served from 1976 to August 1981. He resigned at the Annual Synod of the church and was succeeded by Archbishop Stafford J. Sweeting, its current leader.

The church has affiliated parishes in the West Indies, Nigeria, Uganda, and Ghana, in addition to its small following in the United States. In 1984 one of its strongest parishes, led by Bishop G. Duncan Hinkson, left the church and formed the African Orthodox Church of the West (see narrative).

Group Type: Denomination
Founded: September 2, 1921
Membership: In 1983, 5,100 persons in 17 parishes in the United States
Publications: *The Trumpet*, the Reverend Father Harold Furblur, Box 1925, Boston, MA 02105
Meetings: An annual synod

African Orthodox Church of the West

5831 South Indiana Avenue
Chicago, IL 60637
Bishop G. Duncan Hinkson, Founder

The African Orthodox Church of the West is the result of a split from the African Orthodox Church led by Bishop G.

Duncan Hinkson in 1984. A medical doctor and pastor of St. Augustine's African Orthodox Church on Chicago's southside, he left and formed a new jurisdiction from what had been one of the parent church's strongest parishes.

The doctrine, rituals, and teachings of the church are the same as that of the parent body, but it is independent in administration. Bishop Franzo King, who was consecrated by Bishop Hinkson, is in charge of the home parish and the San Francisco parish.

Group Type: Denomination
Founded: 1984
Membership: Several hundred persons in 2 parishes, 1 in Chicago, IL, and 1 in San Francisco, CA

Ethiopian Orthodox Church in the United States of America

140-142 West 176th Street
Bronx, NY 10451
(212) 299-2741

The Ethiopian Church, under the Patriarch of Alexandria, thrived in the nationalistic consciousness of the early twentieth century. Partially because of Emperor Haile Selassie's diplomacy in 1929, five native Ethiopians were consecrated bishops; however, they had no dioceses and had limited powers and functions. The Theological College in Addis Ababa was established by the Emperor in 1944. After World War II, an agreement with the Egyptians led to the establishment of the Statute of Independence of the Ethiopian Orthodox Church in 1948. This action freed it from the jurisdiction of Alexandria, as well as from the Coptic Orthodox Church in Egypt. The Ethiopian Orthodox Church joined the World Council of Churches the same year. The church's actual autonomy was realized in 1939, when the bishop of Addis Ababa was made patriarch.

After Haile Selassie was overthrown in 1974, the church came under attack, especially from the Marxist government established in Addis Ababa. The Patriarch, His Holiness Abuna Theopolis, was arrested and removed from office in 1976, and he has not been seen since. Other religious leaders were exiled and several remain detained in Ethiopia. Archbishop Abba Mattheas (head of the Ethiopian Monastery in Jerusalem) defected to the United States in 1978 and began to bring attention to the religious oppression in Ethiopia.

Laike Mandefro, an Ethiopian priest, came to study in the United States in 1959. He and several other priests broke with their United States sponsor, Abuna Gabre Kristos Mikeal of the Ethiopian Coptic Church of North and South America. They began to form a congregation of Ethiopian Americans, first in Brooklyn and later in the Bronx, under the authority of His Grace Archbishop Theopolis. Mandefro was raised to the position of Archmatrite as his work progressed, and he was put in charge of the Ethiopian Church in the West. He moved to Jamaica in 1970 and had established congregations all over the island and missions throughout the Caribbean by 1977. He has since been consecrated bishop and made Archbishop of the Western Hemisphere Diocese.

The American branch of the church became an affiliated communion with the National Council of Churches in 1974, and the Jamaican branch belongs to the Jamaica Council of Churches and the Caribbean Council of Churches. As of 1984,

there were thirty-four parishes and missions with five thousand members and fifteen clergy in the United States, and approximately ten thousand persons in seven parishes and three missions in Jamaica.

Group Type: Denomination
Founded: 1959/early 1960s
Membership: In 1984, 5,000 persons in 34 parishes and missions, and 15 clergy in the United States; approximately 10,000 persons in 7 parishes and 3 missions in Jamaica
Publications: *The Structure of the Church*, 140-142 West 176th Street, Bronx, NY 10453

Ethiopian Orthodox Coptic Church of North America

Church:
2018 7th Avenue
P.O. Box 5573
New York, NY 10027
(212) 220-1885

Archdiocese:
204 W. 121st Street
New York, NY 10027
His Eminence Abuna Nathaniel Joshua Shilohsalem, Metropolitan Archbishop Primate
Bishop George Reeder Apollo, Church Contact

This religious body was formed by the Most Reverend Abuna Gabre Kristos Mikael, an Ethiopian American who established his jurisdiction under the authority of Archbishop Walter M. Propheta of the American Orthodox Catholic Church. The Most Reverend Mikael traveled to Ethiopia in 1959 and was ordained and elevated to the position *Chorepiscopos* by Abuna Basilios, the late patriarch of Ethiopia. He then sponsored three priests and five deacons, who were sent by Abuna Basilios to the United States for advanced study. There they were also to develop a branch of the Ethiopian Orthodox Church. Father Laike Mandefro led the priests in a break from Mikael and formed what would become the Ethiopian Orthodox Church in the United States of America. The parish was under the jurisdiction of the patriarch in Addis Ababa. The Ethiopian Orthodox Coptic Church is still in communion with the American Orthodox Catholic Church, from which some clergy came.

According to the church, the Archbishop of the Archdiocese of the Ethiopian Orthodox Coptic Church of North America inherited the ecclesiastical apostolic line of both the Coptic and Royal Ethiopian lines of succession from the founding fathers of the Ethiopian and Coptic churches in North America. The (African American) Egyptian Coptic branch was founded by His Holiness Archbishop Edwin H. Collins between 1945 and 1947 with permission from the Coptic Orthodox Church of Alexandria, Egypt, by the pope of the church. This authorization came through Ethiopia before Emperor Haile Selassie I decided to establish the Independent Ethiopian Orthodox Church. Archbishop Collins remained under the ecclesiastical authority of the Coptic Pope of Alexandria, Egypt. Collins, a native of British Guyana, was a chaplain in Marcus Garvey's Universal Negro Improvement and Conservation Association (UNIA). He was granted permission from the mother church in Egypt and was subsequently ordained by the bishop of the African Orthodox

Church, which was chartered between 1945 and 1947 in Harlem. He was later consecrated as the archbishop of the African American branch of the Coptic Orthodox Church.

Bishop Collins met with many Ethiopian envoys at their embassy in the United States during the Italian invasion of Ethiopia and secretly with Selassie himself when the Emperor visited Abyssinia Baptist Church in Harlem. Before "Abuna" (archbishop) Gabre Kristos Mikael succeeded Bishop Collins, he was an ordained Coptic priest for seven years under Collins's tutorship. After Collins's death, he received the archbishopric Coptic succession. He entered the Melchizedek priesthood of the church to pursue further study, and he was ordained at the age of twenty-three.

Abuna Mikael chose Abuna Nathaniel Joshua Shilohsalem as his successor because of the preserved union of the two African mother churches of Ethiopia and Egypt of the Ethiopian Orthodox Coptic Church. After gaining approval from the board of clergy of the synod, he became the metropolitan archbishop coadjutant under Mikael, the metropolitan archbishop. Before his death, Archbishop Mikael began the process to open Trinity University Theological College with professor Kassa of Ethiopia. After the forty days of traditional obligatory mourning following Abuna Mikael's death, the Holy Ethiopian Orthodox Coptic Synod declared Abuna Nathaniel the metropolitan archbishop primate of the Ethiopian Orthodox Coptic Church of North and South America.

The women's ministry in the church is made up of the messianic order of Ethiopian royalty. The mothers of the church are called "queen mother abbess." In August, 1988, Abuna Nathaniel established the Royal House of Candace Queen Mother Abbess, named after Queen Candace in Acts 8:27. In the order, there are archabbesses, grand abbesses, and abbesses. The grand archabbess, equivalent to the archbishop of the church, is queen mother over all women auxiliaries and missions. There are also other orders, such as the Royal Sacred Order of the Daughters of the Queen of Sheba (in charge of the cultural/educational institutes of women), the Royal Sacred Order of the Daughters of Zion (in charge of missionary work and clergy), and the Royal Sacred Order of the Sacred Shrine of the Black Madonna and Child. The orders were established in order to give back to black women of all nationalities their royal heritage, stripped from them during slavery, because they are considered the mothers of the nation.

The church maintains a collection of African sculpture, paintings, messianic and ancient paintings and scrolls that record the church's history. The collection has been on display and is currently touring the country. Future plans include establishing an African museum for the arts.

Also known as the Church of the Ark of the Covenant of Redemption, the church had branches in Brooklyn and Queens, New York, and in Florida. There are approximately three archbishops, thirteen bishops, thirty unmarried priests, twenty deacons and subdeacons, and eight abbesses. The polity of the church is episcopal, and male officers of the church (in descending order) are: metropolitan archbishop primate, metropolitan archbishop, house of archbishops, Echege (over all orders of the church), archmandarites, archpriests, priests, archdeacons, deacons, and subdeacons.

As of 1987, there were churches in Trinidad, Mexico, and Pennsylvania. There are two churches in Brooklyn, one using Latin rites and the other using the rite most common in the church, the Coptic Ethiopian rite. Worship services are conducted in English for the predominantly African American congregants. All bishops are celibate, in the tradition of the Eastern church, but priests may be either celibate or married. The church was in the spotlight when it raised a white man to the episcopate as bishop of Brooklyn in 1972. The two Ethiopian churches do not maintain a good relationship, as each questions the other's legitimacy.

Group Type: Denomination
Founded: 1940s
Membership: An estimated several hundred persons in the 3 parishes in New York and Pennsylvania

Pan African Orthodox

Shrines of the Black Madonna of the Pan-African Orthodox Christian Church

944 Gordon Street, SW
Atlanta, GA 30310
(404) 752-5490
The Reverend Jaramogi Abebe Agyeman, Holy Patriarch and Founder
Cardinal Donald B. Lester, Southern Regional Bishop

In 1953, three hundred members of St. Mark Presbyterian Church in Detroit left that congregation over issues relating to its community involvement. These members formed St. Mark Congregational Church, which changed its name in 1954 to Central Congregational Church. They purchased their first piece of property that year and, in 1957, purchased a church building on Linwood and Hogarth streets.

During the late 1950s, the theology and philosophy emphasizing the sociocultural mission of the church and the development of its youth began to evolve within the congregation. In 1962, the church, together with Pastor Albert B. Cleage, Jr., became very active in Detroit community affairs, including school system issues. Also in that year, the church began publishing the *Illustrated News*, a biweekly newspaper specifically concerned with issues confronting the African American community. Very active politically, the Reverend Cleage ran for governor of Michigan on the "Freedom Now" ticket in 1962.

In 1966, Central Congregational Church formed the Inner City Organizing Committee that, in turn, spawned other organizations: the Inner City Housing Conference; the Black Retail Employees Association; the Inner City Parents Council; the Black Teacher's Workshop; the Inner City Student's Organization; the Afro-American Committee Against Racist Wars; and the Michigan Inner City Organizing Committee.

The unveiling of a fifteen-foot painting of the Black Madonna and Child in the church building in 1966, coupled with the Reverend Cleage's assertion that Jesus was black, marked the launch of the Black Christian Nationalist Movement (BCN). The Reverend Cleage began preaching a series of sermons consistent with a revolutionary Black Christian Ministry that were published in 1968 as *Black Messiah*. In 1969, the concept of a "Black Nation" evolved from the church, and a Black Christian Ministry creed was developed and implemented. The church changed its name to the Shrine of the Black Madonna, opened a BCN Training Center and Residence Hall, which housed a bookstore and cultural center, and began publishing a monthly newspaper, *The Black Nation News*. In 1970, the Reverend Cleage changed his name to Jaramogi Abebe Agyeman. In 1972, Agyeman published a second book: *Black Christian Nationalism: New Directions for the Black Church*.

In 1974, the church implemented plans for geographic expansion by forming a cadre to open a center in Atlanta. Southern Region Shrine #9 Regional Offices and Training Center opened in 1975. A shrine in Kalamazoo, Michigan, and Houston, Texas, followed in 1977. Then, in 1978, the first Pan African Synod was held in Houston. There, the Shrine of the Black Madonna was established as a new denomination and the name Pan African Orthodox Christian Church was adopted. The Reverend Cleage, however, continues to hold affiliation with the United Church of Christ, Inc.

Pan African Orthodox Christian Church expansion continues. It operates a meditation, educational, and technological center in Detroit, and a communications and technological center in Atlanta. In Houston, it operates the BCN Missionary Training Center, Shrine of the Black Madonna Cultural Center and Bookstore, Meditation Center, and Retreat Center. There are Shrine Community Service Centers in all three of the regional locations. The church is particularly proud of its Youth Technological Training Program in Detroit (which is fully computer-equipped), where young people between the ages of nine and fifteen are being trained to survive in modern, technological society.

The church practices a revolutionary black Christian ministry, based upon the teachings of the Black Messiah, Jesus Christ. It interprets the ministry of Jesus as a movement toward the liberation of black people. It emphasizes that through submission to the will of God, people can be changed and self-realized in order to actualize their maximum human potential. These changes are necessary in order to overcome the black conditions of oppression, exploitation, and powerlessness present worldwide. The Black Nationalist Creed of the church maintains that these things exist because the world now stands in opposition to the will of God. The ministry of the church is directed toward social transformation and empowerment for the black person. Guidance toward these ends is perceived as coming from the Holy Spirit. Pan African Orthodox Christianity emphasizes the well-being of the total community. Survival and salvation are understood to be dependent upon rejection of individualism.

The conclave of the church meets annually in October. In the southern region, the denomination is headed by Cardinal Donald B. Lester, Regional Bishop and First Cardinal.

Group Type: Denomination
Founded: 1953
Publications: *The Black Messiah* (1968) by the Reverend Cleage and *Black Christian Nationalism: New Directions for the Black Church* (1972) by the Reverend Agyeman (formerly the Reverend Albert B. Cleage)
Meetings: Annual conclave in October

Presbyterian

Second Cumberland Presbyterian Church

226 Church Street, NW
Huntsville, AL 35801
(205) 536-7481
The Reverend Dr. Robert S. Wood, General Secretary
The Reverend McKinley Jones, Moderator, General
  Assembly

In 1869, freed slaves chose to separate from the Cumberland Presbyterian Church and constituted a new denomination that expressed their freedom. This new body called itself the Colored Cumberland Presbyterian Church. Since 1874, it has grown to encompass 153 congregations in eleven states, with concentrations in Tennessee, Texas, Alabama, and Kentucky. In 1957, the name was officially changed to Second Cumberland Presbyterian Church. The present organization is divided into sixteen presbyteries and four synods (Alabama, Kentucky, Tennessee, and Texas), with membership in excess of 15,458 communicants. This is the only predominantly African American denomination in the United States adhering to the Reformed theology.

The Second Cumberland Presbyterian Church and the (predominantly white) Cumberland Presbyterian Church are partners in ministry in a variety of ways. The two groups have been discussing unification since 1967 and are on schedule to reunite in 1992. Through its membership in the World Alliance of Reformed churches, the denomination engages in a variety of ministries with other Reformed churches.

The church headquarters are in Huntsville, Alabama. It meets in General Assembly (a delegated assemblage) annually. There is also an annual ministers' conference (in the fall) and an annual conference of church officers, both are held in Huntsville, Alabama. The Reverend Dr. Robert S. Wood, General Secretary of the church, also serves as editor of the monthly publication, *The Cumberland Flag*.

Group Type: Denomination
Founded: 1874
Membership: 15,458 persons, 16 presbyteries, 143 congregations, and 210 ordained clergy in 4 synods (Alabama, Kentucky, Tennessee, and Texas)
Publications: *The Cumberland Flag*
Meetings: An annual General Assembly beginning the second Wednesday in June and church leadership conference every fall, both held in Huntsville, AL

Spiritualist

"Although the origins of the African American spiritual movement remain uncertain, it would seem to have originated in large cities in the North and the South toward the first quarter of the twentieth century. African American spiritual churches combine elements of Vodoun, spiritualism (a belief system based on regular communication with the dead and the spirit world), Roman Catholicism, black Protestantism, and other belief systems."

—Father Elias Farajajé-Jones, Dr. Theol.
   Assistant Professor of World Religions
   Howard University School of Divinity
   Washington, D.C.

Metropolitan Spiritual Churches of Christ, Inc.

4315 S. Wabash Avenue
Chicago, IL 60653
(312) 373-7700
the late Dr. I. Logan Kearse, International President
The Reverend Eugene Gray

The Metropolitan Spiritual Churches of Christ, Inc., was founded in 1925 by Bishop William Frank Taylor and Elder Leviticus Lee Boswell in Kansas City, Missouri. It was subsequently led by The Reverend Clarence H. Cobbs, founder and pastor of the First Church of Deliverance in Chicago. After his death in 1979, Dr. I. Logan Kearse, founder and pastor of the Cornerstone Church of Christ in Baltimore, became the international president. The church is made up of a conglomerate of churches bearing the titles Church of Christ, Church of Deliverance, or Spiritual Church. Its purpose is to educate and facilitate a ministry that will cause people to become self-actualized through an understanding of their spirituality.

The Metropolitan Spiritual Churches of Christ, Inc., do not consider themselves a denomination, but rather a unit of churches that share a similar way of life—that of the life of the spirit. To be spiritual is to have direct contact with one's inner being as well as with the ultimate reality that is viewed and accepted to be God who manifests Himself throughout God's creation. The organization has taken principles of the Pentecostal and Christian Science faiths and baptizes in the name of Jesus and in the name of the Father and the Son. It teaches reincarnation, and the Gospel is considered "foursquare"—preaching, teaching, healing, and prophesy. It also accepts the Apostles' Creed, replacing "catholic" with "universal."

There are approximately eighty-nine congregations, primarily in the Midwest and on the East and West coasts. The organization has enjoyed widespread growth in Africa, with congregations in Liberia, Ghana, and Sierra Leone. There are several congregations in Europe as well. The body meets twice annually, the major conference being held in the third week of July and the midyear congress in the first week of November. A manual is published that includes information on the group's purpose, departments, and meetings.

Group Type: Council of churches; lay/clergy
Founded: 1925
Membership: Approximately 89 churches worldwide
Publications: A manual
Meetings: An annual conference is held during the third week in July, and the midyear congress is held in the first week of November

National Colored Spiritualist Association of America

14228 Wisconsin Street
Detroit, MI 48238

Group Type: Denomination

National Colored Spiritualist Association of Churches

1245 West Watkins Road
Phoenix, AZ 85007
The Reverend Nellie Mae Taylor

The National Colored Spiritualist Association of Churches was formed in 1922 following a split of African American members from the National Spiritualist Association of Churches soon after World War I. Its doctrine is taken from the parent body. Member churches are located in Detroit, Phoenix, New York City, Miami, St. Petersburg, Chicago, Columbus (OH), and Charleston (SC).

Group Type: Denomination
Founded: 1922
Publications: *The Nationalist Spiritualist Reporter*, 1245 West Watkins Road, Phoenix, AZ 85007

Universal Church, the Mystical Body of Christ

No current address
Bishop R. O. Frazier, Founder

The Universal Church, the Mystical Body of Christ, was founded in 1970 by its current leader, Bishop R. O. Frazier, in Saginaw, Michigan, in 1970. The church publishes *The Light of Life Herald*.

Group Type: Denomination
Founded: 1970
Publications: *The Light of Life Herald*

BODIES OTHER THAN CHRISTIAN

Black Hebrews

Church of God and Saints of Christ

3927 Bridge Road
Suffolk, VA 23435
(804) 484-1161
The Reverend Levi S. Plummer, Executive Bishop
The Reverend Ezra Locke, General Secretary

The Church of God and Saints of Christ was founded in Lawrence, Kansas, in 1896 by William S. Crowdy. Members of this denomination celebrate all Jewish Holy Days and Feast Days that have biblical authority and support. The Sabbath is also observed on the seventh day (Saturday). It is believed that the congregation is built upon the patriarchs, prophets, and apostles of the Jewish traditions. The denomination differentiates between prophetic Judaism—following the living insight into the spiritual ideal to its fullest implication—as opposed to legalistic Judaism. The Decalogue is accepted as the standard of conduct for all mankind. Also known as the Church of God Temple Beth El, the church holds its annual meeting the first week in April.

Group Type: Denomination
Founded: 1896
Meetings: Annual meeting first week in April

Church of God (Black Jews)

No current address

Prophet F. S. Cherry, the founder of the Church of God (Black Jews), claimed to have received a vision calling him to the ministry. Although no information is extant concerning his early years, he was sent to America to begin the church in Philadelphia in the early twentieth century. He educated himself and became proficient in both Yiddish and Hebrew. He became known for his speaking ability.

According to the *Encyclopedia of American Religions* (3rd ed.), the Church of God is open only to African Americans whose identity is traced to the Jews of the Bible. White Jews are not considered legitimate. The church's teachings include the belief that God and Jesus were black and that the first men were also black. Blacks came from Jacob. The first white man was Gehazi, who received his whiteness as a curse (see II Kings 5:27). The yellow race resulted from the continued mixing of whites and blacks. Esau is considered the first red man (see Genesis 25:25).

Passover begins the church's new year in April, and Saturday is considered the true Sabbath. The church also believes that speaking in tongues is nonsense. The observation of Christian holidays, consumption of pork, taking of photographs, and divorce are forbidden. Believers also espouse that the end of the period that started with creation is coming soon, and Black Jews will return in the year A.D. 2000 to institute the millennium.

Group Type: Denomination

Commandment Keepers Congregation of the Living God

1 E. 123rd Street
New York, NY 10035
Rabbi David M. Dore

The Commandment Keepers Congregation of the Living God was founded in the West Indian black community of Harlem, New York. Arnold Josiah Ford, a leader in Marcus Garvey's Universal Negro Improvement Association, renounced Christianity, adopted Judaism, and learned Hebrew. He subsequently founded the Beth B'nai Abraham congregation in Harlem in 1924.

Soon after the organization of the group he met Arthur Wentworth Matthew (1892-1973). According to the *Encyclopedia of American Religions* (3rd ed.), Matthew was born in Lagos, Nigeria, and subsequently moved with his family to St. Kitts, British West Indies, and finally to New York in 1911. He later became a minister in the Church of the Living God, the Pillar and Ground of the Truth. The denomination, founded by Mother Mary Lena Lewis Tate, had endorsed Garvey's Universal Negro Improvement Association. In 1919, Matthew and eight other men founded the Commandment Keepers Church of the Living God, and he became bishop of the denomination. He first met white Jews in Harlem, and in the 1920s he met Ford. It is believed that Matthew learned Orthodox Judaism and Hebrew from Ford and also acquired ritual materials.

The two men learned of and began to identify with the Falashas, the black Jews of Ethiopia. Ford's congregation had financial troubles in 1930, and he subsequently turned his membership over to Matthew's care. He then moved to Ethiopia, where he remained for the rest of his life. Matthew's identification with Ethiopian Jews continued to grow, and he declared himself and his followers the Falashas in America when Haile Selassie was crowned emperor in 1935. The Falashas are members of a Hamitic tribe living in Ethiopia and practicing Judaism. He also claimed credentials from Haile Selassie.

The Commandment Keepers believe blacks are really the Ethiopian Falashas as well as the biblical Hebrews, whose knowledge of their name and religion was taken during slavery. Followers believe that the biblical patriarchs were black, and Christianity is considered to be the religion of Gentiles or whites and thus rejected.

The Commandment Keepers make an earnest attempt to align themselves with Orthodox Jewish practices and teach Hebrew, which is revered as a sacred language. The Sabbath is observed on Friday evenings and Saturday mornings, and Jewish holidays are observed. The group also keeps kosher food laws. Leaders are trained in the Mishnah, Josephus, the Talmud, legalism, and Jewish history through an Ethiopian Hebrew Rabbinical college. Elements traditionally associated with Christianity and the African American religious experience—footwashing, healing, and gospel hymns—are a part of the religion. However, services are free of the emotion commonly found in that experience. Matthew called this emotional feeling "niggeritions."

He also taught a practice taken from conjuring (the traditional folk magic attributed to southern African Americans) known as Kabbalistic Science. He believed that he could heal and change situations by conjuring, which was accomplished through four angels. The right angel must be called upon for results.

Rabbi David M. Dore, the current leader, is the grandson of Arthur Wentworth Matthew and a graduate of Yeshiva University. As of the early 1970s, there were approximately three thousand persons in several congregations in the New York metropolitan area and in the Northeast.

Group Type: Denomination
Founded: 1924
Membership: As of the early 1970s, approximately 3,000 persons in several congregations in metropolitan New York and the Northeast

House of Judah

Wetumpka, AL 36092

The House of Judah was founded by Prophet William A. Lewis in 1965. He was converted to Judaism by a street preacher in Chicago in the 1960s. He converted a small following, which worshipped in a storefront building on the southside of Chicago. In 1971, the group moved to a twenty-two-acre tract near Grand Junction, Michigan.

In 1983, the House of Judah gained attention when a young boy in the group was beaten to death. According to the *Encyclopedia of American Religions* (3rd ed.), the incident focused attention on the body because of its advocacy of corporal punishment. The boy's mother was sentenced to prison for manslaughter, and by 1985 the group relocated to a farm in rural Alabama, which is where Lewis was born.

The beliefs of the body are similar to those of the Church of God and Saints of Christ. It teaches that the Old Testament Jews were black and were derived from Jacob and his son, Judah, who were both black (Jeremiah 14:2). It also believes that Jesus and Solomon were black. According to the body, Jerusalem is the real land of blacks, rather than Africa, and the white Jew (the devil, Revelation 2:9), who currently occupies it, will be driven out. The biblical reference of Revelation 2:9 is used to support the group's belief that the white Jew is the devil. The House of Judah believes God will send a deliverer to take blacks from the United States to Jerusalem, and this person will be a second Moses to lead his people to the promised land.

As of 1985, there were approximately eighty members living communally on the farm in Wetumpka, Alabama.

Group Type: Denomination
Founded: 1965
Membership: As of 1985, approximately 80 members

Nation of Yahweh

Temple of Love
2766 NW 62nd Street
Miami, FL 33147
Yahweh ben Yahweh, Founder and Spiritual Leader

The Nation of Yahweh, also known as the Hebrew Israelites or the Temple of Love, was founded by Yahweh ben Yahweh in the 1970s. Formerly known by his slave name, Hulon Mitchell, Jr., and also called Moses Israel, Yahweh was raised in a Pentecostal church where his father was a minister. He later left the church and became the leader of a mosque in the Nation of Islam.

According to the *Encyclopedia of American Religions* (3d ed.), the Nation of Yahweh teaches that there is one God whose proper name is Yahweh. According to scriptural references found in Daniel 7:9, Revelation 1:13-15, and Deuteronomy 7:21, members believe that God is black with woolly hair. Blacks are considered to be the true lost tribe of Judah and will soon return to Israel. God's son, Yahweh ben Yahweh, has been sent to be the savior and deliverer of God's chosen people.

Members of the Nation of Yahweh renounce their slave names upon joining the body and take the surname "Israel." They are noted for wearing white robes (as stated in Ecclesiastes 9:8 and Revelation 3:4-5, 18) to show that they know God. White people are considered to be the devil, the adversary of God, and the product of Eve's adulterous relationship with the serpent in the Garden of Eden. All people, regardless of race, who oppose God or who are wicked, immoral, or evil are considered devils. They also believe that any person can be saved by faith in Yahweh ben Yahweh, regardless of race. Family unity, charity, chastity, peace, love, and harmony are stressed by the body. Members also support such efforts as education, health care, better housing, and voter registration.

The Nation of Yahweh has been under investigation for crimes committed in the Miami area. In 1981, Aston Green, a former member who had publicly criticized the Temple of Love, was decapitated in western Dade County after being apprehended at the temple and beaten. The two persons he lived with (also former members of the body) were attacked a few days later. A man was shot to death, and an attempt to kill a woman was made by cutting her throat and shooting her.

On November 7, 1990, Yahweh ben Yahweh, his chief lieutenant, Judith Israel (also known as Linda Gaines), and several other members of the organization were arrested in New Orleans and Lafayette, Louisiana; Atlanta, Georgia; and Durham, North Carolina. These arrests were the result of a four-year investigation by the FBI and police in Miami, Dade County, and Delray Beach, Florida. The three-count federal indictment naming Yahweh and sixteen followers listed extortion, racketeering, and racketeering conspiracy among the charges for crimes committed from 1981 to 1987 in Dade and Palm Beach counties. Yahweh faces up to sixty years in prison for directing the illegal acts. The indictment charges that approximately fourteen murders have been committed, among them some former members of the Nation of Yahweh who dissented from the leader. Other crimes have been described as acts of retaliation against persons who interfered with activities of the body, such as the acquisition of property, the collection of donations, and the selling of Yahweh products. The arrests follow information from a former member of the body, Robert Rozier, who pled guilty to committing four murders, including those of two tenants who resisted eviction from an apartment building bought by the Nation of Yahweh. In exchange for his twenty-two-year sentence, he guaranteed the FBI that he would reveal Yahweh for them.

There is also an inner circle of the Nation of Yahweh known as the "Brotherhood." Members were only initiated into this secret society after killing a "white devil"—a white person—and bringing a severed body part to the leader as proof. One suspect still at large, Ardmore Canton III, has been accused of killing a homeless white man, Clair Walters, in May 1986 and cutting off his ear.

In 1988, there were reputedly temples or congregations in thirty-seven cities as well as followers across the country and in sixteen countries around the world. Accounts associated with the body's recent activities place the membership at approximately 2,000 persons, mostly in the Miami area. As of 1988, there were also more than forty businesses owned through the corporate entity, the Temple of Love, which supported the organization and its members. The Nation of Yahweh publishes the *Yahweh Magazine*.

Group Type: Denomination
Founded: 1970s
Membership: Approximately 2,000 persons, mostly in the Miami area
Publications: Yahweh Magazine

Original Hebrew Israelite Nation

Communicators Press
Box 19504
Chicago, IL 60649

The Original Hebrew Israelite Nation, also known as the Black Israelites or Black Hebrews, was organized in the 1960s by its current leader, Ben Ammi Carter. Formerly known as G. Parker, Carter studied Judaism with a rabbi and also with Shaleah Ben-Israel. Carter and Ben-Israel incorporated the concept of Black Zionism, or a movement to reestablish or support the Jewish national state of Israel by blacks, into prevalent concepts of Black Jewish ideas. The headquarters of the movement was the A-Beta Cultural Center on Chicago's southside, where membership grew rapidly.

According to the *Encyclopedia of American Religions* (3rd ed.), the body first gained recognition when some of its members attempted to migrate first to Africa and then to Israel in the late 1960s. Their initial move to Liberia was considered reminiscent of the Hebrews' loss in the desert for forty years to rid themselves of the effects of slavery. Members were not successful in their negotiations with the Israeli ambassador to Liberia to make a further move to Israel. In 1968, Carter and thirty-eight of his followers flew directly to Israel from Chicago and were given temporary sanctions and work permits. The Liberian faction soon joined them. However, by the time strict immigration sanctions were employed against the group in 1971, over three hundred had migrated. Many of the members came to the country by using tourist visas and subsequently destroying them when they moved to the colony at Dimona. As of 1980, between fifteen hundred and two thousand members had moved to Israel.

The group maintains a communal life-style, although under harsh conditions and a persistent threat of deportation because of its illegal alien status. Members who immigrated illegally cannot get housing, and children are not allowed to attend public schools. The Original Hebrew Israelite Nation has asked Israel for land to create their own community. Its illegal and unorthodox ways of reaching Israel have hindered the group's aspirations. In 1980 it gained notoriety as members in the United States were charged with methodical theft of airline

tickets, credit cards, and money to aid its members in moving to Israel. Additional attention was brought to the group's plight on television's "60 Minutes" news program.

The members of the body believe that they are the descendants of the ten lost tribes of Israel and as such, Jews by birth. Jewish rituals are celebrated and the Sabbath is kept. Carter, the chief rabbi, is aided by a divine council of twelve princes, each for one of the twelve ancient tribes of Israel. There are seven princes under the princes who are responsible for distributing food, clothing, and shelter; providing education; economics; transportation; recreation and entertainment; sports; life preservation; and sanitation. The American segment of the group was led by Prince Asiel Ben Israel during the early 1980s. One distinctive variation from traditional Judaism is the practice of polygamy by the body, with men allowed to have as many as seven wives. It has also abandoned the synagogue structure.

As of 1980, the membership was estimated to include fifteen hundred persons in Israel—nine hundred at Dimona, four hundred at Arad, one hundred at Mitzpe Ramon, and one hundred at Eilat. There are also approximately three thousand followers scattered in the United States in cities such as Atlanta, Chicago, and Washington, D.C. On July 3, 1990, Israel and the United States reached an agreement on the status of the Black Israelites illegally residing in Israel. Israel was to offer work permits to members of the Original Hebrew Israelite Nation, and the United States will consider annulling the members' renunciation of their U.S. citizenship and renewing their passports. According to the report by the Religious News Service, Israeli officials hope that many members will return to the United States as soon as possible.

Group Type: Denomination
Founded: 1960s
Membership: As of 1980, approximately 1,500 hundred persons in Israel and 3,000 persons in the United States

Rastafarians

No central address

The Rastafarian movement traces its origins to Jamaica and the activities of the Maroons, Marcus Garvey, and the ascent of Haile Selassie I to the throne of Ethiopia in 1930. Garvey had been exposed to the history of Africa, particularly Egyptian and Ethiopian. He and others embraced "Ethiopianism," the belief that Ethiopia (which came to mean all of Africa) was the cradle of the black race and that its contributions to the development of civilization were paramount to the realization of racial equality for the black diaspora. His writings and speeches contained numerous references to the history of Ethiopia and biblical references to the same. Garvey came to the United States to promote his ideology of black nationalism and the return of blacks to Africa—their true homeland—particularly through his organization, the Universal Negro Improvement Association (UNIA). In 1927, Garvey prophesied that a black prince would be crowned king of Africa and that this would be a sign that the oppression of blacks would begin to dissipate.

Ras Tafari Makonnen was crowned Emperor of Ethiopia in 1930 and took as his title *Haile Selassie I, King of Kings, Lord of Lords, His Imperial Majesty the Conquering Lion of the Tribe of Judah, Elect of God*. The name Haile Selassie means power or might of the Holy Trinity. He was the great grandson of King Saheka Selassie of Shoa, claiming to be a direct descendant of David, and was the 225th in an unbroken line of Ethiopian kings beginning with King Solomon and the Queen of Sheba (some believe that he placed himself in the legendary line of King Solomon). His name and titles combined led many to believe that he was indeed the savior of blacks around the world. Important to this belief was biblical verification and support, found in Revelation 5:2-5 and 19:16, about the Lion of Judah breaking the seven seals and opening the Book of Life. Selassie's divinity and the redemption of the black race were also supported in Ezekiel 37:19, 22-25; Isaiah 43: 1-15, 24-28, and 65:9; and Revelation 1 and 19:20 (the latter of which was fulfilled when Selassie returned to power from exile in 1941).

Several Jamaicans—Archibald Dunkley, Joseph Hibbert, Robert Hinds, and Leonard Howell—began to take Selassie's ascension seriously, and each independently promoted the fact that Selassie was the Messiah of black people within their own group of followers. In 1934, a more secular group developed with its foundation based on Garvey's teachings and Selassie's divinity, as espoused by Dunkley, Hibbert, and Howell. It was led by Vernal Davis and Paul Ervington. Dunkley used the King James version of the Bible to promote his teachings, whereas Hibbert began to develop the Ethiopian Coptic Church. Howell, however, attracted the most followers.

Howell sold more than five thousand pictures of Haile Selassie to Jamaicans, claiming that they were passports to Ethiopia. In addition, his movement began to take on a revolutionary, nationalist position. According to Dr. Leonard Barnett, who has done extensive research on Rastafarians, Howell publicly advocated six points: 1) hatred of the entire white race; 2) complete superiority of the black race; 3) revenge on whites for their wickedness; 4) the negation, persecution, and humiliation of Jamaica's government and legal bodies; 5) a move toward returning to Africa; and 6) the acknowledgment of Emperor Haile Selassie I as the Supreme Being and the only ruler of blacks. Howell was arrested on December 16, 1933, and spent two years in prison for fraud.

After his release, he bought an abandoned estate near Kingston and founded the "Pinnacle," a commune of from 500 to over 1,600 Rastafarians, who worked on behalf of the Ethiopian Salvation Society. The movement was less aggressive and somewhat covert at this time. Its life-style was patterned after that of the Maroons, many of whom were their ancestors. Howell reportedly served as "chief" in the African tradition and was said to have as many as thirteen wives. There was trouble with the law again, primarily for the growth and marketing of marijuana (ganja) and acts of violence against Jamaicans who were harassed for paying their taxes to the government instead of to the Rastafarians in the name of Selassie. The police were made aware of their existence and location, and about seventy members of the commune were arrested in 1941, but Howell was not among them. He was finally apprehended and served another prison sentence. When he was released in 1943, Howell began a security force of Rastafarian men known as "locksmen," or "Ethiopian warriors." The men began to let their hair grow long in the now familiar "dreadlocks," which resemble a lion's mane. Police raids continued, resulting in the arrest of 163 persons in 1954, but by this time Howell's position was faltering. He had begun to declare that he was divine (even claiming to be Haile Se-

lassie), but those of the Pinnacle compound began to doubt his divinity. He was committed to a mental hospital in 1960.

After the destruction of the Pinnacle by the police and the loss of leadership, the movement operated primarily in Kingston in splinter groups. Although the organization was detested by the police and the government, it soon began to flourish throughout Jamaica. The Ethiopian World Federation, Inc., of New York (EWF) was established in 1937 as a lobbying organization for support of Ethiopia's fight against Italy. A branch of the organization was founded in Jamaica in 1938, and it is believed that Howell and his group, the Ethiopian Salvation Society, knew of it and were possibly supported by it. Mrs. Mamie Robinson, a leader of the EWF, came to Jamaica in 1955 and infused the Rastafarian movement with new life. She announced that Emperor Haile Selassie was developing a merchant navy whose ships would soon sail from Addis Ababa to American ports, and it was also possible that they would come to Jamaica. Soon after her announcement, Jamaicans were informed that the emperor had granted 500 acres of land (that belonged to him personally) to the black people of the West (actually to those Africans abroad who had aided Ethiopia during the Italian-Ethiopian war). This, in the eyes of many, was a sure sign of a coming return to Africa, and both the Rastafarian movement and the EWF virtually doubled in membership immediately. This happened at a time when many Jamaicans were going to England to seek a better way of life. The call for repatriation was much like a religious revival.

In 1958, there was a month-long convention of over 300 members in Kingston at the Back-O-Wall headquarters in order to attempt to unite the various factions that had developed. It has since been called the *Nyabingi*, an East African term referring to a religiopolitical cult that resisted colonial domination from roughly 1890 to 1928 (*Nyabingi*, or meetings, have since become a part of the Rastafarian life-style and are defined as gatherings of the brethren for inspiration, feasting, social contact, exhortation, and smoking). The meeting received much press attention and became progressively militant, culminating in the attempted takeover of Kingston by bolder members. Police raids and arrests followed. By this time, Prince Emmanuel had become a leader of one of the segments of the community, and it was he, in fact, who called the meeting. He, like Howell, spoke of his own divinity and was eventually arrested along with several followers in a police raid.

In 1959, the Reverend Claudius Henry, "the Repairer of the Breach," became involved in eradicating the national emergency that resulted from the activities of the Rastafarians. He was founder of the African Reformed Church, which drew large numbers of former Rastafarians, and became, in essence, the leader of a large segment of the organization. He sold cards to the masses inviting them to an emancipation jubilee to be held on August 1, 1959, the anniversary of the end of slavery in Jamaica. The celebration was to be a meeting about the repatriation movement. October 5, 1959 was to be the date that Jamaicans would return to their homeland, with the cards serving as their unnecessary passports. Hundreds of Rastafarians came to the church headquarters, and having sold their possessions, they were ready to return to Africa. Henry explained that October 5 was the date when the government would explain how it would meet the demands of the people, not the day when there would be an actual return to Africa.

Henry was arrested and on his release, he was ordered to

keep the peace for a year and fined 100 pounds. He became hostile and radical toward the government, taking a revolutionary stance. In April 1960, in response to rumors of a military takeover of Jamaica by Henry and his followers, the police raided the African Reformed Church headquarters and found an arsenal of machetes, dynamite, detonators, guns, and conch shells filled with marijuana. Henry was arrested and served six years for breach of the treason laws. After his imprisonment, his son was discovered training a guerrilla band in the hills, and many Rastafarians believed it to be a part of the same mission.

As a result of these troubles, Rastafarian leaders asked Dr. Arthur Lewis of the University of the West Indies to send scholars to study the "doctrines and special conditions" of the Rastafarians. Among the ten recommendations made to the prime minister of Jamaica on their behalf were that the government should send representatives to arrange for the immigration of Jamaicans to Africa, including members of the Rastafarian community. It was also recommended that the Jamaican community should recognize that most of the Ras Tafari brethren were peaceful, honest, and willing to work. They encouraged the swift completion of police inquiries and an end to police harassment. Low-income housing and civic centers with facilities for clinics, meetings, and classes were needed, and the acquisition of sites for homeless and destitute people should be implemented. The team also recommended that the churches and University College of the West Indies should assist in these efforts and that the Ethiopian Orthodox Coptic Church should be invited to establish itself in the West Indies.

The recommendations, although the result of only a month's research, were accepted by the government, and each has been implemented to some degree. The immigration of Jamaicans to Africa caused some controversy. Only a few leaders of the Rastafarian movement went, but the harsh realities of African life might have put an end to the widespread desire to return to Africa. On this trip however, they were met by the Abuna, Archbishop of the Ethiopian Orthodox Church, who advised the group that Selassie was a devout, practicing Christian. Their belief in the divinity of Haile Selassie did not change, strengthened by the notion that if Selassie did not believe he was "God," then, in fact, he was, for "God" would never display his divinity. When Selassie visited Jamaica on April 21, 1966, Rastafarians were more convinced than ever that he was divine (this day is now celebrated as a holy day of the movement). It is interesting to note that Selassie himself never commented on the movement or on the idea of his being considered "God." The study resulted in the Jamaican community recognizing the relevance of the movement, and in many ways, the Rastafarian community is credited with striving for social change and equality on the island.

Added to the mystique created by Selassie's 1966 visit is the belief that he said the Rastafarians should liberate themselves in Jamaica before they came back to Ethiopia. The call, especially among younger members of the group, is currently "liberation before repatriation." Members of the Rastafarian community have migrated to the United States, but numerous other Jamaicans and non-Jamaicans have adopted the dreadlocks hairstyle that readily identifies them, without adopting the life-style. In addition to this, reggae music has become the major form of expression, not only of the Rastafarian community, but of many Jamaicans and Americans as well. There are major Rastafarian communities in New York, Miami, Chicago, and Brooklyn.

The Rastafarian community's beliefs can be summarized as follows: 1) Haile Selassie is the living God (at least of the black race); 2) the black person is the reincarnation of ancient Israel and, because of the white person, has been in exile in Jamaica; 3) the white person is inferior to the black person; 4) the Jamaican situation is a hopeless hell; Ethiopia is heaven; 5) the Invincible Emperor of Ethiopia is now arranging for expatriated persons of African origin to return to Ethiopia; and 6) in the near future, blacks will rule the world. The movement is considered to be a messianic-millenarian one. According to Dr. Donald Hogg of the University of Puerto Rico, messianic movements consider the Messiah as the Divine Savior transformed into human flesh and emphasize the move to a future golden age here on earth. Rastafarians also believe that they are like God—both black and divine simultaneously. They believe that Jesus of the Bible was Haile Selassie. Their religious perspective is that of black Judaism, identifying with many characters of the Old Testament and the children of Israel. *Israelite* and *Ethiopian* are one and the same, referring simply to a holy people. The Bible is considered a holy book but not infallible because it is open to various interpretations. Exegesis occurs, however, without full understanding of historical context.

There is much symbolism among the Rastafarians. They adhere to a strict dietetic and hygienic code as adapted from Old Testament laws, and they are primarily vegetarians, consuming only certain animal flesh, excluding swine, shellfish, scaleless fish, or snails. The use of liquor (especially rum) and cigarettes is prohibited, and the members will not drink coffee or milk, nor will they take patent medicines. Anything natural or made from herbs can be consumed. They refrain from the use of instruments that desecrate the body, such as in shaving, tattooing, and cutting the skin. The Prince Emmanuel group (the Ethiopian National Congress) is the only one that practices ritual sacrifice, and it has moved away from the central tenets of the movement toward a new church. The name *Rastafarian* is the Jamaican version of *Ras Tafari*, although it is not known why this name was chosen over *Haile Selassie*. *Ras* is Amharic for the title of nobility given to Ethiopian royalty and can be equated with the title of duke in England. *Tafari* is the family name. *Rastafarian* is also a ritual invocation for the group, and *Haile Selassie* is used mostly in prayers and songs. *Jah*, believed to be a shortened version of the biblical *Jehovah*, is also used to refer to God and is often combined in *Jah-Ras-Tafari* in prayers and rituals. *Ganja*, or marijuana, is used as a crucial part of worship and a ritual aid for meditation. Its use is biblically supported in Genesis 1:12 and 3:18, Exodus 10:12, Proverbs 15:17, and Psalms 104:14.

The colors of the movement are those of the original Garvey movement and of the Jamaican flag—red, black, green, and yellow—signifying the blood of martyrs of Jamaican history, the color of Africans, Jamaican vegetation, and the hope of victory over oppression, respectively. The lion is symbolic of Haile Selassie, the Conquering Lion of Judah. It also represents the dominant maleness of the group and is interpreted as aggressiveness, strength, and dominance. The "locks" are representative of the lion's mane. *I and I* is frequently used in speech to represent the presence of the divine and the human existing as one.

Group Type: Denomination
Founded: 1930
Membership: Estimated at 3,000 - 5,000 persons in the United States
Publications: *Arise*, a magazine, Creative Publishers, Ltd., 8 Waterloo Avenue, Kingston, Jamaica, West Indies; *Jahugligman*, a magazine, c/o Carl Gayle, 19C Annette Crescent, Kingston 10, Jamaica, West Indies

United Hebrew Congregation

No current address

This body was composed of approximately six congregations of black Jews centered in the Ethiopian Hebrew Culture Center in Chicago in the mid 1970s. It was led by Rabbi Naphtali Ben Israel. According to the *Encyclopedia of American Religions* (3rd ed.), the group believed that the sons of Ham were black and that the biblical Hebrews were included in this number. It was also believed that Abraham came from Chaldea and that these people were black. Based upon Song of Solomon 1:5, members also believe that Solomon was black. Saturday was observed as the Sabbath by the group. There has been no sign of activitiy in the 1980s.

Group Type: Denomination
Founded: 1970s

Islam

Islam is the Arabic term for "the surrendering of oneself to God" (Nielsen, et al. 1983, 583). This religious movement developed during the seventh century A.D. and is considered one of the world's great religions. It is a monotheistic religion that holds that God transcends the limits of the material universe. It demands high standards of ethical behavior from its adherents.

God in Islam is addressed by the Arabic word *Allah*, which means one who is not bound by limitations of time and space. The sacred book of the religion is the Qur'an, or Koran. The religion teaches that God is independent of human conceptual models. As Nielsen, et al. (1983, 585) note:

God cannot be properly represented by a graven image, as his infinite Being cannot be likened to anything that human beings can see or touch. In the core tradition of Islam, God created the universe *ex nihilo* (out of nothing). Having created it, he sustains and judges it . . .

Humankind is considered to be the ultimate of creation, and humans are perceived as being blessed with the ability to comprehend their reality and to act in a responsible way to establish a moral relationship with God. The "surrendering of one's life to Allah" conveys the attitude and means by which all believers should respond in homage to God. It is seen as a complete act of devotion and praise to God (i.e., Allah). As Nielsen (1983, 587) notes, Islam is a response to the moral imperative or command of God: "The person who surrenders his or her life to the will of God is a Muslim (*Muslimah* in the feminine)."

Islam, like Judaism and Christianity, is a religion that developed from a revelation. In this regard, prophets or spiritual leaders have played a significant role in interpreting the faith. The Islamics believe that Muhammad was the greatest prophet of the religion, and he is considered to be the special messenger of Allah and the last prophet. As observed by Nielson, et al. (1983, 587):

Almost all Muslims have held that Muhammad was the last of the prophets and that the Qur'an was the last scripture to be sent down to humanity. Since revelation is now complete, there is no need for further prophecy; rather, what remains is for people to accept, understand, and live the revealed Truth.

Muslims accept the Old Testament and New Testament, but maintain that the Qur'an is the ultimate scriptural reference to assess the validity of other religious literature. Although accepting many of the basic premises of the Judeo-Christian religious traditions, the Muslims contend that the non-Muslim religious traditions are incomplete. Building upon the monotheistic model exemplified through the prophet Ibrahim (Abraham), they consider the role that Ibrahim (Abraham) played in establishing the Arab ancestry through his son Ismail (Ishmael). Accepting Issa (Jesus) as a great prophet and messenger of God, Muslims do not adhere to the trinitarian doctrine that He is God incarnate, nor do they accept the Christian thesis of Jesus as being essential to salvation.

The religious obligations of persons committed to the Muslim religion center on five divine worship ordinances. They are known as the five pillars of Islam. They are: 1) the profession of faith (*Shahadah*); 2) ritual prayer (*Salah*); 3) the Ramadan fast; 4) almsgiving (*Zakah*); and 5) the Pilgrimage to Mecca (*Hajj*).

Muslims affirm their religious belief (*iman*) through a declaration of faith: "There is no God but God, and Muhammad is the messenger of God." This phrase is repeated numerous times during the course of the day to affirm the symbolic relationship between God and man. The Islamic faith is distinguished by a formalized prayer ritual that is required five times a day. When praying, all Muslims must face toward Mecca, the city where the Prophet Muhammed was born and which serves as the center of the faith. During the ninth month of the Islamic lunar calendar (Ramadan), all members fast. This commemorates the first revelation of the Qur'an and the holy Battle of Badr. During the entire lunar month, believers must abstain from food, drink, tobacco, and sexual activity between first light and the onset of full darkness. Almsgiving (*Zakah*) is the practice of sharing material resources. Believers are required to share a portion of their wealth. This was instituted as a means by which the community of believers could develop a collective sense of social responsibility. The final pillar of Islam is the Pilgrimage to Mecca (*Hajj*). This ultimate act of worship is the once-in-a-lifetime goal of every believer. It is a highly symbolic and ritualized religious exercise that serves as the most fundamental unifying ceremony in the religion.

There are two major variations in the Islamic religious tradition. They are the Sunna (i.e., the normative Islamic tradition) and the Shiah (the official Islam of Iran). As noted by Ellwood (1976, 327):

> In Sunna the fundamental authority is shari'ah, Muslim law. It is interpreted not by a single individual, but by consensus of learned men who base their decisions on tradition, hadith, and analogy. Although the University of Cairo has long been considered the most venerable repository of such learning, Sunna is more or less decentralized. Its tone is one of putting most emphasis on the basic Five Pillars of Islam, and on a rather formal—though deeply felt—style of devotion. Its legal bent stresses putting all of life under God and the Koran. Different schools of law interpretation obtain within Sunna, though they are not competitive but recognized alternatives. Sunna also embraces some submovements; one is Wahhabi, dominant in Saudi Arabia, a conservative, puritanical reform dating from the eighteenth century.
>
> Shiah is different in tone and more complex. Shiites believe that after Muhammad there was intended to be a succession of *Imams*, divinely appointed and authoritative teachers of Islam, to guide the faithful. The first was Ali, Muhammad's cousin, and after him Ali's eldest son, Hasan, and then Ali's second son, Husain. There were then nine others in family succession, down to the twelfth, who was born in 869.

In addition to these two major branches of Islam, there is a more mystical tradition known as Sufism. Sufis adhere to the teachings of the Koran and the religious traditions of Islam. They strive further to obtain an intimate and integral relationship with the divine through practices of mediation, chanting, and dance. Their focus is to find an inner state of existence that mirrors the qualitative experience of Muhammad. Hence, emphasis is placed on techniques for inducing trances and means of experiencing rapture. The Sufis attach primary importance to the inwardness of the religious experience. This inward quality is built around acknowledged Islamic traditions and adherence to religious-cultural practices.

The African American role in Islam is best distinguished through the establishment of the Black Muslims. The American Muslim Mission (formerly known as the Nation of Islam) refers to itself as the "lost nation of Islam." It was founded by the Honorable Prophet Elijah Muhammad, who was born in Georgia as Elijah Poole (1897-1975). Poole changed his name to Elijah Muhammad as a sign of his conversion to Islam. While working on a Detroit automobile assembly line, Poole met W. D. Fard, a salesman, who instructed him in Islam, then mysteriously disappeared in 1934, leaving Elijah Muhammad to serve as the self-proclaimed messenger of Allah.

The religious teachings of Elijah Muhammad were radical. He emphasized that African Americans descended from the ancient tribe of Shabazz, which initially settled Mecca, the Holy City. He taught his followers that all people of color—black, red, brown, and yellow—were descendants of a great nation that had one common enemy, the white race. This doctrine stressed the need for African Americans and all people of color to strive collectively to overthrow the white, racist society that dominates people of color throughout the world.

The Black Muslims were not initially received as a legitimate branch of Islam, although their members were allowed to go on the pilgrimage to Mecca. Malcolm X (1925-1965) was a notable leader of the movement. After a break with the Honorable Prophet Elijah Muhammad and a pilgrimage to Mecca, where Malcolm X learned how the Black Muslim movement departed from some of the major principles of Islam, he converted to Orthodox Islam and established the Organization of Afro-American Unity. This group supported black nationalism but departed from the teachings of Elijah Muhammad with respect to racial separation. Following the death of Elijah Muhammad, the Black Muslims' name was changed to the World Community of Islam in the West, under the leadership of Elijah Muhammad's son, Wallace D. Muhammad. The group has reversed its position on racial segregation and now admits whites to membership. It is now known as the American Muslim Mission.

References

Ellwood, Robert S., Jr. *Many Peoples, Many Faiths: An Introduction to the Religious Life of Mankind.* Engelwood Cliffs, NJ: Prentice-Hall, Inc., 1976.

Nielsen, Niels C., Jr., Norvin Hein, Frank E. Reynolds, Alan L. Miller, Samuel E. Karff, Alice C. Cochran, and Paul McLean. *Religions of the World.* New York: St. Martins Press, 1983.

Ahmadiyya Movement in Islam, Inc., U.S.A.

2141 Leroy Place, NW
Washington, DC 20008
(202) 232-3737
Imam Sheikh Mubarak Ahmad, Chief Missionary Resident
Mr. Mubasher Ahmad

The Ahmadiyya Movement in Islam, Inc., U.S.A., came to the United States in 1921, when a center was established in Chicago by its founder, Dr. Mufti Muhammad Sadiq. The movement began in March, 1889, when Mirza Ghulam Ahmad of the small town of Qadian (India) claimed that he was the Reformer of the fourteenth century of the Islamic era and that he was the Promised Messiah of Christians and Madhi, the expected returning Savior of Muslims. Thus he laid the foundation of the Ahmadiyya Movement.

Sadiq had spent years in study of the holy Qur'an and scriptures of other faiths. He realized that Islam was in decline and believed that he had been appointed by Allah to demonstrate its truth, a belief that resulted in his writing the book *Barahin-i-Ahmaditah*. He took on the title of *mujaddid*, the renewer of faith for the present age. He also stated that he had been the recipient of divine revelation and that the revival of Islam would be brought about through him. Ahmad believed that Jesus had not died on Calvary but had merely fainted on the cross, escaped the tomb, and fled to Kashmir, India, where His ministry was continued for many years. The organization considers Jesus to be a great prophet who is buried at Srinagar, India, where the legendary Tomb of Issa (Jesus) is a pilgrimage site. Christianity is considered tritheistic, and Jesus is not considered divine, which is consistent with the belief that Allah is the one true God.

In the United States, Dr. Sadiq's efforts to recruit immigrants resulted in the exceptional conversion of African Americans. Since the repeal of the Asian Exclusion Act in 1965 and the influx of Indian and Pakistani immigrants, the organization's constituency has begun to include a significant Asian population.

Also known as the American Ahmadiyya Muslim Association and the American Ahmadiyya Muslim Community, the organization has the most aggressive missionary program in Islam. It is not, however, considered to be true Islam by orthodox Muslims because its founder is portrayed as the Promised Messiah and the Coming One of all major Indian faiths. This has resulted in published *mubahalas*, documents debating the allegations made by orthodox Muslims and others against the group. *Mubahala* is a term of the Holy Qur'an in which claimants of God are rejected without recourse to debate. Both the accusers and the accused invoke the curse of Allah on the willful liars.

There are several publications by the Ahmadiyya Movement in Islam: *Muslim Sunrise* (started by Dr. Sadiq); the *Ahmadiyya Gazette*; *The Review of Religions*; *Ayesha*; and *Misbah*. In addition there is literature on the superiority of Islam to Christianity and about the organization's purpose and beliefs. At this time, there are twenty-six local branches in the United States. The organization numbers approximately 10 million followers worldwide. The American headquarters moved to Washington, D.C., in 1950 after having been located in Chicago for twenty-five years. Imam Sheikh Mubarak Ahmad is the Chief Missionary-Resident at the American headquarters.

Group Type: Denomination
Founded: 1889 in India and established in the United States in 1921
Membership: 26 branches in the United States; over 10,000,000 followers worldwide
Publications: *Muslim Sunrise*; the *Ahmadiyya Gazette*; *The Review of Religions*; *Ayesha*; and *Misbah*

Al-Hanif, Hanafi Madh-Hab Center, Islam Faith, United States of America, American Mussulmans

7700 16th Street, NW
Washington, DC 20012
(202) 291-5392
Khalifa Hamaas Abdul Khaalis, Imam

The Al-Hanif, Hanafi Madh-Hab is one of the four Madh-Habs (schools of the Sunnah of the Holy Prophet Muhammad) that comprise the Sunni Path of Islam. The other three Madh-Habs are the Hanbali, Safi, and Malaki. It recognizes Allah as the author of Islam and believes that the Holy Prophet Muhammad, born in Makkah (Mecca) in A.D. 570, is the ultimate of the prophets and prophecy. According to their religious beliefs, the 124,000 prophets of Islam were all Al-Hanif Mussulmans (Muslims), including Adam, the first man and prophet, and Prophet Ibrahim (Abraham). Several of the many references to the authenticity of the Hanafi Madh-Hab in the Holy Qur'an include these *suras* (chapters) and *ayats* (verses): Baqara (2:135); Al-i-Imran (3:95); Nisaa (4:125); An'am (6:79); Yunus (10:105); Hajj (22:31); and Rum (30:30). The four Madh-Habs follow the same Sunni Path of Islam.

The American segment of Al-Hanif Hanafi Mussulmans traces its founding to Dr. Tasibur Uddein Rahman, a Sunni Al-Hanif Mussulman from Pakistan. Dr. Rahman established the Al-Hanif Hanafi Madh-Hab in America in the early 1920s. The leader of American-born Al-Hanif Hanafi Mussulmans is Khal-

ifa Hamaas Abdul Khaalis (formerly called Ernest Timothy McGhee). He accepted Islam in the latter part of 1949 through his *Murshid* (teacher), Dr. Rahman. Following the directives of his *Murshid*, Khaalis became a member of the Nation of Islam in 1950 in order to show its leader, Elijah Muhammad (formerly Robert or Elijah Poole) that the ideology of that organization did not embrace true Islam. By 1956, Khaalis was the national secretary of the Nation of Islam. Khaalis was critical of the nationalistic tendencies of black Muslim groups because they conflicted with his beliefs that Allah was the only true god and that Mohammed was his prophet, not Elijah Muhammad or Wallace Fard as the Nation of Islam believed (*see* American Muslim Mission).

In 1958, after attempting to guide the Nation of Islam to the Sunni Path with little success, Khaalis established the American headquarters of the Al-Hanif Hanafi Madh-Hab in Washington, D.C. A home, provided by the basketball star Kareem Abdul-Jabbar (formerly Lew Alcindor), who had been a member of this organization since his conversion in the early 1970s, currently serves as both the headquarters of the organization and the residence for Khaalis's family.

In 1972, Khalifa Hamaas Abdul Khaalis wrote and published a book on the Islam faith, *Look and See*. On January 18, 1973, seven members of the organization—including five of Khaalis's children and one grandchild—were brutally murdered in the house that served as their home and the organizational headquarters. His wife was shot and remains paralyzed. Five members of the Philadelphia Nation of Islam were eventually convicted of the murders, but were lightly punished. Blame continues to be aimed at the Nation of Islam, which it denies.

In order to stop the screening of the film *Mohammad, Messenger of God*, Khaalis and several followers took over three buildings in the District of Columbia. The film showing was perceived as *Shirk-O-Bidat*, a sacrilegious outrage to a sincere Mussulman. The takeover was a defense of the Islamic faith against this egregious act, but was mistakenly perceived as revenge for the 1973 killings. The District Building, Washington, D.C.'s, seat of city government and operation, was the site of the only casualty of the takeover. Howard University's Radio (WHUR) District reporter, Maurice Williams, was fatally wounded. City Councilman, Marion S. Barry, Jr., (who later became Washington, D.C.'s mayor) was also shot while in the District Building assisting with negotiations. The B'nai B'rith Building was also taken over because it was felt that Jews understood Islam better than followers of other religions. The Islamic Center, headquarters of the Islamic faith in the Washington, D.C. area, was also seized. These buildings were held by the Hanafi organization for thirty-eight hours in March, 1977. Khaalis's sentence was from forty-one to 120 years in prison for his role in the takeover, and he and several followers are currently serving prison terms. The family and other followers remain in the family home/headquarters.

Believers in the Faith Islam number over one billion worldwide, and Mussulmans use two standards as their guide—the Holy Qur'an as revealed by Allah to the Holy Prophet Muhammad, and the Hadiths, the eyewitness accounts of the Prophet's deeds and words. A literal interpretation of the Qur'an is accepted. In addition, the revealed books—the Torah (Old Testament) revealed to Musa (Moses); the Zabur (Psalms) revealed to Daud (David); and the Injil (Bible) revealed to Isa (Jesus)—are recognized. Mussulmans, as do true Christians, await the return of Hazrat Isa ibn Maryam—Jesus, the son of Mary.

The proliferation of sects outside of the Sunnah was prophesied by the Holy Prophet Muhammad. In Sura An'Am (6:159) and throughout the Qur'an, Allah never condones sectarianism. Rather, Allah commands humankind to accept the Faith Islam as perfected through the Holy Prophet Muhammad (Sura Maidas, 5:3). According to their doctrine, Al-Hanif cannot be sectarian and is not a sect. It is considered to be Islam as practiced by the Prophets, and Allah is the author of Al-Hanif.

All Sunni Mussulmans who follow the way of the Prophets pray five times a day and recognize all of the Spiritual Holy days of the Sunni Mussulmans. All bear witness to the five principles: 1) the *Kalima* (profession of faith); 2) *Salat* (prayer); 3) *Sakat* (alms to the poor); 4) fasting; and 5) *Hajj* (the pilgrimage to Mecca, if physically and financially able, once in life). Sunni Mussulmans also bear witness to the seven cardinal Articles of Faith: 1) to believe in the oneness of Allah; 2) to believe in all His Angels; 3) to believe in all His books; 4) to believe in all His Prophets; 5) to believe in the Day of Resurrection; 6) to believe in the Day of Judgment; and 7) to believe in the predestination of good and evil and the fact that we are all responsible for our own actions. They obey the *Shariat*, which is Islamic law, the fundamental principles of Islam, and the 130 principles of Hiqmat (or Hikmat).

The *Imam* (spiritual leader) of the *masjid* is appointed. Anyone who is a sincere believer, knows his prayers, and lives a clean life under the guidance of the Qur'an and Hadiths can become the *Imam*. The Faith Islam accepts anyone, regardless of racial or ethnic origin. Membership has been offered to whites, but few have joined.

The Al-Hanif, Hanafi Madh-Hab Center seeks "to continue to work in our country America, as American Mussulmans to build a bridge of trust and friendship in all affairs with other peoples of the world that are Non-Mussulmans."

The current membership is unknown. In 1977, there were fewer than one thousand members in the organization in Washington, D.C., Los Angeles, Chicago, and New York.

Group Type: Denomination
Founded: 1958
Membership: As of 1977, fewer than 1,000 persons
Publications: Look and See by Khalifa Hamaas Abdul Khaalis

American Muslim Mission

7351 S. Stony Island Avenue
Chicago, IL 60649
(312) 667-7200
Warith Dean Muhammad, Imam

The American Muslim Mission is probably the most familiar of the black Muslim groups in America both because of its leadership and its celebrated members.

The Nation of Islam was started by Master Wallace Drew Fard Muhammad in the summer of 1930 in Detroit. This followed the death of Noble Drew Ali, founder and leader of the Moorish Science Temple of America. Fard had been one of Ali's followers, and after Ali's death in 1929, Fard appeared in Detroit claiming to be the reincarnated Ali. He appealed to the many southern-born African Americans new to the city who not only sought refuge from the mystic, but also support, having been the first persons to be fired from many jobs and suffering

from the effects of the Depression. Fard believed he had been sent from Mecca to awaken his "uncle"—blacks in the United States—and to denounce their treatment by the "white devils." The movement started as a house-to-house meeting, with Fard selling raincoats and silks that he claimed were from the black homeland. He slowly gained a following, began to condemn Christianity, and pushed the acceptance of Islam as the proper religion for African Americans, as it had been for their ancestors.

Fard's racial and social background is a mystery (especially because he used several aliases) and stories of his background abounded, but his following did not diminish. There were about 8,000 members in the first Temple of Islam in Detroit. Within three years, he had formed such an effective organization that his direct leadership was unnecessary. The Fruit of Islam (FOI), a military/police group that trained men in self-defense and firearm use, was begun. He also started the Muslim Girls' Training Corps Class (which taught girls how to be proper wives and mothers through home economics) and the University of Islam, which was really an elementary and high school. Members substituted "X" for their surnames to disavow their slave ancestry. Fard also wrote two manuals. *The Secret Ritual of the Nation of Islam* was and continues to be an oral tradition. It is memorized verbatim by students of the organization's schools. *Teaching for the Lost Found Nation of Islam in a Mathematical Way* was written in Fard's symbolic language and required his interpretation. It was distributed to his followers.

Fard's infrequent appearances, his personal belief in his divinity, and his outspoken hatred for the United States government took its toll on his leadership, and schisms resulted, led by the most faithful and powerful leaders. According to C. Eric Lincoln—whose 1961 book *The Black Muslims in America* is highly regarded as the authoritative account of the Muslim movement—the organization also faced several attempts to infiltrate it or take it over as early as 1932, when the Communist party tried to do so. The Japanese followed, trying to gain a secure springboard for further action. Major Takahashi tried to persuade members to swear allegiance to the Mikado, which some did, thus he succeeded in splitting off some members. By 1934, the Ethiopians were also interested. Wyxzewixard S. J. Challouehliczilczese sought to use the group to promote several financial schemes that would benefit his homeland. Domestically, union busters tried to take advantage of the poverty of urban blacks in a war against the Congress of Industrial Organizations (CIO). Although all these efforts failed, collectively, they diminished the strength and energy of the organization.

Elijah Muhammad, born Elijah or Robert Poole, was greatly influenced by Fard. His family migrated from Georgia in the 1920s, and several years later joined Fard's ranks. Poole became a devoted follower and, by 1934, had moved up in the leadership ranks to become a minister of Islam. In June same year, Fard mysteriously disappeared, never to be seen again. Subsequently, disagreements and factions developed, and Muhammad moved the headquarters to Chicago, Illinois. He began to restructure the movement under his own militant leadership. Fard soon became identified with Allah; thus deified, he was worshipped with sacrifice and prayer. It was at this time that Muhammad was accorded the position of "Prophet" because he had served "Allah" (that is, Fard) and because Fard, or Allah, had himself been thus called while on his earthly mission. Muhammad was referred to as both the Prophet and the Messenger of Allah.

Under Muhammad's leadership, the organization grew into a strong, cohesive group that, at the time of his death in 1975, numbered approximately 100,000 in seventy temples across the country. He wrote the authoritative *Message to the Blackman in America, a summary statement of the Nation of Islam's position.* Essentially, the teachings of the Nation of Islam stressed dignity, racial pride, thrift, and discipline. Members were expected to contribute a fixed percentage of their income to the central body as well as to other endeavors. Many were able to enjoy a reasonable standard of living by saving money that might otherwise have been spent on things forbidden by the organization, such as gambling, smoking, liquor, rich foods, and credit purchases. The Nation of Islam promoted a more sophisticated, in-depth study of black history than did its parent organization, the Moorish Science Temple of America. Malcolm X and Muhammad Ali are among its most well-known followers.

Wallace D. Muhammad succeeded his father upon his death in 1975 and moved the organization toward Orthodox Islam and decentralization. The weekly newspaper, *Muhammad Speaks*, was renamed *Bilalian News*. The organization itself went through two name changes, from the World Community of Islam in the West to, in 1980, its present name, the American Muslim Mission. Wallace Muhammad resigned as leader of the American Muslim Movement, with the approval of the Council of Imams (ministers) in 1985. The movement's corporate structure was disbanded as well, and property owned by the corporation was to be sold. Thus, its polity has moved to a fully congregational one, with *Imams* providing guidance. Wallace Muhammad remains the *Imam* of Chicago's southside temple. The organizational changes have slowly led to the beginning of its acceptance by the Orthodox Islamic communities, which previously had not regarded any of the black Muslim groups as true Muslims. There are several segments, which split off in the 1960s and 1970s, that want to maintain the political, nationalistic tone. These include the Nation of Islam, led by Louis Farrakhan, the Nation of Islam [The Caliph], and the Nation of Islam led by John Muhammad. The Calistran, another splinter group of the Nation of Islam, formed in the 1970s, was short-lived. According to the *Encyclopedia of American Religions* (2nd ed.), two members of the group were shot by a "disciplinarian" in Pasadena, California in 1973, supposedly for "stepping out of line" from the parent body. This was during the period of tension and internal strife in the black Muslim community. The Calistran has not been active in the 1980s.

At the time of the organization's decentralization, there were about two hundred centers in the mission, located across the United States and in Trinidad, St. Thomas, Jamaica, Bermuda, Canada, the Bahamas, Guyana, and Belize.

Group Type: Denomination
Founded: 1934
Membership: 200 centers
Publications: Bilalian News

ANSAARU ALLAH Community

719 Bushwick Avenue
Brooklyn, NY 11221
(718) 443-4414
The Reverend Isa Al Haadi Al Mahdi, Founder (Al Imaam)

The ANSAARU ALLAH Community was begun in 1970

under the guidance of As Siddid Al Imaan, Isa Al Haahi Al Mahdi, in New York. The members of the organization believe that the Sudanese leader, Muhammed Ahmed Ibn Abdullah (1844-1885), was the predicted "Khaliyfah" or "Expected One"—the successor—to the Prophet Mohammad. Al Mahdi was buried in the Sudan upon his death, and the group continued under his successors. They were As Sayyid Abdur Rahman Al Madhi, As Sayyid Al Haadi Abdur Rahmaan Al Mahdi, and As Sayyid Isa Al Haadi Al Mahdi. The last is the current leader and the great-grandson of the founder.

The beliefs of the organization reflect a mix of Christian, Hebraic, and Islamic principles. The Suhufan (Pure Pages of the Prophets), the Old Testament, the Psalms of David, the New Testament, and the holy Qur'an are used for teaching by the organization. It is believed that the last testament, the Holy Qur'an, was given to Mustafa Muhammad Al Amin (A.D. 570-632). It is also believed that "ALLAH is Alone in His power, the All." God is not used as a reference to a superior being.

According to the *Encyclopedia of American Religions* (2nd ed.), the organization believes that the origin of the black, or Nubian, race is traced from Adam and Hawwah (Eve), who are believed to have been Nubians. Ham, the son of the prophet Nuwh (Noah), had desired to commit sodomy while watching his father naked, and this resulted in Ham's fourth son, Canaan, being cursed with leprosy, which turned his skin pale. Thus, were the pale races born, including the Hittites, Jebusites, Amorites, Sidonites, and the other sons of Canaan (which are all Canaanites) and their descendants (see Genesis 9:25, 10:15-18). To mix blood with these "subraces," or impure Nubians, is believed unlawful for Nubians. Some Nubians have mixed their seed with the cursed sons of Canaan and, as a result, created Sicilians, Malayans, Koreans, Eskimos, Japanese, some Chinese, Indonesians, East Indians, and Pakistani—*they are all black*! Even though Nubians mixed their blood with the sons of Canaan and violated the commandments of the Most High, their children are not the sons of Canaan.

The ANSAARU ALLAH Community also believes that two nations came from the seed of Ibraahiym (Abraham), those of Isaac and Ishmael. Isaac's descendants became known as the Israelites, and Ishmael's descendants became known as the Ishmaelites. As the Israelites were held in bondage in Egypt for over four hundred years (Galatians 3:17), the nation of Ishmael was predicted to be held captive in a foreign land for four hundred years (Genesis 15:13). It is believed that the nation of Ishmael resulted in the Nubians of the United States, West Indies, and in other places around the world. Thus, they are considered Hebrews. Peoples with pale skin and straight hair are Turks, according to the teachings of Al Mahdi, but this does not include people of color such as the Japanese and Latins, who are also Nubians.

The prophesies of the "Opening of the Seventh Seal" as recorded in Revelation 8:1 commenced with the opening of the ANSAARU ALLAH Community in 1970 and the publication of their literature. By 1972, communities had also been established in Albany, Connecticut, Philadelphia, Pittsburgh, and Texas. In 1973, centers were opened in Trinidad and Tobago. Since that time, others have been established in Canada, Delaware, England, Florida, Georgia, Ghana, Guyana, Jamaica, Louisiana, Maryland, Michigan, Ohio, South Africa, South Carolina, Tennessee, Virginia, and Washington, D.C.

Also known as the *Nubian Islamic Hebrew Mission*, the

organization's symbol is a six-pointed star in an inverted crescent, considered the symbol of Allah.

Group Type: Denomination
Founded: 1970

Moorish Science Temple Divine and National Movement of North America, Inc.

P.O. Box 7213
Baltimore, MD 21218
(301) 366-3591
Grand Sheik Louis Richardson Dingle-El, Prophet Noble
    Drew Ali III, Reincarnated
Grand Sheik Joel Bratton-Bey, National Chairman

The Moorish Science Temple Divine and National Movement of North America, Inc., traces its beginnings to 1913, when Timothy Drew, also known as Noble Drew Ali, began to preach in Newark, New Jersey, about the Moorish identity of blacks. Drew, born among the Cherokee tribe on January 8, 1886, in Simpsonbuck County, North Carolina, investigated the heritage of African Americans and concluded from reading and traveling that they were not Ethiopians as claimed by early black nationalists, but rather that they were Asiatics, specifically Moors. He believed that blacks descended from the Moabites and that their homeland was Morocco. He believed that the Continental Congress had stripped American blacks of their nationality and placed them in the menial role of slave. According to the movement's historical account, he was taught by Egyptian masters and earned the title Egyptian Adept, becoming a master in his own right. He also went to Mecca and received his ancient birthright title Os Ali from Sultan Abdul Aziz Ibn Saud, giving him the authority to teach the true religion of Islam to the lost tribes of Israel in the North, South, and Central Americas.

Noble Drew Ali's movement spread slowly from Newark to Pittsburgh, Detroit, and into the South. He moved to Chicago in 1925, and the movement was reestablished as the Moorish Temple of Science. It was registered as a legally chartered, nonprofit organization by the secretary of the state of Illinois on November 29, 1926. Noble Drew Ali published *The Holy Koran of the Moorish Science Temple of America*, now known to members of the movement as the *Holy Koran of the Moorish Science Temple Circle Seven*, and a pamphlet collection of Moorish beliefs conceived largely from *The Aquarian Gospel of Jesus Christ*, a book received through automatic writing by spiritualist Levi Dowling in the 1890s. Ali's book concerns the origin, creation, and fall of blacks, the opposition of Christianity to God's people, and the modern predicament of the Moorish people. Through use of select tenets from the Koran, it teaches the members to master the self and distinguish the higher self from the lower self. The ''circle seven'' refers to the book of the seven seals in the book of Revelation in the Bible. Ali's book is used as a preliminary study tool for its members before they study the Koran, or the Qur'an, the holy book of Orthodox Islamic groups.

Ali's followers took on names indicative of their Moorish heritage and were known as Moorish-Americans. The suffixes ''Bey'' or ''El'' are hyphenated to each member's surname. In the early days of the movement, each person had an iden-tification card that made clear his political and religious status, and the more ornamental elements of Islam were employed, such as wearing the fez. The movement combines elements of black nationalism, Christian revivalism, and the teachings of the Prophet Muhammad, a commonality found in many African American Islamic traditions.

On May 2, 1928, the name of the organization was again changed from the Moorish Holy Temple of Science to the Moorish Science Temple of America, Inc., and its status was changed to a profit organization. This change became official on May 19, 1928. A religious affidavit containing articles of religion and articles of national corporation was recorded in Cook County, Illinois, on August 1, 1928.

Noble Drew Ali died mysteriously on July 20, 1929, possibly as a result of injuries received in a beating by the Chicago police. According to the records of the organization, he was succeeded by his personal chauffeur, Sheik Timothy Givens-El, in August 1929, who was the second reincarnation of the prophet (other accounts list R. German Ali as his successor). Taking the title Prophet Noble Drew Ali Reincarnated Mohammed III, his ministry included personal appearances and use of mail. According to the organization, he also saved the organization from being sold to whites for a million dollars. He authorized Sheik Richardson Dingle-El to expand the work of the founder.

In 1944, Dingle-El, with the help of his younger brother, Timothy Dingle-El, placed ''Our Authority'' and all pertinent literature in the national headquarters and requested that all erroneous terms (racial identifications such as Negro, colored, mulatto, etc.) be removed from all public and private records. He also established through the national headquarters of the Selective Service System the Moorish Bureau of Vital Statistics, under which everyone must register according to their true nationality (this information has not been confirmed by the National Archives, but is based on information from the movement).

On November 30, 1945, Grand Sheik Richardson Dingle-El became the leader of the movement and legally began to resurrect the initial Thirteenth Amendment with its twenty sections and the executive will of President Abraham Lincoln, which guarantees financial compensation and the restoration of land and former names to blacks. Timothy Dingle-El died on March 21, 1982, but left the book *Resurrection of the Moorish Science Temple*, a chronicle of the movement.

On September 25, 1975, the articles of incorporation of the Moorish Science Temple Divine and National Movement of North America, Inc., No. 13, were registered in the Maryland State Department of Assessments and Taxation as a profitable organization. A copy of the articles of incorporation were submitted to the national headquarters of the National Archives and the Judiciary Committee of the House of Representatives. According to the *Encyclopedia of American Religions* (3rd ed.), Sheik Richardson Dingle-El proclaimed himself Noble Drew Ali III in 1975, but the organization's accounts trace his involvement in the movement back at least to the 1940s.

Another person also claimed to be the reincarnated Ali in the 1930s, Noble Drew Ali II (d. 1945). Wallace Drew Fard Muhammad (d. 1934?), a follower of Noble Drew Ali, appeared in Detroit and also claimed to be the reincarnation of Noble Drew Ali. Wallace Fard Muhammad began the Nation of Islam, now known as the American Muslim Mission.

Marcus Garvey, the black nationalist, was seen as a forerunner of Ali. Because Ali believed that blacks are Asiatic, then, Islam, being the religion of the Moors, was that of black Americans. He believed that Jesus was a black who tried to redeem black Moabites but was executed by white Romans. He further believed that Moorish (black) Americans must and could be united only under Allah and his holy prophet. The followers of the organization consider Friday to be the holy day because the first man was formed in flesh and departed out of flesh on Friday, the sixth day. Its worship form, especially musical, is taken from popular black culture. Islamic content has been given to the worship experience and practices. Its major principles are love, truth, freedom, peace, and justice. The movement considers Moses, Jesus, Mohammed, Buddha, and Confucius divine prophets.

The organization has headquarters in Baltimore with several temples throughout the United States.

Group Type: Denomination
Founded: 1975

Moorish Science Temple of America

762 W. Baltimore Street
Baltimore, MD 21201

The movement that came to be known as the Moorish Science Temple of America traces its beginnings to 1913, when Timothy Drew, also known as Noble Drew Ali, began to preach in Newark, New Jersey, about the Moorish identity of blacks. Drew, born among the Cherokee tribe on January 8, 1886, in Simpsonbuck County, North Carolina, investigated the heritage of African Americans and concluded from reading and traveling that they were not Ethiopians as claimed by early black nationalists, but rather that they were Asiatics, specifically Moors. He believed that blacks descended from the Moabites, their homeland was Morocco, and that the Continental Congress had stripped American blacks of their nationality and placed them in the menial role of slave.

Noble Drew Ali's movement spread slowly from Newark to Pittsburgh, Detroit, and into the South. He moved to Chicago in 1925, and the movement was reestablished as the Moorish Temple of Science. It was registered as a legally chartered, nonprofit organization by the secretary of the state of Illinois on November 29, 1926. Noble Drew Ali published *The Holy Koran*, a collection of Moorish beliefs conceived largely from *The Aquarian Gospel of Jesus Christ*, a book received through automatic writing by spiritualist Levi Dowling in the 1890s, and the Koran, the holy book of Islam. Ali's book concerns the origin, creation, and fall of blacks, the opposition of Christianity to God's people, and the modern predicament of the Moorish people.

Ali's followers took on names indicative of their Moorish heritage and were known as Moorish-Americans. The suffixes ''Bey'' or ''El'' are hyphenated to each member's surname. In the early days of the movement, each person had an identification card that made clear his political and religious status, and the more ornamental elements of Islam were employed, such as wearing the fez. The movement combines elements of black nationalism, Christian revivalism, and teachings of the Prophet Muhammad, a commonality found in many African American Islamic traditions.

On May 2, 1928, the name of the organization was again changed from the Moorish Holy Temple of Science to the Moorish Science Temple of America, Inc., and its status was changed to a profit organization. This change became official on May 19, 1928. A religious affidavit containing articles of religion and articles of national corporation was recorded in Cook County, Illinois, on August 1, 1928. Noble Drew Ali died mysteriously on July 20, 1929, possibly as a result of injuries received in a beating by the Chicago police. He was succeeded by R. German Ali.

Another person also claimed to be the reincarnated Ali in the 1930s, Noble Drew Ali II (d. 1945). Wallace Drew Fard Muhammad (d. 1934?), a follower of Noble Drew Ali, appeared in Detroit and also claimed to be the reincarnation of Noble Drew Ali. Wallace Fard Muhammad began the Nation of Islam, now known as the American Muslim Mission.

Marcus Garvey, the black nationalist, was seen as a forerunner of Ali. Because Ali believed that blacks are Asiatic, then, Islam, being the religion of the Moors, was that of black Americans. He believed that Jesus was a black who tried to redeem black Moabites but was executed by white Romans. He further believed that Moorish (black) Americans must and could be united only under Allah and his holy prophet. The followers of the organization consider Friday to be the holy day, and its worship form, especially musical, is taken from popular black culture. Islamic content has been given to the worship experience and practices.

By the 1940s, the movement had spread across the United States, but in more recent years its following has declined. The organization has headquarters in Baltimore with several temples throughout the United States.

Group Type: Denomination
Founded: 1913

Nation of Islam [Farrakhan]

734 West 79th Street
Box 20083
Chicago, IL 60620
(312) 994-5775
Minister Louis Farrakhan

The Nation of Islam [Farrakhan] is the result of a schism from the American Muslim Mission (formerly the Nation of Islam) led by Prophet Elijah Muhammad until his death in 1975, then led by his son, Wallace D. Muhammad, until the decentralization of the group in 1985. Louis Farrakhan, born Louis Eugene Walcott, joined the Nation of Islam in the 1950s when he was a nightclub singer and became Minister Louis X, having dropped his slave surname. He first became minister of the Boston mosque, partly because of his oratorical and musical skills, then he led the Harlem center, once led by Malcolm X after Malcolm split with Elijah Muhammad. Farrakhan also became Elijah Muhammad's official spokesman.

Upon the death of Elijah Muhammad, many believed Farrakhan would assume the leadership of the organization, but Muhammad's son was selected. Farrakhan took a national post upon Muhammad's request and moved to Chicago. Over the next few years, the Nation of Islam moved toward Orthodox Islam and jettisoned many of its black nationalistic positions, opening membership to whites and accepting integration. Farrakhan, among others, began to speak against this new stance and, in 1978, withdrew to form a new Nation of Islam, which went back to the traditional stances of the parent group. Discipline, as expressed in the reinstituted Fruit of Islam (FOI) and strict dress and moral codes, was made an important part of the group's program.

Since then, Farrakhan has built a following of between five thousand and ten thousand persons and has earned the respect of many through outreach by way of the media, personal appearances, and *The Final Call*, the organization's periodical. The group is probably the most well-known of those that split from the parent body, much of it due to Farrakhan's personal popularity, which was bolstered by his involvement in the Reverend Jesse Jackson's 1984 presidential campaign and the perceived "radical," nationalistic, and separatist position he takes.

Group Type: Denomination
Founded: 1978
Membership: Between 5,000 and 10,000 persons
Publications: The Final Call

Nation of Islam [John Muhammad]

Temple Number One
19220 Conat Street
Detroit, MI 48234
Minister John Muhammad, Imam

The Nation of Islam [John Muhammad] is the result of a schism from the American Muslim Mission (formerly the Nation of Islam) lead by the Prophet Elijah Muhammad until his death in 1975. His brother, John Muhammad, like Minister Louis Farrakhan and Caliph Emmanuel Abdullah Muhammad, rejected the shift toward Orthodox Islam that the American Muslim Mission embraced under the leadership of Elijah Muhammad's son, Wallace, who resigned in 1985 when the organization was decentralized.

Minister John Muhammad left in 1978 to continue the work and position of the parent group, as outlined in two books written by Elijah Muhammad, *Our Savior Has Arrived* and *Message to the Blackman*. He believes that "Minister" or "Prophet" Elijah Muhammad was the last messenger of Allah sent for the purpose of teaching blacks a new Islam.

The organization publishes *Minister John Muhammad Speaks*,

a periodical. There is one temple in Detroit, and Muhammad is said to have support across the United States.

Group Type: Denomination
Founded: 1978
Publications: Minister John Muhammad Speaks

Nation of Islam [The Caliph]

No current address
Caliph Emmanuel A. Muhammad

The Nation of Islam [The Caliph] is the result of several schisms in the late 1970s within the American Muslim Mission (formerly the Nation of Islam) lead by Prophet Elijah Muhammad. After his death in 1975, and the succession of Wallace D. Muhammad, his son, as leader, the organization moved toward acceptance and practice of Orthodox Islam and away from its more nationalistic stance. Among those who opposed this move was Emmanuel Abdullah Muhammad, a prominent follower of Elijah Muhammad. He affirmed his position as caliph—the title taken by Mohammed's successors as secular and religious heads of Islam—in order to lead and guide the people in the absence of Allah (who, according to the beliefs of the American Muslim Mission, was believed to be in the person of Wallace Fard Muhammad) and his messenger, Elijah Muhammad. According to Islamic tradition, a caliph always follows a messenger.

This group had retained the traditional beliefs of the American Muslim Mission, those in place before the Mission's move toward Orthodox Islam. It reinstituted the Fruit of Islam (FOI), the disciplined security and protection force of black Muslim men, and formed a new school, the University of Islam. The group also promotes economic self-sufficiency through businesses and programs. It publishes *Muhammad Speaks*, a periodical. In 1982, there were two mosques, located in Baltimore and Chicago.

Group Type: Denomination
Founded: 1978
Membership: 2 mosques
Publications: Muhammad Speaks

Vodoun

Afro-American Vodoun

No central address

"Vodoun, which is usually mistakenly referred to as 'voodoo,' is a complex and highly sophisticated religion, chiefly African in origin, which is practiced by the majority of people in Haiti. Because of the dispersion of Haitians in recent years, Vodoun has spread to areas outside of the geographical confines of the republic of Haiti. In the United States, Miami and New York are now important centers of Vodoun.

Vodoun is not the practice of 'Black Magic,' as is commonly believed. The very name *Vodoun* means *god* and comes from Benin (formerly Dahomey).

Its liturgy centers around the *loa* (also known as *les mys-*

teres), spirits primarily drawn from the Fon of Benin and the Yoruba of Nigeria. However, there are also *loa* that come from Central Africa as well as from other regions of the continent. It is helpful to think of Vodoun as a form of 'decentralized monotheism': there is one Supreme Being, but the human world enters into contact with the world of the *loa*, rather than into direct contact with the Supreme Being.

Because African slaves could legally gather for Roman Catholic worship only, the practice of any African religion was strictly forbidden during the colonial period. However, the Haitians soon discovered similarities between the archetypes represented by the *loa* and those represented by the saints in the Roman Catholic Church. Furthermore, the slaves discovered that Roman Catholicism, because of its beliefs and practices, provided the perfect mantle under which to practice the religion of the *loa*. Outsiders thought that the Africans were practicing Roman Catholicism, when they were practicing what came to be known as Vodoun. This explains the prominence of Roman Catholic elements in Vodoun.

The Vodoun priests (*houngan*) and priestesses (*mambo*) head the liturgies, which can include ceremonial spirit possession. The *loa* 'mount' certain believers and manifest through them. In this way they communicate their instructions, advice, and commentaries; therefore, in the state of ceremonial spirit possession, it is the *loa* who act and speak, not the possessed person.''

—Father Elias Farajajé-Jones, Dr. Theol., Assistant Professor of World Religions, Howard University School of Divinity, Washington, D.C.

Group Type: Denomination

First Church of Voodoo

No current address

The First Church of Voodoo was incorporated in 1973 by Robert W. Pelton, a freelance photographer who studied voodoo practitioners throughout the United States in the early 1970s. This resulted in several books on voodoo practices. Pelton formed the church and met at the home of Francis and Candy Torrance (a voodoo priest and priestess who taught a course in voodoo magic at the University of Tennessee) in North Knoxville, Tennessee. The church's teachings mesh elements of voodoo, Christianity, and ''hoodoo'' (conjuremen), and it offers ordination by mail.

Group Type: Denomination
Founded: 1973

Yoruba Theological Archministry

No current address
John Mason

The Yoruba Theological Archministry began in the early 1980s in Manhattan. The leader, John Mason, has written several books on the ministry. The last available information indicated that there was one center in New York.

Group Type: Denomination
Founded: 1980s
Publications: *Sin Egun (Ancestor Worship)*, 1981; *Osanyin*, 1983; *Ebo Eje (Blood Sacrifice)*, 1981; and *Onje Fun Orisa*, 1981, all by John Mason, Yoruba Theological Archministry, New York

Yoruba Village of Oyotunji

P.O. Box 51
Sheldon, SC 29941
(803) 846-8900
Oba Efuntola Oseijeman Adelabu Adefunmi I, Founder
Her Royal Grace Iya Orite Olasowo, Chief Minister, Royal Ministry of Tourism

The Yoruba Village of Oyotunji is the result of Walter Eugene King's study of Haitian voodoo and African religion. He was born on October 5, 1928, in Detroit, Michigan. Now known as Oba (King) Efuntola Oseijeman Adelabu Adefunmi I, he left his family's traditional Baptist teachings while in his teens and began to search for ancient African gods. Although he began African studies at the age of fourteen, his first exposure to African religion came during his association with the Katherine Dunham Dance Troupe in 1948. After joining the African Nationalist Movement in 1954, he went to Haiti, where he discovered voodoo. King returned to the United States and founded the Order of Damballah Hwedo Ancestor Priests in 1955.

During a trip to Cuba in 1959, he became the first African American fully initiated into the Orisha-Vodu (Santeria) African priesthood by Cubans of African descent at Matanzas, Cuba. This event marked the beginning of the spread of the Yoruba religion and culture among African Americans. The Order of Damballah Hwedo Ancestor Priests was subsequently dissolved and replaced by the Shango Temple, which was eventually renamed the Yoruba Temple. In 1960, the African Theological Archministry was incorporated.

According to the organization, the ''dashiki,'' a loosely fitting, brightly colored robe or tunic modeled after traditional African attire, was introduced by King Adefunmi to the United States in the summer of 1960. The dashiki was popularized by the civil rights, black power, and student movements of the 1960s. King Adefunmi also opened the Ujamaa African Market in 1962, which began a trend toward African boutiques that spread across the country. In 1961, he founded the Yoruba Academy for the study of Yoruba history, religion, and language. King Adefunmi also fostered the establishment of houses of Orisha-Vodu worship in Gary, IN, and Philadelphia.

In the late 1960s, the African Nationalistic Independence Partition Party was established by King Adefunmi with the goal of establishing an African state in America by 1972. A flag was designed for the new state consisting of red, gold, and green bars. The gold bar was emblazoned with an ankh, the ancient Egyptian symbol of life.

Most of the group moved with King Adefunmi to Beaufort County, South Carolina in 1970 and established the Yoruba Village of Oyotunji, modeled after Nigerian communities. It was here that the Afro-Cuban Santeria priesthood was altered to conform to Nigerian principles of Orisha-Vodoun worship. King Adefunmi went to Abeokuta, Nigeria, in 1972 and was initiated into the Ifa priesthood by the Oluwa of Ijeun. He was subsequently declared the ''oba-king'' of Oyotunji. In 1973, he organized several traditional societies to establish rules for the community, based on an African model. These include the first official Ogboni Parliament of Oyotunji chiefs and landowners, and the *Igbimolosha*, the priests' council. The community has a palace for the king, his seven wives, and nineteen children. There are temples dedicated to different deities. Only the Yoruba language is spoken before noon each day. As the African American delegate to the first International Congress on Orisha Tradition and Culture at Ile-Ife University in Nigeria, King Adefunmi was handed royal emblems and given the title ''Bale'' (town king) by the *Ooni* (king) of Ife, His Royal Majesty Okunade Sijuwade Olubushe II. He is now addressed as ''His Royal Highness Adefunmi I.'' King Adefunmi I became the first of a line of New World Yoruba kings consecrated at and to the *Ooni* of Ife.

Worship is centered on reverence for the deities and ancestors, which are considered the closest spiritual entities to humankind. Polygamy is practiced. Partially due to King Adefunmi's connection to the African nationalist movement, many persons have continued to come to the village regardless of their personal beliefs. The founder has published a book on the Yoruba religion, as have others.

The group has received continual national news attention since 1973 and more recently on "The Oprah Winfrey Show," which was coordinated by his now headwife and public relations director, Her Royal Grace Iya Orite Olasowo. Visitors and tourists are welcome to the village to see the king, his queens, chiefs, and members of the community. They are also welcome to witness the Yoruba Temple dancers and drummers, the African market, and the voodoo festival. African shell readings are available by mail or in person.

Group Type: Denomination
Founded: 1970
Membership: As of 1982, approximately 2,000 persons nationally; the Oyotunji village has a population of 110 persons
Publications: *Olorisha, A Guidebook into Yoruba Religion*, Oba Efuntola Oseijeman Adelabu Adefunmi I, 1982; *Oyotunji*, Carlos Canet, Editorial AIP, Miami, FL, n.d.; *Oyotunji Village*, Carl M. Hunt, University Press of America, Washington, D.C., 1979; *Ancestors of the Afro-Americans*, Baba Oseijeman Adefunmi, Aims of Modzawe, Long Island City, NY, 1973

Part 2

African American Religious Councils, Ecumenical Organizations, and Service Agencies

The following listing includes religious councils, ecumenical organizations, music resources, and service agencies and organizations.

Religious Councils

African American Religious Connection

c/o Fellowship Baptist Church
4543 Princeton Avenue
Chicago, IL 60609
(312) 924-3232
The Reverend Clay Evans, President and Founder

The African American Religious Connection was founded in February, 1989 by the Reverend Clay Evans to promote interdenominational fellowship and support for church broadcasts and to establish a stronger communications ministry among all denominations.

Group Type: Ecumenical/nondenominational; worship resource
Founded: February 1989

American Women's Clergy Association and Male Auxiliary

214 P Street, NW
Washington, DC 20001
(202) 797-7460 or 275-3318
The Reverend Imagene Bigham Stewart, Founder and National President
The Reverend Mozelle James Fuller, Co-Founder

The American Women's Clergy Association and Male Auxiliary is a group of lay and ordained female and male ministers who operate the "House of Imagene," a twenty-four-hour shelter for homeless persons in northwest Washington, D.C. The group was founded by the Reverend Imagene Bigham Stewart in October, 1969, as the "Women Ministers of Greater Washington." Today, the Reverend Stewart is the national president. The American Women's Clergy Association and Male Auxiliary meets every third Saturday at various designated locations.

Group Type: Ecumenical/nondenominational; ministerial; women
Founded: 1969
Meetings: Meets every third Saturday

Faith Hope Charity in Christ Outreach Center, Inc.

2501 Waters Avenue
Savannah, GA 31404

Group Type: Ecumenical/nondenominational

Hampton University Ministers Conference and Choir Directors and Organists Guild Workshop

Office of the Chaplain
Hampton University
Hampton, VA 23668
(804) 727-5340
Dr. A. C. D. Vaughn, President
The Reverend M. A. Battle, Executive Secretary/University Chaplain

Begun in 1914 on the campus of what was then Hampton Institute, the Hampton University Ministers Conference brings together ministers and church music professionals in full session during the first week in June and in minisessions in February. Meetings include lectures and worship services. The Annual Choir Directors and Organists Guild Workshop portion of the Conference started in 1934.

The Hampton University Ministers Conference is an active and growing entity. Because its numbers have begun to exceed the capacity of the Memorial Church and Ogden Hall, its traditional meetings places, the Conference is raising funds for building an 8,000-seat Convocation Center. It will be used for Conference meetings and many Hampton University programs. The president is Dr. A. C. D. Vaughn, and the executive secretary is the Reverend M. A. Battle. Charles W. Green is the chairman of the Convocation Center Committee.

Group Type: Ecumenical/nondenominational; ministerial; worship resource
Founded: 1914 (Ministers Conference); 1934 (Choir Directors and Organists Guild Workshops)
Meetings: Annual meeting the first week in June

Interdenominational Women's Ministerial Alliance

716 Charing Cross Road
Baltimore, MD 21229
(301) 744-1996
The Reverend Eva Sapp, President

The goal of the Interdenominational Women's Ministerial Alliance (IWMA) of Baltimore, Maryland, is "to develop strong bonds as women called by God and as Christian women to facilitate open and honest dialogue as it relates to our spiritual, personal and professional journeys." Toward these ends, the organization seeks to: 1) stimulate networking and sharing among women ministers and Christian women; 2) promote acceptance of women in the ministry and emphasize their ministry on all levels in the community; and 3) acquaint the Baltimore area with the uniqueness of women ministers.

IWMA has sponsored concerts, workshops, and its own convention. It publishes the *IWMA Journal*. The president is the Reverend Eva Sapp.

Group Type: Ecumenical/nondenominational; ministerial; women
Publications: *IWMA Journal*, a newsletter

Marin City Ministerial Alliance

c/o Village Baptist Church
825 Drake Avenue
Marin City, CA 94965
The Reverend Emmanuel Akognon, President

Group Type: Ecumenical/nondenominational; ministerial; council of churches/group

National Black Evangelical Association

5736 North Albina Avenue
Portland, OR 97217
(503) 289-0143
Bishop George McKinney, President
The Reverend Aaron M. Hamlin, Executive Director

From its founding in 1963, the National Black Evangelical Association (NBEA) has concerned itself with reconciliation, inspiration, and education. An umbrella organization of individuals and groups representing several different denominations, the NBEA has worked to "facilitate communication and understanding between Christians from different geographical areas as well as different traditions." The purposes of the

organization are to: 1) increase fellowship among others with like goals; and 2) minister to the African American community, reaching community members with the message of Jesus Christ, so that they might affirm our Lord in the totality of their being, in every aspect of their lives.

Currently, the NBEA is turning its attention to young people's issues and issues of the African American family. Their 1988 annual convention included such topics as "Evangelizing Urban Youth," "Parenting in the Black Family," "The Plight of Black America," "Black Female Roles in the Light of Biblical Teaching," and "Critical Issues of the Aged." The Institute of Black Evangelical Thought and Action was inaugurated at that convention. The NBEA publishes a monthly newsletter, *The NBEA Outreach*.

The National Black Evangelical Association works through nine commissions and numerous local chapters. The entire body meets annually in a five-day convention. A Board of Directors provides leadership and guidance. The President is Bishop George McKinney and the Executive Director is the Reverend Aaron M. Hamlin. The organization is based in Portland, Oregon.

Group Type: Ecumenical/nondenominational; lay
Founded: 1963
Publications: *The NBEA Outreach*, a monthly newsletter, Dr. Ruth Lewis-Bentley, editor
Meetings: Annual meeting is held from Wednesday through Sunday after Easter

North Carolina Association for Women in the Ministry, Inc.

P.O. Box 37253
Raleigh, NC 27502
(919) 362-5381
The Reverend Mary M. Heggie, Organizer

Organized in 1984 by the Reverend Mary Heggie, assistant pastor of the Progressive Missionary Baptist Church, the North Carolina Association for Women in the Ministry, Inc., is an interdenominational group for women ministers.

The purposes and objectives of the group are to: 1) enhance the spiritual and intellectual well-being of women ministers throughout the state; 2) encourage and promote a better working Christian relationship with one another and the brothers in the ministry; 3) promote and encourage ministerial professional participation in all areas of church life available to the clergy, regardless of sex; 4) promote harmony, spiritual, and Christian development with one another and all members of the clergy; 5) carry out the Christian Commission as stated by Christ in Luke 4:18-19; and 6) sensitize the general public to the anointing of God's hands on women to become members of the clergy.

The group is organized on the state (convention), county, and area group level and was incorporated in Raleigh, North Carolina, in 1985.

Group Type: Ecumenical/nondenominational; ministerial; women
Founded: 1984
Meetings: Annual meeting in December in Raleigh, NC

Ecumenical/Nondenominational Organizations

African Peoples' Christian Organization

415 Atlantic Avenue
Brooklyn, NY 11217
(718) 596-1991
The Reverend Dr. Herbert Daughtry, President

The African Peoples' Christian Organization (APCO) was founded in October, 1982. At the fifty-second convocation of the House of the Lord Pentecostal Churches, its General Assembly adopted a resolution put forth by the Reverend Dr. Herbert Daughtry (its national presiding minister and pastor of the House of the Lord Church in Brooklyn, New York) to create an organization that would foster the development of an African Christian nation. APCO was launched with an inaugural program on March 20, 1983, attended by approximately 1,000 persons. A special address was delivered by Ambassador Omaru Yosoufou, executive secretary of the Organization of African Unity. Dr. Daughtry gave his initial major address as the first president of the group at the same meeting.

Since its inception, APCO has added several ongoing programs to its program. These include the Timbuktu Learning Center, a voting block, a prison ministry, a lecture series, Nation Time rallies (held at the Brooklyn church), radiobroadcasts, a research division, a college division, borough chapters, APCO enterprises, and membership meetings. In addition, it has sponsored health fairs, cultural music programs, and other activities to enrich the community.

APCO has four major thrusts: 1) to adhere to fundamental biblical Christianity; 2) to affirm African identity and heritage; 3) to advance the cause of human rights; and 4) to assert the rights to self-determination and nationhood.

The growing organization is composed of twelve ministers, one hundred fifty adults, and a youth division of one hundred in the New York City and tri-state area. The general membership meets monthly, as does the executive board. It publishes a quarterly newsletter, *The Horizon*, and has published *Look for Me in the Whirlwind*, a biographical sketch of Marcus Garvey by secretary general Charles Barron. Its current president is the Reverend Dr. Herbert Daughtry.

Group Type: Ecumenical/nondenominational; lay/clergy
Founded: 1982
Membership: 150 adults, 100 youth, 12 ministers
Publications: *The Horizon*, a quarterly newsletter; *Look for Me in the Whirlwind*, a biographical sketch of Marcus Garvey
Meetings: General membership and executive board both meet monthly

Black Light Fellowship

P.O. Box 5369
Chicago, IL 60680
(312) 722-1441
The Reverend Walter A. McCray, Founder and Director
Mrs. Walter A. McCray, Founder

The Black Light Fellowship was founded by the Reverend and Mrs. Walter A. McCray in the fall of 1976, in Chicago,

Illinois. It seeks "to disciple black people into Christ-centered black nationhood through a complete and full Bible-based program." Approximately fifteen black Christians compose the volunteer force that sponsors and supports seminars in the Chicago area. Among the group's publications are *Black Folks and Christian Liberty*, *Reaching and Teaching Black Young Adults*, and *How to Stick Together During Times of Tension*. A new manual, *The Black Presence in the Bible*, has recently been released. The Reverend McCray serves as the director.

Group Type: Ecumenical/nondenominational; publishing
Founded: 1976
Membership: Approximately 15 volunteers
Publications: *Black Folks and Christian Liberty*; *Reaching and Teaching Black Young Adults*; *How to Stick Together During Times of Tension*; and *The Black Presence in the Bible*

Campus Crusade for Christ, International

National Headquarters:
Arrowhead Springs
San Bernardino, CA 92414
(714) 886-5224
Dr. Bill Bright, Founder and President

Here's Life Black America
4651 Flat Shoals Road, Suite 1-A
Union City, GA 30291
(404) 969-7278
Mr. Crawford Loritts, Jr., National Director

Intercultural Resources Ministry
4651 Flat Shoals Road, Suite 1-A
Union City, GA 30291
(404) 969-7278
Mr. Thomas Fritz, National Director

Campus Crusade for Christ, International (CCC), was founded by Bill and Vonette Bright on the campus of the University of California, Los Angeles (UCLA), in 1951. Its purpose is to "help change the world" by introducing people to Jesus Christ and training them to encourage others to accept Him as their personal Savior. Through this process, deemed "spiritual multiplication," the organization seeks to spread the Gospel throughout the world. It functions as an interdenominational para-church group, not seeking to replace the traditional role of the church, but rather assisting the ministry of congregations through the resources of those involved in ministry. It achieves these objectives through several programs aimed at specific audiences.

Here's Life Black America (HLBA) is a CCC program "serving the black church and community as a catalyst towards spiritual awakening, a great harvest of souls and the sending of laborers with the Gospel." Founded in 1982, and headquartered in Union City, Georgia, HLBA is a resource for the black church, providing culturally relevant video and audiocassette training in various areas of ministry, as well as sponsoring pastors', women's leadership, and urban family life conferences nationwide. The organization publishes a newsletter, the *HLBA Update* and the *Legacy Letter*. The national director is Crawford Loritts, Jr.

The *Intercultural Resources Ministry* (ICRM) was formalized as a component of Campus Crusade for Christ, International, in 1974. It seeks to facilitate effective ministry to and through African American and other minority college students. The purpose of the ministry is to "win, build and send" black and other minority college students to help fulfill the Great Commission of Jesus Christ in the United States. Its scope is international. Staff teams are located at the historically black Howard University, Jackson State University, and the Atlanta University Center, as well as on several predominantly white college campuses. There are also ministries in Africa, Asia, and Latin America. It produces the *Gospel Grapevine*, a newsletter, and has produced a workbook, *Reaching and Involving Black Students in the Movement of Campus Crusade for Christ*. In January 1991, the "Black Student Leadership Conference" will be offered to train students in evangelism and spiritual development. In December, 1991, the "Black Student Christmas Conference" will be held, the first conference of its kind. The national director of ICRM is Thomas Fritz.

Group Type: Ecumenical/nondenominational; student; lay
Founded: 1951
Membership: Ministries located on over 200 U.S. college campuses and at over half the college campuses in Africa; also ministries in churches, businesses, and Third World nations
Publications: Legacy Letter, HLBA Update, Gospel Grapevine, and Reaching and Involving Black Students in the Movement of Campus Crusade for Christ
Meetings: Black Student Leadership Conference, January 1991; the Black Student Christmas Conference, December, 1991; conference held in April

Center for Black Church Development

16776 Southfield Road
Detroit, MI 48235
(313) 534-2773
Mr. Matthew Parker, Chief Executive Officer and Chairman of the Board

Formed in the fall of 1984 by individuals who had attended the first National Summit on Black Church Development, the Center for Black Church Development (CBCD) was designed to address the need for evangelism, discipleship, church planning, leadership, and community development within the African American community. Developing programs with pastors and church leaders, the Center seeks to meet the spiritual and physical needs of the people of Detroit, Michigan.

There are three divisions of CBCD. The *Christian Business and Professional Committee* presents the message of Jesus Christ to business and professional people and helps them develop skills to carry out the Great Commission (Matthew 28:16-20). The *Detroit Institute for Biblical Studies* prepares students for Christian ministries or church vocations through Bible studies. *Christian Discipleship Unlimited* presents the message of Jesus Christ to college students and trains them to become involved in the Great Commission. CBCD sponsors seminars, work-

shops, conferences, Bible classes, and specialized community outreach programs. It also functions as a resource for the Detroit urban Christian community, particularly for white Christian organizations seeking to work with African American leadership in reaching the African American community. Toward this end, the Center works in partnership with the Christian Business Men's Committee, the InterVarsity Christian Fellowship, the Metropolitan Detroit Child Evangelism Fellowship, and Prison Fellowship.

The Center is headed by Mr. Matthew Parker, its Chief Executive Officer. There is also a twenty-five member board of directors, composed of clergy and laity. There are seventeen churches affiliated with the Center for Black Church Development.

Group Type: Ecumenical/nondenominational; lay/clergy; Christian education
Founded: 1984
Membership: 17 churches

Clergy Interracial Forum—GRACE

38 West Fulton Street
Grand Rapids, MI 49503
(616) 774-2042
The Reverend David P. Baak, Executive Director

In 1983, a meeting of more than fifty African American and white clergy was organized by the Church Community Relations Committee of the Inter-Denominational Ministerial Alliance in response to a crisis regarding the Grand Rapids public school's superintendency. It was felt that "positive racial relationships needed to begin with members of the clergy" and that "black and white clergy must end [their] 'separateness' first." Accordingly, a planning committee was formed and the Grand Rapids Area Center for Ecumenism (GRACE) agreed to act as convener of both the planning group and the larger forum.

Clergy Interracial Forum meetings were held in November, 1983, March, 1984, and September, 1984, and were planned by representatives of the Inter-Denominational Ministerial Alliance, the Grand Rapids Ministerial Association, and the Grand Rapids Urban Fellowship. The chief concern was to provide "a means to foster communications among clergy persons regarding issues of importance to our community, especially as it relates to interfaith, interracial issues, and to do so in a context that promotes 'contact, dialogue, and fellowship.'"

In 1984, activities such as congregational pairing and pulpit exchanges were implemented, involving some forty congregations and resulting in lasting relationships. Since 1985, sessions of the Clergy Interracial Forum have been held on a regular basis, and in addition, several interracial activities have been held as a result of the friendships established through the organization.

Currently, the Clergy Interracial Forum's monthly meeting is co-chaired by both an African American and a white clergyperson, and is composed of approximately seventy-five people, both clergy and lay (predominantly male). The need for fellowship and action are stressed, usually through discussion of issues. Special emphases are congregational exchanges and Black History Month. The Clergy Interracial Forum also sponsors an annual multiracial service on the National Day of Prayer.

GRACE maintains the organization's mailing list, continues to convene the forum, and provides staff support.

Group Type: Ecumenical/nondenominational; lay/clergy
Founded: 1983
Membership: Approximately 75 persons
Meetings: Monthly meetings

Coalition for Christian Outreach—Black Campus Ministry

6740 Fifth Avenue
Pittsburgh, PA 15208
(412) 363-3303, x32
The Reverend James E. Hunt, Director, Urban/Cross-
  Cultural Ministry

The Coalition for Christian Outreach (CCO), a campus ministry organization, was founded in 1971 to meet the needs of college students who will be future leaders. Its goals are to reach students with the message of Jesus Christ and to help them reflect the Gospel message in their lives. Toward these ends, the Coalition seeks to unite with churches, colleges, and universities. It functions in western Pennsylvania, northern West Virginia, and eastern Ohio, serving approximately forty-five campuses.

Black Campus Ministry is a component of the Coalition for Christian Outreach's Urban/Cross-Cultural Ministry. Of the 400,000 students in the area the Coalition serves, approximately 45,000 are African American. The Black Campus Ministry believes that its ministry should be threefold: 1) it should be based in the African American church; 2) it should maintain an African American fellowship group on campus with its own identity; and 3) it should provide opportunities for African American students to relate to other Christian groups in order to break down cultural, racial, and social barriers. In light of this, the Black Campus Ministry's goals include equipping African American students to proclaim the Gospel and to develop a Christian view of life. It also promotes student involvement to encourage future leadership in the African American church and community and stresses the importance of African American history and contemporary African American life. The Black Campus Ministry publishes *Focus on Black Campus Ministry*, a newsletter.

Group Type: Ecumenical/nondenominational; student
Founded: 1971
Membership: Approximately 45 campuses
Publications: Focus on Black Campus Ministry

Congress of National Black Churches

600 New Hampshire Avenue, NW, Suite 650
Washington, DC 20037
(202) 333-3060
The Reverend Dr. Charles W. Butler, Chairman, Board of
  Directors
The Reverend H. Michael Lemmons, Executive Director
Bishop John Hurst Adams, Founder and Chairman Emeritus

The Congress of National Black Churches (CNBC) was founded in 1978, in Washington, D.C., to strengthen and enhance the ministry in the black churches. The Congress is a representative organization through which six major African American denominations (the African Methodist Episcopal Church, the Christian Methodist Episcopal Church, the Progressive National Baptist Convention, Inc., the National Baptist Convention of America, Inc., the Church of God in Christ, and the National Missionary Baptist Convention of America) share in common ventures designed to enlarge their witness. Funding was provided by the Lilly Endowment, Inc., during the formative years of the Congress. The Lilly grants were augmented by membership dues from the constituent church groups and by contributions from individual congregations, conferences, and other judicatories.

The initial emphases of the CNBC were evangelism, theological education, economic development, and the development of media and communication resources. Since its inception, other projects have been implemented, including programs addressing the problems of substance abuse, casualty insurance for churches, African American families, the enhancement of the churches in order to address areas of community concern, and a broad-based program to inform the churches about justice and freedom issues. With the support of the Ford Foundation, the Carnegie Endowment, the Lilly Endowment, and the U. S. Department of Justice, these efforts are yielding significant results. The casualty insurance program is a cooperative undertaking with the Aetna Life Insurance Company.

One of the programs seeks to aid African American churches, together with parents and schools, to foster the intellectual and emotional growth of inner-city primary schoolchildren. Project SPIRIT (strength, perseverance, imagination, responsibility, integrity, and talent) offers after-school academic tutoring, morale-building, and instruction in practical living skills.

Project SPIRIT has a three-pronged approach. Students identified as "underachievers" are targeted for involvement in Project SPIRIT. Sixty-five percent of these students have been referred by their schools, and the others have been referred by concerned parents. The complementary "parent education" program teaches parents about child development and how to provide youngsters with emotional support and discipline. Project SPIRIT is currently being pilot-tested in five African American churches in Oakland, Atlanta, and Indianapolis, serving 350 youngsters. Funding for the project was obtained from the Carnegie Endowment is part of its support of church-based programs on behalf of children, families, and black-run institutions that specifically address African American family needs.

The Congress also sponsors the National Fellowship Program for Black Pastors. This program allows ministers to gain practical experience in various fields, from social work to communications, in numerous sites across the country. This experience is then applied in the field of ministry. The National Fellowship Program for Black Pastors places ministers in secular, capacity-building institutions to develop a cadre of practicing and prospective pastors who will serve as advocates in areas of critical concern for future generations. Pastors are nominated for the program by the member denominations of the Congress of National Black Churches, Inc. The fellowship is awarded for a ten-month period. The fellows develop a project at their worksite that addresses a critical need within the African American community.

The Congress of National Black Churches, Inc., is governed by a Board of Directors that seeks the advice and counsel of individuals expert in particular dimensions of mission or African American church life. The board meets quarterly; the operational program units meet at the call of their respective directors in concert with their advisory committees.

The Congress of National Black Churches has a combined membership of fifteen million persons and approximately fifty thousand churches in its six constituent bodies. The chairman of the Board of Directors of the Congress, the Reverend Dr. Charles William Butler, pastor of the New Calvary Baptist Church in Detroit, assumed his responsibilities in September 1988. The founder and chairman emeritus of the organization is Bishop John Hurst Adams, senior bishop of the African Methodist Episcopal Church. The Reverend H. Michael Lemmons serves as the executive director.

Group Type: Ecumenical/nondenominational; council of churches/groups
Founded: 1978
Membership: 15,000,000 persons in 50,000 churches in its 6 constituent bodies
Meetings: Board meets quarterly; operational program units meet as necessary

Interreligious Foundation for Community Organization

402 W. 145th Street
New York, NY 10031
(212) 926-5757
The Reverend Lucius Walker, Jr., Executive Director

The Interreligious Foundation for Community Organization (IFCO) was founded in July, 1967 in New York City by a group of clergy and lay community workers from nine national religious organizations and one civic foundation. From its inception, it has sought to assist the poor and disenfranchised by developing community organizations to fight for human and civil rights. IFCO coordinates, promotes, and funds these efforts. It became the first and only national ecumenical foundation committed exclusively to the support of community organization.

Composed of hundreds of community organizations, clergy, community organizers, professionals, young and old, IFCO currently assists more than one hundred community organizations and public policy groups through technical assistance and fiscal agent grants, when possible. Its programs and activities include fundraising training, fiscal agent services, education on justice issues, consultation and coordination services, Nicaragua/Honduras study tours, state-by-state Central America Information Week campaigns, and Pastors for Peace.

During the *Central America Information Week Project*, initiated in 1983, resource people from that region and Americans who have traveled there conduct a week's program of hundreds of educational and cultural events to give information, analysis, context, and a call to action for the case against U.S. intervention in Central America. The group is interested in launching a similar project for South Africa, based on the Central America program.

In addition, IFCO is planning its *Church Partnership Program*, whose purpose will be to promote community growth and hope by visiting communities nationwide to address domestic social justice issues such as poverty, drug abuse, peace, health, crime, and local organizing; and to help tie these issues to global concerns. Efforts are currently underway to establish

the Dr. Negail R. Riley Memorial Scholarship Fund to provide overseas sabbaticals for grassroots community organizers.

Currently IFCO publishes the *IFCO News*, a quarterly newsletter for its five thousand supporters in the United States, Europe, and many Third World countries; an annual report of IFCO concerns; and the Central America Information Week Campaign reports. Its Board of Directors meets twice a year. It also hosts periodic Organizers' Conferences to discuss a variety of social justice issues. IFCO's executive director is the Reverend Dr. Lucius Walker, Jr.

Group Type: Ecumenical/nondenominational; lay/clergy; research/education
Founded: July, 1967
Membership: Hundreds of lay and clergy
Publications: IFCO News, a quarterly newsletter; an annual report; and the Central America Information Week Campaign reports
Meetings: Meets in May and October; hosts periodic organizers' conferences

National Association of Black Seminarians

1400 Shepherd Street, NE
Washington, DC 20017
(202) 806-0500
Miniard Culpepper, President

The National Association of Black Seminarians (NAOBS), formerly known as the National Conference of Black Seminarians, is the only interdenominational organization of African American theological students in the United States. It was established in 1978 at the Interdenominational Theological Center in Atlanta, Georgia. Since its inception, it has sought to foster fellowship, coalitions, and dialogues pertinent to the needs of African American seminarians and graduate theology students.

Its mission incorporates the following: 1) to maintain a network of communication among African American seminarians that will allow for continuing dialogue on issues germane to their respective academic and social settings; 2) to work in conjunction with persons of other disciplines and social settings toward the common objective of facilitating change wherever such change is deemed necessary; 3) to ensure that African American seminarians maintain close contact with the African American community, so that theological training remains relevant to the realities of the African American experience.

In 1986, NAOBS became a nonprofit organization. It established a National Board of Advisors to provide organizational stability. This board includes: Dr. Charles Adams, Hartford Memorial Baptist Church, Detroit, Michigan; Dr. Delores Williams, Drew University, Madison, New Jersey; Dr. Clarice Martin, Princeton Theological Seminary, Princeton, New Jersey; Dr. W. Franklyn Richardson, General Secretary, The National Baptist Convention, U.S.A., Inc.; Dr. H. Beecher Hicks, Jr., Metropolitan Baptist Church, Washington, D.C.; Dr. Peter Paris, Princeton Theological Seminary, Princeton, New Jersey; Dr. Joe Thomas, Pacific School of Religion, Berkeley, California; Bishop H. H. Brookins, African Methodist Episcopal Church; Dr. Henry Young, Garrett-Evangelical Theological Seminary, Evanston, Illinois; Dr. Robert Franklin, Candler School of Theology, Atlanta, Georgia; Dr. Praethia Hall-Winn,

United Theological Seminary, Dayton, Ohio; and Dr. Cain H. Felder, Howard University School of Divinity, Washington, D.C.

NAOBS sponsors national conferences that focus on substantive issues confronting African American religious institutions. Its major conferences have been held at: Interdenominational Theological Center, Atlanta, Georgia (1979); Duke University, Durham, North Carolina (1980); Association of Chicago Theological Schools, Chicago, Illinois (1981); Harvard Divinity School, Cambridge, Massachusetts (1982); Interdenominational Theological Center, Atlanta, Georgia (1983); Virginia Union University, Richmond, Virginia (1986); Vanderbilt University, Nashville, Tennessee (1987); Garrett-Evangelical Theological Seminary, Evanston, Illinois (1988); Graduate Theological Union, Berkeley, California (1989); and Princeton Theological Seminary, Princeton, New Jersey (1990).

The NAOBS operates on both national and regional levels. The national officers are: Miniard Culpepper, Howard University School of Divinity (president); Samuel Nixon, Jr., Harvard University Divinity School (vice-president); Durant K. Harvin III, Colgate Rochester Divinity School/Bexley Hall/Crozer Theological Seminary (chaplain); Perry E. Davis, Princeton Theological Seminary (treasurer); and Bonita Kitt, Graduate Theological Union (secretary). The regional offices are directed by vice-presidents. The geographic subdivisions are: Far West (California, Oregon, and Washington); Southwest/Rocky Mountain (Colorado, Louisiana, Oklahoma, and Texas); Plains (Iowa, Kansas, Minnesota, and South Dakota); Mideast (District of Columbia, Maryland, New Jersey, New York, and Pennsylvania); New England (Connecticut, Maine, and Massachusetts); Southeast (Florida, Georgia, Kansas, North Carolina, South Carolina, Tennessee, Virginia, and Puerto Rico); and Great Lakes (Illinois, Indiana, Michigan, Ohio, and Wisconsin).

Group Type: Ecumenical/nondenominational; student
Founded: 1978

National Black Christian Students Conference

P.O. Box 4311
Chicago, IL 60680
(312) 722-1441
The Reverend Walter McCray, Chairperson
(312) 722-0236
Dr. Ruth Lewis Bentley, Founder and Co-Chairperson

The National Black Christian Students Conference (NBCSC) was established at the convention of the National Black Evangelical Association in Dallas, Texas in April, 1974, by Dr. Ruth Lewis Bentley, its current co-chairperson, and Wyn Wright Potter. Composed of African American high school, college, and graduate students, as well as community workers across the country, the group seeks "to challenge black students to a deeper relationship with and understanding of Jesus Christ as Lord and Liberator . . . to call black students to commitment to the black community by struggling for our holistic liberation."

The organization has five aims: 1) to foster understanding among African American students and challenge them to live out the conviction that Jesus Christ is Lord over all; 2) to assist African American students in maintaining a deep relationship with Jesus through Bible study, prayer, and fellowship; and enabling them to cope with the liberating implications, transformations, and consecration that will result from such a relationship; 3) to lead and call, in accord with God's thoughts and ways, African American students and groups into a definitive individual and corporate commitment to the African American community in terms of location, finances, time, and resources; 4) to help African American students in knowing, loving, securing, and abounding in a holistic liberation of African American people that is religious, cultural, familial, communal, social, educational, financial, political, and geographical, and that has as its base a liberating African American theology and spirituality that permeates all; and 5) to aid African American students in realizing, overcoming, and guarding against the struggles and opposition—both personal and public—of Satan, whites and blacks, non-Christians and Christians, which are diametrically set against the total liberation of African American people.

Currently, the organization is endowing the William Hiram Bentley Chair of Black Theology, which awards scholarships to students of black theology. The chairperson is the Reverend Walter McCray. The National Black Christian Students Conference meets monthly and annually. It conducts an annual conference in November.

Group Type: Ecumenical/nondenominational; student
Founded: 1974
Meetings: Meets annually in November and on a monthly basis

United Black Church Appeal

c/o Christ Church
860 Forrest Avenue
Bronx, NY 10456
(212) 665-6688
The Honorable Reverend Wendell Foster, President

The United Black Church Appeal was founded in 1980. It is a nondenominational foundation designed to provide leadership for the African American church. Its programs focus on economic development, political empowerment, and institution building (especially the family and the church).

Group Type: Ecumenical/nondenominational; lay/clergy; racial/social justice
Founded: 1980

Wednesday Clergy Fellowship

1325 Maryland Avenue, NE
Washington, DC 20002
(202) 397-4333
The Reverend Charles W. Green

Group Type: Ecumenical/nondenominational; ministerial
Founded: 1988

Music Resources

Consortium of Musicians of the Metropolitan Area, Inc.

5212 Lansing Drive
Temple Hills, MD 20748
(301) 449-5127
Mr. John F. Waters, President

The Consortium of Musicians of the Metropolitan Area, Inc., is committed to providing current, accurate information about musical resources in the metropolitan Washington, D.C. area. It publishes *Tutti*, a directory of area musicians classified by category (teacher, vocalist, director, instrumentalist, etc.); type of music, locations, or occasions; and organizations or groups. In addition, the Consortium provides current listings of musical resources to match particular interests and requirements of inquiries. The president is John F. Waters.

Group Type: Ecumenical/nondenominational; lay; music resource
Founded: 1987
Publications: *Tutti*, a directory of musicians, with a concentration in the Washington, D.C., metropolitan area

Edwin Hawkins Music and Arts Seminar, Inc.

1229 Holman Road
Oakland, CA 94610
Mr. Edwin Hawkins, Founder and Presiding Officer
The Reverend Walter Hawkins, Founder

Edwin Hawkins Music and Arts Seminar, Inc., was founded by Edwin Hawkins and his brother, the Reverend Walter Hawkins, in 1981. There are more than ten chapters of the Seminar nationwide. The organization meets annually in April. Edwin Hawkins is the presiding officer.

Group Type: Ecumenical/nondenominational; music resource
Founded: 1981
Membership: Over 10 chapters in the United States
Publications: Gospel music albums and music collections
Meetings: Meets annually in April

Gospel Music Ministries International

P.O. Box 1182
Pittsburgh, PA 15230
(412) 488-7191
The Reverend Robert J. Fulton, President and Founder

Gospel Music Ministries International (GMMI) was chartered as a corporation in the Commonwealth of Pennsylvania in 1978. It is a nonprofit, interdenominational religious ministry for all aspects of Christian talent. Its mission goals are: 1) to fulfill the Great Commission of Jesus Christ; 2) to help others use their talents in Christian service; and 3) to serve human needs. It is the parent ministry of the Gospel Music Ministries International Institute, the Christian Talent Search Crusade, and Gospel Connection World Outreach Ministries.

The Institute uses an interdisciplinary approach in ministry combining the Bible, music, and missionary outreach. Persons seeking to become "outreach missionaries" are offered the preministry training program. The Christian Talent Search Crusade is the organization's primary vehicle for "discovery, development, and presentation of Christian talent." It is an arts education program that assists in building character and communication skills through Christian-based recreation and the study of Bible literature. The music department is involved in presenting the talent discovered through the Christian Talent Search Crusade. The Gospel Connection World Outreach conference is held each September in the Poconos.

Group Type: Ecumenical/nondenominational; music resource
Founded: 1978
Meetings: Gospel Connection World Outreach conference each September

Gospel Music Workshop of America, Inc.

P.O. Box 4632
Detroit, MI 48234
(313) 989-2340
The late Reverend James Cleveland, Founder and President

The Gospel Music Workshop of America, Inc., was organized in 1966 in Detroit, Michigan, by its president, the late Reverend James Cleveland. The Workshop is interdenominational, with more than fifty chapters, and produces gospel music record albums. The organization meets annually in the fourth week in August.

Currently, the Workshop is engaged in Gospel United to Save America's Youth (GUTSAY). GUTSAY is a multifaceted project that brings together the Gospel Music Workshop of America, Inc., the Michigan Department of Public Health, and the Detroit Health Department, among others, in an effort to confront some of the social/health problems affecting youth. This project was begun in August, 1987.

Group Type: Ecumenical/nondenominational; music resource
Founded: 1966
Membership: Over 50 chapters in the United States
Publications: Gospel music record albums; souvenir bulletin at annual convention
Meetings: Annual convention fourth week in August

Gospelrama Gospel Expo, Inc.

P.O. Box 1342
Washington, DC 20013
(301) 369-7071
Dr. Henry A. Thomas, Founder

Gospelrama Gospel Expo, Inc., was organized by Deacon Henry A. Thomas in September, 1982. Its motto is: "Jesus Christ, Gospel Music, and Telecommunications." Gospelrama has more than twenty-five fellowships located mainly in the East, South, and Midwest. A monthly newspaper, *Gospelrama News* is published. The national convention is held annually during the third week in June.

Gospelrama focuses primarily on gospel presentation, vocal techniques, and instruction for musical directors and musicians. There are twenty-one national departments within the organization. The purpose of its music department is: "to unite gospel choirs, community groups, church choirs, and other entities and persons affiliated with the business of gospel music for the betterment of Christian ideals and growth. . . . [and] further engage to maintain a degree of authenticity and promulgate the message of Christ through music." Long-range goals of the organization include providing classes to teach songwriting skills and establishing a publishing vehicle for aspiring songwriters.

Group Type: Ecumenical/nondenominational; music resource
Founded: September, 1982
Publications: *Gospelrama News*, a monthly newspaper
Meetings: National Board meeting held each January; national convention held each June; and National Gospel Women's Caucus held each October

Hampton University Ministers Conference and Choir Directors and Organists Guild Workshop

Office of the Chaplain
Hampton University
Hampton, VA 23668
(804) 727-5340
Dr. A. C. D. Vaughn, President
The Reverend M.A. Battle, Executive Secretary/University
    Chaplain

Begun in 1914 on the campus of what was then Hampton Institute, the Hampton University Ministers Conference brings together ministers and church music professionals in full session during the first week in June and in minisessions in February. Meetings include lectures and worship services. The Annual Choir Directors and Organists Guild Workshop portion of the Conference started in 1934.

The Hampton University Ministers Conference is an active and growing entity. Because its numbers have begun to exceed the capacity of the Memorial Church and Ogden Hall, its traditional meetings places, the Conference is raising funds for building an eight-thousand seat convocation center. It will be used for Conference meetings and the many programs of Hampton University. The president is Dr. A. C. D. Vaughn, and the executive secretary of the Conference is the Reverend M. A. Battle; Charles W. Green is chairman of the Convocation Center Committee.

Group Type: Ecumenical/nondenominational; music resource
Founded: 1914 (ministers conference); 1934 (Choir Directors and Organists Guild Workshop)
Meetings: Annual meeting the first week in June

International Praise Gospel Music Workshop, Inc.

1985 Glencrest Lane
Annapolis, MD 21401
Minister Jeff Jacobs, Founder

The International Praise Gospel Music Workshop, Inc., was established in 1982 and incorporated in Maryland in 1985. Its founder is Minister Jeff Jacobs. International Praise has chapters in Maryland, Pennsylvania, and Virginia. It meets annually during the third week in July.

Group Type: Ecumenical/nondenominational; music resource
Founded: 1982
Meetings: Meets annually the third week in July

Middle Atlantic Regional Gospel Music Festival

5211 A Street, SE
Washington, DC 20019
Elder Dr. E. Myron Noble, Founder and Director

The Middle Atlantic Regional Gospel Music Festival (MARGMF) is an extension of the National Youth Convention of the Apostolic Faith Church of God, Inc. MARGMF was begun in June, 1972 by Elder Dr. E. Myron Noble, who continues as its director. Its emphasis is interdenominational and it seeks to provide a comprehensive Christian music education ministry for all people. Meeting every year in April, MARGMF hosts guest speakers and includes workshops on church music administration, choir directing techniques, advertising and promotion and copyright procedures, as well as sales of books, records, and literature. Fifteen workshops and seminars are sponsored annually by the organization. It publishes *The Founder's Sounder*.

Group Type: Ecumenical/nondenominational; music resource
Founded: 1972
Publications: *The Founder's Sounder*
Meetings: First week in April, unless that is Easter Week, in which case annual meeting held second week in April

National Coalition of Black Church Musicians

No current address
Albert Knight, President

Group Type: Ecumenical/nondenominational; music resource

National Convention of Gospel Choirs and Choruses, Inc.

650 Parkwood Drive
Cleveland, OH 44108
(216) 851-8600
Dr. Earl Preston, Jr., Chairman, Board of Trustees

12525 Nacogdoches, Suite 125
San Antonio, TX 78217
Dr. Thomas A. Dorsey, Founder and President
Ms. Lorraine R. Williams, Executive Officer

Founded in Chicago, Illinois, by Dr. Thomas A. Dorsey in 1932, the National Convention of Gospel Choirs and Choruses, Inc., concerns itself with music education, awarding academic scholarships, and publishing sheet music. The Convention has more the twenty-five chapters and meets annually the first week in August. Dr. Earl Preston, Jr., is the chairman of the board of directors, and Ms. Lorraine R. Williams is an executive officer.

Group Type: Ecumenical/nondenominational; music resource
Founded: 1932
Meetings: Annual meeting is held the first week in August

Youth Unlimited Community Christian Club, Inc.

3401 Holly Street
Denver, CO 80207
(303) 322-9446
The Reverend Mother Sidney Adams, Founder and National
   Director

Founded on June 23, 1972, by the Reverend Mother Sidney Adams in Denver, Colorado, the Youth Unlimited Community Christian Club, Inc., has chapters in Colorado and California. It concentrates on providing youth-focused street ministry and teenage pregnancy prevention, among other programs. It is a community ecumenical group that uses music ministry as the base of its operation. It sponsors retreats, Bible study, and drama teams and holds an annual convention. The Club publishes a monthly newsletter, *Youth Unlimited*, and has issued four gospel record albums.

Group Type: Ecumenical/nondenominational; youth; music resource
Founded: June 23, 1972
Publications: *Youth Unlimited*, a monthly newsletter
Meetings: Annual meeting third weekend in July

Service Agencies and Organizations

Apostolic Community Organization, Inc.

1572 E. 66th Street
Cleveland, OH 44103
(216) 361-0960
District Elder Jesse James, Founder and
   President

The Apostolic Community Organization (ACO) was founded in February, 1980 by District Elder Jesse James, an Apostolic pastor in Cleveland, Ohio. Since its inception, ACO has succeeded in reaching its primary goal—providing nurture, support, and homes to ward children under the care of the Cuyahoga County Department of Human Services.

This organization of community volunteers has used daily radiobroadcasts to spread its message since July 13, 1981. The appeal airs from 9:10 a.m. to 9:30 a.m. weekdays on WABQ-AM 1540 in the Cleveland area, targeting the inner-city neighborhoods on the east side of the Cuyahoga River. Through this communication, many families have been reached who are willing to adopt or provide foster care to African American and biracial youth under the county's supervision. The organization is supported financially through donations from local businesses and individuals and works cooperatively with the Cuyahoga County Department of Human Services.

ACO also serves children of the Bessie Benner Metzenbaum Children's Center through parties, Sunday School visits, and the formation of the Young Voices of Faith Choir, composed of children from the home who have been organized and trained by ACO. They have performed in several public programs. In addition, ACO provides necessary equipment to chronically ill children in Health Hill Hospital. The work of the organization has been recognized through various awards and citations to both the Reverend James and ACO for outstanding contributions to the youth of the area. District Elder Jesse James serves as the president of the organization.

Group Type: Denomination specific; lay/clergy
Founded: February, 1980
Membership: Community volunteers

Association of Black Directors of Christian Education

1439 West 103rd Street
Chicago, IL 60643
(312) 275-1430
Dr. Colleen Birchett, President

The Association of Black Directors of Christian Education (ABDCE) founded in October 1989, is a national, interdenominational association of African American directors of Christian education. The organization will provide a support network for directors of Christian education serving African American churches. Its primary concern is to prepare the church for its work in the 1990s and for the coming twenty-first century. ABDCE plans to conduct workshops and provide a clearinghouse of information to achieve its goal.

ABDCE is divided into eleven regions, and each region has a particular focus, such as genocide, drug abuse, evangelism, black history, and the black family. The organization meets annually, and regional and local groups will meet more frequently as needed. The national president of ABDCE is Dr. Colleen Birchett, who is an editor at Urban Ministries, Inc., in Chicago.

Group Type: Ecumenical/nondenominational; Christian education; research/education
Founded: October 1989
Membership: 35 persons
Publications: *ABDCE Newsletter*, a quarterly newsletter
Meetings: An annual meeting of the body and regional meetings as called

Black Church Magazine

P.O. Box 2216
Baltimore, MD 21203
(301) 338-1523
Mr. Joseph Green-Bishop, Publisher

   The Black Church Magazine is a monthly publication geared

toward the rapidly growing, primarily African American church population in the Baltimore, Maryland/Washington, D.C. area. It presents profiles on ministers, laypersons, and historic church figures, as well as articles of importance to the church community. In addition, it produces a church calendar that gives dates of local activities, as well as information about denominational meetings and conferences, both regional and national. It also intends to start a "vacant pulpit column."

The Black Church Magazine supports corporate tithing, and its owners donate ten percent of the annual net revenues to charitable organizations. Subscriptions to the magazine are available. The current readership is thirty-five thousand persons. The magazine was started in 1982.

Group Type: Ecumenical/nondenominational; publishing
Founded: 1982
Publications: *The Black Church Magazine*, a monthly magazine with a readership of thirty-five thousand persons (yearly subscription rate of $10 per year)

Black Religious Broadcasters Association

2416 Orcutt Avenue
Newport News, VA 23607
(804) 380-6118
Bishop Samuel L. Green, President

Group Type: Ecumenical/nondenominational; worship resource

Interdenominational Church Ushers Association of Washington, D.C., and Vicinity

1923 16th Street, NW
Washington, DC 20009
(202) 265-4188
Mrs. Mabel R. Milton, President

The Interdenominational Church Ushers Association (ICUA) is composed of church ushers from all denominations, including Roman Catholic. They support the Stoddard Baptist Home in Washington, D.C., the YWCA, and the NAACP. The organization represents more than 175 churches in the metropolitan Washington, D.C., vicinity. It has senior, young adult, and junior boards.

Group Type: Ecumenical/nondenominational; worship resource
Publications: *Ushers Bulletin*, Vernise Seals, editor, 4920 11th Street, NE, Washington, DC 20017, (202) 832-2412
Meetings: Business meetings held the second Monday of each month; national convention last full week in July

Martin Luther King, Jr., Center for Nonviolent Social Change

449 Auburn Avenue, NE
Atlanta, GA 30312
(404) 524-1956
Mrs. Coretta Scott King, Founding President and Chief Executive Officer

The Martin Luther King, Jr., Center for Nonviolent Social

Change was established in 1968 to preserve and continue the work of the late Reverend Dr. Martin Luther King, Jr. The Center is the only official national and international memorial dedicated to the life and legacy of Dr. King. It is a part of the forty-four acre Martin Luther King, Jr., National Historic Site and Preservation District (a federal historic site) and is located between his childhood family home and the Ebenezer Baptist Church (which was pastored by King's maternal grandfather, his father, and himself) on Auburn Avenue in Atlanta, Georgia. Dr. King's final resting place is at the Center.

The programs of the King Center are numerous and diverse. Among them is an annual summer workshop on nonviolence that focuses on Dr. King's six-step process for nonviolent change. The Early Learning Center in the King Community Center provides day-care for preschool children of low-income families. The Scholars Internship Program trains undergraduate and graduate students in nonviolent social change and leadership skills, and provides academic instruction, work placement, leadership development, and student housing for program participants. The Cultural Affairs Program "develops and experiments with projects that create new expressions affirming and celebrating the humanity which all people share." This is done through a series of cultural performances. In conjunction with this program, the Martin Luther King, Jr., Trumpet of Conscience Award is presented annually to artists who consistently demonstrate their personal and professional commitment to the goals of Dr. King. The center is also involved in voter education, housing and community development, a small city and rural economic development project, the federal prisons project, and the chaplain's program.

In addition to these programs, the King Center houses a library and archives, which comprise the world's largest collection of primary source material on the life of Dr. King and the civil rights movement. Most of Dr. King's personal papers are included. At this time, the library has undertaken the King Papers Project, a fifteen-year effort to organize and publish his writings and papers. The Center also houses a community library, family and children services, an Olympic-size swimming pool, and arts and crafts facilities. Additionally, there is the chapel of all faiths, a multipurpose auditorium, meeting rooms with multilingual capabilities, a giftshop/bookstore, and a cafeteria. There are also outdoor facilities for sports events.

More than one million persons visit the King Center and the National Historic Site every year. Various materials on the life of Dr. King (speeches, films, photographs, etc.) as well as a catalog of memorabilia are available through the Center. Dr. King's younger son, Dexter Scott King, became president of the King Center in April, 1989, but resigned his position in July, 1989. Mrs. Coretta Scott King serves as the chief executive officer.

Group Type: Ecumenical/nondenominational; racial/social justice
Founded: 1968

Middle Atlantic Regional Press

100 Bryant Street, NW
Washington, DC 20001
Elder Dr. E. Myron Noble

The Middle Atlantic Regional Press (a nonprofit Christian partners ministry) is an independent subsidiary of the Middle

Atlantic Regional Gospel Music Festival of the Apostolic Faith Churches of God. In 1977, the Music Festival began to print *Statement On* . . . , a pamphlet. It then began to publish a newsletter, *The Founder's Sounder*. With the commitment to expand its literature ministry, the Music Festival began plans to copublish a book begun in 1985. In 1986, *The Gospel of Music: A Key to Understanding a Major Chord of Ministry* by Elder E. Myron Noble was published. The success of this book launched the Press. The Press's inauguration and premier release, *Fire in the Soul*, were celebrated on February 21, 1987.

The Middle Atlantic Regional Press is dedicated to publishing works on biblical themes and Christian subjects of parochial, national, and international interest. It publishes three to five titles annually and makes special efforts to assist minority and unpublished writers. It also accepts manuscripts from both beginning and established authors.

Group Type: Ecumenical/nondenominational; publishing
Founded: 1987
Publications: The Founder's Sounder, a newsletter

National Baptist Publishing Board, Inc.

6717 Centennial Boulevard
Nashville, TN 37209-1000
(615) 350-8000

Business Development and Marketing Divisions
1917 Heiman Street
Nashville, TN 37209

Dr. T. B. Boyd III, President and Chief Executive Officer
The Reverend Kenneth H. Dupree, Acting Director of
Publications

The National Baptist Publishing Board, Inc., founded in 1896, has a rich history of service and commitment to the education of the African American religious community. Also known as the Boyd Publishing Board, it prides itself as being the oldest and largest minority-owned and -operated religious publishing company in the world, producing literature written by and for African Americans reflective of their experience in American society.

The Reverend Richard Henry Boyd, a former slave born in 1843, became a cowboy as a free man and taught himself to read and write by studying the Bible he carried in his saddlebags. He became an ordained minister and eventually opened an office in San Antonio, Texas, where he produced and supplied religious books and materials to black Baptist Sunday schools. This early preparation resulted in shaping the religious education for African Americans around the country for years to come.

On November 24, 1880, the Baptist Foreign Mission Convention of the United States was founded in Montgomery, Alabama. In 1895, it merged with two other conventions—the National Baptist Educational Convention, founded in 1893, and the American National Baptist Convention (founded in 1886)—to form the National Baptist Convention, U.S.A., Inc. In 1896, the National Baptist Convention, U.S.A., instructed its Home Mission Board to establish a publishing house and begin printing a series of Sunday School materials for use in its various churches. The publishing house was established in Nashville, Tennessee, with the Reverend Boyd in charge. Before the turn of the century, the company had purchased property at the corner of Second Avenue, North and Locust Streets, which covered almost an entire city block. It was here that the first African American dolls were manufactured.

When the National Baptist Convention, U.S.A., met in Chicago for its annual meeting in 1915, there was confusion relating to the publishing house, then alleged to be worth some $350,000. A series of efforts to bring the publishing house more closely under the control of the convention had revealed that the publishing house and its copyrights were probably not the property of the convention but of the Reverend Boyd, chairman of the board of the publishing house. The publishing house was incorporated under Tennessee law, and the convention, which was not incorporated at all, was hard-pressed to elect members to the board or to control it.

Under this shadow, Boyd's supporters began meeting at Salem Baptist Church in Chicago, Illinois. They successfully sought an injunction against the convention members led by the Reverend E. C. Morris, but it was subsequently overturned; the Boyd faction was eventually ruled a "rump" convention. Nevertheless, on September 9, 1915, the National Baptist Convention, Unincorporated, was born out of the Boyd faction and now carries the name National Baptist Convention of America, Inc. (the directorate of the organization was incorporated in Shreveport, Louisiana, in 1987). One of the first acts of the National Baptist Convention of America, Inc., was to determine that the publishing house was not the property of any convention.

Dr. Richard Henry Boyd continued to run the publishing company until 1922, when he was succeeded by his son, Dr. Henry Allen Boyd, who served as the executive secretary of the publishing board until 1959. He was the first African American appointed as a postal clerk in Texas. His involvement in the company began by working as a janitor, and he learned all aspects of the business firsthand from his father. His keen business acumen and implementation of new operational procedures made the company flourish. He was also one of the persons responsible for having Tennessee State Agricultural and Industrial University located in Nashville.

Dr. Henry Allen Boyd was succeeded by his nephew, Dr. T. B. Boyd, Jr., who served as the secretary-treasurer of the National Baptist Publishing Board from 1959 to 1979. The grandson of the founder, Dr. T. B. Boyd, Jr., saw the company grow to its most prosperous state since its inception. This period of growth included the construction of a modern, million-dollar facility in 1974 and the installation of larger, more efficient machinery. The current president and chief executive officer, Dr. T. B. Boyd III, succeeded his father in 1979. He is the great-grandson of the founder.

Over the summer of 1988, control of the National Baptist Sunday Church School and Baptist Training Union Congress and publishing house became controversial, as it had in 1915. This congress was a part of the National Baptist Convention of America, Inc. Some members of the convention wanted to gain greater control over the planning, execution, and profits of the convention's annual Sunday School leader training meeting. This resulted in the formation of a new convention—the National Missionary Baptist Convention of America—in November 1988.

This division resulted from an official convention session of the National Baptist Convention of America, Inc., in San Antonio, Texas, in 1988 attended by over seven hundred church leaders from across the country. It was determined that the National Baptist Convention of America, Inc., would start a Sunday school congress to be controlled by the convention itself. This, in effect, severed ties with the Boyd-controlled congress and publishing house. Five hundred church leaders subsequently met in Dallas, Texas, in November 1988 to form the new organization, intended to remain committed to the National Baptist Publishing Board, Inc., and the National Baptist Sunday Church School and Baptist Training Union Congress, still controlled by the Boyd family. The parent body—the National Baptist Convention of America, Inc.—thus attempted to gain control over the publishing aspect of the convention, ironically after declaring upon its own inception that the publishing house would not be the property of any convention. The National Baptist Publishing Board is now aligned with the National Missionary Baptist Convention of America and has returned to its true mission.

The National Baptist Sunday Church School and Training Union Congress, begun in 1906 by Dr. Richard Henry Boyd, is sponsored annually in June by the National Baptist Publishing Board, Inc., in a major city and is attended annually by over twenty thousand clergy and laity alike. The Congress features national speakers and offers classes to enhance Christian education in the church.

The T. B. Boyd, Jr. Endowment Fund was established in 1982 to insure the continued tradition of contribution to groups, individuals, and non-profit organizations by the National Baptist Publishing Board, Inc. The Fund has given scholarships and grants to numerous churches, church organizations, seminaries, colleges and universities, medical research efforts, and the United Negro College Fund. Additionally, it produces special radio and television programs of religious and cultural interest for the community.

With a customer base of approximately 4,700,000 persons and standing accounts with 22,000 churches around the world, the National Baptist Publishing Board produces and distributes 14,000,000 books and periodicals annually. These publications include: Sunday school and vacation Bible school materials; books on religion; commentaries; programs for special occasions; anthems and music materials; mission materials; audiovisual materials; and histories. Additionally, the National Baptist Publishing Board offers religious products ranging from Bibles and badges to baptismal pools and choir robes. The company has distribution points in over 2,000 religious bookstores in addition to its catalog. A video, "Journey of the Watchman," chronicles the history of the company.

Five levels of concentration—operations, marketing, business development, publications, and finance—with five division directors, guide the company's future service capabilities. A nine-member Board of Directors assists Dr. T. B. Boyd III in managing the Publishing Board.

Group Type: Denomination specific; publishing
Founded: 1896
Membership: Approximately 4,700,000 customers with standing accounts of 22,000 churches worldwide
Publications: *The New National Baptist Hymnal*; *The Union Review*, a newsletter; numerous religious educational materials
Meetings: National Baptist Sunday Church School and Baptist Training Union Congress meets every June

National United Church Ushers Association of America, Inc.

1431 Shepherd Street, NW
Washington, DC 20011
(202) 722-1192
Ms. Alberta Jones

The National United Church Ushers Association of America, Inc., was founded in 1919 by Philly Elijah Hamilton to bring a uniform system of ushering. It is interdenominational and has representation in thirty-two states. Its membership includes more than thirty thousand ushers, supervisors, and church groups in four regions. It provides scholarships and publishes a quarterly newsletter, *The National Doorkeeper*.

Group Type: Ecumenical/nondenominational; worship resource
Founded: 1919
Membership: Over 30,000 ushers, supervisors, and church groups
Publications: *The National Doorkeeper*, a quarterly newsletter

Operation PUSH

930 East 50th Street
Chicago, IL 60615
(312) 373-3366
The Reverend Jesse L. Jackson, Founder
The Reverend Otis Moss, Chairman of the Board
The Reverend Tyrone Crider, Former National Executive Director

Operation PUSH began as Operation Breadbasket, the economic arm of the Southern Christian Leadership Conference (SCLC) led by Dr. Martin Luther King, Jr. The Reverend Jesse L. Jackson served as the leader of this component of the SCLC. Operation PUSH—People United to Save Humanity—was founded on December 25, 1971, by the Reverend Jackson and a group of seventy nationally prominent African American leaders. There are currently over twenty affiliates in large and small cities across the country.

The program of the organization is focused on three areas: 1) *economic development*, seeking a renegotiated relationship between corporate America and African America; 2) *political empowerment*, specifically fighting to get the 1965 Voting Rights Act enforced and to increase voter registration and education; and 3) *international peace and justice*, putting particular focus on stopping and de-escalating the arms race. PUSH has challenged the majority vote and dual registration voting impediments in Mississippi by filing suits in the Federal District Court of Mississippi. It continues to render a significant impact in arenas such as voter registration, prison ministries, world peace, jobs, education, and African American businesses, and it works for racial equality in professions such as education, sports, and business.

PUSH seeks to be "a positive moral force" to keep the spirit of hope and the spirit of resistance and noncooperation with injustice alive. This is in keeping with the love ethic of its Judeo-Christian tradition and the militant, nonviolent traditions of Thoreau, Gandhi, and Martin Luther King, Jr. PUSH is also helping to change the current national climate by interpreting the change in focus from civil rights as the cutting issue of social change—targeted in the 1950s and 1960s—to "silver" or economic rights as the fundamental issue of the 1970s, 1980s and 1990s. It is attempting to push the nation beyond economic and political liberalism—"white benevolence"—to self-reliance and self-determination—"black liberation."

Operation PUSH Magazine is the organization's quarterly magazine. The chairman of the board is the Reverend Otis Moss, pastor of Olivet Institutional Baptist Church in Cleveland, Ohio. The former national executive director and chief executive officer, the Reverend Willie T. Barrow, retired in December, 1989. She was succeeded by the Reverend Tyrone Crider who resigned in 1991.

Group Type: Ecumenical/nondenominational; racial/social justice
Founded: December 25, 1971
Publications: *Operation PUSH Magazine*, Walter M. Perkins, editor

Opportunities Industrialization Centers of America, Inc.

100 West Coulter Street
Philadelphia, PA 19144
(215) 951-2200
The Reverend Leon H. Sullivan, Founder
Robert C. Nelson, Executive Director
James M. Talton, Chairman, Board of Directors
Ann Hannibal, President, Auxiliary

The Opportunities Industrialization Center (OIC) was initiated on January 24, 1964, in Philadelphia, Pennsylvania, by the Reverend Leon H. Sullivan. Since its founding, OIC has evolved into a national organization with approximately seventy centers in the United States, twelve African countries, the Caribbean, and Birmingham, England. The organization has helped over forty thousand persons in the Philadelphia area alone in the last twenty-five years, and in 1989, took on its one-millionth client.

OIC began in 1959 as an effort by the Reverend Sullivan (then pastor of Zion Baptist Church) to make more jobs available to Philadelphia's unemployed blacks. Ministers from four hundred African American churches in the city began to ask companies to hire more black workers. Those that refused were boycotted by church members. Between 1959 and 1963, the Reverend Sullivan estimates that more than two thousand skilled jobs opened to African Americans as the result of twenty-nine selective patronage campaigns. This technique was adopted by the Reverend Martin Luther King, Jr., the Reverend David Abernathy, and the Reverend Jesse Jackson in many parts of the country in the early days of the civil rights movement.

However, it was found that many blacks did not have the necessary skills for the newly available jobs, thus the training program was begun. OIC was initially funded with $100,000 raised through donations from church members, a grant from the William Penn Foundation, a $50,000 donation from the Otto and Phoebe Haas Foundation, and a second mortgage on Sullivan's home. The city donated an unused, dilapidated police station at 19th and Oxford streets for the headquarters of OIC for rent of one dollar for 99 years. President Lyndon Johnson visited the program's headquarters because it was so unusual and successful. Job training given by the community rather than through vocational schools was unheard of at the time.

The program taught basic arithmetic and reading skills, and used black history books instead of standard texts, providing a sense of pride in many blacks. Finally, the organization found employment for its students. OIC's methods were so successful that many of the concepts it initiated were incorporated in the federal Comprehensive Education and Training Act of 1972, which was the major training initiative of the Nixon administration.

OIC is a training and employment remedial education program that seeks to customize its training programs to meet the specific needs of businesses. Its key to "positive personnel development" includes three steps: 1) diagnosis of educational deficiencies and provision for remediation; 2) encouragement of positive, appropriate workplace attitudes and behaviors; and 3) provision of vocational skills through training and job placement. Its programs include adult education, summer jobs for youth, stay-in-school projects, computer and secretarial skills training, banking and business training, as well as several specific programs designed to meet the needs of certain areas.

The organization's services are free of charge. Although the initial funding of OIC came from church members of Philadelphia, it is now principally supported through federal and corporate funding. Funding has dropped, however, due to federal budget cuts. In 1989, a five-year plan was initiated to increase corporate gifts from one million dollars to five million dollars. The Reverend Sullivan continues to serve as a member of the Board of Directors, which is chaired by James M. Talton. Ann Hannibal serves as president of the Auxiliary.

Group Type: Ecumenical/nondenominational; research/education
Founded: January 24, 1964

Southern Christian Leadership Conference

334 Auburn Avenue, NW
Atlanta, GA 30312
(404) 522-1420
The Reverend Dr. Joseph E. Lowery, President
The Honorable Walter E. Fauntroy, Chairman of the Board
The late Reverend Dr. Ralph D. Abernathy, President Emeritus

The Southern Christian Leadership Conference (SCLC) was founded in a series of meetings in Atlanta, Georgia, New Orleans, Louisiana, and Montgomery, Alabama, in 1957, following the 381-day Montgomery Bus Boycott of 1955-1956. From its inception, SCLC has pursued equality and just treatment for the oppressed and disadvantaged people of African descent. It has broadened its scope to embrace and support all oppressed peoples of the world who use the tactics of nonviolent protest to change society.

By 1958, the SCLC had organized affiliates in ten states and began organizing for massive southern protest action. A huge voter-registration drive, "Crusade for Citizenship," was launched in rallies in twenty-two cities, and workshops for development of grassroots community leadership were held across the South. In 1959, it sponsored the Institute of Nonviolent Resistance to Segregation in Atlanta, which was attended by leaders from sixteen states. African American college students had also begun sit-ins at lunch counters and other public facilities, and the following year the Student Nonviolent Coordinating Committee (SNCC) was founded with the SCLC's support and participation at Shaw University in Raleigh, North Carolina. In 1961, the Freedom Rides moved throughout the South, and in 1962, two new programs were established by the group. Operation Breadbasket, beginning in Atlanta, concentrated on the organization of ministers to gain new and better jobs for African Americans through community-wide boycotts and negotiations. The Citizen Education Program trained southern adults in literacy, voting rights, African American history, community organization, and economic development.

In 1963, the largest African American uprising in modern history took place in Birmingham, Alabama, where SCLC marchers were attacked daily by police using fire hoses, dogs, and clubs. Over thirty-three hundred persons were arrested. The marches and boycotts led to an eventual settlement on racial discrimination. The entire civil rights movement (but particularly the activities in Birmingham) forced Congress to move on civil rights legislation. On August 28 of that same year, the historic March on Washington culminated at the Lincoln Memorial. The march, supported by over 250,000 people, was sponsored by numerous civil rights, civic, religious, and social organizations, and is remembered for the "I Have a Dream" oration delivered by the SCLC president, Dr. Martin Luther King, Jr.

The year 1964 saw Congress complete action on the Civil Rights Act, the most comprehensive civil rights law since Reconstruction. It abolished legal segregation and provided equality in education, jobs, and federal programs, and was the result of nonviolent protest. Dr. King also received the Nobel Peace Prize that year for his work in the movement. The drive for federal protection of voting rights culminated in the Selma movement in 1965. Fifty thousand people answered SCLC's appeal for a fifty-mile march to Montgomery. The resulting nationwide pressure again forced Congress to pass the Voting Rights Act of 1965. This act had a direct impact on the political revolution of the South.

In 1966, the SCLC moved into the North and began a long-range program to examine urban problems in Chicago. After James Meredith was shot on a highway in Mississippi, the civil rights movement mobilized national support for the March Against Fear in Mississippi. Operation Breadbasket also began a comprehensive economic development program in Chicago, and by the next year the program had expanded nationwide. In 1967 the SCLC also became involved in the movement against the Vietnam war.

On April 4, 1968, Dr. King was assassinated while in Memphis to lead a strike of sanitation workers. He was succeeded by Dr. Ralph David Abernathy, his close friend. Dr. Abernathy announced the Poor People's Campaign, which brought thousands of poor and homeless to "Resurrection City," a tent city erected on the Mall in Washington, DC. The organization also began its Ministerial Leadership Training Program in fifteen cities across the country. On the first anniversary of Dr. King's death, the Poor People's Campaign, Chapter 2, was begun with local campaigns protesting poverty and hunger held nationwide.

The 1970s brought continued efforts on the part of the Southern Christian Leadership Conference to bring the plight of the oppressed to the attention of the nation. It lead the March Against Repression following student killings at Jackson State and Kent State universities in 1970. It continued its program of voter registration, especially in rural areas. In 1972, the National Black Political Convention was held in Gary, Indiana. The 1970s saw the SCLC organize and engage in numerous marches, protests, and political movements aimed at changing governmental policies. The decade witnessed great success in these efforts. In 1977, Dr. Abernathy stepped down as president, and Dr. Joseph E. Lowery took the helm.

Dr. Lowery and the national board of SCLC met with President Jimmy Carter in 1977 to sensitize the new administration to the needs of African Americans and the poor. In 1978, SCLC commemorated the tenth anniversary of Dr. King's death in a "Memorial March for the Right to Live" in Gadsden, Alabama. Over twenty-five hundred persons participated. After the mass suicide/murder of nine hundred followers (most of whom were African Americans) of the People's Temple in Jonestown, Guyana, Dr. Lowery, the Reverend Nelson Smith, the Reverend Harry Gibson, and others went to Jonestown to investigate the incident. This resulted in "A Consultation on the Implications of Jonestown for the Black Church and the Nation," held in San Francisco and cosponsored by the National Conference of Black Churchmen.

In late 1979, SCLC broadened its scope to include international as well as domestic issues. On August 15, it protested the resignation of United Nations Ambassador Andrew Young. As a result of this protest, a meeting was initiated with the U.N. Observer for the Palestine Liberation Organization (PLO), Sehdi Labib Terzi, and an invitation was issued by Yasser Arafat to meet in Lebanon. Dr. Lowery became the first African American leader to head a delegation to the Middle East. He presented Arafat with a plan to end the conflict in Palestine. During this year, the SCLC also denounced the seizing of American hostages at the American embassy by Iranian students, and the resurgence of the Ku Klux Klan. Dr. Lowery called for the Shah of Iran to be turned over to the World Court at the Hague and for denial of permanent asylum for the Shah in the United States. He also called for a hearing before the International Tribunal, wherein the Iranian people could address their differences before the world.

With the coming of the 1980s, the organization continued its efforts, commemorating the twelfth anniversary of the death of Dr. King during the first annual Martin Luther King, Jr. Memorial Awards Dinner in Atlanta. In 1981, it pushed for the extension of the Voting Rights Act of 1965. SCLC and Operation PUSH staged a massive march across the Edmund Pettus Bridge in Selma, Alabama, to demonstrate that support. SCLC also met with Atlanta police in an effort to solve the Atlanta child killings. As a result, the Metro Atlanta Black Clergy organized programs for the community to cope with the killings. In 1982, a pilgrimage was made through several cities and states to Washington, D.C. As the protesters arrived at the Capitol, the House was voting unanimously to extend the Voting Rights Act. The "pilgrims" immediately began construction on Resurrection City II as a reminder of the nation's poor.

On August 9, 1982, a memorial march was led by three of SCLC's founders—Dr. Lowery, Dr. Abernathy, and the Reverend Fred Shuttlesworth. From August 10 to 13, the twenty-fifth anniversary of the organization's founding was celebrated at the national convention in Birmingham, Alabama. Birmingham's first African American mayor, Richard Arrington, Jr., welcomed the delegation, and Alabama history was made when George Wallace, gubernatorial candidate, addressed the convention. In a culmination of the year's activities, the SCLC and the Martin Luther King, Jr., Center for Nonviolent Social Change joined in a commemoration of the original March on Washington, held at the King Center in Atlanta.

In 1983, the SCLC and the King Center joined in a march of more than one thousand persons to the Georgia State Capital to commemorate the fifty-fourth birthday of Dr. King and to call for a national holiday to mark his birth and life's work. In May, Dr. Lowery and Minister Louis Farrakhan of the Nation of Islam made history by meeting at SCLC's headquarters to discuss their differences and find ways to work together in the continuing fight for dignity and political and economic justice. On November 2, 1983, President Ronald Reagan signed into law the bill making Dr. King's birthday a national holiday.

In 1987, there was great media coverage as SCLC led the "Coalition of Conscience," an international, multifaceted coalition, through Forsyth County, Georgia, to protest racial violence and widespread discrimination in the all-white county. At the 1988 Democratic National Convention in Atlanta, the SCLC held a rally and prayer vigil seeking help for the homeless at the convention site—the first public protest of the convention. Dr. Lowery gave the opening invocation at Wednesday night's session, before the speech of presidential nominee Michael Dukakis. Dr. Lowery also celebrated forty years in the ministry in 1988.

In 1989, Dr. and Mrs. Lowery were invited by the German Democratic Republic Peace Council to participate in the sixtieth birthday celebration of Dr. King. On the eve of the twenty-first anniversary of Dr. King's assassination, the SCLC national office took over a vacant house seized by foreclosure in southwest Atlanta to protest the lack of federal housing programs and insensitivity to the lack of available housing. The late housing activist Mitch Snyder, Dr. Lowery, and others cleaned and repaired the home throughout the night to prepare it for occupancy and eventual ownership by a homeless family. On May 16, an agreement was reached by SCLC and the First Federal Savings and Loan of Largo, Florida (which owned the house), to sell the property without a down payment for $10,000 at ten percent fixed interest over thirty years. It was also agreed that if it should go into foreclosure in the future, the house would be sold to SCLC until another family could be identified as purchaser. In 1989, a rally and prayer vigil was sponsored by SCLC at Dr. King's tomb in support of the Chinese students' movement.

The Southern Christian Leadership Conference has chapters in cities and states across the country, and each is active in protesting injustices in its region. Mrs. Evelyn Lowery is very active in the organization, serving as SCLC/WOMEN National Convener. There is a fifty-four member National Board of Directors, which includes Mrs. Coretta Scott King, Martin Luther King III, the Honorable Andrew Young, the Honorable Walter Fauntroy, the Reverend C. T. Vivian, and numerous others of prominence, especially in the realms of politics, religion, and academia.

Group Type: Ecumenical/nondenominational; racial/social justice
Founded: 1957
Publications: *Southern Christian Leadership Conference National Magazine*, Ms. Cheryl Lowery-Esborne, editor

Successful Stewardship for Life Ministries, Inc.

409 K Street, NE
Washington, DC 20002
(202) 547-8782
The Reverend William H. Bennett II, Founder, Chairman and President
Ms. Lewoner Winfield, Senior Counselor

Successful Stewardship for Life Ministries, Inc. (SSFL), a nonprofit organization, was founded in April 1987 by its chairman and president, the Reverend William H. Bennett II. As a service center for pastors and their congregations, it assists Christians in utilizing financial and material resources according to God's principles. When financial and material resources are used in an optimal manner, giving increases geometrically. SSFL believes that the church is able to provide better services to its members and the community as a result.

To meet its objectives, SSFL offers several services, among them debt counseling to individuals and families and consumer education to prevent the recurrence of heavy indebtedness. SSFL also offers counseling in home purchasing, investments, small business establishment, and retirement planning. The organization conducts stewardship workshops and seminars for churches, concentrating on God's plan for giving, the care of pastor and church, and development of a successful stewardship life-style. Because it employs a holistic approach, SSFL can also offer pastoral and personal development counseling.

Group Type: Ecumenical/nondenominational; Christian education
Founded: April 1987
Publications: *The Christian's Financial Clinic*, a monthly newsletter

Tom Skinner Associates

505 8th Avenue
New York, NY 10018
(212) 563-5454
The Reverend Tom Skinner, Founder

Tom Skinner Associates (TSA), an interdenominational leadership development ministry, was founded in 1964 by Tom Skinner in New York City. The organization seeks to raise a new generation of African American leaders—especially from among the poor—who are both technically excellent and spiritually and morally mature. These goals will be met by: 1) working with current leaders; 2) working with future leaders on historically African American college campuses; and 3) focusing on youth and adults in the city of Newark, New Jersey, to provide needed skills for improvement and self-advancement.

The Campus Division of the ministry is located at Norfolk State College, under the direction of Steven Davis, and at Howard University, under the direction of the Reverend Michael Worsley. The Howard group, also known as the Igbimo Otito Christian Fellowship, was founded by the Reverend Eric Payne in 1973. Both campus ministries seek to educate and support the student body's spiritual growth through numerous activities such as leadership training, Bible study, fellowship, and special seminars presented by Tom Skinner and his wife, Barbara W. Skinner, who is very active in the ministry.

TSA works with current leaders in business, politics, sports, and entertainment to enhance their leadership skills and potential. Skinner has worked with the Washington Redskins, the New York Yankees, and several Fortune 500 businesses such as IBM and the Xerox Corporation, the New York Stock Exchange, as well as to counsel and bring together leaders from various arenas for cooperative action.

In Newark, New Jersey, TSA works with members of the community through the TSA Learning Center, giving needed skills to direct the futures of the community. These include skills for basic education, coping, employability, leadership, and moral excellence. These are taught during the evening. Four days a week for three classes a day, the ministry works with eleventh graders from Weequahic High School in preparation for the Scholastic Aptitude Test.

Tom and Barbara Skinner serve on the Board of Directors of several organizations such as the Martin Luther King, Jr. Center for Nonviolent Social Change, Urban Ministries, Inc., and the Congressional Black Caucus Foundation. TSA publishes *The News in Black and White*, a quarterly magazine.

Group Type: Ecumenical/nondenominational; student; research/education
Founded: 1964
Publications: *The News in Black and White*, a quarterly magazine

United Outreach for Christ Mission Team, Inc.

P.O. Box 56035
Washington, DC 20011
(202) 829-7837
The Reverend Elizabeth Hawkins, Founder

Founded by Elizabeth Hawkins, United Outreach for Christ Mission Team, Inc. (UOCMT), is a nonprofit, interdenominational, Christian prison ministry responding to the call in Matthew 25:36 ('' . . . I was in prison and ye came unto me'' [KJV]). Organized in 1975 and incorporated in 1982, UOCMT members visit prisons, where they provide worship services and counseling and teach Bible classes. They also provide support services for families of prisoners and assist former offenders to adjust to life outside of prison. The organization publishes *Good News from Prison Cells*, a quarterly newspaper.

Group Type: Ecumenical/nondenominational; lay/clergy; mission/philanthropic
Founded: 1975
Publications: *Good News from Prison Cells*, a quarterly newspaper
Meetings: Annual meeting first weekend in October

Urban Ministries, Inc.

1439 West 103rd Street
Chicago, IL 60643
(312) 233-4499
The Reverend Melvin E. Banks, Sr., President

Urban Ministries, Inc., was founded in 1970. It publishes Sunday school and vacation Bible school literature, in addition to training books. It also produces training and educational videos. Urban Outreach is the nonprofit, leadership development arm of the parent organization. It sponsors a national leadership training conference each year and contributes literature to foreign missions. The president is the Reverend Melvin E. Banks.

Group Type: Ecumenical/nondenominational; publishing
Founded: 1970
Publications: Bible study guide for all age-levels, Sunday school literature, vacation Bible school material, training manuals, and educational videos

Women's International Religious Fellowship

6458 32nd Street, NW
Washington, DC 20015
(202) 686-0312
Mrs. Sakin Mohammed, President

The Women's International Religious Fellowship (WIRF) was founded by Norma E. Boyd (1888-1985), a 1910 graduate of Howard University and a founder and incorporator of Alpha Kappa Alpha Sorority, Inc. It was founded with the cooperation of All Souls Unitarian Church of Washington, D.C., and the United Nations Social and Economic Council (UNESCO). As a teacher always interested in the welfare of children and public policy, she also initiated the National Non-Partisan Council on Public Affairs (a congressional lobbying group sponsored by African American sororities and fraternities) in 1938 and managed this project for the sorority until 1948. In 1946, she was accredited as an official observer at the United Nations on behalf of the sorority's council, and in 1949 she traveled to Brazil and Argentina to publicize UNESCO activities. These activities, as well as her occupation as a teacher, encouraged the formation of this organization.

Miss Boyd became the leader of the Inter-Faith Committee of the Women's Alliance of All Souls Church with the proviso that the group would not only study different religions but would also become an action organization. Several leaders from various religions and women from other countries were contacted to begin this endeavor. The first meeting on March 13, 1959, had as a theme ''World Religions and World Peace.'' The organization decided to become more aware of the work of the United Nations Committee on Human Rights to correlate its activities with this organization and to work to mobilize public opinion for international fellowship. On June 12, 1959, numerous persons representing various embassies, countries, and branches of the United Nations were present at an afternoon tea where the name ''Women's International Religious Fellowship'' was chosen. WIRF then became an entity separate from All Souls Church.

The organization sought to promote the first citywide celebration of Human Rights Day in Washington, D.C. on December 10, 1959. Several embassies, the U.S. Committee for UNESCO, and two television networks made this endeavor successful. With the passing of the United Nations Declaration of the Rights of the Child in November, 1959, WIRF sought to ensure its implementation, and a meeting was called to plan for this. This resulted in a joint international bazaar held with the Temple of Understanding (a proposed temple for all faiths led by Mrs. Judith Hollister) on December 2, 1960, and a television show taped at the Indian embassy in 1961. Other activities were conducted with the Temple of Understanding because of this successful venture.

WIRF has continued to sponsor an annual bazaar, supported by various organizations and the international community in Washington, D.C. Participants donate their proceeds to children's charities in their countries. It also sponsors an annual international dinner and folk festival and a school enrichment program. Over fifty countries continue to participate in WIRF's programs for children. The *WIRF Newsletter* began publication in 1970.

Group Type: Ecumenical/nondenominational; women; lay
Founded: June 12, 1959
Publications: WIRF Newsletter

Part 3
African American Religious Education Institutions

The following listing includes academic seminaries, Bible colleges, research projects, research/professional organizations, and colleges, universities, and seminaries that are historically African American. An *academic seminary* (often referred to as a "school of religion," "school of theology," or "school of divinity") is generally considered to be a school or college that prepares persons for the ministry. Most of these seminaries offer advanced professional degrees (beginning at the master's level), and their programs are accredited. *Bible colleges* may also be accredited and generally offer training or study in biblical literature, practical ministry, Christian education, and religious studies, as well as general education courses. Most offer certificate programs for lay church leaders or a program leading to the bachelor's degree. This training may be considered preparatory to seminary study.

Seminaries

Bay Ridge Christian College

P.O. Box 726
Kendleton, TX 77451
(409) 532-3982
The Reverend Dr. Robert C. Williams, President

The Bay Ridge Christian College provides training for ministers and church leaders. It is a Christian institution of higher education affiliated with the Church of God, Anderson, Indiana. It provides opportunities for quality education, development of Christian leadership, and preparation for professional ministries, both urban and rural.

The Bay Ridge Christian College offers two degree programs leading to the Bachelor of Religious Education degree or the Bachelor of Theology degree. The first is a four-year program. The second requires a fifth year designed to intensify the biblical/theological/Christian ministries concentration area. In addition, the college offers four certificate programs, Christian Business and Christian Leadership (two-year programs), and Christian Education and Ministerial (three-year programs).

Group Type: Denomination specific; research/education

Endich Theological Seminary

New York, NY

The Endich Theological Seminary was founded in June, 1922, by the Reverend George Alexander McGuire of the African Orthodox Church in order to train the church's ministry. There were twelve persons in the first class and three faculty members at its inception. Commencement exercises were usually held on Founder's Day, on the Sunday nearest September 14, which is the Feast of Title, the Exaltation of the Holy Cross. The present circumstances or existence of the seminary are unknown. It is located in New York City, New York.

Group Type: Denomination specific; research/education

Hood Theological Seminary

Livingstone College
701 W. Monroe Street
Salisbury, NC 28144
(704) 638-5644
Dr. William F. Lawrence, Jr., Dean

Founded by the African Methodist Episcopal Zion Church in 1879 and affiliated with Livingstone College, Hood Theological Seminary has an enrollment of approximately thirty-six students (twenty-seven are full-time), a faculty of ten, and library resources of twenty-five thousand items. The Seminary offers the Master of Divinity and the Master of Religious Education degrees and is located in Salisbury, North Carolina. The dean is Dr. William F. Lawrence, Jr.

Group Type: Denomination specific; research/education
Founded: 1879
Membership: 36 students and 10 faculty

Howard University School of Divinity

1400 Shepherd Street, NE
Washington, DC 20017
(202) 806-0500
Dr. Lawrence N. Jones, Dean
Dr. Clarence G. Newsome, Associate Dean

The idea that culminated in the establishment of Howard University was germinated during a "season of prayer for missions" at the First Congregational Church in Washington, D.C. It was the intention of the founders to establish an institution to train preachers and teachers for service to the persons freed from bondage by the Civil War. This vision culminated in the issuance of a charter establishing Howard University on March 2, 1867. Education of "preachers and others looking forward to that work" began on January 6, 1868; the Theological Department was established in 1870. Today, Howard University has grown to include eighteen schools and colleges, nine institutes and research centers, and a variety of less formally structured educational programs.

The School of Divinity (called the School of Religion until 1981) currently enrolls more than two hundred students, one-third of whom are female. It has a faculty of eighteen full- and part-time members, an adjunct faculty of fifteen members, and library holdings numbering more that ninety-six thousand serials and volumes (in addition to the University's holdings). The School has no formal denominational affiliation. Its student body, faculty, and staff are interracial and international. Students are drawn from a broad spectrum of denominations. Graduates of the School of Divinity are involved in pastoral ministry, chaplaincies, denominational leadership, educational institutions, and in non-religious institutions and activities.

The formal mission of the School of Divinity is three-pronged: 1) the preparation of professional religious leaders for service in religious or educational institutions and for service to underserved rural and urban African American communities; 2) inquiry into international, cross-cultural humane values; and 3) preparation of students to pursue advanced studies in the theological disciplines and in the cultural and religious heritage of African Americans. The School of Divinity offers the Master of Divinity, the Master of Arts in Religious Studies, and the Doctor of Ministry degrees.

In addition to its formal degree programs, the School provides a broad spectrum of educational opportunities to clergy and lay persons who seek to strengthen their ministerial skills, to deepen their theological understanding, or to strengthen their personal faith. Such persons enroll in the Urban Institute for Religious Studies.

The extracurriculum of the School includes the annual convocation convened each year in November, as well as numerous public lectures, workshops, and training sessions. The School has published the highly respected *Journal of Religious Thought* for nearly half a century and has, with the publication of the *Directory of African American Religious Bodies*, culminated a research project conducted by its Research Center on Black Religious Bodies.

The School of Divinity is a member school in the Washington Theological Consortium. The Consortium consists of The Catholic University, School of Religious Studies; the Cluster of Independent Theological Schools; the Episcopal Theological Seminary in Virginia; Howard University School of Divinity; the Lutheran Theological Seminary at Gettysburg in Gettysburg, Pennsylvania; the Washington Theological Union; and the Wesley Theological Seminary. The School of Divinity is a member of the Association of Theological Schools. The dean of the Howard University School of Divinity is Dr. Lawrence N. Jones.

Group Type: Ecumenical/nondenominational; research/education

Founded: 1870

Membership: Over 200 students and 60 faculty and staff members

Publications: *The Journal of Religious Thought*, Dr. Cain H. Felder, editor; *Directory of African American Religious Bodies: A Compendium by the Howard University School of Divinity*, Dr. Wardell J. Payne, editor

Interdenominational Theological Center

671 Beckwith Street, SW
Atlanta, GA 30314
(404) 527-7700
Dr. James H. Costen, President

The Interdenominational Theological Center (ITC), Atlanta, Georgia, is a professional graduate school of theology composed of six seminaries and under the direction of a president, Dr. James Hutton Costen, and a forty-member Board of Trustees. The Center was established in 1958 with four participating seminaries: Morehouse School of Religion (Baptist, 1867); Gammon Theological Seminary (United Methodist, 1869); Turner Theological Seminary (African Methodist Episcopal, 1885); and Phillips School of Theology (Christian Methodist Episcopal, 1944). Since 1969, two more seminaries have joined the Center: Johnson C. Smith Theological Seminary (Presbyterian Church, U.S.A., 1867) and Charles H. Mason Theological Seminary (Church of God in Christ, 1970). ITC is a part of the Atlanta University Center, which also consists of Clark College, Atlanta University, Spelman College, Morris Brown College, and Morehouse College.

The primary mission of ITC is to "provide quality theological education for the predominantly black Christian churches." There are approximately three hundred students (eighteen percent are women) from forty-one states and fourteen countries; thirty-nine full- and part-time faculty, and library resources of ninety-three thousand items. The Center offers a Master of Divinity, Doctorate of Ministry, Master of Arts in Religion, Master of Arts in Religion with concentration in Church Music, and, through Atlanta Theological Association, a Doctorate in Sacred Theology.

The Interdenominational Theological Center also offers the program "Black Women in Church and Society." In the program, means of expanding the roles of women in church and society are explored through church structure and seminary/theological education models. The Center also offers a program in continuing education. It is a member of the Association of Theological Schools. ITC publishes *The Journal of the Interdenominational Theological Center*.

Group Type: Ecumenical/nondenominational; research/education

Founded: 1958

Membership: 300 students and 39 faculty members

Publications: *The Journal of the Interdenominational Theological Center*, Dr. Gayraud Wilmore, acting editor

Payne Theological Seminary

P.O. Box 474
Wilberforce, OH 45384-0474
(513) 376-2946
Dr. Louis Charles Harvey, President
Dr. John I. Kampen, Academic Dean

Payne Theological Seminary is an interdenominational, interracial graduate school of theology of the African Methodist Episcopal Church. Its origin can be traced to 1844, when the Ohio Conference of the church decided to erect a seminary. Traditionally, emphasis has been on "educating and preparing blacks for Christian service and community leadership."

Payne Theological Seminary offers the Master of Divinity degree. Its student body is twenty-five, and there are six full- and part-time faculty members. The library holdings are eighteen thousand items. Payne is a member of the Association of Theological Schools. Located in Wilberforce, Ohio, Payne broadens the opportunities available to its students through cooperation with Central State University, Wilberforce University, and United Theological Seminary. The president is Dr. Louis Charles Harvey; the academic dean is Dr. John Kampen.

Group Type: Denomination specific; research/education
Founded: 1844
Membership: 25 students and 6 faculty members

Richmond Virginia Seminary

801 N. 23rd Street
Richmond, VA 23223
(804) 780-0103
The Reverend Dr. Benjamin W. Robertson, Founder and
   President

The Richmond Virginia Seminary was founded in 1981 in Richmond, Virginia. Its mission is "to serve all persons who have been called to the gospel ministry as preachers, pastors, ministers, directors, or workers in the outreach programs of the church, by providing programs of study in an intellectual atmosphere in which student needs, student growth, and student success are the main objects of the school's attention." Its major objectives are to provide guidance, religious training, and specialized preparation to the students. Many of its faculty members and trustees were trained at the Virginia Union University School of Theology. The school offers the Bachelor of Arts degree in religion and the Master of Divinity degree and offers arrangements for course work for those outside of the locale, as well as some financial aid.

The school, located on Richmond's historic Church Hill, is accredited by the Accrediting Association of Religious Schools for Pastors and Evangelists, and its programs are approved for veterans. Its founder, Dr. Benjamin W. Robertson, serves as president of the school.

Group Type: Denomination specific; research/education
Founded: 1981

R. R. Wright School of Religion

Johannesburg, South Africa

Founded in 1938 and named after Bishop R. R. Wright, this A.M.E.-sponsored institution specializes in "training ministers in the tradition and heritage of African Methodism." The R. R. Wright School of Religion is located near Johannesburg, South Africa. The only black theological school on the African continent, R. R. Wright School of Religion is interested in exchange programs with American schools of theology.

Group Type: Denomination specific; research/education
Founded: 1938

Shaw Divinity School

P.O. Box 2090
Raleigh, NC 27602
(919) 832-1701
The Reverend Dr. Talbert O. Shaw, President
The Reverend Dr. Gregory T. Headen, Provost and Dean of
   Academic Affairs
Dr. G. Franklin Wiggins, Chairman, Board of Trustees

The founder of Shaw University, Henry Martin Tupper, taught its first class in religious instruction in 1865. This evolved into Shaw University in 1875. In 1933, the university established the Graduate School of Religion. In 1969, due to the threat of losing its accreditation, the university established the School of Religion as a separate legal entity. At that time, a separate board of trustees was elected. That entity is currently known as the Shaw Divinity School.

In 1987, the boards of trustees of both Shaw University and Shaw Divinity School initiated plans for a reconsolidation or merger of the two institutions. Because of the reaccreditation process of the Southern Association of Colleges and Schools, the merger must take place in stages. The administrative elements merged first, and the programmatic merger is ongoing. As of July 1, 1989, there were no longer two presidents, and Dr. Talbert O. Shaw assumed the leadership of both institutions. Dr. Gregory T. Headen, the former president of the Divinity School, reassumed his position as Provost and Dean of Academic Affairs and Dr. G. Franklin Wiggins is Chairman of the Board of Trustees.

The Shaw Divinity School's new home is a three-and-one-half-acre campus in southeast Raleigh, North Carolina. It includes a chapel with capacity for four hundred persons, a three-story educational annex, a library, three brick houses, parking facilities, and room for expansion. The university is in the process of securing funding to purchase this property.

The programs of Shaw Divinity School are diverse, reasonable in cost, and meet the needs of both clergy and laity, educated and uneducated. The school offers the Master of Divinity degree for professional training for those who have earned a baccalaureate degree, and the Diploma in Theology (which replaced the Bachelor of Theology program) for those who do not have a baccalaureate degree. The courses taken for the Diploma in Theology program may be transferred to Shaw University toward a Bachelor of Arts degree. Shaw also seeks to accommodate its students by scheduling classes on Saturdays and weeknights.

Laypersons who do not seek ordination or do not wish to earn a theological degree may enroll as special students or enter the Church Vocations Certificate Program. This is a nongraduate program. For persons who have received the call to ministry later in life after establishing themselves in another profession, the school offers the Certificate in Theology for Professionals, a one-year program at the graduate level, which is designed to be flexible. For those without a high school diploma, there is an in-service class for ministers and laity that meets on Tuesday evenings and is taught by the Dean of Continuing Education. Additionally, there is the Seminary Extension Program with over twenty centers across the state of North Carolina. Basic- and college-level programs are offered. A teacher is provided through the program (at minimal cost to students) for at least ten persons interested in a course who can meet in a central location. To encourage women in the ministry, there is a Director of Women's Concerns and an organization of women in the ministry. The Divinity School also recognizes the relationship between black religion, politics, and economics, and offers the course "The Black Church in Economic and Political Empowerment." The Divinity School has also enlisted the assistance of "development associates," persons who volunteer their public relations and fundraising skills and talents on behalf of the school. Finally, it offers the expertise of its faculty and staff to benefit local churches, which may call upon the school to provide special workshops.

Shaw Divinity School is an Associate Member of the Association of Theological Schools. The School is Baptist by tradition and association, but welcomes persons of all denominations. Its programs are supported by the General Baptist State Convention of North Carolina.

Group Type: Denomination specific; research/education
Founded: 1933
Membership: Approximately 100 students
Publications: *The Seminarian*, a newsletter

Southern California School of Ministry

2941 West 70th Street
Los Angeles, CA 90043
(213) 757-1804 or 753-3950
The Reverend Dr. Benjamin F. Reid, Executive Director

The Southern California School of Ministry is designed to equip, primarily but not exclusively, African American men and women for Christian ministry. It is supported by the Church of God (Anderson, Indiana) Board of Church Extension and Home Missions. The school operates under the auspices of the Southern California Black Ministers' Fellowship of the Church of God, and the Interstate Association of the Church of God.

The Southern California School of Ministry provides instruction in biblical and practical theology, in-service training for pastors, study disciplines for ministers with limited formal training, ethnic studies, and urban evangelism. It offers the following programs: certificate in ministry; diploma in ministry; Associate in Ministry; Bachelor of Theology; and Master in Ministry.

Group Type: Denomination specific; research/education

Virginia Union University School of Theology

1605 W. Leigh Street
Richmond, VA 23220
(804) 257-5715
Dr. Allix B. James, Chancellor
Dr. John W. Kinney, Dean

Virginia Union University was begun as a merger of several schools founded for African Americans following the Civil War. The School of Theology is a graduate professional school within the University. It is American Baptist and enjoys the support of six national Baptist bodies.

Virginia Union University School of Theology offers a Master of Divinity degree and takes special pride in its efforts to prepare its students for ministry in the African American cultural community. The School has an enrollment of 127 students; twenty-two percent of them are women. There are thirteen full- and part-time faculty and library resources in excess of 234,000 items. The dean is Dr. John W. Kinney.

Virginia Union University School of Theology sponsors the John M. Ellison Convocation (lectures) each year in addition to the Evans-Smith Institute of Leadership Education, which is a joint endeavor with the state Baptist convention and the church leadership conference.

Group Type: Denomination specific; research/education
Membership: 127 students and 13 faculty members

Bible Colleges

American Baptist College of the American Baptist Theological Seminary

1800 Whites Creek Pike
Nashville, TN 37207
(615) 228-7877 or 262-3433
Dr. Odell McGlothian, Sr., President
Ms. Georgia Larnes, Director of Admissions/Registrar

The American Baptist College, in Nashville, Tennessee, was formally opened on September 14, 1924. It is the result of a unique interracial venture by the National Baptist Convention, U.S.A., Inc., and the Southern Baptist Convention. The concept of a seminary to train African American Baptist ministers resulted from discussions between National Baptist leaders and Dr. O. L. Hailey, a "founding father" of the school. At its 1913 annual meeting, the National Baptist Convention, U.S.A., appointed a committee to discuss the establishment of a seminary to train its ministers. The Southern Baptist Convention acted in like manner after a resolution was adopted upon presentation by Dr. E. Y. Mullins that same year. That convention appointed a similar committee and pledged its support and cooperation. After meeting together, the two committees recommended to their respective organizations the establishment of the seminary in Memphis, Tennessee.

The college's present site of fifty-three acres was purchased with assistance from both conventions in 1921, and a plan for the seminary's management by both a holding board and a governing board representative of the two conventions was adopted. The deeds of the college were transferred to the sixteen National Baptists and sixteen Southern Baptists who constitute the board of trustees, which, in turn, governs the college. The college's first building, Griggs Hall, was erected in 1923, and in 1924, it became the formal home of the American Baptist Theological Seminary.

The first ten years of the school's existence were difficult, as its support diminished during the Depression. To ease the financial burden, the trustees proposed to sell the property to Roger Williams University (which moved to Memphis in 1929) and move the school to rented space at Meharry Medical College. The seminary remained there from 1931 to 1934. Trevecca College later agreed to purchase the property and occupied it from 1932 to 1936, but relinquished it when it could not fulfill its contract. The school's full support resumed in 1933, and it moved back to its former home in September, 1934.

Upon the election of Dr. James M. Nabrit, Sr., to the seminary's presidency in April 1936, the school began eight years of prosperity (Dr. Nabrit was the brother of Sam Nabrit, former president of Texas Southern University and the father of James M. Nabrit, Jr., former president of Howard University). In the same year, the National Baptist Convention opened a Missionary Training School for women on the acquired site of the former Roger Williams University. The two schools had separate administrations but a cooperative program between them made possible a full program of Christian training for both women and men. Summer sessions and a night school also began that year, and extension classes were organized under the direction of Dr. J. C. Miles. In 1937, the Southern Baptist Convention agreed to share half of the operation costs for the seminary. Dr. R. W. Wiley, who succeeded Dr. Nabrit in 1944, expanded the physical plant substantially during his term. Victor T. Glass succeeded him as acting president in 1956.

Associate membership in the Accrediting Association of Bible Colleges was granted in 1962. In 1963, Dr. Charles E. Boddie was installed as president, and under his administration, the physical plant was renovated and improved. The evening credit program was reestablished in 1970. After a self-evaluation submitted in October 1970, the American Baptist College of the American Baptist Theological Seminary was granted full membership in the Accrediting Association of Bible Colleges (now the American Association of Bible Colleges) in 1971. In 1980, Dr. Boddie was elevated to chancellor of the college. He was succeeded by Dr. Odell McGlothian, Sr., on June 1, 1980, and was made president emeritus in 1982.

Today, the American Bible College is a four-year, coeducational Bible college with a strong liberal arts orientation. It prepares men and women for the Christian ministry, offering the Bachelor of Arts and Bachelor of Theology degrees and a certificate in Bible. The American Baptist College has a faculty of fifteen members, approximately half of whom hold the Doctor of Philosophy degree, and the other half of whom hold advanced degrees. There is a ratio of eleven students per faculty member. In addition to its accreditation by the American Association of Bible Colleges, it is approved by the Department of Justice for the education of foreign students; by the Department of Education to participate in federal financial aid programs; and by the Tennessee State Department of Education for the education of veterans and others eligible for veterans' benefits. As of the summer of 1990, the support of the Southern Baptist Convention was

discontinued. The college is now solely supported by the National Baptist Convention, U.S.A.

The college has established the Charles E. Boddie Chair of Excellence. It meets at the conventions of both the Southern Baptist Convention and the National Baptist Convention, U.S.A.

Group Type: Denomination specific; research/education
Founded: September 14, 1924
Membership: Approximately 160 students and 15 faculty members
Publications: *The Vision*, a newspaper; *American Baptist College* faculty journal
Meetings: Annual meeting at the National Baptist Convention, U.S.A.

American Bible College

13821 Waterfront Drive
Pineland, FL 33945
(813) 283-0519
Dr. G. W. Hyatt, President

The interracial American Bible College (ABC) was founded during World War II as a means of training laymen to manage congregations whose pastors or spiritual leaders had been called to serve in the armed forces as chaplains. It was recognized that the men at home could not attend the numerous Bible colleges or schools that were primarily residential and geared toward training young people, because they had to work five or six days a week to support their families. An alternative was needed.

Dr. G. W. Hyatt, a trained student of religion, with the assistance of several dedicated ministers, developed a curriculum that was free of denominational doctrines and tendencies; he incorporated and began the school in Chicago on September 2, 1942. Initially, the work was designed to assist those laymen who were filling in at the pulpits, but shortly thereafter, a great number of men and women of all ages were engaged in intensive study through the program, many through correspondence. Before the war ended, ABC lessons were being sent to servicemen throughout the world and many army chaplains were recommending the program to others, especially their assistants.

The school seeks to educate those called to the ministry or interested in intensive study, regardless of race, creed, or origin. Strictly expressed through a home-study, correspondence program, its curriculum has expanded over the years to provide more intense study for those who wish to continue their previous training in religion. Many evangelical churches in the United States, Canada, and Great Britain use the college's program for training their ministers, missionaries, and laity, as has the Salvation Army in order to fulfill required field study.

Among its supporters are Dr. Smallwood Williams, founder and Senior Bishop of the Bible Way Church of Our Lord Jesus Christ, World Wide, himself a graduate who recommends it to the ministers of the church, and the late Bishop O. T. Jones of the Church of God in Christ, Inc., who also encouraged church members to accept the college as the training school for ministers. The American Bible College was the first school of its kind to be recognized by Florida's Department of Education for the granting of theological degrees for off-campus training.

Currently located in Pineland, Florida, the American Bible College operates training centers in the United States and has affiliates in several foreign countries. It is licensed by the Florida State Board of Independent Colleges and Universities. The American Evangelical Christian Churches, a denominational ecclesiastical body headquartered in Pineland, Florida, supervises the work of the school.

Group Type: Ecumenical/nondenominational; research/education
Founded: 1942

Apostolic Overcoming Holy Church of God Theological Seminary

1120 North 24th Street
Birmingham, AL 35234
(205) 324-2202
Dr. Juanita R. Arrington, President

The Apostolic Overcoming Holy Church of God Theological Seminary offers a range of courses in Bible and pastoral studies. It was founded by the A.O.H. Church of God, and it is located on the same site as the A.O.H. Cathedral in Birmingham, Alabama. The seminary offers a summer session in addition to its fall and spring semesters. Dr. Juanita R. Arrington, secretary of the A.O.H. Church of God, also serves as the president of the seminary.

Group Type: Denomination specific; research/education

Central Baptist Theological Seminary in Indiana

1535 Dr. Andrew J. Brown Avenue, N.
Indianapolis, IN 46202-1997
(317) 636-6622
The Reverend Dr. F. Benjamin Davis, President/Dean

The Central Baptist Theological Seminary in Indiana was organized in 1942. Its purpose is to serve the needs of the denomination and to prepare students for all phases of Christian service. It is committed to the historic, evangelical Christian faith, as understood and witnessed by the Missionary Baptist Churches and summarized in the New Hampshire Confession of Faith. It offers the Bachelor of Theology, Bachelor of Religious Education, and Bachelor of Missionary Training degrees, as well as a graduate degree in theology.

Group Type: Denomination specific; research/education
Founded: 1942

Crenshaw Christian Center School of Ministry

P.O. Box 90000
Los Angeles, CA 90009
(213) 758-3777
Dr. Frederick K. C. Price, Founder and Pastor
Ms. Angela M. Evans, Executive Vice-President

The Crenshaw Christian Center School of Ministry is an outgrowth of the Crenshaw Christian Center, led by Dr. Frederick K. C. Price. Located in Los Angeles, California, the school opened in 1985 to instruct those who felt a call to the Christian ministry. The three-year program includes intensive Bible study as well as special ministerial preparation in the third year. It operates concurrently with the School of the Bible (begun in September, 1988), which offers one- or two-year courses in intensive Bible study. Two of the eight ministerial assistants of the church primarily teach in the school.

Group Type: Ecumenical/nondenominational; research/education
Founded: 1985

Crenshaw Christian Center School of the Bible

P.O. Box 90000
Los Angeles, CA 90009
(213) 758-3777
Dr. Frederick K. C. Price, Founder and Pastor
Ms. Angela M. Evans, Executive Vice-President

The Crenshaw Christian Center School of the Bible is an outgrowth of the Crenshaw Christian Center, led by Dr. Frederick K. C. Price. Located in Los Angeles, California, the school held its first classes in September, 1988 for those interested in intensive Bible study. The one- or two-year program will run concurrently with the church's School of Ministry, which differs through the addition of a third year geared toward special training in the ministry. Two of the eight ministerial assistants of the church primarily teach in the school.

Group Type: Ecumenical/nondenominational; research/education
Founded: 1988

Jackson Theological Seminary

604 Locust Street
North Little Rock, AR 72214
(501) 375-2406
Dr. Rufus K. Young, President

Group Type: Ecumenical/nondenominational; research/education

Saint Paul's Bible Institute

37 West 116th Street
New York, NY 10026
(212) 722-5488
Minister Jerome King, Dean

Saint Paul's Bible Institute is one of five Bible colleges founded and supported by the Salvation and Deliverance Church (see narrative on Salvation and Deliverance Church).

Group Type: Denomination specific; research/education

Simmons Bible College

1811 Dumesnil Street
Louisville, KY 40210
(502) 776-1443
Dr. W. J. Hodge, President
Mr. Charles E. Price, Academic Dean

Simmons Bible College was founded by the General Association of Baptists in Kentucky (formerly known as the State Convention of Colored Baptist Churches in Kentucky). In 1866, the year following its founding, the convention met in Frankfort, Kentucky, and considered the establishment of a college to train Negroes. At that time, there was no institution of higher learning for African Americans in the state. After securing land in Frankfort, the trustees of the state convention were empowered to open a normal and industrial school. In 1869, the convention met in Lexington, Kentucky, and the decision to move the school to Louisville was made. On November 25, 1879, the property in Frankfort was sold, and additional property was purchased in Louisville. The school was renamed the Kentucky Normal Theological Institute and opened under the direction of the Reverend Elijah P. Marrs and his brother, H. C. Marrs.

Dr. W. J. Simmons succeeded the Reverend Marrs, and the school prospered under his administration. In 1884, it became a university and expanded its departments to include liberal arts, a normal (teaching) or college preparatory course, a medical law department, business, music, and theological departments. There were three graduates in the first class in 1886, one of whom was a woman. In 1930, the campus was forced to sell its property due to foreclosure. By 1935, however, its present location was secured through the beneficence of Mr. Wood F. Axton.

In 1982, it was renamed Simmons Bible College to define more adequately its focus and mission. It is a full member of the Southern Accrediting Association of Bible Colleges, Inc., and is licensed by the Council on Higher Education, Commonwealth of Kentucky. It is also approved for training veterans and nonimmigrant-status students.

Simmons Bible College offers four academic programs: 1) a certificate in Christian ministry studies (nondegree), emphasizing the Bible or missions; 2) a diploma in Christian ministry studies (nondegree), emphasizing the Bible, theology, pastoral ministry, or Christian education; 3) the Bachelor of Arts degree in Biblical and Theological studies; and 4) the Bachelor of Theology degree (a postbaccalaureate degree).

Group Type: Denomination specific; research/education
Founded: 1879

Universal Bible Institute and Training School

19-23 Park Street
Orange, NJ 07050
(201) 673-4424
The Reverend Robert C. Jiggetts, Jr., Founder and President

A program of the Universal Church of Christ, Inc., the Universal Bible Institute and Training School offers courses for ministers (to awaken and develop the inner potential of those called of God to deliver the Good News) and Christian workers (to prepare to witness for Jesus Christ in evangelism and mission ministries). Courses rotate between the Brooklyn, New York, and Orange, New Jersey, locations of the Church. There are three instructors.

Group Type: Denomination specific; research/education
Membership: Unknown for student body; 3 instructors

Virginia Seminary and College

2058 Garfield Avenue
Lynchburg, VA 24501
(804) 528-5276
Melvin R. Boone, L.H.D., President
Ada M. Palmer, L.H.D., Dean of Education and Registrar

Organized in May, 1886 by the Virginia Baptist State Convention, acting in response to the initiative of the Reverend Phillip F. Morris, the cornerstone of what was then Lynchburg Baptist Seminary was laid in July, 1888. The school opened under the leadership of Professor R. P. Armstead on January 13, 1890, with an enrollment of thirty-three students. Technically, however, the Reverend Morris was the first president of the institution. The name of the school has been changed three times: in 1890 to Virginia Seminary, in 1900 to Virginia Theological Seminary and College, and to Virginia Seminary and College in 1962.

Today, Virginia Seminary and College prepares students to enter four-year institutions of higher learning and trains ministers and pastors. Its enrollment is mainly from Virginia and Maryland, but students from Texas, Washington (state), and New York attend as well. It maintains a mailing list of more than fifteen hundred churches, businesses, and individuals.

In 1988, the Board of Managers of the Virginia Seminary and College renamed the two school divisions. The M. C. Allen School of Religion is named in honor of the school's ninth president, Dr. M. C. Allen (1946-1966). The G. W. Hayes School of Arts and Sciences is named in honor of Professor Gregory W. Hayes, the school's second president (1890-1906). In September, 1989, a high-school program for dropouts of all ages was initiated. The president of the school is Dr. Melvin R. Boone.

Group Type: Denomination specific; research/education
Founded: 1886

Washington Baptist Seminary

1600 13th Street, NW
Washington, DC 20009
(202) 387-6290
The Reverend Dr. Andrew Fowler, President

The Washington Baptist Seminary was founded in October, 1926 through the administrative leadership of the Reverend W. H. Jernagin and the General Baptist Convention of the District of Columbia. The school offers a diploma in biblical studies, with course offerings in Christian education, church history, systematic theology, geography, Sunday school exposition, Baptist Training Union, English, and literature. The facility housing the seminary is the only edifice located in the District of Columbia that is owned and operated by African American Baptist churches of the city. Classes are offered in the evenings. It is under the control of a fifteen-member board of trustees. The students represent a variety of Christian denominational backgrounds. The board is composed of persons representing Baptist churches throughout the District of Columbia.

Group Type: Denomination specific; research/education
Founded: October, 1926

Research Projects

African American Worship Traditions Research Project—Interdenominational Theological Center

671 Beckwith Street, SW
Atlanta, GA 30314
(404) 527-7729
Dr. Melva Wilson Costen, Co-Chair, Consultation Project
   Committee
Dr. Darius Swann, Co-Chair, Consultation Project
   Committee
Ms. Carolyn McFarlin, Director, Worship Projects

The African American Worship Traditions Research Project was initiated in 1984 at the Interdenominational Theological Center (ITC) in Atlanta, Georgia, by Dr. Melva Wilson Costen, Helmar Nielsen Professor of Worship and Music, and Dr. Darius Swann, professor of missiology (theology of missions) and world religions. A portion of the $450,000 gift to ITC by Boston businessman Helmar Nielsen has been used to sponsor a series of consultations that will provide opportunities to examine sociological, historical, aesthetic, ethical, psychological, theological, and biblical dimensions of worship in African American congregations. Participants and leaders in these consultations have included those involved in the worship experience such as ministers, artists, musicians, dramatists, teachers, writers, and researchers.

The project hopes to affect positively as many African American churches as possible across denominational lines. Thus, the participants are from most major denominations with a large or significant African American population in the United States and from African and Caribbean cultures; the project has included both clergy and laity alike. After three consultations, over a two- or three-year period, the data will be published and used for teaching. A major interdenominational worship conference was held at ITC July 25-27, 1990. Worship conferences will also be planned periodically across the country in order to demonstrate and exemplify what has been learned and shared.

The first consultation was held in the fall of 1985 with fifty participants from a cross section of churches with African American constituencies, using the denominations that compose ITC as a starting point. Several elements emerged from the first consultation. Several scholarly papers were presented concerning various areas of African American worship, and these formed the basis for discussions. The provision of an ongoing annotated bibliography of articles and books about African American worship written by African Americans was formulated. Plans included the development of a scholarly resource from papers on worship for use in education. This was an important step in light of the development of the church music degree program initiated in the fall of 1988. Following the consultation, persons will be commissioned to develop a liturgy that could be used for discussion at subsequent consultations. Services would then be field-tested in churches around the country.

A final objective is an annual consultation or conference on worship in the African American church to continue work in conservation, refinement, and creation of worship in the Af-

rican American tradition. The Helmar Nielsen Chair in Worship, which Dr. Melva W. Costen holds, was established with some of the Nielsen funds. A church music degree program was started in 1987, with eight students enrolled in 1990. Currently available is the *Journal of the Interdenominational Theological Center* (Vol. 14, Fall 1986/Spring 1987, nos. 1 and 2), featuring papers on African American worship. Dr. Melva Costen and Dr. Darius Swann co-chair the Nielsen consultation project committee. Ms. Carolyn McFarlin is director of the worship projects.

Group Type: Ecumenical/nondenominational; research/education
Founded: 1984

Black Church Family Project

Department of Family and Community Development
University of Maryland
Family Research Center
4310 Knox Road
College Park, MD 20742
(301) 454-4146
Dr. Andrew Billingsley, Principal Investigator
Dr. Cleopatra Howard Caldwell, Study Director

With funding from the Ford Foundation and the Lilly Endowment, Inc., the Black Church Family Project (BCFP) is conducting a comprehensive national study of family-support programs sponsored by African American churches. The African American church has traditionally played a very important role in the evolution of African American family life in America. Because of the many challenges facing the African American community today, it is important to understand the institutional supports available to assist in sustaining and enhancing these families.

The purpose of this study is to identify and describe family-oriented community-outreach programs sponsored by African American churches that are designed to enhance the functioning of African American family and community life. The outreach programs of interest for this study are those that include services for people who are *not* church members. Through a pilot study, it was found that some of these programs are designed to assist with functions typically provided within the family, such as the provision of food, shelter, clothing, and access to health care. They may also include such expressive functions as imparting a sense of acceptance, self-worth, culture, and pride.

Phase I of the study involves a telephone survey of fifteen hundred African American churches throughout the country to gather information on the history, structure, and characteristics of African American churches across various denominations, as well as the nature of outreach programs offered by these churches. Phase II will focus on a selected sample of one hundred African American churches nationwide that operate exemplary family-support programs. Interviews will be conducted with representatives from each church including the senior minister, coordinators of outreach programs, and program participants. Direct observations of outreach programs in action will also be made.

Dr. Andrew Billingsley is the principal investigator. Dr. Victor Rouse is the co-principal investigator. Dr. Robert Hill is the senior consultant, and Dr. Cleopatra Howard Caldwell is the study director.

Group Type: Ecumenical/nondenominational; research/education

Black Church Project—American Association for the Advancement of Science

Office of Opportunities in Science
1333 H Street, NW
Washington, DC 20005
(202) 326-6670
Treopia G. Washington, Coordinator

The Directorate for Education and Human Resources Programs of the American Association for the Advancement of Science began its Black Church Project in 1988 to promote effective informal mathematic, science, and computer education in churches that serve the African American community. It was initiated because of the very small percentage of African American scientists, engineers, and mathematicians in the current work force; the weak background in the sciences that minorities generally have; and the predicted need for scientifically trained persons in the twenty-first century. The project is based on the belief that support systems (such as the church) that bring family and community together can help counteract negative influences and encourage young people to pursue successful careers in the sciences and technologies of the future.

The project is facilitated through fifteen local networks. Each is headed by a local organization in participating cities. These organizations include churches, universities and colleges, the National Urban League, and science museums. The cities where the program will be conducted are: Atlanta, Georgia; Birmingham/Huntsville, Alabama; Chicago, Illinois; Cleveland, Ohio; Detroit, Michigan; Indianapolis, Indiana; Jackson, Mississippi; Los Angeles, California; New Orleans, Louisiana; New York City, New York; Pittsburgh, Pennsylvania; Philadelphia, Pennsylvania; Raleigh/Durham, North Carolina; San Francisco/Oakland, California; and Washington, D.C./Baltimore, Maryland/Richmond, Virginia. Initial training for site coordinators was held in November, 1989 and included planning for parent workshops/career days, math and science after-school programs, and public science days. In January 1990, workshops began in each city, with city coordinators holding three workshops of thirty participants each. Each of the ninety participants will then conduct activities for at least ten members of their own churches. Other workshops, such as math and science training for Girl and Boy Scout leaders, science training for preschool staffs, and advocacy training for ministers to encourage effective in- and out-of-school math, science, and computer education, will be held at the AAAS headquarters in Washington in the near future. These will be open to all churches around the country.

In addition, the Black Church Project conducts a minigrant competition to fund math, science, or computer programs in churches. It works with two major African American religious organizations: the Congress of National Black Churches (especially through Project SPIRIT); and the Progressive National Baptist Convention. Treopia G. Washington is the project coordinator.

Group Type: Ecumenical/nondenominational; research/education

Founded: 1988

Black Family Ministry Project—National Council of the Churches of Christ in the U.S.A.

P.O. Box 603
Wayne, PA 19087
(215) 688-0629
FAX (215) 964-1381

The Reverend Joe Leonard, Contract Staff
Dr. Edgar J. Mack, Project Chairperson and Executive Committee
Dr. Virginia Sargent, Executive Committee
Dr. Louise Bates Evans, Executive Committee
Ms. Dorothy Savage, Grant Administrator

The Black Family Ministry Project is designed to strengthen African American congregations in their family ministries. It will assess families' needs, look for effective ministries, and share these ministries among African American congregations across denominational and geographical boundaries. Supported by a grant from the Lilly Endowment, the project will be administered through the Ministries in Christian Education, one of the National Council of Churches' educational program areas.

As a part of the National Council of Churches' broader "Families 2000" project, the Black Family Ministry Project's participant bodies include the African Methodist Episcopal Church, the African Methodist Episcopal Zion Church, the Christian Methodist Episcopal Church, the American Baptist Churches in the U.S.A., the Christian Church (Disciples of Christ), the Evangelical Lutheran Church in America, the Presbyterian Church (U.S.A.), and the United Methodist Church. The project will focus on the church's central role in the African American community, where it seeks to counter the forces of racism, poverty, and oppression that are conspiring to pull these families apart.

The "Families 2000" project will have a major ecumenical event in April 1991, where family service agency representatives and a broad range of representatives of the churches will meet for further exploration of issues and new models of church support for families. The conference will include a major Black Family Ministry Conference, where twenty-four persons will be trained. These consultants will be drawn from congregations and seminaries of the participating denominations. Teams of the Black Family Ministry planning consultants will work with at least three local congregations for a year, assisting congregations in planning collaborative ministries of support with families. In May 1992, the teams will meet to begin training a second group of consultants. A planning manual will be developed by December 1992. It is hoped that the project will give rise to an ongoing Ecumenical Community on Black Families, which will continue to address issues and promote cooperative programs.

The Reverend Joe Leonard serves as contract staff for the

project. Dr. Edgar J. Mack, executive director of the African Methodist Episcopal Church's Christian education department, serves as project chairperson. Ms. Dorothy Savage, director of ministries in Christian education of the National Council of the Churches of Christ in the U.S.A., serves as grant administrator.

Group Type: Ecumenical/nondenominational; research/education

Founded: 1990

Black Religion Collection Development Project—Schomburg Center for Research in Black Culture

The New York Public Library
515 Malcolm X Boulevard
New York, NY 10037-1801
(212) 862-4000
Mr. Victor Smythe, Project Archivist
Mr. Howard Dodson, Director and Principal Investigator

The Schomburg Center for Research in Black Culture, an African American archival and research facility and a division of the New York Public Library, has established a Black Religion Collection Development Project to document the role of religion in African American life. The project is supported by a three-year grant from the Lilly Endowment, Inc. The research effort seeks to create a more comprehensive base of African American religion resources within its Special Collection units. The Center plans to develop a strong foundation for the study of the African American church and to define the role of the church in African American economic, political, and social life.

The primary focus of the Black Religion Collection Development Project is to gather documentation on organized religious bodies on the local, state, regional, and national levels that have predominantly African American membership. This includes the collection of primary materials from local congregations, conferences, conventions, synods, dioceses, and other such divisions of Protestant and Catholic churches in the United States. The project will gather data on non-Christian religious organizations whose membership is predominantly African American, as well as existing Christian and non-Christian religious organizations, such as ushers, gospel choirs, and ministerial associations.

An innovative aspect of the project is its use of the microfiche camera to produce microform reproductions where acquisition of original materials is not possible. The Center will also seek to make resources and interpretive programs accessible to seminaries involved with training African American religious leaders, as well as to scholars and other interested parties. In 1990, the Center convened a research symposium of scholars, librarians, and other representatives of seminaries and divinity schools offering graduate-level instruction to identify research priorities and complementary resource materials needed in the study of African American religion.

The Black Religion Collection Development Project is under the general direction of Howard Dodson, the principal investigator and director of the Schomburg Center for Research in Black Culture. The project archivist is Victor Smythe. Assisting the Center in this undertaking is a distinguished national Black Religion Advisory Committee composed of scholars in the field.

Group Type: Ecumenical/nondenominational; research/education

Founded: 1989

Black Religious Studies Network

3045 Douglas Drive
Yorktown Heights, NY 10598
(914) 245-4994
The Reverend James T. Roberson, Jr., Project Manager and President

The Black Religious Studies Network (BRSNET) was created in 1989 by the Reverend James T. Roberson in cooperation with the faculty of the Interdenominational Theological Center (ITC). The Empire State Missionary Baptist Convention of New York and the executive committee of the Society for the Study of Black Religion (SSBR) were also involved in the development of the network.

BRSNET is a computer-conferencing network, which promotes the development and dissemination of information and data related to the study of African American religion. It currently has a working relationship with the SSBR, the Empire State Convention, and ITC. Plans are underway to coordinate computer conferencing between the three accredited, predominantly black graduate seminaries—Howard University, Virginia Union, and ITC—and New York Theological Seminary and Colgate Rochester Divinity School/Bexley Hall/Crozer Theological Seminary. Other seminaries will also be invited to join the network.

BRSNET has the capacity to sponsor exchanges on curriculum, research, papers, journal articles, indexes, and bibliographies. To this end, regional groups and local associations of clergy are constituent parts of the network. BRSNET can also serve local congregations with programmatic counseling, small group meetings on management and administrative problems, and the collection and analysis of sociological data on denominations, congregations, caucuses, ecumenical groups, etc. The network also seeks connections with research institutions, libraries, museums, and study centers that are interested in African American religion. A user's guide is available. In addition to the Reverend Roberson, Dr. Gayraud Wilmore, chair of the SSBR conferencing committee, is involved in the project.

Group Type: Ecumenical/nondenominational; research/education

Founded: 1989

Black Women in Church and Society—Interdenominational Theological Center

671 Beckwith Street, SW
Atlanta, GA 30314
(404) 527-7740
Dr. Jacquelyn Grant, Founder and Director

The Black Women in Church and Society project, housed at Interdenominational Theological Center, seeks to: 1) provide leadership training for African American women in church and society; 2) bridge the gap between African American women in church (laity and clergy) and society; 3) research questions and issues pivotal to African American women in the church and society; and 4) provide a resource center for the gathering of materials on African American women in church and society.

Founded in 1981, Black Women in Church and Society provides leadership training and develops support structures to help women fulfill responsibilities brought on by their increased participation in religious and nonreligious activities in the United States and the Third World. The center has developed a research-resource center on the subject "Black Women and Religion." As part of its activities, the Black Women in Church and Society publishes the *Directory of Black Women in Ministry*.

Group Type: Ecumenical/nondenominational; women; research/education
Founded: 1981
Publications: Directory of Black Women in Ministry

Black Women in the Church, 1780–1970—Center for African American History and Culture, Temple University

Weiss Hall, Suite B18
Philadelphia, PA 19122
(215) 787-4851
Dr. Bettye Collier-Thomas, Project Historian

This project was initiated in October 1990 at Temple University's Center for African American History and Culture to research and write the first comprehensive history of "Black Women in the Church, 1780–1970." It will trace the historic involvement of African American women in the development of primarily, but not exclusively, Protestant and Catholic churches. Issues to be investigated include the role and status of black women in the church and their historical struggle for ordination.

The Center for African American History and Culture is one of Temple University's cross-disciplinary research and training centers that focuses upon the development of research and scholarship in areas of African American history and culture.

Over the next five years, the Center will focus on women, religion, and African Americans in Pennsylvania. The project is funded by a grant from the Lilly Endowment. Dr. Bettye Collier-Thomas, the Center's director, serves as project historian.

Group Type: Ecumenical/nondenominational; research/education
Founded: October 1990

Research Center on Black Religious Bodies—Howard University School of Divinity

1400 Shepherd Street, NE
Washington, DC 20017
(202) 806-0750
Dr. Wardell J. Payne, Research Director

The Howard University School of Divinity Research Center on Black Religious Bodies was initiated in 1985 to produce this landmark volume, the *Directory of African American Religious Bodies: A Compendium by the Howard University School of Divinity*. The purpose of this initial study has been to identify the scope of the African American religious experience through its history, leadership, and programs. The Center maintains information on more than nine hundred "religious bodies"—denominations; ecumenical, nondenominational, or independent ministries; religious organizations; educational and research facilities; and support organizations. It has been funded by a grant from the Lilly Endowment, Inc. The research director is Dr. Wardell J. Payne.

Group Type: Ecumenical/nondenominational; research/education
Founded: 1985
Publications: Directory of African American Religious Bodies: A Compendium by the Howard University School of Divinity, Wardell J. Payne, editor

Research/Professional Organizations

Biblical Institute for Social Change

409 K Street, NE
Washington, DC 20002
(202) 547-0992
The Reverend Dr. Cain Hope Felder, Founder and Chairman
The Reverend Frank E. Drumwright, Jr., President

The Biblical Institute for Social Change (BISC) was incorporated in April 1990 to promote self-esteem and social change through value classification among persons of African descent around the world. These objectives are achieved principally by the development of a deeper understanding of the role of persons of African descent in biblical history in African American churches, challenging Eurocentric theology and its historical distortions, which have undermined the psychological confidence of the African race.

Founded by Dr. Cain Hope Felder, professor of New Tes-

tament Language and Literature at the Howard University School of Divinity and author of the award-winning book, *Troubling Biblical Waters: Race, Class, and Family*, BISC seeks to change the perceptions of Christians by conducting mini-classes across denominational lines that highlight the roles played by people of African descent in biblical history and the critical importance of the Bible for blacks today. Books, pamphlets, working papers, and curriculum materials, as well as video- and audiotapes, films, and learning materials are produced and distributed to educate and enhance black pride, motivation, and solidarity. Additionally, BISC is introducing these ideas into novels, films, television, and plays.

The Reverend Dr. Cain Hope Felder is founder and chairman of the board. The other officers of BISC are the Reverend Frank E. Drumwright, Jr., president; Dr. Betty J. Watson, secretary; the Reverend William H. Bennett II, treasurer; and Dr. Dionne Jones, editor of the *BISC Quarterly*.

Group Type: Ecumenical/nondenominational; Christian education; research/education
Founded: April 1990
Membership: Approximately 250 persons
Publications: *Study Guide to Dr. Cain Hope Felder's Troubling Biblical Waters: Race, Class and Family*; *BISC Quarterly*, a quarterly newsletter
Meetings: Executive board meets monthly on the third Friday

Black Theology Project

c/o Trinity United Church of Christ
532 W. 95th Street
Chicago, IL 60628
Dr. Iva E. Carruthers, Executive Director

The Black Theology Project (BTP), organized in 1976, is an ecumenical association of African American Christians who are "devoted to the discovery, development, and promotion of historic and contemporary black religious thought and action." It is a national organization open to those interested in its mission. The project collaborates with the Ecumenical Association of Third World Theologians and Theology in the Americas. It has also established ongoing exchange programs with international organizations. A delegation of the BTP met with black Christians of Brazil and members of Mantida Pelo Instituto Educacional Piracicabano in Brazil in November, 1988.

On the national level, essays, sermons, songs, monographs, and curricula developed at the local and regional levels are published and disseminated. An annual convocation on the current status of the African American church and target areas engaged in the struggle for justice is held (the 1989 convocation was held in Newark, NJ). In addition to the convocation, periodic symposia, workshops, and conferences are held. Local reflection groups of students, laypersons, clergy, and others interested in social analysis and promotion of the African American church are organized by individual members. Dialogue is also promoted between African American theologians and other Christians engaged in the struggle for equality and liberation.

The Black Theology Project publishes *Doing Black Theology*, a quarterly newsletter and periodic bulletins. Its membership is in excess of six hundred persons. The executive director is Dr. Iva E. Carruthers.

Group Type: Ecumenical/nondenominational; research/education; racial/social justice
Founded: 1976
Membership: Over 600 persons
Publications: *Doing Black Theology*, a quarterly newsletter, and periodic bulletins

Ecumenical Association of Third World Theologians

Union Theological Seminary
3041 Broadway
New York, NY 10027
(212) 662-7100, x356
The Reverend Dr. James H. Cone

The Ecumenical Association of Third World Theologians was founded in August, 1976, in Dar es Salaam, Tanzania. Twenty-two theologians from Africa, Asia, Latin America, and a representative from black North America met at the founding conference. It is an ecumenical group of Catholic and Protestant theologians, both lay and ordained. The General Assembly meets once every five years, and various continental meetings are held in between the general meeting. The group has published several books and articles concerning Third World theology.

Group Type: Ecumenical/nondenominational; research/education
Founded: August 1976

Martin Luther King Fellows, Inc.

c/o Metropolitan Baptist Church
1225 R Street, NW
Washington, DC 20009
(202) 483-1540
The Reverend Dr. H. Beecher Hicks, Jr., President

The Martin Luther King Fellows, Inc., began in 1971 after the 1968 assassination of Dr. King, when black seminarians at Colgate Rochester Divinity School felt the need to remember the legacy of Dr. King. They pushed for establishment of a professorship and program in African American church studies, which was implemented in 1969, after fundraising drives and a closedown of the school to encourage immediate attention to the matter. Dr. Henry H. Mitchell was the first professor to fill the King Chair in Black Church Studies on July 1, 1969, and the program began that September.

A graduate of the school, the Reverend Granville Seward, proposed an advanced program in writing that would produce a bibliography in black-culture church practice, which was deficient. A proposal was submitted to a foundation that subsequently withdrew from supporting religious education. Finally in 1970, a formal proposal was funded by the Irwin-Sweeney-Miller Foundation, allowing a coast-to-coast consultation among experts. The first draft request was increased from $25,000 to $113,000, with an eventual total assistance of $180,000.

By the time the grant was awarded in November, 1971, Colgate Rochester had been joined by the faculties of Bexley Hall (Episcopal) and Dr. King's alma mater, Crozer Theological Seminary (Baptist). Twenty King Fellows were chosen from seventy-five applicants by a committee of African American students and faculty. They were to study in Africa in the summer of 1972, while the three combined faculties worked on the academic processing of the program. The men selected represented a cross-section of African American pastors from different denominations and geographic locations. They varied in age and were also selected based upon their special gifts. Each had a Bachelor of Divinity or Master of Divinity degree and were considered effective in the African American community. Eight Baptists from two national conventions, seven Methodists from four denominations, two Pentecostals, two Episcopalians, one United Church of Christ, one A.M.E. Zion Fellow/Professor, one Disciple of Christ, one Presbyterian professor, and two nonchurchmen from the fields of the media and economics were chosen. Two Roman Catholic consultants were added to the program at a later date.

The overall purpose of the project was to produce a series of books, journal articles, and monographs on the professional practice of ministry in the African American community. In addition, recommendations about the curriculum needs of African American students in the ministry were to be submitted in the form of a design. This was to be done in three summers, with additional work throughout the year. The Master of Theology degree would be awarded in 1975, but it was hoped that, by this time, the Doctor of Ministry degree would be approved.

The Fellows and faculty consultants left from New York for Cotonou, Dahomey (now Benin), on July 1, 1972, for five weeks of intensive study in Ghana and Nigeria in order to find and identify African influences in contemporary African American folk religion, as opposed to the European bias that permeated theological training. They were also made aware of the similarities and compatibility of Christian and traditional African religions. They then attended six weeks of colloquia at the Interdenominational Theological Center in the summer of 1973 and six weeks of colloquia and writing at the sponsoring seminaries in Rochester in the summer of 1974. In January 1974, they spent a week in Jamaica and Haiti and witnessed a ring shout in an A.M.E. Zion conference and an authentic Vodoun ritual. During the course of study, they also visited the Sea Islands off the coast of South Carolina, which emphasized the continuity of West African religion and life-style in African America. By the end of the project, the Doctor of Ministry degree had been approved at Colgate Rochester/Bexley Hall/Crozer Seminary, and nineteen Fellows received the degree on May 9, 1975. Several persons who participated in the program in various capacities—instruction, administration, and so forth—were also made fellows.

The Martin Luther King Fellows were incorporated in the summer of 1975, and since that time, numerous books, monographs, and journal articles have resulted in the growth of material on the African American church experience and community. In 1978, at its annual meeting, the organization adopted a feasible way to publish materials. It provided for the exclusive use of two options that had been included in the funding contract, book publication and journal articles. Materials whose public demand would be too small for general press publication would be produced by the organization's own press, so that they would indeed be available to seminaries and to the public. Shorter pieces would also be published in the *Bulletin of the Martin Luther King Fellows, Inc.*

The Fellows are continuing to publish material to increase the available information on the African American church experience. Currently, they are in the process of producing a biblical commentary written from an African American perspective. The organization continues to meet annually and reserves the right to add other members. The president is the Reverend Dr. H. Beecher Hicks, Jr.

Group Type: Ecumenical/nondenominational; ministerial; research/education
Founded: 1971
Membership: Approximately 30 persons

Society for the Study of Black Religion

c/o Howard University School of Divinity
1400 Shepherd Street, NE
Washington, DC 20017
(202) 806-0500
Dr. Clarence G. Newsome, President

The Society for the Study of Black Religion was established in 1971. It was founded by African American religious scholars, who were primarily members of the American Academy of Religion and who sought to develop a closer network for exchange of information on the role and status of scholarship in African American religious studies. Its organizational purpose and structure developed out of a series of formal and informal discussions between African American theologians who met at Gammon Seminary in Atlanta, Georgia, during the weekend of February 20-21, 1971.

Its organizational goals and purpose have remained consistent with its original intent. They are: 1) to provide an intellectual forum for African Americans in religion; 2) to stimulate African American religious scholarship and research; and 3) to provide fellowship for African American scholars and teachers in religion. The organization conducts an annual meeting, which is designed to enlighten its constituents. Members read scholarly papers and share their reflections on trends and issues pertaining to the African American religious experience in the United States.

The Society for the Study of Black Religion summarizes its vision through five basic elements: 1) the discovery and reclamation of an African American heritage that has been lost, unrecognized, or ignored as an entity of little or no value; 2) the development of a sense of dignity, worth, and pride in the African American heritage on the part of African American people; 3) the increase of knowledge and the development of skills that will free African American people from oppression and dehumanization and enable them to survive in an unjust society; 4) the dissemination of information to persons of African American descent; and 5) the investigation and analysis of the African American religious experience.

The Society for the Study of Black Religion is under the leadership of the Reverend Dr. Clarence G. Newsome, associate dean, Howard University School of Divinity. The other officers include: Dr. Louis-Charles Harvey, secretary, United Theological Seminary, Dayton, Ohio; Dr. Vincent Wimbush, treasurer, Claremont School of Theology, Claremont, California; and Dr. Lillian Ashcraft-Eason, historian, Clark Atlanta University.

Group Type: Ecumenical/nondenominational; research/education
Founded: 1971

Historically African American Colleges, Universities, and Seminaries Founded or Supported by Major Denominations

African Methodist Episcopal

Allen University—*founded 1870*
 1530 Harden Street
 Columbia, SC 29204

Daniel Payne College—*founded 1877*
 Birmingham, AL (closed)

Edward Waters College—*founded 1866*
 1658 Kings Road
 Jacksonville, FL 32209

Morris Brown College—*founded 1881*
 643 Martin Luther King Drive, SW
 Atlanta, GA 30314

Paul Quinn College—*founded 1872*
 1020 Elm Street
 Waco, TX 76704

Payne Theological Seminary—*founded 1844*
 Box 474
 Wilberforce, OH 45384

R. R. Wright School of Religion—*founded 1938*
 Johannesburg, South Africa

Shorter College—*founded 1886*
 604 Locust Street
 North Little Rock, AR 72114

Turner Theological Seminary (ITC)—*founded 1885*
 671 Beckwith Street, SW
 Atlanta, GA 30314

Wilberforce University—*founded 1856*
 Wilberforce, OH 45384

African Methodist Episcopal Zion

Hood Theological Seminary—*founded 1879*
 800 West Thomas Street
 Salisbury, NC 28144

Livingstone College—*founded 1879*
 701 West Monroe Street
 Salisbury, NC 28144

American Missionary Association (these schools were founded by the AMA)

Albany State College—*founded 1903*
 504 College Drive
 Albany, GA 31705

Atlanta University—*founded 1867*
 223 Chestnut Street, SW
 Atlanta, GA 30314

Dillard University—*founded 1869*
 2601 Gentilly Boulevard
 New Orleans, LA 70122

Fisk University—*founded 1866*
 17th Avenue, North
 Nashville, TN 37203

Hampton University—*founded 1868*
 East Queen Street
 Hampton, VA 23668

Talladega College—*founded 1867*
 627 West Battle Street
 Talladega, AL 35160

Tougaloo College—*founded 1869*
 Tougaloo, MS 39174

Baptist

American Baptist College of the American Baptist Theological Seminary—*founded 1924*
 1800 Whites Creek Pike
 Nashville, TN 37207

Arkansas Baptist College—*founded 1901*
 1600 Bishop Street
 Little Rock, AR 72202

Benedict College—*founded 1870*
 Harden and Blanding Streets
 Columbia, SC 29204

Bishop State Junior College—*founded 1927*
 351 North Broad Street
 Mobile, AL 36603

Central Baptist Theological Seminary in Indiana—*founded 1942*
 1535 Dr. Andrew J. Brown Avenue, N.
 Indianapolis, IN 46202-1997

Florida Memorial College—*founded 1879*
 15800 NW 42nd Avenue
 Miami, FL 33054

Friendship Junior College—*founded 1891*
 Rock Hill, SC

Morehouse College—*founded 1867*
 830 Westview Drive, SW
 Atlanta, GA 30314

Morehouse School of Religion (ITC)—*founded 1867*
 671 Beckwith Street, SW
 Atlanta, GA 30314

Morris College—*founded 1908*
 North Main Street
 Sumter, SC 29150

Natchez Junior College—*founded 1884*
  1010 N. Union
  Natchez, MS 39120

Norfolk State College—*founded 1935*
  2401 Corprew Avenue
  Norfolk, VA 23504

Selma University—*founded 1878*
  Selma, AL 36701

Shaw University—*founded 1865*
  118 East South Street
  Raleigh, NC 27611

Shaw Divinity School—*founded 1933*
  118 East South Street
  Raleigh, NC 27611

Simmons Bible College—*founded 1879*
  1811 Dumesnill Street
  Louisville, KY 40210

Spelman College—*founded 1881*
  350 Spelman Lane, SW
  Atlanta, GA 30318

Virginia Seminary and College—*founded 1888*
  2058 Garfield Avenue
  Lynchburg, VA 24501

Virginia Union University—*founded 1865*
  1205 Palmyra Avenue
  Richmond, VA 23227

Christian Methodist Episcopal

Lane College—*founded 1882*
  545 Lane Avenue
  Jackson, TN 38301

Miles College—*founded 1905*
  P.O. Box 3800
  Birmingham, AL 35208

Mississippi Industrial College—*founded 1905*
  Holly Springs, MS
  (closed)

Paine College—*founded 1882*
  1235 Fifteenth Street
  Augusta, GA 30901

Phillips School of Theology (ITC)—*founded 1944*
  671 Beckwith Street, SW
  Atlanta, GA 30314

Texas College—*founded 1894*
  2404 North Grand Avenue
  Tyler, TX 75702

Church of God in Christ

Charles H. Mason Theological Seminary (ITC)—*founded 1970*
  671 Beckwith Street, SW
  Atlanta, GA 30314

Disciples of Christ

Jarvis Christian College—*founded 1912*
  P.O. Box G
  Hawkins, TX 75765

Tougaloo College—*founded 1869*
  Tougaloo, MS 39174

Ecumenical/Nondenominational

Howard University School of Divinity—*founded 1870*
  1400 Shepherd Street, NE
  Washington, DC 20017

Interdenominational Theological Center—*founded 1958*
  671 Beckwith Street, SW
  Atlanta, GA 30314

Episcopal

St. Augustine's College—*founded 1867*
  1315 Oakwood Avenue
  Raleigh, NC 27611

St. Paul's College—*founded 1888*
  406 Windsor Avenue
  Lawrenceville, VA 23868

Voorhees College—*founded 1897*
  Voorhees Road
  Denmark, SC 29042

Lutheran

Alabama Lutheran Academy and College—*founded 1922*
  Selma, AL
  (closed)

Presbyterian

Barber-Scotia College—*founded 1867*
  145 Cabarrus Avenue
  Concord, NC 28025

Johnson C. Smith Theological Seminary (ITC)—*founded 1867*
  671 Beckwith Street, SW
  Atlanta, GA 30314

Johnson C. Smith University—*founded 1867*
  100-300 Beatties Ford Road
  Charlotte, NC 28216

Knoxville College—*founded 1875*
  901 College Street
  Knoxville, TN 37921

Lincoln University—*founded 1854*
  Lincoln, PA 19352

Mary Holmes Junior College—*founded 1892*
  West Point, MS

Stillman College—*founded 1876*
  P.O. Box 1430
  Tuscaloosa, AL 35403

Quaker

Cheyney State College—*founded 1837*
  Cheyney, PA 19313

Roman Catholic

Xavier University—*founded 1915*
7325 Palmetto Street
New Orleans, LA 70125

Seventh-Day Adventist

Oakwood College—*founded 1896*
Oakwood Road
Huntsville, AL 35806

United Church of Christ/Congregational

Atlanta University—*founded 1867*
223 Chestnut Street, SW
Atlanta, GA 30314

Dillard University—*founded 1869*
2601 Gentilly Boulevard
New Orleans, LA 70122

Howard University—*founded 1867*
2400 Sixth Street, NW
Washington, DC 20059

Huston-Tillotson College—*founded 1876*
1820.East 8th Street
Austin, TX 78702

Le Moyne-Owen College—*founded 1870*
807 Walker Avenue
Memphis, TN 38126

Southwestern Christian College—*founded 1949*
Box 10
Terrell, TX 75160

Talladega College—*founded 1867*
627 West Battle Street
Talladega, AL 35160

United Methodist

Bennett College—*founded 1873*
900 East Washington Street
Greensboro, NC 27420

Bethune-Cookman College—*founded 1904*
640 Second Avenue
Daytona Beach, FL 32015

Claflin College—*founded 1869*
College Street, NE
East Orangeburg, SC 29115

Clark College—*founded 1869*
(now Clark Atlanta University)
223 James P. Brawley Drive, SW
Atlanta, GA 30314

Dillard University—*founded 1869*
2601 Gentilly Boulevard
New Orleans, LA 70122

Gammon Theological Seminary (ITC)—*founded 1869*
671 Beckwith Street, SW
Atlanta, GA 30314

Huston-Tillotson College—*founded 1876*
1820 East 8th Street
Austin, TX 78702

Meharry Medical College—*founded 1876*
1005 18th Avenue, North
Nashville, TN 37208

Morgan State University—*founded 1867*
Cold Spring Lane and Hillen Road
Baltimore, MD 21239

Morristown College—*founded 1881*
(now Knoxville College-Morristown Campus)
417 North James Street
Morristown, TN 37814

Paine College—*founded 1882*
1235 Fifteenth Street
Augusta, GA 30901

Philander Smith College—*founded 1877*
812 West 13th Street
Little Rock, AR 72202

Rust College—*founded 1866*
1 Rust Avenue
Holly Springs, MS 38635

University of Maryland, Eastern Shore—*founded 1886*
Princess Anne, MD 21853

Wiley College—*founded 1873*
711 Rosborough Springs Road
Marshall, TX 75670

Part 4

Selected Listing of African Americans with Scholarly Interest in Religion or Cognate Religious Studies

The following list includes African Americans who have made significant contributions to and achievements in the realms of religious education, publication, or ministry. Most have received the Doctor of Philosophy degree in religion or its cognate areas, and the listing does not generally include persons whose highest earned degree is the Doctor of Ministry degree, a professional rather than a scholarly degree (there are some exceptions). The information presented was collected primarily from questionnaires based on recommendations from persons in the religious realm, interviews, and the *Directory of Faculty of Departments and Programs of Religious Studies in North America*, produced by the Council of Societies for the Study of Religion, Watson E. Mills, editor. The directory represents all currently available information on each individual.

The entries are arranged in alphabetical order according to last name. The format for each entry (in paragraph form) is as follows:

(1) ASHCRAFT-EASON, Lillian E.; (2) Dr.; (3) f; (4) assistant professor, Department of History, Bowling Green State University, Bowling Green, OH 43403, (419) 372-8120; associate professor, on leave (1990–91), De-partment of Religion and Philosophy, Clark Atlanta University, 240 James P. Brawley Drive, SW, Atlanta, GA 30314, (404) 681-8234; (5) B.S., history and education, Hampton University, 1962; M.Ed., teaching (social science), University of Virginia, 1967; Ph.D., history, College of William and Mary, 1975; (6) history of religion, African American history, African American church history, African traditional religions; (7) AAR, SSBR, ASALH; (8) United Methodist; (9) member; (10) 7350 Nightingale Drive, Apt. 6, Holland, OH 43528, (419) 866-5584.

Key

(1) Name; (2) title; (3) gender; (4) academic title/position and institutional affiliation [address and phone number]; (5) education [degree, major, institution, year]; (6) areas of specialization; (7) professional affiliations; (8) denominational affiliation; (9) position in denomination; (10) home address and telephone number.

The following list is abbreviations of professional affiliations that appear in item seven in the entries. Immediately following this listing is the list of scholars.

Abbreviations for Professional Affiliations

AH—Academy of Homiletics

AAHP—African-American Hermeneutics Project

AAMA—African American Museums Association

AfSA—African Studies Association

ARAK—Afrikan Religiographic Association of Kenya

AKD—Alpha Kappa Delta National Sociology Honor Society

AKM—Alpha Kappa Mu Honor Society

AAAS—American Academy of Arts and Sciences

AAR—American Academy of Religion

AAA—American Anthropological Association

AAHE—American Association of Higher Education

AAMFT—American Association of Marriage and Family Therapists

AAPC—American Association of Pastoral Counselors

AARS—American Association of Religious Studies

AAUP—American Association of University Professors

ABA—American Bar Association

ACHS—American Catholic History Society

ACHA—American Church History Association

ACE—American Council on Education

AHA—American Historical Association

AHuA—American Humanist Association

APGA—American Personnel and Guidance Association

APhA—American Philosophical Association

APA—American Psychological Association

ASOR—American School of Oriental Research

ASCE—American Society of Christian Ethics

ASCH—American Society of Church History

ASM—American Society of Missiology

ASA—American Sociological Association

ATS—American Theological Society

ARCIC II—Anglican/Roman Catholic International Commission II

AEA—Applied Education for Africa

AAS—Association for Asian Studies

ACS—Association for Case Study

ACPE—Association for Clinical Pastoral Counseling

AID—Association for International Development

ASSSR—Association for Social Scientific Study of Religion

ASR—Association for the Sociology of Religion

ASALH—Association for the Study of Afro-American Life and History

ASCAC—Association for the Study of Classical African Civilizations

AAABS—Association of African American Biblical Scholars

ABA—Association of Black Anthropologists

ABS—Association of Black Sociologists

ABWHE—Association of Black Women in Higher Education

ACAS—Association of Concerned African Scholars

AFE—Association of Field Educators

APRRE—Association of Professors and Researchers in Religious Education

ASCD—Association of Supervision and Curriculum Development

ACUS—Atlantic Council of the U.S.

BWA—Baptist World Alliance

BAS—Biblical Archeology Society

BT—Biblical Theologians

BTC—Black Theology Coalition

BTP—Black Theology Project

BWCS—Black Women in Church and Society

BPTCSTC—Board of Philosophical Theology, Coppin State College

CSA—Caribbean Studies Association

CBA—Catholic Biblical Association

CTSA—Catholic Theological Society of America

CLA—College Language Association

CMS—College Music Society

CTS—College Theology Society

CAT—Conference of Anglican Theologians

CFH—Conference of Faith and History

CNBC—Congress of National Black Churches

CCAS—Council of the Colleges of Arts and Sciences

DCSA—D.C. Sociological Association

DMA—Decatur Ministerial Alliance

EATWOT—Ecumenical Association of Third World Theologians

FOCNCC—Faith and Order Commission, National Council of Churches

FOCUCC—Faith and Order Commission, United Church of Christ

FOCWCC—Faith and Order Commission, World Council of Churches

FREE—Foundation for Religious and Educational Exchange, Inc.

FAA—Fulbright Alumni Association

GMFTA—Georgia Marriage and Family Therapists Association

GPA—Georgia Psychological Association

GTF—Graduate Theological Foundation

HSGBJ—Historical Society of Great Britain and Jamaica

HSP—Historical Society of Pennsylvania

HBA—Houston Bar Association

HTET—Howard Thurman Educational Trust

IABS—International Association of Buddhist Studies

IOSCS—International Organization for Septuagint and Cognate Studies

IOSOT—International Organization for the Study of the Old Testament

ISRAS—Institute for the Study of Religion in the Age of Science

JFKL—John F. Kennedy Library (Honorary Fellow)

JWTA—John Wesley's Thought on Africa

LHS—Langston Hughes Society

MLKBCF—Martin Luther King, Jr. Black Church Fellows

MFPMME—Midwest Fellowship of Professors of Mission and Mission Executives

MLA—Modern Language Association

MENC—Music Educators National Conference

NAACP—National Association for the Advancement of Colored People

NACUC—National Association of College and University Chaplains

NAPT—National Association of Poetry Therapy

NAPH—National Association of Professors of Hebrew

NBCCE—National Baptist Congress of Christian Education

NBA—National Bar Association

NBCCC—National Black Catholic Clergy Caucus

NBCET—National Black Church Education Team

NCBS—National Council for Black Studies

NCC—National Council of Churches

NFMAWL—National Fellowship of Musicians, Artists, and Worship Leaders

NAKS—North American Kant Society

NAPTS—North American Paul Tillich Society

NCBT—North Carolina Baptist Teachers

NSAACH—Northeast Society for African American Church History

NWCTS—Northwest Council for Theological Studies

OHA—Oral History Association

OAH—Organization of American Historians

PBK—Phi Beta Kappa

PST—Phi Sigma Tau National Honor Society for Philosophy

PCTE—Presbyterian Committee on Theology Education

PWTE—Presbyterian Women in Theological Education

PCMRA—Project on Christian-Muslim Relations in Africa

REA—Religious Education Association

RESI—Religious Education Search Institute

RRA—Religious Research Association

SAC—Society for the Anthropology of Consciousness

SCEM—Society for Continuing Education in Ministry

SE—Society for Ethnomusicology

SHHV—Society for Health and Human Values

SPEP—Society for Phenomenology and Existential Philosophy

SPC—Society for Philosophy of Creativity

SITE—Society for the Internationalization of Theological Education

SSSR—Society for the Scientific Study of Religion

SSBR—Society for the Study of Black Religion

SSCE—Society for the Study of Christian Ethics

SPT—Society for Pastoral Theology

SVHE—Society for Values in Higher Education

SVA—Society for Visual Anthropology

SAA—Society of American Archivists

SBL—Society of Biblical Literature

SBS—Society of Biblical Scholarship

SCE—Society of Christian Ethics

SECP—South East College Professors

SBHS—Southern Baptist Historical Society

SCLC—Southern Christian Leadership Conference

SCAAS—Southern Conference on Afro-American Studies, Inc.

SNTS—Studiorum Novi Testamenti Societas

SSHR—Swiss Society for the History of Religions

TC—Tennessee Clericus

UBCUCC—United Black Christians, United Church of Christ

WIGUT—West Indian Group of University Teachers

Listing of Scholars

ARNOLD, Lionel A., Rev. Dr.; m; professor emeritus, Oklahoma State University; A.B., Latin, Thiel College, 1943; B.Th., Anderson College Theological Seminary, 1944; M.A., Oberlin College Graduate School of Theology, 1946; B.D., Oberlin College Graduate School of Theology, 1947; S.T.M., Harvard University Divinity School, 1955; Ph.D., Drew University, 1969; religion and literature, modern drama, African American literature; AAR; United Church of Christ; 2132 University Avenue, Stillwater, OK 74074, (405) 372-0103.

ASHBY, Homer U., Jr., Rev. Dr.; m; professor of pastoral care and director of the African American Ministries Program, McCormick Theological Seminary, 5555 South Woodlawn Avenue, Chicago, IL 60637, (312) 947-6300; A.B., history, Princeton University, 1968; M.Th., Christian ministry, University of Chicago, 1970; D.Min., Christian ministry, University of Chicago, 1972; Ph.D., pastoral psychology, Northwestern University, 1978; pastoral care, aging, faith development, African American religious experience, health and wholeness; APA, AAPC; United Methodist; ordained elder; 5219 South Dorchester Avenue, Chicago, IL 60615, (312) 643-9890.

ASHCRAFT-EASON, Lillian E., Dr.; f; assistant professor, Department of History, Bowling Green State University, Bowling Green, OH 43403, (419) 372-8120; associate professor, on leave (1990–1991), Department of Religion and Philosophy, Clark Atlanta University, 240 James P. Brawley Drive, SW, Atlanta, GA 30314, (404) 681-8234; B.S., history and education, Hampton University, 1962; M.Ed., teaching (social science), University of Virginia, 1967; Ph.D., history, College of William and Mary, 1975; history of religion, African American history, African American church history, African traditional religions; AAR, SSBR, ASALH; United Methodist; member; 7350 Nightingale Drive, Apt. 6, Holland, OH 43528, (419) 866-5584.

AYMER, Albert J. D., Rev. Dr; m; associate dean, associate professor, program director/coordinator for D.Min. program and continuing education, Drew University, Theological School, Madison, NJ 07940, (201) 408-3419; Dip. Th., University of London, 1963; B.D. (preliminary), University of London, 1964; M.Div., Lancaster Theological Seminary, 1970; M.A., Drew University, 1980; Ph.D., Drew University, 1983; New Testament, professional ministry, continuing education for ministry; SBL, SCEM, SITE; United Methodist; elder; 112 Reynolds Place, South Orange, NJ 07079, (201) 763-8698.

AYMER, Birchfield C. P., Rev. Dr.; m; L.Th., early church history, University of the West Indies, 1971; Dip. Th., early church history, University of London, 1973; M.T.S., New Testament, Boston University School of Theology, 1981; Ph.D., New Testament and Christian origin, Boston University Graduate School, 1986; New Testament and Christian origins, early church history, sociology of knowledge, liberation theology; SBL, AAR; United Methodist; elder; Marshfield United Methodist Church, 185 Plain Street, Marshfield, MA 02050, (617) 837-2746; P.O. Box 536, 1818 New Main Street, Marshfield, MA 02051, (617) 837-9262.

BAILEY, Randall C., Rev. Dr.; m; associate professor, Interdenominational Theological Center, 671 Beckwith Street, SW, Atlanta, GA 30314, (404) 527-7754; A.B., sociology, Brandeis University, 1969; A.M., social service, University of Chicago School of Social Service, 1972; M.Div., Bible, Candler School of Theology, 1979; Ph.D., Old Testament, Emory University, 1987; Old Testament—Samuel and Psalms, ancient Israelite history, history of ancient Egypt, African influence on Old Testament; SSBR, SBL, BTP; Baptist (Progressive and American Baptist Churches in the U.S.A.); minister; 2473 Glenrock Drive, Decatur, GA 30032, (404) 284-0512.

BALDWIN, Lewis V., Rev. Dr.; m; assistant professor, Vanderbilt University Department of Religious Studies, Nashville, TN 37240, (615) 322-6358; B.A., history, Talladega College, 1971; M.A., African American church studies, Colgate-Rochester Divinity School, 1973; M.Div., theology, Colgate-Rochester Divinity School, 1975; Ph.D., American Christianity, Northwestern University, 1980; history of African American religion, American evangelicalism, Black nationalism, Martin Luther King, Jr.; JWTA; United Methodist; ordained deacon; 2006 26th Avenue South, Nashville, TN 37212, (615) 298-2317.

BANNER, William A., Dr.; m; graduate professor of philosophy (emeritus), Howard University; 5719 1st Street, NW, Washington, DC 20011, (202) 291-6736.

BARNETT, Joanne A. Jones, Dr.; f; B.S., communications, Boston University, 1976; Ph.D., history of religions (early Christianity), Brown University, 1989; New Testament literature and languages, history of early Christianity, African presence in antiquity, Greco-Roman history; SBL, AAR; African Methodist Episcopal Zion; member; 19 Terrell Lane, Willingboro, NJ 08046.

BARRETT, Leonard, Dr.; m; professor emeritus, Temple University, Department of Religion, C/o Ms. Linda Jenkins, Philadelphia, PA 19122; African American religions, Caribbean religions.

BEANE, Wendell C., Rev. Dr.; m; associate professor and chair, University of Wisconsin, Oshkosh, Department of Religious Studies, 800 Algoma Boulevard, Oshkosh, WI 54901, (414) 424-4406/7; B.A., French/history, Howard University, 1958; B.D., practical theology, Howard University, 1961; M.A., history of religions, University of Chicago, 1966; Ph.D., history of religions, University of Chicago, 1971; history of religions, myth and mysteries, comparative religious worldviews, faith and healing; AAR, AAS, IABS; United Methodist; elder; 2500C Village Lane, Oshkosh, WI 54904, (414) 235-2347.

BENNETT, Robert A., Rev. Dr.; m; professor, Episcopal Divinity School, 99 Brattle Street, Cambridge, MA 02138, (617) 868-3450; A.B, philosophy, Kenyon College, 1954; S.T.B., Scripture, General Theological Seminary, 1958; S.T.M., Old Testament, General Theological Seminary, 1966; Ph.D., Near Eastern languages, Harvard University, 1974; Hebrew scriptures, wisdom literature in Bible, Africa and the Bible, archaeology and the Bible; SBL, PBK; Episcopal;

ordained clergy; 49 Hawthorn Street, Cambridge, MA 02138, (617) 661-5904.

BETHEL, Leonard Leslie, Rev. Dr.; m; associate professor, Rutgers University, Department of Africana Studies, Beck Hall 112, New Brunswick, NJ 08903, (201) 932-3335, 932-4023; B.A., political science, Lincoln University (PA), 1961; M.Div., theology, Johnson C. Smith University School of Theology, 1964; M.A., theology, New Brunswick Theological Seminary, 1971; Ed.D., philosophy of education, Rutgers University, 1975; philosophy, theology, history, political science; AAUP; Presbyterian; pastor, Bethel Presbyterian Church, 500 E. 5th Street, Plainfield, NJ 07060; 146 Parkside Road, Plainfield, NJ 07060, (201) 756-2737.

BOYER, Horace C., Dr.; m; professor and associate director, Fine Arts Center, University of Massachusetts, Amherst, Department of Music and Dance, Amherst, MA 01003, (413) 545-2279, 545-0109; B.A., music, Bethune-Cookman College, 1957; M.A., music theory, Eastman School of Music, University of Rochester, 1964; Ph.D., music theory, Eastman School of Music, University of Rochester, 1973; African American sacred music, music theory, jazz, European art and music; EMS, MENC; Episcopal; member, standing commission of church music; 92 Grantwood Drive, Amherst, MA 01002, (413) 549-1484.

BROWN, Charles S., Rev. Dr.; m; adjunct professor, United Theological Seminary, 1810 Harvard Boulevard, Dayton, OH 45406, (513) 278-5817; voluntary associate professor, Wright State University School of Medicine; A.B., Morehouse College, 1956; M.Div., theology (cum laude), United Theological Seminary, 1962; Th.D., Boston University, 1973; social ethics, sociology of religion, church and society, Black religion; SVHE, ASALH; Baptist (National, U.S.A.); pastor, Bethel Baptist Church, 401 South Paul Laurence Dunbar Street, Dayton, OH 45407, (513) 222-4373; 2nd VP, Ohio Baptist General Convention, moderator, Western Union Association; 625 Ridgedale Road, Dayton, OH 45406, (513) 275-7828.

BROWN, Kelly D., Rev. Dr.; f; assistant professor, Howard University School of Divinity, 1400 Shepherd Street, NE, Washington, DC 20017, (202) 806-0500; B.S., psychology (summa cum laude), Denison University, 1979; M.Div., Union Theological Seminary (NY), 1982; M.Phil., Union Theological Seminary (NY), 1985; Ph.D., Union Theological Seminary (NY), 1988; liberation theology, Black theology, womanist theology; EATWOT, AAR; Episcopal; priest; 733 Sligo Avenue #507, Silver Spring, MD 20910, (301) 589-6164.

BURNIM, Mellonnee U., Dr.; f; associate professor, Indiana University, Department of Afro-American Studies and Ethnomusicology, Memorial Hall E, Bloomington, IN 61701, (812) 855-3874; B.M., music education, North Texas State University, 1971; M.M., ethnomusicology, University of Wisconsin-Madison, 1976; Ph.D., ethnomusicology, Indiana University, 1980; African American religious music, aesthetics; SE, SSBR, NCBS; African Methodist Episcopal; minister of music, Bethel A.M.E. Church, Bloomington, IN; 3628 S. Sowder Square, Bloomington, IN 47401, (812) 339-4906.

BURROW, Rufus, Jr., Dr.; m; asssistant professor, Christian

Theological Seminary, 1000 W. 42nd Street, Indianapolis, IN 46208, (317) 924-1331, x262; B.A., criminial justice, Anderson College, 1974; M.T.S., social ethics, Boston University School of Theology, 1977; Ph.D., social ethics, Boston University, 1982; Black liberation theology, metaphysics of personalism, philosophy of religion; Christian Church (Disciples of Christ); elder-in-training; 2862 N. Medford Avenue, Indianapolis, IN 46208, (317) 925-1382.

BUSH, Evelyn L., Rev.; f; Ph.D. student, Temple University Department of African American Studies, 810 Gladfelter Hall, Philadelphia, PA 19121, (215) 787-5651; B.A., mass media, Wilberforce University, 1980; M.A., rhetorical theory, Ohio State University, 1982; African religion and spirituality, African cultural retention among African Americans; ASCAC, SCAAS; African Methodist Episcopal; itinerant elder; 1619 W. Butler Street, Philadelphia, PA 19140, (215) 225-6593.

BYRD, Alicia D., Rev. Dr.; f; program director, Congress of National Black Churches, 600 New Hampshire Avenue, NW, Suite 650, Washington, DC 20037, (202) 333-3060; A.B., psychology, Wheaton College, 1975; M.A., human development counseling, Sangamon State University, 1977; M.Div., religion, Howard University School of Divinity, 1985; Ph.D., sociology and religion, American University, 1988; religion, sociology, philanthropy, human relations; ASA, DCSA; African Methodist Episcopal; pastor, St. Stephens A.M.E. Church, Elkridge, MD; 7436 Shady Glen Terrace, Capitol Heights, MD 20743.

CANNON, Katie G., Rev. Dr.; f; associate professor, Episcopal Divinity School, 99 Brattle Street, Cambridge, MA 02138, (617) 868-3450; B.S., elementary education, Barber-Scotia College, 1971; M.Div., Biblical studies, Johnson C. Smith Seminary (ITC), 1974; M.Phil., Christian ethics, Union Theological Seminary (NY), 1983; Ph.D., Christian ethics, Union Theological Seminary (NY), 1983; Christian social ethics, womanist ethics/theology, Afro-Christian culture, preaching in Black idiom; SCE, AAR, SSBR, ABWHE; Presbyterian; clergywoman; 9 Phillips Place, Cambridge, MA 02138, (617) 661-8606.

CARPENTER, Delores H. Causion, Rev. Dr.; f; associate professor, Howard University School of Divinity, 1400 Shepherd Street, NE, Washington, DC 20017, (202) 806-0500; B.A., sociology, Morgan State University, 1966; M.Div., sociology of religion, Howard University School of Divinity, 1969; M.A., sociology, Washington University, 1972; Ed.D., sociology of education, Rutgers University, 1986; religious education, African American women in ministry, faith development, spiritual formation; APRRE, REA; Christian Church (Disciples); pastor, Michigan Park Christian Church, South Dakota Avenue and Taylor Street, NE, Washington, DC 20017; 13203 Glasgow Way, Fort Washington, MD 20744, (301) 292-7101.

CARSON, R. Logan, Rev. Dr.; m; professor, Gardner Webb College, Bolling Springs, NC 28017, (704) 434-2361, x328; B.A., Bible and social studies, Shaw University, 1957; B.D., Old Testament and Hebrew, Hartford Seminary, 1960; Th.M., Old Testament, Louisville Presbyterian Seminary, 1961; Ph.D., theology and culture, Drew University, 1988; Old Testament and Hebrew, Judaism and sacred writings, mission and New Testament; NCBT, SECP; Baptist; pastor,

Green-Bethel Baptist Church, Bolling Springs, NC 28017; 1100 Stanton Drive, Shelby, NC 28150, (704) 487-8532.

CARTER, Lawrence E., Sr., Rev. Dr.; m; professor and dean, Morehouse College, 830 Westview Drive, SW, Atlanta, GA 30314, (404) 681-2800, x208; B.A., social sciences, Virginia State College, 1964; M.Div., theology, Boston University, 1968; S.T.M., pastoral care, Boston University, 1970; Ph.D., pastoral psychology/counseling, Boston University, 1978; social ethics, psychology of religion, introduction to religion, Martin Luther King, Jr.'s, life and thought; NCC, AAR, BWA, HTET; Baptist; ecumenical officer; 3708 Cherry Ridge Boulevard, Decatur, GA 30034, (404) 244-0073.

CHEEK, James E., Rev. Dr.; m; president emeritus, Howard University, 2400 Sixth Street, NW, Washington, DC 20059; B.A., Shaw University, 1955; M.Div., Colgate-Rochester Divinity School, 1958; Ph.D., religion, Drew University, 1962; Ed.D., Providence College, 1972; Baptist; 8035 16th Street, NW, Washington, DC 20012.

CHILDS, Robert G., Rev.; m; lecturer, Howard University School of Divinity, 1400 Shepherd Street, NE, Washington, DC 20017, (202) 806-0500; B.A., religion, Bishop College, 1978; M.Div., Old Testament, Howard University School of Divinity, 1981; Th.M. candidate, Old Testament studies, Harvard University Divinity School; Old Testament, Hebrew language; Baptist (National, U.S.A.); pastor, Berean Baptist Church, 924 Madison Street, NW, Washington, DC 20011, (202) 829-8454; 1624 Webster Street, NW, Washington, DC 20011, (202) 291-5025.

CLARK, Isaac R., Rev. Dr.; m; Fuller E. Callaway Professor of Homiletics, Interdenominational Theological Center, 671 Beckwith Street, SW, Atlanta, GA 30314, (404) 527-7700; B.A., Wilberforce University, 1951; B.D., Payne Theological Seminary, 1952; Th.D., Boston University School of Theology, 1958; postdoctoral study, Union Theological Seminary; homiletics.

COAN, Josephus, Rev. Dr.; m; professor emeritus, Interdenominational Theological Center, 671 Beckwith Street, SW, Atlanta, GA 30314, (404) 527-7700; B.A., Howard University; B.D., Yale University Divinity School; M.A., Yale University Graduate School; Ph.D., Hartford Seminary Foundation; Christian education and mission.

COLLIER, Karen Y., Rev. Dr.; f; former acting chair, Department of Religious and Philosophical Studies, Fisk University, former acting director, Black Church Studies, Duke University; B.A., history, Fisk University; M.Div., church history, Gammon Theological Seminary (ITC); Ph.D., American church history, Duke University; American religious studies, American church history, African American church history; SSBR; United Methodist; ordained elder and pastor, Seay-Hubbard, United Methodist Church, Nashville, TN; P.O. Box 100574, Nashville, TN 37224.

CONE, James H., Rev. Dr.; m; Briggs Distinguished Professor of Systematic Theology, Union Theological Seminary, 3041 Broadway at Reinhold Niebuhr Place, New York, NY 10027, (212) 280-1369; B.A., Philander Smith College, 1958; B.D., Garrett Theological Seminary, 1961; M.A., Northwestern University, 1963; Ph.D., Northwestern University, 1965; African American church history, liberation theology, systematic theology; SSBR, AAR, BTP, EATWOT; African

Methodist Episcopal; 606 West 122nd Street, New York City, NY 10027, (212) 662-9402.

COPELAND, M. Shawn, Sister; f; assistant professor, Yale University Divinity School, 409 Prospect Street, New Haven, CT 06511, (204) 432-6158; B.A., English, Madonna College, 1969; Ph.D., systematic theology, Boston College, 1991; systematic theology, political philosophy, African American critical thought; CTSA, AAR, SVHE; Roman Catholic; nun; 70 Hubinger Street, New Haven, CT 06511.

COPHER, Charles B., Rev. Dr.; m; professor emeritus, former vice-president for academic affairs and former dean of faculty, Interdenominational Theological Center, 671 Beckwith Street, SW, Atlanta, GA 30314, (404) 527-7700; A.B., Clark College, 1938; B.D., Gammon Theological Seminary (ITC), 1939; B.D., Oberlin Graduate School of Theology, 1941; Ph.D., Boston University, 1947; Old Testament; United Methodist; 3340 Lake Valley Road, NW, Atlanta, GA 30331.

COSTEN, James H., Rev. Dr.; m; president, Interdenominational Theological Center, 671 Beckwith Street, SW, Atlanta, GA 30314, (404) 527-7702; A.B., philosophy/social science, Johnson C. Smith University, 1953; B.D., philosophy/theology, Johnson C. Smith University Seminary, 1956; Th.M., Christian education, Southeastern Theological Seminary, 1964; theology, Christian education; AAR, SSBR, PCTE; Presbyterian (U.S.A.); ordained minister and former moderator of the General Assembly, 1982-1983; 3360 Laren Lane, SW, Atlanta, GA 30311, (404) 696-5900.

COSTEN, Melva Wilson, Dr.; f; Helmar Neilson Professor of Music and Worship and co-chair, consultation project committee, African American Worship Traditions Research Project, Interdenominational Theological Center, 671 Beckwith Street, SW, Atlanta, GA 30314, (404) 527-7700; A.B., Johnson C. Smith University, 1953; advanced studies, Atlanta University; M.A.T.M., music, University of North Carolina, 1964; Ph.D., Georgia State University, 1978; Presbyterian (U.S.A.); ordained elder, chairperson, Presbyterian Church Hymnbook committee, Presbyterian Office of Worship, Administrative Committee; 3360 Laren Lane, SW, Atlanta, GA 30311, (404) 696-5900.

CRAWFORD, Evans E., Rev. Dr.; m; dean of the chapel, Office of the Chapel, Carnegie Building, room 104, Howard University, Washington, DC 20059, (202) 806-7280, professor, Howard University School of Divinity, 1400 Shepherd Street, NE, Washington, DC 20017, (202) 806-0500; B.A., sociology, Huston-Tillotson College, 1943; S.T.B., Boston University School of Theology, 1946; Ph.D., theological studies/ethics, Boston University Graduate School, 1957; social ethics, homiletics, preaching; AH, SSBR, NACUC; United Methodist; ordained elder; 4130 Arkansas Avenue, NW, Washington, DC 20011, (202) 726-2468.

DAVIS, Cyprian, O.S.B., Rev. Dr.; m; professor, St. Meinrad School of Theology, St. Meinrad Archabbey, St. Meinrad, IN 47577, (812) 357-6611; A.B., history, St. Meinrad College, 1953; S.T.L., theology, Catholic University of America, 1957; license, historical sciences, Catholic University of Louvain (Belgium), 1963; Ph.D., historical sciences, Catholic University of Louvain (Belgium), 1977; African American Catholic history, medieval church history, history of African American spirituality; SAA, ACHS, NBCCC;

Roman Catholic; Benedictine monk/priest; St. Meinrad Archabbey, St. Meinrad, IN 47577, (812) 357-6611.

DAVIS, Donald H. Kortright, Rev. Dr.; m; professor, Howard University School of Divinity, 1400 Shepherd Street, NE, Washington, DC 20017, (202) 806-0500; certificate, Central Advisory Council for Training in Ministry (Church of England), general ordination, 1964; B.D., theology, London University, 1965; M.A., history, University of West Indies, 1976; D.Phil., religious studies, Sussex University, 1979; systematic theology, development, ecumenism, evangelism; ARCIC II, SSBR, BTP; Anglican; priest, rector, Holy Comforter Episcopal Church (St. Andrew's Parish), 701 Oglethorpe Street, NW, Washington, DC 20011, (202) 726-1862); 11414 Woodson Avenue, Kensington, MD 20895, (301) 942-2327.

DAVIS, Grady D., Rev. Dr.; m; professor, Shaw University Divinity School, P.O. Box 2090, Raleigh, NC 27602-2090, (919) 781-1837; A.B., education, Shaw University, 1942; M.Div., religion, Andover-Newton Theological Seminary, 1949; Ph.D., psychology of religion, Boston University, 1953; postdoctorate work, University of California-Berkeley, University of Michigan-Ann Arbor; education, psychology, counseling; APA, NAACP; Baptist; pastor; 5520 Sweetbriar Drive, Raleigh, NC 27609, (919) 781-1837.

DeVEAUX, William P., Rev. Dr.; m; B.A., philosophy, Howard University, 1962; S.T.B., religion, Boston University, 1968; M.A., ethics, Vanderbilt University, 1976; Ph.D., ethics, Vanderbilt University, 1979; public policy, medical ethics; African Methodist Episcopal; pastor, Metropolitan A.M.E. Church, 1518 M Street, NW, Washington, DC 20005, (202) 331-1426; 2257 Sudbury Road, NW, Washington, DC 20012, (202) 723-1314.

DIAMOND, John D., Jr., Rev. Dr.; m; Andrew W. Mellon Professor of Systematic Theology and editor, *The Black Church Scholars Series*, Interdenominational Theological Center, 671 Beckwith Street, SW, Atlanta, GA 30314, (404) 527-7700; B.S., biology, Hampton University, 1951; S.T.B., systematic theology, Boston University School of Theology, 1958; Ph.D., systematic theology, Boston University, 1969; metaphysics, science and religion, Black theology, liberation theology; SSBR; Baptist.

DICKERSON, Dennis C. Rev. Dr.; m; professor, Williams College, Department of History, P.O. Box 301, Williamstown, MA 01267, (413) 597-2484; B.A., Lincoln University (PA), history, 1971; M.A., Washington University, St. Louis, history, 1974; Ph.D., Washington University, St. Louis, history, 1978; African American religious history; ASCH, AHA, OAH, Executive Committee of the World Methodist Historical Society, HSP; A.M.E.; historiographer; (413) 458-4994.

DIXON, L. Rita, Dr.; f; program director, Black Congregational Enhancement, Presbyterian Church, U.S.A., 100 Witherspoon Street, Louisville, KY 40202-1396, (502) 569-5697; Ed.D., education, Harvard University, 1972; M.Div., Harvard University Divinity School, 1978; postgraduate work, theological studies, Emory University, 1979; African American religious studies, theology and human development; BTP, NBCET; Presbyterian (U.S.A.); national staff member; 2834 Toney Drive, Decatur, GA 30032, (404) 288-5952.

DODSON, Jualynne E. White, Dr.; f; Ford Foundation Fellow and Scholar-in-Residence, Schomburg Center for Research on Black Culture, 515 Lennox Avenue, New York, NY 10037-1801, (212) 491-2200; B.S., social science, University of California-Berkeley, 1969; M.A., sociology, University of California-Berkeley, 1973; Ph.D. sociology, University of California-Berkeley, 1984; African American behavior and culture, sociology of religion, women in religion, black religious history, world ecumenism; SSSR, AAR, ASA, NSAACH, ABS; Baptist (Progressive); ecumenical liaison for PNBC; 7 Fordham Hill, Apt. 8-G, New York, NY 10468.

EARL, Riggins R., Jr., Rev. Dr.; m; associate professor, Interdenominational Theological Center, 671 Beckwith Street, SW, Atlanta, GA 30314, (404) 527-7700; A.B., religion and philosophy, American Bible College, 1966; M.Div., ethics and Bible, Vanderbilt University, 1969; Ph.D., ethics and society, Vanderbilt University, 1978; postdoctorate work, Harvard University; African American history, theology, ethics, phenomenology; AAR, SCE, SSBR; Baptist; lecturer/consultant; 1409 Martin Luther King Drive, SW, Atlanta, GA 30314, (404) 755-1691.

EUBANKS, John B., Rev. Dr.; m; visiting professor, Howard University School of Divinity, 1400 Shepherd Street, NE, Washington, DC 20017, (202) 806-0500; Th.B., sociology and religion, Howard University, 1935; A.B., philosophy, Howard University, 1936; M.A., philosophy of religion, University of Chicago, 1938; Ph.D., history of religions, University of Chicago, 1947; anthropology of religion, African traditional religions, religion, anthropology of modern social issues; SSSR, SHHV, NAPT, JFKL; Christian Church (Disciples of Christ); minister; 654 Girard Street, NW, Washington, DC 20001, (202) 387-0880.

EUGENE, Toinette M., Dr.; f; associate professor of practical theology and culture, Chicago Theological Seminary, 5757 S. University Avenue, Chicago, IL 60637, (312) 752-5757; B.A., English literature, University of San Francisco; M.A., theology and education, Jesuit School of Theology, Berkeley, 1979; Ph.D., religion and society, Graduate Theological Union, 1983; African American family, church, African American women in theology, Christian education; AAR, APRRE; Roman Catholic; laywoman.

EVANS, James H., Rev. Dr.; m; president, Colgate Rochester Divinity School, 1100 S. Goodman Street, Rochester, NY 14620, (716) 271-1320; A.B., English and political science, University of Michigan, 1971; M.Div., theology and ethics, Yale University Divinity School, 1975; Ph.D., systematic theology, Union Theological Seminary, 1980; African American theology, religion, and theology; AAR, SSBR; Baptist (American Baptist Churches in the U.S.A.).

FARAJAJE'-JONES, Elias, Rev. Dr.; m; assistant professor, Howard University School of Divinity, 1400 Shepherd Street, NE, Washington, DC 20017, (202) 806-0500; B.A., history of religions (cum laude generali), Vassar College, 1972; M.Div., Eastern Christian Orthodox Theology (magna cum laude), St. Vladimir's Graduate School of Orthodox Theology, 1975; D.Th., history of religions (magna cum laude), University of Bern (Switzerland), 1986; African religions, Native American religions, African religions in the Americas, liberation theology, womanist theology, anthropology of liturgy, sociology of religion; SSBR, SSHR; Orthodox Church of France (Patriarchate of Rumania); priest; founder and pastor, St. Moses the Black Orthodox Church, 1223 Girard Street, NE, Washington, DC 20017, (202) 526-5153.

FELDER, Cain Hope, Rev. Dr.; m; professor and editor, *Journal of Religious Thought*, Howard University School of Divinity, 1400 Shepherd Street, NE, Washington, DC 20017, (202) 806-0500; B.A., philosophy, Howard University, 1966; Dip. Theol., New Testament/Greek, Oxford University, 1968; M.Div., theology, Union Theological Seminary, 1969; M.Phil., Biblical languages/literature, Columbia University, 1978; Ph.D., Biblical languages/literature, Columbia University, 1982; New Testament studies, early Christian history and Islam, Greek language, Africa of the Biblical period; SBL, AAR, SSBR, BTP; United Methodist; ordained elder; 1247 Delaware Avenue, SW, Washington, DC 20024, (202) 479-4565.

FLUKER, Walter E., Rev. Dr.; m; assistant professor, Vanderbilt University Divinity School, Box 25, Station B, Nashville, TN 37235, (615) 343-3973; B.A., philosophy/Bible, Trinity College, 1977; M.Div., Garrett-Evangelical Theological Seminary, 1980; Ph.D., social ethics, Boston University, 1988; Howard Thurman, Martin Luther King, Jr., community, social transformation, and spirituality; AAR, UBCUCC; Baptist and United Church of Christ; 616 Dunston Drive, Nashville, TN 37211, (615) 781-8367.

FORBES, James, Rev. Dr.; m; B.S., chemistry, Howard University, 1957; M.Div., Union Theological Seminary, 1962; D.Min., Colgate-Rochester Divinity School, 1975; liberation praxis, ministries of spirituality and stewardship in local congregations, homiletics; CNBC, AH; American Baptist Churches in the U.S.A.; senior minister, Riverside Church, 490 Riverside Drive, New York, NY 10027, (212) 222-5900, x282; 99 Claremont Avenue, New York, NY 10027, (212) 864-7337.

FRANKLIN, Robert M., Rev. Dr.; m; assistant professor and program director, Black Church Studies Program, Candler School of Theology, Emory University, Atlanta, GA 30322, (404) 727-0818; overseas scholar, University of Durham, 1974-1975; B.A., political science, Morehouse College, 1975; M.Div., social ethics, Harvard University Divinity School, 1978; Ph.D., religion/social science/ethics, University of Chicago, 1985; social ethics, African American religion, religion and social science, homiletics; AAR, SCE, SSBR; Church of God in Christ; ordained elder; 4700 Guilford Forest Drive, Atlanta, GA 30331, (404) 691-8733.

GILKES, Cheryl Townsend, Dr.; f; associate professor, Colby College, Department of Sociology, Waterville, ME 04901, (207) 872-3133; B.A., sociology, Northeastern University, 1970; M.A., sociology, Northeastern University, 1973; Ph.D., sociology, Northeastern University, 1979; M.Div., Boston University, expected 1991; Pentecostal/Holiness denominations, African American women, social change, African American experience; ASA, AAR; Baptist (National, U.S.A.); parliamentarian for state convention, assistant dean, congress of Christian education, associate minister, Union Baptist Church, Cambridge, MA 02139.

GOODWIN, Bennie E., Rev. Dr.; m; associate professor, Interdenominational Theological Center, 671 Beckwith Street,

SW, Atlanta, GA 30314, (404) 527-7739; diploma, Moody Bible Institute, 1955; B.A., Barrington College, 1956; M.R.E., Gordon-Conwell Theological Seminary, 1965; M.Ed., University of Pittsburgh, 1972; M.A., Pittsburgh Theological Seminary, 1973; Ph.D., University of Pittsburgh, 1974; Christian education, youth ministry, Martin Luther King, Jr., as social educator; NAACP, SCLC; Church of God in Christ; elder, special assistant to pastor, Cathedral of Faith Church of God in Christ, Atlanta, GA; 542 Lynnhaven Drive, SW, Atlanta, GA 30310, (404) 755-5039.

GRANT, Jacquelyn, Rev. Dr.; f; assistant professor and project director, Black Women in Church and Society, Interdenominational Theological Seminary, 671 Beckwith Street, SW, Atlanta, GA 30314, (404) 527-7740; M.Div., systematic theology, Interdenominational Theological Center, 1973; M.Phil., systematic theology, Union Theological Seminary (NY), 1980; Ph.D., systematic theology, Union Theological Seminary (NY), 1985; womanist theology, Black theology, feminist theology, liberation theology, systematic theology; BTP, EATWOT, AAR; African Methodist Episcopal; assistant minister and dean of board of examiners.

GREEN, Junior E., Rev. Dr.; m; M.A.R.S., religious studies, Howard University School of Divinity, 1978; D.Min., religion and culture, Howard University School of Divinity, 1979; M.A., philosophy, Drew University, 1983; Ph.D., philosophy, Drew University, 1987; philosophical theology, modern and enlightenment philosophy and theology, history of philosophy, religion and culture Africana studies; NAKS, ISRAS, AAR, APR; Unitarian; 37 Old Oregon Road, Peekskill, NY 10566, (914) 528-9268.

GREENE, John T., Dr.; m; associate professor, Michigan State University, 304 Linton Hall, East Lansing, MI 48824, (517) 353-2930 (dept.) or 353-0830 (direct); B.A., German, University of Detroit, 1972; M.A., humanities, University of Detroit, 1973; Ph.D., history of religions, Boston University, 1980; archaeology of Near East, languages of Near East, history of religions, sociology of religions; SBL, AAR, NAPH, ASOR; 1109 S. Genesee Drive, Lansing, MI 48915.

GRIFFIN, Paul R., Rev. Dr.; m; assistant professor, Wright State University, Department of Religion, Dayton, OH 45435, (513) 873-2914 or 873-2274; A.A., liberal arts, Sinclair College, 1971; B.A., sociology, Wright State University, 1973; M.Div., United Theological Seminary, 1976; Ph.D., church history, Emory University, 1983; African American religious history, American religion, church history, sociology of religion; AAR, AHA, ASCH; African Methodist Episcopal; ordained elder; 1913 North Longview Drive, Dayton, OH 45432, (513) 429-3174.

HALL, Benjamin L., III, Rev. Dr.; m; instructor, University of Houston Law Center, Calhoun Street, Houston, TX 77002, (713) 651-2052; B.A., religious studies, University of South Carolina, 1977; M.Div., philosophy and ethics, Duke University Divinity School, 1979; Ph.D., philosophy and theology, Duke University Graduate School, 1985; J.D., law, Harvard University Law School, 1986; law, theology, philosophy; ABA, AARA, HBA, NBA; Apostolic; minister; 7843 Chinon Circle, Houston, TX 77071, (713) 728-9837.

HARRIS, James H., Dr.; m; B.S., business, Virginia State University, 1974; M.Div., Virginia Union University School of Divinity, 1976; M.A., philosophy and religion, Old Dominion University, 1981; Ph.D., urban studies, Old Dominion University, 1985; D.Min. candidate, United Theological Seminary; pastoral theology; African American church and social structure, urban church and society, preaching and liberation, religion and the social sciences; NBCCE; American Baptist Churches in the U.S.A.; senior minister, Second Baptist Church, 1400 Idlewood Avenue, Richmond, VA 23220, (804) 353-7682; 3311 Northview Place, Richmond, VA 23225, (804) 272-6114.

HAYES, Diana L., Dr.; f; assistant professor, Georgetown University, 120 New North Building, Washington, DC 20057, (202) 687-5846; J.D., George Washington Law Center, 1973; Ph.D., religious studies, Catholic University of Louvain, (Belgium), 1988; S.T.D., systematic theology, Catholic University of Louvain (Belgium), 1988; systematic theology, African American Catholic theology, Black theology, African American religions, liberation theology; CTSA, CTS, AAR; Roman Catholic; layperson.

HAYNES, Roland E., Rev. Dr.; m; associate professor, University of South Carolina, Department of Psychology, Barnwell College, Columbia, SC 29208, (803) 777-2379 or 777-4137; A.B., psychology, Clark College, 1949; S.T.B., theology, Boston University, 1952; S.T.M., psychology and pastoral counseling, Boston University, 1953; Ph.D., psychology and pastoral counseling, Boston University, 1961; psychology of religion, psychology of the African American experience, community psychology, social psychology; Baptist; minister; P.O. Box 210798, Columbia, SC 29221.

HODGES, John O., Dr.; m; associate professor and acting chair of department (1989–1990), University of Tennessee, Department of Religious Studies, 501 McClung Tower, Knoxville, TN 37996-0450, (615) 974-2466; B.A., English and French, Morehouse College, 1968; M.A., English, Atlanta University, 1971; M.A., religion and literature, University of Chicago, 1972; Ph.D., religion and literature, University of Chicago, 1980; African American religion, African American literature, religion and literature, American studies; AAR, MLA, LHS, CLA; Baptist; layperson; 4815 Skyline Drive, Knoxville, TN 37914, (615) 673-0989.

HOOD, Robert E., Rev. Dr.; m; professor, General Theological Seminary, 175 Ninth Avenue, New York City, NY 10011-4924, (212) 243-5150; A.B., philosophy/religion, Ohio Wesleyan University, 1957; S.T.B., theology, General Theological Seminary, 1960; D.Phil., theology, Oxford University, 1981; Karl Barth's theology, Afro-Caribbean and African religions, Christian ethics, Christian theology and churches in Afro cultures; AAR, SSBR, SCE, FOCUCC; Episcopal; priest.

HOPKINS, Dwight N., Rev. Dr,; m; assistant professor, Santa Clara University, Department of Religious Studies, Santa Clara, CA 95053, (408) 554-4547; B.A., Afro-American studies/political economy, Harvard University, 1976; M.Div., systematic theology, Union Theological Seminary (NY), 1984; M.Phil., systematic theology, Union Theological Seminary (NY), 1987; Ph.D., systematic theology, Union Theological Seminary (NY), 1988; Black theology, liberation theology, systematic theology; AAR, BTP, NCBS, ACAS; Baptist; 8180 Hansom Drive, Oakland, CA 94605, (415) 569-2044.

HOYT, Thomas E., Jr., Rev. Dr.; m; professor, Hartford Seminary, 77 Sherman Street, Hartford, CT 06105, (203) 232-4451; B.A., sociology, Lane College, 1962; M.Div., New Testament, Interdenominational Theological Center, 1965; S.T.M., New Testament, Union Theological Center, 1967; Ph.D., New Testament, Duke University, 1975; New Testament, theology, ecumenics, liberation ethics; SSBR, FOCNCC, FOCWCC, SBL, AAR; Christian Methodist Episcopal; minister; 80 Girard Avenue, Hartford, CT 06105, (203) 232-6252.

JACKSON, Jonathan, Rev. Dr.; professor and area chairperson, Interdenominational Theological Center, 671 Beckwith Street, SW, Atlanta, GA 30314, (404) 527-7700; B.A., Clark College, 1953; M.Div., Gammon Theological Seminary (ITC), 1956; M.A., Scarritt College, 1957; Th.D., Boston University School of Theology, 1964.

JEFFERSON, Frederick D., Jr., Dr.; m; executive, the Martin Luther King Center, 290 Troup Street, Rochester, NY 14608, (716) 328-5464; B.S., education, French, Wilberforce University, 1950; B.D., pastoral theology, Yale University, 1956; Th.M., systematic theology, Harvard University, 1958; M.A., constructive theology, University of Chicago, 1968; Ph.D., constructive theology, University of Chicago, 1973; Black theology, systematic theology, constructive theology, theological ethics; SSBR, AAR; Presbyterian Church, U.S.A.; 415 Kimberly Drive, Rochester, NY 14610 (716) 244-3549.

JOHNSON, Edgar A., Rev. Dr.; m; administrator and lecturer, Capitol Region Conference of Churches, 30 Arbor Street, Hartford, CT 06106, (203) 236-1295; M.Div., Andrews University Theological Seminary, 1972; M.A., biblical languages, Andrews University Theological Seminary, 1975; Ph.D., New Testament, Andrews University, 1985; exegesis, biblical, theological cognate studies; SBL, AAR; Seventh Day Adventist; 36 Cottage Grove Circle, Bloomfield, CT 06002, (203) 243-0446.

JONES, Lawrence N., Rev. Dr.; m; dean and professor, Howard University School of Divinity, 1400 Shepherd Street, NE, Washington, DC 20017, (202) 806-0500; B.S., education, English, West Virginia State College, 1942; M.A., American history, University of Chicago, 1948; B.D., Oberlin Graduate School of Theology, 1956; Ph.D., religion, Yale University Graduate School, 1961; African American church history, American religious history; SSBR, ACHA; United Church of Christ; clergy and educator; 1206 Devere Drive, Silver Spring, MD 20903, (301) 439-2579.

JONES, William R., Rev. Dr.; m; professor, Florida State University, Black Studies Program, 172 Bellamy Building, Tallahassee, FL 32306, (904) 644-5512; B.A., philosophy (magna cum laude), Howard University, 1955; M.Div., Harvard University Divinity School, 1958; Ph.D., philosophy/religion, Brown University, 1969; liberation theology, humanism, neofundamentalism, ethnic studies; AAR, APhA, SSBR, SSCE; Unitarian Universalist (Humanist); ordained minister; 2410 Limerick Drive, Tallahassee, FL 32308, (904) 893-3519.

KINNEY, John W., Rev. Dr.; m; dean and associate professor, Virginia Union University School of Theology, 1601 W. Leigh Street, Richmond, VA 23220, (804) 257-5715; B.A., social studies, Marshall University, 1969, M.Div., theology,

Virginia Union University School of Theology, 1972; M.Phil., religion, Columbia University, 1978; Ph.D., theology, Columbia University/Union Theological Seminary (NY), 1979; theology, philosophy, history; Baptist; P.O. Box 757, Ashland, VA 23005, (804) 798-5331.

LEATHERS, Kim Q. B.; f; senior research assistant and associate editor, *Directory of African American Religious Bodies*, Research Center on Black Religious Bodies, Howard University School of Divinity, 1400 Shepherd St., NE, Washington, DC 20017, (202) 806-0750; B.A., sociology (administration of justice), Howard University, 1983; M.A., sociology, Howard University, 1987; Ph.D. student, sociology, Howard University; African American women's history, race relations, African American church history, sociology of religion; AKD, AAMA, ASA; Baptist (Progressive); lay person; 4243 Colorado Avenue, NW, Washington, DC 20011, (202) 291-4638.

LEWIS, Lloyd A., Rev. Dr.; m; associate professor, Virginia Theological Seminary, 3737 Seminary Road, Alexandria, VA 22304, (703) 370-6600; A.B., classics, Trinity College (Hartford, CT), 1969; M.Div., theology, Virginia Theological Seminary, 1972; M.A., religious studies (New Testament), Yale University, 1975; M.Phil., religious studies (New Testament), Yale University, 1981; Ph.D., religious studies (New Testament), Yale University, 1985; New Testament, classics, ancient history, sociology; SBL, ACS, CAT; Episcopal; priest; 3737 Seminary Road, Alexandria, VA 22304, (703) 370-0559.

LINCOLN, C. Eric, Rev. Dr.; professor, Duke University, Department of Religion, P.O. Box 4735, Durham, NC 27706, (919) 684-3453; A.B., social science, LeMoyne College (TN), 1947; A.M., religion and philosophy, Fisk University, 1954; B.D., general studies, University of Chicago, 1956; Ph.D., social ethics, Boston University, 1960; M.Ed., counseling and guidance, Boston University, 1960; cults and sects, African American church, sociology of religion, sociology of the African American church; AAAS, SSBR, AAR, ASA; United Methodist and African Methodist Episcopal; clergyman; 2507 Tanglewood Drive, Durham, NC 27705, (919) 493-4386.

LONG, Charles H., Dr.; m; professor and director of humanities doctoral program, Syracuse University, Department of Religion, 501 Hall of Languages, Syracuse, NY 13244, (315) 443-3861; B.D., University of Chicago, 1953; Ph.D., University of Chicago, 1962; history of religion, African American religions, religions of the New World; AAR, SSBR, IAHR; Baptist; layperson; 1608 Jefferson Tower, Syracuse, NY 13202, (315) 424-1715.

LONG, Jerome, Rev. Dr.; m; associate professor, Wesleyan University, Department of Religion, Middleton, CT 06457, (203) 347-941, x2689 or 2598; B.A., religion/philosophy, Knox College, 1956; B.D., University of Chicago, 1960; M.A., University of Chicago, 1962; Ph.D., University of Chicago, 1973; religion of hunters and gatherers, African American religions, religions of African peoples, myth and ritual, autobiographies/biographies of African Americans; SSBR, AAR, NAACP, AfSA; African Methodist Episcopal Zion; 16 Brainerd Avenue, Middletown, CT 06457, (203) 344-0724.

MABRY, Eddie L., Rev. Dr.; m; associate professor, Augustana College, Rock Island, IL 61201, (309) 794-7000, former dean, Oklahoma School of Religion, Tulsa, OK; A.B., religion, Millikin University, 1966; M.Div., church history, Princeton Theological Seminary, 1969; Ph.D., church history, Princeton Theological Seminary, 1982; history of Christianity, African American studies, Christian ethics; DMA; Baptist (National, U.S.A.); lecturer, advanced studies division, National Baptist Congress of Christian Education; 327 East Garfield Avenue, Decatur, IL 62526, (217) 422-6434.

MAFICO, Temba L., Dr.; m; associate professor, Interdenominational Theological Center, 617 Beckwith Street, SW, Atlanta, GA 30314, (404) 527-7700; B.A., University of London (at University College of Rhodesia), 1970; Th.M., Harvard University Divinity School, 1973; M.A., Harvard University, 1977; Ph.D., Harvard University, 1979; Old Testament.

MARTIN, Clarice J., Rev. Dr.; f; assistant professor, Princeton Theological Seminary, CN 821, Princeton, NJ 08540, (609) 921-8300, x7725 or 7925; B.A., psychology, University of California-Riverside, 1972; M.A., New Testament, Wheaton Graduate School, 1974; teaching credential, University of California-Riverside, 1977; M.Div., San Francisco Theological Seminary, 1981; Ph.D., New Testament, Duke University, 1985; New Testament literature and exegesis, social world of New Testament, synoptic Gospels, classical rhetoric, New Testament and hermeneutics, history of exegesis; AAR, SBL, SSBR, AAABS, PWTE; Presbyterian (U.S.A.); ordained clergy; 15 Alexander Street, Princeton, NJ 08540, (609) 924-1162.

MARTIN, Sandy D., Dr.; m; associate professor, University of Georgia, Department of Religion, Athens, GA 30602, (404) 524-5356; B.A., philosophy and religion, political science, Tougaloo College, 1973; M.A., religion, Columbia University, 1975; M.Phil., religion, Columbia University/Union Theological Seminary (NY), 1978; Ph.D., religion, Columbia University/Union Theological Seminary (NY), 1981; church history, American religious history, African American religious history, modern Christianity; ASCH, AAR, SBHS, SSBR, SBL; Baptist; layperson; 700 Fourth Street, #D-146, Athens, GA 30601, (404) 353-3686.

McCLAIN, William B., Rev. Dr.; m; professor, Wesley Theological Seminary, 4500 Massachusetts Avenue, NW, Washington, DC 20016, (202) 885-8600, x8644; A.B., English, religion, philosophy, Clark College, 1960; M.Div., theology, Boston University, 1962; Ph.D., systematic theology, Boston University, 1975; liturgy, preaching, Black theology and history, African American Methodist history; SSBR, AH, AR, NFMAWL; United Methodist; ordained elder; 500 Round Table Drive, Fort Washington, MD 20744, (301) 839-5009.

McFARLANE, Adrian A., Rev. Dr.; m; B.A., philosophy, religion (cum laude), Millikin University, 1971; M.Div., theology, Princeton Theological Seminary, 1974; M.Phil., philosophy of religion, Drew University, 1983; Ph.D., philosophy of religion, Drew University, 1985; continental philosophy, philosophical theology, epistemology/philosophy of mind, philosophical hermeneutics; APhA, AAR, SCP, SBE; Presbyterian; senior minister, Witherspoon Street Presbyterian Church, 124 Witherspoon Street, Princeton, NJ 08540,

(609) 924-1666; 453 Walnut Lane, Princeton, NJ 08540, (609) 921-7897.

McKINNEY, Richard I., Dr.; m; distinguished scholar in philosophical theology, Coppin State University, 2500 West North Avenue, Baltimore, MD 21216, (301) 333-5302; A.B., philosophy, Morehouse College, 1931; B.D., philosophy of religion, Andover Newton Theological School, 1934; S.T.M., philosophy of religion, Andover Theological School, 1937; Ph.D., educational philosophy, Yale University, 1942; philosophy of religion, philosophy, educational administration; APhA, SPEP, PST, SVHE, AAR, AAUP, PBK, AKM; Baptist; 2408 Overland Avenue, Baltimore, MD 21214, (301) 426-0741.

McNAIR, Alice G., Rev. Dr.; f; adjunct lecturer, Howard University School of Divinity, 1400 Shepherd Street, NE, Washington, DC 20017, (202) 806-0500, Pastoral Ministries Institute, 1760 Reston Parkway, Reston, VA 22090, (703) 834-5521; B.A., sociology and history, Spelman College, 1967; M.Div., Garrett-Evangelical Theological Seminary, 1977; Ph.D., pastoral psychology and counseling, Garrett-Evangelical Theological Seminary, 1983; pastoral counseling and care, women's issues (professional women), cross-cultural research, ministerial development; AAPC; African Methodist Episcopal; elder, member, Board of Examiners, Washington Annual Conference; 2423 Ansdel Court, Reston, VA 22091, (703) 860-2975.

McNAIR, Clinton, D., Rev. Dr.; m; associate professor and D.Min. program coordinator, Howard University School of Divinity, 1400 Shepherd Street, NE, Washington, DC 20017, (202) 806-0500; B.A., history and education, Virginia Union University, 1966; M.Div., pastoral ministry, Crozer Theological Seminary, 1969; Ph.D., psychology and pastoral counseling, Northwestern University, 1978; practical theology, pastoral psychology, research; AAPC, ACPE; Baptist (Progressive and American Baptist Churches in the U.S.A.); minister, member, PNBC Home Mission Board; 2423 Ansdel Court, Reston, VA 22091, (703) 860-2975.

MICHAEL, Stanley R., Rev. Dr.; m; A.A., theology, Caribbean Union College, 1969; B.A., religion, Oakwood College, 1977; M.A., religion, Andrews University, 1978; Ph.D., sociology of religion, Boston University, 1985; sociology of religion, psychology of religion, anthropology, African American studies; ASR, SSSR; Seventh-day Adventist; pastor, Flatbush Seventh-day Adventist Church, 261 E. 21st Street, Brooklyn, NY 11226, (718) 693-9169; 259-66 147 Drive, Rosedale, NY 11422, (718) 949-5410.

MITCHELL, Ella Pearson, Rev. Dr.; f; former dean of Sisters Chapel, Spelman College, Atlanta, GA 30318; visiting professor of homiletics, Interdenominational Theological Center, 671 Beckwith Street, SW, Atlanta, GA 30314, (404) 527-7700; A.B., early childhood education, Talladega College, 1939; M.A., Columbia University and Union Theological Seminary, 1943; D.Min., School of Theology at Claremont, 1974; SSBR, MLKF; Baptist; 411 Angier Court, NE, Atlanta, GA 30312, (404) 827-9095.

MITCHELL, Henry H., Rev. Dr.; m; former dean, Virginia Union University School of Theology; acting chair of homiletics, Interdenominational Theological Center, 671 Beckwith Street, SW, Atlanta, GA 30314, (404) 527-7700; D.

Min. mentor, United Theological Seminary, Dayton, OH; A.B. (cum laude), Lincoln University, 1941; M.Div., Union Theological Seminary, 1944; M.A., California State University, 1966; Th.D., School of Theology at Claremont, 1973; SSBR, MLKF; Baptist; 411 Angier Court, NE, Atlanta, GA 30312, (404) 827-9095.

MITCHELL, Mozella G., Rev. Dr.; f; associate professor, University of South Florida, Religious Studies Department, 310 CPR, Tampa, FL 33620, (813) 974-2221; A.B., English, LeMoyne College, 1959; M.A., English, University of Michigan, 1963; M.A.R.S., religion, Colgate-Rochester Divinity School, 1973; Ph.D., literature and theology, Emory University, 1980; mysticism, African American religious history, liberation theology, ecumenism; AAR, SSBR, BWCS; African Methodist Episcopal Zion; presiding elder and pastor, Mt. Sinai A.M.E. Zion Church, Tampa, FL; 2605 South Kings Avenue, Brandon, FL 33511, (813) 685-2280.

MORRIS, Calvin S., Rev. Dr.; m; associate professor, Howard University School of Divinity, 1400 Shepherd Street, NE, Washington, DC 20017, (202) 806-0500; B.A., history (cum laude), Lincoln University (PA), 1963; M.A., history, Boston University Graduate School, 1964; S.T.B., Boston University School of Theology, 1967; Ph.D., history, Boston University Graduate School, 1982; African American church history, African American literature and history, American social and political history, pastoral theology; SSBR, ASCH, ASALH, AFE, AAR; United Methodist; ordained elder and assistant pastor, Gibbons United Methodist Church, Brandywine, MD; 917 Hamlin Street, NE, Washington, DC 20017, (202) 635-8535.

MORRISON, Roy D. II, Dr.; m; professor, Wesley Theological Seminary, 4500 Massachusetts Avenue, NW, Washington, DC 20016, (202) 885-8600; B.A., philosophy and psychology, Howard University, 1947; B.D., epistemology in theology and science, Northern Baptist Seminary, 1950; M.A., University of Chicago, 1969; Ph.D., philosophical theology, University of Chicago, 1972; African American religions, philosophy of science in relation to religion; AAR, NAPTS, IRAS; Unitarian Universalist; 2611 Evans Drive, Silver Spring, MD 20902, (301) 649-5132.

MOSELEY, Romney M., Rev. Dr.; m; associate professor and assistant dean, Candler School of Theology, Emory University, Atlanta, GA 30322, (404) 727-6317; B.A., biology, Boston University, 1968; B.D. (magna cum laude), Harvard University Divinity School, 1971; Ph.D. (with distinction), Harvard University, 1978; ethics, theology, psychology of religion, sociology of religion; AAR, SSSR, SCE; Anglican; priest; 2498 Williamswood Court, Decatur, GA 30033, (404) 320-1548.

MURPHY, Larry G., Rev. Dr.; m; associate professor, Garrett-Evangelical Theological Seminary, 2121 Sheridan Road, Evanston, IL 60201, (312) 866-3977; B.A., religion, Michigan State University, 1967; Ph.D., historical studies, Graduate Theological Union, 1973; American religious history, African American religious history, women in religion, oral history; SSBR, OHA, AAR; African Methodist Episcopal; ordained elder; 1709 South Boulevard, Evanston, IL 60202, (312) 491-0742.

MURRELL, Nathaniel Samuel, Dr.; m; assistant professor,

Glassboro State College, Glassboro, NJ 08028, (609) 863-6048; B.A. (honors), Bible/religion, Jamaica Theological Seminary, 1978; M.A. (honors), theology, Wheaton College, 1981; Pre.M.Phil., Caribbean studies, University of the West Indies, 1982; M.Phil., Drew University, 1986; Ph.D., Drew University, 1988; biblical studies, African Americans in Bible, liberation theologies, feminist interpretation/scripture; AAR, SBS, SSSR, AAABS, BAS; Presbyterian; interim pastor; 42J Loantaka Way, Madison, NJ 07940, (201) 408-4364.

MYERS, William H., Dr; m; professor of New Testament, Ashland Theological Seminary, 910 Center Street, Ashland, OH 44805, director, McCreary Center for African American Religious Studies, 1508 E. 71st Street, Cleveland, OH 44103; M.A., Ashland Theological Seminary, 1976; M.Div., Ashland Theological Seminary, 1984; D.Min, Ashland Theological Seminary, 1984; Ph.D., New Testament, University of Pittsburgh, 1991; biblical studies, African American studies; AAR, SBL, AAHP; Baptist; 6768 Smith Road, Middleburg Heights, OH 44130, (216) 267-4543.

NDIRANGO-KIHARA, Nehemy, Rev. Dr.; m; senior lecturer, Department of Philosophy and Religious Studies and Department of Sociology, Kenyatta University, P.O. Box 438441, Nairobi, Kenya; L.Th., theological education and counseling, St. Paul's College, 1971; B.Th., biblical literature and history, Christian International College, 1977; M.Div., psychology and sociology, Interdenominational Theological Center, 1977; Ph.D., sociology of religion, anthropology, and political science, Emory University, 1984; Afrocentric social theory, liberation theology, social scientific study of social ethics, empirical research in African belief systems, religions of the African diaspora; ASSSR, ISA, AID, ARAK; Presbyterian Church of East Africa; ordained minister, university chaplain; P.O. Box 55016, Atlanta, GA 30308.

NEWSOME, Clarence G., Rev. Dr.; m; associate professor and associate dean, Howard University School of Divinity, 1400 Shepherd Street, NE, Washington, DC 20017, (202) 806-0500; B.A., religious studies, Duke University, 1972; M.Div., church history, Duke University, 1975; Ph.D., religious studies, Duke University, 1982; church history, American religious thought, African American experience in America; SSBR, AAR, ASCH; Baptist (National, U.S.A.); minister, chairman, General Baptist State Convention of North Carolina Foundation; 6761 Sewells Orchard Drive, Columbia, MD 21045, (301) 290-9380.

OGLESBY, Enoch, Dr.; m; professor of Christian ethics and theology and director of the Black Church Studies Program, Eden Theological Seminary, 475 E. Lockwood Avenue, St. Louis, MO 63119-3192, (314) 961-3627 or 831-2126; Christian ethics and theology.

OGUNYEMI, Emmanuel S., Bishop; m; assistant dean, Methodist Church Nigeria, P.O. Box 4502, Ilorin, Kwara State, Nigeria, West Africa; B.A., religion and philosophy, Virginia Wesleyan College, 1971; M.Div., New Testament studies, Interdenominational Theological Center, 1973; Ph.D., sociology of religion, Emory University, 1976; sociology of religion, philosophy of religion; Methodist; bishop; Bishop's House, Methodist Church Nigeria, P.O. Box 4502, Ilorin, Kwara State, Nigeria, West Africa.

O'NEAL, Eddie S., Rev. Dr.; m; professor, Andover Newton Theological School, 210 Herrick Road, Newton Centre, MA 02159, (617) 964-1100; B.A., religion and philosophy, Tougaloo College, 1963; B.D., Andover Newton Theological School, 1967; S.T.M., Andover Newton Theological School, 1969; D.Min., Andover Newton Theological School, 1972; homiletics, theology; SSBR; American Baptist Churches in the U.S.A.; minister.

PARIS, Peter J., Rev. Dr.; m; professor and department chair, Princeton Theological Seminary, CN 821, Princeton, NJ 08542, (609) 921-8300; B.A., English, Acadia University, 1956; B.D., Acadia University, 1958; M.A., social ethics, University of Chicago, 1969; Ph.D., social ethics, University of Chicago, 1975; religion, ethics, and politics in black America, African American religious leadership, black American and African theologies; AAR, SCE, SSBR, SVHE; Baptist; minister; 92 Stockton Street, Princeton, NJ 08540.

PAYNE, Wardell J., Dr.; m; research director and editor, *Directory of African American Religious Bodies*, Research Center on Black Religious Bodies, Howard University School of Divinity, 1400 Shepherd St., NE, Washington, DC 20017, (202) 806-0750; B.S., psychology, DePaul University, 1970; M.A., sociology, DePaul University, 1974; Ph.D., sociology, University of Southern California, 1978; demography, race and ethnicity, social deviance, organizations, sociology of religion; ASA, NAACP, ABS; Baptist (Progressive); licensed minister; 4705 6th Place, NE, Washington, DC 20017, (202) 269-6258.

PERO, Albert, Jr., Dr.; m; professor, Lutheran School of Theology at Chicago, 1100 East 55th Street, Chicago, IL 60615, (312) 753-0700; Th.D., Lutheran School of Theology at Chicago, 1975; systematic theology, cross-cultural studies, Black theology.

PETERS, Melvin K. H., Dr.; m; associate professor, Duke University, Department of Religion, P.O. Box 4735, Durham, NC 22706, (919) 684-3261; B.A., theology, Andrews University, 1966; M.A., religion, Andrews University, 1968; Ph.D., Near Eastern studies, University of Toronto, 1975; Hebrew Bible, Septuagint studies, textual criticism, Coptic versions; AAR, SBL, IOSOT, IOSCS.

PHELPS, Jamie T., Dr.; f; assistant professor, Catholic Theological Union, Department of Theology, 5401 S. Cornell, Chicago, IL 60615, (312) 324-8000; B.A., sociology, Siena Heights College, 1969; M.S.W., social work, University of Illinois (Chicago), 1972; M.A., scripture and systematics, St. John's University, 1975; Ph.D., systematic theology, Catholic University of America, 1989; systematic theology, African American religion, feminine studies, theology of missions; CTSA, BTC, MFPMME, SSBR, AAR, ASM; Catholic; 5346 S. Cornell, Chicago, IL 60625, (312) 288-7474.

POLLARD, Alton, B., III, Rev. Dr.; m; assistant professor, Wake Forest University, Department of Religion, Box 7212, Winston-Salem, NC 27109, (919) 761-5462; B.A., religion, philosophy, business management, Fisk University, 1978; M.Div., religion, Harvard University Divinity School, 1981; Ph.D., religion and culture, Duke University, 1987; sociology of religion, African American church and religion, religion in America, history of religions; AAR, ASR, RRA,

SSSR; Baptist (American Baptist Churches in the U.S.A., Progressive, National); minister; 2026 Storm Canyon Road, Winston-Salem, NC 27106 (919) 922-1965.

PRESSLEY, Arthur L., Rev. Dr.; m; assistant professor, Drew University Theological School, Box R-22, Madison, NJ 07940, (201) 408-3594; B.A., religion, Allegheny College, 1972; M.Div., theology, Garrett-Evangelical Theological Seminary, 1975; Ph.D., pastoral care, Northwestern University, 1986; psychology, pastoral care, ethics, pastoral formation; AAPC, APA; United Methodist; minister; 36 Ralph Place, Morristown, NJ 07960, (201) 984-8842.

PROCTOR, Samuel D., Rev. Dr.; m; Martin Luther King Memorial Professor, Rutgers University, New Brunswick, NJ 08903, professor emeritus and former president, Virginia Union University and North Carolina A and T University; A.B., English, Virginia Union University, 1942; M.Div., religion, Crozer Theological Seminary, 1945; Th.D., New Testament and ethics, Boston University, 1950; New Testament, ethics, moral education, higher education; Baptist (Progressive); pastor emeritus, Abyssinian Baptist Church, 132 Odell Clark Place (W. 138th Street), New York City, NY 10030, (212) 862-7474/5, associate general secretary, National Council of Churches; 63 McAfee Road, Somerset, NJ 08873, (201) 246-1416.

PUGH, Thomas J., Rev. Dr.; m; professor and department chair, Interdenominational Theological Center, 671 Beckwith Street, SW, Atlanta, GA 30314, (404) 527-7713; B.A., religious education and social science, Clark College, 1940; B.D., New Testament, Gammon Theological Seminary, 1942; M.A., educational administration, Atlanta University, 1947; Ph.D., psychology, pastoral counseling, Boston University, 1955; education and statistics, psychology and educational theory, pastoral counseling, marriage and family therapy; APA, AAPC, AAMFT, GPA, GMFTA; Baptist; member; 2806 Engle Road, NW, Atlanta, GA 30318, (404) 794-0068.

RABOTEAU, Albert J., Dr.; m; Putman professor, Princeton University, Department of Religion, 613-1879 Hall, Princeton, NJ 08544, (609) 258-4481; B.A., English, Loyola-Marymount College, 1964; M.A., English, University of California-Berkeley, 1966; Ph.D., religious studies, Yale University, 1974; African American religion, religion in America; AAR, ASCH, AHA, OAH; Catholic.

REID, Stephen B., Rev. Dr.; m; associate professor, Pacific School of Religion, 1798 Scenic Avenue, Berkeley, CA 94709, (415) 848-0528; B.S., religion, Manchester College, 1973; M.Div., Bethany Theological Seminary, 1976; Ph.D., Bible, Emory University, 1981; Hebrew scriptures, biblical theology; SBL, CBA, ASOR; Church of the Brethren; 829 Shattuck, Berkeley, CA 94707, (415) 527-1989.

RICHARDSON, Harry V., Dr.; m; professor emeritus, Interdenominational Theological Center, 671 Beckwith Street, SW, Atlanta, GA 30314, (404) 527-7700; A.B., Western Reserve University; S.T.B., Harvard University Divinity School; Ph.D., Drew University.

RIGGS, Marcia Y., Dr.; f; The Theological School, Drew University, 36 Madison Avenue, Madison, NJ 07940, (201) 408-3271; A.B., religion, Randolph-Macon Woman's College, 1980; M.Div., Yale University Divinity School, 1983; Ph.D., Vanderbilt University, 1991; African American re-

ligious history, African American women and religion in America, religious ethics; AAR, SCE; African Methodist Episcopal Zion; ordained elder; 2 Seven Oaks Circle, Madison, NJ 07940, (201) 822-8098.

ROBERTS, J. Deotis, Rev. Dr.; m; Distinguished Professor of Philosophical Theology, Eastern Baptist Seminary, Lancaster and City Line Avenues, Philadelphia, PA 19151, (215) 896-5000; former professor, Howard University School of Divinity (1958–80); former editor, *Journal of Religious Thought* (1974–80); former president, Interdenominational Theological Center (1980–83); A.B., religious education and English, Johnson C. Smith University, 1947; B.D., religion, Shaw University, 1950; B.D., Hartford Seminary, 1951; S.T.M., philosophy of religion (magna cum laude), Hartford Seminary, 1952; Ph.D., philosophical theology, Edinburgh University, 1957; theology, philosophy, ethics, world religions; ATS, AAR, SSBR, BT, and president, FREE; Baptist; minister; 7 Appleby Court, Silver Spring, MD 20904, (301) 384-0614.

ROBERTS, Samuel K., Rev. Dr.; m; professor, Virginia Union University School of Theology, 1500 N. Lombardy Street, Richmond, VA 23220, (804) 257-5715; Diploma, French civilization, Université de Lyon, France, 1966; A.B., English, Morehouse College, 1967; M.Div., Union Theological Seminary, 1970; Ph.D., ethics, church and society, Columbia University, 1974; Christian social ethics, African American social history, political/ economic structures, history of ideas in African American religion; AAR, SSSR; Baptist (American Baptist Churches in the U.S.A.); member, Commission on Recruitment and Guidance in Ministry; 1209 Westbrook Avenue, Richmond, VA 23227, (804) 266-8850.

ROBERTS, Wesley A., Rev. Dr.; m; adjunct professor, Gordon College, Wenham, MA 01984; B.A., history, Wilfrid Laurier University (Ontario), 1965; M.Div., Toronto Baptist Seminary, 1965; Th.M., apologetics, Westminster Theological Seminary, 1967; M.A., University of Guelph, (Ontario), 1968; Ph.D., University of Guelph (Ontario), 1972; African American religious history, the Reformation, eighteenth- and nineteenth-century British and European history; ASCH, CFH, SSBR; Baptist; pastor, People's Baptist Church of Boston, 134 Camden Street, Boston, MA 02118, (617) 427-0424; 1 Enon Road, Wenham, MA 01984, (508) 921-0225.

ROCK, Calvin B., Dr.; m; B.A., religion, Oakwood College, 1954; M.A., sociology, University of Detroit, 1966; D.Min., ethics (religion), Vanderbilt University, 1978; Ph.D., ethics (religion), Vanderbilt University, 1984; ethics (religion); Seventh Day Adventist; vice-president, General Conference of Seventh Day Adventists, 12501 Old Columbia Pike, Silver Spring, MD 20904-1608, (301) 680-6000; 1001 Spring Street, Silver Spring, MD 20910, (301) 585-5816.

ROGERS, Cornish R., Rev.; m; professor, School of Theology at Claremont; 1325 North College Avenue, Claremont, CA 91711, (714) 626-3521; B.A., botany, Drew University, 1951; S.T.B., theology, Boston University School of Theology, 1955; pastoral theology, urban studies, spirituality studies, religious journalism; AAUP, AAR, SSBR; United Methodist; ordained elder; 465 E. Concha Street, Altadena, CA 91001, (818) 794-3423.

ROOKS, Charles Shelby, Rev. Dr.; m; executive vice-president, United Church Board for Homeland Ministries, 132 W. 31st Street, New York, NY 10001; A.B., Virginia State College, 1949; M.Div., Union Theological Seminary, 1953; United Church of Christ; ordained minister; 83 Riverbend Drive, North Brunswick, NJ 08902.

RUSSELL, Horace O., Rev. Dr.; m; professor and dean of the chapel, Eastern Baptist Theological Seminary, Lancaster and City Avenues, Philadelphia, PA 19096, (215) 896-5000; B.D. (honors), church history, London University, 1954; B.A., (honors), Honors School of Theology, Oxford, 1957; M.A., Regent's Park College and St. Catherine's College, Oxford, 1960; D.Phil., West Indian/West African history, missions, Regent's Park College and St. Catherine's College, Oxford, 1972; African and Caribbean missions, ecumenics, Caribbean church history and religions, early church and reformation studies, ministerial training; SSBR, WIGMT, HSGBJ; Baptist; Eastern Baptist Theological Seminary, Philadelphia, PA 19151, (215) 642-2944.

SANDERS, Boykin, Dr.; m; associate professor, Virginia Union University School of Theology, 1601 W. Leigh Street, Richmond, VA 23220, (804) 257-5715; B.S., mathematics, Morris College; M.Div., New Testament and church history, Interdenominational Theological Center; Th.M., New Testament, Harvard University Divinity School; M.A., New Testament and Christian origins, Harvard University; Ph.D., New Testament and Christian origins, Harvard University; New Testament and Christian origins, African history and religion, African American history and traditions, contemporary socioreligious movements; SSBR, SBL; Baptist (Progressive).

SANDERS, Cheryl J., Rev. Dr.; f; associate professor, Howard University School of Divinity, 1400 Shepherd Street, N.E, Washington, DC 20017, (202) 806-0500; B.A., mathematics, Swarthmore College, 1974; M.Div., Harvard University Divinity School, 1980; Th.D., applied theology, Harvard University Divinity School, 1985; ethics, African American religion; AAR, SSBR; Church of God (Anderson, IN); minister; 7704 Morningside Drive, NW, Washington, DC 20012, (202) 829-7638.

SANNEH, Lamin, Dr.; m; professor, Yale University Divinity School, 409 Prospect Street, New Haven, CT 06510, (203) 432-5336; B.A., history, Union College, 1967; M.A., Arabic and Islamic studies, University of Birmingham (U.K.), 1968; Ph.D., Islamic history, University of London, 1974; history of Islam with special reference to Africa, history of religion, interreligious dialogue, African studies; AAR, AfSA, PCMRA; Methodist; 47 Morris Street, Hamden, CT 06517.

SCOTT, Thomas M.; Rev.; m; visiting assistant professor of religious studies, Knox College, Department of Religious Studies, Galesburg, IL 61401-4999, (309) 343-0112; B.A., history, Lincoln University, 1970; M.Div., Interdenominational Theological Center, 1973; Th.M., New Testament, Harvard University Divinity School, 1974; Th.D. candidate, New Testament and Christian origins, Harvard University Divinity School, expected 1991; New Testament and Christian origins, Ancient African culture and languages, psychology of religion; SBL; United Methodist 1971–1990; ordained minister 1971–1990; 304 S. Fitzhugh Street, Rochester, NY 14608-2437, (716) 232-7979.

SHANNON, David T., Rev. Dr.; m; professor and vice-president for academic services/academic dean, Interdenominational Theological Center, 671 Beckwith Street, SW, Atlanta, GA 30314, (404) 527-7704; B.A., Virginia Union University, 1954; B.D., Virginia Union University, 1957; S.T.M., New Testament, Oberlin College, 1959; D.Min., New Testament, Vanderbilt University, 1974; Ph.D., higher education (focus on theological education), University of Pittsburgh, 1975; Old Testament—wisdom literature, New Testament—Pauline studies; AAR, SSBR, SBL; Baptist; ordained clergy; 3640 Rolling Green Ridge, SW, Atlanta, GA 30331, (404) 349-5097.

SHAW, Talbert O., Rev. Dr.; m; president, Shaw University, 118 E. South Street, Raleigh, NC 27611, (919) 546-8300; A.B., history and religious studies, Andrews University; M.A., ethics and society, University of Chicago, 1968; Ph.D., ethics and society, University of Chicago, 1973; ethics and society, ethics and religion, religion and social policies; AAR, ASHE, ACE, AAC, CCAS, ASCE, ACUS; Baptist; president of Baptist-affiliated university; 9400 Owls Nest Court, Raleigh, NC 27613, (919) 846-5146.

SHOPSHIRE, James M., Rev. Dr.; m; professor and coordinator of Urban Ministries track, Wesley Theological Seminary, 4500 Massachusetts Avenue, NW, Washington, DC 20016-9990, (202) 885-8600; B.A., social science, Clark College, 1963; B.D., Gammon Theological Seminary (ITC), 1966; Ph.D., sociology of religion and ethics, Northwestern University, 1975; sociology of religion, urban ministry, congregational studies; SSBR, SSSR, RRA, ASR; United Methodist; ordained elder; 6215 Sligo Mill Road, NE, Washington, DC 20011-1527, (202) 291-0419.

SMITH, Luther E., Jr., Dr.; m; associate professor, Candler School of Theology, Emory University, Atlanta, GA 30322, (404) 727-4176; B.A., sociology/anthropology, Washington University, 1969; M.Div., Eden Theological Seminary, 1972; Ph.D., American studies, St. Louis University, 1979; Howard Thurman, religion and society, Christian spirituality; SSBR; Christian Methodist Episcopal; ordained elder; 2892 Greenspan Court, Decatur, GA 30034, (404) 288-1044.

STEWART, Carlyle F., Rev. Dr.; m; assistant professor, Wayne State University, College of Lifelong Learning, Detroit, MI 48202; B.A., psychology, humanities, Wilberforce University, 1973; M.A., social science, religion, University of Chicago, 1974; M.Div., ethics, Christian education, Chicago Theological Seminary, 1977; D.Min., ethics, Christian education, Chicago Theological Seminary, 1978; Ph.D., sociology of religion, ethics, Northwestern University, 1982; Christian ethics, sociology of religion, U.S. literature, European-Third World; SSBR; United Methodist; pastor, Hope United Methodist Church, Southfield, MI, (313) 356-1020; 23731 Civic Center Drive, Southfield, MI 48034, (313) 356-4069.

SWANN, Darius L., Dr.; m; professor and area chairperson, Interdenominational Theological Center, 671 Beckwith Street, SW, Atlanta, GA 30314, (404) 527-7700; A.B., Johnson C. Smith University, 1945; M.Div., Johnson C. Smith University, 1948; S.T.M., Union Theological Seminary, 1959; Ph.D., University of Hawaii, 1974; missiology (theology of missions), world religions.

TAYLOR, Joseph E., Rev. Dr.; m; assistant professor, Howard University School of Divinity, 1400 Shepherd Street, NE, Washington, DC 20017, (202) 806-0500; B.A., sociology and anthropology, Bowie State College, 1972; M.Div., Princeton Theological Seminary, 1975; D.Min., church administration, Howard University School of Divinity, 1980; pastoral theology, church administration; AFE; United Church of Christ; pastor, Faith United Church of Christ, 4900 10th Street, NE, Washington, DC 20017, (202) 635-1508; 1790 Verbena Street, NW, Washington, DC 20012, (202) 829-4672.

THOMPSON, George W. M., Rev. Dr.; m; professor, East Stroudsburg State College, Department of Philosophy and Religious Studies, East Stroudsburg, PA 18301, (717) 424-3602; B.A., history, Virginia Union University, 1954; M.Div., philosophy of religion, Southern Baptist Theological Seminary, 1957; M.A., ethics and society, University of Chicago, 1962; Ph.D., ethics and society, University of Chicago, 1974; technology, African American religion, theology, philosophy; SSSR, SPC, SSBR, AAR, APhA; Baptist; pastor, New Horizon Baptist Church, Philadelphia, PA; P.O. Box 177, Glenside, PA 19088, (215) 247-4643.

TIMITY, Roland J. R., Rev. Dr.; m; adjunct lecturer, Howard University School of Divinity, 1400 Shepherd Street, NE, Washington, DC 20017, (202) 806-0500; R.S.A., economics, University of London, 1961; L.B.Div., divinity, Fourah State College, University of Sierra Leone, 1965; M.Div., divinity, Howard University School of Divinity, 1970; M.Th., theology, Howard University School of Divinity, 1971; M.Ed., psychological counseling, Howard University, 1972; Ph.D., education, Catholic University of America, 1982; theology, psychology, education, economics; BPT, CSTC, ASCD, APGA, FAA; United Methodist; pastor, member of the board of ordained ministry; 1851 Statesman Court, Severn, MD 21144, (301) 551-2707.

TRIBBLE, Sherman Roosevelt, Rev. Dr.; m; B.A., religion and business management, Fisk University, 1978; M.Div., Howard University School of Divinity, 1981; Ph.D., African American religious history, Northwestern University, 1990; African American religious history, history of the Baptist church, worship and music of the black church, American religious history; Baptist (National Baptist Convention, U.S.A., Inc., and American Baptist Churches in the U.S.A.); pastor, Star of Bethlehem Baptist Church, 148 Spring Street, Ossining, NY 10562, (914) 762-1360 and corresponding secretary, Central Hudson Baptist Association; 15 Overton Road, Ossining, NY 10562, (914) 762-8453.

TRULEAR, Harold Dean, Rev. Dr.; m; dean of first professional programs and professor, New York Theological Seminary, 5 W. 29th Street, New York, NY 10001, (212) 532-4012; B.A., religion, music, Morehouse College, 1975; M.Phil., sociology of religion, Drew University, 1979; Ph.D., sociology of religion, Drew University, 1983; sociology of religion, pastoral theology, African American church studies, African American worship; AAR, SSBR, SPT; Baptist (Progressive and American Baptist Churches in the U.S.A.); pastor, Mt. Zion Baptist Church of Germantown, 41 W. Rittenhouse Street, Philadelphia, PA 19144, (215) 844-7614; 912 Church Lane, Yeadon, PA 19050, (215) 623-3066.

TURNER, Otis, Rev. Dr.; m; B.S., biology, Albany State College, 1962; B.D., social ethics, Emory University, 1969; Ph.D., social ethics, Emory University, 1974; social ethics, African American history, liberation theology, race relations; AAR, NAACP, SSBR; Presbyterian (U.S.A.); coordinator for Racial Justice Policy Development, Presbyterian Church (U.S.A.) Racial Ethnic Unit, 100 Witherspoon Street, room 2008, Louisville, KY 40202-1398, (502) 569-5698; 8904 Gonewind Court, Louisville, KY 40299, (502) 491-2408.

TURNER, William C., Jr., Rev. Dr.; m; assistant professor, Duke University Divinity School, Durham, NC 27706, (919) 684-6795; B.S., electrical engineering, Duke University, 1971; M.Div., Duke University, 1974; Ph.D., religion, Duke University, 1984; African American church in the U.S., Christian theology, homiletics, Pentecostalism; SSBR, AAR; United Holy Church of America, Inc.; ordained elder and pastor; 41 Sedgewood Court, Durham, NC 27713, (919) 544-4769.

TWESIGYE, Emmanuel K., Rev. Dr.; m; professor, Ohio Wesleyan University, Department of Religion and Philosophy, Delaware, OH 43105, (614) 368-3827; Dip. Th., theology, University of East Africa, 1970; M.A., religion and philosophy, Vanderbilt University, 1972; B.A. (honors), Dip., Ed., history and education, Makerere University, 1973; Ph.D., religion and philosophy, Vanderbilt University, 1973; M.A. (honors), communications, Wheaton Graduate School, 1978; S.T.M., theology, University of the South, 1979; philosophy, theology, African religion and philosophy, African American history and religion; AAR, APhA, TC, AEA; Episcopal/Anglican; priest; 651 Governors Street, Delaware, OH 43015, (614) 363-2670.

TYMS, James Daniel, Rev. Dr.; m; professor (retired), Howard University School of Divinity, 1400 Shepherd Street, NE, Washington, DC 20017, member, Religious Education Association, 409 Prospect Street, New Haven, CT 06511-2177; B.A., English, Lincoln University (MO), 1934; B.D., Howard University School of Religion, 1937; M.A., Howard University, 1938; Ph.D., Boston University, 1942; theological studies, religious education; REA; Baptist; retired minister; 1729 Varnum Street, NW, Washington, DC 20011, (202) 882-9184.

WALKER, J. Lynwood, Rev. Dr.; m; founder and president, Northwest Theological Union, 914 E. Jefferson Street, Seattle, WA 98122, (206) 329-7878; B.A., psychology, North Carolina Central University, 1963; M.Div., pastoral psychology, Pacific School of Religion, 1967; Ph.D., religion, clinical psychology, Graduate Theological Union/ University of California-Berkeley, 1970; psychology of religion, pastoral theology, interrelations of theology and psychology, human development, values, and religion; SVHE, SSBR, MLKBCF, NWCTS; Christian Church (Disciples of Christ); ordained ministry; 3303 E. Valley Street, Seattle, WA 98112, (206) 324-6207.

WALKER, Sheila, S., Dr.; f; professor, Department of Anthropology, College of William and Mary, Williamsburg, VA 23185, (804) 221-1068; B.A., political science, Bryn Mawr College, 1966; M.A., anthropology, University of Chicago, 1969; Ph.D., anthropology, University of Chicago, 1976; Afro-Brazilian religion and culture, African Christianity, Africa to African American cultural continuum; AAA, ABA, SAC.

WASHINGTON, James Melvin, Rev. Dr.; m; professor, Union Theological Seminary, 3041 Broadway, New York, NY 10027, (212) 280-1383; B.A., religious studies and American history, University of Tennessee, Knoxville, 1970; M.T.S., social ethics, Harvard University Divinity School, 1972; M.Phil., church history, Yale University, 1979; modern and American church history; ASCH, AAR, SSBR, SVHE, ASALH; Baptist (Progressive and American Baptist Churches in the U.S.A.); member, Home Mission Board, PNBC; 99 Claremont Ave., New York, NY 10027, (212) 222-8039.

WASHINGTON, Joseph R., Jr., Rev. Dr.; m; professor, Department of Religious Studies, Box 36 College Hall, University of Pennsylvania, Philadelphia, PA 19104; B.A., University of Wisconsin (Madison), 1952; B.D., Andover Newton Theological School, 1958; Th.D., social ethics, Boston University, 1961; christian social ethics, black religion; 350 Grays Lane, Haverford, PA 19041.

WATERS, John W., Rev. Dr.; m; former professor, Interdenominational Theological Center, Boston University School of Theology, University of Detroit; B.A., chemistry, Fisk University, 1957; Certificate, French thought, University of Geneva (Switzerland), 1962; S.T.B., Hebrew studies (cum laude), Boston University School of Theology, 1967; Ph.D., Biblical studies—Old Testament, Boston University, 1970; Hebrew studies, Egyptology, African American religions, ancient Near Eastern studies; SBL, AAR, AHuA, AAUP; Baptist; pastor, The Greater Solid Rock Baptist Church, 6280 Camp Road, Riverside, GA 30296-2803, (404) 997-4666; P.O. Box 310416, Atlanta, GA 30331-0416, (404) 344-8104.

WEEMS, Renita J., Rev. Dr.; f; assistant professor, Vanderbilt University Divinity School, Nashville, TN 37240; (625) 343-7516; B.A., economics, Wellesley College, 1976; M.Div., Old Testament, Princeton Theological Seminary, 1983; Ph.D., Old Testament, Princeton Theological Seminary, 1989; biblical hermeneutics, Old Testament theology, prophetic literature, Old Testament history; SBL; African Methodist Episcopal; elder.

WEST, Cornel R., Dr.; m; professor, Princeton University, Department of Religion, 1879 Hall, Princeton, NJ 08540, (609) 258-4718; A.B., Near Eastern languages, Harvard University, 1973; M.A., philosophy, Princeton University, 1975; Ph.D., philosophy, Princeton University, 1980; philosophy, Near Eastern languages; Baptist; layperson; 188 Prospect Avenue, Princeton, NJ 08540, (609) 497-1903.

WILEY, Dennis W., Rev. Dr.; m; A.B., African American studies, Harvard University, 1972; M.Div., Howard University School of Divinity, 1981; M. Phil., systematic theology, Union Theological Seminary (NY), 1985; Ph.D., systematic theology, Union Theological Seminary (NY), 1988; Black theology, ecclesiology, Howard Thurman; AAR; Baptist (Progressive); pastor, Covenant Baptist Church, 3845 South Capital Street, SW, Washington, DC 20032, (202) 562-5576; 9006 Hewlett Drive, Fort Washington, MD 20744, (301) 248-2377.

WILLIAMS, Preston N., Rev. Dr.; m; professor, Harvard University Divinity School, 45 Francis Avenue, Cambridge, MA 02178, (617) 495-5766; A.B., English, Washington and Jefferson College, 1947; M.A., history, Washington and Jefferson College, 1948; B.D., Johnson C. Smith Theological Seminary, 1950; S.T.M., Yale University Divinity School, 1954; Ph.D., Harvard University, 1967; ethics, history, theology; SCE, AAR, SSBR; Presbyterian Church, U.S.A.; minister; 36 Fairmont, Belmont, MA 02178, (617) 484-3857.

WILMORE, Gayraud, S., Rev.; m; professor and acting editor, *Journal of the Interdenominational Theological Center*, Interdenominational Theological Center, 671 Beckwith Street, SW, Atlanta, GA 30314, (404) 527-7747; B.A., English, Lincoln University, 1947; B.D., Lincoln University Theological Seminary, 1950; S.T.M., Temple University School of Religion, 1952; doctoral studies, social ethics, Drew University, 1960-1963; African American religious history, social ethics, ecumenism, Presbyterian history; BTP, SSBR, EATWOT; Presbyterian; ordained minister; 710 McGill Place, SW, Atlanta, GA 30312, (404) 524-2888.

WIMBUSH, Vincent L., Rev. Dr.; m; associate professor, School of Theology at Claremont, 1325 North College Avenue, Claremont, CA 91711, (714) 626-3521, (714) 681-2800, x208; B.A., philosophy, Morehouse College, 1975; M.Div., Yale University Divinity School, 1978; A.M., New Testament, Harvard University, 1981; Ph.D., New Testament, Harvard University, 1983; New Testament—early Christianity, history of biblical interpretation, African American religious history; SBL, AAR, SNTS, HTET; Baptist; 738 Santa Barbara Drive, Claremont, CA 91711, (714) 621-9686.

WRIGHT, Leon E., Dr.; m; professor emeritus, Howard University School of Divinity; A.B., Boston University, 1934; A.M., Boston University, 1937, S.T.B., Harvard University Divinity School, 1943; Ph.D., Harvard University, 1945; New Testament; United Church of Christ; 1726 Varnum Street, NW, Washington, DC 20011, (202) 726-4262.

YOUNG, Henry J., Rev. Dr.; m; professor, Garrett-Evangelical Theological Seminary, 2121 Sheridan Road, Evanston, IL 60201, (312) 866-3865; B.A., philosophy and religion, Tougaloo College, 1967; Th.M., systematic theology, Boston University School of Theology, 1970; Ph.D., systematic theology, Hartford Seminary, 1973; systematic theology, theology and ethics, philosophical theology; AAR, GTF, SCE, SSBR; United Methodist; elder; 8922 Ewing Avenue, Evanston, IL 60203, (312) 675-7809.

YOUNG, Josiah U., III, Dr.; m; associate professor, Wesley Theological Seminary, 4500 Massachusetts Avenue, NW, Washington, DC 20016, (202) 885-8600; B.A., English, Morehouse College, 1975; M.Div., Union Theological Seminary (NY), 1981; M.Phil., theology, Union Theological Seminary (NY), 1984; Ph.D., theology, Union Theological Seminary (NY), 1985; systematic theology, black and African theologies, African American religion, African traditional religion; United Methodist; elder; 11748 Carriage House Drive, Silver Spring, MD 20904, (301) 680-0352.

Persons for Whom Information Is Incomplete

ALLEN, Benjamin W. P., Theological School, Drew University, Ph.D., 1953.

ANDERSON, Moses B., Bishop; m; 1234 Washington Boulevard, Detroit, MI 48826.

ARULEFELA, J. Olu, Dr.; m; Obafemi Awolowo University, Ile-Ife, Department of Religious Studies, Ile-Ife, Oyo, Nigeria.

AUGMAN, William J., Dr.; m; United Theological Seminary, 1810 Harvard Boulevard, Dayton, OH 45406; Ph.D., Drew University, 1983.

BAILEY, Joyce, Dr.; f; last known address: United Theological College of the West Indies, Mona, Kingston 7, Jamaica, West Indies.

BAKER-FLETCHER, Garth; m; 263 Beverly Hill Road, Portsmouth, NH 03801, (603) 433-5863.

BAKER-FLETCHER, Karen; f; 263 Beverly Hill Road, Portsmouth, NH 03801, (603) 433-5863.

BOKEMBYA, R. Nkanga, Dr.; m; 1625 16th Avenue, South, Nashville, TN 37212.

BOOKER, Sue (Thandeka), Claremont, Ph.D., 1988.

BRADLEY, Fulton O., Dr.; m; New Hope Missionary Baptist Church, 5403 South Wayne Road, Wayne, MI 48184 (313) 728-2180.

BRONSON, Oswald P., Garrett Theological Seminary, Ph.D., 1965.

CARTWRIGHT, John, Dr.; m; 745 Commonwealth Avenue, Boston, MA 02215.

CONE, Cecil W., Dr.; m; president, Edward Waters College, 1658 Kings Road, Jacksonville, FL 32209; Ph.D., Emory University, 1974.

CROCKETT, Roosevelt David, Boston University School of Theology, Ph.D., 1953.

CUMMINGS, George C. L., Dr.; m; professor, Pacific School of Religion, 1798 Scenic Avenue, Berkeley, CA 94709, (415) 848-0528; Ph.D., Union Theological Seminary, 1989; 2516 Benevenure Avenue, Berkeley, CA 94704, (415) 841-1905.

DAVIS, Henderson, Dr.; m; P.O. Box 783, Indianapolis, IN 46206, (317) 546-9654.

DELPINO, Jerome K., Boston University, Ph.D., 1980.

DELPINO, Julius E., Garrett/Northwestern, Ph.D., 1976.

DUNNE, Ernest, Dr.; m; Rutgers University, New Brunswick, NJ 08903.

EDWARDS, Herbert O., Dr.; m; 2733 Sevier Street, Durham, NC 27705, (919) 489-0893.

ERSKINE, Noel, Dr.; m; associate professor, Candler School of Theology, Emory University, Atlanta, GA 30322, (404) 727-6322; theology.

EVERSLEY, Walter V. L., Rev. Dr.; m; Virginia Theological Seminary, 3737 Seminary Road, Alexandria, VA 22304, (703) 370-6600.

GABA, Octavius, Dr.; m; no current address.

HARRIS, Michael W., Harvard University, Ph.D., 1980.

HARVEY, Louis-Charles, Dr.; m; president, Payne Theological Seminary, P.O. Box 474, Wilberforce, OH 45384-0474, (513) 376-2946; Ph.D., Union Theological Seminary, 1978.

HIGGINBOTHAM, Evelyn Brooks, Dr.; f; assistant professor, University of Pennsylvania, Department of History, 3400 Spruce Street, Philadelphia, PA 19104, (215) 898-5704; Ph.D., University of Rochester; American church history.

HOLMES, Zan, Dr.; m; adjunct professor, Perkins School of Theology, Southern Methodist University, 201 Kirby Hall, Dallas, TX 75275, (214) 692-2138; United Methodist; pastor, St. Luke "Community" United Methodist Church, 5170 East R. L. Thornton Freeway, Dallas, TX 75223, (214) 821-2970.

HORTON, Frank L., Southern California School of Theology, Claremont, Rel.D., 1968.

HURST, David T., Dr.; m; Th.D., School of Theology at Claremont, 1981; Missionary Church, 2343 N. San Antonio Avenue, Pomona, CA 91767, (714) 621-5369.

JACKSON-BROWN, Irene V., Dr.; f; the Episcopal Church Center, 815 Second Avenue, New York, NY 10017.

JAMES, Allix B., Dr.; m; chancellor and dean, Virginia Union University School of Theology, 1601 W. Leigh Street, Richmond, VA 23220, (804) 257-5715; Th.D., Union Theological Seminary (VA); 2956 Hathaway Road, Richmond, VA 23225, (804) 320-3655.

JOHNSON, J. Dell, Harvard University, Ph.D., 1980.

JONES, E. Theodore, Dr.; m; Temple University, Philadelphia, PA 19122 (215) 787-7000.

JONES, Major J., Dr.; m; Woodruff Library, Atlanta University, Atlanta, GA 30314.

JONES, Miles, Dr.; m; Virginia Union University School of Theology, 1601 W. Leigh Street, Richmond, VA 23220, (804) 257-5715; 468 E. Ladies Mile Road, Richmond, VA 23227.

KIRBY, James Louis; m; 515 Park Drive, Apt. 5, Boston, MA 02215, (617) 266-7447.

LAKEY, Othal H., Bishop; m; 2815 Melrose Avenue, Cincinnati, OH 45206.

LATIMORRE, Vergel, Dr.; m; no current address.

LAWRENCE, William F., Jr., Union Theological Seminary, Ph.D., 1984.

LOVETT, Leonard, Dr.; m; Pastor, Church of the Crossroads, P.O. Box 762, Inglewood, CA 90307, (213) 566-5615; Ph.D., Emory University, 1979.

MANGRAM, John D., Pacific School of Religion, Ph.D., 1966.

MARBURY, Carl H., Harvard Divinity School, Ph.D., 1968.

MASON, Elliott, Rev. Dr.; m; Ph.D., Old Testament, School of Theology at Claremont.

MAULTSBY, Herbert, Dr.; m; no current address.

MAXEY, Lee Z., Dr.; m; Institute for Antiquity and Christianity, 831 Dartmouth, Claremont, CA 91711, (714) 621-8000, x3224; Ph.D. candidate, New Testament, Claremont Graduate School.

McCREARY, Edward D., Rev. Dr.; m; Virginia Union University School of Theology, 1601 W. Leigh Street, Richmond, VA 23220, (804) 257-5715; Th.D., Union Theological Seminary (VA); 2416 Northumberland Avenue, Richmond, VA 23220, (804) 321-7482.

McLAUGHLIN, Wayman B., Dr.; m; North Carolina A and T University, Greensboro, NC, (919) 767-6245.

MILLER, George, Dr.; m; no current address.

MOSES, Jesse, Southern California School of Theology, Claremont, Th.D., 1955.

MURRAY, Cecil L., Southern California School of Theology, Claremont, Rel.D., 1965.

PANNELL, William, Dr.; m; professor of evangelism and director of black church studies, Fuller Theological Seminary, Pasadena, California.

PARKER, Aaron, Dr.; m; Morehouse College, P.O. Box 56, Atlanta, GA 30314, (404) 681-2800.

REWOLINSKI, Edward T., Dr.; m; Th.D., New Testament, Harvard University; no current address.

ROBINSON, William, Dr.; m; 1315 Yerkes Street, Philadelphia, PA 19119, (215) 224-7496.

ROSS, Jerome C., Dr.; m; Virginia Union University School of Theology, 1601 W. Leigh Street, Richmond, VA 23220, (804) 257-5715; Ph.D. candidate, Old Testament studies; 310 N. Birdneck Road, Virginia Beach, VA 23451, (804) 422-5048.

RUGAYO, John, Dr.: m; 21 Lindsay House, Mutare, Zimbabwe, Africa.

SCOTT, James E.; no current address.

SCOTT, Julius S., Jr., Boston University School of Theology, Ph.D., 1968.

SEWELL, George Alexander, Boston University School of Theology, Ph.D., 1957.

SHOCKLEY, Grant Sneed, Union Theological Seminary, New York, Ed.D., 1953.

SITHOLE, Robinnah, Dr.; f; Rutgers University School of Communication Information, 4 Huntington Street, New Brunswick, NJ 08903.

SMITH, Archie, Dr.; m; Pacific School of Religion, 1796 Scenic Avenue, Berkeley, CA 94709.

SMITH, Ervin, Garrett/Northwestern, Ph.D., 1976.

SMITH, Thee, Dr.; m; Emory University, Atlanta, GA 30322.

SPAULDING, Olivia T., Hartford Theological Seminary, Ed.D., 1967.

STORRS, Walter Lennett, Jr., Harvard Divinity School, Ph.D., 1958.

THOMAS, Herman E., Dr.; m; University of North Carolina at Charlotte, UNCC Station, Charlotte, NC 28223.

TITUS, Noel, Dr.; m; principal, Codrington College, Barbados, West Indies.

TURNER, Richard B., Dr.; m; assistant professor, University of California at Santa Barbara, Department of Religion and Department of Black Studies, Santa Barbara, CA 93106; B.A., Boston University; M.A., Boston University; Ph.D., religion, Princeton University.

WALKER, Theodore, Dr.; m; assistant professor, Perkins School of Theology, Southern Methodist University, 201 Kirby Hall, Dallas, TX 75275, (214) 692-2138; Christian ethics.

WASHINGTON, Preston, Dr.; m; New York Theological Seminary, 5 W. 29th Street, New York, NY 10001.

WELCHEL, L. Henry, Dr.; m; Los Angeles, CA.

WHEELER, Edward L., Emory University, Ph.D., 1982.

WHITELOCK, Lester T., Boston University, Ph.D., 1968.

WILLIAMS, Delores S., Dr.; f; assistant professor, Drew University, The Graduate School, Madison, NJ 07940, (201) 408-3261; Ph.D., Union Theological Seminary, 1990; 39 Green Village Road #306, Madison, NJ 07940, (201) 377-6212.

WILLIAMS, Kenneth R., Boston University School of Theology, Ph.D., 1962.

WOODS, Virgil, Dr.; m; Ed.D., education, Harvard University; Providence, RI.

YOUNG, James R., Dr.; m; no current address.

Part 5

White Religious Bodies and Agencies with Significant African American Membership

The following religious bodies represent the African American presence in predominantly white denominations and religious institutions.

Adventist

General Conference of Seventh-day Adventists

World Headquarters
12501 Old Columbia Pike
Silver Spring, MD 20904-1608
(301) 680-6000
Elder Neal Wilson, President
Elder Meade C. Van Putten, Associate Secretary

The Seventh-day Adventists emerged from an interdenominational movement that started in the early nineteenth century. It was formally organized in 1863. It stresses the imminence of the Second Advent of Christ. The Bible is used as the only rule for the faith. The major points of distinction in the faith are belief in the personal, imminent, premillennial return of Christ, and the observance of the seventh day as the Sabbath.

The Seventh-day Adventists is an interracial body that has a significant African American constituency. The church is organized into geographically defined areas called unions. There are nine groups (seven black conferences and two offices of regional affairs), which focus on the concerns of African Americans and foster communication with African Americans. Each conference is directed by an elder. The two unions have a director. These leaders comprise the Regional Presidents Council, which meets twice a year. The spring session is usually held in February at Oakwood College in Huntsville, Alabama, and the fall session is generally held in August on the West Coast. All members of the Regional Presidents Council serve as members of the Oakwood College Board. The Reverend Neal Wilson is the president of the denomination. Elder Meade C. Van Putten is the Associate Secretary of the Northern American Division of Seventh-day Adventists and the Associate Secretary of the General Conference. In addition, Elder Van Putten has served as the contact person for information on African American groups within the denomination.

Group Type: Denomination
Founded: 1863

Conferences of the Seventh-day Adventists

Allegheny East Conference of Seventh-day Adventists

P.O. Box 266
Pine Forge, PA 19548
(215) 326-4610
Elder Charles Cheatam, Executive Secretary

Group Type: Denomination specific; district association/annual conference
Geographic Areas: Delaware, District of Columbia, Eastern Pennsylvania, Eastern Virginia, Maryland, and New Jersey

Allegheny West Conference of Seventh-day Adventists

1339 East Broad Street
Columbus, OH 43205
(614) 252-5271
Elder Willie J. Lewis, President

Group Type: Denomination specific; district association/annual conference
Geographic Areas: Allegheny and Garrett counties in Maryland, Ohio, Western Pennsylvania, Western Virginia, and West Virginia

Central States Conference of Seventh-day Adventists

P.O. Box 1527
Kansas City, MO 64141
(816)361-7177
Elder J. Paul Monk, Jr., President

Group Type: Denomination specific; district association/annual conference
Geographic Areas: Colorado, Iowa, Kansas, Minnesota, Missouri, Nebraska, North Dakota, San Juan County in New Mexico, South Dakota, and Wyoming

Lake Region Conference of Seventh-day Adventists

8517 South State Street
Chicago, IL 60619
Elder Luther R. Palmer, President

Group Type: Denomination specific; district association/annual conference
Geographic Areas: Illinois, Indiana, Michigan, Minnesota, and Wisconsin

Northeastern Conference of Seventh-day Adventists

115-50 Merrich Boulevard
St. Albans, NY 11434
(718) 291-8006
Elder Stennett H. Brooks, President

Group Type: Denomination specific; district association/annual conference
Geographic Areas: Connecticut, Maine, Massachusetts, New Hampshire, New York, Rhode Island, and Vermont

Office of Regional Affairs–North Pacific Union Conference of Seventh-day Adventists

P.O. Box 5005
Westlake Village, CA 91359

Group Type: Denomination specific; district association/annual conference
Geographic Areas: Alaska, Idaho, Montana, Oregon, and Washington

Office of Regional Affairs–Pacific Union Conference of Seventh-day Adventists

P.O. Box 16677
Portland, OR 97216
(503) 255-7300
Elder E. Wayne Sheppard, Director

Group Type: Denomination specific; district association/annual conference
Geographic Areas: Arizona, California, Hawaii, Johnston Island, Nevada, and Utah

South Atlantic Conference of Seventh-day Adventists

P.O. Box 92447
Morris Brown Station
Atlanta, GA 30314
(404) 792-0535
Elder Ralph Peay, President

Group Type: Denomination specific; district association/annual conference
Geographic Areas: Georgia, North Carolina, and South Carolina

South Central Conference of Seventh-day Adventists

P.O. Box 24936
Nashville, TN 37202
(615) 226-6500
Elder Charles E. Dudley, President

Group Type: Denomination specific; district association/annual conference
Geographic Areas: Alabama, Florida west of the Appalachicola River, Kentucky, Mississippi, and Tennessee

Southeastern Conference of Seventh-day Adventists

P.O. Box 160067
Altamont Spring, FL 32716
Elder Jackson Doggette, President

Group Type: Denomination specific; district association/annual conference
Geographic Areas: Florida and southern Georgia

Southwest Region Conference of Seventh-day Adventists

P.O. Box 226289
Dallas, TX 75203
(214) 943-4491
Elder Richard E. Barron, President

Group Type: Denomination specific; district association/annual conference
Geographic Areas: Arkansas, Louisiana, New Mexico, Oklahoma, and Texas

Jehovah's Witnesses

25 Columbia Heights
Brooklyn, NY 11201
(718) 625-3600
Frederick W. Franz, President

Jehovah's Witnesses (legally known as the Watchtower Bible and Tract Society of Pennsylvania, Inc.) started in the early 1870s as a Bible study group in Allegheny, Pennsylvania (now a part of Pittsburgh), and has grown into an international religious organization. Its membership exceeds 3.6 million and as of 1988, members were found in 212 countries worldwide. The headquarters relocated to Brooklyn, New York, in 1909 as its ministry became international. Its literature is translated into 289 languages and is distributed by members throughout the world. The body is committed to the work of preaching the good news (gospel) of God's Kingdom. Allegiance to this heavenly government has created unity among its members, who represent many races, cultures, and backgrounds. The number of African American members is significant, although the body does not have a specific administrative unit that focuses on African American issues. Persons interested in obtaining additional information about the organization should address their inquiries to the headquarters.

Group Type: Denomination
Founded: Early 1870s
Publications: *Awake!* and *The Watchtower* journals and bound books explaining the Bible
Membership: In excess of 3.6 million persons worldwide

Baptist

American Baptist Black Caucus— American Baptist Churches in the U.S.A.

34 W. Pleasant Street
Springfield, OH 45506
(513) 323-3504
The Reverend Jacob Chatman, President

The American Baptist Black Caucus is affiliated with the American Baptist Churches in the U.S.A. It elects a president who serves a one-year term. The administrative office is located with the incumbent. In addition to contacting the incumbent through the direct address, correspondence can be transmitted through the headquarters of the American Baptist Churches in the U.S.A., P.O. Box 851, Valley Forge, PA 19482.

Group Type: Denomination specific; ministerial

Black Church Extension Division—Home Mission Board, Southern Baptist Convention

1350 Spring Street
Atlanta, GA 30367
(404) 898-7400
Dr. Emmanuel L. McCall, Director

The Southern Baptist Convention has had ministries with African Americans since its formation in 1845. During its first 120 years, the Convention took a rather paternal approach to its African American constituents, but from 1965 through 1980, efforts were made to bring about racial reconciliation and co-operative efforts with the three major African American Baptist conventions (the National Baptist Convention of America, Inc.; the National Baptist Convention, U.S.A., Inc.; and the Progressive National Baptist Convention, Inc.). By 1976, African Americans were enjoying full inclusion in the programs and life of the Southern Baptist Convention.

Today there are more than twelve hundred African American member churches in the Southern Baptist Convention. In addition, the Convention works and cooperates with all four of the major African American Baptist conventions (the National Missionary Baptist Convention of America, in addition to the three listed above). The Black Church Extension Division concerns itself, particularly, with starting churches and church growth in African American communities. The Division emphasizes theological education and other educational support programs, including scholarships, intern opportunities, work in institutes, and seminary extension. The Black Church Extension Division has periodic statewide fellowship meetings, regional conferences, and an annual conference.

Group Type: Denomination specific; administrative; mission/ philanthropic
Founded: 1845
Membership: Over 1,200 churches

Church of Christ

Church of Christ

No central headquarters

The interracial Church of Christ is an outgrowth of the Restoration Movement. In 1793, James O'Kelly, a member of the Methodist Episcopal Church, withdrew from the Baltimore conference of the church, requesting others to join him and take the Bible as the only creed. His following was primarily in North Carolina and Virginia, where about seven thousand persons followed his example and leadership, returning to primitive New Testament Christianity. In England in 1802, Baptists under the leadership of Elias Smith and Abner Jones decided to accept the Bible as their only guide and began to refer to themselves as Christians, eschewing any denominational names and creeds.

In 1904, Barton Stone and other Presbyterian ministers denied denominational alignment and declared the Bible as the "only sure guide to heaven." Alexander and Thomas Campbell are well known for a similar crusade in West Virginia in 1809, believing that "nothing should be bound upon Christians as a matter of doctrine which is not as old as the New Testament." These four movements, although in different locations, soon led to a renewed interest in returning to the church of Christ as described in the Bible, free from denominational restraints and unrealistic creeds. It should be noted that many African Americans, slaves and former slaves, were influenced by Stone and the Campbells, who were against slavery.

The Church of Christ does not conceive of itself as a new church, but rather the movement of the church is a contemporary reproduction of the church established on Pentecost. The body is composed of approximately fifteen thousand congregations with a membership totaling two million persons and over seven thousand persons who preach regularly. The church, although located across the country and in more than eighty foreign countries, is concentrated in the South, especially Texas and Tennessee. Its missionary program was expanded after World War II to Africa, Europe, Asia, and other foreign countries, where more than 450 workers are supported.

The congregations are autonomous, following the organizational plan found in the New Testament. There is no central headquarters nor any structural hierarchy above that within each congregation. No conventions or annual meetings are held, and there are no official publications. About forty periodicals are published by individual members of the church. One congregation, the Highland Avenue Church in Abilene, Texas, sponsors "The Herald of Truth," a nationwide radio and television program. It is heard on over eight hundred radio stations and one hundred fifty television stations across the country, and

WHITE RELIGIOUS BODIES AND AGENCIES

much of its budget is donated freely by other congregations. In addition, "World Radio," an extensive radio network, has twenty-eight stations in Brazil alone, and operates in the United States and several foreign countries, with programs produced in fourteen languages. The common thread that ties the churches together is loyalty to the principles of the restoration of New Testament Christianity.

The Church of Christ believes that the Bible was divinely inspired and that it is, therefore, infallible and authoritative. It practices baptism by immersion, and the Lord's Supper, served each Sunday, is considered a binding appointment for the members. Only *a cappella* singing is used in the worship, because it is believed that this conforms to the music of the early Apostolic church. For the same reason, incense and candles are not used. The church's financial support comes strictly from its members' gifts, each giving as they have prospered. No assessments are made on the membership, and money-making activities such as dinners and bazaars are not allowed. There is no creed such as those in the Catholic church or other Protestant denominations, and members do not pray to saints or confess to ministers. The relationship is directly between God and the individual.

All congregations have elders as their leaders, and they are assisted by deacons, teachers, and evangelists or ministers. Ministers are referred to as "brother." The church's position on the role of women in the ministry is not known. Local congregations are named "Church of Christ" and according to streets, cities, or neighborhoods. Forty colleges and secondary schools and seventy-five homes for the aged and orphanages are operated by members of the church. The Church of Christ has made great strides in the integration of its congregations, and continues to seek true New Testament Christianity.

Group Type: Denomination
Membership: Two million persons in fifteen thousand congregations with over seven thousand preachers

Episcopal

Office of Black Ministries— The Episcopal Church

The Episcopal Church Center
815 Second Avenue
New York, NY 10017
(212) 867-8400
The Reverend Canon Harold T. Lewis, Staff Officer

The Office of Black Ministries of the Episcopal Church serves as a clearinghouse for the deployment of African American clergy, and is responsible for compiling an annual directory of African American clergy in the church, together with an annual report of the Episcopal Commission for Black Ministries. The office is also responsible for convening the Black Diocesan Executives (BLADE) on an annual basis. In fulfilling its mission, the office is supported by the African American bishops of the Episcopal church. They are:

Bishop John M. Burgess, retired Bishop of Massachusetts, 401 Whitney Avenue, Apt. 1, New Haven, CT 06511, (203) 777-2833;

Bishop Clarence Coleridge, Suffragan Bishop of Connecticut, 1335 Asylum Avenue, Hartford, CT 06105, (203) 233-4481, (800) 842-0126;

Bishop Walter D. Dennis, Jr., Suffragan Bishop of New York, 1047 Amsterdam Avenue, New York, NY 10025, (212) 316-7411 or 316-7436;

Bishop Sturdie Downs, Bishop of Nicaragua, Apartado 1207, Managua, Nicaragua, 011-505/2-2-5174;

Bishop Herbert D. Edmondson, Assisting Bishop, Diocese of Central Florida, 381 Lincoln Street, Daytona Beach, FL 32014, (904) 255-2016;

Bishop Jean Rigal Elisee, Assisting Bishop, Diocese of New York, 516 Pleasant Valley Way, West Orange, NJ 07052, (201) 669-8114;

Bishop Luc Anatole Garner, Bishop of Haiti, Boite Postale 1309, Port-au-Prince, Haiti 011-509/1-7-1624;

Bishop Barbara Harris, Suffragan Bishop of Massachu-setts, Diocese of Massachusetts, 138 Tremont Street, Boston MA 02111, (617) 482-5800;

Bishop Telesforo A. Isaac, Bishop of the Dominican Republic, Apartado 764, Santo Domingo, Dominican Republic, (809) 682-7208 or 533-5673;

Bishop Richard Beamon Martin, Retired Suffragan Bishop of Long Island, 1388 Union Street, Brooklyn, NY 11213;

Bishop H. Irving Mayson, Suffragan Bishop of Michigan, 4800 Woodward Avenue, Detroit, MI 48201, (313) 832-4400 or 393-2838;

Bishop Cedric E. Mills, retired Bishop of the Virgin Islands, 2235 West 25th Street, San Pedro, CA 90732, (213) 547-9573;

Bishop James H. Ottley, Bishop of Panama, Apartado R, Balboa CZ, Panama, 011-507/62-4558/52;

Bishop Quintin E. Primo, Jr., retired Suffragan Bishop of Chicago, 3322 Morningside Drive, Wilmington, DE 19810, (302)478-7149;

Bishop James H. Shirley, retired Bishop of Panama, Apartado R., Balboa CZ, Panama, 011-507-62-4558-52;

Bishop E. Don Taylor, Bishop of the Virgin Islands, P.O. Box 7488, St. Thomas, USVI 00801, (809) 776-1797 or 775-4409;

Bishop Herbert Thompson, Jr., Coadjutor Bishop of Southern Ohio, 412 Sycamore Street, Cincinnati, OH 45202, (513) 421-0311;

Bishop Franklin D. Turner, Suffragan Bishop of Pennsylvania, 1700 Market Street, Philadelphia, PA 19103, (215) 567-6650 or 572-6459;

Bishop Orris G. Walker, Jr., Coadjutor Bishop of Long Island, 36 Cathedral Avenue, Garden City, Long Island, NY 11530, (516) 248-4800;

Bishop Arthur B. Williams, Suffragan Bishop of Ohio, 2230 Euclid Avenue, Cleveland, OH 44115, (216) 771-4815 or 531-7742; and

Bishop Cornelius J. Wilson, Bishop of Costa Rica, Apartado 2773, San Jose, Costa Rica, 011-506/25-0209 or 011-506/53-0790.

Group Type: Denomination specific; administrative

Organization of Black Episcopal Seminarians

The Episcopal Church Center
815 Second Avenue
New York, NY 10017
(800) 334-7626
The Reverend Canon Harold T. Lewis, Staff Officer

Group Type: Denomination specific; student

Union of Black Episcopalians

Washington Cathedral
Mt. Saint Alban
Washington, DC 20016
The Reverend Canon Kwasi A. Thornell, National President

First organized in 1968 as the Union of Black Clergy and Laity, the Union of Black Episcopalians is now a confederation of more than twenty chapters and ten interest groups throughout the continental United States and Hawaii. The purpose of the organization is to ''encourage the involvement of Black people in the total life of the Church''—in mission, stewardship, evangelism, education, sharing, liberation, empowerment, leadership, governance, and politics. The eradication of racism within the Church membership in the Episcopal Church is a major goal of the Union.

The Union of Black Episcopalians is headed by a National Board of Directors that performs functions of communication, advocacy, representation, lobbying, and promotion. The Board of Directors helps organize the chapters, but each chapter develops its own priorities.

Group Type: Denomination specific; lay/clergy
Founded: 1968
Membership: Over 20 chapters and 10 interest groups in the United States

Islam

Ahmadiyya Anjuman Ishaat Islam, Lahore, Inc.

36911 Walnut Street
Newark, CA 94560
(415) 791-6449

This branch of the Ahmadiyya organization in Islam was established in 1914 by Maulawi Muhammad Ali and four other members of the Anjuman out of ten original members nominated by the founder, Hazrat Mirza Ghulam Ahmad, when he formed the Anjuman in 1905 and declared that Anjuman would be his successor. The followers of Ali considered Ahmad the Promised Messiah and the renewer of Islam or *mujaddid*. However, they denied that Ahmad had claimed the status of prophet, as the followers of Ahmad's family believed and declared. Ali believed that Ahmad used the term *prophet* in a symbolic sense only. Because of the belief that Ahmad was a prophet, the entire community of Ahmadiyya Muslims is not regarded as authentic, and they have suffered persecution for their beliefs in many Muslim countries. Ali's branch of the Ahmadiyya Muslims came to the United States in the 1970s and was incorporated in California.

Group Type: Denomination
Founded: 1914
Publications: *The Islamic Review*, Masud Akhtar Choudry, editor, 1376 Lytelle Street, Hayward, CA 94544

Council of Islamic Organizations of America

676 St. Marks Avenue
Brooklyn, NY 11216
Hajj Amir Hassan, President

Group Type: Denomination specific; council of churches/groups

Islam, Orthodox

The Islamic Center
2551 Massachusetts Avenue, NW
Washington, DC 20008
(202) 332-8343

Group Type: Denomination

Sunni Muslims

The Islamic Center
2551 Massachusetts Avenue, NW
Washington, DC 20008
(202) 332-8343

Group Type: Denomination

Lutheran

African American Lutheran Association—Evangelical Lutheran Church in America

122 W. Franklin Avenue, Suite 600
Minneapolis, MN 55404
(612) 870-3610
The Reverend James R. Thomas, President

The African American Lutheran Association (AALA), formerly United Lutherans for Black Concerns, renamed in July, 1989, is a reflection of the merger of three Lutheran bodies. In January, 1988, the American Lutheran Church, the Lutheran Church in America, and the Association of Evangelical Lutheran Churches merged into the Evangelical Lutheran Church in America. Prior to 1988, African American Lutherans in the American Lutheran Church had been represented by the Coalition of Black Lutherans, whereas African American Lutherans in the Lutheran Church in America had been represented by the Association of Black Lutherans. In a meeting at Loyola University in Chicago, July 22-24, 1987, African American Lutherans agreed to combine the two groups as the African American Lutheran Association.

The African American Lutheran Association seeks to celebrate diversity in the human family. Toward that end, it encourages its members to become fully involved with the affairs of the church assembly, synod, regions, and congregations. The group also encourages African American Lutherans to contribute to theological discussions as writers.

At the national level, the African American Lutheran Association meets biennially. The group is also organized into chapters based in Teaneck, New Jersey; New York City; Carson, California; Philadelphia, Pennsylvania; Minneapolis, Minnesota; Oakland-San Francisco, California; Baltimore, Maryland; Chicago, Illinois; and St. Louis, Missouri. The chapters hold monthly meetings. The group publishes a newsletter, *Ujamaa*.

Group Type: Denomination specific; lay/clergy; racial/social justice

Founded: July 1987
Publications: Ujamaa, a newsletter

Association of Black Lutherans

1744 North 26th Street
Philadelphia, PA 19121
(215) 236-2090
Grover Wright, Coordinator

Group Type: Denomination specific; lay/clergy
Publications: TieLine, a newsletter, 813 West Lehigh Avenue, Philadelphia, PA 19133

Commission for Multicultural Ministries—Evangelical Lutheran Church in America

8765 West Higgins Road
Chicago, IL 60631-4185
(312) 380-2840
The Reverend Herbert W. Chilstrom, Bishop
The Reverend Craig J. Lewis, Executive Director

The Commission for Multicultural Ministries works to overcome racism and develops programs with African Americans, Hispanic Americans, Asian Americans, and Native Americans. Through the Division of Outreach, the Commission is working to ensure new ministry development in these four communities. The goal of the Commission is the full partnership of people of color and primary language other than English within the church.

The Commission is one of the churchwide agencies of the Evangelical Lutheran Church in America, which was formed in 1987 by the union of the Lutheran Church in America, the American Lutheran Church, and the Association of Evangelical Lutheran Churches. The executive director of the Commission for Multicultural Ministries is the Reverend Craig J. Lewis.

Group Type: Denomination specific; lay; administrative
Founded: 1987
Meetings: A biennial convention

Methodist

Black Methodists for Church Renewal, Inc.

601 West Riverview Avenue, Suite 325
Dayton, OH 45406
(513) 227-9460
Ms. Carolyn M. Anderson, Executive Director
Mr. Ernest Swiggett, National Chairperson

Black Methodists for Church Renewal, Inc. (BMCR), was organized in Cincinnati, Ohio, in 1968, when former members of the Central Jurisdiction realized that if African American

Methodists were to make an impact on the United Methodist Church, they must organize and become united, addressing those issues that most concern African American people. Since that time, BMCR has been actively opposing racism, while assisting the United Methodist Church to become the inclusive body as mandated by its own legislation and by the Scripture in which it is grounded.

Black Methodists for Church Renewal serves as a forum where African American Methodists may discuss problems, define issues, develop and adopt strategies for meaningful change, and develop new ways to affect the ministry. BMCR has expressed to the general church its concerns regarding the involvement of African Americans within the structure and the conduct of the church as it relates to social issues and its investment policies.

As the legitimate African American caucus recognized by the general United Methodist Church, BMCR is governed by a Board of Directors representative of five geographic jurisdictions within United Methodism in the United States. It includes lay and clergy, youth and young adults, and persons of both genders.

Black Methodists for Church Renewal have a commitment toward: 1) maximum involvement of African American persons in the total life of the church; 2) strengthening African American churches; 3) increasing the number of African American pastors to serve African American churches; 4) increasing African American membership in United Methodist churches; 5) continued support of the eleven historically African American United Methodist institutions of higher learning; and 6) encouraging dialogue and exchanges between African American sisters and brothers in the Caribbean and Africa.

Meeting annually in March, BMCR maintains offices in Dayton, Ohio, headed by the Executive Director, Ms. Carolyn Anderson. It publishes a newsletter, *NOW*. Their national chairperson is Mr. Ernest Swiggett of Brooklyn, NY.

Group Type: Denomination specific; administrative; lay/clergy
Founded: 1968
Membership: Five jurisdictional chapters/caucuses; forty-seven annual conference chapters/caucuses; and the Inter-Ethnic Strategy Development Group
Publications: NOW, a newsletter, c/o Carolyn M. Anderson, Executive Director, 601 W. Riverview, Suite 325, Dayton, OH 45406
Meetings: Annual meeting in March

Commission for Coordination of Ethnic Minority Ministries—West Ohio Conference, United Methodist Church

218 East Sandusky Street
Findlay, OH 45840
(419) 422-4131
The Reverend Joseph Pilate, Chair

Black Church Development Committee
P. O. Box 15264
Columbus, OH 43215
(614) 249-7648
Mr. Clemenzo Fox, Chair

Ethnic Minority Committee
249 East Center Street
Marion, OH 43302
(614) 387-8344
The Reverend Joseph Sprague, Chair

The Commission for Coordination of Ethnic Minority Ministries is an administrative unit in the West Ohio Conference of the United Methodist Church. Operating under this unit are the Black Church Development Committee and the Ethnic Minority Committee.

The Black Church Development Committee funds proposals and projects pertaining to the enhancement of African Americans in the church and community. The Ethnic Minority Committee funds projects and scholarships for minority persons and is interested in increasing the participation of all minorities in the United Methodist Church.

Group Type: Denomination specific; lay/clergy; racial/social justice

Council on Ethnic Affairs—Free Methodist Church of North America

P.O. Box 369
North Chili, NY 14514
(716) 594-2500
Bishop Gerald Bates, Chairman

The Council on Ethnic Affairs is an advisory body of the Free Methodist Church of North America. It concerns itself with all ethnic and minority groups, including African Americans. Its tasks are to enhance visibility of ethnic groups and ministries, to facilitate access to the higher councils of the church, and to encourage full participation of ethnic groups in general church life. Composed of laity and clergy from all over the United States, the Council works throughout the year and meets once annually. Bishop Gerald E. Bates is the chairman.

Group Type: Denomination specific; administrative; racial/social justice
Meetings: An annual meeting

General Commission on Religion and Race—United Methodist Church

110 Maryland Avenue, NE, Box 48
Washington, DC 20002
(202) 547-2271
Ms. Barbara Ricks Thompson, General Secretary
Bishop Calvin D. McConnell, President

The General Commission on Religion and Race of the United Methodist Church was formed in April, 1968. Its primary purpose is to challenge the general agencies, institutions, and connectional structures of the denomination to bring about a full and equal participation of their varied racial and ethnic constituencies in the total life and mission of the church. The Commission achieves this through advocacy and by reviewing and monitoring the practices of the entire church in order to ensure further racial inclusiveness. It is one of thirteen general agencies within the United Methodist Church.

Group Type: Denomination specific; administrative; racial/social justice
Founded: April, 1968

Pentecostal/Apostolic/Holiness

Assemblies of the Lord Jesus Christ, Inc.

875 N. White Station Road
Memphis, TN 38122
(901) 685-1969
Mr. Ray Vance, General Manager

The interracial Assemblies of the Lord Jesus Christ, Inc., is the result of the merger of three Apostolic bodies—the Assemblies of the Church of Jesus Christ, the Church of the Lord Jesus Christ, and the Jesus Only Apostolic Church of God—in 1952. Although the church is predominantly white, it has several African American and integrated churches, particularly around Memphis and Chicago. The church is congregational in polity and has an annual general conference. There is a general board that guides the church through the year, and the church is separated into state districts by geographic location. It has foreign mission programs in Colombia and Uruguay.

The denomination believes in justification and the baptism of the Holy Spirit and practices tithing, healing, and footwashing. Membership in unions and secret societies is not allowed, nor is participation in service that would demand the carrying of arms or war; however, the government is respected for its leadership. In addition, the church is fundamental in its beliefs about frivolous or immodest activity, and amusements considered worldly as well as immodest clothing and participation in school social activities and gymnastics are specifically forbidden in its articles of faith, which were partially extracted from those of the United Pentecostal Church. It publishes the *Apostolic Witness*.

Group Type: Denomination
Founded: March, 1952
Doctrine: Oneness/Apostolic
Membership: In 1971, about three hundred fifty churches
Publications: Apostolic Witness
Meetings: An annual general conference

Church of God (Anderson, Indiana) Board of Church Extension and Home Missions, Urban Ministry Division

5819 Georgia Avenue
Kansas City, KS 66104
(913) 596-1599
The Reverend Sethard A. Beverly, Director of Urban
   Ministries

Within the administrative organization of the Church of God (Anderson, IN) there are two primary offices for communication with African Americans: Urban Ministries, directed by the Reverend Sethard A. Beverly, under the Board of Church Extension and Home Missions; and the National Association of the Church of God. Urban Ministries provides guidance to pastors and congregations in the metropolitan areas. It addresses the concerns of African Americans, Hispanic Americans, Native Americans, Appalachians, and other minorities. The Urban Ministries program provides opportunities for congregations and individuals to focus on the concerns and problems of the church and the broader concerns of the community.

Group Type: Denomination specific; administrative

Church of God (Cleveland, Tennessee) Office of Black Evangelism

Keith and 25th Streets
Cleveland, TN 37311
(615) 478-7829
Dr. C. C. Pratt, Evangelism Director and Director of Black
   Affairs

The Church of God was organized on August 19, 1886, at a meeting at Barney Creek Meetinghouse in Tennessee. Under the leadership of a licensed Baptist minister, R. G. Spurling, the young organization adopted the name "Christian Union." The name was later changed to the Church of God. Although a predominantly white religious body at its inception, since 1909 the Church of God has had African American members and ministers. During 1909, Edmond S. Barr, a native of the Bahamas, attended the autumn camp meeting in Pleasant Grove, Florida, and with his wife Rebecca, received the Baptism of the Holy Ghost. Barr was licensed by the church in 1909 and ordained in 1913. He was joined by R. M. Evans on January 4, 1910. Evans is credited to be the first missionary of the Church of God.

The minutes of the Eighth General Assembly, January 7-12, 1913, lists four African American churches in Florida—Coconut Grove, Jacksonville, Webster, and Miami—and six in the Bahamas. By 1915, there were nine African American congregations in Florida. Until 1915, the supervision of African American congregations was under the white State Overseer, but at the Assembly of that year, Edmond S. Barr was appointed Overseer of the black work of the Church. Other African American leaders in the Church of God who have served in a similar capacity include: Thomas J. Richardson (1922); David LaFleur (1923-1928); J. H. Curry (1928-1938); N. S. Marcelle, Sr. (1939-1945); Bishop W. L. Ford (1945-1950); Bishop George A. Wallace (1950-1954); Bishop W. L. Ford (1954-1958); Bishop J. T. Roberts (1958-1965); Bishop David Lemons (1965-1966); H. G. Poitier (1966-1968); the Reverend Wallace J. Sibley (1968-1972); and Dr. C. C. Pratt, Director of Black Affairs and Evangelism Director.

Group Type: Denomination specific; lay/clergy
Founded: August 19, 1886
Publications: Church of God Evangel

Church of God (U.S.A.)

1207 Willow Brook Drive, SE, #2
P.O. Box 13036
Huntsville, AL 35802
(205) 881-9629
Bishop Voy M. Bullen, General Overseer

In 1884, R. G. Spurling, a Baptist minister in Monroe County, Tennessee, began to seek Scripture as an answer to problems of formality, "modernism," and a lack of spirituality. At a meeting in August, 1886, a new movement that would reform and revive churches as well as preach primitive church holiness was organized, and thus the Christian Union was begun. Most of the Pentecostal churches with the name "Church of God" can be traced back to this meeting. Spurling soon died, and his son, R. G. Spurling, Jr., succeeded him.

After ten years and little growth, three laymen influenced by the Spurlings claimed a "deep religious experience," similar to that of John Wesley of Methodism, and began to preach sanctification. They began to hold services at Camp Creek, Cherokee County, North Carolina. Spurling and the Christian Union joined with them, and during the following revival, spontaneous speaking in tongues occurred. The group saw this as a biblical occurrence and as a new outpouring of the Holy Spirit (Acts 2:1-4).

After community complaints about the noisy services and lack of restraint of the members speaking in tongues, several leaders of the Christian Union decided to make the services more orderly. The group changed its name to the Holiness Church. Ambrose J. Tomlinson, an agent of the American Bible Society with a Quaker background, came to the revival in 1896 to sell his wares. He joined the group in 1903 and became pastor of the Camp Creek Church. This event is seen as the beginning of the Church of God movement. Tomlinson was influenced by the Church of God (Anderson, Indiana), and persuaded the group to accept the biblical name Church of God. Tomlinson started a publishing enterprise and printed the doctrines of the church for distribution. He became the dominant leader, and the church's headquarters was moved to his home in Culbertson, Tennessee. He and the church's headquarters later moved to Cleveland, Tennessee.

The first assembly of the churches resulting from its quick expansion was held in 1906 at Camp Creek, North Carolina. It was decided that footwashing should be observed at least annually, and midweek family services were promoted. The name of the church was officially changed to the Church of God at the 1907 assembly.

G. B. Cashwell attended the 1908 assembly and introduced the idea of baptism of the Holy Spirit and speaking in tongues as witnessed at the Azusa Street Revival in Los Angeles. Tomlinson subsequently was baptized by the Holy Spirit and spoke in tongues. He was made general moderator of the church in 1909 and was elected general overseer for life in 1914.

Before Tomlinson's death in 1943, he appointed his eldest son, Homer, his successor; however, the General Assembly selected his younger son, Milton, as the new general overseer. A meeting of his followers was called by Bishop Homer Tomlinson in New York. The church was reorganized and distinguished from its predecessor and others by the addition of "World Headquarters." After a court decision, Bishop Homer Tomlinson continued to lead his loyal followers and rebuilt the church. He remained general overseer until his death in 1968 and was succeeded by the current general overseer, Voy M. Bullen.

The doctrine of the church, sometimes known as the Church of God (World Headquarters), is similar to that of other Church of God bodies with the exception of premillennialism. In the minutes of the 81st General Assembly of 1986, the body reaffirmed its belief that a government without God has no lasting peace and that which is obtained is through force. The body upholds the following basic beliefs:

1) People get into God's Kingdom by being born again;
2) Jesus gave the prayer to his disciples and instructed them to pray according to Matthew 6:10, "Thy Kingdom come, thy will be done, in earth as in Heaven."
3) The end will come when this gospel of Jesus is preached to all nations;
4) All Christians who believe in Jesus Christ as the Son of God and are born again are part of the Kingdom of Christ and will surely be just as much a part of bringing the Kingdom of God in earth as the Church of God;
5) Through the Gospel of Jesus Christ evil forces will be overturned and God's Kingdom will fill the whole earth.

According to the *Encyclopedia of American Religions* (2nd ed.), these beliefs are based on the Bible as interpreted by A. J. Tomlinson. The pacifist emphasis found in many Pentecostal churches is also attributed to him.

The interracial Church of God is episcopal in administration and is considered evangelical in its doctrines of justification by faith, sanctification as a second work of grace, and of baptism by the Holy Ghost as witnessed by speaking in other tongues and healing.

The Church of God operates mission programs in Barbados, Canada, Egypt, England, Haiti, Ghana, Greece, Jamaica, Kenya, Liberia, Nigeria, Panama, and Scotland. Its mission work has been extended to the Philippines and the U.S. Virgin Islands. The Church of God publishes a newsletter, its book of doctrine, and a Sunday school quarterly.

Group Type: Denomination
Founded: 1903
Publications: Day by Day, a history of the denomination by A. J. Tomlinson; The Church of God (newsletter), and a book of doctrine
Meetings: Annual meeting at Chaffee, Missouri in August

General Assembly of the Church of God (Anderson, Indiana)

P.O. Box 2420
1303 East Fifth Street
Anderson, Indiana 46018
(317) 642-0255 or (202) 347-5889
The Reverend Dr. G. David Cox, Chairman of the Executive Board

The Church of God (Anderson, Indiana) was founded in 1881 by Daniel S. Warner and several others who were disappointed in denominational structures and their emphasis on formal creeds. The early pioneers sought to restore unity and holiness to the church by promoting primary allegiance to Jesus Christ and reducing denominational distinctions. It has developed into a denomination that strives to promote spiritual fellowship with minimal emphasis on formal institutional structures. As such, the body is Congregational in structure and Holiness in doctrine. Congregations determine their own programs and activities. Ministers are ordained. There are national and state organizations that support the operation of the church.

The Church of God (Anderson, Indiana) is predominantly a

white religious body, but highly integrated in its operational administration. African Americans occupy prominent leadership positions throughout all facets of the church. The General Assembly of the Church of God is composed of ordained ministers, unordained ministers who are full-time pastors, and laypersons who are elected or appointed to membership on the Executive Council, one of the subordinate boards, commissions, or committees. The General Assembly determines policy for the general business of the church, elects membership on the subordinate boards and units of its work, and approves the World Service budget. It is the most representative decision-making body in the Church of God (Anderson, Indiana). The Reverend Dr. G. David Cox is chairperson of the Executive Committee.

Within the administrative organization of the denomination there are two primary offices for communication with African Americans: Urban Ministries, directed by the Reverend Sethard A. Beverly, under the Board of Church Extension and Home Missions; and the National Association of the Church of God.

The Church of God (Anderson, Indiana) operates several seminaries and Bible colleges. African American students are enrolled in all these institutions, but two institutions are especially noteworthy. They are: Bay Ridge Christian College in Kendleton, Texas, and Southern California School of Ministry in Los Angeles, California. These two institutions generally serve African Americans. Both are supported by the national body.

Group Type: Denomination specific; administrative; lay/clergy
Founded: 1881

National Association of the Church of God (Anderson, Indiana)

P.O. Box 357
West Middlesex, PA 16159
(412) 528-9347
Alvin Lewis, Executive Secretary

The National Association of the Church of God is a primarily African American constituency affiliated with the Church of God (Anderson, Indiana) which, guided by the vision of Elisha Wimbush, mobilizes ministries and resources through national forums to remind, inspire, renew, equip, and enable persons to live in obedience to Jesus Christ. It sponsors an annual camp meeting in August at West Middlesex, Pennsylvania. It conducts other auxiliary functions throughout the year. It operates a youth summer camping program. A national inspirational youth convention is held annually in December between Christmas and New Year's Day.

The National Association of the Church of God publishes *The Shining Light*, Wilfred Jordan, editor, 1612 E. 10th Street, Anderson, Indiana 46012, (317) 644-1593.

Group Type: Denomination specific; lay/clergy
Publications: The Shining Light
Meetings: Annual camp meeting in August in West Middlesex, Pennsylvania; national inspirational youth convention held in December between Christmas and New Year's Day; each convention averages an attendance of approximately 4,000–5,000 persons

Presbyterian

National Black Presbyterian Caucus

2923 Hawthorne Avenue
Richmond, VA 23222
(804) 321-3433
Mrs. Willie Dell, President
The Reverend Elias Hardge, Vice President

Presbyterian Church (U.S.A.)
100 Witherspoon Street, Room 2008
Louisville, KY 40202-1396
(502) 569-5698
The Reverend Dr. Otis Turner, Staff Liaison

The National Black Presbyterian Caucus traces its beginning to 1807, with the founding of the First African Presbyterian Church in Philadelphia, Pennsylvania. By the 1850s, members of the African American Presbyterian clergy had acted in conjunction with members of the Congregational denomination to fight slavery and injustices against African Americans. From these early efforts, the Afro-American Presbyterian Council was formed in Philadelphia in 1894. It served to provide mutual support and fellowship for African American Presbyterians and assisted or encouraged the integrationist forces. This organization became known as the Presbyterian Council of the North and West in 1947. Presbyterians Concerned was formed in 1964 and Black Presbyterians United in 1968. These groups addressed the needs and the conditions of each era.

The National Black Presbyterian Caucus, formerly known as Black Presbyterians United, serves to use its influence and power to achieve equal and full participation in the United Presbyterian Church. It provides educational programs that promote African American history, and it produces educational resources that present positive images of the African American experience. The organization acts as an advocate within the church and monitors the participation of African Americans at all levels of the church.

The sixty-five thousand-member-strong National Black Presbyterian Caucus holds its national annual meeting in April. Regional and chapter meetings are also held annually. Members are found in 450 congregations nationwide, with approximately ten thousand participating in predominantly white congregations. The president is Mrs. Willie Dell, and the vice-president is the Reverend Elias Hardge. Staff support for the National Black Presbyterian Caucus is provided through the Racial Ethnic Ministry Unit. The Reverend Dr. Otis Turner, coordinator of social justice policy development for the Presbyterian Church (U.S.A.), serves as the staff liaison.

Group Type: Denomination specific; lay/clergy; racial/social justice

Founded: 1807
Membership: 65,000 persons in 450 congregations
Meetings: An annual meeting in April; annual regional and chapter meetings

Racial Ethnic Ministry Unit—Presbyterian Church (U.S.A.) Racial Justice Ministry

Racial Justice Ministry
100 Witherspoon Street, Room 2001
Louisville, KY 40202-1396
(502) 569-5688
The Reverend Dr. Wesley Woo, Coordinator

Group Type: Denomination specific; administrative; racial/social justice

Racial Ethnic Ministry Unit—Presbyterian Church (U.S.A.) Social Justice Policy Development

Social Justice Policy Development
100 Witherspoon Street, Room 2008
Louisville, KY 40202-1396
(502) 569-5698
The Reverend Dr. Otis Turner, Coordinator

Group Type: Denomination specific; administrative; racial/social justice

Reformed Church in America

Black Council—Reformed Church in America

475 Riverside Drive
New York, NY 10115
The Reverend M. William Howard, Jr., Executive Director
(212) 870-2538

The Reformed Church (called "Presbyterian" in Scotland) had its earliest roots in a split between Ulrich Zwingli and Martin Luther over whether the glorified Christ is present in the bread and wine of Communion. Insisting that bread and wine were simply symbols, Zwingli reformed his group into a separate branch of Protestantism. The Reformed Church first immigrated to the United States from the Netherlands, where it was the official church.

The Dutch were active participants in the slave trade from Africa to the New World. In America, Reformed Protestant Dutch Church ministers and laity owned slaves, and there is some evidence that they did not consider blacks to be people. But in 1783, a significant change was noted when the Church agreed to receive blacks into membership without consent of their masters and mistresses, citing that the Bible stated no such condition and because "care should be taken 'for the promotion and establishment of households.' "

The Reformed Protestant Dutch Church was more squarely faced with the question of slavery in 1855, when the North Carolina Classis of the German Reformed Church sought to unite with the church. Questions raised at the General Synod resulted in tabling of the motion.

After the Civil War, toward the end of the nineteenth century, the Church (from 1867, called the Reformed Church in America) considered the possibility of doing mission work among African Americans. This discussion came about because of the efforts of a Reformed minister, Dr. W. L. Johnson, the first African American to graduate from the Reformed Seminary, in New Brunswick, New Jersey. There is some debate over Johnson's graduation. A historic survey of black presence in the Dutch Reformed Church conducted by Dr. Noel Erskine indicated that Dr. Johnson was one of the first graduates of

Brunswick Seminary. This account is also supported in the denominational minutes. There is no record of protest from the seminary regarding Johnson's claim during his lifetime.

Johnson did eventually find the Classis of Philadelphia to be somewhat receptive to his concerns, and the General Synod of the Reformed Church in America did, in 1902, accept the two African American churches (both located in South Carolina) begun by Johnson as member churches of the denomination. However, the African American churches were transferred over to the Presbyterian Church in 1926 (after the death of Johnson, in 1913).

In 1919, the Reformed Church assumed responsibility for the Southern Normal School at Brewton, Alabama. Southern Normal had been founded in 1911 and recruited most of its teachers from Tuskegee Institute. When the active and productive work among African Americans being conducted by the Presbyterians was pointed out, it effectively quelled early opposition to this decision. Over the years, the denomination did undertake to aid Brewton School students in their efforts to attend Reformed colleges and New Brunswick Theological Seminary.

In the 1950s, the Reformed Church became interested in inner-city and storefront ministries. African Americans began to join Reformed churches, particularly those in the New York area. The problem often was that as African Americans joined, whites left. A 1964 request by the Board of North American Mission that the General Synod authorize it to form a "Commission on Race," resulted in the establishment of the Commission on Race Relations.

In 1900, the Reformed Church in America expressed kinship with the Dutch Reformed Church in South Africa. In 1967, however, the Reformed Church stated that the Dutch Reformed Church's continued support of its government's policy toward the eleven million African Americans of South Africa was a cause of "anguish, shame and embarrassment."

On June 6, 1969, James Foreman of the National Black Economic Development Conference (NBEDC) led a group that occupied the Reformed Church in America national headquarters in New York and presented a "Black Manifesto." The manifesto came out of the NBEDC meeting held in Detroit, April 25-27, 1969. An Ad Hoc Committee appointed by the Reformed Church to respond to Foreman's demands recommended, among other things, that a caucus of African American leadership within the church be called together as a Black Council, which would share in program and capital development formulation; that $100,000 be transferred to them to fund their proposals; and that the power to make decisions having to do with current and future programs affecting minorities be entrusted to minorities. The Black Council was formed in August, 1969, by Elders Clyde Watts, John Ashley, and Edgar Dillard.

Since that time, the Black Council has served as a monitor and advocate of African American concerns within the denomination. Composed of clergy, laity, and young people and representing more than forty-five churches, the primary thrust of the Black Council is to ensure the full participation of people of African descent in the life of the Reformed Church in America. The Council has emphasized leadership development, self-reliance for local congregations, and a wide range of social issues. Through its efforts, the Reformed Church in America has taken a leadership role in opposition to South African apartheid.

African Americans comprise approximately 2.5 percent of the membership in the Reformed Church in America. The church has a strong connection to the Black Dutch Reformed Church in South Africa, which opposes apartheid. The Reformed Church in America has just had its first African American president. Dr. Wilbur T. Washington, pastor of the First Reformed Church in Jamaica, Queens, New York, served his one-year term from 1988 to 1989. Prior to that, he served as vice-president. The tenure for the presidency is one year, with the vice-president automatically elected to the presidency in the succeeding year.

The Black Council meets regularly four times yearly, with its annual meeting taking place in October. In 1989, its twentieth anniversary year, their meetings included a national assembly in the New York metropolitan area.

The Black Council publishes a monthly newsletter, *Black Caucus RCA*. It also publishes an annual lectureship in honor of its first chairperson, the Reverend B. Moses James (an alumnus of the Howard University School of Divinity). The Executive Director of the Black Council is the Reverend M. William Howard, Jr.

Group Type: Denomination specific; lay/clergy; racial/social justice
Founded: 1969
Membership: Representatives from 45 churches
Publications: *Black Caucus RCA*, a monthly newsletter
Meetings: Meets four times yearly; annual meeting in October; 20th anniversary meeting, 1989

Roman Catholic

Knights of Peter Claver

The National Headquarters
1825 Orleans Avenue
New Orleans, LA 70116
(504) 821-4225
Mr. Paul C. Condoll, Supreme Knight
Mr. W. Charles Keyes, Jr., Executive National Secretary

The Knights of Peter Claver was founded in Mobile, Alabama, in 1909, by four Josephite priests—Fathers C. F. Rebesher, S. J. Kelly, P. Van Baast, and John H. Dorsey—and three laymen—G. Faustina, F. Collins, and F. Trenier. It was incorporated two years later. It is a national fraternal organization of more than 100,000 Catholic families in the United States. The name refers to Peter Claver, a Jesuit priest from Spain assigned to Cartagena, Colombia, in the early 1600s. As a port in the "Middle Passage," Cartagena (located on the Caribbean Sea) was the arrival point of some one thousand slaves monthly. Father Claver took upon himself an "apostolate of presence," ministering to the newly arrived slaves in defiance of local custom. During his forty years of service, he is said to have converted 300,000 people to Christianity. The elite group of believers, for whom the organizational name is taken, was organized by Father Claver to assist him in his work. They were considered to be the first Knights of Peter Claver. Father Claver died on September 8, 1654, and was canonized by Pope Leo XIII on January 15, 1888.

Today, the Knights of Peter Claver concern themselves with educational, recreational, and athletic events; they come together to share the eucharist at mass; they contribute monies to many causes including the NAACP, the National Urban League, and the Southern Christian Leadership Conference; and they staunchly support their local parishes. They have established the Thomas R. Lee, Jr., Memorial Scholarship (1970) and the Willie Polk, Jr., Memorial Scholarship (1977). They have conducted a sickle-cell program, and since 1978 they have maintained a development fund at Xavier University in New Orleans. It is an interracial lay organization. The National Office Building, located in New Orleans, was dedicated in 1976.

The Knights of Peter Claver meet on the state, district, and national levels. The Junior Knights (a division for boys) was founded in 1917, and the Junior Daughters (a division for girls) was established in 1930. The Ladies Auxiliary was authorized in 1922 and later recognized as a division of the Knights of Peter Claver in 1926. In 1980, the Ladies of Grace, Fourth Degree Division, was established.

Group Type: Denomination specific; lay
Founded: 1909
Membership: Over one hundred thousand Catholic families in the United States

Knights of Peter Claver, Ladies Auxiliary

1127 W. Gilman Road
Lafayette, LA 70501
(318) 235-7982
Ms. Dorothy Henderson, Supreme Lady

The Knights of Peter Claver, Ladies Auxiliary, was authorized in 1922 and later recognized as a division of the Knights of Peter Claver in 1926. In 1980, the Ladies of Grace, Fourth Degree Division, was established.

Group Type: Denomination specific; women; lay
Founded: 1922; reorganized in 1926

National Association of Black Catholic Administrators

50 North Park Avenue
Rockville Center, NY 11570
(516) 678-5800, x615 or 616
Mrs. Barbara Horsham-Brathwaite, Chairperson

The National Association of Black Catholic Administrators (NABCA), established in 1976 by the Reverend Jerome Robinson, is dedicated to addressing the spiritual and social needs of African American Catholics and the question of oppression in the African American communities it serves. As an influential association within the African American Catholic community, NABCA's commitment extends to the world needs of its brothers and sisters in their struggle against oppression. It is comprised of vicars for African American Catholics and diocesan directors of Offices for Black Ministry. It also includes African American Catholic leadership from diocesan agencies or programs ministering to the African American Catholic community from over fifty Roman Catholic archdioceses and dioceses around the country.

NABCA meets twice a year. In addition, there is a retreat in the spring and an in-service training session in the fall. The fall program is designed to assist both the professional and neophyte manager to become proficient in managerial skills. These skills include, but are not limited to: planning; implementation and evaluation of goals and objectives for various programs; communication techniques; budget administration, negotiation and conflict resolution skills; and a functional understanding of the Revised Code of Canon Law. The peer support and collaborative efforts of the group assist its members, many of whom are laity, to understand church structure and how to work productively within the strata of the church.

An important activity of NABCA is its leadership of the National Black Catholic Congress. The last Congress (1987) focused on evangelization in the African American community, an effort NABCA regards as a way of expanding the communities its members serve. The next Congress, Congress VIII, will be held in 1992.

The officers of NABCA are chairperson, vice-chairperson, secretary, and treasurer. The organization is governed by a board of directors that includes the four officers and seven regional coordinators elected by representatives of their respective region.

Group Type: Denomination specific; administrative
Founded: 1976

National Black Catholic Clergy Caucus

1419 V Street, NW, Suite 400
Washington, DC 20009
(202) 328-0718

Brother Roy Smith, C.S.C., President
(219) 233-8273
The Reverend Warren Savage, Vice-president
(413) 732-1422

The National Black Catholic Clergy Caucus is a fraternal organization that supports the spiritual and theological education of African American clergy and laypersons within the Catholic Church. The Caucus is a means through which the many contributions of African Americans to the Catholic Church may be noted and appreciated, and the effectiveness of African Americans within the Church may be perceived. In addition, the Caucus takes a stand in the battle against institutional and societal racism. The Caucus sponsors the Institute of Black Catholic Studies at Xavier University in New Orleans, Louisiana, each summer. The Master of Theology degree may be granted upon completion of this program. Brother Roy Smith is the current president. The organization meets annually in late summer (July/August).

Group Type: Denomination specific; ministerial
Publications: A newsletter, a directory of African American clergy revised annually, and through a joint effort, *The African American Catholic Hymnal*, GIA Publications, 7404 South Mason Avenue, Chicago, Illinois 60638
Meetings: Annual joint conference held in late summer (July/August) in conjunction with the National Black Sisters' Conference and the National Black Catholic Seminarian Association

National Black Catholic Congress, Inc.

320 Cathedral Street
Baltimore, MD 21201
(301) 547-5330
Bishop John H. Ricard, S.S.J., National Coordinator
Ms. Leodia Gooch, Executive Director

The National Black Catholic Congress (NBCC) was established in Washington, D.C., in response to the need for greater communication among African American Catholics throughout the United States. In April 1986 the organization was incorporated in Baltimore, Maryland, where it maintains its national headquarters. Stemming from the tradition of convening African American Catholics together to address issues pertinent to the collective presence of African Americans in the Catholic Church, the National Black Catholic Congress, Inc., demonstrates the continuing African American interest in Catholicism. It serves as a communications network for persons interested in understanding the role, function, and status of African Americans in the Catholic Church.

The organizational autonomy of the NBCC was created through the administrative aegis of Bishop John H. Ricard, S.S.J., who in 1985 called for the establishment of a permanent office to facilitate and coordinate the planning efforts to convene African American Catholics in their first national meeting of the twentieth century. This meeting, Congress VI, was held at The Catholic University of America, May 21-24, 1987. It was the sixth Congress of African American Catholics to be held in the United States. The previous congresses were: Congress I, January 1-4, 1889 (Washington, DC); Congress II, July 8-11, 1890 (Cincinnati, OH); Congress III, January 5-7, 1892 (Philadelphia, PA); Congress IV, September, 1893 (Chicago, IL); and Congress V, October 8-11, 1894 (Baltimore, MD). Congress VII is scheduled for 1992. Additional information on the specific time and place for this event is unavailable.

The NBCC consists of representatives from 110 dioceses throughout the United States. It operates in conjunction with the five major national African American Catholic organizations: the National Black Clergy Caucus; the National Black Sisters' Conference; Knights of Peter Claver and the Ladies Auxiliary; the National Association of Black Catholic Administrators; and the Black Catholic Bishops of the United States. Administrative oversight is provided by the Executive Director of the Secretariat for Black Catholics, Ms. Beverly A. Carroll, under the direction of the African American Catholic bishops in the United States. These Bishops are:

Bishop Moses B. Anderson, S.S.E, Detroit, Michigan;
Bishop Carl A. Fisher, S.S.J., Los Angeles, California;
Bishop Joseph Francis, S.V.D., Newark, New Jersey;
Bishop Wilton D. Gregory, Chicago, Illinois;
Bishop Curtis Guillory, S.V.D., Galveston, Texas;
Bishop Joseph L. Howze, Biloxi, Mississippi;
Archbishop James P. Lyke, O.F.M., Atlanta, Georgia;
Archbishop Eugene A. Marino, S.S.J.;
Bishop Emerson J. Moore, New York, New York;
Bishop Leonard Olivier, S.V.D., Washington, DC;
Bishop Harold R. Perry, S.V.D., New Orleans, Louisiana;
Bishop John H. Ricard, S.S.J., Baltimore, Maryland; and
Bishop J. Terry Steib, S.V.D., St. Louis, Missouri.

The first NBCC Executive Director was Therese Wilson-Favors, who served in this capacity until November 1988. Bishop John H. Ricard, S.S.J., Ph.D., is the national coordinator.

Group Type: Denomination specific; administrative; lay/clergy

National Black Catholic Seminarian Association

St. Joseph's Seminary
1200 Varnum Street, NE
Washington, DC 20017
(202) 526-4231
The Reverend Donald Goodley, S.S.J., President

Established in 1969 by Father Clarence Williams, CPPS (Congregation of the Most Precious Blood), as a fraternity for African American Catholic seminarians (candidates for the priesthood and brotherhood), the National Black Catholic Seminarian Association (NBCSA) includes seminarians from throughout the United States and the Virgin Islands. The primary purpose of the organization is to provide supportive and formative experiences for its approximately 300 members, the majority of whom are being educated in predominantly white environments. The NBCSA has a maintenance and sustenance program designed to assist individuals in becoming more responsible for their own education and formation. The goal of the program is that seminarians be affirmed, as well as retained, in their educational situations. This program is the group's first attempt to work with church authority.

The National Black Catholic Seminarian Association is a subsidiary of the National Black Catholic Clergy Caucus and is affiliated with the National Black Sisters Conference. The group meets annually in the summer; there are also biannual

regional meetings and quarterly board meetings. They publish a quarterly newsletter.

Group Type: Denomination specific; student
Founded: 1969
Membership: Approximately three hundred men
Publications: A quarterly newsletter
Meetings: Annual joint conference held in July in conjunction with the National Black Catholic Clergy Caucus and the National Black Sisters' Conference; biannual regional meetings and quarterly board meetings

National Black Lay Catholic Caucus

3015 4th Street, NE
Washington, DC 20017
(202) 635-1778
Mr. Walter T. Hubbard, Executive Director

Founded in 1970, the National Black Lay Catholic Caucus is one of several groups under the umbrella of the National Office of Black Catholics. The organization concerns itself with the efforts of African American Catholics in the areas of liturgy, education, pastoral ministry, international programs, local leadership development, social and political issues, and evangelization.

Group Type: Denomination specific; lay
Founded: 1970

National Black Sisters' Conference

1001 Lawrence Street, NE, Suite 102
Washington, DC 20017
(202) 529-9250
Sister Barbara Spear, O.S.P., President
Sister Gwynette Proctor, S.N.D., Executive Director

Established in August 1968, the National Black Sisters' Conference (NBSC) is an organization of African American religious women from across the United States. Its purpose is to strive to provide ongoing communication and dialogue that focus on the education and support of African American nuns. The NBSC holds an annual meeting and conducts an annual joint conference of African American priests, nuns, brothers, seminarians, and deacons. It also conducts a ministry clearinghouse for African American women who want to minister within the African American community and a resource center for statistical research of African American sisters throughout the United States. The overall organizational mission is to foster: education and support of African American sisters toward effective ministry; education toward community control of African American communities; training of others in community organization and development; development of religious education from an African American perspective; development of African American spirituality; and identification of African American sisters throughout the United States.

The organizational goals of the National Black Sisters' Conference are:

1) to develop the personal resources of individual sisters for the deepening of spirituality and promotion of unity and solidarity among African American religious women;

2) to study, speak, and act on conditions and issues in the social, educational, economic, and religious milieus in the United States that involve moral, Christian principles;

3) to urge our society, especially the Roman Catholic Church and religious congregations, to respond with Christian enthusiasm to the need for eradicating the powerlessness, the poverty, and the distorted self-image of victimized African American people by responsibly encouraging white people to address themselves to the roots of racism in their own social, professional, and spiritual milieus;

4) to help promote a positive self-image among African American religious women and African American people through knowledge of and appreciation of the beauty of our rich historic, religious, and cultural heritage;

5) to give impetus to boldly innovative forms of community action and to participate in existing programs in the civic communities that comprise the respective communities in which the members are present;

6) to initiate, organize, and participate in self-help programs through which the African American community can be further educated, and to encourage the utilization of these resources within the African American community;

7) to develop and utilize the existing organizations within the African American Catholic Church community to enhance the growth of African American religious leadership within the church and in religious communities; and

8) to establish and maintain consultative, contributing, and cooperative relationships with the National Conference of Catholic Bishops, the Secretariat for Black Catholics, all national organizations of religious women, national African American Catholic organizations, and national African American organizations working for the liberation of African American people.

In August, 1983, the NBSC established Sojourner House in Detroit, Michigan, to assist in developing the spiritual needs of African American lay and religious women ministering in the church. It serves as a resource for religious congregations preparing to minister within or seeking vocations from the African American community. Sojourner House provides support, respite, and healing that enables women to regain perspective and restore balance.

Group Type: Denomination specific; women
Founded: 1968
Membership: Approximately seven hundred women
Publications: *Signs of Soul*, a newsletter; ''Tell It Like It Is''—Catechetics from the Black Perspective
Meetings: Annual joint conference held in July in conjunction with the National Black Catholic Clergy Caucus and the National Black Catholic Seminarian Association

National Catholic Conference for Interracial Justice

3033 4th Street, NE
Washington, DC 20017
(202) 529-6480
Mr. Jerome Ernst, Executive Director

The National Catholic Conference for Interracial Justice (NCCIJ), established in 1958, is an independent racial and social justice organization that focuses on the Catholic Church. It addresses the issues of civil rights and racism. It specifically focuses on the problems of exclusion of minorities from the institutional church. Its goal is to create an inclusive church by combating institutional racism.

The National Catholic Conference for Interracial Justice fosters collaboration among all races by promoting activities and programs to raise the consciousness within the church. As part of its mission it addresses crises caused by racial tensions. It conducts annual and regional conferences and develops and disseminates information/resource packets designed to promote cultural diversity. Among these packets is the ''Martin Luther King, Jr., Celebration Packet,'' which provides meaningful examples on how the church could observe the national holiday commemorating the slain civil rights leader. Included are recommendations for liturgy, parish bulletins, and other related activities. Portions of the packets are translated into several languages and written from the cultural perspective of diverse groups. In addition, the NCCIJ provides resource materials to assist local dioceses in developing and implementing affirmative action plans and in identifying mechanisms that may be adopted to create more inclusive religious orders.

Group Type: Denomination specific; lay/clergy; racial/social justice
Founded: 1958
Publications: *Commitment*, a quarterly newsletter

National Office for Black Catholics

3025 4th Street, NE
Washington, DC 20017
(202) 635-1778
Mr. Walter T. Hubbard, Executive Director

The National Office for Black Catholics was begun in 1970 as a result of a movement involving priests, religious brothers and sisters, and laity who were advocates for African American Catholics within the Church. The goals of this service organization are: 1) to share with U.S. Catholics the rich religious, intellectual, and cultural tradition of the African American Catholic community; 2) to enable African American Catholics to assume a greater responsibility for and participation in the Catholic Church and the African American community; 3) to assist African American Catholics and the Church in general in making effective contributions to the total African American community; and 4) to influence the Catholic Church in America to recognize, take action, and eradicate racism within its own structure and assume a more forceful stand on this issue in American society.

The National Office for Black Catholics conducts workshops, assists parishes and schools, and distributes books, records, and other materials. The Office joins with other organizations, such as the Leadership Conference on Civil Rights and the Congressional Black Caucus, in its social action and advocacy efforts.

Representing more than one million African American Catholics, the National Office for Black Catholics is governed by a Board of Directors and run by a central staff that, together with consultants, concerns itself with evangelism, education, liturgy, vocations, and lay ministry. More than sixty percent of its operating budget is provided through the contributions of the membership. The National Office maintains contact with the National Conference of Catholic Bishops through an Ad Hoc Committee that represents it before that body.

Group Type: Denomination specific; state group or convention
Founded: 1970
Membership: Represents more than one million persons

Secretariat for Black Catholics

3211 4th Street, NE
Washington, DC 20017
(202) 541-3177
Ms. Beverly A. Carroll, Executive Director

This office represents African Americans in the Roman Catholic Church in the United States. It provides communication and information on African American Catholics throughout all of the dioceses in the United States. It is the major national office of the National Conference of Catholic Bishops for communication with its African American constituency.

The official activities of the Secretariat for Black Catholics are coordinated by an executive director appointed by the Bishops' Committee. The Bishops' Committee is composed of the American Catholic Bishops in the United States, who are elected by the general body of bishops. They include:

Bishop Moses B. Anderson, S.S.E., Detroit, Michigan;
Bishop Carl A. Fisher, S.S.J., Los Angeles, California;
Bishop Joseph Francis, S.V.D., Newark, New Jersey;
Bishop Joseph Florenza, Galveston-Houston, Texas;
Bishop Joseph Gozman, Raleigh, North Carolina;
Archbishop Eugene A. Marino, S.S.J.;
Bishop John H. Ricard, S.S.J., Baltimore, Maryland.

Group Type: Denomination specific; administrative
Founded: 1988
Meetings: The Bishops' Committee (comprising Roman Catholic bishops in the United States) meets three times a year, generally in January and during the Spring and November General Meetings of the U.S. Catholic Bishops

Unitarian Universalist

African American Unitarian Universalist Ministry

25 Beacon Street
Boston, MA 02108
(617) 742-2100
Mark Morrison-Reed and William E. Jones, Co-conveners

The African American Unitarian Universalist Ministry (AAUUM) was founded in November 1988 in Washington, D.C. by Mel Hoover and Mark Morrison-Reed. It was conceived by the Affirmative Action Task Force for African American Ministers of the Unitarian Universalist Association's Department of Ministry. The twenty-member organization is composed of religious professionals (ministers, directors of religious education, denominational employees, etc.) from the United States and meets annually.

AAUUM is developing African American–oriented worship material to be included in the 1991 Unitarian Universalist Association Meditation Manual, in addition to a resource notebook. Its future plans include the development of African American–focused historical brochures and resources as well as archival material. A theological convocation on the meaning of liberation theology for liberal religion is also planned. Its annual meeting is held in the fall. Mark Morrison-Reed and William E. Jones serve as co-conveners of the organization.

Group Type: Denomination specific; lay/clergy

Founded: November 1988
Membership: Approximately twenty-five persons
Meetings: An annual meeting in the fall

Department for Social Justice— Unitarian Universalist Association

25 Beacon Street
Boston, MA 02108
(617) 742-2100
Ms. Loretta Williams, Director

Together with the Department for Extension, the Department for Social Justice of the Unitarian Universalist Association seeks to counter the color line on all levels of the denomination and in society in general. The department, founded in 1961, concerns itself primarily with advocacy and education and works on projects ranging from opposition of white supremacist groups to civil rights legislation. The department is based in the denominational headquarters in Boston and also works through a Washington, DC office. The department's director, Ms. Loretta Williams, is also a member of the National Interreligious Commission on Civil Rights.

Group Type: Denomination specific; administrative; racial/social justice
Founded: 1961

United Church of Christ

Commission for Racial Justice—United Church of Christ, Inc.

700 Prospect Avenue
Cleveland, OH 44120
(216) 241-5400
The Reverend Dr. Benjamin F. Chavis, Jr., Executive
   Director

The Commission for Racial Justice (CRJ) is a national body of the United Church of Christ, Inc., created at the Sixth General Synod in 1967. It provides leadership in mobilizing the membership of the church to continue in the struggle for racial justice; assists the national African American community and other minority communities in becoming self-determined, self-directed, and self-controlled; and assists African Americans and other ethnic constituencies of the United Church of Christ to organize effectively and maximize their impact and influence upon the church and its decision-making processes. It also serves as a coordinating consultative unit for local churches and entities of the United Church of Christ and develops new policies and practices to meet the needs of minority persons. Finally, it provides a national denominational liaison with ecumenical, interfaith, secular, and other concerned efforts seeking to effect social change wherein racial justice becomes reality.

Among its national programs is the Community Organization Program, which provided a national voter registration and education program in cooperation with Operation PUSH. It also sponsored a successful "Freedom Riders 1987" campaign to mobilize voters in Chicago. The youth development component of the program sponsors "Project Hotel," a leadership development project for African American and Hispanic American youth in New York City's welfare hotels. The Information and Resource Development Program is responsible for publishing *Racial Justice Alerts*, which are sent to conferences, associations, and various churches of the United Church of Christ. It is also responsible for the weekly publication and audiotape distribution of *Civil Rights Journal* commentaries, which are published in over three hundred newspapers and aired over two hundred fifty radio stations weekly. The Leadership, Development, and Training Programs provide assistance to Ministers for Racial and Social Justice and United Black Christians in regional and national organizational development. Leadership training is also provided to church and community groups as requested.

CRJ has also implemented a national study on the issue of toxic hazards occurring in defenseless, poor, and minority communities. The project ended with a national computer-based study and report, "Toxic Waste and Race in the United States," which made recommendations to municipal, state, and federal governments concerning this issue. Several communities particularly affected have been assisted through this project. Through the Developing Field Program, CRJ has assisted in the organizational development and coordination of the National Black Leadership Roundtable (NBLR), a national umbrella organization of over five hundred national, community, church-related, civil rights, and professional organizations located in Washington, DC. NBLR meets periodically to focus on the national agenda of African America. In 1967, CRJ initiated its Special Higher Education Program, which recognizes minority students with marginal academic and/or economic backgrounds and helps them realize their potential through college education and a support system of placement, funding, referral, and counseling. Financial assistance has been given to over five thousand college students since the program began.

There are three field offices, located in Washington, DC, Enfield, North Carolina, and Chicago, Illinois. In addition to coordinating programs and activities with the national office, they assist the local United Church of Christ membership in involvement with programs and issues of racial justice. The Commission for Racial Justice offers various resources such as publications, videotapes, and posters through its offices. The Reverend Dr. Benjamin F. Chavis, Jr., is the executive director.

Group Type: Denomination specific; administrative; racial/social justice
Founded: 1967
Publications: *Civil Rights Journal*, a weekly commentary by the executive director on issues related to racial justice; *Like a Ripple on a Pond: Crisis Challenge, Change*, a resource book on the plight of displaced homemakers; *The Black Family: An Afro-Centric Perspective*; racial justice position papers
Meetings: National convention every two years (on even years) with the Ministers for Racial and Social Justice and United Black Christians

Council for Racial/Ethnic Ministries— United Church of Christ, Inc.

700 Prospect Avenue
Cleveland, OH 44120
(216) 241-5400

The Council for Racial/Ethnic Ministries of the United Church of Christ, Inc., was established in 1983 during its Fourteenth General Synod to advocate concerns pertaining to racial and ethnic groups within the church.

Group Type: Denomination specific; racial/social justice
Founded: 1983

Ministers for Racial and Social Justice— United Church of Christ, Inc.

7223 16th Street, NW
Washington, DC 20012
The Reverend John S. Fortt, President

A meeting of African American clergy within the United Church of Christ who wanted to organize the African American lay constituency as well as the clergy was held in March 1966. The groundwork for United Black Churchmen (later United Black Christians) was laid at this time. The African American clergy coalition evolved into the Ministers for Racial and Social Justice (MRSJ) in the spring of 1967.

MRSJ was instrumental in pushing for the establishment of

the Commission for Racial Justice at the Sixth General Synod in 1967 and has worked cooperatively with the Commission for Racial Justice and United Black Christians in numerous programs since their respective inceptions. MRSJ was also instrumental in the nomination of and subsequent campaigning for the election of the late Reverend Dr. Arthur D. Gray to be the first African American clergyman of any major denomination in the United States to the office of president of the United Church of Christ. Although his election failed by an extremely narrow and crucial margin, his stature and influence (as well as that of the MRSJ) increased within the church.

Group Type: Denomination specific; ministerial; racial/social justice
Founded: Spring, 1967
Meetings: National convention every two years (on even years) with the Commission for Racial Justice and United Black Christians

United Black Christians—United Church of Christ, Inc.

332 South Michigan, Suite 1242
Chicago, IL 60604
(312) 786-9205
Ms. Patricia J. Eggleston, Esq., President

United Black Christians (UBC) was the result of a meeting of African American clergy within the United Church of Christ in March, 1966, who wanted to organize the clergy as well as the African American lay constituency (the clergy organized into the Ministers for Racial and Social Justice by the spring of 1967). Originally known as the United Black Churchmen, the organization was formally launched in November, 1970,

in Washington, DC. The name was changed to be nonsexist and totally inclusive in 1976. It is an officially recognized special-interest group of the United Church of Christ, serving as a voice for the more than fifty thousand African American clergy and lay members of the church.

UBC works with all components of the United Church of Christ in implementing programs and strategies that have a positive impact on the African American community, such as the Council of Racial and Ethnic Ministries, the Office for Church in Society, the Commission for Racial Justice, United Church Board for Homeland Ministries, and the Ministers for Racial and Social Justice, as well as with the other agencies of the United Church of Christ. Its own programs include the Black Youth and Young Caucus, UBC Black Women's Caucus, UBC Regional Leadership Workshops, UBC Quarterly Newsletter, UBC General Synod Briefings, a UBC Regional Black Church Development Program, a biennial dinner for African American churches at synod, and a Black Seminary Student Network. There are regional chapters of the organization throughout the country, and it meets in a national convention every two years with the Ministers for Racial and Social Justice. In 1990, UBC will host its first biennial youth and young adult leadership event in Greensboro, NC. The president for the 1988-1990 biennium is Patricia R. Eggleston, Esq.

Group Type: Denomination specific; administrative; lay/clergy
Founded: November, 1970
Publications: A quarterly newsletter
Meetings: National convention is held every two years (on even years) with the Ministers for Racial and Social Justice; in 1990, UBC will host its first biennial youth and young adult leadership event in Greensboro, NC

Councils of Churches

Christian Council of Metropolitan Atlanta, Inc.

465 Boulevard, SE
Atlanta, GA 30312-3498
(404) 622-2235
Dr. Perry Ginn, Executive Director

Founded in 1879 by a group of Atlanta ministers, the interracial, intercultural Christian Council of Metropolitan Atlanta, Inc. (CCMA) is one of the oldest and most ecumenically inclusive organizations in the United States. On the Council, Roman Catholic, Greek Orthodox, and Protestant individuals, congregations, and denominations work together, focusing their talents, energies, and resources to help those who are suffering. The purpose of the Council is "to witness to and enhance the mutual commitment of its membership to Jesus Christ, and to express our unity in Christ; to serve as a resource, coordinator, enabler, and prophetic leader for working together to meet the material and spiritual needs of all people in the metro Atlanta area and beyond; and to facilitate and provide special compassionate ministries to those in need in our society."

Approximately five hundred churches are involved in participation and support of the various activities of the CCMA. In addition, the CCMA is in contact with over thirteen hundred churches in the seven-county metropolitan Atlanta area. This is accomplished, in part, through the publication of a bimonthly newsletter, *Together*, which has a circulation of eleven thousand.

The Christian Council of Metropolitan Atlanta directly administers fifteen programs: *Achor Center*—a transitional housing, day-care and training center for women and children; *Action Information Ministry*—a statewide network of churches and other nonprofit groups that provide advocacy for mentally ill persons, the homeless population, women and children, and elderly citizens; *Airport Ministry to Refugees*—counseling, interpretation and guidance for refugees in transit; *Christian Emergency Help Centers, Inc.*—a metropolitan area computer and telephone system that shares information on resources and referrals and gives direct assistance to persons in need; *Commission on Disability Concerns*—an effort to foster awareness of the needs of disabled and handicapped persons; *Community Breakfast*—an annual sharing experience for local Christians and a recognition of special ministry achievements; *Conferences, Workshops and Symposiums*—such as leadership training for the pastor/staff of local churches; *Education for Peace and Justice*—education and advocacy on domestic and international peace and justice efforts; *Emergency Shelters for Homeless Persons*—five large area shelters; *Evangelism*—stimulation, assistance, and coordination of local evangelism efforts; *Mental Health Ministries*—three personal care homes and a twelve-unit apartment facility; *Metro Planning for Ministry*—planning with denominations to meet human needs and assist in church development in new and old churches; *Refugee Resettlement Program*—assistance to congregations sponsoring refugee families; *Together*—a bimonthly newsletter; and *Work/Study and Internship Programs*—For graduate students of all disciplines to provide personal experience in ministry to persons in need and to provide for biblical and spiritual reflection on the experience.

The Christian Council of Metropolitan Atlanta is run by a Board of Directors (headed by a President), Board of Trustees (headed by a Chairman), and an Executive Director. The General Assembly of the Council meets annually in November of each year. The Board of Directors meets monthly, and various committees and task forces meet regularly. The Executive Director of CCMA is Dr. Perry Ginn.

The Christian Council of Metropolitan Atlanta has been a racially inclusive organization for more than thirty years. African Americans are well represented on the Board of Directors, Board of Trustees, and within the membership of CCMA. The immediate past president of the Council, the Reverend Dr. Harold E. Moore, Sr., is pastor of Newberry Chapel A.M.E. Church. The 1990 president of the CCMA is Mr. Joe Beasley, a staff layperson with Antioch Baptist Church, North. Mr. Beasley is the first lay, African American religious leader to serve as president.

Group Type: Ecumenical/nondenominational; council of churches/groups
Founded: 1879
Membership: Over five hundred churches and many individual Christians
Publications: *Together*, a bimonthly newsletter

Church Council of Greater Seattle

4759 15th Avenue, NE
Seattle, WA 98105
(206) 525-1213
The Reverend William B. Cate, Director

Group Type: Ecumenical/nondenominational; council of churches/groups

Churches United of Scott County, Iowa, and Rock Island County, Illinois

630 9th Street
Rock Island, IL 61201
(309) 786-6494
Mr. Thomas N. Kalshoven, Executive Director

Group Type: Ecumenical/nondenominational; council of churches/groups

Church Federation of Greater Chicago

18 S. Michigan Avenue, Suite 900
Chicago, IL 60603-3208
(312) 977-9929
The Reverend Nathaniel Jarrett, Jr., President
The Reverend David M. Whitermore, Executive Director

At the turn-of-the-century, a greater emphasis on Christian unity throughout the United States was sought. An Inter-Church conference held in November, 1905, in New York City, explored the idea of church federation. An actual association took root in the Chicago area, and, in 1907, the Church Federation of Greater Chicago was founded. The Federation began as a loose clergy association that met monthly to hear guest speakers. The Federation continued to grow and now includes twenty-three denominations and 2,109 churches.

The Federation is a shared ministry, working together to meet the needs of the community. Member organizations include the A.M.E. Church, the A.M.E. Zion Church, the C.M.E. Church, the Church of God in Christ, the National Baptist Convention of America, the National Baptist Convention, U.S.A., Inc., and the Progressive National Baptist Convention.

Today, the interracial Federation supports an award-winning radio and television broadcast ministry and ecumenical/interfaith programming, including citywide human relations programs to combat racism. Its Anti-Hunger Program was established in 1975. Through that program, fresh fruits and vegetables and other nutritionally balanced products are distributed through some of Chicago's 116 food pantries and soup kitchens to more than one million people a year.

The Church Federation of Greater Chicago is headed by a president, the Reverend Nathaniel Jarrett, Jr., and an executive director, the Reverend David M. Whitermore. The Executive Board meets monthly, as do all standing committees.

Group Type: Ecumenical/nondenominational; council of churches/groups
Founded: 1907
Membership: Twenty-three denominations and 2,109 churches
Meetings: Executive Board and standing committees meet monthly

Council of Churches of Greater Washington

411 Rittenhouse Street, NW
Washington, DC 20011
(202) 722-9248
The Reverend Frank D. Tucker, President
The Reverend Ernest R. Gibson, Executive Director

Group Type: Ecumenical/nondenominational; council of churches/groups
Founded: 1929
Publications: *Capital Counciler*, a quarterly newsletter

Council of Churches of the City of New York

475 Riverside Drive, Suite 456
New York, NY 10115
(212) 749-1214
The Reverend Robert L. Polk, Executive Director

Group Type: Ecumenical/nondenominational; council of
churches/groups

Ecumenical Council of the Pasadena Area Churches

444 E. Washington Boulevard
Pasadena, CA 91104
(818) 797-2402
The Reverend Charles B. Milburn, Executive Director

Group Type: Ecumenical/nondenominational; council of
churches/groups

Ethnic Cooperation and Institutional Ministries—Pennsylvania Council of Churches

900 South Arlington Avenue, Room 100
Harrisburg, PA 17109
(717) 545-4761
The Reverend Debra L. Moody, Director

In November, 1986, the Pennsylvania Council of Churches
determined that there was a need for greater outreach by and
participation of the minorities churches in the work of the
Council. It was decided that a minority person should be selected to work actively toward fostering ecumenical minority
church cooperation on social and political issues relevant to the
minorities in Pennsylvania. The first director was the Reverend
Andrew Holtz, Jr. The Reverend Debra L. Moody has held the
position since March 1988.

Already, the work of the Office of Ethnic Cooperation has
lead to member churches assisting in the establishment of a
Family Center in Chester, Pennsylvania. Future plans include
organizing a counseling program for teenagers, building homes
for the homeless population, and strengthening the family life
of minorities throughout the state.

The Pennsylvania Council of Churches, which initiated this
undertaking, is a combined effort of forty-five denominations
(including seven African American denominations). Additional
information about the work of the Office of Ethnic Cooperation
can be obtained from the Council's yearly report.

Group Type: Ecumenical/nondenominational; council of
churches/groups; racial/social justice
Founded: November, 1986
Membership: Representatives from forty-five denominations
Meetings: Ministries meet approximately every three months

Greater Dallas Community of Churches

2800 Swiss Avenue
Dallas, TX 75204
(214) 824-8680
The Reverend Thomas H. Quigley, Executive Director

Group Type: Ecumenical/nondenominational; council of
churches/groups

Illinois Conference of Churches

615 S. 5th Street
Springfield, IL 62703
(217) 544-3423
The Reverend James P. Ebbers, Executive Secretary

Group Type: Ecumenical/nondenominational; council of
churches/groups

Indiana Council of Churches

1100 W. 42nd Street, Room 225
Indianapolis, IN 46208
(317) 923-3674
The Reverend Scott J. Schiesswohl

Twenty-five denominational bodies compose the interracial
Indiana Council of Churches. The group was formed in 1942
and incorporated in 1948, with the express purpose of being a
visible symbol and an instrument of unity and mission among
the churches in Indiana. Member churches include A.M.E.;
A.M.E. Zion; C.M.E.; National Baptist Convention of America; National Baptist Convention, U.S.A., Inc.; and the Progressive National Baptist Convention. The Council includes
the Department of Social Ministries, which disseminates information and explores social issues before the state legislature.
The Department of Peace and Justice conducts workshops and
conferences and studies and plans action on peace and justice
issues in the United States and worldwide.

The Council is governed by a biennial assembly of delegates
elected by member denominations. The assembly meets on the
second Friday and Saturday of November in even years. A
board of directors meets three times yearly and carries on the
interim business of the Council.

Group Type: Ecumenical/nondenominational; council of
churches/groups; racial/social justice
Founded: 1942
Membership: Twenty-five denominational bodies are represented

Indiana Interreligious Commission on Human Equality

1100 W. 42nd Street, Suite 320
Indianapolis, IN 46208
The Reverend James E. Taylor, Executive Director
Ms. Dorothea S. Green, Program Consultant

The Indiana Interreligious Commission on Human Equality
(IICHE) was founded in response to the 1968 President's National Advisory Commission on Civil Disorders ("Kerner Commission"), which recognized that the United States "is moving
toward two societies, one black, one white—separate and un-
equal." Leaders in the Jewish, Catholic, and Protestant faiths
joined to develop, operate, and fund programs designed to
remove racism and other forms of discrimination from the institutional structures of religion and society.

Its mission is fourfold: 1) to stimulate interreligious dialogue
in issues pertaining to human equality; 2) to bring religious
congregations and institutions to a greater understanding of
racism and human inequality, sufficient enough to result in
individual and group action toward achieving human equality
and dignity; 3) to aid in the empowerment of minorities and

to make common cause with other groups involved in the empowerment of minorities; and 4) to provide on a statewide basis, whenever needed, staff, resources, and workshops that will promote a better understanding of issues of human equality.

IICHE offers workshops to promote awareness and analysis of barriers against overcoming racism and other forms of discrimination. For groups wanting to act on racism, it provides consultant and human equality services that include specific programs, resource information, and referral to national groups involved in human equality issues. Resource information is provided on racism, extremism, interfaith dialogue, and related issues. A resource library is also maintained. In addition, public forums on a variety of topics are offered. In November, the organization sponsors an annual forum on South Africa to inform the public about apartheid, economic injustice, and brutality. This forum features speakers such as Dr. Allan Boesak. The organization also sponsors the statewide Dr. Martin Luther King, Jr., Essay Contest each year in conjunction with several other organizations. There are over five hundred student participants in the contest each year.

Of the twenty-one member religious organizations, four are historically African American—the A.M.E. Church, the A.M.E. Zion Church, the C.M.E. Church, and the Martin Luther King, Jr., Memorial Baptist State Convention of Indiana. The president, the Reverend E. Anne Henning Byfield, is from the A.M.E. Church. The Reverend James E. Taylor is the executive director.

Group Type: Ecumenical/nondenominational; council of churches/groups; racial/social justice
Founded: 1968
Membership: Twenty-one member religious organizations

Interfaith Conference of Metropolitan Washington

1419 V Street, NW
Washington, DC 20009
(202) 234-6300
The Reverend John V. O'Connor, President
The Reverend Clark Lobenstine, Executive Director

Founded in 1978 by leaders of the Protestant, Roman Catholic, Jewish, and Islamic faith communities, the interracial Interfaith Conference of Metropolitan Washington is composed of thirty-one faith groups, judicatories, and organizations of historically African American churches, as well as the predominantly white Protestant, Catholic, Islamic, Jewish, and Mormon faith communities. In 1989, the Sikh faith community was unanimously voted to full membership, making this conference the first interreligious body in the nation to include the Sikh religion.

The Interfaith Conference of Metropolitan Washington seeks to promote interfaith dialogue among persons of different faiths, races, and cultures. It also serves as a vehicle for education, advocacy, and action on issues of social and economic justice and importance in the metropolitan Washington area.

Among the Conference's annual events are the uniting of choirs and soloists from many diverse religious traditions for a combined concert and the public interfaith dialogue, held in the spring, on an issue of current concern. Of particular importance is the Conference's interest in AIDS. The Task Force on AIDS, founded in the spring of 1987, addresses the issue of AIDS and how the religious community can compassionately respond to those with the disease as well as to their families and friends.

The General Assembly of the Conference meets three times yearly in January, May, and September. The Executive Board meets monthly. The Interfaith Conference publishes a newsletter, *The Interfaith Connector*, and a comprehensive directory of emergency food and shelters. The president of the Interfaith Conference of Metropolitan Washington is the Reverend John V. O'Connor; the executive director is the Reverend Clark Lobenstine.

Group Type: Ecumenical/nondenominational; council of churches/groups; racial/social justice
Founded: 1978
Membership: Thirty-one religious faith communities
Publications: *The Interfaith Connector*; a directory of emergency food and shelters
Meetings: The Assembly meets three times a year—January, May, and September; Executive Board meets monthly

International Council of Community Churches

900 Ridge Road, Suite LL1
Homewood, IL 60430
(312) 798-2264
J. Ralph Shotwell, Executive Director

The International Council of Community Churches is duly aligned with the Consultation on Church Union, the National Council of the Churches of Christ of the U.S.A., and the World Council of Churches. It publishes *The Christian Community* and *The Pastor's Journal*. The organization meets annually in mid-July. Its executive director is J. Ralph Shotwell.

Group Type: Ecumenical/nondenominational; council of churches/groups
Publications: *The Christian Community*, J. Ralph Shotwell, editor, and *The Pastor's Journal*, Robert Puckett, editor, Community Church Press, 900 Ridge Road, Suite LL1, Homewood, IL 60430
Meetings: Annual conference is held in July

Kentuckian Interfaith Community

P.O. Box 4671
Louisville, KY 40204
The Reverend Kenneth D. MacHarg, Executive Director

The Kentuckian Interfaith Community is an ecumenical, interfaith organization serving the denominations of metropolitan Louisville. It combines the major Protestant, Catholic, Greek Orthodox, and Jewish bodies in cooperative efforts such as media, social justice, racism and discrimination concerns, poverty issues, interfaith dialogue, and inter-Christian cooperation.

Group Type: Ecumenical/nondenominational; council of churches/groups; racial/social justice

Kentucky Council of Churches

1039 Goodwin Drive
Lexington, KY 40505
(606) 253-3027
Dr. John C. Bush, Executive Director

The Kentucky Council of Churches is a statewide ecumenical organization comprising fifteen member denominations, both Protestant and Catholic. The A.M.E., A.M.E. Zion, and C.M.E. churches are member denominations. The council was established in 1947, continuing the work of several previous bodies dating back as far as 1865. It is active in working for social and racial justice, equitable public policy, and economic justice.

Group Type: Ecumenical/nondenominational; council of churches/groups; racial/social justice
Founded: 1947
Membership: 15 member denominations

Martin Luther King, Jr., Scholarship/ Memorial Service Committee Capital Area Council of Churches, Inc.

901 Madison Avenue
Albany, NY 12208
(518) 489-8441
Ms. Nell Stokes-Holmes, Committee Chair
The Reverend Fred L. Shilling, Executive Director

The Martin Luther King, Jr., Scholarship/Memorial Service Committee is a function of the Board of Directors of the Capital Area Council of Churches, Inc., in Albany, New York. The first interfaith memorial service was held at the Union Missionary Baptist Church in 1968, shortly after the assassination of Dr. King. The scholarship awards began in 1973. Presently, the service is held annually on January 15, and the scholarship is awarded at the June assembly of the Capital Area Council of Churches.

The Scholarship/Memorial Service Committee consists of lay-people and clergy representing the interfaith and interracial community of the Albany area. Funds for the scholarship are obtained through a love offering at the memorial service and through donations from groups and individuals. The chairperson of the Martin Luther King, Jr., Scholarship/Memorial Service Committee is Ms. Nell Stokes-Holmes. The Executive Director of the Capital Area Council of Churches is the Reverend Fred L. Shilling.

Group Type: Ecumenical/nondenominational; council of churches/groups; mission/philanthropic
Founded: 1968

Minnesota Council of Churches

122 W. Franklin Avenue, #100
Minneapolis, MN 55404
(612) 870-3600
The Reverend Margaret J. Thomas, Executive Director

Group Type: Ecumenical/nondenominational; council of churches/groups

Ohio Council of Churches, Inc.

89 E. Wilson Bridge Road
Columbus, OH 43085
(614) 885-9590
The Reverend Carlton N. Weber, Executive Director

The Ohio Council of Churches, Inc., was founded in 1919 by representatives from ten different denominations. The goal of what was then the Federal Council of Churches was to enhance Christian unity by drawing in the state's small communities. Concern was expressed about those small churches that lacked well-trained, full-time ministerial attention.

Today the Council is interracial and includes representation from the A.M.E., A.M.E. Zion, C.M.E. churches, and the National Baptist Convention of America. The Council operates six commissions, including one on Black Church and Community and one on Poverty and Economic Justice. The chairpersons of these two commissions are, respectively, the Reverend Irvin Moxley of the Presbyterian Church (U.S.A.), Synod of the Covenant (Columbus); and Mr. John Crawford of the Roman Catholic Church, Diocese of Columbus (Worthington).

Christian unity continues to be the chief concern of the Ohio Council of Churches. Its mission is to: 1) establish ways to participate and experience the essential oneness in the Body of Christ; 2) express advocacy in a united way on behalf of those who are experiencing need, oppression, or injustice; and 3) foster united opportunities to grow in understanding and participate in meaningful forms of Christian discipleship. Biblical and theological study, the meeting of human needs, the development of responsible citizenship, upholding human justice, and building world peace and ecumenical partnership are considered priorities.

The Council is composed of nearly three million members from 11,500 congregations, representing seventeen Christian denominations. An Assembly of two hundred delegates from the member denominations sets priorities and overall direction of the Council, and an eighty-five-member General Board sets policy and oversees the Council's work. The Assembly and the General Board each meet annually.

The Ohio Council of Churches publishes a monthly newsletter, *Ohio Christian News* and, when the state legislature is in session, a weekly summary, *Ohio Brief*.

Group Type: Ecumenical/nondenominational; council of churches/groups; racial/social justice
Founded: 1919
Membership: Approximately three million persons in 11,500 congregations representing seventeen denominations
Publications: *Ohio Christian News*, a newsletter, and *Ohio Brief*, a weekly summary during legislative sessions
Meetings: Assembly (two hundred delegates) meets annually in November; General Board (eighty-five members) meets annually in October

Oklahoma Conference of Churches

P.O. Box 60288
Oklahoma City, OK 73146
(405) 525-2928
Dr. William Moore, Executive Director

The Oklahoma Conference of Churches is a community of sixteen denominations that confess Jesus Christ as Savior and Lord. These include the historically African American A.M.E., A.M.E. Zion, C.M.E., and Second Cumberland Presbyterian churches and major predominantly white denominations with significant African American membership.

The major activities of the Oklahoma Conference of Churches include church and unity concerns with Baptism, Eucharist, and Ministry studies (BEM), produced by the World Council of Churches; community building among denominations, church, and society; disaster response; minority affairs; refugee resettlement; and concern for poverty. The Conference has been particularly instrumental in working with farm families in crisis, providing suicide, emotional, and financial counseling, and serving as a mediator with financial lenders.

Group Type: Ecumenical/nondenominational; council of churches/groups

Pomona Valley Council of Churches

1753 N. Park Avenue
Pomona, CA 91768
(714) 622-3806
The Reverend Richard Landrum

Group Type: Ecumenical/nondenominational; council of churches/groups

Trenton Ecumenical Area Ministry

2 Prospect Street
Trenton, NJ 08618
(609) 396-9166
The Reverend Angelique Walker-Smith

The Trenton Ecumenical Area Ministry (TEAM) is a Christian council of churches in the capital area of New Jersey concerned with a number of ecumenical and justice issues, including those in the African American community and church. It is the result of the merger of two organizations in 1977: the Council of Churches, founded in 1941, and the United Trenton Ministry, founded in 1970.

TEAM serves as an advocate and a coordinating agency of the churches in the greater Trenton area in cooperation with other community efforts. It provides and participates in programs such as the summer program for children and youth, clergy gatherings, a hunger coalition, a housing coalition, and CROP WALK—monies raised for the hungry. It also sponsors seminary and youth interns, ecumenical gatherings and celebrations, and hospital chaplaincies.

Group Type: Ecumenical/nondenominational; council of churches/groups
Founded: 1977

Ecumenical/Nondenominational Organizations

Community Renewal Society

332 South Michigan Avenue
Chicago, IL 60604-4302
(312) 427-4830
Roy Larson, Acting Executive Director
Bennie E. Whiten, Jr., Director, Metropolitan Mission

The Community Renewal Society (CRS) began as the Chicago City Missionary Society in Chicago, Illinois, in 1882, an organization founded by clergy and laity of twenty-three Congregational churches. Caleb Foote Gates served as the first president. Its major concern was the poor living conditions of immigrants (primarily European), growing lawlessness and immorality, and children. Its initial goals were ''to serve the poor, to work with and for the distressed and neglected in order to better their lives, and to serve the churches, especially in areas where churches had little chance of being self-sufficient''— the fulfillment of the social gospel. These goals were achieved through language classes; provision of day-care for working mothers; schools for vocational education; and food, clothing, and employment for the homeless.

Victor Lawson, the publisher of the *Chicago Daily News*, left a generous bequest to the organization in 1925, thus ensuring its future. Its work turned to the needs of newer immigrants—African Americans, Asian Americans, and Hispanic Americans—between World Wars I and II. During this period, CRS also established or assisted in establishing more than one hundred thirty churches in Chicago. Its focus shifted from social

welfare programs to a greater emphasis on stimulating systematic change in the 1960s, and during this time its commitment to racial equality was confirmed. The organization adopted its present name in 1967.

The Community Renewal Society's current program includes the provision of seed grants and technical assistance to community-based groups that seek to improve the community, and the initiation of model programs to address issues of health, education, housing, and employment. The Metropolitan Mission Division gives program and financial aid to local congregations and specialized ministries. The Offices of Studies and Research provide the basis for the organization's response to pressing urban issues through research and publication, collaborative studies, workshops, and conferences. Pleasant Valley Outdoor Center provides residential camping programs that emphasize self-reliance training for disadvantaged children and families in the Chicago area. In addition to these, the Community Renewal Chorus and All God's Children provide a musical message of justice through performance in the Chicago area.

The Community Renewal Society is a private, nonprofit, tax-exempt mission agency integrally related to the United Church of Christ. In 1987, it published *Race and Politics in Chicago*, a history of the influence of race on Chicago politics from the riots of 1919 to Mayor Harold Washington's election in 1983. It also publishes *The Chicago Reporter*, a monthly newsletter specializing in investigating issues of race and poverty in metropolitan Chicago. The acting executive director of CRS is Roy

Larson, and the director of the Metropolitan Mission is Bennie E. Whiten, Jr.

Group Type: Ecumenical/nondenominational; lay/clergy; racial/social justice
Founded: 1882
Publications: *The Chicago Reporter*, a monthly newsletter; *Race and Politics in Chicago*, a history of Chicago politics

Endowment for Community Leadership

4601 N. Fairfax Drive, Suite 708
Arlington, VA 22203
(703) 243-7844
Mr. Spencer Brand, President
Dr. Pattie L. Harris, Director of Research and Evaluation

The Endowment for Community Leadership, formerly known as the Special Ministry Assistance Fund, was founded by its president, Spencer Brand, in 1983 in Arlington, Virginia. The interracial organization's purpose is to recruit, develop, and sustain ethnic Christian leadership who make known the Gospel of Jesus Christ and who instill the moral, ethical, and lawful values necessary to transform the urban community. It was conceived after ten years of ministry experience in the African American, Hispanic American, and Asian American communities in Washington, DC and from the awareness of the evident need and perennial difficulties that many ethnic Christian workers experienced in raising and sustaining financial support.

The recipients of the fund are men and women from the African American, Hispanic American, and Asian American communities who are involved in full-time Christian ministries both nationally and internationally. The number of recipients are determined by the level of available funds. There are regular board and staff meetings, and the organization publishes *Urban Breakthrough*, a quarterly newsletter. The director of research and evaluation is Dr. Pattie L. Harris.

Group Type: Ecumenical/nondenominational; mission/philanthropic
Founded: 1983
Publications: *Urban Breakthrough*, a quarterly newsletter

Greensboro Urban Ministry

407 N. Eugene Street
Greensboro, NC 27401
(919) 271-5959
The Reverend Mike Aiken, Executive Director

The Greensboro Urban Ministry is an interfaith outreach agency founded in 1967. It is supported by volunteers from more than one hundred forty congregations who cooperate in expressing "the love of God through practical action to people in need" throughout the Greensboro area.

There are several projects carried out by the volunteers. *Project Independence* matches low-income, welfare-dependent families to places of worship for sponsorship and assistance in securing employment, housing, and child care. The *Emergency Assistance Program* provides food, clothing, and financial aid (such as interest-free loans for bill payment and grants for essential medical services) for individuals and families in emergency situations. The *Night Shelter* offers year-round shelter

to the homeless. *Pathways* is a temporary shelter for up to seventeen families who have been made homeless due to unforeseen circumstances. The *Food Bank* redistributes wholesome food salvaged from area markets, restaurants, wholesalers, and other vendors to local, nonprofit, charitable agencies. The *Potter's House* serves nutritious, well-balanced meals to more than 240 people daily. *H.A.V.E. (Housing Assistance through Volunteer Effort)* helps low-income families rehabilitate their housing in order to avoid condemnation of their properties. Finally, *Marriage and Family Therapy* provides free or low-cost therapy to individuals, couples, and families by skilled therapists working toward certification by the American Association for Marriage and Family Therapy.

In addition, the organization provides additional services for senior citizens and works with the Department of Social Services and other agencies in providing services to the community. Its volunteers also coordinate CROP WALK, an effort to raise money for the hungry. It also produces the *GUM Newsletter*. The Reverend Mike Aiken is the executive director.

Group Type: Ecumenical/nondenominational; council of churches/groups
Founded: 1967
Publications: *GUM Newsletter*

Joint Educational Development

12221 Marne Lane
Bowie, MD 20715
(301) 464-5906
Lorey Hodgson

Joint Educational Development (JED) is an ecumenical partnership for the development of educational systems and resources. It is comprised of the Christian Church (Disciples of Christ), the Episcopal Church, Presbyterian Church in the United States, Reformed Church in America, United Church of Christ, and United Presbyterian Church in the U.S.A.

Group Type: Ecumenical/nondenominational; worship resource; Christian education

National Council of the Churches of Christ in the U.S.A.—Office of Racial Justice

475 Riverside Drive
New York, NY 10115
(212) 870-2298
Dr. Kenyon C. Burke, Associate General Secretary

Group Type: Ecumenical/nondenominational; administrative; racial/social justice

National Interreligious Commission on Civil Rights

1442 N. Farwell Avenue, Suite 210
Milwaukee, WI 53230
(414) 272-2642
Ms. Betty J. Thompson, Founder and Director

On January 25, 1984, meeting under the auspices of Project Equality of Wisconsin, Inc., a task force undertook to address the urgent need for the establishment of a national interreligious commission on the status of civil rights. The group was particularly concerned with what it perceived as a "perceptible weakening of civil rights law enforcement mechanisms and an insensitivity to civil rights in general."

Once known as Project Equality of Wisconsin, Inc., the National Interreligious Commission on Civil Rights (NICCR) is now independent and incorporated with its own bylaws. It works nationally through state, community, and religious groups to identify and explore civil rights issues; cooperate with other concerned groups (such as the Urban League) in improving opportunities for minorities; expand use of minority-owned businesses; improve health care and education for minorities; and encourage congregations to detect discrimination in their communities and act to alleviate it.

Much of the work of the NICCR is conducted through hearings. Since its formation, the Commission has held hearings on the status of civil rights in Montgomery, Alabama; Kansas City, Missouri; Louisville, Kentucky; and in Indiana and Wisconsin. The goal of the hearings is to monitor civil rights enforcement and to enable the religious community to gain greater involvement in decision making on civil rights issues in different areas around the country where civil rights are violated. Reports on testimony received at the hearings are available from the Commission.

The membership of the NICCR is composed of national interfaith religious leaders from Alabama; Illinois; Kentucky; Massachusetts; New Jersey; New York; Virginia; Washington, DC; and Wisconsin. The Board of the Council meets twice yearly. Its director, Ms. Betty J. Thompson, works in the Milwaukee office.

Group Type: Ecumenical/nondenominational; lay/clergy; racial/social justice
Founded: January 25, 1984

New York City Mission Society

105 E. 22nd Street, 6th Floor
New York, NY 10010
(212) 674-3500
Calvin O. Pressley, Executive Director

Group Type: Ecumenical/nondenominational; mission/philanthropic

Programme to Combat Racism—World Council of Churches

475 Riverside Drive, Room 915
New York, NY 10115
(212) 870-2533
The Reverend Dr. Yvonne Delk, Commission Chairperson

From its first assembly in 1948, the World Council of Churches (WCC) has been particularly concerned about the evil of racism, recognizing it as a denial of the truth that every human being is created in the image of God, and as a means of perpetuating oppression, domination, and injustice. In 1969, the Central Committee of the Council proposed the Programme to Combat Racism (PCR) as an integral part of its witness and efforts to work for unity, renewal, justice, and service. In 1979, the entire membership of the WCC (three hundred churches in more than one hundred countries, representing four hundred million Chris-

tians) joined in a process of consultation on combating racism in the 1980s, and the program was formed.

The commitment of the PCR is to: 1) end discrimination based on race; 2) end exploitation of women and men and to expose the racism often used to justify that exploitation; 3) support the struggle of the racially oppressed; and 4) help the churches understand and live out their Christian commitment to the unity of the church and the unity of humankind. Member churches of the World Council of Churches are called "to move beyond charity, grants and traditional programming to relevant and sacrificial action leading to new relationships of dignity and justice among all and to become agents for the radical construction of society."

The Programme to Combat Racism has three major elements: programmatic categories; research, publications and consultations; and the Special Fund. As a channel of communication between WCC member churches and local groups struggling against racism, the PCR initiates and assists with programs (including small grants given as a symbolic act of solidarity). The Programme to Combat Racism publishes a newsletter, *PCR Information* four times yearly, undertakes research on a variety of issues, and uses consultations and seminars to engage the churches and organizations of the racially oppressed in dialogue and mutual action. Racism in children's books, racism and theology, and women under racism have been topics of particular concern. Finally, through the PCR, the WCC annually makes grants to organizations of racially oppressed groups and organizations that support victims of racial injustice.

Although the PCR is a global program with a global agenda, it has concerned itself, particularly, with South African apartheid (including selling its holdings in corporations that invest in South Africa and closing its accounts with three major banks that refused to stop making loans to the South African government and its agencies). The PCR has also found the international problem of land rights to be of great concern, particularly among Native Americans, the Aborigines in Australia, and the Maoris in New Zealand. The position of the Tamils in Sri Lanka; the Dalit ("untouchable") in India; Burakumin and Koreans living in Japan; African Americans, Hispanic Americans, and Asian Americans in the United States; migrant workers and other racial minorities living in Western Europe; and the links between racism and the international economic system are also areas of major concern for the PCR.

The Programme to Combat Racism encourages local churches to support their efforts by identifying racial issues in their own society, listening to what the victims of racial injustice have to say, and seeing how they can cooperate with them; finding out how their country and organizations in their country are involved in international systems that support and perpetuate racial injustice and taking action on it; finding out what churches and church-related bodies in their country have done about the PCR and stimulating their involvement in the issue of the program; and informing the PCR about their activities while helping to support the activities of the program.

In the United States, the PCR is headed by five U.S. commissioners: the Reverend Dr. Yvonne Delk, chairperson, United Church of Christ; the Reverend Joseph Agne, United Methodist Church; Dr. Carol Hampton, Episcopal Church (U.S.A.); the Reverend Jovelino Ramos, Presbyterian Church (U.S.A.); and the Reverend Wyatt Tee Walker, Progressive National Baptist Convention, Inc. The international headquarters are in Geneva,

Switzerland, at the World Council of Churches: 150 route de Ferney; 1211 Geneva 20, Switzerland, Telephone (022) 91 61 11.

Group Type: Ecumenical/nondenominational; council of churches/groups; racial/social justice

Founded: 1969

Membership: Over three hundred churches worldwide representing over four hundred million persons in more than one hundred countries

Publications: *PCR Information*, a quarterly newsletter

Project Equality, Inc.

1020 E. 63rd Street, Suite 102
Kansas City, MO 64110
(816) 361-9222
Mrs. Barbara Thompson, Chairperson
The Reverend Maurice E. Culver, President/Chief Executive Officer

With the involvement of fifty judicatories of religious organizations, eleven national religious organizations, sixteen congregations and parishes, and two hundred twenty other supporters, Project Equality is a national interracial, interfaith program that monitors the equal employment opportunity practices of the suppliers of goods and services for religious bodies. The project was initiated in 1965 as an affirmative action program by the National Catholic Conference for Interracial Justice. Within a year, it had expanded beyond local programs in Detroit, Michigan; St. Louis, Missouri; and San Antonio, Texas, to a national focus, which included Protestant and Jewish groups.

From the beginning, the approach of the project was twofold: 1) to attack racism on the institutional level by attempting to remedy a basic cause of inequality—lack of economic and employment opportunity; and 2) to call upon the interfaith community to use its considerable spending to accomplish the mission of the project. Originally concerned mainly with racial discrimination, the project now investigates issues of sex, age, disability, and national origin. Project Equality prides itself on being the only independent, nongovernment agency focusing solely on affirmative action and equal employment opportunity.

Project Equality is based in Kansas City, Missouri, with local programs in that state and Illinois, Kansas, the metropolitan New York area, and Wisconsin. The chairperson is Mrs. Barbara Thompson, and the president/chief executive officer is the Reverend Maurice E. Culver.

Group Type: Ecumenical/nondenominational; lay/clergy; racial/social justice

Founded: 1965

Membership: Fifty judicatories of religious organizations, eleven national religious organizations, sixteen congregations and parishes, and two hundred twenty other organizations and individuals

Rochester Committee for Justice in Southern Africa, Genesee Ecumenical Ministries

17 S. Ritzhugh Street
Rochester, NY 14614
James A. Rice, Chairman
Richard S. Gilbert, Editor

The Rochester Committee for Justice in Southern Africa, Genesee Ecumenical Ministries, publishes *Time Running Out*, a quarterly newsletter linking people of the United States and South Africa. It contributes financial support to the struggle against apartheid and is composed of volunteers. James A. Rice serves as chairman of the organization, and Richard S. Gilbert is the editor of the newsletter.

Group Type: Ecumenical/nondenominational; racial/social justice

Membership: Volunteers

Publications: *Time Running Out*, a quarterly newsletter

Part 6

Selected Historical Overviews of African American Religious Traditions

A Synoptic Survey of the History of African American Baptists

Clarence G. Newsome

The history of African American Baptists in the United States, like that of most New World Baptists, is rooted in the Puritan movement of seventeenth-century England. "Some Baptists maintain that there has been a continuous succession of Baptist congregations since the time of John the Baptist, Jesus, and the Apostles. Other Baptists cite the continental Anabaptists of the sixteenth century as the major progenitors of the Baptist movement."[1] But extant historical data support the view that the Baptist tradition originated with a conclave of English Puritans who emphasized believers' baptism and a congregational polity.[2]

The Puritan movement in the Church of England began around 1550-1560, during the reign of Elizabeth I. Inspired by one of the Protestant Reformation's brightest and most prolific writers, John Calvin, the leaders of the movement sought to reform the church by "purifying" it theologically and liturgically of its Roman Catholic influence. Those Puritans who later were identified with the Baptist movement insisted that only believers should be admitted to church membership. Favoring the concept of a "gathered" church over that of a "parish church," they contended that church membership was not a birthright.[3] They opposed, therefore, infant baptism, a common practice in the Anglican church, and lobbied for the position that church rolls should be filled with "only those persons who could testify to their own Christian experience."[4] The "visible" church should be populated with "visible" saints (i.e., the earthly church should be composed of believers and practitioners of the faith, and not just everyone, as was the practice).

Ironically, the Baptist movement among English Puritans began on Dutch soil. By the time that James I succeeded to the British throne in 1603, the push of some Puritans to separate from the Anglican church was in full force. Foremost among these Separatists, as they were called, was John Smyth, the pastor of a "gathered" congregation at Gainsborough, England.[5] Convinced that the Anglican church would continue to resist substantive reform, he and a likeminded group fled to Amsterdam, Holland, in 1608, thereby escaping persecution. Within a year, Smyth adopted the position of believers' baptism and "baptized himself by pouring."[6] Convinced that his

action was consistent with the New Testament canon, others in his congregation soon followed his lead, thus bringing into existence the first English Baptist church, albeit outside England.

Under the leadership of Thomas Helwys, several members of Smyth's flock returned to England sometime around 1611 or 1612 and organized "the first permanent Baptist congregation on English soil."[7] The Helwys church deviated from the Calvinistic posture of limited atonement (i.e., that Christ died for a chosen few) in favor of the general atonement viewpoint (i.e., that Christ died for all) advanced by the Dutch theologian Jacobus Arminius (1560-1609). They and others who took the latter view subsequently became known as General, or Arminian, Baptists.

In 1609, on the heels of the Smyth group, another Puritan congregation left England for Holland. Led by John Robinson, they settled in Leyden. Unlike the Smyth fellowship, this "gathered church" departed England committed to a nonseparating form of Congregationalism. They proved to be of equal importance in the eventual presence of Baptists in the American colonies, particularly through the labors of Henry Jacobs and John Spilsbury.

Henry Jacobs, a member of Robinson's Leyden fellowship, returned to England and organized a church in 1616.[8] By the 1630s, this church was composed of people of both Congregational and Baptist sympathies. In 1633, a small group withdrew, convinced that believers' baptism was clearly the scriptural norm.[9] Under the guidance of John Spilsbury, who promptly had himself rebaptized, this "communion of saints" organized the first Particular (limited atonement) Baptist congregation in England.[10] "By them immersion was adopted as the proper mode of baptism about 1641."[11] Thereafter, it was extensively practiced by English Baptists, both General and Particular.[12]

Baptist Background: Early Colonial America

In 1620, the tradition of the "gathered church" was planted in New England by a contingent from Robinson's congregation. Within a single decade, the Baptist viewpoint was visible among the Massachusetts Bay Colonists committed to the "Congregational Way."[13] The first Baptist church was constituted in Providence, Rhode Island, in 1638 or 1639 by Roger Williams and Ezekiel Holliman. The second was organized in Newport, Rhode Island, in 1648 by John Clarke. Despite the numerical advantage of General Baptists, who were scattered throughout the Congregationalist churches of New England, these two churches were established in the emerging Particular Baptist tradition.[14]

During the eighteenth and nineteenth centuries, the number of General and Particular Baptists increased significantly. This was largely due to the widespread revivalism of the First and Second Great Awakenings. Although Sydney Ahlstrom perhaps more accurately pinpoints 1738 as the beginning of the revivalistic period called the First Awakening, the 1720s are very often cited. The 1760s are frequently noted as its time of decline. The next period of heightened revivalistic activity, often called the Second Great Awakening, can be said to have occurred roughly between the 1790s and the 1830s. None of these dates, however, is final; there is considerable disagreement among scholars.[15]

Typical of subsequent Baptist developments, growth spawned controversy and schism.[16] The revivalism that helped to foster expansion engendered division. For example, "in New England the [First] Awakening produced the Separate Baptists."[17] Sometimes referred to as "New Light" Baptists, these men and women generally regarded the free expression and outward emotionalism of revivalistic meetings as authentic signs of a true and efficacious work of God through the activity of the Holy Spirit. Those who dismissed the notion of paroxysms as genuine evidence of God's grace were often referred to as Regular Baptists.[18] The emergence of the New Lights proved to be a determining factor in the genesis of the African American Baptist church in America.

Equally important was the emergence of "missionary" Baptists. At the outset of the nineteenth century, a controversy over missions erupted among Baptists. It is ironic that almost from the start "the very existence of the denomination (in America) was dependent upon the maintenance of [a] missionary spirit,"[19] fueled over the years by the evangelical fervor of the First, and especially the Second, Awakening. Prior to 1814, this zeal was evident in work that, although extensive enough to include African and Native Americans, was randomly and haphazardly organized.[20] In 1814, the Baptist missionary spirit led to the creation of a national organization, the General Missionary Convention of the Baptist Denomination in the United States for Foreign Missions.[21]

The Triennial Convention, as this organization was known,[22] brought denominational status to American Baptists, but not without controversy and eventually more schisms in the ranks of the Baptist faithful. Some groups, such as the Chemung Association, which included churches on both sides of the New York-Pennsylvania boundary, had long opposed systematic missionary activity.[23] Although its members acknowledged the value of "evangelistic preaching of a sort,"[24] they believed organized endeavors such as Bible societies, Sunday schools, and state conventions were not supported by Scripture. By 1835, the difference in opinion was pronounced enough for the emergence of another Baptist denomination, the Primitive Baptist church (PBC).

Sometimes referred to as Old School or Anti-Mission Baptists, this communion of Particular or Calvinistic Baptists arose when the Chemung Association "urged a disunion with those associations which had begun missionary societies on a monied (or organized) basis."[25] Other splinter groups preceded and followed the PBC, but the organization of the PBC essentially rounded out the historical context within which African American Baptist organizations emerged and developed.

Emergence and Evolution of the African American Baptist Movement

The African American Baptist movement originated around the Revolutionary War era. Prior to the mid-1700s, most slave-owners resisted proselytization of their labor force. However, by the 1750s, they tended to be more permissive. They felt confident that neither their control, nor the productivity of their bondsmen, would be jeopardized by their slaves' participation in church. Consequently, a significant number of slaves were able to attend revival or evangelistic services. In this way, blacks were introduced en masse to the Christian religion, and the Baptist faith in particular, because many evangelists were New Light Baptists.

Few slaves joined churches of their own accord before the 1770s. "But the preaching of the new wave of revivalists who emerged during the political revolutionary mood of the 1770s emboldened them [to establish] their own congregations."[26] Many of these congregations were Baptist and in the early years, oriented toward the Particular stance.[27] The reasons for the move toward separate and independent churches were several. But, for the most part, they were related to the discrimination inherent in white-controlled churches and the concomitant desire of blacks to participate in church life unfettered. This was rooted in a profound difference in theological assumptions implicit in the social reality of slavery.

Although Baptists on the whole are said to profess a noncreedal theology, over the years several "confessions of faith" have shaped and reflected a Baptist theological perspective.[28] With regard to these "confessions," both African American and white Baptists have seldom, if ever, differed. Both groups have subscribed to the basic principles of their tradition. For example, "of the true God," both believe that "there is one, and only one, living and true God [an infinite, intelligent Spirit], whose name is JEHOVAH, the Maker and Supreme Ruler of heaven and earth."[29] But black/white social relationships during slavery (and afterward) betrayed the pivotal difference in their concepts about equity of divine endowment, both spiritually and corporally. At best, white Baptists equivocated on this issue, whereas black Baptists stood firm in the belief that all people are created equal in every respect. This difference in theological presupposition was a determining factor in the rise of the African American Baptist movement.[30]

Perhaps the move toward separate, if not altogether independent, African American Baptist churches was underway as early as 1758. In that year, a congregation was formed on the plantation of William Byrd in Mecklenburg County, Virginia, with the assistance of two separatist white Baptists, Philip Mulkey and William Murphey.[31] Reputedly, the first African American Baptist church was not organized until 1775, in Silver Bluff, South Carolina, or possibly not until 1777 or 1788 in Savannah, Georgia.[32] At any rate, from the mid-1770s on, the number of separate African American Baptist churches proliferated.[33]

By 1822, approximately thirty-seven African American Baptist churches were in existence. By 1834, some of these had begun to organize themselves into all-black associations. "In general black Baptist associations arose with much the same aim as white Baptist associations: cooperative endeavor in such activities as domestic missions, mutual aid, and education."[34] However, in contrast to most white associations, all the black associations were actively opposed to slavery. Moved, in part, by commitment to the antislavery cause, six churches in southeastern Ohio organized the Providence Association (later the Providence Anti-slavery Colored Baptist Association) in 1834. Two years later, the Union Association was formed when churches in Cincinnati, Columbus, Chillicothe, and Brush Creek banded together. A third group, the Colored Baptist Association and Friends to Humanity, was organized in 1839 by three churches in southwestern Illinois. In 1849, this association divided (ostensibly for geographic reasons), giving rise to the Colored Baptist Association and the Mount Olive Association.[35] In 1856, the Colored Baptist Association changed its name to the Wood River Colored Baptist Association. A Canadian-based association, the Amherstburg Association, was formed in 1841. "Originally called the Baptist Association for Colored People,"[36] this organization united black Baptist churches in southern Ontario and Detroit, Michigan. The final association organized during the antebellum period was the Colored Baptist Association of Indiana, established in 1857.[37] Altogether, six associations were organized during the pre-Civil War years. Collectively, they helped to prepare the way for a truly national organization, following emancipation.

A significant step toward denominational status was the organization of two conventions prior to the Civil War, both of which enjoyed wide regional influence.[38] In 1840, the American Baptist Missionary Convention was created at the Abyssinian Baptist Church in New York City. The convention consisted of Zion Baptist in New York and Union Baptist of Philadelphia along with Abyssinian.

The convention resulted largely from a disagreement between black and white Baptists over slavery. In addition to lobbying for more missions to Africa, blacks pressed the General Missionary Convention of the Baptist Denomination in the United States for Foreign Missions (the Triennial Convention) for a stronger stand against slavery. "The abolition issue came to a head in April 1849 with the gathering in New York [of blacks and whites] of the American Baptist Antislavery Convention, the first Baptist abolitionist convention of national scope."[39] The meeting succeeded in voting "to bar slaveholders from being Baptist missionaries."[40] However, black Baptists wanted a more comprehensive policy. "They were also annoyed that they were blocked from significant influence in the Antislavery Convention and that the Triennial Convention discouraged strong antislavery voices in an effort to keep its Southern members."[41] Consequently, the American Baptist Missionary Convention (ABMC) was brought into being in August of that year, beginning the racially motivated splintering process among Baptists at the national level that has not been reversed to this day.

It is worth noting that five years after the organization of the ABMC, "most white southerners withdrew anyway,"[42] despite the efforts of the leadership in the Triennial Convention to softpedal the slavery issue. In 1845, the Southern Baptist Convention was formed, further dividing Baptists, not only along racial lines, but regional lines as well.

In 1853, the Western Colored Baptist Convention was "organized for trans-Mississippi church extension under the auspices of the Wood River Association."[43] In 1864, it was reorganized and renamed the Northwestern and Southern Baptist Convention, encompassing twenty-six churches representing eight states: Arkansas, Illinois, Indiana, Louisiana, Mississippi, Missouri, Ohio, and Tennessee.[44] "The major difference between this convention and its forerunner was the new commitment to missions among the 'freed brethren in the valley of the lower Mississippi' and 'in the states of Tennessee, Arkansas, and Missouri.' "[45]

In 1866, the ABMC and the Northwestern and Southern Baptist Convention merged to form the Consolidated American Baptist Missionary Convention (CABMC). This marked the first organization of denominational proportions among African American Baptists. Anticipating a rising tide of white supremacism and the disenfranchisement of most southern blacks, the two groups deemed it wise to join forces in the interest of black solidarity. The move toward union was significantly aided by William P. Normans, pastor of Union Baptist Church, Cincinnati, who "declared that black people must 'look out for our own interest in common with that of others, and stand by the people, who stand by God and the right.' "[46]

Unfortunately, the organization was plagued with internal and external problems from the outset. Internally, divisive issues sprang from regional attitudes, national politics, financial support, and internal governance. Externally, the problems were largely related to white denominational paternalism.[47] The demise of the CABMC was signaled in 1874, when the northern membership organized the New England Baptist Missionary Convention. The following year, the southern group formed the Southwestern and Southern Missionary Baptist Convention. The Consolidated Convention dissolved in 1879.[48]

The next attempt at national, if not denominational, organization took place the following year (1880) with the creation of the Baptist Foreign Mission Convention (BFMC). The mostly southern-based BFMC was an attempt to rally black Baptists to the cause of African missions. The effort met with limited success, because the New England Baptist Missionary Convention and the Western Baptist Foreign Mission Convention were entirely outside its aegis throughout its fourteen-year existence.

"The most ambitious attempt to found a black Baptist national denomination"[49] following the dissolution of the CABMC was the American National Baptist Convention. Led by such men as William J. Simmons, a Kentucky minister and educator,[50] and Richard de Baptiste, former president of the CABMC, black Baptists gathered in St. Louis, Missouri, in August 1886 "to devise and consider the best methods possible for bringing us [themselves] more closely together as a church and as a race."[51] Proponents were convinced that " 'race confidence' in black leadership would be enhanced through the union of black Baptist forces" and that "unity . . . would stand as a testimony against the . . . charge that blacks could not be amalgamated into American society."[52] They also believed that unity would help to dispel the belief of black and white ecclesiastics that black Baptist ministers, particularly in the South, were mostly an ignorant lot.[53] At the 1888 meeting of the American National Baptist Convention in Nashville, Tennessee, D. W. Wisher (pastor of Olivet Baptist Church, New York City), was eloquent in his plea for all black Baptist organizations to unite under one banner.[54]

Despite the passion and eloquence of Wisher's speech, it was clear at the 1889 gathering that the American National Baptist Convention could not claim the degree of loyalty needed to bring about unity. There were many black Baptists who felt a stronger allegiance to foreign missions than to home missions and who believed that the need to Christianize Africa was a higher calling, one that superseded the appeal for denominational unity on the basis of race.[55]

Four years later, at the convention's meeting in 1893, another fervent appeal for unity was made when it was argued that black Baptists should at least consolidate their foreign mission commitments. The representatives present received the appeal favorably. They agreed that all the organizations should meet with the American National Baptist Convention (as was customary) at its next meeting in Montgomery, Alabama. At that assembly, in 1894, the way was finally cleared for a permanent denominational structure when Albert W. Pegues, a prominent North Carolina preacher, tendered a motion that the Education Convention, the Baptist Foreign Mission Convention, and the American National Baptist Convention be reconstituted as boards of a single organization. They would become the Boards of Education, Foreign Mission, and Home Mission, respectively. "The national bodies agreed to take Pegues's proposal under advisement by appointing a joint committee that was asked to report at the 1895 meeting."[56] The committee endorsed the idea, thereby creating the National Baptist Convention, U.S.A., Inc. (NBCUSA). With the birth of this convention, African American Baptist denominationalism, of whatever root or branch, was firmly established in American ecclesiastical soil. In addition to NBCUSA, today's major African American Baptist bodies and organizations include the National Baptist Convention of America, Inc.; the Progressive National Baptist Convention, Inc.; the Lott Carey Baptist Foreign Mission Convention; the National Primitive Baptist Convention of the U.S.A.; the United American Free Will Baptist Denomination, Inc.; and the National Missionary Baptist Convention of America.

National Baptist Convention, U.S.A., Inc.

The National Baptist Convention, U.S.A., Inc. (NBCUSA), was organized on September 28, 1895, in Atlanta, Georgia.[57] Elias C. Morris of Helena, Arkansas, a pastor of national reputation, was elected president. Under his leadership, the Baptist Convention of Western States and Territories joined NBCUSA in 1896, making the convention the most comprehensive body of African American Baptists to that date. An able administrator, Morris served for twenty-seven years. During this time, additional boards and auxiliaries were organized to complement the work of the original three (i.e., the Boards of Education, Foreign Missions, and Home Missions). The Baptist Young People's Union (BYPU), the Women's Auxiliary, and the National Baptist Benefit Association, or Benefit Board, were organized in 1899, 1900, and 1903, respectively. The Sunday School and Baptist Young People's Union Congress was formed out of the Baptist Young People's Union Board in 1905.

NBCUSA has sometimes been referred to as a "corporation of corporations."[58] From its inception, it has largely been a confederation of organizations, each with its own distinct identity and loyal following. The conduct and success of its work has depended heavily upon strong leadership of its boards and auxiliaries, and the willingness of these men and women to keep the bodies under their charge "anchored in the Convention proper."[59] By virtue of Baptist polity, Baptists as a group have historically favored localized authority. For this reason, the individual units of the NBCUSA have tended to function semiautonomously. This has fostered a situation integrally linking the success of the Convention's work to the persuasive leadership skills of the national president. Often the national president must exhibit charismatic leadership qualities in order to transcend this tradition of local control.

President Lacey Kirk Williams, elected in 1922, met this requirement. Pastor of Olivet Baptist Church in Chicago, Williams's eighteen-year tenure was marked by his ability to promote cooperation between the various units and the parent body.[60] He is credited with granting the boards "the latitude and the freedom to perform their work creatively,"[61] while simultaneously commanding their allegiance and commitment to the convention as a cooperative enterprise.

In 1940, Williams was succeeded by David V. Jemison, who presided for many years over the Alabama Baptist State Convention. Until he retired in 1953, Jemison worked to maintain the emphasis on cooperation that characterized Williams's administration.[62] Jemison's foremost objective was to maintain a strong fellowship.

Joseph H. Jackson was elected to the presidency in 1953. This was the second time that a pastor of Olivet Baptist Church, Chicago, had been so honored. For nearly thirty years the activity of the convention was synonymous with his name. During the early years of his administration, considerable attention was directed to clarifying constitutional issues and reeducating members about the convention's structure and mission. In an effort to enhance the convention's effectiveness, Jackson orchestrated the most significant modification of its structure since its origination. A number of commissions were organized to broaden the scope of its work and to allow for more extensive participation. They included commissions on business, theological education, church-supported colleges, international and intercultural relationships, labor and management, ecumenical christianity, denominational coordination, rural life, public affairs, united nations, evangelism, undergraduate scholarships, and race relations.[63] Jackson also succeeded in gaining representation for the convention in the Baptist World Alliance.

A popular leader until his death in August 1990, Jackson took a controversial stand during the civil rights movement of the 1950s and 1960s. He opposed the strategies of civil disobedience and nonviolent protest as popularized by the Baptist activist, the Reverend Martin Luther King, Jr. He favored the cause of civil rights, but contended that it should be pursued according to the laws of democratic government. Another sore point during his administration was the question of presidential tenure. During the late 1950s and early 1960s, a vocal minority voiced strong opposition to his remaining in office beyond four years. Together with the civil rights issue, the tenure debate was a factor precipitating the creation of another national Baptist organization (the Progressive National Baptist Convention, Inc.) in 1961.

In 1982, Jackson was succeeded by Theodore J. Jemison, the son of David V. Jemison. Jemison currently presides over three auxiliaries and three boards. The auxiliaries include the National Baptist Laymen's Movement; the National Baptist Congress of Christian Education; and the Women's Convention, which represents four million women and publishes *The National Baptist Women*.The boards include the Sunday School Publishing Board, (which assumed the operation of the National Baptist Temperance Union Board in 1984), the National Baptist Home Mission Board, and the National Baptist Foreign Mission Board.

Consistent with its long-standing commitment to foreign missions, the convention is active in the Bahamas, Barbados, Jamaica, Lesotho, Liberia, Malawi, Nicaragua, Sierra Leone, South Africa, and Swaziland. Its home-missions program includes the support of a number of institutions of higher learning. They include American Baptist Theological Seminary, Central Baptist Theological Seminary, Morehouse School of Religion, National Baptist College, Selma University, Shaw Divinity School, and Shaw University.

NBCUSA represents thirty thousand churches, with membership in excess of 7.5 million.

National Baptist Convention of America, Inc.

The National Baptist Convention of America, Inc. (NBCA), was organized in 1915, the result of a dispute in the NBCUSA over ownership of the Publishing Board. Controversy was presaged as early as 1895, the time of the NBCUSA's founding, when the convention failed to create a separate department for publications.[64] In 1897, the problem was partly resolved when the NBCUSA instructed its Home Mission Board to establish a publishing house to print Sunday school materials. The publishing house was established in Nashville, Tennessee, with the Reverend Richard H. Boyd, who had long pushed the idea, in charge.

When the convention convened its annual meeting in Chicago in 1915, two issues dominated the proceedings. The first concern was whether the Reverend E. C. Morris should continue as president. The second, accentuated by the first, was confusion related to ownership of the publishing house, then alleged to be worth approximately $350,000.

Between 1899 and 1915, Morris attempted repeatedly to bring the publishing house under closer control of NBCUSA. It became clear at the Chicago meeting that the publishing operation and its copyrights were probably not the property of the convention but of the Reverend Richard Boyd, chairman of the board of the publishing house. It was revealed that the publishing house was incorporated under Tennessee law. Unknown to the great majority of the members, the NBCUSA was, itself, not incorporated. Consequently, the convention was hard-pressed to influence the publishing house's board members or, for that matter, control them.

Under the shadow of controversy, the Boyd faction severed its ties to the convention, organizing a meeting at another church in the city. Its members successfully sought an injunction against Morris and his followers, which was subsequently overturned, and the Boyd conclave was eventually ruled a "rump" convention. Nevertheless, on September 9, 1915, Boyd and his followers organized the National Baptist Convention, Unincorporated. A short time later the new body was renamed the National Baptist Convention of America (NBCA).[65] In 1916, the new convention published a document entitled "The Rightful and Lawful Ownership of the National Baptist Publishing House,"[66] which forthrightly declared that the publishing house was not owned by any convention. E. P. Jones was elected the first president. He served until 1923. Among other presidents, J. E. Woods (1923-1930), J. W. House (1930-1933), G. L. Prince (1933-1957), C. D. Pettaway (1957-1967), J. C. Sams (1967-1985), and E. E. Jones (1985 to present) have served.

Today the total membership of NBCA is estimated at between 3.5 to 5 million. It represents more than seven thousand churches and is strongest in Louisiana, Mississippi, North Carolina, South Carolina, and Texas.

Progressive National Baptist Convention, Inc.

The Progressive National Baptist Convention, Inc. (PNBC), was organized on November 14-15, 1961, at Zion Baptist Church, Cincinnati, Ohio. As with the National Baptist Convention of America, Inc., and the Lott Carey Baptist Foreign Mission Convention, its founding is attributable to controversy within the National Baptist Convention, U.S.A., Inc. Central to the discord were the issues of presidential tenure and the ways and means

to achieve civil rights.[67] The issue of tenure had been debated periodically from as early as 1922. After 1925, it had not been officially discussed until 1952, when the membership voted to amend the constitution to read, "[A] president . . . shall not be eligible for reelection after he has served four consecutive terms, until at least one year has elapsed."[68] Questions concerning the constitutionality of such an amendment kept the issue alive during the early years of Jackson's presidency. The debate intensified when it became linked with his position on civil rights. Jackson's stance was in opposition to that of a vocal and influential ministry inspired by the Reverend Martin Luther King, Jr., and his strategy of nonviolent resistance and civil disobedience: "Jackson tended to be more gradual or conservative in his approach to civil rights."[69] This group rallied behind Gardner C. Taylor, pastor of Concord Baptist Church in New York City and, in 1961, mounted a campaign to replace Jackson. When the effort failed, L. V. Booth, pastor of Zion Baptist Church in Cincinnati, Ohio, issued a national news release calling for the creation of another national Baptist organization, one committed to "redeeming the Baptist initiative and restoring a Democratic thrust."[70] Thirty-three delegates from fourteen states responded to the call, and the Progressive National Baptist Convention, Inc., was born.

The preamble to the PNBC's constitution is a clear statement of the organization's doctrine and polity:

The people called Progressive Baptists believe in the principles, tenets, and doctrines proclaimed or advocated in the New Testament as sufficient for their polity and practices. In Church government Baptists believe in the rule of the people, by the people, and for the people, and in the vestment of the authority and power to act in the majority. Therefore, we, the members of the Progressive National Baptist Convention, U.S.A., Inc., federate ourselves together in the name of and under the direction and guidance of God, sharing our common faith in Jesus Christ and our concern for strengthening God's work through our common activities, and establish this Constitution for the Progressive National Baptist Convention, U.S.A., Inc.[71]

Like most Baptists, Progressive Baptists endorse the concept that individuals are able to discern religious truth in communion with God and in fellowship with Jesus. They especially emphasize individual discernment in the life of local, state, and national church structures. Because of this emphasis, they stress sociopolitical involvement.

The PNBC has been very active in protesting South African apartheid and supporting the NAACP; the Urban League; the SCLC; the Martin Luther King, Jr., Center for Social Change; the Baptist World Alliance; the North American Baptist Fellowship; the Baptist Joint Committee on Public Affairs; the National Council of Churches; and the General Commission of Chaplains and Armed Forces Personnel. In addition, the PNBC includes a number of institutions of higher learning in its budget: Central

Baptist Theological Seminary, Howard University School of Divinity, Morehouse School of Religion, Morris College, Shaw Divinity School, Shaw University, Virginia Union Divinity School, and Virginia Union University.

The PNBC is divided into four regions: southern, southwestern, midwestern, and eastern. Each region conducts its own annual meetings in addition to participating in the annual meeting of the convention.

In contrast to the NBCUSA, which has had only five presidents since its founding, fourteen presidents have served the PNBC since 1961: Dr. T. M. Chambers, Los Angeles, California (1961-1966); Dr. Gardner C. Taylor, Brooklyn, New York (1967-1968); Dr. E. R. Searcy, Sr., Atlanta, Georgia (1968-1970); Dr. Earl L. Harrison, Washington, D.C. (1970-1971, who died in office); Dr. L. Venchael Booth, Cincinnati, Ohio (1971-1974); Dr. Nelson H. Smith, Jr., Birmingham, Alabama (1974-1976); Dr. Thomas Kilgore, Los Angeles, California (1976-1978); Dr. William A. Jones, Jr., Brooklyn, New York (1978-1980); Dr. Ralph W. Canty, Sumter, South Carolina (1980-1982); Dr. Charles W. Butler, Detroit, Michigan (1982-1984); Dr. Marshall L. Shepard, Jr., Philadelphia, Pennsylvania (1984-1986); Dr. J. Alfred Smith, Sr., Oakland, California (1986-1988); Dr. Fred C. Lofton, Memphis, Tennessee (1988-1990); and Dr. Charles G. Adams, Detroit, Michigan (1990-1994).

From modest beginnings, the PNBC has grown remarkably. Its churches now total more than eighteen hundred, with membership in excess of 1.8 million persons in forty-six states and the District of Columbia, its national headquarters.

Lott Carey Baptist Foreign Mission Convention

The Lott Carey Baptist Foreign Mission Convention (generally known as the Lott Carey Convention) was named in honor of the Reverend Lott Carey, a former slave born near Richmond, Virginia. Carey sailed for West Africa on January 16, 1821, as the first African American missionary to Africa. Originally called the First District Foreign Mission Convention,[72] the organization, founded at Shiloh Baptist Church in Washington, D.C., December 1897,[73] was renamed the "Lott Carey Foreign Missionary Society" in 1899.[74] In 1903, the name was modified a final time to the Lott Carey Baptist Foreign Mission Convention.[75] The founders included Calvin S. Brown, Albert W. Pegues, and Samuel N. Vass of North Carolina; John M. Armistead and Anthony Binga, Jr., of Virginia; W. M. Alexander and W. J. Howard of Maryland; and Walter H. Brooks, pastor of the Nineteenth Street Baptist Church, Washington, D.C.[76]

The founders were moved to organize the convention during the September 1897 annual meeting of the National Baptist Convention, U.S.A. Meeting in Boston, Massachusetts, at the Ebenezer Baptist Church, NBCUSA delegates found themselves embroiled in a vigorous debate centering on three interrelated and emotionally charged issues: 1) the relocation of the Foreign Mission Board office from Richmond to Louisville; 2) the use of American Baptist literature and cooperation with white Baptists in general; and 3) the primacy of foreign missions as a greater emphasis for the convention. These issues, in turn, were rooted in tensions arising from the consolidation of the national bodies in 1895 to form the NBCUSA.[77] "The majority of the delegates to the convention favored an independent spirit from white Baptist bodies."[78] A highly influential minority group, however, opposed relocating the Foreign Mission Board, as well as disassociation from the American Baptist Convention. Moreover, this group fervently believed that foreign missions should be the major focus of the convention's work. Unable to effect a consensus of their view, "this faction of clergymen (largely from North Carolina and Virginia) held a caucus session at Boston to evaluate the strength of their idea and to plan a strategy for the realization of their goal."[79] The result was the organizational meeting at Shiloh Baptist Church in Washington, D.C., "exactly three months" later.[80]

Almost from its inception, efforts were made to reunite the leadership of the Lott Carey Convention with NBCUSA. In 1903, "a proposal of cooperation"[81] was presented at the fifth annual meeting of the Lott Carey Convention; however, it was not until 1905 that an "organic relationship"[82] was reestablished. The arrangement was limited "to the foreign mission program of the two conventions . . . [with] the Lott Carey Convention enrolled as the First District Convention of the National Baptist Convention, U.S.A."[83]

In 1924, the Lott Carey Convention signed an agreement with NBCA (1915) to represent its commitment to foreign missions. In its formative years, the NBCA was unable to mount a strong foreign-missions program on its own. The Lott Carey Convention, under the leadership of Calvin Scott Brown, believed the new compact to be "more in keeping with the original philosophy of the [Lott Carey Baptist Foreign Mission Convention] than the earlier one with the National Baptist Convention, U.S.A."[84]

Following the agreement between the Lott Carey Convention and the NBCA, an attempt was made to reunite the group with NBCUSA. The effort failed, however, leading to a period of decline for both the Lott Carey Convention and the NBCA.[85]

The fate of the Lott Carey Convention was reversed when Wendell C. Somerville, nephew of Calvin Scott Brown, was appointed executive secretary-treasurer in the early 1940s. Somerville, who had already distinguished himself as a leader of the General Baptist State Convention of North Carolina, introduced a fundraising program that turned a nearly defunct operation into perhaps the most viable foreign mission organization ever created by African Americans. Titled "The Magnificent Men and Women of Troas," the program was aimed at motivating "black Baptist church leaders to contribute $1,000 or more annually to the convention."[86] By means of this program, Somerville, noted for his fervent, passionate appeals, has raised millions of dollars for "the cause of Christian missions."[87]

Today the membership of the Lott Carey Convention includes individuals and representatives from local Baptist congregations, associations, and state organizations. Sixteen states and the District of Columbia are affiliated and support 133 missionaries in Guyana, India, Kenya, Liberia, and Nigeria. The work of the convention is performed through evangelism, education, hospitals and leprosaria, and alleviation of hunger in crisis areas.

The Lott Carey Convention consists of the parent body, the Women's Auxiliary, the Laymen's League, the Youth Department, and the Annual Christian Youth Seminary. The parent body and auxiliaries jointly meet annually.

National Primitive Baptist Convention of the U.S.A.

The National Primitive Baptist Convention of the U.S.A. (also referred to as the National Primitive Convention) was organized in Hunstville, Alabama, in 1907. It was an outgrowth of the Primitive Baptist movement, which began about a century earlier. This movement was essentially a response to a growing trend among Baptists to embrace organized missionary activity, principally through affiliation with the Triennial Convention. Although the Triennial Convention could claim the allegiance of most Baptists, "there remained a minority who viewed the missionary movement as an innovation."[88] By 1827, this group was strongly represented in the Kehukee Association, which, as a spin-off from the Philadelphia Association, was the second-oldest Baptist association in America. In that year, the Kehukee Association resolved to withdraw support from all missionary societies, Bible societies, and theological seminaries, stating that the association saw these as the "inventions of men, and not warranted from the Word of God."[89]

The action of the Kehukee Association precipitated the organization of a number of new Baptist associations that regarded themselves as representative of the "'true,' 'primitive,' or 'old school'" way.[90] Thirteen years later, "Primitive Baptist associations covered what was then the United States, reaching north into Pennsylvania and west to Missouri and Texas."[91] Among their ranks were a number of black Primitive Baptists who worshiped with whites in segregated meetinghouses. It was not until after the Civil War that African Americans organized separate churches and, subsequently, separate associations. Among the first of these was the Indian Creek

Association, which was founded in northern Alabama around 1869.

Toward the end of the nineteenth century, the African American associations began pushing for a national convention. Although such a body deviated from a principal Primitive Baptist belief that no organization should exist above the loosely structured associations covering several counties, black Primitive Baptists believed that their collective interests would be best met and safeguarded through a national organization.[92] In 1906, approximately eighty-five elders responded to a call by Elders Clarence Francis Sams, George S. Crawford, and James H. Carey, to meet in Hunstville the following year to unite black Primitive Baptists throughout the country, albeit mainly in the South.

The doctrines of the National Primitive Baptist Convention of the U.S.A. include belief in the Trinity, in the Bible as the only rule of faith and practice, divine election, original sin, human depravity (i.e., the inability of people to recover from their fallen state by means of their own free will), perseverance of the saints, baptism by immersion, closed communion, the resurrection, and ordination.[93] Baptism, the Lord's Supper, and footwashing are regarded as ordinances (i.e., the formally institutionalized religious observances, rituals or practices that are basic to membership). The polity is congregational. There are two offices at the local level: pastor or elder; and deacon or deaconess. "The convention meets annually and sponsors a publishing board. In 1975, it claimed 606 churches with 250,000 members and 636 ministers."[94]

United American Free Will Baptist Denomination, Inc.

The history of the United American Free Will Baptist church can be traced to a general conference of Free Will Baptists, organized in 1827 as a result of cooperation between the southern-based Original Free Will Baptists and the Free Will Baptists in the North.[95] "In 1827 the General Conference, in one of its first sessions, decided to ordain Negroes to the ministry."[96] In so doing, the conference acted wholly in accord with the spirit of the Arminian principles it espoused: "1) the universal love of God to men, 2) the universal atonement in the work of redemption by Jesus Christ, 3) the universal appearance of Grace to all men, and 4) the universal call of the Gospel."[97] The action was also "a significant forecast of the strong position which [the Conference] was to take against slavery in later years."[98]

The antislavery posture of the conference, together with its work among the freedmen at Storer College, "which was established by the Home Mission Society at Harper's Ferry,"[99] attracted a number of African Americans to its ranks during the nineteenth century. However, not even its thoroughgoing Arminian theology could withhold the encroachment of racism within its fold. Consequently, in 1901, the African American membership established its own denomination, the United American Free Will Baptist church.

The United American Free Will Baptist Denomination, Inc., is similar to its parent body (the Free Will Baptists) in many respects. For example, "It is Arminian in theology and practices footwashing and anointing the sick with oil."[100] Moreover, "the local church is autonomous in regard to business, elections, and form of government, [although] the conferences have the power to decide the questions of doctrine."[101] The United American Free Will Baptist church differs, however, in that "the congregational polity was modified within a system of district, quarterly, annual, and general conferences."[102] As of 1952, the most recent year for which figures are available, there were 836 churches and 100,000 members.[103] The denominational headquarters are in Kinston, North Carolina.[104]

National Missionary Baptist Convention of America

The National Missionary Baptist Convention of America (NMBCA) was organized in November 1988 in Dallas, Texas. Reminiscent of the events that led to the founding of the National Baptist Convention of America (NBCA) in 1915, the NMBCA resulted from controversy concerning the Sunday school congress and publishing house and the desire on the part of some to restore the organizational structure as envisioned in the creation of the National Baptist Convention, U.S.A., Inc. (NBCUSA). Ironically in 1988, the NBCA attempted to gain legal control over the publishing house, after declaring at its 1915 founding that the publishing house was not the property of any convention. From the inception of the NBCA both had remained largely under the direction and immediate supervision of the Boyd family. At its 1988 meeting in San Antonio, Texas, attended by over seven hundred messengers from across the nation, the convention resolved to organize a Sunday school congress, which it would indisputably control. This move effectively severed ties with the Boyd-controlled congress and publishing house. Approximately five hundred church leaders met subsequently in Dallas to create a new organization, the NMBCA, electing S. M. Lockridge of San Diego, California, president, and S. J. Gilbert, general secretary. The NMBCA consists of a membership of 2,142,150 persons representing 14,281 churches.

Conclusion

Although substantive African American Baptist organizational development took place prior to 1895, no fewer than six major bodies have emerged since then. For the most part, they have a common emphasis on believers' baptism, baptism by immersion, congregational polity (although in a modified form within the United Free Will Baptist church), and separation of church and state. None officially endorses the ordination of women, believing it not to be justified in Scripture, but together they believe that African Americans should participate equally in the life and work of the church with other racial and ethnic groups.

Beyond what they have in common, they differ on which ordinances they recognize, on their commitment to systematic missionary activity, and on their theological stand on atonement. The NBCUSA, the NBCA, the PNBC, the NMBCA, and the Lott Carey Convention regard only baptism and the Lord's Supper as ordinances. To these, the National Primitive Baptist Convention of the U.S.A. adds footwashing, and the United American Free Will Baptist Church holds yet another ordinance, anointing the sick. NBCUSA, NBCA, PNBC, NMBCA, and the Lott Carey Convention are explicitly missionary-oriented. As the United Free Will Baptist church does, they believe in general atonement, although it is not a matter of primary emphasis. By contrast, the National Primitive Baptist Convention, U.S.A., posits limited atonement. In varying degrees, a fraternal relationship exists among the NBCUSA, the NBCA, the PNBC, and the Lott Carey Convention. Collectively, the six organizations represent more than forty thousand churches with thirteen million congregants.

Notes

1. James M. Washington, *Frustrated Fellowship: The Black Baptist Quest for Social Power* (Macon, Ga.: Mercer University Press, 1986), 4. Winthrop Hudson, *A Baptist Manual of Polity and Practice* (Valley Forge, Pa.: Judson Press, 1981), 8-9. *Anabaptists*, or "rebaptizers," is a name applied to a number of related groups that emerged during the sixteenth century. Called Anabaptists by opponents, their name was derived from their declaration that infant baptism was invalid and their insistence that those who had been baptized in infancy must be rebaptized. The Anabaptist movement is often characterized as the radical "Left Wing" of the Reformation. Many Anabaptists pressed far beyond the reforms proposed for the Catholic church by Martin Luther (1483-1546) in Germany, and Huldreich Zwingli (1484-1531) in Switzerland. Historically, Anabaptist groups have subscribed to: 1) literal interpretation of Scripture; 2) baptism of adults, or believers' baptism; 3) separation of church and state; 4) congregational autonomy; and 5) pacifism. Today the largest group of Anabaptists are the Mennonites, founded by Menno Simons (1492-1559) in the Netherlands. For more information see F. H. Littell, *The Free Church* (Boston: Beacon Press, 1957); G. H. Williams, *The Radical Reformation* (Philadelphia: Westminster Press, 1962); and Hudson, 11-12. Contrary to popular opinion, baptism by immersion, as opposed to aspersion (sprinkling) or affusion (pouring), was not one of the initial emphases of Anabaptists. See William H. Brackney, ed., *Baptist Life and Thought: 1600-1980* (Valley Forge, Pa.: Judson Press, 1983), 37.
2. Hudson, 11-12.
3. Hudson, 9.

234

4. Ibid., 9-10. On the issue of congregational polity, Puritans were strongly influenced by one of the foundational principles of the Reformation: the "priesthood of all believers," that is, the tenet that all true believers are of equal estate in matters of faith. They posited that true believers should covenant to form a congregation. Having done so, they should be self-governing, relying upon holy Scripture as the ultimate source of authority. In the final analysis, they believed that true believers should answer to God only.

5. Willison Walker, *A History of the Christian Church* (New York: Charles Scribner's Sons, 1970), 408.

6. Ibid., 408-9.

7. Ibid., 409. This group was a remnant of Smyth's congregation. Smyth died of tuberculosis in 1612.

8. Ibid., 409. Brackney, ed., *Baptist Life and Thought: 1600-1980*, 29. This is the first Congregational church to remain in continuous existence.

9. Walker, 409; Brackney, ed., *Baptist Life and Thought: 1600-1980*, 29.

10. Brackney, 6. William Kiffin (1616-1701) joined the Spilsbury church five years later and subsequently became one of the leading polemicists for the Particular viewpoint.

11. Walker, *A History of the Christian Church*, 409.

12. Evidence suggests that prior to the 1640s, Baptists practiced sprinkling, pouring, dipping, and plunging. By the 1640s, study and debate inclined most to adopt immersion. Article 40 of the Leiden Confession of 1644 defined the practice; for quote, see Brackney, 37.

13. Ibid., 97. Brackney also notes that General Baptists in New England had actually organized an association as early as 1670. During the 1630s English Baptists increased steadily in numbers. Until the mid-eighteenth century, General Baptists were more numerous than the Particular Baptists in New England and the southern colonies. Particular Baptists were probably in the majority in the middle colonies, especially around Philadelphia and southern New Jersey, where they organized the first Calvinistic association in 1707.

14. In the 1680s, two Baptist churches were constituted in the middle colonies. "A short-lived congregation was founded in 1684, and, in 1688, the Pennepack Church in Philadelphia was founded." See J. Gordon Melton, ed., *The Encyclopedia of American Religions*, 2d ed. (Detroit: Gale Research Inc., 1987), 61. During the late 1600s Baptists also began to appear in the South. The first Baptist church was formed in this region in 1714, in Burleigh, Isle of Wight County, Virginia. It was straightforwardly of Arminian, or General, Baptist persuasion. Compare Robert G. Torbet, *A History of the Baptists* (Valley Forge, Pa.: Judson Press, 1963), 215. According to Torbet, a group of English General, or Arminian, Baptists had settled in Isle of Wight County, Virginia, as early as 1700. They appealed to their fellowship in London to send them an ordained preacher. Two men, Thomas White and Robert Nordin, were sent, but only Nordin survived the voyage. Nordin organized the church just across the James River from Jamestown. Today this congregation is known as the Mill Swamp Church in the Blackwater Association.

15. See Sydney Ahlstrom, *A Religious History of the American People* (New Haven: Yale University Press, 1972), 282. However, two helpful, full-length studies are Edwin Scott Gaustad, *The Great Awakening in New England* (New York: Harper & Brothers, 1957), and Wesley M. Gewehr, *The Great Awakening in Virginia, 1740-1790* (Durham, N.C.: Duke University Press, 1930). By the mid-eighteenth century, however, Particular Baptists surpassed General Baptists, largely because of "the efficient missionary work of the Philadelphia Association" (Washington, *Frustrated Fellowship*, 5). This work, coupled with the enthusiasm for organized religion stimulated by the Awakenings, produced the second-largest single denomination in America (See Torbet, *A History of the Baptists*, 243-46, 253).

16. Throughout the years, the free church, or nonjurisdictional character, of Baptist organizational life has resulted in separations over diverse matters.

17. Washington, *Frustrated Fellowship*, 5.

18. "Separate Baptists were known also as 'New Lights' because of their emphasis upon the possibility of individual inspiration and enlightenment through the Holy Spirit." Torbet, *A History of the Baptists*, 223-24. Regular Baptists believed that a reserved and constrained manner was a more reliable indication of divine favor. Frequently, New Lights separated themselves from the Regulars, thereby giving rise to two distinctive camps of Particular Baptists.

19. Ibid., 246.

20. Ibid., 245.

21. Ibid., 249.

22. This popular name for the convention derived from the fact that it met every three years. See Torbet, 250.

23. Ibid., 263.

24. Ibid.

25. Ibid.

26. Washington, *Frustrated Fellowship*, 8.

27. Over the years there occurred a gradual, barely perceptible drift toward the Arminian point of view. The reasons for this shift remain to be identified. It is likely that the trend was evident during the last thirty years of the nineteenth century. It was around this time that African American Baptists began organizing Primitive Baptist, or Old School, associations. Perhaps by the turn of the century, when African American Primitive Baptists began the slow process of organizing nationally, most were essentially of General Baptist persuasion. See the section on the National Primitive Baptist Association of the U.S.A., this volume.

28. Torbet provides a helpful overview of early Baptist confessions of faith in *History of the Baptists*, 45. Most important for American Baptists is the New Hampshire Confession of Faith of 1833. Melton points out that this confession became the working document for the majority of Baptists in America. Amended versions have been adopted by a number of Baptist groups, including the Southern Baptist Convention, in 1925. For a reading of the New Hampshire Confession with its 1853 additions, see Melton, *Encyclopedia of American Religions*, 2d ed., 59-60.

29. From the New Hampshire Confession of Faith with its 1853 additions. See Melton, 59.

30. I agree with James Washington's illuminating statement that the emergence of "some kind of community" among the slaves was due to their total life situation, or "sitz im leben." But I want to emphasize that theological issues and considerations, even when they function as parts of political discourse, as Washington correctly asserts, were central to the situation in which African Americans found themselves.

31. Mechal Sobel, *Trabelin' On: The Slave Journey to an Afro-Baptist Faith* (Westport, Conn.: Greenwood Press, 1979), 102, 296. There is considerable debate about the first African American Baptist congregation. Questions as to whether a particular congregation was officially constituted, legally recognized, wholly separate, actually independent, or pastored by an ordained African American person complicate the discussion. All these questions aside, I have chosen to adopt Sobel's view as to the likelihood of the congregation on the Byrd plantation being the first. In this regard, it is helpful to note that both Mulkey and Williams were inspired by Shubal Stearns (1706-1771), who had been inspired by the "Grand Itinerant," George Whitefield. According to Sobel, Stearns was ordained in 1751 in Toland, Connecticut. That same year, he evangelized throughout New England, Virginia, and then North Carolina, where at Sandy Creek, a legendary revival meeting took place. In 1755, he began a revival that spread through parts of North Carolina, South Carolina, Virginia, Geor-

gia, and Mississippi. Stearns's evangelism is integrally related to African American Baptist beginnings in the South. See Sobel, 84ff.

32. Sobel, *Trabelin' On*, cites 1777 as the founding date for the First Colored Baptist Church, Savannah, while acknowledging that there is a historical dispute over the continuity of the church until 1788. See Sobel, 319. Leroy Fitts, *A History of Black Baptists* (Nashville: Broadman Press, 1985), 33, favors 1788 as the date of origin.

33. Sobel, *Trabelin' On*, provides a very helpful chronology of African American Baptist church development. Some of the dates are open to question, but the chronology remains quite useful. See Appendix B, this volume.

34. Washington, *Frustrated Fellowship*, 38.

35. Sobel, *Trabelin' On*, 364.

36. Washington, *Frustrated Fellowship*, 36.

37. Sobel, *Trabelin' On*, 364.

38. Washington, *Frustrated Fellowship*, 38.

39. Ibid., 39.

40. Ibid.

41. Ibid.

42. Ibid.

43. Ibid., 44.

44. Sobel, 365, cites 1866 as the year of reorganization. See *Trabelin' On*.

45. Washington, *Frustrated Fellowship*, 44.

46. Ibid., 78.

47. Ibid., 81.

48. Washington, *Frustrated Fellowship*, 130. Sobel, 365, cites 1871.

49. Washington, *Frustrated Fellowship*, 138.

50. Simmons was also president of the black State University of Kentucky; see Washington, *Frustrated Fellowship*, 139.

51. Ibid.

52. Ibid., 141.

53. Ibid., 142.

54. Ibid., 145-46.

55. Ibid., 171.

56. Ibid., 183

57. Perhaps it is helpful to quote Fitts, *A History of Black Baptists*, 94: "Strangely enough, neither . . . [the National Baptist Convention, U.S.A. nor the National Baptist Convention of America] was organized in 1880. The black Baptist convention that was organized in Montgomery, Alabama, in 1880 . . . was named the Baptist Foreign Mission Convention. However, black Baptist leaders, from the outset of the cooperative movements of a national scope, developed the habit of claiming the organizational date of antecedent black Baptist conventions."

58. J. H. Jackson, *A Story of Christian Activism: The History of the National Baptist Convention, U.S.A., Inc.* (Nashville: Townsend Press, 1980), 169.

59. Joseph H. Jackson, quoting L. K. Williams, second president of the National Baptist Convention, U.S.A., Inc., 169.

60. Ibid.

61. Ibid.

62. Jackson, *A Story of Christian Activism*, 179.

63. Ibid., 240-50. According to Jackson, a program committee and a committee on place were also constituted for the first time.

64. Washington, *Frustrated Fellowship*, 185.

65. Fitts, *A History of Black Baptists*, 93.

66. Ibid.

67. Ibid., 99-100.

68. Jackson, *A Story of Christian Activism*, 212.

69. Fitts, *A History of Black Baptist*, 101.

70. Ibid., 104.

71. Progressive National Baptist Convention, Inc., 1. Press Release (n.d.).

72. Jackson, *A Story of Christian Activism*, 82.

73. Washington, *Frustrated Fellowship*, 195.

74. Jackson, *A Story of Christian Activism*, 82.

75. Washington, *Frustrated Fellowship*, 195.

76. Ibid., 194-195.

77. Fitts, *A History of Black Baptists*, 84-85.

78. Ibid., 85.

79. Ibid., 86.

80. Washington, *Frustrated Fellowship*, 195.

81. Fitts, *A History of Black Baptists*, 89.

82. Ibid.

83. Ibid.

84. Ibid., 95.

85. Ibid., 97.

86. Ibid.

87. Ibid.

88. Melton, *Encyclopedia of American Religions*, 2d ed., 62.

89. Ibid., 63.

90. Ibid.

91. Ibid.

92. J. Gordon Melton, ed., *The Encyclopedia of American Religious Creeds*, 1st ed., (Detroit: Gale Research, Inc., 1988), 529.

93. Melton, *Encyclopedia of American Religions*, 2d ed., 63.

94. Ibid., 398.

95. The Original Free Will Baptists were organized in 1729 in Virginia and North Carolina. Perhaps their emergence is indirectly due to Thomas Nordin who, in 1714, organized the first Baptist church in Virginia (Isle of Wight County) and directly to Paul Palmer who, in 1727, organized the first Baptist church in North Carolina, near the Virginia border (Chowan County). Both Nordin, a native of England, and Palmer, a native of Maryland, were Arminian in their theology. Torbet does not mention either contact between Nordin and Palmer or their possible connection to the Original Free Will Baptists, who believed themselves to be historically descended from the church Helwys organized in England in 1611 or 1612. Nonetheless, it is quite likely that this organization resulted from their ministrations, given the close proximity of their followers (a distance of seventy miles). See Torbet, *A History of the Baptists*, 218-19, 256-61. With particular regard to Palmer, it is interesting to note that the National Association of Free Will Baptists, organized in 1935 and headquartered in Nashville, Tennessee, traces its history through the general conference to him. See Melton, *Encyclopedia of American Religions*, 2d ed., 403.

The presence of Free Will Baptists in the North, cited in Melton, *Encyclopedia of American Religions*, 2d ed., 403, is probably connected to Benjamin Randall, a seaman turned tailor and evangelist. Randall organized a Free Will Baptist Church in New Durham, New Hampshire, in 1780. According to Torbet, 258-61, between 1781 and 1792, Randall organized the churches into "Quarterly Meetings and a Yearly Meeting." Torbet clearly links Randall to the events leading to the formation of the general conference nineteen years following his death.

96. Torbet, *A History of the Baptists*, 259.

97. Torbet, *A History of the Baptists*, quoting Randall, 258, n.100.

98. Ibid., 259.

99. Ibid., 261.

100. Melton, *Encyclopedia of American Religions*, 2d ed., 404.

101. Ibid.

102. Ibid.

103. Ibid.

104. Ibid. Melton indicates Kingston rather than Kinston.

Bibliography

Ahlstrom, Sydney. *A Religious History of the American People*. New Haven: Yale University Press, 1972.

Brackney, William H., ed., *Baptist Life and Thought: 1600-1980*. Valley Forge, Pa.: Judson Press, 1983.

Fitts, Leroy. *A History of Black Baptists*. Nashville: Broadman Press, 1985.

Gaustad, Edwin S. *The Great Awakening in New England*. New York: Harper & Brothers, 1957.

Gewehr, Wesley M. *The Great Awakening in Virginia, 1740-1790*. Durham, N.C.: Duke University Press, 1930.

Hudson, Winthrop. *A Baptist Manual of Polity and Practice*. Valley Forge, Pa.: Judson Press, 1981.

Jackson, Joseph H. *A Story of Christian Activism: The History of the National Baptist Convention, U.S.A., Inc*. Nashville: Townsend Press, 1980.

Littell, F. H. *The Free Church*. Boston: Beacon Press, 1957.

Melton, J. Gordon, ed., *The Encyclopedia of American Religions*, 2d ed. Detroit: Gale Research Co., 1987.

————. *The Encyclopedia of American Religious Creeds*, 1st ed. Detroit: Gale Research Inc., 1988.

Sobel, Mechal. *Trabelin' On: The Slave Journey to an Afro-Baptist Faith*. Westport, Conn.: Greenwood Press, 1979.

Torbet, Robert G. *A History of the Baptists*. Valley Forge, Pa.: Judson Press, 1963.

Walker, Willison. *A History of the Christian Church*. New York: Charles Scribner's Sons, 1970.

Washington, James M. *Frustrated Fellowship: The Black Baptist Quest for Social Power*. Macon, Ga.: Mercer University Press, 1986.

Williams, G. H. *The Radical Reformation*. Philadelphia: Westminster Press, 1962.

African Americans and Methodism

Calvin S. Morris

Methodism was introduced to America from England in 1766 by Charles and John Wesley and their associates. As students at Oxford University in 1729 these brothers stressed the importance of developing a religious lifestyle that seriously and methodically manifested religious devotion in work, prayer, study, and Bible reflection. In 1739 John Wesley initiated a program in England that provided instruction to his followers on the principles of the faith through exchanges in small groups known as class meetings. These class meetings were informal gatherings that served as the primary vehicle for promoting fellowship, stewardship, and understanding of the church's doctrine and met under lay leadership in the absence of ordained persons. These groups later became known as "societies."[1] The Methodist movement reached America in the fall of 1766 through class meetings held in the home of Barbara Heck and Philip Embury in New York City. This group later evolved into the John Street Methodist Episcopal Church.

African Americans have been associated with the Methodist church from its earliest beginnings in America. Africans, including one woman named Betty, an African female who was most likely a slave, were among the pioneering members of the John Street Methodist Episcopal Church. By the end of the century, Africans numbered 211, or almost a third of the total membership. Although it is generally thought that Maryland might have been the site of Methodism's earliest society in the colonies, Norwood and McClain maintain that Methodism's emergence in New York City predated similar developments in Maryland by at least a decade.[2]

Early Development: An Egalitarian Movement

Methodism as a religious movement in the American colonies did not make distinctions between blacks and whites in its evangelism. This revolutionary theology was associated with the Great Awakening, a series of religious revivals that spread throughout the American colonies about the middle of the eighteenth century. The early evangelists, most of whom were laypersons, were fired with a zeal to bring the saving message of redemption in Christ to those who were "lost in sin" and to persuade them of the forgiving mercy of God. As the movement matured, traveling preachers carried the Gospel throughout the inhabited parts of the developing nation. Africans who heard these preachers' messages of repentance and salvation responded with enthusiasm, submitted to the disciplines of the societies, and were active participants in the class meetings. There is little evidence to suggest that Methodism promoted any overt or intentional acts of discrimination among the races in its early years.[3]

In *The African Methodist Episcopal Zion Church: Reality of the Black Church*, William J. Walls provides an insightful reflection on African Americans in the early development of Methodism. Walls reviews the emergence of Methodism in America and its attenuating institutional restrictions. He documents the extensive acts of racial oppression and bigotry that gave New York the largest slave population among the nonplantation English colonies. His most critical commentary on the limitations of Methodism as they pertained to the treatment of African Americans between 1766 and 1796 considers the legal restrictions placed on both freed and enslaved African Americans. The civil laws restricted the freedom of assembly for both groups of African Americans. Black worshipers were required to use the gallery and to attend classes led by white male class leaders. Walls concludes that whether the adjustments were due to societal restrictions or racism (in spite of John Wesley's strong opposition to slavery), African Americans were discontented with the harsh realities of a segregated society. As a result of these racial restrictions, some African Americans became especially skeptical of the church's role and mission.[4]

The egalitarian nature of Methodism in America was sustained during its first two decades, dating from 1744 to 1764.[5] Although Africans were frequently organized into separate societies and classes, there was ample opportunity for interracial prayer and praise meetings and integrated class meetings. Richard Allen, who was converted under the preaching of Freeborn Garrettson while he was a slave in Delaware, described how Africans shared in the early spread of the Gospel:

. . . [T]he colored people were their [Methodist traveling preachers'] greatest support; for there were but few of us free; but the slaves would toil in their little patches many a night until midnight to raise their little truck and sell to get something to support them more than what their masters gave them, but we used often to divide our little support among the white preachers of the Gospel. This was once a quarter.[6]

There were a number of reasons that account for the African Americans' affirmative responses to Methodist ministrations. Primarily, the Methodist preachers appeared to have genuine interest in and concern for the spiritual welfare of their black brothers and sisters. African Americans also found the spontaneity and freedom in Methodist worship to be congenial. Richard Allen put the matter succinctly:

The Methodists were the first people that brought glad tidings to the colored people. I feel thankful that ever I heard a Methodist preach. We are beholden to the Methodist, under God, for the light of the Gospel we enjoy; for all other denominations preached so high-flown that we were not able to comprehend their doctrine. Sure am I that reading sermons will never prove beneficial to the colored people as spirited or extermpore [sic] preaching. I am well convinced that the Methodist have proved beneficial to thousands and ten times thousands.[7]

Organized religion, and Methodism in particular, provided an arena in which some African Americans could exercise their leadership talents. Access to the preaching ministry was a principal venue through which some pioneer African American Methodists rose to positions of prominence in the community. The best-known black preacher in Methodism prior to 1800 was Harry Hosier, sometimes known as "Black Harry." A close associate and traveling companion of Bishops Thomas Coke and Francis Asbury, Hosier was known for his powerful and moving preaching. His preaching and example were prototypes for many who would follow him, including Richard Allen, James Varick, Peter Spencer, and Daniel Coker, who all later gained fame as leaders of African American Methodist denominations.[8]

The Methodist church was reluctant to elevate African American preachers formally to the itinerant ministry, and did not agree to ordain them as deacons until the General Conference of 1800. Even this action was not incorporated in the Discipline as an established policy of the church.[9] The practice of ordaining African Americans as deacons became the de facto policy of the church, and it was adhered to, despite the vigorous opposition of proslavery forces within the church.[10]

Abolition: The Divisive Issue

African Americans, both slave and free, were attracted to Methodism because of its opposition to slavery. John Wesley, the founder, had boldly denounced slavery and the African slave trade on the grounds that they were contrary to the will of God. Following his example, many clergy and lay Methodists opposed human bondage, called

upon all persons within the church to desist from traffic in human beings, and urged them to free their bondsmen. As Methodists became more and more numerous in the South, the church's opposition to slavery became less and less prominent, and its denunciation of the institution as a sin against God was muted.[11]

The Methodist church's retreat from its vigorous opposition to slavery was part of a broader movement in American society, in which the security of property in slaves transcended commitment to the principles of both the Gospel and the Constitution of the United States. Later, the issue of slavery would lead to the formation of separate black Methodist bodies. Donald G. Matthews described the Methodist defection from the antislavery vanguard as follows:

The reasons for the great repudiation of Methodist anti-slavery ideals and action are not difficult to determine. In the first place, recalcitrant Methodist laymen simply did not want to free slaves which they already owned or someday hoped to buy. The Church was growing rapidly not only among the dispossessed Negroes but also among possessing whites, who craved a share of the prosperity which has always been the "American dream." Part of that dream for many Southerners became the owning of slaves as cotton ascended to the throne after 1793. . . . Methodism was a people's movement, and the people either wanted slavery or feared emancipation. Bishop Asbury had concluded by 1798 that slavery would exist in Virginia "for ages; there [was] not sufficient sense of religion or liberty to destroy it; Methodists, Baptists, Presbyterians, in the highest flights of rapturous piety, still maintain and defend it."[12]

African American Methodists were aware of the waning fervor in the church for abolition and noted the growing segregation in individual congregations. They also observed that they were increasingly excluded from significant participation in the life of the worship community by segregated practices such as separate "love feasts" (meals shared in common in a congregation), separate communion services for whites and blacks, segregated reserved seating in the galleries or against the walls in worship services, and hostility expressed by whites relative to the growing number of blacks in the congregations. Some white churchmen were concerned lest the sheer numbers of blacks would enable them to exercise veto power in the politics of the church. The white churchmen's response was to hold special meetings from which African American members were excluded. Despite exclusion and disenfranchisement, the church's black membership continued to expand, and by 1796 constituted one-fifth of the total membership.[13]

The discriminatory practices within the Methodist societies in Philadelphia, Wilmington, and New York were the precipitating reasons for separate African American congregations being organized. Richard Allen put the withdrawal of the Philadelphia group in its most favorable light when he concluded that he and the men and women who followed him withdrew because they felt that their presence was offensive to whites, because they could not worship as they wanted to, and because many African Americans refused to listen to a Gospel that appeared to ratify the cruel practices of slavery.

Although some African Americans withdrew from the Methodist societies in the locations previously cited, they remained Methodists and retained, formally, most aspects of its discipline, polity, hymnody, and order of worship. The emerging African American congregations continued petitioning the Methodist church to be more responsive to the particular needs of their fellows and arguing for a more vigorous antislavery stance. These efforts met with limited success and ultimately resulted in severed ties to the Methodist church. Frederick Norwood, in his authoritative account, *The Story of American Methodism*, delineates seven stages that defined the separating process: 1) integration, 2) segregation, 3) separate meeting time, 4) separate meeting place, 5) autonomous local organization, 6) independent local church, and 7) regional denomination.[14]

The Establishment of Separate African American Traditions

African American Methodists became convinced through segregated practices of the Methodist church that the dominant body was incapable of addressing the particular human and religious needs of oppressed slaves and freedpersons, and so separate African American churches and denominations were established in the late eighteenth and early nineteenth centuries. These African American bodies did not change the Methodist doctrine; rather, they adhered to the basic theological and doctrinal traditions of Methodism. The African American church bodies provided opportunities for their members to worship according to their own preferences, to be involved in their own self-help projects, to exercise the prerogatives of free men and women without the superintendence of whites, and to interpret the Gospel in such ways as to demonstrate its relevance for their redemption both in time and eternity. Above all, they were convinced of the fact that despite their historical circumstances, God cared for them.

In the late eighteenth and early nineteenth centuries, several independent African American congregations were created: the African Methodist Episcopal Church, the Union Church of Africans (now known as the Union American Methodist Episcopal Church), and the African Methodist Episcopal Zion Church. With the split in 1844 in the Methodist Episcopal Church that resulted in the creation of two distinct bodies—the Methodist Episcopal Church (the northern body) and the Methodist Episcopal Church, South—the groundwork was laid for the establishment of the Colored Methodist Episcopal Church. Following the Civil War, the Methodist Episcopal Church, South, created the Colored Methodist Episcopal Church, which later, under its own initiative, adopted the name "Christian Methodist Episcopal Church."

The issue of slavery was indeed divisive. Not only did it result in the establishment of the African Methodist Episcopal Church, but it was also instrumental in the creation of the Christian Methodist Episcopal Church. Methodist Bishop James O. Andrew and his wife, both Georgian slave owners, found themselves in a political quandary. When confronted by church officials who demanded that they cease slaveholding, they found it impossible to manumit their slaves under Georgia laws. The General Conference of 1844, held in New York City, voted to restrain Bishop Andrew in his duties until he desisted. The southern delegates were outraged by this resolve and created the Methodist Episcopal Church, South, that same year. Although there was considerable debate over the procedures that the General Conference should use in order to depose a bishop, this split was not related to theological or doctrinal positions.

Organizational Overview

The governance of the Methodist church is episcopal, and this may also account for much of the church's growth. There is a highly centralized governing authority that operates under the auspices of bishops, who supervise jurisdictional territories called districts. However, decisions affecting the body are made by both clergy and laity. In general, these practices have not changed since the church's inception.

Methodist bodies operate through quarterly, annual, and general conferences. The quarterly conference is under the authority of the district superintendent. It usually consists of the local churches, called "charges," which are generally less autonomous than many local churches in other Protestant bodies. This conference determines such matters as the salary of the pastor, the operational budget for the church, and the selection of church officers and delegates to the annual conference.

The annual conference handles such issues as determination of the geographical boundaries, ordination and certification of ministers, constitutional matters pertaining to the church's governance, and determination of delegates to the general conference. Pastors or elders are also appointed to congregations by the jurisdictional bishop at these meetings. The annual conference is under the authority of the bishop.

The general conference meets quadrennially. It is the organizational entity that enacts the laws governing the church as a collective unit. It operates through committees and is under the supervision of the presiding or senior bishop. The position of presiding bishop is generally rotated among the bishops. Delegates—lay and clergy alike—are elected by and sent from the individual churches and/or annual conferences to the general conference. The general conference is the ultimate ruling authority of the church. Matters adopted by this body constitute the church's laws. Issues pertaining to the church constitution are not changed by the general conference unless every annual conference has acted upon the proposed changes. Bishops are also elected by the membership at general conference meetings, and their tenure is often for life.

Methodist theology perhaps is another factor that accounted for the growth of the Methodist movement. Its theology, Arminian in emphasis as interpreted by Wesley, is generally cohesive and uniform. Arminian theology was introduced by Jacobus Arminius in the late sixteenth century. He emphasized the believer's free will and ability to chose, maintaining that one's fate was not predetermined at birth. The theological position of Methodism does not vary drastically from one body to the next. The Apostles' Creed is generally incorporated in the worship. Methodism preaches and teaches a trinitarian doctrine that emphasizes the natural sinfulness of humankind, the fall of humanity and need for repentance, freedom of choice, justification by faith, sanctification and holiness, and the sufficiency of the Scriptures for salvation. It observes two sacraments—baptism and the Lord's Supper. Baptism is generally administered to both infants and adults by sprinkling.

Numerous independent African American congregations and denominations were established as a result of the social and political consequences of segregation and racism. *The Directory of African American Religious Bodies* has attempted to identify and trace the history of the independent African Methodist denominations and similar organizations that provide communication with African Americans in predominantly white Methodist bodies. Descriptive narratives of the extant Methodist bodies are presented in the respective sections of this book. The descriptions that follow are based on that material.

Union American Methodist Episcopal Church, Inc.

One of the African American groups to separate from the Methodist church as a result of the racial political climate in postrevolutionary America was located in Wilmington, Delaware. This body withdrew from the white Asbury Methodist Church in that city and formed an African American church (then known as Ezion Methodist Episcopal Church) that would later be named the Union American Methodist Episcopal Church, Inc.[15]

The Union American Methodist Episcopal Church, Inc. (UAME), traces its origins to the movement of Peter Spencer, William Anderson, and forty other black members of the Asbury Methodist Church in Wilmington who left that church in 1805 because they had been denied the rites of the church on the basis of race. The group established itself as Ezion Methodist Episcopal Church, under the supervision of Asbury Church.

Since Spencer and Anderson were both lay leaders, a

white elder was appointed to preach at the Ezion Methodist Episcopal Church in 1812. This resulted in another dispute that quickly ended up in court. Lacking sufficient time and money, the African American members abandoned the lawsuit and left Ezion. The group purchased a lot from a Quaker and constructed another building, which was dedicated in the fall of 1813. They severed their ties with the Methodist Episcopal church and established and incorporated the Union Church of Africans three years before Richard Allen incorporated the African Methodist Episcopal (A.M.E.) Church in Philadelphia, Pennsylvania. Spencer was present at the 1816 organizing conference of the A.M.E. church, but decided not to join with the Allen group.

Some time after 1816, thirty congregations of the Union Church of Africans were led out of that denomination by Ellis Saunders and Isaac Barney. Twenty-four of the congregations continued on their own under the same name (Union Church of Africans) for several years, eventually incorporating in 1865, as the Union American Methodist Episcopal Church in the United States of America and Elsewhere. The denomination is known today as the Union American Methodist Episcopal Church, Inc. The other wing of the original group merged in 1866 with the First Colored Methodist Protestant Church and is known today as the African Union First Colored Methodist Protestant Church.

UAME has a strong tradition of lay participation and responsibility. Coupled with this tradition is the church's long-standing position in favor of licensing women to preach. The general conference of UAME, composed of elected delegates representing all UAME churches, meets quadrennially. The first and fourth districts' annual conference is held in April, and the second and third districts convene annually in May.

Today, UAME comprises between twelve thousand and fifteen thousand persons in fifty-five congregations. Its greatest concentrations are in Delaware, Jamaica, Maryland, New England, New Jersey, New York, and Pennsylvania. The church is distinguished by its Pan-Methodist involvement. At the 1986 General Conference, the bishops were authorized by the body to meet with representatives of the African Methodist Episcopal Zion Church to discuss and implement ways and means to strengthen the fellowship and affiliation between the two churches. UAME is headquartered in Camden, New Jersey. The church news is published in *The Union Messenger*; a UAME church catechism is also published.

African Union First Colored Methodist Protestant Church

The African Union First Colored Methodist Protestant Church, also known as the African Union Church or the African Union First Colored Methodist Protestant Church of America and Elsewhere, is the product of the union between the Union Church of Africans and the First Colored Methodist Protestant Church.

The African Union church resulted from the previously mentioned lawsuit between Asbury Methodist Church, (the parent and predominantly white church in Wilmington, Delaware) and Ezion Methodist Episcopal Church, which was a predominantly black Methodist congregation. Peter Spencer, William Anderson, and forty other black members of Asbury withdrew in 1805 and formed Ezion Methodist Episcopal Church after being denied church rites because of their race. They remained under the supervision of Asbury Church. The suit arose when a white elder was appointed to preach at Ezion because Spencer and Anderson were laypersons, and the Ezion congregation rejected this. The suit was quickly abandoned because of the time and expense involved, and the group led by Spencer and Anderson left Ezion to form the Union Church of Africans, which was incorporated three years before Richard Allen incorporated the A.M.E. church in Philadelphia. In 1850 (shortly after Spencer's death), a faction left the Union Church of Africans and formed another church with an episcopal government. This group later became UAME. The schism resulted in the Union Church of Africans becoming the African Union church.

It is believed that the First Colored Methodist Protestant Church resulted from a schism within the A.M.E. church, although little is known of its origin. Its representatives met with those of the African Union church on November 25, 1865, to finalize plans for a merger. The church's polity reflects that of the Methodist Protestant church before 1939. Its doctrine is Wesleyan. The church has no foreign mission program, but home missions are the responsibility of the women of the church. The last reported membership figures, in 1957, listed five thousand members in thirty-three churches.

African Methodist Episcopal Church

The A.M.E. church was founded in Philadelphia on April 12, 1787, as a result of discrimination against the black members of St. George's Methodist Episcopal Church and in protest of slavery. Richard Allen, along with Absalom Jones and others, organized the Free African Society, a beneficial and mutual aid society, which eventually spread to other cities. The society issued a plan for a nondenominational church, which was organized on July 7, 1791, and formalized as the Bethel Church in Philadelphia on July 17, 1794. The denomination was officially established on April 16, 1816, with Richard Allen named as its first bishop on April 11, 1816. Although its ties with the Methodist Episcopal church were questionable, in 1816 the A.M.E. church severed

its ties with the Methodist Episcopal church when the Supreme Court of Pennsylvania issued a writ of mandamus ratifying its independence.

The A.M.E. church has always accepted the standards of Methodism. Its standards of faith are the Twenty-five Articles of Religion adopted by John Wesley from the Thirty-nine Articles of the Church of England, and the Apostles' Creed. The church believes in justification through faith and personal repentance through Jesus Christ. It does not believe in apostolic succession or extreme ritualism in services. Additionally, it proposes faith in the Holy Trinity, belief in Jesus Christ and His resurrection, the sacraments of baptism and the Lord's Supper, law and leadership of the country, and support of the poor.

Based on the principle that local A.M.E. bodies "shall be engaged in carrying out the spirit of the original Free African Society out of which the A.M.E. church evolved," A.M.E. churches seek to find and save the lost and to serve those in need through preaching, caring for the needy, sick, and elderly, and encouraging economic advancement. The denomination emphasizes educational opportunity and mission work; therefore, the A.M.E. church sponsors seven colleges and universities (Wilberforce, Morris Brown, Paul Quinn, Edward Waters, Allen, Shorter, and Bonner Campbell). The church has established and continues to support two seminaries: Payne Theological Seminary in Xenia, Ohio, and Turner Theological Seminary in Atlanta, Georgia (now a part of the Interdenominational Theological Center).

Overseas, the A.M.E. church supports many projects, including Monrovia College and Industrial Training School, Inc., in Monrovia, Liberia; the Jordan Agricultural Institute in Royesville, Liberia; the A.M.E. Church Publishing House in South Africa; the James Center (a multipurpose facility) in Mesuru, Lesotho; schools in Malawi and Zimbabwe; and a school of religion in Johannesburg, South Africa. In the Caribbean, the A.M.E. church sponsors numerous schools in Jamaica, St. Croix, and Haiti. There are also three active A.M.E. congregations in London, England.

The polity of the A.M.E. church is based upon that of the Methodist church. The general conference is the supreme body and meets every four years to address matters of concern to the church. The Council of Bishops, the executive branch of the body, is charged with the general oversight of the church between general conferences. The General Board of Trustees supervises in trust all church property and acts on behalf of the church on such matters when necessary. The General Board serves as the administrative body of the church and is composed of various departmental representatives. The Judicial Council is the highest judiciary body, serving as an appellate court chosen by the general conference and answerable to it. In addition to these, each of the nineteen districts is responsible for annual, district, and quarterly conferences as well as church meetings in each congregation.

Much of the denominational work of the A.M.E. church is handled through its commissions. There are eleven commissions: Finance and Statistics, Pensions, Publications, Minimum Salary, Church Extension and Evangelism, Missions, Higher Education, Research and Development, Christian Education, Social Action, and Lay Organization. The A.M.E. church continues to serve others through its 3,500,000 members and eight thousand churches located in the United States, Africa, Canada, the Caribbean, and South America. The church celebrated its bicentennial in 1987.

African Methodist Episcopal Zion Church

Founded in October 1796, after blacks had been denied the sacraments and full participation in the John Street Methodist Church (a white church in New York City), the African Methodist Episcopal Zion Church became a reality through the efforts of James Varick and others who were dissatisfied with the condition and treatment of blacks in New York City. They petitioned Bishop Francis Asbury for permission to meet among themselves. The bishop visited the black classes. After a series of meetings at the home of James Varick, they met again with Bishop Asbury in August 1796. The bishop gave them his approval to hold separate meetings, and they rented a meetinghouse.

Eventually, from this humble beginning emerged the African Methodist Episcopal Zion (A.M.E. Zion) Church, which was chartered by the name "African Methodist Episcopal Church" in New York City on April 6, 1801. The A.M.E. Zion church finally broke its official ties with the Methodist church in 1821. "Zion" was added to the church's original name by vote of the General Conference in 1848. The addition distinguished this body from the African Methodist Episcopal Church, which emerged in Philadelphia at about the same time with the same name, but under the leadership of Richard Allen. "Zion" refers to the first church of the denomination. The church claims to be the oldest Methodist organization to separate from the Methodist Episcopal church in the United States, having voted itself out of the Methodist Episcopal church on July 26, 1820.

As with most Methodist bodies, the standards of faith for the A.M.E. Zion church are the Twenty-five Articles of Religion extracted from the Thirty-nine Articles of the Church of England by John Wesley. The Apostles' Creed is the only formal creed accepted. Other beliefs of the church include the following: sanctification, a witness of the spirit, a life of joy and obedience, Christian experience, means of grace, and conversion. Love feasts are also practiced. The Articles of Religion are the basis for biblical interpretation and the church's political stance.

From its inception, the A.M.E. Zion church adopted the fundamental polity of the American Methodist church. The church is governed by a general conference, which meets every four years. The A.M.E. Zion church divides its territory into thirteen districts, each of which is presided over by a bishop. The bishops of the church govern the body and interpret its laws and mandates in the interim of the general conference. The presidency of the Board of Bishops changes at six-month intervals. Each district is divided into conferences. Annual meetings are held on the district and conference level. A district convention is established where the church schools' organizations are separate from the district conference. Quarterly conferences are held to assess the condition of the local churches within a specific area. The members' meetings consider business within the local churches.

The church formed the Bureau of Evangelism in 1920 to ensure close adherence to the teachings of Christ and accomplishment of the chief end of the Gospel—the salvation of souls. The church established the A.M.E. Zion Health Center in Hot Springs, Arkansas, in 1956; the Laymen's Council (which became a part of the constitutional structure in 1952) in 1916; the Ministers' and Laymen's Association in 1938; and the Historical Society in 1956. There is also a Woman's Home and Overseas Missionary Society. The A.M.E. Zion church supports Livingstone College and Hood Theological Seminary in Salisbury, North Carolina; Clinton Junior College in Rock Hill, South Carolina; and Lomax-Hannon Junior College in Greenville, Alabama.

There have been several unsuccessful attempts by the African Methodist bodies to merge. The A.M.E. Zion and the Christian Methodist Episcopal (C.M.E.) churches tried to unify from 1902 to 1903, and the A.M.E., A.M.E. Zion, and C.M.E. churches attempted to unite in 1918. After careful consideration of the aborted attempts, the A.M.E. Zion church and the C.M.E. church are in the midst of implementing the union between the two churches. A detailed and multistage plan of union has been developed by the steering committee of each church and the joint commission, and each church body will have an opportunity to ratify the plan's recommendations before moving on to the next stage. Principles of and reasons for union have been established; after final approval of the last phases of the merger by each church's annual conferences in January of 1991 and 1992, it is expected and hoped that the new church will celebrate its inaugural general conference in July of 1992. At this time, a plan to select the new name of the church has not been delineated, but the working title is the "Varick/Miles Methodist Episcopal Church," in honor of James Varick, the founder of the A.M.E. Zion church, and William H. Miles, the first bishop of the C.M.E. church.

The A.M.E. Zion church is distinguished by its ecclesiastical principles. It believes that it is in accord with John 8:32—"And ye shall know the truth, and the truth shall make you free." With a membership of approximately 1,200,000 persons, over 6,275 ordained clergy, and over six thousand churches worldwide, the church has spread far from its humble beginnings in New York City. The church first expanded into the South and West, especially after the Civil War. Then it moved quickly into Canada. After World Wars I and II, migration of African Americans to the North led to the growth of the church in large northern cities. Over the years it expanded also into Haiti, the Bahamas, Liberia, South America, Jamaica, and England.

Christian Methodist Episcopal Church

The issue of slavery created a schism in the Methodist Episcopal church in America. The resulting division of the church into the Methodist Episcopal church and the Methodist Episcopal Church, South (M.E.C.S.), led to greater consideration of the role of blacks in the church, whether free or enslaved. Accordingly, in 1866, the African American members of M.E.C.S. petitioned the main body for a separate church that would be governed by the M.E.C.S. The African American members' petition reflected their desire to remain affiliated with the parent body. At the 1870 General Conference of M.E.C.S., the committee that had studied the question at the previous conference recommended that the black members be constituted as an independent church, rather than a subordinate group. This recommendation reflected the prevailing values, following the Civil War, that urged for independence of African Americans and social reconstruction of American society. Thus, the Colored Methodist Episcopal Church (now Christian Methodist Episcopal Church) was created by agreement between the separating parties on December 15, 1870.

The C.M.E. church adopted the Discipline of M.E.C.S. at its organizing conference in 1870 and made changes to suit its name and the unique circumstances of its membership. Thus, the Twenty-five Articles of Religion as extracted from the Thirty-nine Articles of the Church of England by John Wesley serve as the guiding doctrines. The polity of the church was adopted from the M.E.C.S. and that of American Methodism. It is governed by bishops and holds general, annual, and quarterly conferences.

The evangelization of the black race, primarily by preaching and education, is the C.M.E. church's philosophical goal. Because of its precarious position between the white Methodist body and black Methodists, it took the position that its property would not be used for political purposes or assemblages. However, many of its leaders were prominent in the civil rights movement of the 1960s and serve the church now as administrators of its colleges and schools. The 1970 General Conference approved the establishment of the Department of Christian Social Action and Concerns to address social problems of the era. A Social Creed was adopted in 1966 as well.

Free Christian Zion Church of Christ

The Free Christian Zion Church of Christ was founded by the Reverend E. D. Brown on July 10, 1905, in Redemption, Arkansas. The Reverend Brown, an A.M.E. Zion conference missionary, and several other Methodist ministers disagreed with the assessment of individual churches to support the central church body. Rather, they believed that the church's primary interests should be directed toward support of the poor.

The polity of the church is essentially episcopal, and its doctrine is Wesleyan. The bishop, who is the chief pastor, is the head of the church and appoints ministers and church officers. Each local church has a pastor and deacons as its officers, and evangelists are appointed for communities where there are no churches. No record of the Free Christian Zion Church of Christ's current activity is available.

Reformed Methodist Union Episcopal Church

Withdrawing members of the A.M.E. church founded the Reformed Methodist Union Episcopal Church in 1885. The occasion was a dispute concerning the election of ministerial delegates to the annual conference. The first president of the church was the Reverend William E. Johnson. The new church's nonepiscopal structure was well received, but in 1896 an effort was made to change its polity. After the death of the Reverend Johnson, E. Russell Middleton was elected bishop in 1899; after his death, another bishop was consecrated by seven elders of the church.

The church shares the doctrine of the Methodist Episcopal church. Its polity shifted toward that of an episcopacy, which was adopted in 1899. Love feasts and class meetings, common in traditional Methodism, are held.

United Wesleyan Methodist Church of America

The United Wesleyan Methodist Church of America was founded in 1905 by immigrants from the West Indies. They wanted to continue the practices of the Methodist Church in the Caribbean and the Americas, rather than unite with any of the American Methodist bodies. The Methodist Church in the Caribbean and the Americas had British Methodism as its historical base. The church's doctrine adheres to Wesleyan principles; it does not have a governing episcopacy. According to the *Encyclopedia of American Religions* (2nd ed.), the Methodist Church in the Caribbean and the Americas entered into an agreement with the United Methodist church in 1976, which has led to several jointly supported projects in the Caribbean. The United Wesleyan Church of America belongs to the Caribbean Conference of Churches and the World Council of Churches.

African American Presence in Predominantly White Methodist Bodies

The organization of separate African American Methodist denominations did not have the effect of ending the participation of African Americans in the Methodist church. African Americans are the largest minority constituency in the United Methodist Church at the present time. As of 1989, African Americans constituted approximately 4 percent of the total membership of the church.

There are several organizations within predominantly white Methodist bodies that have a strong commitment to continuing the tradition of service among African Americans within the church. The largest known group of African Americans among predominantly white Methodist bodies is in the United Methodist Church. The United Methodist Church, historically linked with the Methodist Episcopal church, has several key organizations that foster racial unity and exchange. They are: Black Methodists for Church Renewal, Inc. (BMCR); the Commission for Coordination of Ethnic Minority Ministries; and the General Commission on Religion and Race.

Black Methodists for Church Renewal, Inc., was organized in Cincinnati, Ohio, in 1968, when former members of the Central Jurisdiction of the United Methodist Church realized that if African American Methodists were to make an impact on the United Methodist Church, they must organize and become united, addressing those issues that most concern African American people. Since that time, the group has been actively opposing racism, while assisting the United Methodist Church to become an inclusive body, as mandated by its own legislation and by the Scripture in which it is grounded.

BMCR serves as a forum where African American Methodists may discuss problems, define issues, develop and adopt strategies for meaningful change, and develop new ways to affect the ministry. It has expressed to the general church its concerns regarding the involvement of African Americans within the structure and the conduct of the church as it relates to social issues and its investment policies.

As the legitimate African American caucus recognized by the general United Methodist Church, BMCR is gov-

erned by a board of directors that is representative of five geographic jurisdictions within the United Methodist in the United States. It includes lay and clergy, youth and young adults, men and women.

BMCR is committed to 1) involving African American persons fully in the total life of the church, 2) strengthening African American churches, 3) increasing the number of African American pastors to serve African American churches, 4) increasing African American membership in United Methodist churches, 5) continuing support of the eleven historically African American United Methodist institutions of higher learning, and 6) encouraging dialogue and exchanges between African American sisters and brothers in the Caribbean and Africa. Meeting annually in March, the organization maintains offices in Dayton, Ohio, and publishes a newsletter.

The Commission for Coordination of Ethnic Minority Ministries is an administrative unit in the West Ohio Conference of the United Methodist Church. Operating under this unit are the Black Church Development Committee and the Ethnic Minority Committee. The commission's Black Church Development Committee funds proposals and projects pertaining to the enhancement of African Americans in the church and community. Its Ethnic Minority Committee funds projects and scholarships for minority persons and is interested in increasing the participation of all minorities in the United Methodist Church.

The United Methodist Church's General Commission on Religion and Race was formed in April 1968. Its primary purpose is to challenge the general agencies, institutions, and ecclesiastical structures of the denomination to bring about a full and equal participation of their varied racial and ethnic constituencies in the total life and mission of the church. The commission achieves this through advocacy and by reviewing and monitoring the practices of the entire church in order to ensure further racial inclusiveness. It is one of thirteen general agencies within the United Methodist Church.

The Council on Ethnic Affairs is an advisory body of the Free Methodist Church of North America. It concerns itself with all ethnic and minority groups, including African Americans. Its tasks are to enhance visibility of ethnic groups and ministries, to facilitate their access to the higher councils of the church, and to encourage full participation of ethnic groups in general church life. Composed of laity and clergy from all over the United States, the council works throughout the year and meets once annually.

African American Methodist history is replete with examples of transitions and inconsistencies associated with American society. The dynamics of urban migration, rural development, racial intolerance, conflicting moral and ethical standards, and changing social norms mirror the growth and changes of the church. Methodist historical reality is integrally linked with the social and political changes that characterize life in the United States. It is a movement that developed out of a revolutionary idea that promised an inclusive and racially integrated society. It was conceived with an egalitarian theology that continues to shape its development.

Methodist traditions have been tempered by significant forces in the American social structure, especially racial segregation and civil conflicts. Many factions and contradictions have contributed to the development of alternative Methodist traditions. John and Charles Wesley's simple legacy of living and organizing one's personal life in accordance with a biblical method or standard has evolved into diverse communities that reflect different understandings of how this religious community should operate. The theological and doctrinal standards guiding these different faith communities are very similar. The existence of these separate traditions reflects societal influences. As C. Eric Lincoln observes in his review of these inconsistencies, "One of the many ironies of American history is the development of separate churches for Black Christians and white Christians worshiping the same God in essentially the same way."[16]

Out of the segregated history of America has developed significant religious institutions that have fostered the dissemination of the Gospel throughout the world. The growth of independent African American Methodist congregations and denominations reflects the diversity of African American culture and life. The common bond of fellowship, doctrine, and theology remains a link to this vibrant past. The fact that African Americans continue to be active participants in predominantly white Methodist bodies further indicates that the role of African Americans in Methodism is continually evolving beyond the walls of racial segregation. Independent African American Methodist bodies continue to strive for the development of their respective organizations. Some independent bodies are considering possible mergers, while other organizational structures are still evolving. There is a diverse legacy in African American Methodist history. This diversity should be appreciated as an expression of the freedom inherent in the many ways of praising God.

Notes

1. See William J. Walls, *The African Methodist Episcopal Church: Reality of the Black Church* (Charlotte, N.C.: A.M.E. Zion Publishing House, 1974), 32-34.
2. See Frederick A. Norwood, *The Story of American Methodism* (Nashville: Abingdon, 1974), 63-67, especially notes 3 and 4. William B. McClain, *Black People in the Methodist Church* (Cambridge, Mass.: Schenkman Publishing Company, 1984), 5, 15-18, observes that the first organized Methodist Society was located at Sam's Creek in Frederick County, Maryland, and that Betty was a servant in the Heck household.
3. Norwood, 67. Cf. Harry V. Richardson, *Dark Salvation: The Story*

of *Methodism as It Developed among Blacks in America* (New York: Anchor Press, 1976), 117-118.
4. Walls, 38-42.
5. See Norwood, 65-66, and McClain, 16.
6. Richard Allen, *The Life Experience and Gospel Labors of the Right Reverend Richard Allen* (Nashville: Abingdon Press, 1960), 29.
7. Ibid., 30.
8. Richard Allen organized the Bethel A.M.E. Church in Philadelphia, Pennsylvania, in 1794 following his historic departure from the St. George Methodist Episcopal Church in 1787. James Varick organized Mother Zion, one of the earliest African American Methodist congregations, in 1796 in New York City. Other notable African American church leaders include: Daniel Coker, founder of the first African Methodist Episcopal Church in Baltimore, Maryland, and Peter Spencer, founder of the Union Church of Africans, an outgrowth of the Ezion Church in Wilmington, Delaware. This body is now known as the Union American Methodist Episcopal Church, Inc. See Walls, 27-28.
9. The Discipline includes laws that govern the church during the four-year period between general conferences. Norwood, 168; Lewis V. Baldwin, *Invisible Strands in African Methodism: A History of the African Union Methodist Protestant and Union American Methodist Episcopal Churches, 1805-1980* (Metuchen, N.J.: Scarecrow Press, 1983), 35.
10. Baldwin, 32.
11. For a fuller discussion of Wesley's stance on slavery, see McClain, 7-14.
12. Donald G. Matthews, *Slavery and Methodism: A Chapter in American Morality, 1780-1845* (Princeton: Princeton University Press, 1965), 22-23.
13. Further documentation of African American membership in the church is found in McClain, 18.
14. Norwood, 169.
15. Richardson, 79.
16. C. Eric Lincoln, "Change and the Black Church," in Dionne J. Jones and William H. Matthews (eds.), *The Black Church: A Community Resource* (Washington, D.C.: Howard University Institute for Urban Affairs and Research, 1977), 22.

Bibliography

Allen, Richard. *The Life Experience and Gospel Labors of the Right Reverend Richard Allen*. 1887. Reprint. Nashville: Abingdon Press, 1960.

Baldwin, Lewis V. *Invisible Strands in African Methodism: A History of the African Union Methodist Protestant and Union American Methodist Episcopal Churches, 1805-1980*. Metuchen, N.J.: Scarecrow Press, 1983.

Bradley, David H., Sr. *A History of the A.M.E. Zion Church. 1796-1872. Plus a Study about Francis Asbury*. Vol. 1. Nashville: Parthenon Press, 1956.

————. *A History of the A.M.E. Zion Church. 1872-1968*. Vol. 2. Nashville: Parthenon Press, 1970.

Colbert, William. "A Journal of the Travels of William Colbert, 1790-1837." Unpublished manuscript, 13 vols.

Faulkner, John Alfred. *The Methodists*. Rev. ed. New York: The Methodist Book Concern, 1903.

George, Carol V. R. *Segregated Sabbaths: Richard Allen and the Rise of Independent Black Churches, 1760-1840*. New York: Oxford University Press, 1973.

Jones, Dionne J. and William H. Matthews. *The Black Church: A Community Resource*. Washington, D.C.: Howard University Institute for Urban Affairs and Research, 1977.

Lakey, Othal H. *The History of the C.M.E. Church*. Memphis: The C.M.E. Publishing House, 1985.

Matthews, Donald G. *Slavery and Methodism: A Chapter in American Morality 1780-1845*. Princeton: Princeton University Press, 1965.

Norwood, Frederick A. *The Story of American Methodism*. Nashville: Abingdon, 1974.

Richardson, Harry V. *Dark Salvation: The Story of Methodism as It Developed among Blacks in America*. New York: Anchor Press, 1976.

Shaw, J., and F. Beverly Shaw. *The Negro in the History of Methodism*. Nashville: Parthenon Press, 1954.

Walker, Clarence E. *A Rock in a Weary Land: The African Methodist Episcopal Church during the Civil War and Reconstruction*. Baton Rouge: Louisiana State University Press, 1982.

Walls, William J. *The African Methodist Episcopal Zion Church: Reality of the Black Church*. Charlotte, N.C.: A.M.E. Zion Publishing House, 1974.

Wesley, Charles H. *Richard Allen: Apostle of Freedom*. Washington, D.C.: Associated Publishers, Inc., 1935.

Movements in the Spirit
A Review of African American Holiness/Pentecostal/Apostolics

William C. Turner, Jr.

Who are African American Holiness/Pentecostal/Apostolic Believers?

In their classic 1933 study, Benjamin E. Mays and Joseph Nicholson found, through a sample taken in seven southern cities, that some form of "Holy or Sanctified church" ranked just behind the Baptists and the African Methodist Episcopalians in number of churches among African Americans.[1] Not separating them by subfamilies (Holiness, Pentecostal, and Apostolic), they used the name Holiness for them all. What the study unmistakably showed was that African American Christians who emphasized sanctification and spiritual manifestations somewhat differently from the mainstream black churches were gaining greatly in numbers and participating with the older bodies in determining the character of Christian African American religious life.

Other early twentieth-century studies did not differentiate between the three groups, but were forced to note their presence. In his study of sects within American religion, Elmer Clark included a group he called "sanctified sects."[2] Likewise, Carter G. Woodson made a somewhat oblique reference to this group of Christians when he distinguished between the conservatives and the progressives in his classic study of the Negro church in America. Furthermore, E. Franklin Frazier, in his study of the black church, referred to these Christians, subsuming their beliefs and practices under the heading "storefront religion."[3]

What is not always clear in these early studies is whether the people in these groups perceived themselves to be reformers in existing African American Christian denominations, or whether self-understanding was inseparable from denominational identification. For example, in Arthur Huff Fauset's study, *Black Gods of the Metropolis*, the Mount Sinai Holy Church was considered as an alternative to mainstream Christianity. This church, founded by Mother Ida Robinson, alongside other new religious movements—which Fauset labeled as cults—emerged in northern urban black communities in the early twentieth century.

These groups, which included cult leaders Daddy Grace, Prophet Cherry, Father Divine, and Noble Drew Ali, reflected the common experiences of people who were frustrated and nearly crushed by the harshness of African American life during this period. Although some similarities in socioeconomic status and esteem for leadership are shown among all of these bodies, the Mount Sinai Holy Church typifies a segment of the black church that desperately sought restoration and revival through a recovery of latent spirituality rather than resorting either to practices outside the Christian tradition or to blending with other faiths. Bishop Ida Robinson and the Mount Sinai church considered themselves to be as orthodox in their faith as other mainstream groups.

Robinson, along with H. L. Fisher, G. J. Branch, C. H. Mason, C. P. Jones, W. E. Fuller, and G. T. Haywood, was among the black Christians around the turn of the century who "came out" of the mainline black denominational churches, seeking "the deeper life of entire sanctification" and Spirit baptism. Their initial concern was not so much to start a new denomination as to call the existing ones back to the wells of their spirituality. This group often found that its brand of prophetic faith and spiritual exercises were not welcomed by brothers and sisters who regarded existing forms as sufficient. Although they variously left both voluntarily and involuntarily, the departing ones never lost the sense of being part of the true Christian church, and they made every effort to retain purity in their faith. In their own words, they strove to "contend earnestly for the faith once delivered unto the saints."[4]

These people are rarely brought to the attention of scholars, or of the general public, for that matter. Their limited exposure in the scholarly literature is of the sort discussed previously. Alternatively, caricatures of them can be found in the work of novelists such as James Baldwin.[5] Knowing these groups intimately (probably from firsthand experience), he reflected carefully and fairly accurately on the dimension that was of interest to him. This essentially negative portrayal conforms rather closely with the "non-progressive image" projected by C. G. Woodson and others, and shows them as epitomizing the ''folk religion'' that, in Joseph R. Washington's view, must yield to historic Protestantism if black religious life is to become Christian in belief and action.[6]

A major reconsideration of the place of these groups within the larger configuration of African American spiritual life and American religion has come about through the emergence of the Church of God in Christ as a major Protestant denomination and the pervasive influence of gospel music. In his recent study, *Race, Religion and the Continuing American Dilemma*, and in his continuing studies of the African American church, C. Eric Lincoln included the Church of God in Christ along with the three African American Baptist and the three African American Methodist denominations as comprising ninety-five percent of all black Christians in the United States.[7] Outstanding preachers such as James A. Forbes, Jr., and Otho T. Jones, Jr., are esteemed as among the very best preachers in the country. Gospel singers such as Andre Crouch, Shirley Caesar, and Edwin Hawkins and their groups continue to top the charts and set the pace for gospel singing. Other, lesser-known preachers and musicians from other musical groups constantly conduct revivals, assume pastorates, and train the choirs of the more established Baptist and Methodist churches, thus strongly influencing the content of faith and the style of worship.

Emergence from the Historic African American Denominations

African American Holiness/Pentecostal/Apostolics emerged from the historic African American denominations—particularly the Methodist and the Baptists. Indeed, the lines delineating these evangelicals have never been absolutely firm, and there is a sense in which they all truly belong to one family. In many ways, the African American Holiness/Pentecostal/Apostolics repeated a century later many of the same patterns of growth and development as the older groups, who, in their turn, were considered to be sectarians.

The Holiness/Pentecostal/Apostolics' clearest connection with the Methodists is the doctrine of sanctification—the teaching that the Spirit works in the believer subsequent to justification to deliver from the desire to sin. In sanctification one is brought into a state of holiness characterized by moral and spiritual purity that is evident. Numerous prominent Methodists taught that even after justification—the divine act that frees humankind from the penalty of sin and promises eternal life for believers— and the conversion experience, a residue of sin would remain in the believer. This residue, which was a consequence of our sharing of Adam's nature, was inbred.[8] To be freed from it, the believer was required to attend to spiritual disciplines, which included prayer, partici-

pating in preaching services and love feasts, and receiving the sacrament of Holy Communion.[9] The point at which this inbred sin was removed was correlated with an intense religious experience, which brought a deeper inner feeling of ecstasy and joy. This experience, sometimes known as the ''double cure,'' often coincided with release from some tenacious habit. Whereas the doctrine and experience of conversion were for the purpose of assuring repentant sinners of their forgiveness and acceptance by God, the doctrine and experience of sanctification were for the assurance of power to live the holy life.

Less clear is the Baptist contribution, which is not as explicitly doctrinal, and which concerns direct leading and movement of the Holy Spirit.[10] This emphasis from the Baptists was heightened among African Americans by their own notion of the free, unbounded, and unlimited Spirit deeply embedded within their religious consciousness and world view. In their view, the Holy Spirit testifies directly and immediately to the believer's heart, bypassing priest and teacher. The autonomy and free expression that characterized Baptists were joined with the emphasis on holiness among black Methodists, eventually emerging as African American Pentecostalism.

A genuine exchange between African and European evangelicals took place shortly before and following the Revolutionary War.[11] By virtue of this interpenetration at its very inception in the colonies, American Methodism was infused with elements of African religious expressions. The Baptists and other evangelicals, to a lesser degree, were similarly influenced during the Great Awakening.[12]

Africans were drawn to the Methodist ''exercises'' in great numbers, leading to the observation of one detractor that the Africans were influencing the Methodists more than they were being ''elevated'' by their association with the Caucasians.[13] There were mixed churches, such as the one in Wilmington, North Carolina: its official name was the Front Street Church, but because of its large African membership it was commonly referred to as the African Chapel.[14]

A similar interpenetration was present within the Baptists: initially, they were well known for their egalitarian sentiments. Along with the Methodists and Quakers, a significant number of Baptists opposed slavery and all forms of classism and hierarchy. Africans were a clear target for their evangelism. In large measure, this was their way of showing disapprobation for the Anglicans, and to some degree, the Presbyterians and Congregationalists. The stiltedness of Anglican theology and the formality of Anglican worship held limited appeal for African Americans. Unlike other groups' rather stringent requirements for entering the ministry, the Baptists' ministry was open to all who felt inwardly persuaded of a call from God to spread the Gospel.

Although African Americans were especially encouraged to spread the Gospel among their fellows, they occasionally held audiences with whites as well. Indeed, in numerous instances the preaching of African Americans was so popular that it was preferred to that of some whites. One of the most well-known of African American preachers was Harry Hosier, known as "Black Harry."[15]

Thus African American Holiness/Pentecostal/Apostolicism has always had close ties to mainstream Protestantism. More than all else, however, the mothers and fathers of African American Holiness/Pentecostal/Apostolics saw themselves as perpetuating the spirituality of the black church. C. P. Jones, the founder of the Church of Christ Holiness, for instance, was quite clear and explicit in this regard: he was raised a Baptist and was attached to the spirituality of that tradition, and it was this spirituality that he sought to recover.[16] Only after a considerable period of time and tension was his relationship with the Baptist church severed and normalized.

The Five Original African American Holiness/Pentecostal/ Apostolic Groups

Leonard Lovett listed what he called the five original groups as follows: the United Holy Church of America; the Church of Christ Holiness, U.S.A.; the Church of God in Christ, Inc.; the Fire Baptized Holiness Church of God in the Americas; and the Pentecostal Assemblies of the World. Describing their emergence chronologically in the previous order, Lovett argues that the numerous groups that proliferated after the turn of the century can be traced to these five.[17]

Lovett states that the members of these bodies were in the first generation born following the end of slavery in the United States. For them, the power of their religious experiences and their sustaining spirituality shielded them from a vile and inhospitable world. This source of empowerment enabled them to thrive in the midst of the trying times of Reconstruction and disenfranchisement.

Typically, the emergence of a Holiness/Pentecostal/Apostolic body began when an individual or a group of African American Baptists or Methodists involved themselves in some sort of prayer meeting or union service, seeking to recover the intensity and fervor of their spiritual life. They sought the deeper life of entire sanctification. This experience, accompanied by strong emotions such as crying, dancing, shaking, rolling, and speaking in tongues, was said to bring the believer under the Spirit's control in a rapture described as nothing less than sublime.

Henry L. Fisher, formerly of the A.M.E. Zion church and the single most important figure in the early history of the United Holy Church, tells of his first encounter with the Holy People and his exposure to the doctrines of Holiness.[18] During a meeting, Elder Elijah Lowney addressed those gathered at the Sam Jones Tabernacle in Wilmington, North Carolina. As the preacher delivered his discourse, the Reverend Robert White, a local preacher in the A.M.E. church of that city, was moved. Fisher recounts that, as he led the song, "the holy fire" struck White, and White cried, "what I was I am not, and what I was not I am." These words, so reminiscent of those spoken over a century earlier by Richard Allen, followed the pattern of correlating the deeper life of entire sanctification with a discrete religious experience. Fisher became leader of one of the bands of Holy People and led the way for them to unite with others of like faith and commitment.

The founder and leader of the Church of God in Christ, Charles Harrison Mason, followed a similar pilgrimage. After beginning his ministerial career as a Baptist preacher, Mason experienced "sanctification through the word" in 1894. He subsequently preached the doctrine of Holiness in Arkansas, Alabama, and Mississippi. According to Mason's account, significant numbers of people received his preaching, and through his ministry, countless numbers were converted and sanctified. His efforts led him to a short but fruitful cooperative effort with Charles P. Jones of Mississippi, but it also led to tension with the Baptist churches and associations of the area.

The high point of Mason's early career was his five-week visit to the Azusa Street Revival in Los Angeles, California, in 1907, where, under the leadership of Elder Seymour, Mason was satisfied that his prayer to receive the baptism of the Holy Spirit was fulfilled. Recalling his experience, Mason said:

When I opened my mouth to say glory, a flame touched my tongue which ran down to me. My language changed and no word could I speak in my own tongue. O, I was filled with the glory of my Lord. My soul was then satisfied.[19]

Following Mason's return to Memphis, he separated from C. P. Jones over whether speaking in tongues was necessary for Spirit baptism and became the undisputed leader of the Church of God in Christ, which emerged as the largest of all black Holiness/Pentecostal bodies.[20]

The most far-reaching of the religious meetings popular during this era was the Azusa Street Revival, conducted by the African American Holiness preacher William Joseph Seymour in Los Angeles from approximately 1906 to 1909. This meeting, named for the street where it was held; stood out as the great watershed from which nearly all the Pentecostal groups (both black and white) flowed and to which all Holiness groups were forced to respond. The Azusa Street Revival was responsible as no other single historical event for catapulting Pentecostalism onto the world religious scene. People came to this revival from around the world in response to the reports visitors carried. From this protracted meeting, converts to the new way went to enliven their own churches and to spread the Gospel as missionaries. Indeed, this meeting—first held in an old A.M.E. church—was referred to as the new "Upper Room," and Los Angeles was known as the New Jerusalem among believers.

William J. Seymour, the Apostle of Azusa Street, traveled the circuit of the Holiness movement before taking his place as a leader in Los Angeles. Beginning his religious career as a member of the Methodist church in Centerville, Louisiana, he left to travel north. Along the way, he came in contact with Charles P. Jones and Charles H. Mason, as well as with other Holiness leaders. At that time, Jones and Mason were working together as Baptist evangelists who had embraced the doctrines of Holiness. Jones was later to become the leader of the Church of Christ Holiness, and Mason was to head the Church of God in Christ.

Until recently, Seymour was portrayed primarily as a disciple of Charles Fox Parham. Parham was a white Holiness evangelist from Kansas, known as the doctrinal father of modern Pentecostalism. He founded and operated the Topeka Bible College and is credited with articulating the "tongues" doctrine. Through his reading of the Book of Acts, he concluded that speaking with tongues is the necessary initial evidence that one has been baptized with the Holy Spirit. Seymour popularized this doctrine, which fanned the flames of revival at Azusa Street. The supposition of Parham's extensive influence on Seymour must be modified, however, in light of Douglas J. Nelson's monumental study of Seymour's life. Nelson shows that Parham, an avowed and intractable racist, did not permit Seymour to study with his students. At most, Seymour caught the doctrine through the cracks of the door as he sat outside the room—the only place a black man was permitted unless serving in some menial capacity. Seymour utterly rejected Parham's doctrines on race and creation. Parham taught the theory of two creations: that the created race was brought into being on the sixth day and that on the eighth day the Adamic race—from which Caucasians came—was formed. The Adamic race, being the superior race, was defiled through the mixing of blood, and the flood was the punishment for the sin of race mixing and was meant to purge the world.

Seymour, however, believed that the coming together of the races was the act for which the revival was a sign of approbation. Indeed, the approbation of Azusa Street, in Seymour's view, had more to do with the crossing of racial lines and the achievement of unity in the body of Christ than the formal criterion of glossolalia as proof of spirit baptism. In this respect, Seymour was more within the tradition of the African American religious experience than anything else. Parham repudiated Seymour's experiment in racial cooperation as a "darky camp meeting" and refused to conduct the great union revival that Seymour had requested. Seymour was finally forced to repudiate Parham as not being the leader of the Azusa Street Revival.[21]

Things of the Spirit—Common Ground

The point of greatest and clearest common belief among African American Holiness/Pentecostal/Apostolics is the emphasis on the reality and working of the Holy Spirit in clearly evident ways. For African American Holiness/Pentecostal/Apostolics, the Holy Spirit is not viewed primarily as a symbol or a name in the creeds and confessions. Neither is the Spirit seen as being contained within structures, limited by boundaries, or impeded by any human obstacle. Rather, the Spirit is held to be active, alive, and powerful in ways that are manifested within both the invisible and the visible realms of reality. Within the spiritual realm, the Spirit is experienced in intense personal and communal ways. In the visible realm, the Spirit moves upon the material world to effect demonstrations, miracles, and other acts that show God's favor and judgment. In a real sense, the entirety of Christian life is but the movement of the Spirit, according to African American Holiness/Pentecostal/Apostolics.

Among African American Holiness/Pentecostal/Apostolics is a common openness to the Spirit that contrasts with the dominant motifs of Western culture. Where the influence of the Enlightenment remains strong, the overriding emphasis is on what can be known and measured through the senses. Positive knowledge can be acquired through means initiated and controlled by humans. If two individuals make the same observation, the same conclusion can and should be reached. All that is claimed as knowledge can be verified for the sake of upholding or refuting that conclusion. Knowledge begins and ends with laws that are based on regularity and order in nature. The world to which one has access by means of reason is the world that is to be trusted. Claims for knowledge or events outside the world of reason are to be regarded with a high degree of suspicion. Either such knowledge or events represent areas wherein rational explanations are yet to be found, or they are to be relegated to the realm of projection, illusion, fantasy, and myth.

Against, or alongside, this rational world, African American Holiness/Pentecostal/Apostolics find themselves at home in the realm of the Spirit. This world, like that of the Old and New Testament and those cultures not heavily influenced by the Enlightenment, is one in which the deity exercises radical freedom. The Spirit, who is divine, intervenes at will to act directly upon and within the affairs of men and women. Priority is given to this "noumenal" or spiritual realm. Although there may be scientific explanations for phenomena that occur in the visible world, some explanation from within this noumenal realm can be supplied as well. But the logic that inheres within the world of the Spirit is also sufficient for explaining or accounting for events and occurrences that have no rational explanation. Or, to put it another way, the explanation is essentially a spiritual one.

Spirit Baptism

The center of this spiritual vitality is the Spirit-filled church, comprised of members who have experienced Spirit baptism. Spirit baptism is the threshold criterion that cannot be denied. Instead, it is to stand out in the consciousness and memory of each person, allowing for detailed recollection accompanied by physical evidence. Spirit baptism, which supplies the "fullness of salvation," is not achieved through church membership, confession of faith, water baptism, or even conversion. Rather, it is attained through an experience normally regarded as subsequent to conversion, and in some cases, subsequent to sanctification. Even in those exceptional cases where Spirit baptism is simultaneous with conversion or sanctification, it is still held to be distinct. Spirit baptism normally occurs subsequent to the believer's having met conditions that require a considerable degree of devotion and self-denial. Traditionally, these conditions were usually met through tarrying services, which consisted of extended periods of fasting, praying, and subjection to the nurturing influences of the community through teaching and preaching.

Efforts are made to ensure that Spirit baptism conforms to the criteria these communities of believers derive from the Book of Acts. Criteria are regarded as not merely descriptive, but as normative. Spirit baptism, with physical evidence (such as speaking in tongues), is considered the precondition for vitality and continuing manifestations in the church. Without these manifestations the church cannot legitimately claim to have life. In this view, Christian living revolves around Spirit baptism. Everything prior to Spirit baptism is considered as preparation for it. Not conversion, not regeneration, but Spirit baptism is what makes a bona fide Christian. One who does not testify to this event often and convincingly is considered to be either "quasi Christian," or "living beneath his or her privilege"—no matter how pious or esteemed he or she may be. All of the Spirit's work and consequences in the church and the world are either preparation for or outgrowths of Spirit baptism.[22]

Although the doctrines and the formulaic language described previously awaited the Holiness movement and the Pentecostal movement that followed it, the experience known as Spirit baptism has clear antecedents within the evangelical life of the African American church. A soul labored before the Lord; others "tarried" with him or her until he or she "came through" or "prayed through" (i.e., received Spirit baptism by speaking in tongues). On the frontier, in the camp meetings, at the praying ground, and in secret meetings on the plantations, this moment of "coming through" was punctuated with strong emotion and great drama. This can be seen clearly in the testimonies to conversion by Jarena Lee, Richard Allen, and John Marrant.[23]

The African American church—in an attempt to follow the lead of the white church perhaps—placed less emphasis on this highly charged crisis moment. Spirit baptism was said to occur in the rituals of confirmation and chrismation—as part of incorporation into the church. In some cases, the language of Spirit baptism was dropped altogether; in other cases the argument that this act of the Spirit had taken place was strictly a theological proposition, with no emphasis on accompanying experience or evidence. Spirit baptism became objective, not subjective in any significant sense.

Manifestation of the Spirit

Among African American Holiness/Pentecostal/Apostolics, the Spirit is understood as being clearly manifest whenever present. Indeed, the indistinct or nonmanifest presence of the Spirit is regarded as an utter contradiction. Accordingly, the presence of the Spirit makes worship an eventful and exciting occasion. Testimonies are characterized by fervor. Singing is loud, intense, and vivacious. Prayers are offered in the Spirit, with rapture being the sign for those who truly "make contact with heaven." Worship entails both formally structured acts and spontaneous ones, which include dancing, profusion of praise, weeping, laughing, and ecstatic speech. Preaching tends to be sonorous, animated, dramatic, and rhythmic, often breaking into a full-blown chant. In addition, the preacher solicits a verbal response from the listeners and may include or prompt any of the other spontaneous acts of worship.[24] The Spirit's presence in worship may well include prophecy, miracles, healing, and other manifestations known as the exercise of "spiritual gifts."[25]

Of all the physical manifestations credited to the Spirit, none is more crucial for Pentecostals than speaking with tongues, or glossolalia. Indeed, the emphasis placed on tongues-speaking often forms the entire basis for Pentecostal pneumatology, and without a doubt, the doctrine of tongues is the element that most distinguishes Pentecostals from other Christians. African American Holiness/Pentecostal/Apostolics as a group tend to regard speaking with tongues as the sign par excellence that the Spirit has come to abide within the believer. The body is the temple of the Holy Ghost, and the entrance of this heavenly guest is highlighted by ecstatic speech. This ecstasy signals the temporary displacement of the human ego in favor of the divine person, namely, the Holy Spirit. As a consequence of this divine infusion, the individual stands outside of the self in a state of rapture and exultation.

Tongues-speaking is generally regarded as commonplace among African American Holiness/Pentecostal/Apostolics. In most cases, this matchless point of ecstasy is seen as the high point in worship. Along with dancing, it stands as a supreme manifestation of God's presence: in that moment, the tethers to the mundane world are broken. There is perforation of the artificial barrier between the world of the creatures and the world of the Creator that bestows and sustains life. Among the explanations for this incomparable experience are that: 1) it is a form of divinely inspired communication which overcomes the separation of language that keeps human beings apart from one another; 2) it is a language that overcomes the impediments of human speech for the sake of unimpeded communication with God; 3) it is a means of speaking mysteries to God, in tongues of men and angels; and 4) it is a language given as a sign for unbelievers to show them that God is real and concerned with their needs and their salvation.

Tongues Doctrine

The tongues doctrine is the tenet that tongues-speaking is necessary evidence of Spirit baptism. Adherents to the tongues doctrine base their belief on several passages in the Book of Acts that they regard as crucial to its interpretation. Chief among them is the second chapter of Acts, which records the coming of the Spirit in fulfillment of the Lord's promise on the Day of Pentecost. On that occasion, according to Luke, they "all spoke with other tongues" (Acts 2:4). In Acts 10, believers at Caesarea spoke with other tongues, and within the context of that scene, tongues-speaking was the undisputable evidence that the Gentiles had received the gift of the Spirit, as had the Jews. In Acts 19, believers previously baptized by John spoke with tongues following their baptism by Paul in the name of the Lord Jesus. On the basis of these three texts where tongues-speaking is explicitly mentioned, adherents to tongues doctrine conclude that speaking with tongues is the sign that attracts the attention of Simon in Samaria in the eighth chapter of Acts. On the basis of these four texts, they take speaking with tongues to be the scripturally mandated, necessary, and indisputable evidence of Spirit baptism.

A crucial point of disagreement among African American Holiness/Pentecostal/Apostolics is whether a person must speak with tongues to validate his or her Spirit baptism. The tongues doctrine unites Pentecostals and Apostolics, and divides Holiness believers from the former two. Indeed, this threshold criterion for Pentecostals and Apostolics is written into the Articles of Faith of numerous groups. Those who adhere to the tongues doctrine see speaking in tongues as God's way of settling doubt and uncertainty among believers seeking the fullness of the blessing.

Tongues-Speaking without Tongues Doctrine

The group that is hardest to classify is Holiness believers who appreciate and/or practice tongues-speaking without adhering to the tongues doctrine. This group is distinguished from Holiness members who reject tongues-speaking in all forms, limiting legitimate glossolalia to the era of the early church and ascribing contemporary manifestations to the work of the devil or some other form of derangement. The somewhat flexible position of appreciating tongues-speaking, to which a rather considerable number of African American Holiness adherents ascribe, is especially notable when compared with white Holiness adherents, who take a fairly consistent and rigid position against both the tongues doctrine and tongues-speaking.

Indeed, the contact between African American Holiness and Pentecostal adherents is so great that the distinction is practically nonexistent in a large cross-section of the two groups. Many African American Holiness members regard it as quite appropriate for believers to speak in tongues when receiving the Holy Ghost and to speak with tongues periodically—either publicly or privately, causing the names Holiness and Pentecostal to be virtually interchangeable in this group.

Holiness and Pentecostals: A Matter of Emphasis

The most outstanding feature of belief for Holiness adherents is sanctification, or personal holiness. Spirit baptism is related in a definite way to Holiness. The classical Holiness position relates sanctification to Spirit baptism in the following manner: entire sanctification is wrought through the baptism of the Holy Ghost. This entire sanctification—or Christian perfection—is a point at which the believer yields so completely to God that there is no desire for the things that displease God. If a believer makes mistakes or errors in judgment, these are repulsive to the believer, and there is immediate self-condemnation, leading to repentance and restoration. With perfect love toward God, all the believers' dispositions and passions are directed by the single aim to please God with all the heart. Such a disposition is achieved in a moment that is correlated with a definite experience, which is as powerful as conversion, if not more so. In this experience, power and disposition are given by the Spirit to keep the commandments of God.

Among most African American Holiness/Pentecostals, whether of the Holiness or Pentecostal emphasis, sanctification is preparatory to receiving the baptism of the Holy Ghost. The formula most often articulated is this: the baptism of the Holy Ghost is the gift of power to the sanctified life. In other words, once the believer is truly and fully sanctified, the Spirit descends, without effort, without seeking. Tarrying, when it does take place, is not so much for the Holy Ghost as it is to ensure that sanctification is complete. The Holiness emphasis is on sanctification; the Pentecostal emphasis is on power.

Apostolics: The Oneness Issue

Although numerous similarities in faith and practice remain within the family of African American Holiness/Pentecostal/Apostolics, a significant distinction exists between those known as Apostolic and the others. In many ways, all share the common heritage within African American Christianity and evangelical religion in America. The orientation to the Spirit, the patterns of worship, and numerous other matters pertaining to faith and practice make Apostolics hardly distinguishable. This often leads outsiders to make no differentiation among the subfamilies, with the consequence that the integrity of each subfamily is overlooked. Hence, although Apostolics are closely related to Holiness believers and Pentecostals, they differ from the other two groups on a significant point of theology. Unlike Pentecostals and Holiness believers, who may disagree on the importance of the tongues doctrine, the Apostolics differ about the doctrine of the Trinity and the formula for baptism.

African American Holiness believers and Pentecostals join mainline Protestants in affirming the doctrinal consensus of the early ecumenical councils of the church, which confessed the trinitarian mystery that Father, Son, and Holy Spirit are the three persons constituting the Godhead. These three mutually dwell in one another; they are equal in eternity, power, and glory; and they always work in agreement, according to this confession. Despite the numerous problems of translating this ancient formula into modern times, those who consider trinitarian doctrine crucial to Christian faith refuse to abandon their dogmatic position. Apostolics, adhering to the "oneness" of God, reject the trinitarian formula, holding that there is but one God, whose name is revealed in the New Testament as Jesus. Furthermore, they show from the Book of Acts that the consistent formula for baptizing believers in the early church was in the name of Jesus.[26]

African American Holiness/Pentecostal/Apostolics and the World

The development among African American Holiness/Pentecostal/Apostolic bodies since their inception and early stages of the movement is considerable. During the early decades of the century, the majority of the African American Holiness/Pentecostal/Apostolics came from among the poor, the uneducated, and the outcasts of society. Despite the sprinkling of moderately well-trained persons within the leadership and the membership, a large proportion of drunks, derelicts, and criminals among the converts clearly marked this brand of religion as a movement of the underclass. Frequently, the places of worship were abandoned buildings, warehouses, sheds, old movie theaters, and stores. This is largely what led to Frazier's designation of the Holiness movement among African Americans as "storefront religion." Furthermore, where no building was available, meetings were held in tents, brush arbors, or on street corners. Due to the intense emotions and vigorous exercises within worship services, Holiness believers and Pentecostals were often referred to with the pejorative labels of "that mess" or "holy rollers." Because of the rather large exodus from the Baptists and Methodists to Holiness and Pentecostal and Apostolic bodies, tensions were sometimes high between these evangelical bodies.

Marked changes from the early days of the Holiness/Pentecostal/Apostolic movement are notable from the standpoints of the physical structures and of the makeup of membership. African American Holiness/Pentecostal/Apostolics now worship in modern, stately, attractive structures, as do other Christian bodies. In some cases, the facilities are buildings purchased from other groups, including Protestants, Catholics, and Jews. Many children of African American Holiness/Pentecostal/Apostolics have remained within these bodies after acquiring their educations, thus giving impetus to reform and development from within, and making it easier to attract people from among the well-trained and professional classes. Consequently, many local churches and most connected bodies among African American Holiness/Pentecostal/Apostolics have a good share of school teachers, businessmen and women, lawyers, doctors, university professors, and so forth.

African American Holiness/Pentecostal/Apostolics join with other African American Protestants in holding elective offices and assuming their share of the leadership within the African American community. This includes holding such positions as the presidency of NAACP chapters, PTAs, ministerial alliances, and other community organizations and corporations, and being elected to mayorships and city councils. An example of such participation occurred during the strike of sanitation workers in Memphis at the time of the Reverend Dr. Martin Luther King, Jr.'s, assassination, when the rallying point was the Mason Temple, headquarters for the Church of God in Christ.

Despite this development within individual bodies and African American Holiness/Pentecostal/Apostolics as a whole, there remains a dynamic that causes the movement to gravitate to the lowest socioeconomic level. As a whole, African American Holiness/Pentecostal/Apostolics take pride in being able to reach the downcast, the despised, and the wretched. In some cases, the goal is to bring people into a community that elevates them socially, making them part of an organization that takes pride in its heritage, development, and achievement. However, some pockets of Pentecostals literally despise churches that are large, buildings that are ornate, or services that are formal. Their aim is to remain small, narrowly focused, and uncomplicated. Among this element the charge made against evangelicals some one hundred years ago is often heard—that the church has become worldly, ashamed to praise the Lord, and has backslid. Or, there is the charge of trying to be like the Baptists and the Methodists, sometimes leading to further proliferation of reform groups within the Holiness and Pentecostal churches.

There can be no denying that development within these groups is much like that of the older Protestant denominations, which began essentially as reform movements. Clear evidence of this is the spiritual renewal within the mainline denominations that has now begun to draw former Holiness and Pentecostal believers into the ranks of their membership and leadership. Such an interpenetration has the effect of making the three major groups within African American Protestant churches—Baptist, Methodist, and Pentecostal—more and more like one another.

Notes

1. See Benjamin E. Mays and Joseph W. Nicholson, *The Negro's Church* (New York: Institute of Social and Religious Research, 1933; New York: Arno Press, 1969), 209-10.
2. See chapter 4, "Charismatic and Pentecostal Sects" in Elmer T. Clark, *Small Sects in America* (Nashville: Abingdon-Cokesbury Press, 1937); also 98. Clark's references to black Holiness and Pentecostal groups are scarce and sketchy. Where black Pentecostals are discussed, they are referred to as ignorant sorts who indulge in shouting, visions, trances, prophecy, and other forms of ecstasy.

   Carter G. Woodson in his *History of the Negro Church* (Washington, D.C.: Associated Publishers, 1921) does not identify any black Holiness/Pentecostal groups as such. But in chapter 12, "The Conservatives and the Progressives," he draws a portrait of conservatives in the black church who opposed the progressives following the Civil War. The way the conservatives are depicted is clearly parallel to the description of Holiness/Pentecostals found in Clark.
3. E. Franklin Frazier and C. Eric Lincoln, *The Negro Church in America/The Black Church Since Frazier* (New York: Shocken Books, 1974).
4. See Arthur Huff Fauset, *Black Gods of the Metropolis* (Philadelphia: University of Pennsylvania Press, 1944). In chapter 2, Fauset offers a portrait of Mount Sinai Holy Church, which is very typical of African American Holiness/Pentecostal/Apostolics. When he makes his comparisons in Chapter 6, it becomes clear that the Mount Sinai group stands out from the others.
5. In particular, see Baldwin's *Amen Corner*. *The Fire Next Time* is also quite descriptive.
6. See Joseph R. Washington, *Black Religion: The Negro and Christianity in the United States* (Boston: Beacon Press, 1964), ch. 2.
7. C. Eric Lincoln, *Race, Religion and the Continuing American Dilemma* (New York: Hill & Wang, 1984), 103.
8. See Thomas A. Langford, *Practical Divinity: Theology in the Wesleyan Tradition* (Nashville: Abingdon Press, 1983) and Vinson Synan, *The Holiness Pentecostal Movement in the United States* (Grand Rapids, Mich.: W. B. Eerdmans Publishing Co., 1977).
9. See Colin W. Williams, *John Wesley's Theology Today* (Nashville: Abingdon Press, 1960) for a discussion of how the order of salvation was bound up with attending to the means of grace—both instituted and prudential means.
10. See Mechal Sobel, *Trabelin' On: The Slave Journey to an Afro-Baptist Faith* (Westport, Conn.: Greenwood Press, 1979).

11. Luther P. Jackson chronicled the waves of revivals in Virginia, showing the influx of Africans into the church in "Religious Development of the Negro in Virginia from 1760-1860." *Journal of Negro History*, 16(April 1931): 168-239.
12. In his study of black Methodism, *Dark Salvation*, (New York: Doubleday, 1976), Harry Richardson shows that blacks were part of the development of Methodism from its very inception in the United States.
13. Bishop Francis Asbury referred to African Methodists as the "African part of the family" and made mention in his letters of the "black people's exercises." In one letter he told of how a "thoughtless young lady" found the Lord among the Africans one night, and the next day she jumped the pew during morning prayer. See Potts, Clark, and Payton, eds., *The Journal and Letters of Francis Asbury*, (Nashville: Abingdon Press, 1958), 3: 218-19.

    Also see Albert J. Raboteau, *Slave Religion* (New York: Oxford University Press, 1978), 67, for an excerpt from John Fanning Watson's "Methodist Error," in which he described the influence of Africans on Methodists.
14. See the Directory of St. Steven's A.M.E. Church, Wilmington, N.C., for a brief history of how the St. Steven's Church evolved from the Front Street Church.
15. Richardson, 171ff.
16. Otho B. Cobbins, *History of Church of Christ (Holiness) U.S.A. 1895-1965.* (New York: Vantage Press, 1966), ch. 2.
17. Lovett made his list in his dissertation, "Black Holiness-Pentecostalism: Implications for Ethics and Social Transformation" (Emory University, 1978), 13. The United Holy Church of America was founded ca. 1886, and several persons are associated with its beginnings in Method, North Carolina. Church of Christ Holiness, U.S.A., was founded about 1894-96 by Charles P. Jones, in Jackson, Mississippi. Church of God in Christ was founded in 1895-97 by Charles H. Mason in Lexington, Mississippi. Fire Baptized Holiness Church of God in the Americas was founded in 1889 by W. E. Fuller, leader of the black faction between 1900 and 1922, which grew out of the predominantly white Fire Baptist Holiness Church originally founded by Benjamin H. Irwin. Pentecostal Assemblies of the World was founded by Garfield Thomas Haywood, leader of the black faction, which was originally said to have split from the Assemblies of God (ca. 1914-24).
18. Henry L. Fisher, "The History of the United Holy Church of America" (Duke University, Durham, N.C., 1945), 1, ff. Also see a dissertation by William C. Turner, "The United Holy Church of America: A Study in Black Holiness Pentecostalism" (Duke University, Durham, N.C., 1984).
19. Milton C. Sernett, *Afro-American Religious History: A Documentary Witness* (Durham, N.C.: Duke University Press, 1985), 293. See also J. O. Patterson, German R. Ross, and Julia Atkins, eds., *History and Formative Years of the Church of God in Christ with Excerpts from the Life and Works of Its Founder—Bishop C. H. Mason* (Memphis: Church of God in Christ Publishing House, 1969).
20. Sernett, 294; Cobbins, 50-52, 86.
21. References made to W. J. Seymour in most studies of the Pentecostal movement rely on early and unfavorable accounts. Many of these works perpetuate a portrait of Seymour as an insignificant figure who was untidy, ineffective as a leader, and a retiring, mysterious sort of character. However, Nelson's study of Seymour's life and work shows him to be a pivotal figure in the movement. See Nelson's dissertation, "For Such a Time as This: The Story of Bishop William J. Seymour and the Azusa Revival" (The University of Birmingham, England, 1981), in which he makes use of primary materials—the writings of Seymour himself.
22. See Andrew W. Lawson, *The Holy Spirit in Action* (Durham, N.C.: Service Printing Company, 1980), and *The Doctrine of the United Holy Church* (Durham, N.C.: United Holy Church, 1964).
23. See Richard Allen, *The Life Experience and Gospel Labors of the*

Right Reverend Richard Allen (Nashville: Abingdon Press, 1960),
15-16, for an account of Allen's conversion. See Sernett, 160ff.,
for Jarena Lee's testimony of her conversion. See Sobel, 103-4,
for John Marrant's testimony of his conversion.

24. For descriptions of African American Pentecostal worship, see
Melvin D. Williams, Community in a Black Pentecostal Church:
An Anthropological Study (Pittsburgh: University of Pittsburgh
Press, 1974); Arthur E. Paris, Black Pentecostalism: Southern
Religion in an Urban World (Amherst, Mass.: University of Mas-
sachusetts Press, 1982); and James Baldwin, Amen Corner.

25. Although several New Testament passages list spiritual gifts (e.g.,
Romans 12, Ephesians 4), African American Holiness/Pentecostal/
Apostolics tend to regard the enumeration of I Corinthians 12:7-
10 as normative. They place special emphasis on the necessity of
all ''nine gifts'' in a church that is Spirit filled.

26. See James C. Richardson, Jr., With Water and Spirit: A History
of Black Apostolic Denominations in the U.S. (Washington, D.C.:
Spirit Press, 1980).

Bibliography

Allen, Richard. The Life Experience and Gospel Labors of the Right
Reverend Richard Allen. Nashville: Abingdon Press, 1960.

Baldwin, James. Amen Corner. New York: Dial Press, 1968.

————— . The Fire Next Time. New York: Dial Press, 1963.

Clark, Elmer T. Small Sects in America. Nashville: Abingdon-Cokesbury Press, 1937.

Cobbins, Otho B. History of Church of Christ (Holiness) U.S.A. 1895-
1965. New York: Vantage Press, 1966.

Directory of St. Steven's A.M.E. Church. Wilmington, N.C.: St.Steven's
A.M.E. Church, n.d.

Fauset, Arthur Huff. Black Gods of the Metropolis. Philadelphia: University of Pennsylvania Press, 1944.

Fisher, Henry L. ''The History of the United Holy Church of America.'' Ph.D. diss., Duke University, 1945.

Frazier, E. Franklin, and C. Eric Lincoln. The Negro Church in Amer-
ica/The Black Church Since Frazier. New York: Shocken Books,
1974.

Jackson, Luther P. ''Religious Development of the Negro in Virginia
from 1760-1860.'' Journal of Negro History, 16 (April 1931): 168-
239.

Langford, Thomas A. Practical Divinity: Theology in the Wesleyan
Tradition. Nashville: Abingdon Press, 1983.

Lawson, Andrew W. The Doctrine of the United Holy Church. Durham, N.C.: United Holy Church, 1964.

————— . The Holy Spirit in Action. Durham, N.C.: Service Printing
Company, 1980.

Lincoln, C. Eric. Race, Religion and the Continuing American Dilemma. New York: Hill & Wang, 1984.

Lovett, Leonard. ''Black Holiness-Pentecostalism: Implications for Ethics
and Social Transformation.'' Ph.D. diss., Emory University, 1978.

Mays, Benjamin E., and Joseph W. Nicholson. The Negro's Church.
New York: Institute of Social and Religious Research, 1933. Reprint.
New York: Arno Press, 1969.

Nelson, Douglas J. ''For Such a Time as This: The Story of Bishop
William J. Seymour and the Azusa Revival.'' Ph.D. diss., University
of Birmingham, England, 1981.

Paris, Arthur E. Black Pentecostalism: Southern Religion in an Urban
World. Amherst, Mass.: University of Massachusetts Press, 1982.

Patterson, J. O., German R. Ross, and Julia Atkins, eds. History and
Formative Years of the Church of God in Christ with Excerpts from
the Life and Works of Its Founder—Bishop C. H. Mason. Memphis:
Church of God in Christ Publishing House, 1969.

Potts, J. Manning, Elmer T. Clark, and Jacob S. Payton, eds. The
Journal and Letters of Francis Asbury. 3 vols. Nashville: Abingdon
Press, 1958.

Raboteau, Albert J. Slave Religion. New York: Oxford University
Press, 1978.

Richardson, Harry. Dark Salvation. New York: Doubleday, 1976.

Richardson, James C., Jr. With Water and Spirit: A History of Black
Apostolic Denominations in the U.S. Washington, D.C.: Spirit Press,
1980.

Sernett, Milton C. Afro-American Religious History: A Documentary
Witness. Durham, N.C.: Duke University Press, 1985.

Sobel, Mechal. Trabelin' On: The Slave Journey to an Afro-Baptist
Faith. Westport, Conn.: Greenwood Press, 1979.

Synan, Vinson. The Holiness Pentecostal Movement in the United
States. Grand Rapids, Mich.: W. B. Eerdmans Publishing Co., 1977.

Turner, William C. ''The United Holy Church of America: A Study
in Black Holiness Pentecostalism.'' Ph.D. diss., Duke University,
1984.

Washington, Joseph R. Black Religion: The Negro and Christianity in
the United States. Boston: Beacon Press, 1964.

Williams, Colin W. John Wesley's Theology Today. Nashville: Abingdon Press, 1966.

Williams, Melvin D. Community in a Black Pentecostal Church: An
Anthropological Study. Pittsburgh: University of Pittsburgh Press,
1974.

Woodson, Carter G. History of the Negro Church. Washington, D.C.:
Associated Publishers, 1921.

History of the African American Catholic Church in the United States
Evangelization and Indigenization

Cyprian Davis, O.S.B.

In 1866, the Catholic bishops of the United States came together just after the morrow of the Civil War in the Second Plenary Council of Baltimore. On that occasion, they issued a pastoral letter, the second pastoral letter of the American bishops since the founding of the hierarchy. The bishops had this to say in their pastoral letter regarding the abolition of slavery:

> We must all feel, beloved Brethren, that in some manner a new and most extensive field of charity and devotedness has been opened to us, by the emancipation of the immense slave population of the South. We could have wished, that in accordance with the action of the Catholic Church in past ages, in regard to the serfs of Europe, a more gradual system of emancipation could have been adopted, so that they might have been in some measure prepared to make a better use of their freedom, than they are likely to do now. . . .
>
> We urge upon the Clergy and people of our charge the most generous co-operation with the plans which may be adopted by the Bishops of the Dioceses in which they are, to extend to them that Christian education and moral restraint which they so much stand in need of. Our only regret . . . is that our means and opportunity . . . are so restricted.[1]

One must admit that with a less-than-enthusiastic acknowledgment of the new status achieved by African Americans in this country, the bishops did seem to agree upon the necessity of some efforts at evangelization. The rather unmagnanimous gesture on the part of the bishops of the Second Plenary Council masked their very hostile reception to the suggestion of the Holy See for a structured plan for the evangelization of the freed slaves. This hostile reception is not to be found in the quiet phrases of the Acts of the Council as published. Rather, one must look for the acts of the extraordinary session of the council, held after the council had officially closed, on October 22, 1866.[2]

Martin J. Spalding, former bishop of Louisville and,

by 1866, archbishop of Baltimore, first proposed the idea of a national council. One of his objectives was the formulation of a program for the newly emancipated slaves by the American Catholic church as a whole. Spalding, who was from a slaveholding southern family, had been a Confederate sympathizer during the Civil War.[3] Nevertheless, he had a genuine concern for the evangelization of the freed blacks. In a letter to Archbishop McCloskey of New York, he wrote:

> . . . It is . . . the most urgent duty of all to discuss the future status of the negro. [sic] Four million of these unfortunates are thrown on our Charity, and they silently but eloquently appeal to us for help. It is a golden opportunity for reaping a harvest of souls, which neglected may not return.[4]

At the end of the Civil War, there were 4 million African Americans in the country, and some 100,000 were Catholic.[5]

In submitting his project for a national council to the Sacred Congregation of the Propaganda, Spalding also made concrete proposals for the evangelization of African Americans. In fact, he suggested that, among several possibilities, one project might be the establishment of a national ordinariate to coordinate all activity for African American evangelization. The congregation leaped at the opportunity for encouraging some sort of ministry to the freed blacks. It took Spalding's proposal as its own and presented it for consideration to the bishops at the Second Plenary Council. In fact, Spalding never indicated to the bishops that he was the one who had originally thought of the establishment of an ordinariate or an ecclesiastical coordinator on the national level.[6]

The debate over the proposed national director was a bitter one. Many bishops severely criticized the Curia for its mandate that an arrangement be made. Peter Kenrick, the archbishop of St. Louis, was one of the most outspoken in his opposition to such an appointment. It was his opinion that the appointment of such an ecclesiastic for the evangelization of freed African Americans would suggest that the bishops had been remiss in their duties.[7] There was sarcasm. One bishop urged in jest

"The History of the Black Catholic Church in the U.S.: Evangelization and Indigenization" by the Reverend Dr. Cyprian Davis, O.S.B, is a revision of a paper originally presented at the National Black Catholic Symposium, "Unless Someone Explains. . .," April 29, 1985, sponsored by the Archdiocese of Detroit, Detroit, Michigan.

that the director, who was to be an ''ecclesiastic'' should be qualified as a ''Negro ecclesiastic.'' Another wanted to know what the Congregation of the Propaganda would do for white people. Spalding, however, persevered in urging the adoption of the plan. One bishop, the French-born Augustin Verot, bishop of Savannah, who had publicly defended slavery in a sermon during the Civil War, gave his wholehearted support to the plan envisioned by the congregation.[8] Verot was genuinely concerned about the evangelization of African Americans in the South, and he had made several attempts to get a religious order (i.e., a community of monks, nuns, etc.) to come to his diocese for that purpose.

With the exception of Verot, there was little support for Spalding's efforts. The northern bishops did not consider the newly liberated population their problem. The southern bishops did not want to share their authority with a national director, or even worse, an ordinary for African Americans. All were unwilling to raise money for the purpose of African American evangelization if it would hurt fundraising for their churches in general. As a result, the bishops did not appoint a national director for African American evangelization, but left it to each bishop to do what he considered best for his diocese. It was mandated, however, that efforts be made to bring an order of priests or brothers from Europe who would work among the African American population. This project was realized when the Mill Hill Fathers (later known as the Josephites when the American branch was formed) arrived in Baltimore in 1871. Nevertheless, it must be admitted that, in the words of Archbishop Spalding, ''the golden opportunity'' had slipped away.

The Response of African American Catholics

In their 1984 pastoral letter on evangelization, the African American bishops wrote:

> At every turning point of American history, we come face to face with the Black man and Black woman. What is true of our national history is even truer of American Catholic history.[9]

This is especially true upon examination of the church and the evangelization of African Americans. In 1866, when the bishops at the Second Plenary Council considered the question of how to minister to the newly freed African Americans, the Oblate Sisters of Providence had already been in existence some thirty-seven years. It was four African American women, French-speaking for the most part, who, with the aid of Jacques Joubert and under the leadership of Elizabeth Lange, established the first congregation of African American sisters in this country. The sisters were dedicated to the education and care of African American children at a time when, in the South, these children were inured to slavery at a tender age and,

in the North, were often neglected and abandoned on the streets. Again, it was French-speaking African American women, Henriette Delille and Juliette Gaudin, who brought the Gospel and material aid to the African American poor of New Orleans when they formed the Sisters of the Holy Family, the second-oldest African American Catholic sisterhood in this country, already in existence for twenty-four years at the time of the Second Plenary Council. It says a lot about the faith and the sense of mission among African American Catholics in the pre-Civil War period, when we note the existence of two religious orders of African American women who managed to survive the dark days of slavery.[10] An even greater tribute to the faith of these African American women is shown in the person of Sister Therese Maxis Duchemin, one of the original members of the Oblate Sisters, who founded the Sisters of the Immaculate Heart of Mary in Monroe, Michigan, in 1845.[11] African American Catholic women preserved the faith not only for the African American community, but also for the church at large.

The Vision of an African American Catholic Layman

Perhaps the most significant response by African American Catholics to the need for evangelization among African Americans came in the person of Daniel Rudd, an Ohio newspaperman, who organized the first nationwide lay movement among African American Catholics. Twenty-two years after the bishops in the Second Plenary Council demonstrated their inability to deal successfully with the plight of freed Americans, Daniel Rudd, a former slave, born in Bardstown, Kentucky, who, at the age of thirty-three, was already the editor of an African American Catholic weekly newspaper, addressed a convention of young Catholic men in Cincinnati in June 1888. Rudd's tone was optimistic and reassuring. He explained to his audience his hopes and his vision for the future of African Americans:

> It may seem strange to you, possibly, to hear me talking about colored Catholics, or any other sort of Catholics, yet it must be so; we have in this country a large number of our own race, many of whom are Catholics. . . . I believe that there are about two hundred thousand practical Catholics in the United States of my race.
>
> That is indeed a grand showing, considering that we have done nothing ourselves to promote and facilitate a knowledge of the church among our own race, except possibly to attend to our own duties. According to the statistics there are seven millions of negroes in the United States. My friends, this race is increasing more rapidly than yours, and if it continues to increase in the future as it has in the past, by the middle of the next century they will outnumber your race.
>
> We have been led to believe that the church was inimical to the negro race. . . . I owe it to myself, my God, and my country to refute the slander.
>
> We are publishing a weekly newspaper. . . . A meeting

of our people will be held somewhere: the time and place has not yet been fixed. . . .

When that convention meets, I trust that many of you will . . . show your interest in this work. I believe that within ten years . . . there will be awakened a latent force in this country.[12]

The "latent force," of whose imminence Rudd was convinced, related to a massive conversion of African Americans to Catholicism. His purpose in editing the weekly newspaper, which, with the exception of a short-lived African American Catholic weekly in Philadelphia, was the only Catholic newspaper edited and published by African Americans, was to explain and defend Catholicism to a nationwide African American readership.[13] Rudd edited his newspaper in Cincinnati until 1894, when he moved to Detroit, where he published the newspaper until almost 1899. Surprisingly, there is no historical record either in the archdiocesan archives or in the Detroit historical society of Rudd's presence in Detroit. There is only a mention of Rudd's address in the Detroit Street Directory from 1895 to 1897.[14]

Yet Daniel Rudd was pivotal in the history of African American Catholicism. Not only did he edit an informative newspaper and lecture extensively throughout the North and South, but Rudd also organized and launched a series of Black Catholic Lay Congresses. The initial congress, in Washington, D.C., at the beginning of January 1889, was the first of its kind in the nation, although lay congresses, as such, were common in Belgium and Germany.[15] In fact, Rudd would be on the planning committee for the first two national Black Catholic Lay Congresses, the first of which was held in November 1889.

The five Black Catholic Lay Congresses, from 1889 to 1894, brought together leading African American members of the Catholic laity from all parts of the United States.[16] The first such congress was a celebration of unity and solidarity with greetings from Pope Leo XIII and a visit with President Grover Cleveland. There was tremendous support for Father Augustus Tolton, the only publicly acknowledged African American priest in the country,[17] who had been ordained in Rome only three years before. There was also a stirring address in which the delegates called for an end to racial injustice and professed their faith that the Catholic Church "will, by the innate force of her truth, gradually dispel the prejudices unhappily prevailing amongst so many of our misguided people."[18] In this address, the delegates called for more Catholic schools; called for literary societies among their young; exhorted fellow Catholics "to practice the self-sacrificing virtue of temperance"; demanded the admission of African American men into the labor unions and urged the full employment of African American men and women; turned again to the question of education by urging the establishment of industrial schools for the vocational training of African American youth; called for orphanages, hospitals, and asylums for the care of African American children and the sick and indigent; and deplored housing conditions for African Americans in the cities and discrimination against African Americans seeking to buy real estate.[19]

During the next four congresses—Cincinnati (1890), Philadelphia (1892), Chicago (1893), and Baltimore (1894)—the delegates became more determined in their demands and more articulate about their expectations of the church. The delegates made plans to document acts of prejudice within the American Catholic church, and set up a grievance committee within the framework of what was to become a permanently structured organization. A very dedicated, determined, independent-minded African American Catholic laity began to emerge. This laity was at the same time highly devoted to the Catholic church, extremely proud of what it saw as the African roots within this church and very pointed about what it expected the Catholic church to accomplish in the areas of social concern and racial justice. All of this becomes clear when one reads the almost lyrical outpourings of challenge and praise in the address to the Catholics of the United States by the fourth Black Catholic Lay Congress in Chicago in 1893.[20]

Whether the five Black Catholic Lay Congresses were a success or not depends upon one's point of view. One thing is certain: they were a revelation of the faith that existed in the African American Catholic community at the end of the nineteenth century. They were also an indication of the kind of lay leadership that has characterized African American Catholics from that time until now. Further research will show that many of those who took part in the congresses were not only leaders in their local communities, but were also witnesses to their Catholic faith outside the congresses.

Frederick McGhee, for example, born in 1861 in Mississippi, was the son of a blacksmith who, although enslaved, could read and write. McGhee, the first African American admitted to the bar in the upper Midwest, became well-known as a criminal lawyer in St. Paul, Minnesota, and was involved in Democratic politics. He converted to Catholicism in 1891. This author had the good fortune to discover an entire series of letters between him and Booker T. Washington and another series between him and W. E. B. Du Bois. McGhee also worked in the Niagara Movement with Du Bois and helped to found the NAACP; in fact, McGhee established the legal section of the Niagara Movement, which later became the legal arm of the NAACP.[21] McGhee also worked in the last three congresses. It was his desire to lecture on Catholicism in the African American community, as he expressed in one of his letters. Unfortunately, this brilliant man died fairly young, in 1912 at the age of fifty-one.

Another who attended the congresses was Lincoln C. Valle, a newspaperman originally from St. Louis, who collaborated with Daniel Rudd as a traveling correspondent and salesman for Rudd's newspaper. Valle participated in all the congresses, especially the fourth one, held in Chicago in conjunction with the World's Fair of that year. But it was especially in the decade following the congresses that he emerged as a "lay apostle" in the African American community of Milwaukee. Valle went to Milwaukee with his wife in 1908 and, with the approval of the archbishop, began preaching and teaching in the African American community. He opened a mission house named in honor of St. Benedict the Moor, arranged for Mass to be celebrated there, and eventually was instrumental in getting the Capuchin Order to open the first Catholic church in the Milwaukee African American community, also named St. Benedict the Moor. A look at the baptismal register lists Valle and his wife as the sponsor or sponsors for about the first thirty or so baptisms of adults and children in the infant parish. Unfortunately, disagreement between Valle and the first pastor forced the eventual withdrawal of Valle and his wife from this apostolic work. Valle returned to Chicago, where he continued his journalistic activity. He never lost sight of the original ideal of the Black Catholic Lay Congresses, writing in *America* in 1924:

> Unfortunately had the Catholic Church in America immediately after the Negro's Emancipation accepted the burden of caring for his welfare, through her commission, her board for work among the colored people and her societies and several diocesan agencies, as she is doing today, the progress of the Negro race would be more permanent. The Catholic Church which possesses the deposit of Divine Faith is the only organism capable of producing, developing and maintaining in the race an adequate, moral basis, necessary for any noteworthy success.[22]

In a way, this is an African American Catholic leader's commentary on what the Second Plenary Council could have done and did not do. But as part of the African American congress movement of the 1890s, Valle added another consideration: he noted that the present activity (i.e., in the 1920s) of the Catholic Church on behalf of the African American population was being carried out without African American Catholic leadership and thus it was "the play of 'Hamlet' with Hamlet left out."[23] Valle concluded his remarks in the periodical almost as a tragic chorus to a noble dream:

> What a difference it would have made in the life of the Catholic Church in the South if (these converts) had been added to the roll of Catholicism in that section! What a gain, not only to the Negroes themselves, but also to our country, if very large numbers of the race had been led into the Catholic Church![24]

African American Catholic Lay Leadership in the Twentieth Century

With these words, Lincoln Valle seemed to have written the epitaph for African American Catholic evange-

lization. The project of Spalding and the dream of Rudd seemed to have borne no fruit. African American Catholic lay leadership was a dead issue by the first quarter of this century. In fact, when Valle wrote its obituary, it was emerging stronger than ever.

This time, again, an African American layman would emerge as a leader for African American Catholics. Thomas Wyatt Turner, like Daniel Rudd before him, came from an area noted for its traditional African American Catholic roots. Rudd had come from central Kentucky; Turner came from southern Maryland. Born in 1877, he received his degree from Howard University in 1901. He studied at the Catholic University of America in Washington, D.C., in the period before that venerable institution closed its doors to African American students, not to open them again until much later. In his youth, Turner, who had been Catholic from birth, decided to remain in the church and work within it. And work he did! He became a leading educator in the field of biological science, and he also became a leader in the African American Catholic community of Washington, D.C. In 1913, Turner headed a group of African American Catholic leaders in the nation's capital, which met in his home to form the "Black Catholic Community Committee Against the Extension of Race and Prejudice in the Church." A dozen years later the committee evolved into the "Federated Colored Catholics of the United States." Turner always envisioned the group as a black protest organization within the Catholic church under African American leadership. He was a man of breadth and education and had no desire to exclude or be hostile to white Catholics. Nevertheless, he believed strongly in African American leadership and responsibility.

In subsequent years, as the Catholic Interracial councils evolved, what was an action-oriented group of African American Catholics gradually became a study group of whites and African Americans. Turner's action groups continued, however, until 1952. Thomas Wyatt Turner lived to be 101 years old, dying in April 1978.[25] Like the African American Catholic leaders before him, he believed with undying loyalty in the teachings of the Catholic church and the genius of Catholicism, but he was convinced that African American Catholics had the responsibility to demand that the church be loyal to her teachings and traditions in racist America. Turner had no more reason than the Black Catholic Lay Congress leaders before him to apologize for being a Catholic. He had reason, in fact, to be proud of a church that inspired fidelity to a creed and to an ideal that drew to itself people of every race and clime. And Turner lived long enough to see African American Catholics once again be charged with the ideal of responsible lay leadership within the church. In 1970, the National Office of Black Catholics emerged as a clearinghouse and central voice for the African American Catholic community. It seemed that just perhaps a century later the golden opportunity for the Catholic church in this country and the "acceptable time" of God's Harvest had just begun.

African American Catholic History: Future Research

This historical survey of African American Catholicism in the United States has, of necessity, been brief. The Second Plenary Council of 1866 was a watershed in the history of African American Catholicism. What it did not do, others did. It is not possible to praise too much the efforts of the Oblate Sisters, the Josephites (as the Mill Hill Fathers came to be known in the U.S.), the men of the Society of the Divine Word, and other male and female religious communities. Too rarely mentioned are individual diocesan priests who helped form a community of African American Catholics through the force of their own personalities and personal charisma. The purpose here, however, is to highlight the concerted efforts of African American Catholics themselves to make the faith come alive in the African American community. This history, too often ignored, has yet to be written. The research has just begun, and documentation and many sources are in place. As the African American bishops wrote in their pastoral of 1984:

> The historical roots of African American America and those of Catholic America are intimately intertwined. Now is the time for us who are African Americans and Black Catholics to reclaim our roots. . . . [26]

In this section, areas for future research and methodologies that might be employed are proposed. In future studies of African American Catholic history, local research, clearly limited in place and time, is necessary before a grand synthesis can be made.

First, it is important to discover who the African American Catholics were in the nineteenth and early twentieth centuries. It is difficult to obtain pre-Civil War names. One source waiting to be exploited is the membership lists of the two African American sisterhoods of the nineteenth century. If the early sisters in these communities can be identified, the names of parents and siblings, and the baptismal records giving names of sponsors and their geographical locations might be discovered. Then family relationships and the geographical locations of African American Catholics could be established. As an index of persons and places is compiled, conclusions can be drawn regarding socioeconomic situations, education, religious cohesiveness, and so forth.

The identification of persons and families will be facilitated by an exhaustive research of baptismal registers and other parish records. The presence of African Americans in the most unlikely areas has been verified through a search of parish records of the early nineteenth century. The records of slave-owning religious congregations must also be more carefully researched. The Sisters of Charity at Nazareth, Kentucky, for instance, maintained their own baptismal registers for their slaves. The African American Catholic presence is often hidden but emerges with diligent investigation.

Histories of parishes in which African Americans lived should be carefully researched on the grassroots level. It is not only important to study the pastors, assistants, and sisters, but also to look at the surrounding population. Again, the establishment of family connections is important. The Catholic faith survived in many instances because there was a family to whom the faith was transmitted. Who made up the family? Whence did the Catholic influence come? Where did the older family members learn their faith? How was it transmitted? Orally? Through catechism? What kind of prayers were taught? What kind of devotions practiced? We need to have some idea regarding African American cultural expression in African American Catholic churches. What kind of hymns did they sing in the African American parishes established right after the Civil War? Were there particular devotions to St. Peter Claver, St. Benedict the Moor, or Blessed Martin de Porres? Information in parish handbills announcing parish celebrations, musical programs, and lecture titles, and announcements in the local press can give some idea of the depth and characteristics of African American religious expression in the Catholic church. A rich source that needs to be systematically indexed for Catholic news is the extensive African American press that existed in nineteenth-century America. Research indicates that the African American press did not ignore the Catholic presence in the African American community.

The establishment of an oral history archive is long overdue. Soon, living links with the nineteenth century will be gone. The pre-World War I society was vastly different from our own. This is certainly true for African American history. Oral history is especially important for African Americans because relatively few African American families have passed down their papers. Oral history cannot be simply random tape recordings. It is important that historians record older members of the community following the rules of professional historical research. This project can only be realized on the local level, but it can be coordinated with the efforts of local historical associations or local institutions of higher learning. Funds for this sort of research are probably more readily available than funds for others.

Finally, a historical commission for African American Catholic history on the national level should be created. Ideally, it would be supported by the National Office of Black Catholics or the National Association of Black Catholic Administrators. The commission should be able to undertake the following: coordinate the efforts of local historical scholarship; promote scholarship by historians who choose to write in the area of African American Catholic history; and serve as a depository and clearinghouse for such research. It should maintain a file of persons and places culled from the sources of African American Catholic history, and it should maintain a current bibliography of primary and secondary sources related to African American Catholic history. It should be able to set guidelines for local institutions in the African American Catholic community today, as well as for African American Catholic organizations nationwide, for the ongoing maintenance of historical records and the creation of archives.

Four hundred years ago the first black Catholics arrived on these shores. They and their descendants have kept the faith and have fought the fight. Mute witnesses and silent believers in a church that sometimes neglected them, they were the church in chains and they became the church of liberation. Their descendants have a solemn duty to recount their stories and to keep alive the lessons of faith, hope, and love that they so courageously lived.

Notes

1. *Sermons Delivered During the Second Plenary Council of Baltimore, October, 1866, and Pastoral Letter of the Hierarchy of the United States* . . . (Baltimore: Kelly and Piet, 1866). See "Pastoral Letter," Section XII, "The Emancipated Slaves," 237.

2. The official Acts deal with the question of the evangelization of African Americans in Title X. "De Salute Animarum efficacius Promovenda," in *Concilii Plenarii Baltimorensis II* . . . *Decreta*, 243-47 (Baltimore: John Murphy, 1876). The minutes for this extraordinary session held on October 22, 1866, are found in the Baltimore Archdiocesan Archives, 39A-D5, 3-10. For the background of this proposal by the Sacred Congregation of the Propaganda, see Edward Misch, "The American Bishops and the Negro from the Civil War to the Third Plenary Council of Baltimore (1865-1884)" (Ph.D. diss., Pontifical Gregorian University [Rome], 1968).

3. David Spalding, "Martin John Spalding's 'Dissertation on the American Civil War,' " *The Catholic Historical Review* 52 (1966-67): 66-87.

4. Edward Misch, "The American Bishops and the Negro from the Civil War to the Third Plenary Council of Baltimore (1865-1884)" (Ph.D. diss., Pontifical Gregorian University [Rome], 1968), 1889.

5. John T. Gillard, S.J., *Colored Catholics in the United States* (Baltimore: Josephite Press, 1941), 99. The figures given by Gillard are subject to caution.

6. Misch, "The American Bishops and the Negro," 248ff.

7. Baltimore Archdiocesan Archives, 39A-D5, 7.

8. Ibid., 3ff.

9. Black Catholic Bishops of the United States, *What We Have Seen and Heard: A Pastoral Letter on Evangelization from the Black Bishops of the United States* (Cincinnati: St. Anthony Messenger Press, 1984), 17. (Hereinafter referred to as "Black Catholic Bishops.")

10. Maria Lannon, *Mother Mary Elizabeth Lange: Life of Love and Service*, Black Catholic Series no. 2 (Washington, D.C.: The Josephite Pastoral Center, 1976). This is a short account in booklet form of the founding of the Oblate Sisters of Providence and of the foundress. A much older, although more detailed work, is by Grace Sherwood, *The Oblates' Hundred and One Years* (New York: Macmillan, 1931). For the foundation of the Sisters of the Holy Family, see Sister Audrey Marie Detiege, *Henriette Delille, Free Woman of Color: Foundress of the Sisters of the Holy Family* (New Orleans: Sisters of the Holy Family, 1976).

11. Sister M. Rosalita, I.H.M., *No Greater Service: The History of the Congregation of the Sisters, Servants of the Immaculate Heart of Mary, Monroe, Michigan, 1845-1945* (Detroit: 1948). Chapter 3, "Mother Theresa Maxis," 37-46. For more information regarding Therese Duchemin Maxis's tragic circumstances, see Sister Diana Edward Shea, I.H.M., and Sister Marita Constance Supan, I.H.M., "Apostolate of the Archives—God's Mystery through History," *Josephite Harvest* 85 (1983): 10-13.

12. Thomas McMillan, "Knowledge of Public Questions," *Catholic World* 47 (1888): 711-13.

13. The name of Rudd's weekly newspaper was *The American Catholic Tribune*. The most extensive collection of the *Tribune* is in the Archdiocese of Philadelphia Archives and Historical Collections, Overbrook, Pennsylvania. It has been transferred to microfilm and is available from the Microtext Board of the American Theological Library Association. Rudd explained his purpose in an article reprinted in *The Washington Bee*, an African American newspaper in the nation's capital, dated September 11, 1886. This article was reprinted in the *Tribune* editorial page of September 2, 1887. The other African American Catholic newspaper was *The Journal*, also a weekly, which appeared in Philadelphia in 1892 for about eight months. The *Journal's* extant issues can also be found in the Archdiocese of Philadelphia Archives, Overbrook, Pennsylvania.

14. He is listed in the Detroit City Directory of 1895 at 37 Mullett Street. In 1897, he was living at 469 Monroe Avenue.

15. See David Spalding, "The Negro Catholic Congresses, 1889-1894," *Catholic Historical Review* 55 (1969): 337-57. For information regarding the lay congresses, see M. Adele Francis, "Lay Activity and the Catholic Congresses of 1889 and 1893," *Records of the American Catholic Historical Society of Philadelphia* 74 (1963): 3-23.

16. The proceedings for the first three congresses were published by Daniel Rudd and have been reprinted by the Arno Press. See Daniel Rudd, *Three Catholic Afro-American Congresses*. (Cincinnati: The American Catholic Tribune, 1893; reprint, New York: Arno Press, 1978).

17. James Augustine Healy (1830-1900) was ordained a priest in 1854. He became the second bishop of Portland, Maine, and the first African American bishop in the United States in 1875. His younger brother, Alexander Sherwood Healy (1836-1875) was ordained in 1858. Patrick Francis Healy, S.J. (1834-1910), was ordained in 1864. For a brief account of each, see Albert Foley, S.J., *God's Men of Color* (New York: Farrar, Straus, and Co., 1955). The Healy brothers were born slaves on a Georgia plantation, the sons of a slaveowner, Michael Healy, and a slave woman, Mary Elisa. The brothers, although known in a general way to be African American, never identified with the African American community. For an analysis of their mental attitudes, see Joseph Taylor Skerrett, "'Is There Anything Wrong with Being a Nigger?' Racial Identity and Three Nineteenth Century Priests." *Freeing the Spirit* 5 (1977): 27-37. For a review of the life of Augustus Tolton, see Sister Caroline Hemesath, *From Slave to Priest: Biography of Reverend Augustine Tolton, First Afro-American Priest in the United States* (Chicago: Franciscan Herald Press, 1973).

18. Rudd, 68.

19. Ibid., 66-72.

20. William J. Onahan. Columbian Catholic Congress. Speeches, Resolutions, and Miscellaneous Addresses. IX-1-0. University of Notre Dame Archives. "Address of the 4th Congress of Colored Catholics to the Rev. Clergy and Laity of the Catholic Church of America." The address was also published in *The Boston Pilot*, September 23, 1893, 6. The fourth congress was held at the same time as the Columbian Catholic Congress; the two congresses included a joint session.

21. Information about Frederick McGhee can be found in various publications of the Minnesota Historical Society. See, for example *Gopher Historian* (1968-1969): 18-19. Also, A. R. Fenwick, *Sturdy*

Sons of St. Paul (St. Paul, Minn.: 1899). Regarding McGhee's role in the Niagara Movement, see August Meier, *Negro Thought in America, 1880-1915* (Ann Arbor, Mich.: University of Michigan Press, 1964, 241-42. Letters between Washington and McGhee are in *Booker T. Washington Papers, General Correspondence*, Manuscripts Division, Library of Congress. Letters between Du Bois and McGhee are in the Du Bois Papers on microfilm in the Manuscripts Division, Library of Congress. The original collection is in the Library of the University of Massachusetts. Information regarding the legal career of McGhee at St. Paul is found in scattered references in *The Western Appeal* (later named simply *The Appeal*), an African American newspaper with headquarters at St. Paul but with readership throughout the Midwest, from 1889 through the 1890s. The Catholicism of McGhee becomes quite evident in the correspondence of McGhee with the Josephites, Fr. Donovan and Fr. Slattery, found in the Josephite Archives in Baltimore.

22. See L. C. Valle, "The Catholic Church and the Negro," *America* 30 (1923-1924): 327-28. Information regarding Valle's work in Milwaukee is found in a brochure printed in Milwaukee in 1912 entitled *History of St. Benedict the Moor. Catholic Colored Mission. 311 Ninth Street. Milwaukee, Wisconsin* found in the Josephite Archives in Baltimore, Maryland.

23. Ibid., 328.

24. Ibid.

25. Marilyn W. Nickels, *Black Catholic Protest and the Federated Colored Catholics, 1917-1933: Three Perspectives on Racial Justice*, Vol. 24 of *Heritage of American Catholicism*, Timothy Walch, gen. ed. (New York: Garland Publishing, Inc. 1988).

26. Black Catholic Bishops, 17.

Bibliography

Baltimore Archdiocesan Archives, Records of II Plenary Council, 1866, "Biographies of Black Pioneers. Afro-Americans in Minnesota History." *The Goopher Historian* (1968–69): 18–19.

Black Catholic Bishops of the United States. *What We Have Seen and Heard: A Pastoral Letter on Evangelization from the Black Bishops of the United States.* Cincinnati: St. Anthony Messenger Press, 1984.

"De Salute Animarum efficacius Promovenda." *Concilii Plenarii Baltimorensis II. Decreta.* Baltimore: John Murphy, 1876.

Detiege, Sister Audrey Marie. *Henriette Delille, Free Woman of Color: Foundress of the Sisters of the Holy Family.* New Orleans: Sisters of the Holy Family, 1976.

Fenwick, A. R. *Sturdy Sons of St. Paul.* St. Paul: n.p., 1899.

Foley, Albert, S.J. *God's Men of Color.* New York: Farrar, Straus, and Co., 1955.

Francis, M. Adele. "Lay Activity and the Catholic Congresses of 1889 and 1893." *Records of the American Catholic Historical Society of Philadelphia* 74 (1963): 3-23.

Gillard, John T., S.J. *Colored Catholics in the United States.* Baltimore: Josephite Press, 1941.

Hemesath, Sister Caroline. *From Slave to Priest: Biography of Rev. Augustine Tolton, First Afro-American Priest in the United States.* Chicago: Franciscan Herald Press, 1973.

Josephite Archives. Baltimore, Md.

Lannon, Maria. *Mother Mary Elizabeth Lange: Life of Love and Service*, Black Catholic Series, no. 2. Washington, D.C.: The Josephite Pastoral Center, 1976.

McMillan, Thomas. "Knowledge of Public Questions." *The Catholic World* 47 (1888): 711-13.

Meier, August. *Negro Thought in America, 1880-1915.* Ann Arbor: University of Michigan Press, 1964.

Misch, Edward. "The American Bishops and the Negro from the Civil War to the Third Plenary Council of Baltimore (1865-1884)." Ph.D. diss., Pontifical Gregorian University (Rome), 1968.

Nickels, Marilyn W. *Black Catholic Protest and the Federated Colored Catholics, 1917-1933: Three Perspectives on Racial Justice.* New York: Garland Publishing, Inc., 1988.

Onahan, William J., Address of the 4th Congress of the Colored Catholics to the Rev. Clergy and Laity of the Catholic Church of America. Columbian Catholic Congress. Speeches, Resolutions, and Miscellaneous Addresses. IX-1-0. University of Notre Dame Archives.

Rosalita, Sister M., I.H.M. *No Greater Service: The History of the Congregation of the Sisters, Servants of the Immaculate Heart of Mary, Monroe, Michigan, 1845-1945.* Detroit: n.p., 1948.

Rudd, Daniel. *Three Catholic Afro-American Congresses.* Cincinnati: The American Catholic Tribune, 1893; reprint, New York: Arno Press, 1978.

Sermons Delivered during the Second Plenary Council of Baltimore, October, 1866, and Pastoral Letter of the Hierarchy of the United States. Baltimore: Kelly and Piet, 1866.

Shea, Sister Diana Edward, I.H.M., and Sister Marita Constance Supan, I.H.M. "Apostolate of the Archives—God's Mystery through History." *The Josephite Harvest* 85 (1983): 10-13.

Sherwood, Grace. *The Oblates' Hundred and One Years.* New York: Macmillan, 1931.

Skerrett, Joseph Taylor. "'Is There Anything Wrong with Being a Nigger?' Racial Identity and Three Nineteenth Century Priests." *Freeing the Spirit* 5 (1977): 27-37.

Spalding, David. "Martin John Spalding's 'Dissertation on the American Civil War.'" *Catholic Historical Review* 52 (1966-67): 66-87.

————. "The Negro Catholic Congresses, 1889-1894." *Catholic Historical Review* 55 (1969): 337-57.

Valle, Lincoln C. "The Catholic Church and the Negro." *America* 30 (1923-1924): 327-28.

Washington, Booker T. Papers, General Correspondence, Manuscript Division, Library of Congress.

The Western Appeal. St. Paul, Minn.

Part 7

Appendices

APPENDIX A: GLOSSARY

Sources for definitions in this glossary are primarily from the following: *The Dictionary of Religion and Ethics*, edited by Shailer Mathews and Gerald B. Smith (Macmillan Publishing Co.); *Webster's New World Dictionary of the American Language*, edited by David B. Guralnik, (Prentice–Hall Press); *The Oxford Dictionary of the Christian Church* (Oxford University Press); *Dictionary of Ecclesiastical Terms*, by J. S. Purvis (Thomas Nelson, Inc.); *Dictionary of Religious Terms*, by Donald T. Kauffman (Fleming H. Revell Co.); *A Christian's Dictionary*, by James S. Kerr and Charles Lutz (Fortress Press); *Harper's Bible Dictionary*, by Madeleine S. Miller and J. Lane Miller (Harper & Row); and the *Encyclopedia of American Religions* (second edition), by J. Gordon Melton (Gale Research Inc.).

Abuna: The Arabic honorific for a priest, it is the equivalent of "Father." However, in the Ethiopian church it is the honorific for the patriarch.

Adventist: A Christian denomination believing that the Second Coming of Christ and the day of judgment are both imminent.

Affusion: Baptismal process in which water is poured on the baptismal candidate.

African: Persons who claim or trace their sociohistorical roots to Africa.

African American: Persons of color in the United States who trace their historical or cultural heritage to Africa.

Allah: The name applied to the Supreme Being in the Islamic religious tradition.

Anglican: A Protestant religious tradition that developed from the break from Roman Catholicism, resulting in the creation of the Church of England. The administrative structure is hierarchical, as in the Roman Catholic tradition, but it operates under the auspices of the archbishop of Canterbury rather than the pope.

Annual Conference: An ecclesiastical session held annually to address issues pertaining to the aggregate well-being of the church (such as to hear complaints; to adjudicate on behalf of church officials and members; to admit and assign ministers to roles and responsibilities within the denomination; and to send delegates to the General Conference). Its composition, purpose, and representation vary, depending upon the denominational polity.

Anointing: A form of consecration by dropping water or oil (usually olive oil) on the head of the person for whom prayer is offered for spiritual empowerment, ordination, consecration to an ecclesiastical office, healing, or recovery.

Apocrypha: Books included in the Roman Catholic Bible but excluded from the Protestant Bible, because Protestants do not consider them to be authoritative and divinely inspired.

Apostle: A title often given to a missionary, evangelist, or a member of the clergy in Pentecostal, Holiness, or Apostolic bodies.

Apostolic: A religious body practicing and perpetuating the beliefs and doctrines of the original twelve apostles of Jesus Christ. These bodies have traditionally upheld two different positions: 1) Acceptance of the triune Godhead (Trinity), using the water baptism formula: "in the name of the Father and of the Son and of the Holy Ghost"; or 2) Oneness, which advocates a doctrine that refutes belief in the Trinity: Water baptism must be administered "in the name of Jesus Christ." This position advocates that Jesus is Jehovah, God of the Old Testament, as well as Jesus Christ, God of the New Testament. (*See also* Deliverance, Holiness, Penetecostal, and Sanctified Church.)

Apostolic Succession: Doctrine that the chain of authority in the church, from the time of the apostles to the present day, is unbroken. It is a fundamental principle in many Greek, Roman, and Anglican religious bodies.

Arminian: An advocate of the religious teachings and beliefs of the Dutch Protestant theologian Jacobus Arminius (1560–1609). Arminius held that salvation is possible for all and refuted Calvin's positions on unconditional predestination, limited atonement, and irresistible grace.

Articles of Faith: The doctrines or basic teachings of a religious tradition that state the position of the religious body on issues of faith.

Aspersion: Baptismal process wherein water is sprinkled on the baptismal candidate.

Atonement: Restoration process by which the sinner is reconciled to God through the sufferings of Jesus Christ.

Autonomous: A self-governing or independent body that has no legal ties to another organization.

Ban: A declaration by the church that excommunicates or

denounces a person adjudicated by its ecclesiastical authority as guilty of violating the church's standards or doctrine.

Baptism: The ceremony in which a new believer is inducted into the religious family by applying water through aspersion (sprinkling), immersion (submersion), or affusion (pouring). It symbolizes the washing away of sin and admission into the church. In some religious circles, this process is achieved through spirit baptism, which is not by water but by the Holy Ghost. (*See also* Baptism in the Holy Ghost, Spirit Baptism, and Water Baptism.)

Baptism in the Holy Ghost: Doctrine stating that the initial evidence of a believer's conversion is demonstrated through the believer's speaking in unknown tongues as the Spirit gives utterance. (*See also* Glossolalia, Spirit Baptism, Water Baptism, and Xenoglossia.)

Baptist: A protestant denominational group with a congregational church polity. Their fundamental doctrine holds that only believers should be baptized and that baptism should occur by immersion.

Bible College: Institutions offering training or study in biblical literature, practical ministry, Christian education, religious studies, and general education. Most Bible colleges offer certificate programs for lay church leaders or a program leading to the baccalaureate degree. Accreditation of these institutions varies. Bible college training is considered to be preparation for seminary work.

Binitarianism: Religious doctrine that holds there are only two persons in the Godhead. It recognizes the *Father and Son*, as opposed to the *Father, Son, and Holy Ghost* (i.e., the Trinity definition).

Bishop: Title of the religious head or governing individual in churches having hierarchical or episcopal polity.

Black Nationalism: Racial pride and solidarity within the African diaspora, which promotes black self-determination and identity. Racial allegiance is compatible with the highest patriotism. It was popularized by such leaders as Marcus Garvey in his efforts to promote African American pride and self-help through education and the development of independent institutions.

Born Again, To Be: To submit to or to acknowledge a spiritual rebirth by recommitment or baptism into the communion of a religious body. At this rebirth, Jesus Christ is acknowledged as Lord and Savior.

Calvinists: Religious bodies that adhere to the principles espoused by John Calvin (1509–64), who held that God is the ruler of the universe and that man is incapable of independence. Calvin believed that God's elect were predestined to spend eternity with Him and that their wills were not free to choose.

Canon: A law or set of laws of a religious body or church.

Cardinal: A chief clergy official in the Roman Catholic church. A cardinal is appointed by the Pope to serve as an official in his council (i.e., the College of Cardinals).

Catechism: A manual of questions and answers for religious instruction.

Catholic: A non-Protestant group of believers with an episcopal polity and having the pope, the bishop of Rome, as their highest human leader. This term generally refers to the Roman Catholic church and its members. Also refers to the universal Christian church.

Catholic Epistles: A set of seven New Testament Epistles focusing on the universal (or catholic) church. It includes James; I and II Peter; I, II, and III John; and Jude.

Celibacy: The condition of being unmarried or remaining sexually abstinent as a part of the vows of commitment to God and the church.

Chalice: A cup or goblet used at communion (or eucharistic) services to hold the wine or water of Holy Communion.

Charge: To give ecclesiastical responsibilities to a clergyperson or religious official in accordance with their religious duties; one or more congregations entrusted to a minister.

Charisma: A divinely given gift or talent, such as healing or prophecy, that reflects God's grace; qualities of leadership and presence that inspire allegiance and devotion.

Christening: The ceremony of baptism or anointing for infants as practiced by a religious tradition. (*See also* Dedication of Baby.)

Christian: A person who believes in Jesus as the Christ, or a person who follows a religious tradition based on the ministry of Jesus Christ.

Christocentric: The belief that Christ is the center or apex from which all things can be understood.

Christology: The study of the life, work, personhood, and significance of Jesus Christ and the literature pertaining to His ministry.

Church: An organization or congregation of believers who are united in thought and practice to share in worship, fellowship, and mission; the ecclesiastical government of a particular religious group.

Church Conference: A meeting of members and ministers for consideration and transaction of local church business. The minister in charge is the presiding officer.

Church Mother: Senior female in the church selected to promote church growth and the spiritual instruction and nurture of young believers. She is generally a lay member of the congregation.

Circuit: A city, town, district, or area inclusive of several churches or congregations; the regular route of a clergyperson in executing her or his ministry.

Class: Divisions of the congregation into smaller groups to promote spiritual growth, fellowship, and financial support for the church.

Class Leader: Leaders of the classes or bands that promote spiritual growth, fellowship, and financial support of the church.

Clergy: The category of persons authorized by a religious body to perform religious duties. (*See also* Minister)

Collect: A short prayer that requests specific blessings. In Roman and Anglican worship services, it is said before the Gospel and Epistle readings and is meant to condense or gather the teachings.

Communicant: The person who receives Holy Communion; a member of a church that observes the sacrament of the Lord's Supper.

Communion: The Lord's Supper; the sharing of thought and emotion in the sacrament of the Lord's Supper, symbolizing the unity of the recipients in the faith. The Christian celebration or observance of the Holy Eucharist or Holy Communion. Communions can be administered in two different ways—*open* or *closed*. In open communion, all Christians may share in the celebration. In closed communion, only those of a particular faith or belief may receive the Eucharist.

Communion of Saints: A fellowship of persons sharing a common religious faith and belief.

Conference: A meeting of all segments of a church's hierarchy, ranging from the local level to the governing body, in order to exchange opinions on subjects and issues confronting the body.

Confirmation: The initiation ceremony that brings a person into membership with a church (generally following the completion of formal instruction); the formal ratification of a candidate to a position in the church administrative hierarchy.

Congregational: The form of church organizational governance that authorizes members of local congregations to determine their own direction and set their own policies.

Connectional: The form of church organizational governance under which congregations are linked together in a common bond of leadership and organizational practices.

Consecrate: To set apart for a divine purpose or role.

Consubstantiation: A doctrine that the substance of the bread and wine of the Eucharist exists, after consecration, side by side with the substance of the body and blood of Christ, but it is not changed into it. It is usually contrasted with the doctrine of transubstantiation, which maintains that the words of institution in the Lord's Supper create a union that remains unchanged until the consecration is fulfilled; the bread and wine are sacramentally transformed into the body and blood of Christ, and the bread and wine remain visibly unchanged. (*See also* Transubstantiation.)

Contrition: Sincere penitence or sorrow for the commission of sin with a definite and deliberate desire to make a favorable change.

Conversion: Spiritual and moral changes that accompany changes in belief and spirit, generally referred to as a *change of heart*; to become a member of a religious tradition or to adopt a religious belief.

Covenant: An agreement between members of a church to act in cooperation; the agreement between God and man as expressed in the Old and New Testaments.

Creed: A statement of belief that outlines the basic tenets of a religious body.

Cult: A group having an exclusive sacred ideology and a series of rites centering around their sacred symbols.

Curia: The pope and those who comprise the papal authority in the administration of the Roman Catholic Church.

Deacon: A church official who serves the membership and assists clergy in the operation of church duties and responsibilities. The office is generally associated with the establishment of church officers in Acts 6:1–6. Typically, deacons are ordained. Many bodies restrict this office to males, but recently in some churches, it has also been extended to females.

Deaconess: A female church official (usually the wife of a deacon) whose duties are to encourage, foster, and improve the general interests of the church and its membership.

Decalogue: The Ten Commandments as noted in Exodus 20: 3–17.

Dedication of Baby: The acts of anointing (optional), laying on of hands, and praying for babies, invoking divine protection, guidance, and future salvation. (*See also* Christening.)

Defrock: To divest or strip a minister or clergyperson of priestly or clerical responsibilities.

Deism: Belief in the existence of a God on the evidence of reason and nature only, with rejection of supernatural revelation (distinguished from theism).

Deliverance: A religious practice emphasizing the use of spiritual gifts (especially healing and miracles) to address personal problems by spiritual means. (*See also* Apostolic, Holiness, Pentecostal, and Sanctified Church.)

Denomination: A religious group that maintains corporate fellowship and basically shared doctrinal beliefs. Generally considered to represent an established organizational structure that maintains general doctrine and theology with allowances for departure from certain creeds and practices. Its growth and development is generally stable and not under the influence of "charismatic" individual(s).

Diocese: The district or region under the pastoral care and supervision of a bishop.

Dispensation: Various periods of history that order events under divine authority, such as the *old*, *Mosaic*, or *Jewish* dispensation, and the *new*, *gospel*, or *Christian* dispensation; in the Roman Catholic tradition, it refers to the relaxation of church law through case-specific applications that grant exemptions by one with authority.

Dispensationalism: A type of biblical analysis started by a nineteenth-century Irishman, John Nelson Darby, that divides human history into seven basic themes or time periods. These periods present seven eras during which man is tested in respect to obedience to some definite revelation of God's will. They include the following themes: innocence (Gen. 3:24), conscience (Gen. 6-9), human government (Gen. 8:20-9:27), promise (Gen. 12:1; Exod. 19:8), law (Exod. 20:1–31:8), grace (Rom. 3:24–26; 4:24–25), and the kingdom (2 Sam. 7:8–17; Zech. 12:8; and Luke 1:31–33).

District: Geographic division of the church into segments, each governed by a bishop, elder, or a presiding officer of a religious body.

District Conference: A division of the annual conference that is under the supervision of the presiding elder and is considered to be his district meeting. It is made up of the respective traveling, supernumerated, and superannuated ministers, local elders, deacons, preachers, lay leaders, and exhorters under the jurisdictional authority of the presiding elder.

Doctrine: A policy or body of principles; a tenet; a dogma.

Dogma: The system of principles or tenets authoritatively maintained by a church.

Ecclesiastic: A clergyperson or individual in a religious order; a church official.

Ecclesiastical: That which pertains to the clergy or church.

Ecclesiology: Study of the church, church architecture, art, doctrine, etc.

Ecumenical (or Oecumenical): That which pertains to the

general or universal Christian church without regard to denominational distinctions.

Elder: A spiritual leader or minister whose duties may entail preaching, administering the Lord's Supper and baptism, and performing the rite of matrimony. In many religious bodies, only elders can consecrate the elements for Holy Communion.

Election: Selection of an individual by God for salvation.

Episcopal: That which pertains to a bishop or the designation of a Protestant sect governed by bishops.

Eschatology: Refers to the end time and includes consideration of death, heaven and hell, judgment, the Second Coming of Christ, and the millennium (Christ's reign on earth for a thousand years).

Eucharist: The Lord's Supper or Holy Communion.

Evangelical: That which pertains to or is in accordance with the Gospel and its teachings. Also certain Christian churches that emphasize the teachings and authority of the Scriptures, especially the New Testament, over and above church doctrine or reason.

Evangelism: A religious movement to spread vigorously the tenets of the Gospel.

Evangelist: A minister or preacher (i.e., carrier) of the "Good News" who converts people to Christ.

Excommunication: The formal act by which a church severs the membership, rights, and privileges of a person or group of people. It especially prohibits the partaking of sacraments and the fellowship of the church.

Exhorter: Lay helper to preachers, sometimes seen as the first step into the ministry. Generally in Methodism, he or she is licensed by the presiding elder upon the vote of the quarterly conference, which receives candidates upon recommendation of his class leader and pastor. The exhorter should use his or her talents to urge people to become Christians.

Fall of Man: The first departure from innocence and goodness as related in the Genesis account of Adam and Eve's departure from Eden following the "original sin."

Fasting: Refraining from eating as part of a spiritual experience growing out of a desire to gain favor with God or to discipline oneself.

Feast Day: A celebration or commemoration of a religious event that has particular significance to its adherents.

Footwashing (or Feetwashing): The act of washing the feet of fellow church members to demonstrate humility and servitude, generally performed as a ceremonial act of cleansing or in compliance with a church ordinance.

Free Will: Ability to select or chose between good and evil without force.

Fundamentalism: A reaction to modernism, asserting traditional standards against the new theology and its search for scientific compatibility. It is affirmative in nature, asserting certain ideas concerning biblical truth. It began as a movement in the early twentieth century based on literal interpretation of the Bible.

General Conference: The governing body of a church with an episcopal hierarchy, which meets on a regular basis. The bishops rule the church upon charge of the general confer-

ence, which elects the bishops and changes them accordingly. The bishops govern the church and interpret its laws and mandates in the interim of the general conference.

General Confession: An open or public confession of sins, generally recited in unison by pastor and congregation, maintained as a part of the ritual or liturgy of a church.

Genuflection: An act of reverence in which the believer bends the knee in worship, either upon entering the sanctuary or upon approaching the altar.

Gift of Tongues: The exercise of joyous emotional speech during religious excitement or divine presence. It is considered to be a sign of the believer's baptism by the Holy Spirit. (*See also* Baptism, Glossolalia, Spirit Baptism, Water Baptism and Xenoglossia.)

Gifts of the Spirit: As found in I Corinthians 12:4–11, gifts of the Holy Spirit include healing, prophecy, speaking in tongues, wisdom (knowledge unattainable by natural means), and discernment of spirits (seeing nonphysical beings such as angels and demons).

Glossolalia: The common prayer speech heard at Pentecostal churches or the act of speaking in tongues. (*See also* Glossolalia, Speaking in Tongues, Spirit Baptism, and Xenoglossia.)

Grace: The unmerited gift of God to humanity that restores people to God's favor.

Great Commission: The orders given by Christ to his disciples to evangelize and instruct others in the faith: "Go ye therefore, and teach all nations, baptizing them in the name of the Father and of the Son, and of the Holy Ghost: Teaching them to observe all things whatsoever I have commanded you: and, lo, I am with you alway, even unto the end of the world" (Matthew 28: 19–20 KJV).

Hierarchy: An organized body of church officials in successive ranks or orders.

Holiness: The religious tradition that affirms the state of sinlessness characterized by moral and spiritual purity as a second work of grace following salvation or justification; the title reserved for a person whose life has been dedicated to, or set apart for, religious service. (*See also* Apostolic, Deliverance, Pentecostal, and Sanctified Church.)

Holy Orders: The authority granted to church officials (e.g., bishops, priests, ministers, elders, deacons, etc.) to govern and administer the spiritual matters of the church.

Imam: The title for various Moslem spiritual leaders and rulers who may direct prayer or lead worship in a mosque.

Immaculate Conception: In the Roman Catholic church, this doctrine maintains that through the anticipated merits of Jesus Christ, the Virgin Mary was conceived in her mother's womb without the blemish of original sin. Therefore, the Christ child was conceived free of original sin.

Immersion: Baptism by submerging the whole person into the water.

Immortality: Life everlasting after death.

Impanation: The doctrine that maintains that the body and blood of Christ exist as one substance with the bread and wine of the Eucharist after consecration, but without transubstantiation.

Incarnation: The embodiment of God in the form of a man,

Jesus Christ, to manifest divine love and to provide the means for salvation.

Inerrant: Without error or mistake.

Infallibility: Incapable of being incorrect.

Inspiration: The movement of the Holy Spirit in the minds and hearts of chosen persons, which renders them instruments of divine revelation.

Judgment, Judgment Day: The time of accounting for virtuous and sinful behavior followed by reward or punishment.

Justification: The divine act that frees humankind from the penalty of sin and promises eternal life for believers.

Kiss of Peace, or Holy Kiss: A religious ceremonial kiss symbolizing unity and originating in the early church.

Laity: Church members who are not clergy.

Laying on of Hands: The tradition of ministers, apostles, and elders praying for and placing their hands on the heads of believers commissioned for public gospel ministry or some special facet of ministry.

Litany: A set of petitions that are said alternately by the minister and the congregation.

Liturgy, Liturgical: An established form or order for public worship. Churches that place special emphasis on liturgy have different rites and ceremonies for specific occasions.

Lord's Supper: Rite administered to believers using the elements of broken unleavened bread, crackers, or wafers and wine, unfermented grape juice, or water. It is also known as *communion* or the *Holy Eucharist*. (*See also* Communion, Eucharist.)

Love Feast: A remembrance of the early Christian celebration of the Agape meal, usually held every quarter. In the A.M.E. church, it is a prayer and praise service to renew one's spirit and reaffirm the faith in the presence of other believers. Bread is broken with one another to signify fellowship, and water is consumed to signify cleansing of the soul.

Lutheran: The religious group founded by the German biblical scholar and theologian Martin Luther. His treatise, written in the early part of the sixteenth century, led to a break from Roman Catholicism and to the eventual start of the Protestant church.

Mass: The central worship service in the Roman Catholic church, it consists of prayers and ceremonies, and it is always eucharistic.

Methodist: Term first applied to followers of John Wesley, the father of Methodism, who seemingly did everything by a method. Methodist bodies generally have an episcopal hierarchy. It is a recognized Protestant denomination.

Metropolitan: A bishop in the Eastern church.

Minister: One who is licensed and/or ordained by a particular denomination to preach the Gospel and teach the beliefs and traditions of a religious community. The classification of minister varies with religious bodies. Following are some of the designations used: apostle, bishop, chaplain, deacon, elder, evangelist, imam, itinerant elder, licensed or ordained minister, metropolitan, pastor, priest, rabbi, and reverend.

Missionary: One sent by a local church or denominational body to promote the growth of the religious faith, often in foreign countries. Missionaries often make home, hospital, convalescent, and prison visits and give assistance to the community and the indigent.

Monophysitism: The theological position that maintains that in Christ there is but a single nature. This nature is partly divine and partly human. This doctrine is held by the Coptic church of Egypt.

Monotheism: The theological position that maintains that there is but one God.

Mysticism: A doctrine that focuses on the ability to receive direct knowledge of God and of spiritual truth through spiritual insight.

Nicene Creed: A formal statement of the chief principles of Christian doctrine, adopted by the first Nicene Council in A.D. 325.

Oneness: A doctrine that refutes belief in the Trinity, maintaining that water baptism must be administered "in the name of Jesus Christ." It is based on the belief that Jesus is Jehovah, God of the Old Testament, as well as Jesus Christ, God of the New Testament.

Ordinance: A formally instituted religious observance or ritual.

Ordination: The ceremony that sets a person apart to an order or office; it generally signifies the appointment or designation of the person to a ministerial office.

Orthodox: Conforming to the usual beliefs or established doctrines.

Orthodoxy: Beliefs or practices that conform to established or institutional doctrine.

Overseer: A church official in charge of a parish or church program, sometimes denotes the governing role of a bishop.

Pacificism: The belief or policy that stresses the importance of unlimited peace by reducing the distinctions between nations and eliminating the need for war to solve problems.

Passover: An annual Jewish holy feast that observes Jehovah's passing over or sparing the Hebrews in Egypt when he killed the firstborn of the Egyptians (cf. Exodus 12). It is also used to refer to the Feast of Unleavened Bread (Leviticus 23:5–6), which observes the Israelites' deliverance from Egypt.

Pastor: A minister in charge of a parish or congregation.

Paten: A metal plate used at communion (or eucharistic) services to hold the bread of Holy Communion.

Patriarch: The male head of a long family line; a founder of an order or religious body; one of the three distinguished forefathers of the Israelites: Abraham, Isaac, or Jacob. In the Greek Orthodox church, the bishop of the ancient sees of Alexandria, Antioch, Constantinople, and Jerusalem (and in more recent years, Russia, Rumania, and Serbia). The bishop of Constantinople is the highest officer in the church and is called the *ecumenical patriarch*.

Penance: An act of atonement for sin; punishment pronounced by a church official to repudiate the commission of a sin.

Pentecostal: A religious tradition in which believers share in the charismatic experience of speaking in tongues as it occurred on the Day of Pentecost as recorded in Acts 2:4. The doctrine holds that believers must speak in tongues at least once in their lifetimes, after which they are "sanctified."

Speaking in tongues is considered a sign of the baptism of the Holy Spirit. (*See also* Apostolic, Deliverance, and Holiness.)

Perfection: The highest degree of flawlessness or purity possible; holiness; the complete accomplishment of ethical or spiritual potentiality.

Pietism: A movement that began during the latter part of the seventeenth century to awaken and promote spirituality in the German Lutheran churches. Christian movements or programs designed to accentuate the intimate, spiritual, and realistic features of faith over its conventional, ceremonial, and abstract characteristics.

Plenary: Full, complete, or absolute; a plenary council is a meeting where all members of an institution are to be present.

Pneumatology: The study of spirits and spiritual phenomena.

Polity: A specific model or ecclesiastical administrative structure.

Preacher: One who exhorts or treats a religious text systematically to urge people to become believers.

Predestinarian: One who believes in the doctrine or concept of predestination, which maintains that every incident is preordained by God and that every individual's endless destiny is fixed by divine order.

Presbyterian: A Protestant denomination that traces its roots back to the reformer John Calvin and is related to his reformed tradition. The church derives its name from the fact that it is ruled by a presbytery, a court formed of all of the local congregations' elders and ministers in a particular ecclesiastical district.

Presbytery: A body of elders; a church judicatory, court, or assembly having the ecclesiastical or spiritual rule and oversight of a district, or the district itself; that part of the church edifice where the primary altar is generally elevated above the rest of the structure and reserved for clergy only.

Presiding Bishop: Chief administrator and spiritual leader of a religious body.

Pseudepigrapha: A term applied to intertestamental literature falsely attributed to the heroes of the Old Testament that does not fall within the Apocrypha.

Quarterly Conference: A local meeting held every three months to assess the conditions of the local church. This administrative structure is generally associated with Methodist polity.

Rastafarian: A Black Hebrew sect based in Jamaica and the Caribbean, which believed that the Ethiopian monarch Haile Selassie (born Ras Tafari Makonnen) was the promised Messiah, the "Conquering Lion of Judah." The adherents believe that Ethiopia (extended to mean all of Africa) is the cradle of the black race and that its contributions to the development of civilization are paramount to the realization of racial equality for the African diaspora. They also believe that black persons are the reincarnation of ancient Israel, who because of white persons, live in exile in Jamaica; white persons are inferior to black persons; the Jamaican situation is a hopeless hell; Ethiopia is heaven; the Invincible Emperor of Ethiopia is now arranging for expatriated persons of African origin to return to Ethiopia; and in the near future blacks shall rule the world.

Reconciliation: The attainment of good relations between two parties who have been estranged; the reestablishment of fellowship between God and humanity by the removal of all barriers that separate people from God.

Redemption: The deed of setting free or attaining deliverance from sin.

Regeneration: To be born again into a spiritual awareness.

Religious: Person belonging to or connected with a monastic or religious order (i.e., a friar, monk, or nun); persons who are devout adherents to a religion or religious teaching.

Religious Body: An institution or a group of people unified by commitment to the service of God, or the Divine.

Remission of Sin: Pardon or forgiveness for sin.

Repentance: Turning from a sinful life to a godly life.

Reprobation: Eternal condemnation, the fate of those rejected by God and unredeemed.

Revelation: A divine communication to human beings.

Reverend: The title given to a member of the clergy.

Ritual: A stylized voluntary behavior focused on a religious goal or sacred symbol.

Sabbatarian: A person who observes the seventh day as the Christian Sabbath.

Sacrament: A consecrated rite or ceremony in which two elements can be distinguished, a physical sign and a spiritual good.

Salvation: The deliverance of humans from evil or guilt by God's power, that they may gain sanctification.

Sanctification: The redeeming force of the Holy Spirit that saves believers from sin and elevates them to a life of holiness.

Sanctified Church: Religious body that stresses the role of sanctification in transforming the believer. It is generally used to identify Christian groups that departed from traditional doctrine by their emphasis on the manifestation of particular evidence of the believer's inward change as a second work of grace. (*See also* Apostolic, Deliverance, Holiness, and Pentecostal.)

Schism: A split or separation of a religious body into independent organizations, generally as a result of disagreements over doctrine, polity, or leadership.

Second Coming: The bodily return of Jesus Christ to the world.

Sect: A religious organization or body that separates from a more established denomination or religious body. Its growth and development are usually related to "charismatic" leadership and fundamental religious doctrine. It may also refer to an autonomous religious group whose adherents recognize a special set of teachings or practices. Sects may occur in several ways: 1) by division from other religious bodies; 2) by shared revelations of believers; 3) through revivals; 4) around a special analysis or interpretation of Scripture; or 5) in support of additional teachings that elaborate upon traditional religious beliefs.

See: The local seat from which a bishop, archbishop, or the pope exercises jurisdiction.

Seminary: Often referred to as a *school of religion*, *school of theology*, or *school of divinity*; generally, it is a school or college that prepares persons for the ministry. Its programs may be accredited.

Sexton: A church official charged with maintaining the physical church property.

Speaking in Tongues: *See* Gift of Tongues.

Split: *See* Schism.

Spirit Baptism: Baptism not by water but by the Holy Ghost symbolizing the believer's spiritual birth, usually manifested by speaking in tongues as the Spirit gives utterance. (*See also* Baptism, Baptism in the Holy Ghost, Glossolalia, Water Baptism, and Xenoglossia.)

Steward: A church official or trustee who supervises or administrates financial and/or property matters.

Stewardess: A female church official or trustee who supervises or administrates financial and/or property matters.

Storefront Church: Religious institutions or churches that house their congregations in facilities initially designed to serve as commercial establishments. Although identified with Apostolic, Pentecostal, Holiness, and Deliverance traditions, the practice is not limited to any specific denominational group.

Suffragan Bishop: An assistant bishop in an episcopal hierarchy with no direct line to succession of the See.

Superannuated Minister: A minister who is retired because of age or infirmity.

Supernumerary Minister: A minister who is left without an appointment by the bishop either from lack of ability, lack of sufficient charges to supply him, temporarily impaired health, or at the minister's own request.

Synod: An ecclesiastical council either of regular standing or appointed as needed; in Presbyterian churches, the body between the presbyters and the general assembly.

Tonsured: The shaved top of the head that denotes membership in a monastic order or other holy order.

Transcendence: The quality associated with being able to exceed certain natural limitations.

Transfiguration: Change in form or appearance, as in the transfiguration of Jesus (Mark 9:2–10).

Transmutation: The change from one nature, substance, or form to another.

Transubstantiation: The doctrine that maintains that the words of institution in the Lord's Supper create a union that remains unchanged until the consecration is fulfilled. The bread and wine are sacramentally transformed into the body and blood of Christ, with his whole soul and divinity. The bread and wine remain visibly unchanged. (*See also* Consubstantiation.)

Trinity or Trinitarian: The belief that the single substance of the Godhead exists in three separate but equal persons: the Father, the Son, and the Holy Spirit.

Triune: The unity associated with the Godhead's three-person and one-substance identity.

Triune Immersion: A baptism that consists of immersing the candidate three successive times, in the name of the Father, Son, and Holy Ghost.

Trustee: A church official who supervises or administrates financial and/or property matters.

Unction: A ceremonial anointing of a person with oil, especially in cases of illness or imminent death.

Uniat: Persons or churches recognizing the preeminence of the pope but maintaining their own liturgies or rites.

Unitarian: A theology that insists upon the unity or oneness of God, but disavows the trinitarian doctrine.

Universalism: The theology upholding God's universal salvation of all creation and the final harmony of all souls with God.

Unleavened Bread: A relatively flat bread made without yeast (also known as matzo). In many religious traditions it is used in the observance of the communion or passover meal.

Venial Sin: A minor offense committed against a divine law in the Roman Catholic tradition. The term is also given to more serious offenses if a lack of volition can be proved.

Vestment: The robes or outer garments worn by clergy, choirs, or others assisting in religious ceremonies.

Vicar: A church official or minister who represents the pope or bishop.

Virgin Birth: The belief that Jesus was born to Mary without violation of her virginity and that she was His only human parent.

Vocation: The divine call to religious service or the assumption of a duty or task in response to a divine mandate.

Vodoun: Also mistakenly called "voodoo," it is a complex and highly sophisticated religion, chiefly of African origin, practiced by the majority of people in Haiti. It combines elements of traditional West African religion and Roman Catholicism.

Vulgate: The Latin version of the Holy Scriptures prepared by St. Jerome around the end of the fourth century and accepted as the authentic version by the Roman Catholic church.

Warden: A church official charged with maintaining the physical church property. (See also Sexton.)

Water Baptism: A physical rite demonstrating cleansing of sin and admittance into the church. There are three alternate forms of water baptism: 1) the candidate is fully emerged in water in a river, stream, or pool (immersion); 2) the candidate is sprinkled with water on the head (aspersion); or 3) the candidate has water poured over the head (affusion). (*See also* Affusion, Aspersion, Baptism, and Immersion.)

Wesleyan: That which pertains to or derives from Methodism, especially as associated with its founder John Wesley (1703–91).

Western Church: The numerous Christian churches connected with or having their origin in either the Roman Catholic or Anglican church.

Xenoglossia: The utterance of an existent foreign language by one who has no knowledge of it. A rare occurrence, it nevertheless has been noted and recorded in the literature of psychical research. Both telepathy and spirit contact have been hypothesized. (*See also* Glossolalia, Speaking in Tongues, and Spirit Baptism.)

Yahweh: The name of God in the Hebrew text of the Old Testament, commonly transliterated as Jehovah. It is represented by the tetragrammaton (JHVH or JHWH, YHVH, YHWH). Without vowels the tetragrammaton represents the name of God that must not be pronounced in Hebrew, but is commonly substituted with the word Adonai, meaning "the Lord."

Zionism: A movement that sees heaven as the final gathering place of true believers; in the Hebrew tradition, it refers to the establishment of a homeland for the Jews.

APPENDIX B: CHARTS

The following charts are meant to assist in understanding the evolution of several religious bodies that share a historic bond or have similar names. All groups in the *Directory* are not represented in the charts. The charts are:

Figure 1. Evolution of the African Union First Colored Methodist Protestant Church and the Union American Methodist Episcopal Church.

Figure 2. Evolution of Black Baptists.

Figure 3. Evolution of Black Muslims.

Figure 4. Denominational Descendants of the Church of God (Apostolic).

Figure 5. Denominational Descendants of the Church of the Living God (Christian Workers for Fellowship).

Figure 6. Denominational Descendants of the Church of the Living God, the Pillar and Ground of the Truth, Inc. (Lewis Dominion).

Figure 7. Denominational Descendants of the Pentecostal Assemblies of the World.

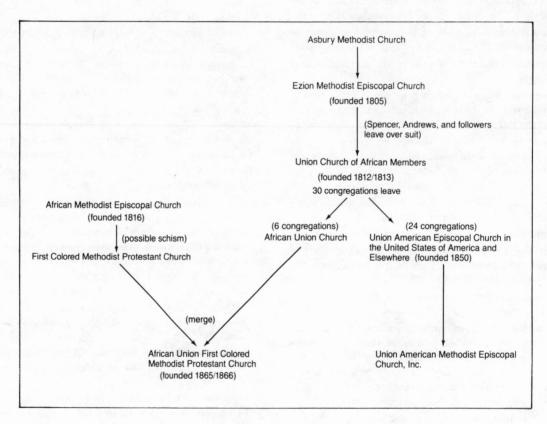

Figure 1   African Union First Colored Methodist Protestant Church and Union American Methodist Episcopal Church

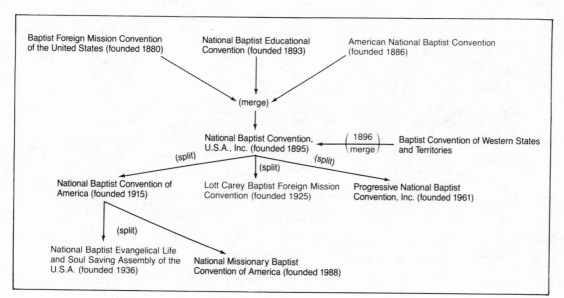

Figure 2
Black Baptists

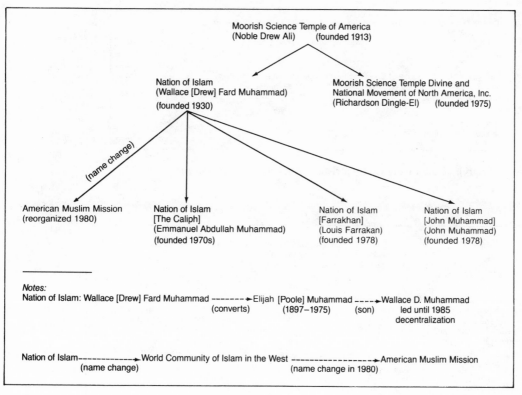

Figure 3
Black Muslims

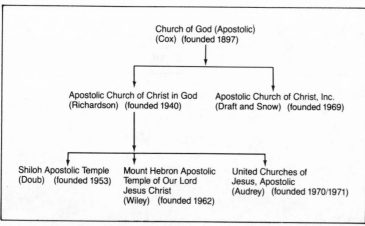

Figure 4   Church of God (Apostolic)

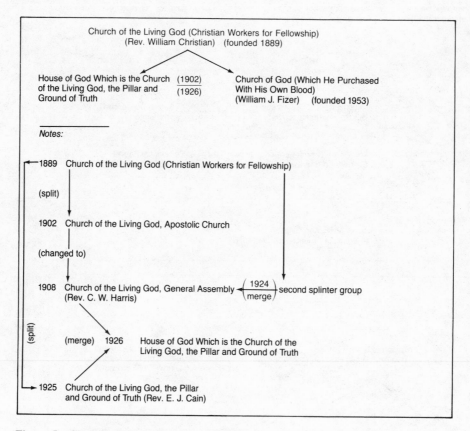

Figure 5   Church of the Living God (Christian Workers for Fellowship)

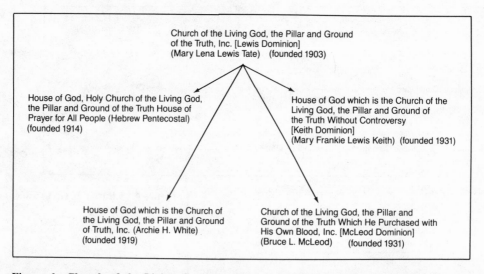

Figure 6   Church of the Living God, the Pillar and Ground of the Truth, Inc. (Lewis Dominion)

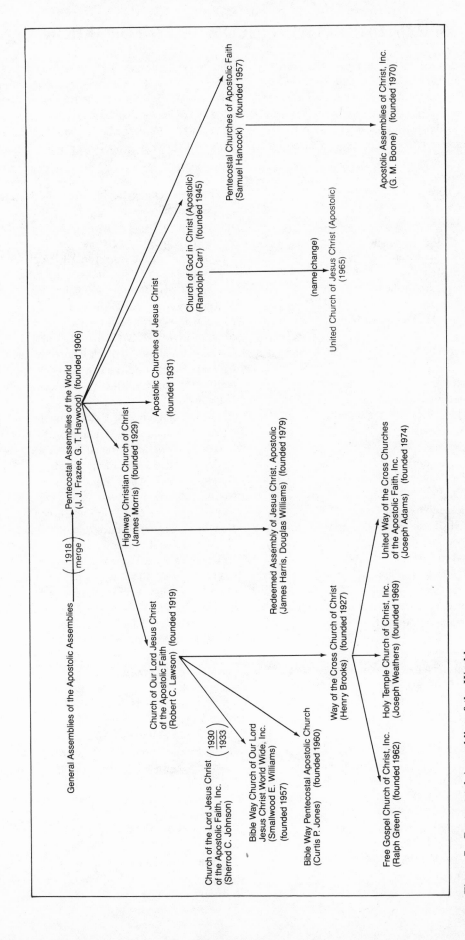

Figure 7   Pentecostal Assemblies of the World

APPENDIX C: ORGANIZATIONS WITH INCOMPLETE INFORMATION

The following organizations are those for which information is incomplete. Each is listed in the text of the *Directory* with all known or available information included. In most cases, there is little or no information on their histories or current activities. Some groups do not have confirmed addresses or information on current leadership.

The list does not include councils of churches, district associations, annual conferences, or organizations connected with larger bodies, such as the Baptist conventions and the Methodist churches. Information on these groups should be sent to the *Research Center on Black Religious Bodies*, Howard University School of Divinity.

African Orthodox Church
African Orthodox Church of the West
Afro-American Vodoun
Apostolic Assemblies of Christ, Inc.
Associations of Black Lutherans
Bible Church of Christ, Inc.
Bible Way Pentecostal Apostolic Church
Church of God [Black Jews]
Church of God Which He Purchased with His Own Blood
Commandment Keepers Congregation of the Living God
Council of Islamic Organizations of America
Deliverance Evangelistic Centers, Inc.
Deliverance Miracle Revival Center, Inc.
Endich Theological Seminary
Evangel Temple, Inc.
Faith Hope Charity in Christ Outreach Center, Inc.
Faith Temple Pentecostal Church, Inc.
Father Abraham Temple
Father Divine's "Kingdom" and Peace Mission
First Church of Love, Faith and Deliverance
First Church of Voodoo
Free Church of God in Christ
Free Church of God True Holiness
Free Temple Revival Center
Glorious Church of God in Christ Apostolic Faith
God's House of Prayer for All Nations, Inc.
Gospel Mission
Greater Emmanuel Apostolic Church, Inc.
Greater Mount Zion Pentecostal Church of America
Holiness Church of God, Inc.
Holiness Community Temple
Holy Temple, First Pentecostal Church of Deliverance
Holy Temple of God
Holy Temple of Jesus Christ Church, Inc.
House of God, Holy Church of the Living God, the Pillar and Ground of the Truth House of Prayer for All People (Hebrew Pentecostal)
House of God Which is the Church of the Living God, the Pillar and Ground of Truth
House of Judah
House of Prayer, Church of God, Inc.
House of Prayer for All Nations
House of the Lord

International Evangelical Church and Missionary Association
International Gospel Center
Jackson Theological Seminary
Latter House of the Lord for All People and the Church of the Mountain, Apostolic Faith
Living Witness of Apostolic Faith, Inc.
Marin City Ministerial Alliance
Missionary Church of America
Mount Calvary Holy Church of America
National Coalition of Black Church Musicians
National Colored Spiritualist Association of America
National Colored Spiritualist Association of Churches
National Conference of Black Churchmen
National Council of the Churches of Christ in the U.S.A.—Office of Racial Justice
Nation of Islam [John Muhammad]
Nation of Islam [The Caliph]
Nation of Yahweh
New Bethel Church of God in Christ (Pentecostal)
New Faith Chapel Holiness Church, Inc.
New Jerusalem Cathedral
New York City Mission Society
Organization of Black Episcopal Seminarians
Original Glorious Church of God in Christ, Apostolic Faith, Inc.
Original Hebrew Israelite Nation
Overcoming Saints of God
Pentecostal Churches of Apostolic Faith
Pentecostal Church of God
Pentecostal Miracle Deliverance Centers, Inc.
Perry Community Holiness Church
Powerhouse of Deliverance Church
Prayer Band Fellowship Union
Racial Ethnic Ministry Unit—Presbyterian Church (U.S.A.), Racial Justice Ministry
Racial Ethnic Ministry Unit—Presbyterian Church (U.S.A.), Social Justice Policy Development
Rastafarians
Saint Paul's Bible Institute
Saints of the Solid Rock Holiness
Sanctuary Church of the Open Door
Sought Out Church of God in Christ and Spiritual House of Prayer, Inc.

Soul Saving Station for Every Nation, Christ
  Crusaders of America Tabernacle of Prayer
True Way Resurrection Pentecost Holiness Church of
  God in Christ
United Christian Evangelistic Association [Rev. Ike]
United Churches of Jesus, Apostolic, Inc.
United Church of Jesus Christ Apostolic, Inc.
United Crusade Fellowship Conference, Inc.

United Hebrew Congregation
United Way of the Cross Churches of Christ of the
  Apostolic Faith
Universal Church, the Mystical Body of Christ
Wednesday Clergy Fellowship
World's Gospel Feast
Yahweh's Temple
Yoruba Theological Archministry

Part 8
Selected Bibliography

Denominational Histories and Profiles

Adams, C. C. and Marshall A. Talley. *Negro Baptists and Foreign Missions*. Philadelphia: The Foreign Mission Board of the National Baptist Convention, U.S.A., Inc., 1944.

Adams, E. A., Sr. *Yearbook and Historical Guide to the African Methodist Episcopal Church*. Columbia, SC: Bureau of Research and History, 1955.

African Methodist Episcopal Church Compilation Committee, ed. *The Book of Discipline of the African Methodist Episcopal Church*. 42nd rev. ed. Nashville: H. A. Berlin, Jr., 1980.

Ali, Muhammad. *The Founder of the Ahmadiyya Movement*. 3rd ed. Newark, CA: Ahmadiyya Anjuman Isha'at Islam, Lahore, Inc., 1984.

Ammi, Ben. *God, the Black Man, and Truth*. Chicago: Communicators Press, 1982.

Anderson, Vinton R., ed. *A Syllabus for Celebrating the 200th Birthday of the A.M.E. Church*. Nashville: African Methodist Episcopal Church Sunday School Union, 1986.

Baldwin, Lewis V. *"Invisible" Strands in Methodism: A History of the African Union Methodist Protestant and Union America Methodist Episcopal Churches, 1805-1980*. Metuchen, NJ: Scarecrow Press, 1983.

————— . *The Mark of a Man: Peter Spencer and the African Union Methodist Tradition, the Man, the Movement, the Message, and the Legacy*. Lanham, MD: University Press of America, 1987.

Barrett, Leonard E. *The Rastafarians: Sounds of Cultural Dissonance*. Rev. ed. Boston: Beacon Press, 1988.

Blyden, Edward W. *Christianity, Islam and the Negro Race*. Edinburgh, Scotland: Aldin Publishing Company, 1967.

Boyd, Ruby Chappelle. *On This Rock . . . The Mother Church of African Methodism*. Philadelphia: Princeton Press, 1982.

Bragg, George F. *History of the Afro-American Group of the Episcopal Church*. Baltimore: Church Advocate Press, 1922.

Brotz, Howard M. *The Black Jews of Harlem*. New York: Schoken Books, 1970.

Christian Methodist Episcopal Church. *The Doctrines and Discipline of the Christian Methodist Episcopal Church*. Memphis: C.M.E. Publishing House, 1986.

Cornelius, Lucille J. *The Pioneer History of the Church of God in Christ*. Private printing, 1975.

Dandridge, Octavia W. *A History of the Women's Missionary Society of the African Methodist Episcopal Church 1874-1987*. Private printing, 1987.

Davis, Cyprian. *The History of Black Catholics in the United States*. New York: Crossroad, 1990.

Demarest, W. H. S., ed. *Tercentary Studies*. Board of Publications, Reformed Church in America, 1928.

Dwelle, J. H. *A Brief History of Black Baptists in North America*. Pittsburgh: Pioneer Printing Company, no date.

Eikerencotter, Frederick. *Health, Happiness and Prosperity for You!* New York: Science of Living Publications, 1982.

Erskine, Noel L. *Black People and the Reformed Church in America*. Reformed Church Press, 1978.

Ewell, John Louis. *A History of the Theological Department of Howard University, Washington, D.C.* Washington, D.C.: Howard University, 1906.

Faruqui, N. A. *Ahmadiyyat in the Service of Islam*. Newark, CA: Ahmadiyya Anjuman Isha'at Islam Lahore, Inc., 1983.

Fauset, Arthur H. *Black Gods of the Metropolis: Negro Religious Cults of the Urban North*. Philadelphia: University of Pennsylvania Press, 1944.

Freeman, Edward A. *The Epoch of Negro Baptists and the Foreign Mission Board*. Kansas City, KS: Central Seminary Press, 1953.

George, Carol V. R. *Segregated Sabbaths: Richard Allen and the Rise of Independent Black Churches, 1760-1840*. New York: Oxford University Press, 1973.

Gerber, Israel J. *The Heritage Seekers*. Middle Village, NY: Johnathan David Publishers, 1977.

Gillard, John T. *The Catholic Church and the American Negro*. 1929. Reprint. New York: Johnson Reprint Corporation, 1968.

Golder, Morris E. *History of the Pentecostal Assemblies of the World*. Indianapolis: Pentecostal Assemblies of the World, 1973.

Gregg, Howard D. *History of the African Methodist Episcopal Church (The Black Church in Action)*. Nashville: African Methodist Episcopal Sunday School Union, 1980.

Gregory, Chester W. *The History of the United Holy Church of America, Inc. 1886-1986*. Baltimore: Gateway Press, 1986.

Hodges, Sloan S. "Black Baptists in America and the Origins of Their Conventions." Progressive National Baptist Convention, no date.

Hood, J. W. *One Hundred Years of the African Methodist Episcopal Church*. New York: A.M.E. Zion Book Concern, 1895.

Jackson, J. H. *A Story of Christian Activism: The History of the National Baptist Convention, U.S.A., Inc.* Nashville: Townsend Press, 1980.

Jones, Lawrence N. *From Conscience to Consciousness: Blacks and the United Church of Christ*. Philadelphia: United Church of Christ Press, 1976.

Jordan, Lewis G. *Negro Baptist History, U.S.A. 1750-1930*. Nashville: Sunday School Publishing Board, 1930.

Krebs, Ervin E. *The Lutheran Church and the American Negro*. Columbus, OH: Board of American Missions, 1950.

Lakey, Othal H. *The Rise of Colored Methodism*. Dallas: Crescendo Books, 1972.

————— . *The History of the C.M.E. Church*. Memphis: C.M.E. Publishing House, 1985.

Lincoln, C. Eric. *The Black Muslims in America*. Boston: Beacon Press, 1961.

Mack, Edgar L. *Our Beginning: Introduction to the African Methodist Episcopal Church*. Nashville: Christian Education Department, no date.

Marsh, Clifton E. *From Black Muslims to Muslims: The Transition from Separatism to Islam, 1930-1980*. Metuchen, NJ: Scarecrow Press, 1984.

Moses, W. H. *The Colored Baptists' Family Tree*. Nashville: The Sunday School Publishing Board of the National Baptist Convention of America, 1925.

Murray, Andrew E. *Presbyterianism and the Negro: A History*. Philadelphia: Presbyterian Historical Society, 1966.

Nicholas, Tracy. *Rastafari: A Way of Life*. Garden City, NY: Anchor Books, 1979.

Payne, Daniel A. *History of the African Methodist Episcopal Church*. 1891. Reprint. New York: Arno Press and the New York Times, 1969.

Patterson, J. O., German R. Ross, and Julia Mason Atkins, *History and Formative Years of the Church of God in Christ with Excerpts from the Life and Works of its Founder—Bishop C. H. Mason*. Memphis: Church of God in Christ Publishing House, 1969.

Pelt, Owen D. and Ralph Lee Smith. *The Story of the National Baptists*. New York: Vantage Press, 1960.

Phillips, C. H. *The History of the Colored Methodist Episcopal Church*. 1898. Reprint. New York: Arno Press and the New York Times, 1972.

Pius, N. H. *An Outline of Baptist History*. Nashville: National Baptist Publishing Board, 1911.

Reynolds, Louis B. *We Have Tomorrow: The Story of American Seventh-day Adventists with an African Heritage*. Hagerstown, MD: Review and Herald Publishing Association, 1984.

Richardson, James C., Jr. *With Water and Spirit: A History of Black Apostolic Denominations in the U.S*. Washington, D.C.: Spirit Press, 1980.

Second Episcopal District, African Methodist Episcopal Church. *200 Years: The Bicentennial History, Second Episcopal District, African Methodist Episcopal Church*. Tappan, NY: Custombook, Inc., 1987.

Seventy-fifth Anniversary Yearbook of The Church of the Living God, the Pillar and Ground of the Truth, Inc., 1903-1978. Nashville: New and Living Way Publishing House, 1978.

Singleton, George A. *The Romance of African Methodism*. New York: Exposition Press, 1952.

Smith, M. G., Roy Augier, and Rex Nettleford. *The Rastafari Movement in Kingston, Jamaica*. Kingston, Jamaica: University College of the West Indies, 1960.

Spencer, Janet D., Celia T. Marcelle, and Catherine J. Robinson, eds. *Black Women in the Church: Historical Highlights and Profiles* [*Church of God*]. Pittsburgh: Magna Graphics, Inc., 1986.

Stanley, A. Knighton. *The Children is Crying: Congregationalism among Black People*. New York: Pilgrim Press, 1979.

Teegarden, Kenneth L. *We Call Ourselves Disciples*. 2nd ed. St. Louis: Bethany Press, 1983.

Terry-Thompson, A. C. *The History of the African Orthodox Church*. New York: African Orthodox Church, 1956.

Tufail, S. Muhammad. *The Ahmadiyyah Movement*. Pakistan: Ahmadiyyah Anjuman Isha'at Islam, 1973.

United Holy Church of America, Inc. *Standard Manual and Constitution and By-laws of the United Holy Church of the America, Inc*. Washington, D.C.: Middle Atlantic Regional Press, 1988.

Walker, Clarence E. *A Rock in a Weary Land: The African Methodist Episcopal Church During the Civil War and Reconstruction*. Baton Rouge: Louisiana State University Press, 1982.

Walls, William J. *African Methodist Episcopal Zion Church: Reality of the Black Church*. Charlotte: A.M.E. Zion Publishing House, 1974.

Whitfield, Thomas. *From Night to Sunlight*. Nashville: Broadman Press, 1980.

Wilmore, Gayraud S. *Black and Presbyterian: The Heritage and the Hope*. Philadelphia: Geneva Press, 1983.

Wright, Richard Robert, Jr., ed. *The Encyclopedia of the African Methodist Episcopal Church*. Philadelphia: A.M.E. Church Book Concern, 1947.

Yehuda, Shaleak Ben. *Black Hebrew Israelites from America to the Promised Land*. New York: Vantage Press, 1975.

Biographical Works

Abernathy, Ralph D. *And the Walls Came Tumbling Down*. New York: Harper and Row, 1989.

Allen, Richard. *The Life Experience and Gospel Labors of Rt. Rev. Richard Allen*. Nashville: Abingdon Press, 1960.

Andrews, William L. *Sisters of the Spirit: Three Black Women's Autobiographies of the Nineteenth Century*. Bloomington: Indiana University Press, 1986.

Ansbro, John J. *Martin Luther King, Jr.: The Making of a Mind*. Maryknoll, NY: Orbis Books, 1982.

Bass, Dorothy C. and Sandra Hughes Boyd. *Women in American Religious History*. Boston: G. K. Hall and Company, 1986.

Bennett, Lerone. *What Manner of Man: A Biography of Martin Luther King, Jr*. Chicago: Johnson Publishing Company, 1964.

Berry, Leonidas H. *I Wouldn't Take Nothing for My Journey*. Chicago: Johnson Publishing Company, 1981.

Branch, Taylor. *Parting the Waters: The King Years, 1954-63*. New York: Simon and Schuster, 1988.

Clarke, John Henrik, ed. *Malcolm X: The Man and His Times*. New York: Collier, 1969.

Clark, John Henrick and Amy Jacques Garvey. *Marcus Garvey and the Vision of Africa*. New York: Random House, 1974.

Cronon, Edmund D. *Black Moses*. Madison: University of Wisconsin Press, 1962.

DuPree, Sherry Sherrod. *Biographical Dictionary of African-American, Holiness-Pentecostals 1880-1990*. Washington, D.C.: Middle Atlantic Regional Press, 1989.

Fax, Elton C. *Garvey: The Story of a Pioneer Black Nationalist*. New York: Random House, 1974.

Foley, A. S. *God's Men of Color: The Colored Catholic Priests of the United States, 1854-1954*. 1955. Reprint. New York: Arno Press, 1969.

Franklin, John Hope and August Meier, eds. *Black Leaders of the Twentieth Century*. Champaign: University of Illinois Press, 1982.

Goldman, Peter. *The Death and Life of Malcolm X*. 2nd ed. Champaign: University of Illinois Press, 1979.

Hamilton, Charles V. *The Black Preacher in America*. New York: William Morrow, 1972.

Harris, Sarah. *Father Divine*. Enl. ed. New York: Collier Books, 1971.

Heard, William H. *From Slavery to the Bishopric in the A.M.E. Church*. Reprint. New York: Arno Press, 1969.

Hoshor, John. *God in a Rolls-Royce: The Rise of Father Divine, Madman, Menace, or Messiah . . . .* New York: Hillman-Curl, 1936.

Hough, J. C., Jr. *Black Power and White Protestants: A Christian Response to the New Negro Pluralism.* New York: Oxford University Press, 1968.

Humez, Jean M., ed. *Gifts of Power: The Writings of Rebecca Jackson.* Amherst: University of Massachusetts Press, 1981.

Jacques-Garvey, Amy. *Garvey and Garveyism.* Kingston, Jamaica: United Printers, Ltd., 1963.

King, Martin Luther, Sr., with Clayton Riley. *Daddy King: An Autobiography.* New York: William Morrow, 1980.

Lewis, David L. *King: A Critical Biography.* Champaign: University of Illinois Press, 1970.

Lincoln, C. Eric, ed. *Martin Luther King, Jr., A Profile.* New York: Hill and Wang, 1970.

Logan, Rayford W. and Michael R. Winston, eds. *Dictionary of American Negro Biography.* New York: W. W. Norton and Company, 1982.

Maglangbayan, Shawna. *Garvey, Lumumba, Malcolm.* Chicago: Third World Press, 1972.

Martin, Tony. *Race First: The Ideological and Organizational Struggles of Marcus Garvey and the Universal Negro Improvement Association.* Westport, CT: Greenwood Press, 1976.

Mason, Mary Esther. *The History and Life Work of Elder C. H. Mason and His Co-Laborers.* Private printing. No date.

Mays, Benjamin E. *Born to Rebel.* New York: Scribner, 1971.

Morris, Calvin S. *Reverdy C. Ransom: Black Advocate of the Social Gospel.* Lanham, MD: University Press of America, 1990.

Oates, Stephen. *Let the Trumpet Sound: The Life of Martin Luther King.* New York: Harper & Row, 1982.

Parker, Robert Allerton. *The Incredible Messiah: The Deification of Father Divine.* Boston: Little, Brown & Co., 1937.

Patterson, W. A. *From the Pen of W. A. Patterson.* Memphis: Deakins Typesetting Service, 1970.

Payne, Daniel A. *Recollections of Seventy Years.* Reprint. New York: Arno Press, 1969.

Ploski, Harry A. *The Negro Almanac: A Reference Work on the Afro-American.* New York: Bellwether Company, 1976.

Ponton, Mungo M. *The Life and Times of Henry McNeal Turner.* Reprint. Westport, CT: Negro Universities Press, 1971.

Sims, Janet L. *Howard Thurman: A Selected Bibliography.* Washington, D.C.: Howard University Press, Moorland-Spingarn Research Center, 1976.

Singleton, George A. *The Autobiography of George A. Singleton.* Boston: Forum Publishing Company, 1964.

Thurman, Howard. *With Head and Heart: The Autobiography of Howard Thurman.* 1st ed. New York: Harcourt Brace Jovanovich, 1979.

Tucker, David M. *Black Pastors and Leaders: The Memphis Clergy, 1819-1972.* Memphis: Memphis State University Press, 1975.

Washington, James M. *A Testament of Hope: The Essential Writings of Martin Luther King, Jr.* 1st ed. San Francisco: Harper & Row, 1986.

Weisbrot, Robert. *Father Divine and the Struggle for Racial Equality.* Champaign: University of Illinois Press, 1983.

Wesley, Charles H. *Richard Allen: Apostle of Freedom.* Washington, D.C.: Associated Publishers, 1935.

Williams, Ethel L. *Biographical Dictionary of Negro Ministers.* 3rd ed. Boston: G. K. Hall, 1975.

Williams, Smallwood Edmond, D.D. *This is My Story: A Significant Life Story. Autobiography of Smallwood Edmond Williams, D.D.* Washington, D.C.: William Willoughby Publishers, Inc., 1981.

Wright, Richard R., Jr. *The Bishops of the A.M.E. Church.* Nashville: A.M.E. Sunday School Union, 1963.

X, Malcolm and Alex Haley. *The Autobiography of Malcolm X.* New York: Ballantine Books, 1964.

Yates, Elizabeth. *Howard Thurman: Portrait of a Practical Dreamer.* New York: John Day Company, 1964.

African American Religious Traditions, Trends, Expressions, and Experiences

Anderson, Robert Mapes. *Vision of the Disinherited: The Making of American Pentecostalism.* New York: Oxford University Press, 1979.

Bach, Marcus. *They Have Found A Faith.* Indianapolis: Bobbs-Merrill, 1946.

Baldwin, James. *Go Tell It on the Mountain.* New York: New American Library, 1953.

Barrett, Leonard E. *Soul-Force: African Heritage in Afro-American Religion.* Garden City, NY: Doubleday, 1974.

Blackwell, James E. *The Black Community: Diversity and Unity.* 2nd ed. New York: Harper & Row, 1985.

Bloch-Hoell, Nils. *The Pentecostal Movement: Its Origins, Development, and Distinctive Character.* Oslo, Sweden: Universitetsforlaget, 1964.

Braden, Charles Samuel. *These Also Believe: A Study of Modern American Cults and Minority Religious Movements.* New York: Macmillan, 1949.

Breitman, George, ed. *Malcolm X Speaks.* New York: Grove, 1965.

Burgess, John M. *Black Gospel/White Church.* New York: Seabury Press, 1982.

Burkett, Randall K. and Richard Newman, ed. *Black Apostles: Afro-American Clergy Confront the Twentieth Century.* Boston: G. K. Hall and Company, 1978.

Burkett, Randall K. *Black Redemption: Churchmen Speak for the Garvey Movement.* Philadelphia: Temple University Press, 1978.

———. *Garveyism as a Religious Movement: The Institutionalization of a Black Civil Religion.* Metuchen, NJ: Scarecrow Press, 1978.

Cannon, Katie G. *Black Womanist Ethics.* Atlanta: Scholars Press, 1988.

Clark, Elmer Talmage. *The Small Sects in America.* Rev. ed. Memphis: Abingdon Press, 1965.

Cleage, Albert B., Jr. *The Black Messiah.* New York: Sheed and Ward, 1968.

———. *Black Christian Nationalism: New Directions for the Black Church.* New York: William Morrow, 1972.

Cone, Cecil W. *The Identity Crisis in Black Theology.* Nashville: A.M.E. Church Press, 1975.

Cone, James H. *Black Theology and Black Power.* New York: Seabury, 1969.

———. *A Black Theology of Liberation.* Philadelphia: J. B. Lippincott, 1970.

———. *God of the Oppressed.* New York: Seabury Press, 1975.

———. *My Soul Looks Back.* Nashville: Abingdon Press, 1982.

———. *For My People: Black Theology and the Black Church.* Maryknoll, NY: Orbis Books, 1982.

———. *Speaking the Truth: Ecumenism, Liberation, and Black Theology.* Grand Rapids: William B. Eerdmans, 1986.

Davis, Gerald A. *I Got the Word in Me and I Can Sing It, You Know: A Study of the Performed African-American Sermon.* Philadelphia: University of Pennsylvania Press, 1985.

Davis, Kortright. *Emancipation Still Comin': Towards a Theology of Liberation for the Caribbean*. New York: Orbis Books, 1990.

Drake, St. Clair and Horace R. Cayton. *Black Metropolis: A Study of Negro Life in a Northern City*. New York: Harcourt, Brace, Jovanovich, 1945.

Drake, St. Clair. *The Redemption of Africa and Black Religion*. Chicago: Third World Press, 1970.

DuBois, W. E. B. *The Negro Church*. Atlanta: Atlanta University Press, 1903.

_____. *The Souls of Black Folk*. 1929. Reprint. New York: Avon, 1965.

_____. *The Gift of Black Folk*. New York: Washington Square Press, 1970.

_____. *Black Reconstruction in America*. New York: Antheneum, 1985.

Ellwood, Robert S., Jr. *Many Peoples, Many Faiths: An Introduction to the Religious Life of Mankind*. Englewood Cliffs, NJ: Prentice-Hall, Inc., 1976.

Evans, James E., ed. *Black Theology: A Critical Assessment and Annotated Bibliography*. New York: Greenwood Press, 1987.

Farajajé-Jones, Elias. *In Search of Zion*. New York: Peter Lang, 1990.

Felder, Cain Hope. *Troubling Biblical Waters: Race, Class and Family*. Maryknoll, NY: Orbis, 1989.

_____, ed. *Stony the Road We Trod: African American Biblical Hermeneutics*. Minneapolis: Fortress Press, 1990.

Forman, James. *The Making of a Black Revolutionary*. New York: Macmillan, 1971.

Franklin, John Hope and Alfred A. Moss, Jr. *From Slavery to Freedom*. 6th ed. New York: Alfred A. Knopf, 1988.

Frazier, E. Franklin. *Black Bourgeosie*. New York: McMillan, 1957.

Frazier, E. Franklin and C. Eric Lincoln. *The Negro Church in America* and *The Black Church since Frazier*. Reprint. New York: Schocken Books, 1974.

Fredrickson, George M. *The Black Image in the White Mind: The Debate on Afro-American Character and Destiny, 1817-1914*. New York: Harper Torchbooks, 1971.

Frodsham, Stanley H. *With Signs Following: The Story of the Pentecostal Revival in the Twentieth Century*. Springfield, MO: Gospel Publishing House, 1946.

Gardiner, James A. and J. Deotis Roberts, eds. *Quest for a Black Theology*. Philadelphia: Pilgrim Press, 1971.

Garrow, David J. *Bearing the Cross: Martin Luther King, Jr. and the Southern Christian Leadership Conference*. New York: William Morrow, 1986.

Genovese, Eugene. *Roll, Jordan, Roll: The World the Slaves Made*. New York: Pantheon, 1974.

Gerlach, Luther P. *People, Power, Change: Movements of Social Transformation*. Indianapolis: Bobbs-Merrill, 1970.

Giddings, Paula. *When and Where I Enter: The Impact of Black Women on Race and Sex in America*. New York: William Morrow and Company, 1984.

Gossett, Thomas F. *Race: The History of an Idea in America*. New York: Schocken Books, 1965.

Hamilton, Michael P., ed. *The Charismatic Movement*. Grand Rapids: Eerdmans, 1975.

Hamlin, Michael et al. *The Political Thought of James Forman*. Detroit: Black Star Publishing Company, 1970.

Haynes, Leonard L., Jr. *The Negro Community within American Protestantism, 1619-1844*. Boston: Christopher Publishing House, 1953.

Hollenweger, Walter J. *The Pentecostals: The Charismatic Movement in the Churches*. Minneapolis: Augsburg Publishing Company, 1972.

Hopkins, Dwight N. *Black Theology USA and South Africa: Politics, Culture and Liberation*. Maryknoll, NY: Orbis Press, 1989.

Hull, Gloria T. *All the Women are White, All the Blacks are Men, But Some of Us are Brave*. New York: The Feminist Press, 1982.

Jacques-Garvey, Amy, ed. *The Philosophy and Opinions of Marcus Garvey*. New York: Arno Press and the New York Times, 1969.

Jones, Charles Edwin. *Black Holiness: A Guide to the Study of Black Participation in Wesleyan Perfectionist and Glossolalic Pentecostal Movements*. Atla Bibliography Series. Metuchen, NJ: Scarecrow Press, 1987.

Jones, Lawrence N. "The Black Churches: A New Agenda." In *Afro-American Religious History*, edited by Milton C. Sernett. Durham: Duke University Press, 1985.

_____. "The Organized Church: Its Historic Significance and Changing Role in Contemporary Black Experience." In *Directory of African American Religious Bodies: A Compendium by the Howard University School of Divinity*, edited by Wardell J. Payne. Washington, D.C.: Howard University Press, 1990.

Jones, Major J. *Black Awareness: A Theology of Hope*. Nashville: Abingdon Press, 1971.

Jones, Raymond J. *A Comparative Study of Religious Cult Behavior among Negroes with Special Reference to Emotional Group Conditioning Factors*. Washington, D.C.: Howard University Press, 1939.

Jones, William R. *Is God A Racist? A Preamble to Black Theology*. Garden City, NY: Anchor Press, 1973.

Jordan, Winthrop D. *White Over Black: American Attitudes toward the Negro, 1550-1812*. New York: Oxford University Press, 1974.

Kelsey, George D. *Racism and the Christian Understanding of Man*. New York: Scribner, 1965.

Kendrick, Klaude. *The Promise Fulfilled: A History of the Modern Pentecostal Movement*. Springfield: Gospel Publishing House, 1961.

King, Martin Luther, Jr. *Stride Toward Freedom: A Leader of His People Tells the Montgomery Story*. New York: Harper & Row, 1958.

_____. *Strength to Love*. New York: Harper & Row, 1963.

_____. *Where Do We Go From Here: Chaos or Community?* New York: Harper & Row, 1967.

Lecky, Robert S. and H. Elliott Wright, eds. *The Black Manifesto*. New York: Sheed and Ward, 1969.

Lincoln, C. Eric, ed. *The Black Experience in Religion*. Garden City, NY: Anchor/Doubleday, 1974.

_____. *Race, Religion, and the Continuing American Dilemma*. New York: Hill and Wang, 1984.

Lincoln, C. Eric and Lawrence A. Mamiya. *The Black Church in the African American Experience*. Durham, NC: Duke University Press, 1990.

Long, C. H. *Significations: Signs, Symbols, and Images in the Interpretation of Religion*. Philadelphia: Fortress Press, 1986.

Lovell, John, Jr. *Black Song: The Forge and the Flame*. New York: Macmillan, 1972.

MacRobert, Iain. *The Black Roots and White Racism of Early Pentecostalism in the USA*. New York: St. Martin's Press, 1988.

Marx, Gary. *Protest and Prejudice: A Study of Belief in the Black Community*. New York: Harper & Row, 1967.

Mays, Benjamin E. and Joseph W. Nicholson. *The Negro's Church*. New York: Arno Press, 1969.

Mays, Benjamin E. *The Negro's God*. Boston: Chapman and Grimes, 1938.

McCall, Emmanuel L., ed. *The Black Christian Experience.* Nashville: Broadman, 1972.

McClain, William B. *Black People in the Methodist Church: Whither Thou Goest?* Cambridge, MA: Schenkman Press, 1984.

Mitchell, Henry H. *Black Preaching.* Philadelphia: J. B. Lippincott, 1970.

————. *Black Belief: Folk Beliefs of Blacks in America and West Africa.* New York: Harper & Row, 1975.

Mitchell, Mozella G. *Spiritual Dynamics of Howard Thurman's Theology.* Briston, IN: Wyndham Hall Press, 1985.

Morris, Aldon D. *The Origins of the Civil Rights Movement: Black Communities Organizing for Change.* New York: Free Press, 1984.

Myrdal, Gunnar. *An American Dilemma.* New York: Harper & Row, 1944.

Nielsen, Niels C. Jr., Norvin Hein, Frank E. Reynolds, Alan L. Miller, Samuel E. Karff, Alice C. Cochran, and Paul McLean. *Religions of the World.* New York: St. Martins Press, 1983.

Nelsen, Hart M., Raytha L. Yokley, and Anne K. Nelsen, eds. *The Black Church in America.* New York: Basic Books, 1971.

Nelsen, Hart M. and Anne K. Nelsen. *Black Church in the Sixties.* Lexington: University Press of Kentucky, 1975.

Nichol, John Thomas. *Pentecostalism.* 1st ed. New York: Harper & Row, 1966.

Ottley, Roi. *'New World A-Coming': Inside Black America.* Boston: Houghton Mifflin, 1943.

Paris, Arthur E. *Black Pentecostalism: Southern Religion in the Urban World.* Amherst: University of Massachusetts Press, 1982.

Paris, Peter J. *Black Leaders in Conflict: Martin Luther King, Jr., Malcolm X, Joseph H. Jackson, Adam Clayton Powell, Jr.* New York: Pilgrim, 1978.

————. *The Social Teaching of the Black Churches.* Philadelphia: Fortress Press, 1985.

Quarles, Benjamin. *The Negro in the Making of American Life.* New York: Macmillan, 1969.

Raboteau, Albert. *Slave Religion: The "Invisible Institution" in the Antebellum South.* New York: Oxford University Press, 1978.

Reimers, David M. *White Protestantism and the Negro.* New York: Oxford University Press, 1965.

Richardson, Harry V. *Dark Salvation: The Story of Methodism as it Developed among Blacks in America.* 1st ed. Garden City, NY: Anchor Press, 1976.

Richardson, Marilyn. *Black Women and Religion: A Bibliography.* Boston: G. K. Hall and Company, 1980.

Roberts, James Deotis. *Liberation and Reconciliation: A Black Theology.* Philadelphia: Westminster Press, 1971.

————. *Quest for a Black Theology.* Philadelphia: Westminster Press, 1971.

————. *A Black Political Theology.* Philadelphia: Westminster Press, 1974.

Ross, B. Joyce. *J. E. Spingarn and the Rise of the NAACP, 1911-1939.* New York: Antheneum, 1972.

Ruether, Rosemary Radford. *Women and Religion in America.* Vol. 3. San Francisco: Harper & Row, 1986.

Schuchter, Arnold. *Reparations: The Black Manifesto and Its Challenge to White America.* Philadelphia: J. B. Lippincott, 1970.

Schwartz, Gary. *Sect Ideologies and Social Status.* Chicago: University of Chicago Press, 1970.

Sernett, Milton. *Black Religion and American Evangelicalism: White Protestants, Plantation Missions, and the Flowering of Negro Christianity, 1787-1819.* Metuchen, NJ: Scarecrow Press, 1975.

————, ed. *Afro-American Religious History: A Documentary Witness.* Durham, NC: Duke University Press, 1985.

Shannon, David T. and Gayraud S. Wilmore, eds. *Black Witness to the Apostolic Faith.* Grand Rapids: William B. Eerdmans, 1985.

Shaw, James B. F. *The Negro in the History of Methodism.* Nashville: Partheon Press, 1954.

Sherill, John L. *They Speak with Other Tongues.* 1st ed. New York: McGraw-Hill, 1964.

Simpson, George Eaton. *Black Religions in the New World.* New York: Columbia University Press, 1978.

Singleton, George A. *The Romance of African Methodism: A Study of the African Methodist Episcopal Church.* New York: Exposition Press, 1952.

Smith, H. Shelton. *In His Image, But...Racism in Southern Religion, 1780-1910.* Durham: Duke University Press, 1972.

Smith, Luther E. *Howard Thurman: The Mystic as Prophet.* Washington, D.C.: University Press of America, 1981.

Smythe, Mabel, ed. *Black American Reference Book.* Englewood Cliffs: Prentice Hall, 1976.

Sobel, Mechal. *Trabelin' On: The Slave Journey to an Afro-Baptist Faith.* Westport, CT: Greenwood, 1979.

Synan, Vinson. *The Holiness-Pentecostal Movement in the United States.* Grand Rapids: William B. Eerdmans Publishing Company, 1971.

Thurman, Howard. *Jesus and the Disinherited.* New York: Abingdon-Cokesbury Press, 1949.

Tinney, James S. "Black Origins of the Pentecostal Movement." *Christianity Today* 16 (October 8, 1971), 4-6.

————. "William J. Seymour: Father of Modern-Day Pentecostalism." *Journal of the Interdenominational Theological Center* 4 (Fall 1976), 38.

Walker, Wyatt Tee. *Somebody's Calling My Name: Black Sacred Music and Social Change.* Valley Forge: Judson Press, 1979.

Washington, Booker T. *Up From Slavery: An Autobiography.* Reprint. New York: Bantam Books, 1963.

————. *The Future of the American Negro.* 1899. Reprint. Chicago: Afro-Am Press, 1969.

Washington, James M. *Frustrated Fellowships: The Black Baptist Quest for Social Power.* Macon, GA: Mercer, 1986.

Washington, Joseph R., Jr. *The Politics of God.* Boston: Beacon, 1967.

————. *Black Sects and Cults.* Garden City, NY: Doubleday, 1972.

————. *Black Religion: The Negro and Christianity in the United States.* 1964. Reprint. Lanham, MD: University Press of America, 1984.

Weems, Renita. *Just a Sister Away: A Womanist Vision of Women's Relationships in the Bible.* San Diego: LuraMedia, 1988.

West, Cornel. *Prophesy Deliverance! An Afro-American Revolutionary Christianity.* Philadelphia: Westminster Press, 1982.

————. *Prophetic Fragments.* Grand Rapids, MI and Trenton, NJ: William B. Eerdmans and Africa World Press, Inc., 1988.

Wheeler, Edward L. *Uplifting the Race: The Black Minister in the New South, 1865-1902.* Lanham, MD: University Press of America, 1986.

Williams, Juan. *Eyes on the Prize: America's Civil Rights Years, 1954-65.* New York: Viking Press, 1987.

Wills, David W. and Richard Newman, eds. *Black Apostles at Home and Abroad: Afro-Americans and the Christian Mission from the Revolution to Reconstruction.* Boston: G. K. Hall and Company, 1982.

Wilmore, Gayraud S. *Black Religion and Black Radicalism.* 2nd ed. Maryknoll, NY: Orbis Books, 1983.

————. *African American Religious Studies: An Interdisciplinary Anthology.* Durham: Duke University Press, 1989.

Wilmore, Gayraud S. and James H. Cone, eds. *Black Theology: A Documentary History, 1966-1979*. Maryknoll, NY: Orbis, 1979.

Williams, Ethel L. and Clifton F. Brown. *Howard University Bibliography of African and Afro-American Religious Studies*. Wilmington: Scholarly Resources, 1977.

Williams, Melvin D. *Community in a Black Pentecostal Church*. Pittsburgh: University of Pittsburgh Press, 1982.

Wilson, Robert L. and James H. Davis. *The Church in the Racially Changing Community*. New York: Abingdon Press, 1966.

Witvliet, Theo. *The Way of the Black Messiah: The Hermeneutical Challenge of Black Theology as a Theology of Liberation*. Oak Park, IL: Meyer Stone Books, 1987.

Woodson, Carter G. *The History of the Negro Church*. 1921. 3rd ed. Reprint. Washington, D.C.: Associated Publishers, 1972.

_____ . *Eighty-seven Years Behind the Black Curtain*. Philadelphia: Rare Book Company, 1965.

Young, Josiah U. *Black and African Theologies: Siblings or Distant Cousins?* Maryknoll, NY: Orbis Books, 1986.

General Works

Association of Theological Schools in the United States and Canada, Bulletin 38 (Part 4), 1989 Directory. Vandalia, OH: Association of Theological Schools, 1989.

Balachandran, M. and S. Balachandran, eds. *State and Local Statistics Sources 1990*. 1st ed. Detroit: Gale Research Company, 1989.

Browne, Ray B., ed. *Contemporary Heroes and Heroines: A Biographical Guide to Heroic Figures of the Twentieth Century*. Detroit: Gale Research Company, 1989.

Burek, Deborah M. and Karin E. Koek, eds. *Encyclopedia of Associations 1990*. 24th ed. 3 vols. Detroit: Gale Research Company, 1989.

Cloyd, Iris, ed. *Who's Who among Black Americans 1990*. 6th ed. Detroit: Gale Research Company, 1989.

Dayton, Donald W. *The Theological Roots of Pentecostalism*. Metuchen, NJ: Scarecrow Press, 1987.

Dieter, Melvin E. *The Holiness Revival of the Nineteenth Century*. Metuchen, NJ: Scarecrow Press, 1980.

Dresser, Peter D. and Karen Hill, eds. *Research Centers Directory 1990*. Detroit: Gale Research Company, 1989.

Geisendorfer, James, ed. *Directory of Religious Organizations in the United States*. 2nd ed. Wilmington, NC: Consortium, 1980.

Hinnells, John R. *The Penguin Dictionary of Religions*. London: Penguin Books, 1984.

Jacquet, Constant H., Jr., ed. *Yearbook of American and Canadian Churches*. 57th ed. Nashville: Abingdon Press, 1989.

Jones, Charles Edwin. *A Guide to the Study of the Holiness Movement*. Metuchen, NJ: Scarecrow Press, 1974.

_____ . *A Guide to the Study of the Pentecostal Movement*. Metuchen, NJ: Scarecrow Press, 1983.

Kauffman, Donald T. *The Dictionary of Religious Terms*. Westwood, NJ: Fleming H. Revell, 1967.

Kerr, James S. and Charles Lutz. *A Christian's Dictionary*. Philadelphia: Fortress Press, 1969.

Livingstone, Elizabeth A. *The Oxford Dictionary of the Christian Church*. 2nd ed. New York: Oxford University Press, 1977.

Mathews, Shailer and Gerald B. Smith, eds. *The Dictionary of Religion and Ethics*. Detroit: Gale Research Company, 1973.

Mead, Frank S. *Handbook of Denominations in the United States*. 4th ed. Nashville: Abingdon Press, 1965.

Melton, J. Gordon, ed. *The Encyclopedia of American Religions: Religious Creeds*. 1st ed. Detroit: Gale Research Company, 1988.

_____ . *The Encyclopedia of American Religions*. 3rd ed. Detroit: Gale Research Company, 1989.

_____ . *The Churches Speak on AIDS*. Issue 1. Detroit: Gale Research Company, 1989.

_____ . *The Churches Speak on Abortion*. Issue 2. Detroit: Gale Research Company, 1989.

_____ . *The Churches Speak on Racial Prejudice*. Issue 3. Detroit: Gale Research Company, 1989.

_____ . *The Churches Speak on Women's Ordination*. Issue 4. Detroit: Gale Research Company, 1989.

Miller, Madeleine S. and J. Lane Miller. *Harper's Bible Dictionary*. New York: Harper & Row, 1973.

Modoc Press, Inc. *Guide to Schools and Departments of Religion and Seminaries in the United States and Canada*. New York: Collier Macmillan Publishers, 1987.

Purvis, J. S. *Dictionary of Ecclesiastical Terms*. New York: Thomas Nelson, 1962.

Richardson, Alan and John Bowden. *The Westminster Dictionary of Christian Theology*. Philadelphia: Westminster Press, 1983.

Smith, Darren L., ed. *Black Americans Information Directory*. 1st ed. Detroit: Gale Research Company, 1989.

Towell, Julie and Charles B. Montney, eds. *Directories in Print 1990*. Detroit: Gale Research Company, 1989.

United States Department of Commerce, Bureau of the Census. *Census of Religious Bodies, 1936*. Washington, D.C.: Government Printing Office, 1940.

Part 9
Indexes

INDEX 1: ALPHABETICAL LISTING

This is a complete listing of the official names of the religious bodies presented in the *Directory*. Any other names by which the religious bodies may be known are also listed. The names are presented in letter-by-letter alphabetical order, ignoring punctuation and spacing. Please note that this is the only index that presents alternate names for organizations.

INDEX 2: CATEGORICAL LISTING

The official names of the religious bodies presented in the Directory are listed in categories based upon their doctrinal orientation or traditional affiliation. They are presented in letter-by-letter alphabetical order, under the administrative heading relevant to each group, ignoring punctuation and spacing. The categories presented are:

African Methodist Episcopal (A.M.E.)

INDEX 3: GEOGRAPHIC LOCATION LISTING

The religious bodies are organized according to the *geographic location of their respective headquarters*, with entries arranged in letter-by-letter alphabetical order within each state or country. The United States is presented first, and bodies outside of the United States are listed in their respective countries. Those organizations without a central headquarters or whose addresses are unknown are presented at the end of the index.

UNITED STATES

Alabama

African Methodist Episcopal Church, 9th Episcopal District, 56

African Methodist Episcopal Zion Church, 1st Episcopal District, 65

African Methodist Episcopal Zion Church, 12th Episcopal District, 66

Alabama Annual Conference, 9th Episcopal District (*A.M.E. Church*), 57

Alabama Baptist Missionary State Convention, 33

Apostolic Faith Mission Church of God, 86

Apostolic Overcoming Holy Church of God, Inc., 87

Apostolic Overcoming Holy Church of God Theological Seminary, 170

Bethlehem Baptist District Association #1, 34

Bethlehem Baptist District Association #2, 34

Birmingham Annual Conference, 5th Episcopal District (*C.M.E. Church*), 77

Birmingham District—North Alabama Annual Conference, 8th Episcopal District (*A.M.E. Zion Church*), 67

Brewton District—South Alabama Annual Conference, 10th Episcopal District (*A.M.E. Zion Church*), 68

Central Alabama Annual Conference, 9th Episcopal District (*A.M.E. Church*), 58

Christian Methodist Episcopal Church, 5th Episcopal District, 77

Church of God (*U.S.A.*), 206–7

Dallas County District Association, 36

East Alabama Annual Conference, 9th Episcopal District (*A.M.E. Church*), 59

East Dallas District Association, 36

East Montgomery District—Central Alabama Annual Conference, 10th Episcopal District (*A.M.E. Zion Church*), 69

Fayette/Jasper District—North Alabama Annual Conference, 8th Episcopal District (*A.M.E. Zion Church*), 70

Florida Annual Conference, 5th Episcopal District (*C.M.E. Church*), 78

Greensboro/Demopolis District—Cahaba Annual Conference, 10th Episcopal District (*A.M.E. Zion Church*), 70

Greenville District—South Alabama Annual Conference, 10th Episcopal District (*A.M.E. Zion Church*), 70

House of God Which is the Church of the Living God, the Pillar and Ground of Truth Without Controversy [Keith Dominion], 103–4

House of Judah, 132

Jackson District—West Alabama Annual Conference, 7th Episcopal District (*A.M.E. Zion Church*), 70

Jefferson District—West Alabama Annual Conference, 7th Episcopal District (*A.M.E. Zion Church*), 71

Mobile District—West Alabama Annual Conference, 7th Episcopal District (*A.M.E. Zion Church*), 72

Montgomery Antioch District Association, 40

Mount Zion Cossa Valley District Association, 28

New Antioch Bethlehem Association, 41

New Bethel District Association, 28

New Era Baptist State Convention of Alabama, 41

New Era Progressive Baptist State Convention of Alabama, 28

North Alabama Annual Conference, 9th Episcopal District (*A.M.E. Church*), 61

North Central Alabama Annual Conference, 5th Episcopal District (*C.M.E. Church*), 79

Opelika District—Alabama Annual Conference, 10th Episcopal District (*A.M.E. Zion Church*), 72

Peace Baptist District Association, 42

Progressive Baptist Missionary and Educational Convention, 53

Second Cumberland Presbyterian Church, 129

Selma District—Cahaba Annual Conference, 10th Episcopal District (*A.M.E. Zion Church*), 74

Snow Creek District Baptist Association, 44

South Alabama Annual Conference, 9th Episcopal District (*A.M.E. Church*), 62

Southeast Alabama Annual Conference, 5th Episcopal District (*C.M.E. Church*), 79

Southeast Alabama District Baptist Association, 44

Tuscaloosa District—North Alabama Annual Conference, 8th Episcopal District (*A.M.E. Zion Church*), 74

Tuskegee District—Alabama Annual Conference, 10th Episcopal District (*A.M.E. Zion Church*), 74

Union Springs District—Alabama Annual Conference, 10th Episcopal District (*A.M.E. Zion Church*), 74

West Alabama Annual Conference, 9th Episcopal District (*A.M.E. Church*), 64

West Montgomery District—Central Alabama Annual Conference, 10th Episcopal District (*A.M.E. Zion Church*), 75

Wills Creek District Missionary Baptist Association, 46

Alaska

Alaska Annual Conference, 11th Episcopal District (*A.M.E. Zion Church*), 67

Greatland State Baptist Convention of Alaska, 39

Arizona

Arizona Annual Conference, 9th Episcopal District (*A.M.E. Zion Church*), 67

Free Church of God in Christ in Jesus' Name, Inc., 99

General Missionary Baptist State Convention of Arizona, 26

National Colored Spiritualist Association of Churches, 130

Salt River Valley General Association of Arizona, 30

Southern Arizona Missionary Baptist District Association, 44

Arkansas

African Methodist Episcopal Church, 12th Episcopal District, 56

Illinois (cont.)

African Methodist Episcopal Church, 4th Episcopal District, 66

African Methodist Episcopal Zion Church, 11th Episcopal District, 66

African Orthodox Church of the West, 126–27

American Muslim Mission, 139–40

Antioch District Association, 49

Association of Black Directors of Christian Education, 156

Baptist Brotherhood District Association, 33

Baptist Ministers Union of Chicago and Vicinity, 33

Baptist State Convention of Illinois, 49

Baptist State Convention of Illinois, Inc., 34

Bethlehem Baptist District Association, 49

Black Light Fellowship, 149

Black Religious Broadcasters Association, 157

Black Theology Project, 176

Canadian Annual Conference, 4th Episcopal District (*A.M.E. Church*), 58

Central Baptist District Association, 24

Chicago Annual Conference, 4th Episcopal District (*A.M.E. Church*), 58

Chicago District—Michigan Annual Conference, 4th Episcopal District (*A.M.E. Zion Church*), 68

Churches United of Scott County, Iowa and Rock Island, Illinois, 217

Church Federation of Greater Chicago, 217

Church of God in Christ, Congregational, 91

Commission for Multicultural Ministries—Evangelical Lutheran Church in America, 204

Community Renewal Society, 221–22

Fellowship Baptist District Association, Inc., 50

Friendship Baptist District Association, 25

God's House of Prayer for All Nations, Inc., 100

Gospel Mission, 124

Holiness Community Temple, 102

Illinois Annual Conference, 4th Episcopal District (*A.M.E. Church*), 59

Illinois Conference of Churches, 218

Illinois District Association, 26

Illinois National Baptist State Convention, 26

Illinois Annual Conference, 4th Episcopal District (*A.M.E. Church*), 59

International Council of Community Churches, 219

Lake Region Conference of Seventh-Day Adventists, 200

Living Witness of Apostolic Faith, Inc., 106

Metropolitan Spiritual Churches of Christ, Inc., 130

Michigan Annual Conference, 4th Episcopal District (*A.M.E. Church*), 60

Mount Olive Baptist District Association, 28

Nation of Islam [Farrakhan], 142–43

National Black Christian Students Conference, 153

New Unity District Association, 29

Northwood River District Association, 29

Operation PUSH, 159–60

Original Hebrew Israelite Nation, 133

Orthodox Woodriver District Association, 29

Progressive Baptist District Association, 52

Progressive Baptist State Convention of Illinois, 53

Progressive National Baptist Convention Youth Department, 53

Union District Association, 54

United Black Christians, United Church of Christ, 216

Universal Foundation for Better Living, Inc. [Johnnie Coleman], 125

Urban Ministries, Inc., 163

Woodriver Baptist District Association, 46

Zion District Association, 47

Indiana

African Methodist Episcopal Church, 4th Episcopal District, 56

Canadian Annual Conference, 4th Episcopal District (*A.M.E. Church*), 57

Capitol City District Association, 24

Central Baptist Theological Seminary in Indiana, 170

Chicago Annual Conference, 4th Episcopal District (*A.M.E. Church*), 58

Church of the Living God, the Pillar and Ground of the Truth, Which He Purchased with His Own Blood, Inc., [McLeod Dominion], 95–96

General Assembly of the Church of God (Anderson, Indiana), 207–8

General Missionary Baptist State Convention of Indiana, Inc., 38

General Missionary Baptist State Convention of Indiana, Inc., #2, 38

Indiana Annual Conference, 4th Episcopal District (*A.M.E. Church*), 59

Indiana Brotherhood Missionary Baptist District Association, 39

Indiana Council of Churches, 218

Indiana Interreligious Commission on Human Equality, 218–19

Indiana Missionary Baptist State Convention, 27

Indianapolis District—Indiana Annual Conference, 9th Episcopal District (*A.M.E. Zion Church*), 70

Indiana State Convention, 50

Madisonville District—Kentucky Annual Conference, 5th Episcopal District (*A.M.E. Zion Church*), 72

Martin Luther King, Jr. State Convention, 51

Michigan Annual Conference, 4th Episcopal District (*A.M.E. Church*), 60

National Association of the Church of God (Anderson, Indiana), 208

National Convocation of the Christian Church (Disciples of Christ), 120

New Era District Association, 51

Northeastern District Baptist Association, 29

Northwestern District Association, 29

Pentecostal Assemblies of the World, Inc., 108–9

Iowa

Iowa Missionary and Educational Baptist State Convention, 39

Kansas

Church of God (Anderson, Indiana) Board of Church Extension and Home Missions, Urban Ministry Division, 206

Free Church of God True Holiness, 99

Kansas General Missionary Baptist State Convention, 27

Kaw Valley District Association, 39

Missionary Baptist State Convention of Kansas, 40

Northeastern District Association, 41

Southeast District Association, 44

Southwestern District Association, 44

Sunflower District Association, 31

United Missionary Baptist District Association of Kansas, 31

Kentucky

Baptist State Missionary Convention, 49

Bluegrass State Baptist Convention, 34

Evansville District—Indiana Annual Conference, 9th Episcopal District (*A.M.E. Zion Church*), 70

General Association of Baptists in Kentucky, 21

Kentuckian Interfaith Community, 219

Kentucky Council of Churches, 220

Kentucky State Baptist Convention, 27

Kentucky State Fellowship, 50

Louisville District—Kentucky Annual Conference, 5th Episcopal District (*A.M.E. Zion Church*), 72

National Black Presbyterian Caucus, 208

OUTSIDE THE UNITED STATES

Africa (cont.)

Northern Transvaal Annual Conference, 19th Episcopal District (*A.M.E. Church*), 61

Orangia Annual Conference, 19th Episcopal District (*A.M.E. Church*), 62

Rivers Annual Conference, 13th Episcopal District (*A.M.E. Zion Church*) (no current address), 73

R. R. Wright School of Religion, 167

West Ghana Annual Conference, 12th Episcopal District (*A.M.E. Zion Church*) (no current address), 75

West Transvaal Annual Conference, 19th Episcopal District (*A.M.E. Church*), 64

England

Birmingham/Manchester District—London/Birmingham Annual Conference, 12th Episcopal District (*A.M.E. Zion Church*), 67

London District—London/Birmingham Annual Conference, 12th Episcopal District (*A.M.E. Zion Church*), 71

Germany

General Baptist Association of West Germany, 38

South America

Central Demerara District—Guyana Annual Conference, 3rd Episcopal District (*A.M.E. Zion Church*), 68

East Demerara/West Berbice District—Guyana Annual Conference, 3rd Episcopal District (*A.M.E. Zion Church*) (no current address), 69

East West Demerara and Essequibo District—Guyana Annual Conference, 3rd Episcopal District (*A.M.E. Zion Church*), 69

Virgin Islands

Virgin Island Annual Conference, 2nd Episcopal District (*A.M.E. Zion Church*), 74

West Indies

Bahamas Annual Conference, 1st Episcopal District (*A.M.E. Zion Church*), 67

Bahamas National Baptist Missionary and Educational Convention, 33

Black River District—Cornwall Jamaica Annual Conference, 7th Episcopal District (*A.M.E. Zion Church*), 67

Grange Hill District—Cornwall Jamaica Annual Conference, 7th Episcopal District (*A.M.E. Zion Church*), 70

Kingston District—Surrey Jamaica Annual Conference, 7th Episcopal District (*A.M.E. Zion Church*), 71

Manchester District—Middlesex Jamaica Annual Conference, 7th Episcopal District (*A.M.E. Zion Church*), 72

May Pen District—Middlesex Jamaica Annual Conference, 7th Episcopal District (*A.M.E. Zion Church*), 72

Osborne Store District—Middlesex Jamaica Annual Conference, 7th Episcopal District (*A.M.E. Zion Church*), 73

Portland District—Surrey Jamaica Annual Conference, 7th Episcopal District (*A.M.E. Zion Church*), 73

Rocky Point District—Middlesex Jamaica Annual Conference, 7th Episcopal District (*A.M.E. Zion Church*), 73

Saint James District—Cornwall Jamaica Annual Conference, 7th Episcopal District (*A.M.E. Zion Church*), 73

Trinidad/Tobago District—Virginia Annual Conference, 4th Episcopal District (*A.M.E. Zion Church*), 74

Address Unknown

African Universal Church, 82

Apostolic Assemblies of Christ, Inc., 83

Baptist Associations and Auxiliaries of Southern Maryland and Vicinity, 33

Bible Way Pentecostal Apostolic Church, 87

Church of God (Black Jews), 131

First Church of Voodoo, 144

Free Church of God in Christ, 99

Fundamental Baptist Fellowship Association, 38

House of God Which is the Church of the Living God, the Pillar and Ground of Truth, 103

House of the Lord, 104

Latter House of the Lord for All People and the Church of the Mountain, Apostolic Faith, 106

National Coalition of Black Church Musicians, 155

Nation of Islam [The Caliph], 143

Original Glorious Church of God in Christ Apostolic Faith, Inc., 108

United Churches of Jesus Apostolic, Inc., 113

United Hebrew Congregation, 136

Universal Church, The Mystical Body of Christ, 130

Yahweh's Temple, 125

Yoruba Theological Archministry, 144

No Central Headquarters

Afro-American Vodoun, 143–44

Church of Christ, 201–2

Rastafarians, 133–36

INDEX 4: ORGANIZATIONAL CLASSIFICATION LISTING

The religious bodies in the *Directory* are listed in letter-by-letter alphabetical order according to their particular type of organization. In order to reflect the diverse nature of the groups, each entry may be listed in as many as three categories. The categories are:

1. **Administrative groups:** These are organizational units designed to facilitate, coordinate, and manage the affairs of the organization or a specific subcomponent of its activities. It is often the corporate head of the organization.
2. **Christian education groups:** Such groups are organizational units devoted to enhancing or increasing information on matters pertaining to the doctrine and literature of each group. Their primary emphasis is to share information about the beliefs and practices of the faith.
3. **Councils of churches/groups:** These organizational units coordinate independent or semi-autonomous organizations in a geographic region or those who share a common interest.
4. **Denominations:** Denominations are religious bodies that may be distinguished by tradition or practice and that identify themselves as separate or autonomous entities. These groups may exist in name only, with or without an administrative support structure.
5. **Denomination specific groups:** Organizations that exist as a subcomponent of a denomination or that incorporate the doctrinal beliefs of a religious body are denomination specific. These organizations may be independent from the religious body.
6. **District associations/annual conferences:** These are organizational subdivisions in connectional churches, which are structured according to geographical regions with varying levels of affiliation.
7. **Ecumenical/nondenominational groups:** These organizational entities have no alliance to a specific doctrine or faith tradition. Their doctrine may be a synthesis of beliefs from various faith traditions.
8. **Episcopal districts:** Organizational subdivisions in hierarchically structured religious bodies that are supervised by designated leadership under the auspices of a bishop or religious leader are known as episcopal districts.
9. **Lay groups:** These organizational units are designed primarily to serve the needs of nonclergy and they generally are staffed by or composed of lay persons.
10. **Lay/clergy groups:** These organizational units are designed to serve the needs of clergy and laity and they may be staffed by or composed of any combination of clergy and laity.
11. **Ministerial groups:** These organizational units are designed to foster communication and information exchange between clergy.
12. **Mission/philanthropic groups:** These organizational units are structured to serve the mission or economic needs of a religious body or community. Included are organizations that focus on preaching, evangelization, charity, education, and social welfare.
13. **Music resource groups:** These organizational units promote communication and information exchange with respect to music; these groups may sponsor music workshops, music publishing forums, and professional associations designed to facilitate developing musicians' networks in religious settings.
14. **Publishing groups:** These organizational units publish religious materials.
15. **Racial/social justice groups:** These organizational units promote and enhance communication and exchanges with minority status groups.
16. **Research/educational/professional organizations and seminaries:** These organizational units are designed to increase the exchange of intellectual ideas in religious communities. These include religion-related research projects, educational institutions in religious and religion-related communities (e.g., Bible colleges, seminaries and schools of religion).
17. **State groups or conventions:** These organizational units serve individuals or groups within designated geographical boundaries.
18. **Student groups:** These organizational units are designed to serve the needs of students and are primarily composed of students.
19. **Women's groups:** These organizational units are designed to facilitate and communicate concerns of women and/or are primarily composed of women.
20. **Worship resource groups:** These organizational units are designed to assist in worship and matters pertaining to the celebration of rites recognized by religious bodies.
21. **Youth groups:** These organizational units are composed of youth and/or designed to address the role, status, and involvement of youth.

Administrative Groups

Black Church Extension Division—
Home Mission Board, Southern
Baptist Convention, 201
Black Methodists for Church Renewal,
Inc.—United Methodist Church,
204–5
Church of God (Anderson, Indiana)—
Board of Church Extension and
Home Missions, Urban Ministry
Division, 206
Commission for Multicultural
Ministries—Evangelical Lutheran
Church in America, 204
Commission for Racial Justice—United
Church of Christ, Inc., 215
Council on Ethnic Affairs—Free
Methodist Church of North America,
205
Department for Social Justice—
Unitarian Universalist Association,
214
General Assembly of the Church of
God (Anderson, Indiana), 207–8
General Commission on Religion and
Race—United Methodist Church, 205
National Association of Black Catholic
Administrators, 211
National Black Catholic Congress, Inc.,
211–12
National Council of the Churches of
Christ in the U.S.A., Office of
Racial Justice, 222
National Office for Black Catholics,
213–14
Office of Black Ministries—The
Episcopal Church Center, 202–3
Racial Ethnic Ministry Unit—
Presbyterian Church (U.S.A.), Racial
Justice Ministry, 208
Racial Ethnic Ministry Unit—
Presbyterian Church (U.S.A.), Social
Justice Policy Development, 208
Secretariat for Black Catholics, 214
United Black Christians—United
Church of Christ, Inc., 216

Christian Education Groups

Association of Black Directors of
Christian Education, 156
Baptist Congress of Christian
Education—Maryland, 33
Biblical Institute for Social Change,
Inc., 175–76
Center for Black Church Development,
150
Joint Educational Development, 222
National Capital Baptist Congress of
Christian Education—D.C., 41
State Congress of Christian Education,
Bluegrass Baptist Convention—
Kentucky, 44
Successful Stewardship for Life
Ministries, Inc., 162

Councils of Churches/Groups

Christian Council of Metropolitan
Atlanta, Inc., 216
Church Council of Greater Seattle, 217
Churches United of Scott County, Iowa
and Rock Island, Illinois, 217
Church Federation of Greater Chicago,
217
Congress of National Black Churches,
151–52
Council of Churches of Greater
Washington, 217
Council of Churches of the City of New
York, 217–18
Council of Islamic Organizations of
America, 203
Ecumenical Council of the Pasadena
Area Churches, 218
Ethnic Cooperation and Institutional
Ministries—Pennsylvania Council of
Churches, 218
Faith Tabernacle Council of Churches,
International, 97–98
Full Gospel Pentecostal Association,
Inc., 100
Greater Dallas Community of Churches,
218
Greensboro Urban Ministry, 222
Illinois Conference of Churches, 218
Indiana Council of Churches, 218
Indiana Interreligious Commission on
Human Equality, 218–19
Interfaith Conference of Metropolitan
Washington, 219
International Council of Community
Churches, 219
Kentuckian Interfaith Community, 219
Kentucky Council of Churches, 220
Marin City Ministerial Alliance, 148
Martin Luther King, Jr. Scholarship/
Memorial Service Committee—
Capital Area Council of Churches,
Inc., 220
Metropolitan Spiritual Churches of
Christ, Inc., 130
Minnesota Council of Churches, 220
National Convocation of the Christian
Church (Disciples of Christ), 120
Ohio Council of Churches, Inc., 220
Oklahoma Conference of Churches,
220–21
Pomona Valley Council of Churches,
221
Prayer Band Fellowship Union, 110
Programme to Combat Racism—World
Council of Churches, 223–24
Trenton Ecumenical Area Ministry, 221
United Fellowship Convention of the
Original Azusa Street Mission,
113–14

Denominations

African American Catholic
Congregation, 117–18
African Methodist Episcopal Church,
54–55
African Methodist Episcopal Zion
Church, 64–65
African Orthodox Church, 126
African Orthodox Church of the West,
126–27
African Union First Colored Methodist
Protestant Church, 75–76
African Universal Church, 82
Afro-American Vodoun, 143–44
Ahmadiyya Anjuman Ishaat Islam,
Lahore, Inc., 203
Ahmadiyya Movement in Islam, Inc.,
U.S.A., 137–38
Al-Hanif, Hanafi Madh-Hab Center,
Islam Faith, United States of
America, American Mussulmans,
138–39
Alpha and Omega Pentecostal Church
of America, Inc., 83
American Muslim Mission, 139–40
ANSAARU ALLAH Community,
140–41
Apostolic Assemblies of Christ, Inc.,
83
Apostolic Assemblies of Our Lord and
Saviour Jesus Christ, 83
Apostolic Church of Christ, Inc., 83
Apostolic Church of Christ in God,
83–84
Apostolic Faith Churches Giving Grace,
Inc., 84
Apostolic Faith Churches of A Living
God, Inc., 84
Apostolic Faith Churches of God, Inc.,
84–85
Apostolic Faith Churches of God in
Christ, Inc., 85
Apostolic Faith Church of God, 85–86
Apostolic Faith Church of God, Live
On, 86
Apostolic Faith Mission Church of God,
86
Apostolic Holiness Church of America,
86
Apostolic Overcoming Holy Church of
God, Inc., 87
Assemblies of the Lord Jesus Christ,
Inc., 206
Bible Church of Christ, Inc., 87
Bible Church of God, Inc., 87
Bible Way Church of Our Lord Jesus
Christ World Wide, Inc., 88
Bible Way Pentecostal Apostolic
Church, 88
Black Primitive Baptists, 21
Christ Holy Sanctified Church of
America, Inc., 88–89
Christian Methodist Episcopal Church,
76
Christ's Sanctified Holy Church, 89
Churches of God, Holiness, 89
Church of Christ, 201–2
Church of Christ (Holiness), Inc.,
89–90
Church of Christ Holiness Unto the
Lord, Inc., 90
Church of Christ (Holiness) U.S.A., 90

Central Oklahoma Annual Conference, 12th Episcopal District (*A.M.E. Church*), 58

Central South Carolina Annual Conference, 7th Episcopal District (*A.M.E. Church*), 58

Central States Annual Conference of Seventh-day Adventists, 199

Central Texas Annual Conference, 8th Episcopal District (*C.M.E. Church*), 78

Central Texas Annual Conference, 10th Episcopal District (*A.M.E. Church*), 58

Central Valley District—California Annual Conference, 11th Episcopal District (*A.M.E. Zion Church*), 68

Chain Lake District Missionary Baptist Association—Michigan, 35

Charleston Association—South Carolina, 49

Charlotte District—Western North Carolina Annual Conference, 1st Episcopal District (*A.M.E. Zion Church*), 68

Chattanooga District—Tennessee Annual Conference, 4th Episcopal District (*A.M.E. Zion Church*), 68

Cheraw/Bennettsville District—Pee Dee Annual Conference, 9th Episcopal District (*A.M.E. Zion Church*), 68

Chicago Annual Conference, 4th Episcopal District (*A.M.E. Church*), 58

Chicago District—Michigan Annual Conference, 4th Episcopal District (*A.M.E. Zion Church*), 68

Christian Fellowship District Association—California, 50

Christian Fellowship Missionary Baptist Association—New Jersey, 35

Christian Methodist Episcopal Church, 1st Episcopal District, 77

Christian Methodist Episcopal Church, 2nd Episcopal District, 77

Christian Methodist Episcopal Church, 3rd Episcopal District, 77

Christian Methodist Episcopal Church, 4th Episcopal District, 77

Christian Methodist Episcopal Church, 5th Episcopal District, 77

Christian Methodist Episcopal Church, 6th Episcopal District, 77

Christian Methodist Episcopal Church, 7th Episcopal District, 77

Christian Methodist Episcopal Church, 8th Episcopal District, 77

Christian Methodist Episcopal Church, 9th Episcopal District, 77

Christian Methodist Episcopal Church, 10th Episcopal District, 77

Christian Ministers Missionary Baptist Association—Louisiana, 24

Church of God (Anderson, Indiana)—Board of Church Extension and Home Missions, Urban Ministry Division, 206

Church of God (Cleveland, Tennessee)—Office of Black Evangelism, 206

Cincinnati District Association—Ohio, 50

Cincinnati, Ohio District Association, 35

City Union Number 1 State of Tennessee District Association, 50

Clarkton District—Cape Fear Annual Conference, 6th Episcopal District (*A.M.E. Zion Church*), 69

Cleveland District of Baptist Women—Ohio, 35, 50

Colorado Annual Conference, 5th Episcopal District (*A.M.E. Church*), 58

Colorado Baptist Southern District Association, 35

Columbia Annual Conference, 7th Episcopal District (*A.M.E. Church*), 58

Columbia/Camden District—Palmetto Annual Conference, 9th Episcopal District (*A.M.E. Zion Church*), 69

Columbus/Cincinnati District—Ohio Annual Conference, 8th Episcopal District (*A.M.E. Zion Church*), 69

Commission for Coordination of Ethnic Minority Ministries—West Ohio Conference, United Methodist Church, 205

Commission for Multicultural Ministries—Evangelical Lutheran Church in America, 204

Commission for Racial Justice—United Church of Christ, Inc., 215

Concord District—West Central North Carolina Annual Conference, 8th Episcopal District (*A.M.E. Zion Church*), 69

Connecticut Baptist Missionary Convention, 50

Consolidated Missionary State Convention of Arkansas, Inc., 36

Council for Racial/Ethnic Ministries—United Church of Christ, Inc., 215

Council of Islamic Organizations of America, 203

Council on Ethnic Affairs—Free Methodist Church of North America, 205

County Line Baptist Convention Association—North Carolina, 50

Creek District Baptist Association—Oklahoma, 36

Cuba Annual Conference, 16th Episcopal District (*A.M.E. Church*), 58

Cumberland River, South Kentucky, Middle Tennessee Baptist District Association—Tennessee, 24

Cypress District Baptist Association—Texas, 36

Dallas County District Association—Alabama, 36

Dallas District—Texas Annual

Conference, 11th Episcopal District (*A.M.E. Zion Church*), 69

Dallas-Fort Worth Annual Conference, 8th Episcopal District (*C.M.E. Church*), 78

Dal-Worth District Association—Texas, 25

D.C. Ministers' Conference, 50

D.C. Progressive Laymen, 50

Delaware Annual Conference, 1st Episcopal District (*A.M.E. Church*), 58

Denver District—Colorado Annual Conference, 6th Episcopal District (*A.M.E. Zion Church*), 69

Department for Social Justice, Unitarian Universalist Association, 214

Detroit District—Michigan Annual Conference, 4th Episcopal District (*A.M.E. Zion Church*), 69

District Federation of Young People—D.C., 50

Dominican Republic Annual Conference, 16th Episcopal District (*A.M.E. Church*), 59

Durham District—Central North Carolina Annual Conference, 5th Episcopal District (*A.M.E. Zion Church*), 69

East Alabama Annual Conference, 9th Episcopal District (*A.M.E. Church*), 59

East Dallas District Association—Alabama, 36

East Demerara/West Berbice District—Guyana Annual Conference, 3rd Episcopal District (*A.M.E. Zion Church*), 69

Eastern Baptist Association of New York, 36

Eastern Cape Annual Conference, 15th Episcopal District (*A.M.E. Church*), 59

Eastern Keystone Baptist Association—Pennsylvania, 50

Eastern Ohio District Association, 36

Eastern Progressive District Association—Michigan, 25

Eastern Seventh District Association—Louisiana, 25

East Florida Annual Conference, 11th Episcopal District (*A.M.E. Church*), 59

East Florida Bethany Baptist District Association—Florida, 25

East Ghana Annual Conference, 12th Episcopal District (*A.M.E. Zion Church*), 69

East Mississippi Annual Conference, 4th Episcopal District (*C.M.E. Church*), 78

East Mississippi Annual Conference, 8th Episcopal District (*A.M.E. Church*), 59

East Mississippi State Baptist Convention, Inc., 36

East Montgomery District—Central

4th Episcopal District (*C.M.E. Church*), 80

South Mississippi Baptist State Convention, 30

South Ohio Annual Conference, 3rd Episcopal District (*A.M.E. Church*), 63

South West Baptist Association—Missouri, 44

Southwestern District Association—Kansas, 44

Southwest Georgia Annual Conference, 6th Episcopal District (*A.M.E. Church*), 63

Southwest Georgia Annual Conference, 6th Episcopal District (*C.M.E. Church*), 80

Southwest Region Conference of Seventh-day Adventists, 200

Southwest Texas Annual Conference, 10th Episcopal District (*A.M.E. Church*), 63

South-West Zimbabwe Annual Conference, 17th Episcopal District (*A.M.E. Church*), 63

South Zambia Annual Conference, 17th Episcopal District (*A.M.E. Church*), 63

Spartanburg District—Palmetto Conference, 9th Episcopal District (*A.M.E. Zion Church*), 74

Spring Hill District Association—Mississippi, 31

Spring Hill Missionary Baptist Association—Mississippi, 44

State Congress of Christian Education, Bluegrass Baptist Convention—Kentucky, 44

Statesville District—Western North Carolina Annual Conference, 1st Episcopal District (*A.M.E. Zion Church*), 74

Stones River District Association—Tennessee, 31

Storm Branch Association—South Carolina, 45

Sunflower District Association—Kansas, 31

Sunshine District Association—Missouri, 31

Surinam-Guyana Annual Conference, 16th Episcopal District (*A.M.E. Church*), 63

Swan Lake Missionary Baptist Association—Mississippi, 45

Swaziland Annual Conference, 18th Episcopal District (*A.M.E. Church*), 63

Tallahatchie-Oxford Missionary Baptist Association, Inc.—Mississippi, 45

Tampa District—South Florida Annual Conference, 7th Episcopal District (*A.M.E. Zion Church*), 74

Tampa, Florida Annual Conference, 11th Episcopal District (*A.M.E. Church*), 63

Tennessee Annual Conference, 13th Episcopal District (*A.M.E. Church*), 63

Tennessee Baptist Missionary and Education Convention, 45, 54

Tennessee Regular Baptist Convention, 45

Texas Annual Conference, 10th Episcopal District (*A.M.E. Church*), 63

Third District Bogue Chitto Baptist Association—Louisiana, 31

Tri-County District Association—California, 45

Trinidad/Tobago District—Virginia Annual Conference, 4th Episcopal District (*A.M.E. Zion Church*), 74

Trinity Valley Missionary Baptist District Association—Texas, 45

True Friendship Missionary Baptist and Educational Association—Louisiana, 45

Tuscaloosa District—North Alabama Annual Conference, 8th Episcopal District (*A.M.E. Zion Church*), 74

Tuskegee District—Alabama Annual Conference, 10th Episcopal District (*A.M.E. Zion Church*), 74

Union District Association—Illinois, 54

Union District Association—Missouri, 31

Union District Association—Ohio, 45

Union District Association—Oregon, 31

Union District Association—Texas, 31

Union General Baptist State Convention—California, 31

Union of Black Episcopalians, 203

Union Springs District—Alabama Annual Conference, 10th Episcopal District (*A.M.E. Zion Church*), 74

United Baptist Convention of Delaware, Inc., 45

United Baptist Convention of Massachusetts, Rhode Island, and New Hampshire, Inc., 46

United Baptist District Association of California, 54

United Baptist Missionary Convention of Maryland, Inc., 46

United Black Christians—United Church of Christ, Inc., 216

United Fellowship Convention of the Original Azusa Street Mission, 113–14

United Missionary Baptist Association—New York, 46

United Missionary Baptist District Association of Kansas, 31

United Progressive District Association—Louisiana, 31

United Shiloh Missionary Baptist Association—North Carolina, 54

Unity District Association—Texas, 31

Universal Bible Institute and Training School, 171

Virginia Annual Conference, 2nd Episcopal District (*A.M.E. Church*), 63

Virginia Baptist State Convention, 31, 54

Virginia Seminary and College, 171

Virginia Union University School of Theology, 168

Virgin Island Annual Conference, 2nd Episcopal District (*A.M.E. Zion Church*), 74

Virgin Islands Annual Conference, 16th Episcopal District (*A.M.E. Church*), 63

Wadesboro Monroe District—West Central North Carolina Annual Conference, 8th Episcopal District (*A.M.E. Zion Church*), 74

Washington Baptist Seminary, 171

Washington, D.C. Annual Conference, 2nd Episcopal District (*A.M.E. Church*), 64

Washington District—North Carolina Annual Conference, 2nd Episcopal District (*A.M.E. Zion Church*), 74

Washington District—Philadelphia/Baltimore Annual Conference, 3rd Episcopal District (*A.M.E. Zion Church*), 74

Washington/Oregon Annual Conference, 11th Episcopal District (*A.M.E. Zion Church*), 75

Washington State Baptist Convention, 31

Wateree Association—South Carolina, 54

West Alabama Annual Conference, 9th Episcopal District (*A.M.E. Church*), 64

West Arkansas Annual Conference, 12th Episcopal District (*A.M.E. Church*), 64

Western District Association—Michigan, 31

Western District Missionary Association, Inc.—Oklahoma, 46

Western North Carolina Annual Conference, 2nd Episcopal District (*A.M.E. Church*), 64

Western States Baptist Convention of Colorado and Wyoming, 46

West Florida Annual Conference, 11th Episcopal District (*A.M.E. Church*), 64

West Ghana Annual Conference, 12th Episcopal District (*A.M.E. Zion Church*), 75

West Kentucky Annual Conference, 13th Episcopal District (*A.M.E. Church*), 64

West Montgomery District—Central Alabama Annual Conference, 10th Episcopal District (*A.M.E. Zion Church*), 75

West Mount Olive District Association—Mississippi, 46

West Nashville District Association—Tennessee, 31

West Pensacola District—Florida

District Associations/Annual Conferences

341

Ecumenical/Nondenominational Groups

Student Groups

Women's Groups

Worship Resource Groups

Youth Groups

INDEX 5: PERSONAL NAME LISTING

All persons in the chapters, essays and contact information of the *Directory* are listed in letter-by-letter alphabetical order, ignoring punctuation and spacing.

INDEX 6: PUBLICATIONS LISTING

The publications produced by the religious bodies presented in the *Directory* are listed in letter-by-letter alphabetical order, ignoring punctuation and spacing.

Directory of African American Religious Bodies: A Compendium by the Howard University School of Divinity

Questionnaire

To update and correct information on any of the groups listed in this *Directory* and to include groups that have been omitted, please complete this form and mail it to the address below.

1. Name of religious body, organization or group: _____
_____

2. Address: _____
_____

3. Telephone number, including area code: _____
_____

4. Name and title of the person(s) heading or directing the organization: _____
_____

5. When and where was the organization or group founded? (If there is a written history or public relations kit for the group please include it) _____
_____
_____
_____

6. What is the scope and focus of the group or organization? How many people/churches are involved? _____
_____
_____
_____

7. Who composes your membership? (Example: ministers, women, young people, musicians, laity, etc.) _____
_____

8. State the purpose of your organization or group: _____
_____
_____
_____

9. Name, address, and telephone number of person completing this form: _____
_____
_____
_____

Please return this information to:

Howard University School of Divinity
Research Center on Black Religious Bodies
1400 Shepherd Street, N.E.
Washington, DC 20017
(202) 806-0750